PHILIP'S

ESSENTIAL
WORLD
ATLAS

CONTENTS

WORLD

8-9 **World: Northern part**
10-11 **World: Southern part**
12-13 **Arctic**
14-15 **Antarctic**

EUROPE

16-17 **Europe: Physical**
18-19 **Europe: Political**

20-21 **British Isles: South**
22-23 **British Isles: North**
24-25 **Southern England**
26-27 **Wales and South West England**
28-29 **Northern England**
30-31 **Southern Scotland**
32-33 **Northern Scotland**
34-35 **Ireland**

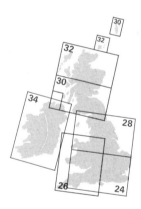

First published in Great Britain in 1994
by George Philip Limited,
an imprint of Reed Consumer Books Limited,
Michelin House, 81 Fulham Road, London SW3 6RB
and Auckland, Melbourne, Singapore and Toronto

ISBN 0 540 05824 6

A CIP catalogue record for this book is available from the British Library

Printed in Hong Kong

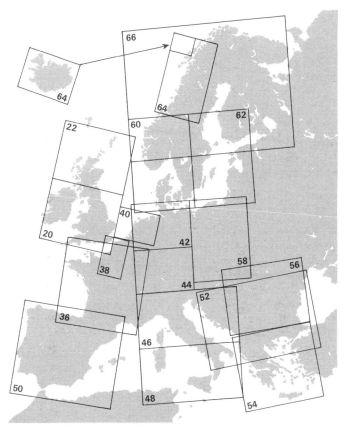

36-37 France
38-39 Northern France
40-41 Netherlands
42-43 Germany and the Low
       Countries
44-45 Alpine Lands
46-47 Northern Italy and
       Corsica
48-49 Southern Italy and
       Sardinia

50-51 Spain and Portugal
52-53 Danube Lands
54-55 Greece and Albania
56-57 Romania
58-59 Central Europe
60-61 Southern Scandinavia
62-63 Baltic Lands
64-65 North West Scandinavia
       and Iceland
66-67 Northern Scandinavia

ASIA

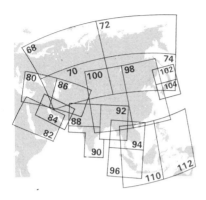

76-77   Asia: Physical
78-79   Asia: Political

80-81   Turkey and the Middle East
82-83   Arabian Peninsula
84-85   The Gulf
86-87   Central Asia and Afghanistan
88-89   Pakistan and North West India
90-91   Central and Southern India, Sri Lanka
92-93   Eastern India, Bangladesh and Burma
94-95   Mainland South East Asia
96-97   The Malay Peninsula
98-99   China: East
100-101 China: West

68-69   Eastern Europe
70-71   Kazakhstan and Central Asia
72-73   North East Russia
74-75   South East Russia and Mongolia

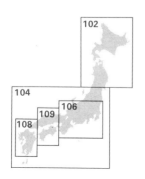

102-103 Japan: North
104-105 Japan: South
106-107 Japan: Tokyo, Kyoto, Osaka
108-109 Japan: Kyushu, West Honshu and Shikoku

110-111 Indonesia: West
112-113 Indonesia: East

AUSTRALASIA

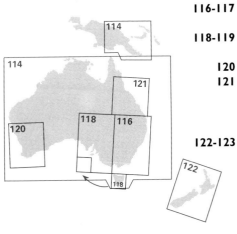

114-115 Australia, New Zealand and Papua New Guinea

116-117 Australia: Brisbane, Sydney and Melbourne

118-119 Australia: Adelaide, Melbourne and Tasmania

120 Australia: Perth

121 Australia: North East Queensland

122-123 New Zealand, Central and South West Pacific

AFRICA

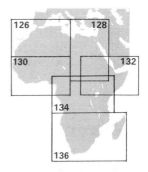

124 Africa: Physical

125 Africa: Political

126-127 Africa: North West

128-129 Africa: North East

130-131 Africa: West

132-133 Africa: East

134-135 Africa: Central

136-137 Africa: South

NORTH AMERICA

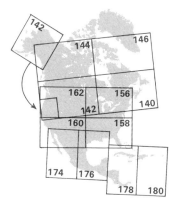

138 North America: Physical
139 North America: Political

140-141 Canada: South East
142-143 Canada: South West and Alaska
144-145 Canada: North West
146-147 Canada: North East
148-149 Canada: Saint Lawrence Estuary
150-151 Canada: The Great Lakes
152-153 Canada: Southern Saskatchewan and Manitoba
154-155 Canada: Southern British Columbia and Alberta

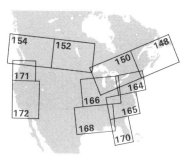

156-157 USA: North East
158-159 USA: South East
160-161 USA: South West
162-163 USA: North West
164 USA: Boston, New York, Washington
165 USA: Washington, Atlanta
166-167 USA: Upper Mississippi
168-169 USA: Lower Mississippi and Gulf Coast
170 USA: Florida
171 USA: Columbia Basin
172-173 USA: California

174-175 Mexico: West
176-177 Mexico: East
178-179 Caribbean: West
180-181 Caribbean: East

SOUTH AMERICA

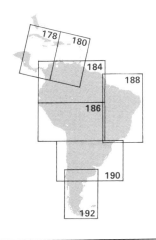

182 **South America: Physical**

183 **South America: Political**

184-185 **South America: North West**

186-187 **South America: West**

188-189 **South America: East**

190-191 **South America: Central**

192 **South America: South**

INDEX

MAP SYMBOLS

Settlement symbols in order of size

⬡ ⬡ ■ ● ◎ ○ ○ ○

──────── International boundary

┄┄┄┄┄┄ Internal boundary

──────── Principal railway

──────── Principal road

┴┴┴┴┴ Canal

☼✈ Principal airport

─┤- - -├─ Tunnel

∿∿∿ Permanent river

╌╌╌╌ Intermittent river

⬭ Permanent lake

⬭ Intermittent lake

░░░░ Marsh

▲ 8848 Altitude above sea level

▼ 10497 Depth below sea level

263 Level of lake

(18) Indicates the adjoining map

As far as possible the de facto situation of international boundaries is shown

Scale note
To the right of each map title there is a number representing the scale of the map for example, 1 : 2 000 000. This means that one centimetre on the map represents 2 million centimetres or 20 kilometres on the ground. Or, if the number is 1 : 40 000 000, one centimetre represents 40 million centimetres or 400 kilometres.

Height and depth colours

Height of land above sea level

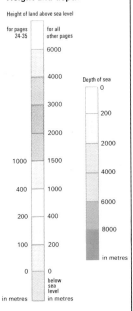

for pages 24-35 | for all other pages
6000
4000   Depth of sea
              0
3000   200
2000   2000
1000   1500   4000
400   1000   6000
200   400   8000
100   200   in metres
0   0
       below
       sea
       level
in metres | in metres

WORLD : NORTHERN PART

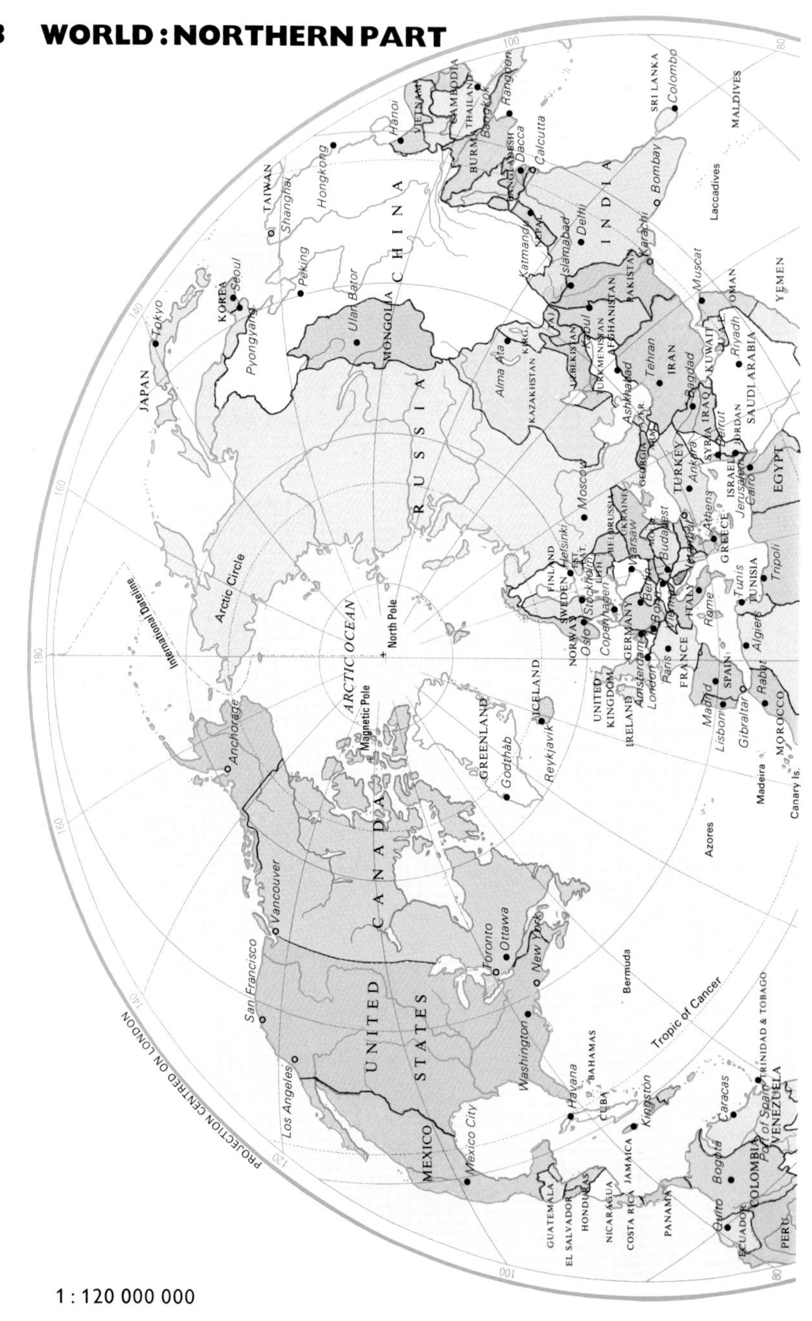
ARCTIC OCEAN
North Pole
Magnetic Pole
Arctic Circle
International Dateline
Tropic of Cancer
PROJECTION CENTRED ON LONDON
R U S S I A
C H I N A
I N D I A
C A N A D A
UNITED STATES
MEXICO
GREENLAND
ICELAND
JAPAN
KOREA
MONGOLIA
TAIWAN
VIETNAM
CAMBODIA
THAILAND
BURMA
BANGLADESH
NEPAL
SRI LANKA
MALDIVES
Laccadives
PAKISTAN
AFGHANISTAN
IRAN
IRAQ
KUWAIT
U.A.E.
OMAN
YEMEN
SAUDI ARABIA
JORDAN
SYRIA
ISRAEL
EGYPT
TURKEY
GEORGIA
ARM.
AZ.
KAZAKHSTAN
KIRG.
TAJ.
UZBEKISTAN
TURKMENISTAN
UKRAINE
BELORUSSIA
LITH.
LAT.
EST.
FINLAND
SWEDEN
NORWAY
GERMANY
UNITED KINGDOM
IRELAND
FRANCE
SPAIN
ITALY
GREECE
TUNISIA
MOROCCO
Madeira
Canary Is.
Azores
Bermuda
BAHAMAS
CUBA
JAMAICA
GUATEMALA
EL SALVADOR
HONDURAS
NICARAGUA
COSTA RICA
PANAMA
COLOMBIA
VENEZUELA
ECUADOR
PERU
TRINIDAD & TOBAGO
Tokyo
Seoul
Pyongyang
Peking
Shanghai
Hongkong
Ulan Bator
Hanoi
Bangkok
Rangoon
Dacca
Calcutta
Colombo
Katmandu
Delhi
Bombay
Karachi
Islamabad
Kabul
Muscat
Riyadh
Tehran
Bagdad
Ashkhabad
Alma Ata
Beirut
Jerusalem
Cairo
Ankara
Athens
Istanbul
Budapest
Moscow
Helsinki
Stockholm
Oslo
Copenhagen
Warsaw
Berlin
Bonn
Amsterdam
London
Paris
Rome
Tunis
Tripoli
Algiers
Rabat
Madrid
Lisbon
Gibraltar
Reykjavik
Godthåb
Anchorage
Vancouver
San Francisco
Los Angeles
Toronto
Ottawa
New York
Washington
Havana
Kingston
Mexico City
Caracas
Port of Spain
Bogota
Quito
100
120
140
160
180
80

1 : 120 000 000

PROJECTION CENTRED ON CAPETOWN

Chagos Arch.

ALGERIA
LIBYA

MAURITANIA
MALI
NIGER
CHAD
SUDAN
ERITREA
DJIBOUTI
Sana
Khartoum
ETHIOPIA
SOMALIA
Addis Ababa
Mogadishu
SEYCHELLES

CAPE VERDE IS.

SENEGAL
Dakar
GAMBIA
Banjul
GUINEA BISSAU
GUINEA
Conakry
SIERRA LEONE
Freetown
LIBERIA
Monrovia
IVORY COAST
BURKINA
GHANA
TOGO
BENIN
Accra
NIGERIA
Niamey
Lagos
CAMEROON
Yaoundé
CENTRAL AFRICA
Bangui
EQUAT. GUINEA
GABON
CONGO
Libreville
Brazzaville
Kinshasa
ZAIRE

UGANDA
KENYA
Kampala
Nairobi
RWANDA
Dar es Salaam
TANZANIA
MALAWI
Lilongwe
MAURITIUS
Réunion
MADAGASCAR
Antananarivo

Luanda
ANGOLA
ZAMBIA
Lusaka
ZIMBABWE
Harare
MOZAMBIQUE
Maputo
NAMIBIA
BOTSWANA
SWAZILAND
Gaborone
Windhoek
Pretoria
Johannesburg
LESOTHO
SOUTH AFRICA
Cape Town

Equator
Tropic of Capricorn

St. Helena
Ascension

Georgetown
Paramaribo
GUYANA
SURINAM
FRENCH GUIANA

BRAZIL
BOLIVIA
Brasília
São Paulo
Rio de Janeiro

West from Greenwich
East from Greenwich

• Capital Cities

TIME ZONES

| 9.00 | 6.00 |

Time Zone in hours fast (+) or
slow (−) of Greenwich Mean Time

Standard Time not the Zone hour

No Official Time

All distances measured through the centre
of the map are correct for scale

PROJECTION CENTRED ON CAPETOWN

ATLANTIC OCEAN
INDIAN OCEAN
PACIFIC OCEAN

Greenwich A +1.00
0.00
+2.00 C −2.00
+3.00
+4.00
−3.30
+5.00
+4.00
+5.30
+3.00 C
+2.00 J
+1.00
+3.00
−3.00
BA −3.00
−4.00
−5.00

East from Greenwich
West from Greenwich

Equator
Antarctic Circle
South Pole

+7.00 J
+8.00 P

PROJECTION CENTRED ON SAN FRANCISCO

West from Greenwich
Greenwich

ATLANTIC OCEAN
PACIFIC OCEAN

M +3.00 +4.00
+5.00 +2.00
+1.00
0.00 A
Greenwich
−2.00
−3.00
−3.30
NY −4.00
−4.00
−5.00
−6.00 C
M −6.00
LA −7.00
−8.00
−10.00
+6.00
+7.00
+8.00
+9.00
+10.00
+11.00
+12.00
T
P
North Pole
−8.00
−9.00
−10.00

International Dateline
Arctic Circle
Equator

East from Greenwich

COPYRIGHT GEORGE PHILIP & SON LTD

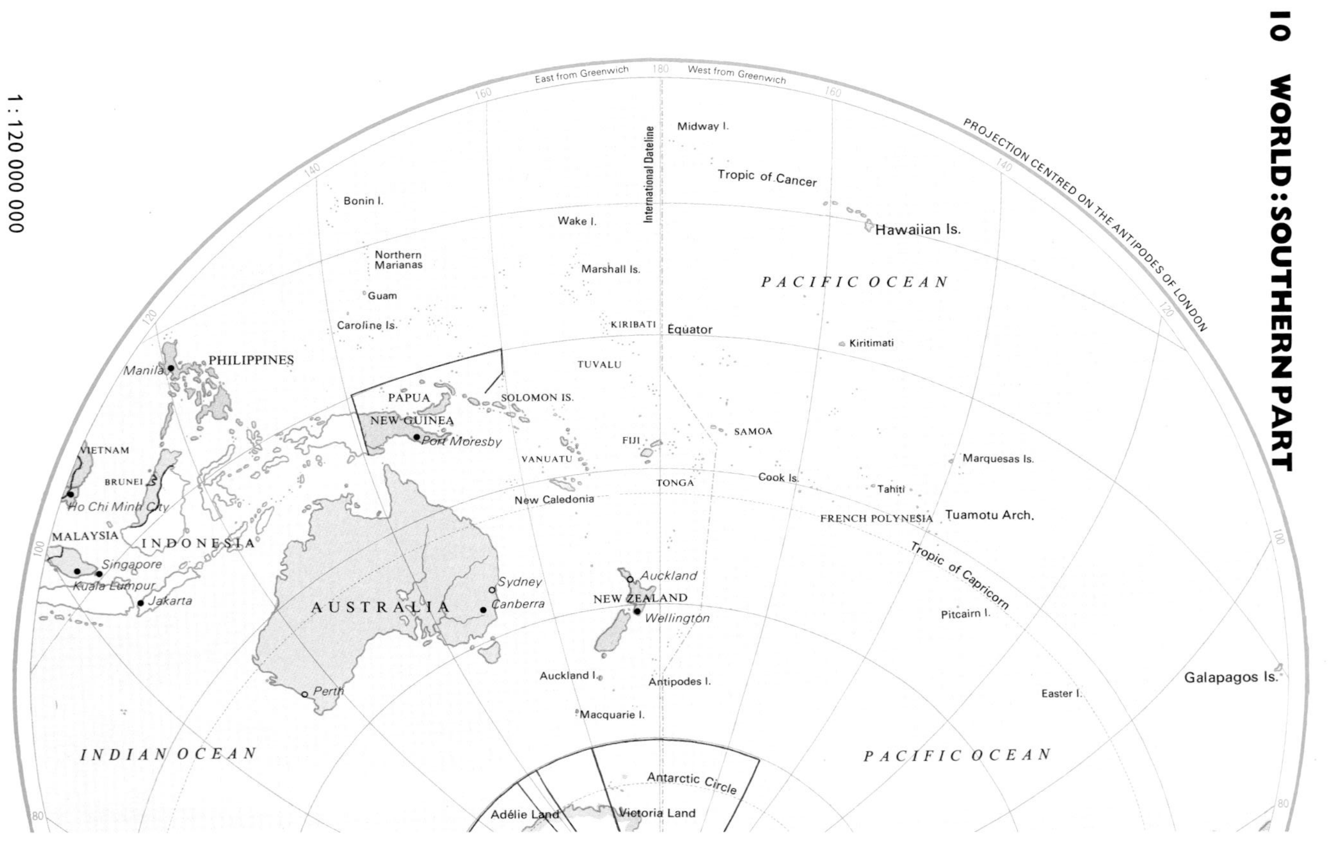

PROJECTION CENTRED ON THE ANTIPODES OF LONDON

Galapagos Is.

Easter I.

West from Greenwich

East from Greenwich

International Dateline

PACIFIC OCEAN

PACIFIC OCEAN

Hawaiian Is.

Tropic of Cancer

Midway I.

Kiritimati

Marquesas Is.

Tuamotu Arch.

Tropic of Capricorn

Pitcairn I.

Tahiti

FRENCH POLYNESIA

Equator

SAMOA

Cook Is.

Wake I.

Marshall Is.

KIRIBATI

TONGA

FIJI

Auckland

Wellington

NEW ZEALAND

Antarctic Circle

Victoria Land

TUVALU

SOLOMON IS.

VANUATU

New Caledonia

Auckland I.

Macquarie I.

Antipodes I.

Adélie Land

Northern
Marianas

Guam

Caroline Is.

PAPUA
NEW GUINEA

Port Moresby

Sydney
Canberra

AUSTRALIA

Perth

Bonin I.

PHILIPPINES

Manila

INDONESIA

Jakarta

INDIAN OCEAN

VIETNAM

Ho Chi Minh City

BRUNEI

MALAYSIA

Singapore

Kuala Lumpur

Dili Timor

1 : 120 000 000

Lima
PERU

CHILE

BOLIVIA

Santiago
ARGENTINA

PARAGUAY

URUGUAY
Buenos Aires
Montevideo

BRAZIL

Falkland Is.

South Georgia

South Sandwich Is.

ATLANTIC OCEAN

Bouvet I.

Pr. Edward I.

Crozet I.

Kerguelen

Heard I.

Ross Sea

Byrd Land

Amundsen Sea

Ellsworth Land

Weddell Sea

Antarctica

Wilkes Land

South Pole

Enderby Land

Queen Maud Land

PROJECTION CENTRED ON SHANGHAI

West from Greenwich

PACIFIC OCEAN

International Dateline

North Pole

Greenwich

Equator

INDIAN OCEAN

East from Greenwich

−10.00
−5.00 −6.00
−7.00 −8.00
−9.00
−2.00
+12.00
+10.00 +11.00
+8.00 +9.00
0.00
+1.00
+2.00 +4.00
+6.00 +7.00
+8.00
+5.30
+9.00 +10.00
+9.00 +10.00
+8.00
+11.00
+2.00
+7.00
+3.00

A
M
C
S
HK
P
J
T
P
C
O

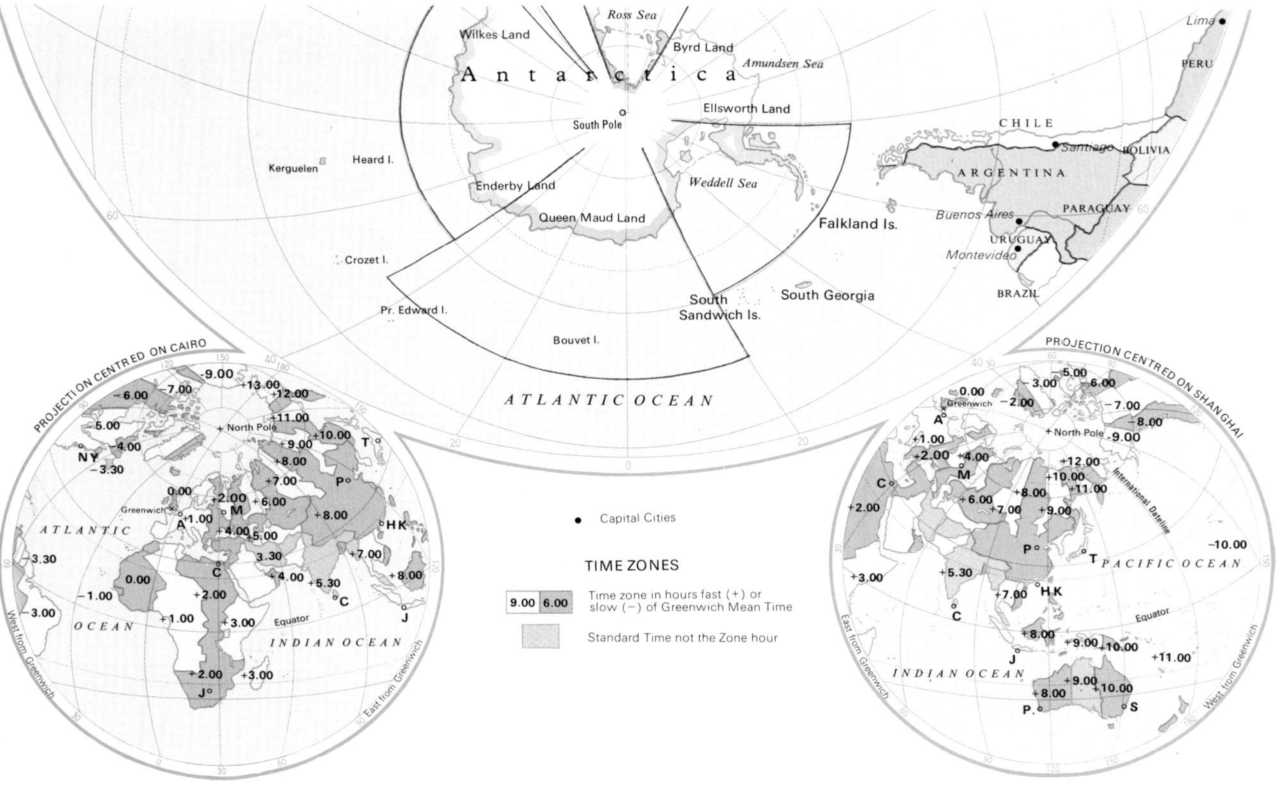

• Capital Cities

TIME ZONES

Time zone in hours fast (+) or slow (−) of Greenwich Mean Time

| 9.00 | 6.00 |

Standard Time not the Zone hour

PROJECTION CENTRED ON CAIRO

East from Greenwich

North Pole

ATLANTIC OCEAN

INDIAN OCEAN

Greenwich

Equator

West from Greenwich

9.00
6.00
+13.00 +12.00
−9.00
−11.00
+10.00
−7.00
+8.00
+7.00
0.00
−1.00 +2.00
+6.00
+4.00 +5.00
+3.30
+3.30
+4.00 +5.30
+8.00
−4.00
−5.00
NY
−3.30
0.00
−1.00
+1.00
+2.00
+2.00
+3.00
+3.00
+7.00

A
M
C
C
J
T
P
HK
J
O

COPYRIGHT GEORGE PHILIP & SON LTD

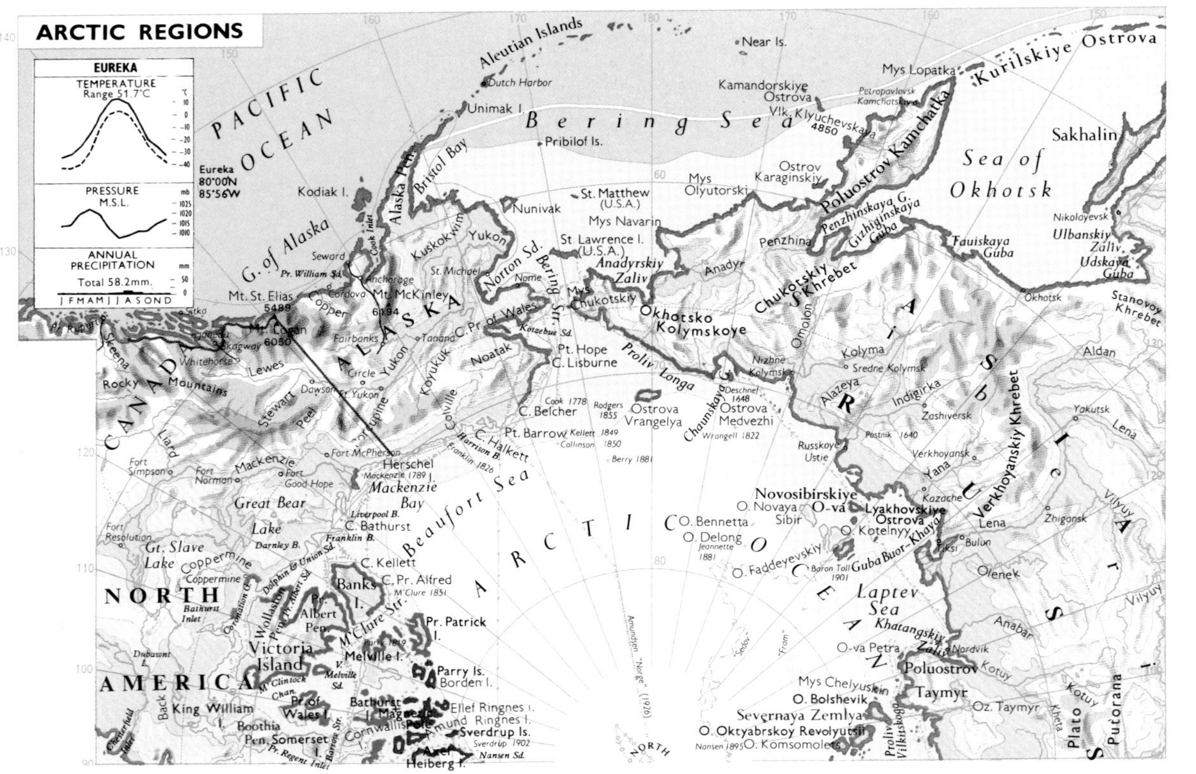

ARCTIC REGIONS

EUREKA
80°00N
85°56W

TEMPERATURE
Range 51.7°C

PRESSURE
M.S.L.

ANNUAL
PRECIPITATION
Total 58.2mm.

J F M A M J J A S O N D

1 : 42 000 000

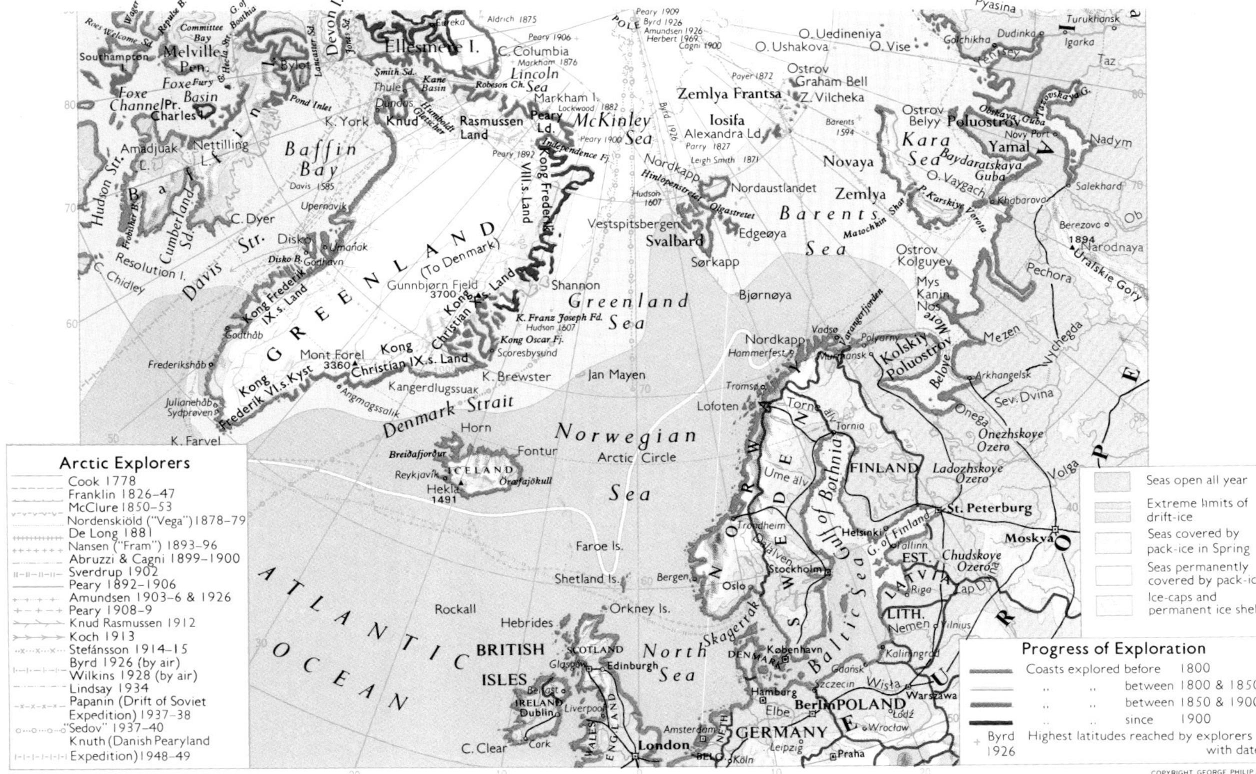

13

Progress of Exploration

Coasts explored before 1800		
,, ,, between 1800 & 1850		
,, ,, between 1850 & 1900		
,, ,, since 1900		

Highest latitudes reached by explorers
+ Byrd 1926   with date

Seas open all year
Extreme limits of drift-ice
Seas covered by pack-ice in Spring
Seas permanently covered by pack-ice
Ice-caps and permanent ice shelf

COPYRIGHT GEORGE PHILIP & SON LTD

Arctic Explorers

Cook 1778
Franklin 1826–47
McClure 1850–53
Nordenskiöld ("Vega") 1878–79
De Long 1881
Nansen ("Fram") 1893–96
Abruzzi & Cagni 1899–1900
Sverdrup 1902
Peary 1892–1906
Amundsen 1903–6 & 1926
Peary 1908–9
Knud Rasmussen 1912
Stefánsson 1914–15
Byrd 1926 (by air)
Wilkins 1928 (by air)
Lindsay 1934
Papanin (Drift of Soviet Expedition) 1937–38
"Sedov" 1937–40
Knuth (Danish Pearyland Expedition) 1948–49

ANTARCTIC

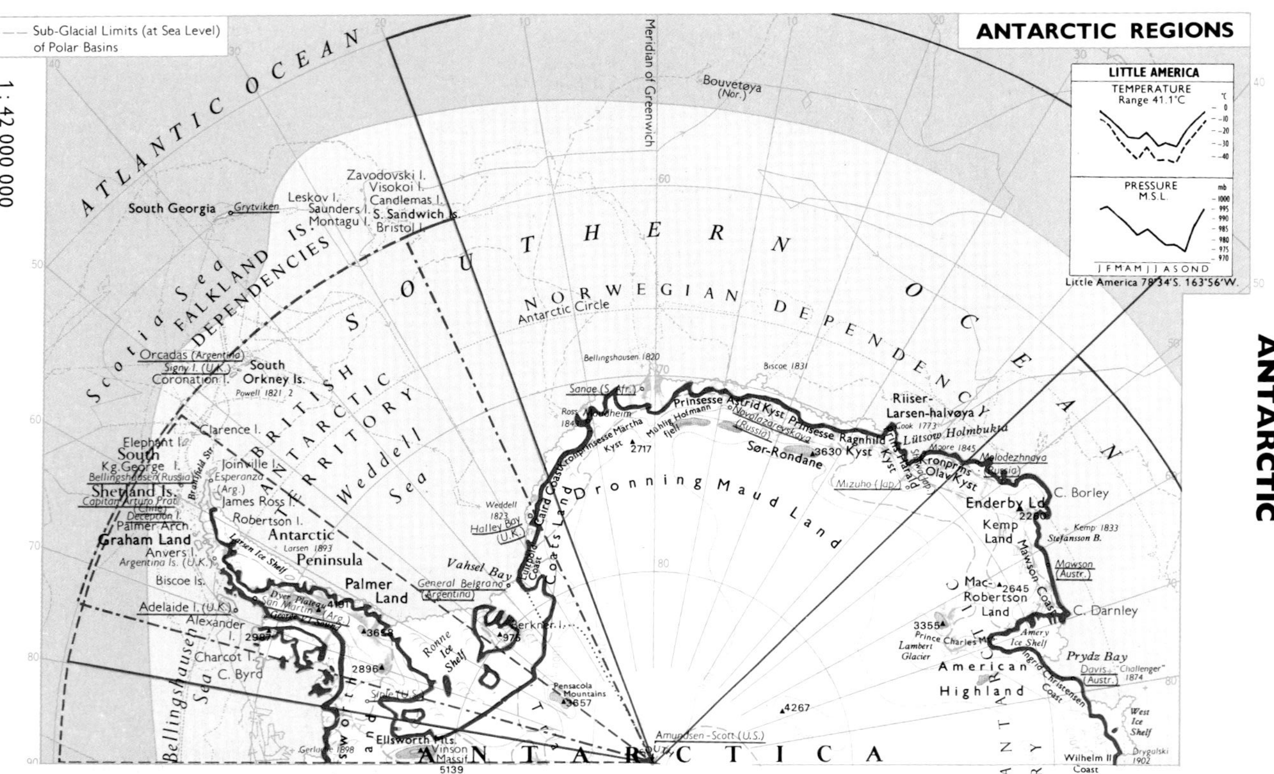

Sub-Glacial Limits (at Sea Level) of Polar Basins

1 : 42 000 000

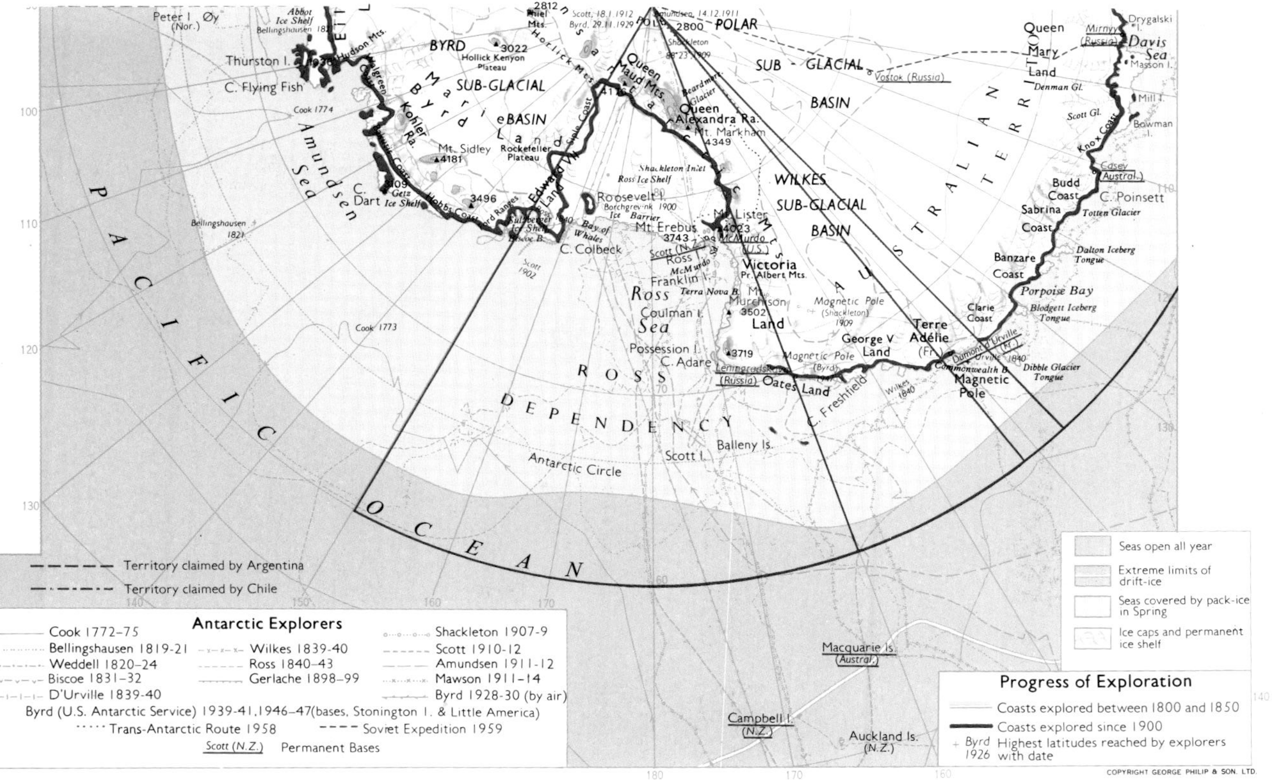

15

Progress of Exploration

[legend:] Seas open all year
Extreme limits of drift-ice
Seas covered by pack-ice in Spring
Ice caps and permanent ice shelf

Coasts explored between 1800 and 1850
Coasts explored since 1900
Byrd Highest latitudes reached by explorers with date
1926

COPYRIGHT GEORGE PHILIP & SON, LTD.

Antarctic Explorers

Cook 1772–75
Bellingshausen 1819-21
Weddell 1820-24
Biscoe 1831–32
D'Urville 1839-40

Wilkes 1839-40
Ross 1840-43
Gerlache 1898-99

Shackleton 1907-9
Scott 1910-12
Amundsen 1911-12
Mawson 1911-14
Byrd 1928-30 (by air)

Byrd (U.S. Antarctic Service) 1939-41, 1946-47 (bases, Stonington I. & Little America)
Soviet Expedition 1959
Trans-Antarctic Route 1958
Scott (N.Z.) Permanent Bases

Territory claimed by Argentina
Territory claimed by Chile

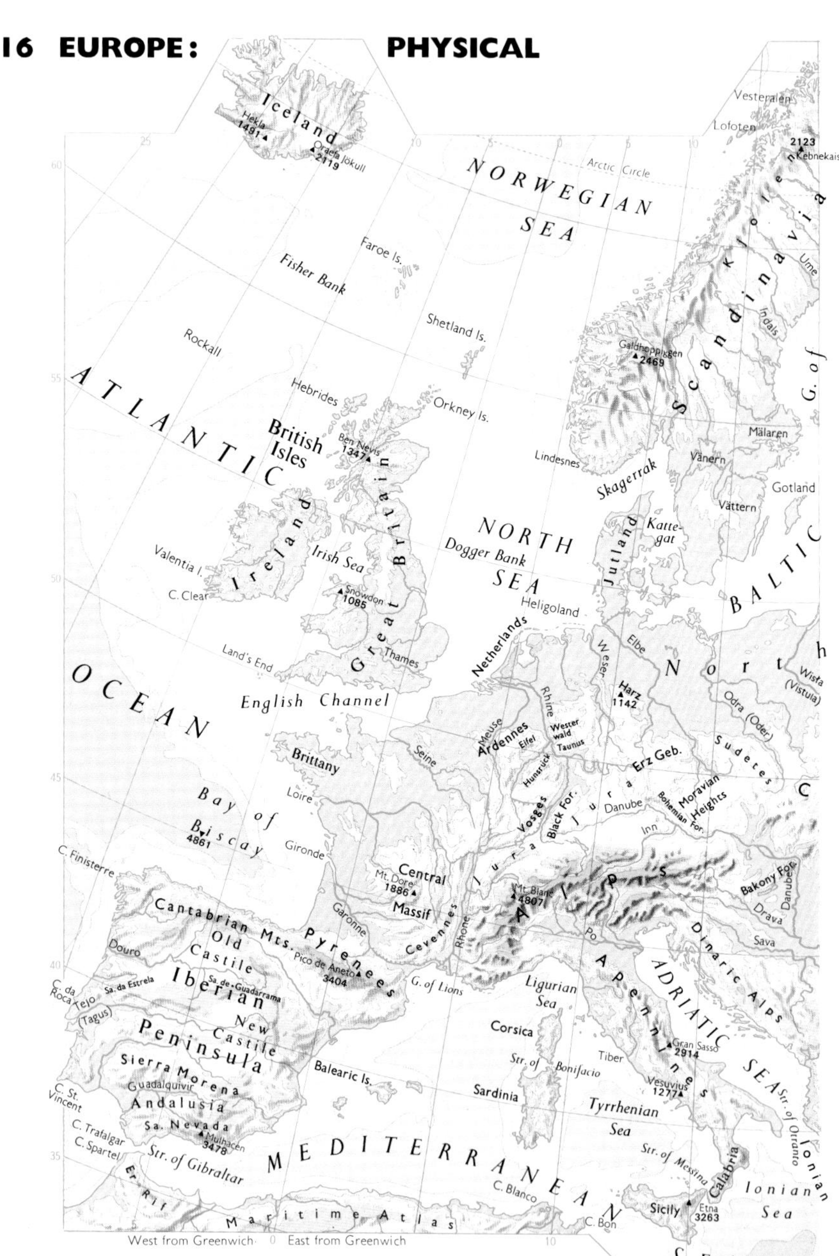

Iceland
Hekla 1491▲ ▲Vatna Jökull 2419

NORWEGIAN SEA

Arctic Circle

Vesterålen
Lofoten
2123 ▲Kebnekaise

Faroe Is.

Fisher Bank

Shetland Is.

Rockall

Hebrides

Orkney Is.

ATLANTIC

British Isles

Ben Nevis 1347▲

Galdhøpiggen ▲2468

S c a n d i n a v i a

Une

G. of

Indals

Mälaren

Vänern

Gotland

Lindesnes

Skagerrak

Kattegat

Vättern

BALTIC

Valencia I.

Ireland

Irish Sea

Great Britain

Snowdon ▲1085

NORTH SEA

Dogger Bank

Jutland

North

Wisla (Vistula)

C. Clear

Land's End

R. Thames

English Channel

Heligoland

Elbe

Weser

Netherlands

Rhine

Harz 1142

Odra (Oder)

Sudetes

OCEAN

Brittany

Seine

Meuse
Ardennes
Eifel
Hunsrück
Westerwald
Taunus

Jura

Vosges

Black For.

Erz Geb.

Moravian Heights

C

Bay of Biscay 4861

Loire

Gironde

Mt. Dore 1886▲

Central Massif

Jura

Danube

Inn

Bohemian For.

Bakony For.

C. Finisterre

Cantabrian Mts.
Old Castile
Douro
Sa. de Estrela
Pico de Aneto 4404
Sa. de Guadarrama
Ibérian
New Castile
Peninsula

Pyrenees

Garonne

Cévennes

Mt. Blanc 4807▲

A L P S

Ligurian Sea

Po

Apennines

Dinaric Alps

ADRIATIC

Drava

Sava

Danube

C. da Roca
Tejo (Tagus)

Sierra Morena
Guadalquivir
Andalusia
Sa. Nevada 3478

G. of Lions

Balearic Is.

Corsica

Str. of Bonifacio

Sardinia

Tiber

Gran Sasso ▲2914

Vesuvius 1277▲

SEA

Str. of Otranto

Ionian

C. St. Vincent
C. Trafalgar
C. Spartel
Er Rif

Str. of Gibraltar

M E D I T E R R A N E A N

Tyrrhenian Sea

Calabria

Etna 3263

Ionian Sea

M a r i t i m e   A t l a s

C. Blanco

C. Bon

Str. of Messina

Sicily

SEA

West from Greenwich   0   East from Greenwich

Malta

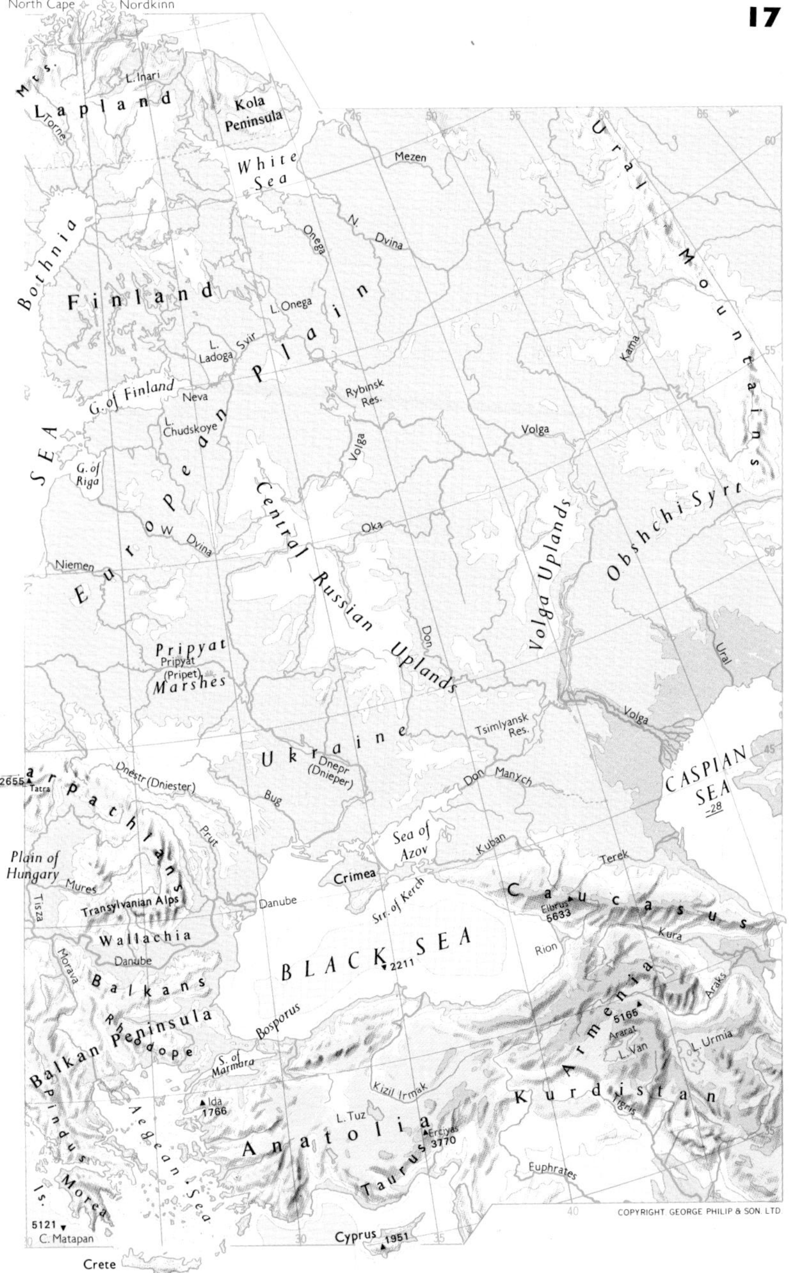

North Cape Nordkinn

Mts.
L. Iorma   L. Inari
Lapland   Kola
                 Peninsula

                    White
                     Sea   Mezen

Bothnia   Onega   N. Dvina

  Finland   L. Onega

           Svir
        L. Ladoga
    G. of Finland   Neva   Rybinsk
                                    Res.
                          Plain
  SEA   L.
        Chudskoye   Volga   Volga

  G. of   Oka
  Riga   European

         O.W. Dvina

  Niemen   Obshchi Syrt

           Pripyat   Ural
        Pripyat
        (Pripet)
        Marshes

              Ukraine   Don

                  Dnepr   Tsimlyansk
                  (Dnieper)   Res.
                                                        Volga
2655 Tatra Dnestr (Dniester)
Carpathians   Bug   Don Manych
                     Prut   CASPIAN
                                  Sea of   SEA
Plain of   Azov   Kuban   -28
Hungary   Terek
        Mures   Transylvanian Alps Crimea Str. of Kerch
Tisza   Danube   Caucasus
        Morava   Rion Elbrus
        Wallachia   5633   Kura
        Danube   Araks
  Balkans   BLACK SEA   2211   Armenia
Balkan Peninsula   5165
        Rhodope   Bosporus Ararat L. Van Urmia
Pindus Morea   S. of Marmara   Kurdistan
  Is.   Kizil Irmak   Tigris
        Ida   L. Tuz
        1766   Anatolia   Erciyas Euphrates
5121   Taurus 3770
C. Matapan   Aegean Sea
          Crete   Cyprus 1951

EUROPE: POLITICAL

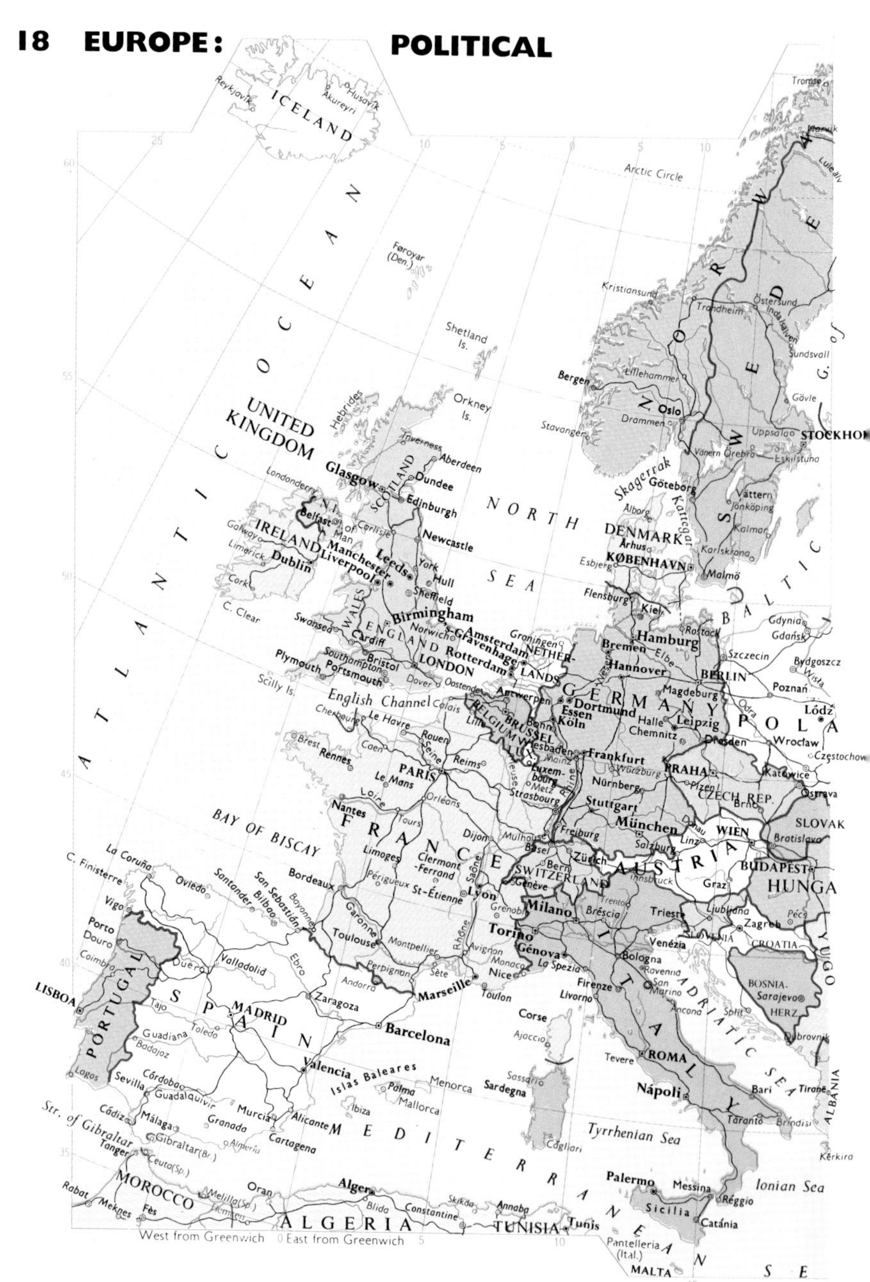
ICELAND
Reykjavík
Akureyri
Húsavík
Arctic Circle
ATLANTIC OCEAN
Føroyar (Den.)
Shetland Is.
Orkney Is.
Hebrides
UNITED KINGDOM
SCOTLAND
Inverness
Aberdeen
Glasgow
Dundee
Edinburgh
Londonderry
N.I.
Belfast
I. of Man
Carlisle
Newcastle
IRELAND
Galway
Limerick
Dublin
Cork
C. Clear
Manchester
Liverpool
Leeds
York
Hull
Sheffield
WALES
Swansea
Birmingham
Norwich
ENGLAND
Cardiff
Bristol
LONDON
Plymouth
Southampton
Portsmouth
Dover
Scilly Is.
English Channel
NORTH SEA
Bergen
Stavanger
Drammen
Oslo
Lillehammer
Kristiansund
Trondheim
NORWAY
Tromsø
Narvik
Luleälv
Östersund
Indalsälven
Sundsvall
Gävle
Uppsala
STOCKHOLM
Vänern
Örebro
Eskilstuna
Skagerrak
Göteborg
Kattegat
Vättern
Jönköping
Kalmar
Karlskrona
Malmö
SWEDEN
G. of
Ålborg
DENMARK
Århus
Esbjerg
KØBENHAVN
Flensburg
Kiel
BALTIC
Rostock
Gdynia
Gdańsk
Hamburg
Bremen
Elbe
Groningen
NETHERLANDS
Amsterdam
's-Gravenhage
Rotterdam
Hannover
BERLIN
Szczecin
Bydgoszcz
Wisła
Poznań
Łódź
Magdeburg
Oostende
Antwerpen
Calais
BRUSSEL
BELGIUM
Lille
GERMANY
Dortmund
Essen
Köln
Bonn
Halle
Leipzig
Chemnitz
Dresden
Odra
POLAND
Wrocław
Częstochowa
LUX.
Luxembourg
Wiesbaden
Mainz
Frankfurt
Würzburg
Nürnberg
PRAHA
Plzeň
CZECH REP.
Brno
Katowice
Ostrava
Cherbourg
Le Havre
Brest
Rennes
Caen
Rouen
Seine
Reims
PARIS
Le Mans
Loire
Orléans
Metz
Strasbourg
Rhein
Meuse
Nantes
Tours
FRANCE
Dijon
Mulhouse
Basel
Freiburg
Stuttgart
München
Donau
Salzburg
Linz
WIEN
AUSTRIA
Bratislava
SLOVAKIA
BAY OF BISCAY
Limoges
Clermont-Ferrand
Périgueux
St-Étienne
Bordeaux
Lyon
Saône
Genève
Bern
Zürich
SWITZERLAND
Innsbruck
Graz
BUDAPEST
HUNGARY
Grenoble
Milano
Trento
Brescia
Trieste
Ljubljana
SLOVENIA
Zagreb
Pécs
CROATIA
La Coruña
C. Finisterre
Oviedo
Santander
Bilbao
San Sebastián
Bayonne
Garonne
Toulouse
Montpellier
Rhône
Avignon
Torino
Genova
Venézia
Bologna
Ravenna
San Marino
Ancona
ADRIATIC SEA
BOSNIA-HERZ.
Sarajevo
Split
YUGO.
Dubrovnik
Vigo
Porto
Douro
Coimbra
Valladolid
Duero
Ebro
Andorra
Perpignan
Sète
Monaco
Nice
La Spezia
Firenze
Livorno
Marseille
Toulon
ITALY
LISBOA
PORTUGAL
Tajo
MADRID
SPAIN
Zaragoza
Toledo
Barcelona
Corse
Ajaccio
ROMA
Tevere
Guadiana
Badajoz
Valencia
Islas Baleares
Menorca
Mallorca
Palma
Ibiza
Sardegna
Sassari
Nápoli
Bari
Tiranë
ALBANIA
Lagos
Sevilla
Córdoba
Guadalquivir
Murcia
Alicante
Cádiz
Málaga
Granada
Almería
Cartagena
Str. of Gibraltar
Gibraltar (Br.)
Tanger
Ceuta (Sp.)
MEDITERRANEAN SEA
Tyrrhenian Sea
Cagliari
Táranto
Brindisi
Kérkira
MOROCCO
Rabat
Meknès
Fès
Melilla (Sp.)
Oran
Tlemcen
Alger
Blida
Constantine
Skikda
Annaba
ALGERIA
TUNISIA
Tunis
Palermo
Messina
Sicilia
Réggio
Catánia
Ionian Sea
Pantelleria (Ital.)
MALTA
West from Greenwich
East from Greenwich

1 : 24 000 000

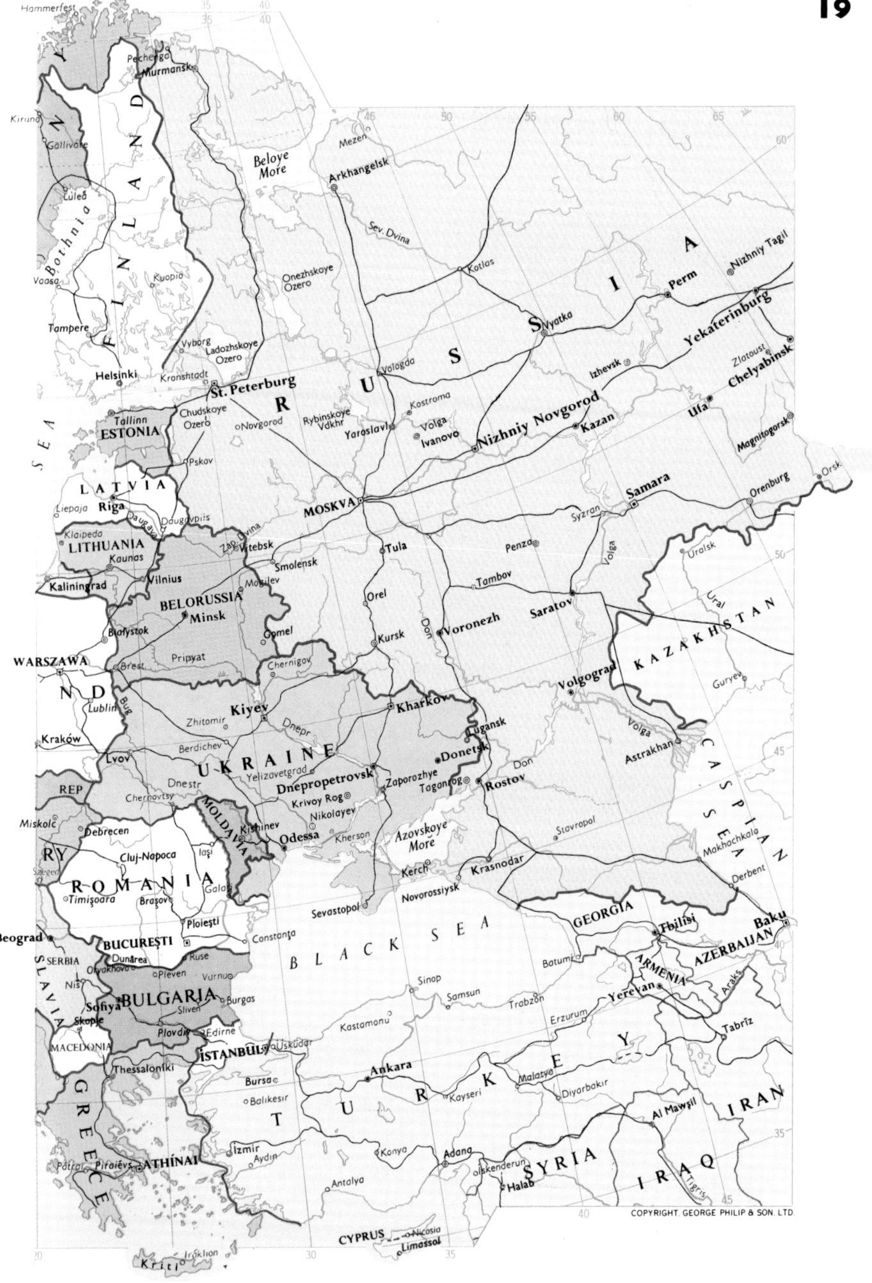
RUSSIA
FINLAND
ESTONIA
LATVIA
LITHUANIA
BELORUSSIA
UKRAINE
MOLDAVIA
ROMANIA
BULGARIA
GREECE
TURKEY
GEORGIA
ARMENIA
AZERBAIJAN
KAZAKHSTAN
SYRIA
IRAQ
IRAN
CYPRUS
MACEDONIA
SERBIA
BLACK SEA
CASPIAN SEA
Beloye More
Onezhskoye Ozero
Ladozhskoye Ozero
Azovskoye More
MOSKVA
St. Peterburg
Arkhangelsk
Murmansk
Nizhniy Novgorod
Kazan
Samara
Perm
Yekaterinburg
Chelyabinsk
Volgograd
Saratov
Voronezh
Rostov
Kiyev
Kharkov
Dnepropetrovsk
Donetsk
Odessa
Minsk
Riga
Tallinn
Vilnius
Helsinki
WARSZAWA
BUCUREŞTI
Sofiya
İSTANBUL
Ankara
ATHÍNAI
Tbilisi
Baku
Yerevan
COPYRIGHT GEORGE PHILIP & SON LTD

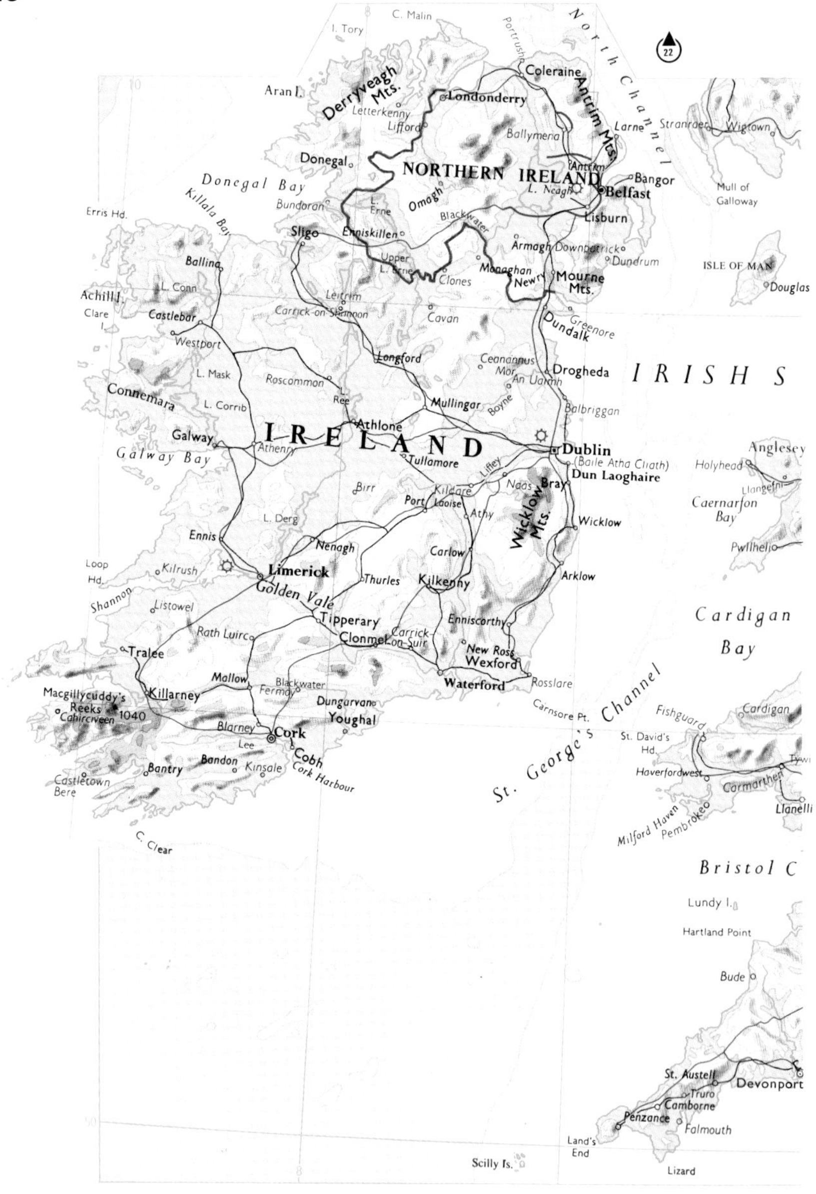

C. Malin
I. Tory
North Channel
C. Malin
Aran I.
Derryveagh Mts.
Londonderry
Coleraine
Antrim Mts.
Letterkenny
Lifford
Ballymena
Larne
Stranraer
Wigtown
Donegal
NORTHERN IRELAND
Antrim
Belfast
Bangor
Donegal Bay
L. Neagh
Lisburn
Mull of
Galloway
Bundoran
Omagh
Blackwater
ISLE OF MAN
Erris Hd.
Killala Bay
Sligo
Enniskillen
L. Erne
Armagh
Downpatrick
Dundrum
Ballina
Clones
Monaghan
Newry
Mourne Mts.
Douglas
Achill I.
L. Conn
Leitrim
Greenore
Clare
Castlebar
Carrick-on-Shannon
Cavan
Dundalk
Westport
L. Mask
Longford
Drogheda
IRISH S
Connemara
Roscommon
Ceanannus Mor/An Uaimh
L. Corrib
Ree
Mullingar
Balbriggan
Galway
Athlone
IRELAND
Boyne
Dublin
Anglesey
Galway Bay
Athenry
Tullamore
Liffey
(Baile Átha Cliath)
Holyhead
Dun Laoghaire
Llangefni
Birr
Kildare
Naas
Bray
Caernarfon Bay
Ennis
L. Derg
Port Laoise
Athy
Wicklow Mts.
Wicklow
Pwllheli
Loop Hd.
Nenagh
Carlow
Arklow
Kilrush
Limerick
Thurles
Kilkenny
Shannon
Golden Vale
Listowel
Tipperary
Enniscorthy
Cardigan Bay
Rath Luirc
Clonmel
Carrick-on-Suir
Tralee
Mallow
New Ross
Wexford
Cardigan
Macgillycuddy's Reeks
Blackwater
Fermoy
Dungarvan
Waterford
Rosslare
Fishguard
Killarney
Youghal
Carnsore Pt.
Cahirciveen 1040
Blarney
Cork
St. David's Hd.
Tywi
Castletown Bere
Bantry
Bandon
Lee
Cobh
Kinsale
Cork Harbour
St. George's Channel
Haverfordwest
Carmarthen
Llanelli
Milford Haven
Pembroke
C. Clear
Bristol C
Lundy I.
Hartland Point
Bude
St. Austell
Devonport
Truro
Camborne
Penzance
Falmouth
Land's End
Scilly Is.
Lizard

22

1 : 4 000 000

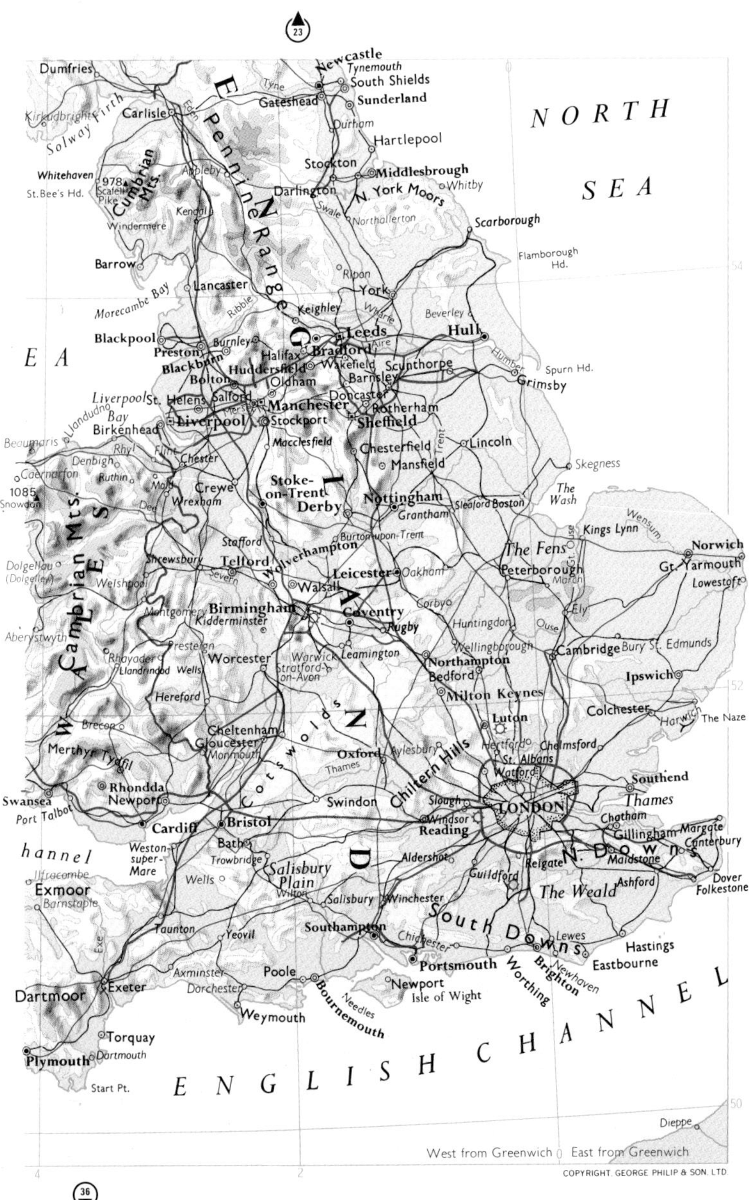
23
NORTH SEA
Dumfries
Newcastle
Tynemouth
South Shields
Gateshead
Sunderland
Carlisle
Kirkcudbright
Solway Firth
Durham
Hartlepool
Pennine Range
Cumbrian Mts.
Whitehaven
St. Bee's Hd.
978 Scafell Pike
Appleby
Stockton
Middlesbrough
Whitby
Darlington
N. York Moors
Northallerton
Kendal
Windermere
Scarborough
Flamborough Hd.
Barrow
Ripon
Lancaster
York
Morecambe Bay
Keighley
Beverley
Blackpool
Leeds
Hull
Preston
Burnley
Halifax
Bradford
Blackburn
Huddersfield
Wakefield
Scunthorpe
Spurn Hd.
Bolton
Oldham
Barnsley
Grimsby
Liverpool Bay
St. Helens
Salford
Manchester
Doncaster
Rotherham
Liverpool
Stockport
Sheffield
Birkenhead
Llandudno
Beaumaris
Rhyl
Flint
Macclesfield
Chesterfield
Lincoln
Denbigh
Chester
Mansfield
Skegness
Caernarfon
Ruthin
Mold
Crewe
Stoke-on-Trent
1085 Snowdon
Wrexham
Derby
Nottingham
The Wash
Sleaford
Boston
Grantham
Kings Lynn
Stafford
Burton-upon-Trent
The Fens
Norwich
Dolgellau (Dolgelley)
Shrewsbury
Telford
Wolverhampton
Leicester
Oakham
Peterborough
Gt. Yarmouth
Welshpool
Walsall
March
Lowestoft
Cambrian Mts.
Corby
Ely
Montgomery
Birmingham
Coventry
Kidderminster
Huntingdon
Aberystwyth
Rugby
Presteign
Wellingborough
Cambridge
Bury St. Edmunds
Rhayader
Worcester
Warwick
Leamington
Northampton
Llandrindod Wells
Stratford-on-Avon
Bedford
Ipswich
Hereford
Milton Keynes
Colchester
Luton
Harwich
The Naze
Brecon
Cheltenham
Gloucester
Hertford
Chelmsford
Merthyr Tydfil
Monmouth
Oxford
Aylesbury
St. Albans
Cotswolds
Chiltern Hills
Watford
Rhondda
Southend
Swansea
Newport
Swindon
Slough
LONDON
Thames
Port Talbot
Cardiff
Bristol
Windsor
Chatham
Reading
Gillingham
Margate
Bath
Canterbury
Weston-super-Mare
Trowbridge
Aldershot
N. Downs
Maidstone
Salisbury Plain
Guildford
Reigate
Dover
Ilfracombe
Exmoor
Wells
Wilton
Salisbury
Winchester
The Weald
Ashford
Folkestone
Barnstaple
Taunton
Southampton
South Downs
Lewes
Yeovil
Chichester
Hastings
Axminster
Poole
Portsmouth
Worthing
Brighton
Newhaven
Eastbourne
Exeter
Dorchester
Bournemouth
Newport
Isle of Wight
Dartmoor
Needles
Weymouth
Torquay
Plymouth
Dartmouth
Start Pt.
ENGLISH CHANNEL
Dieppe
West from Greenwich
East from Greenwich
36

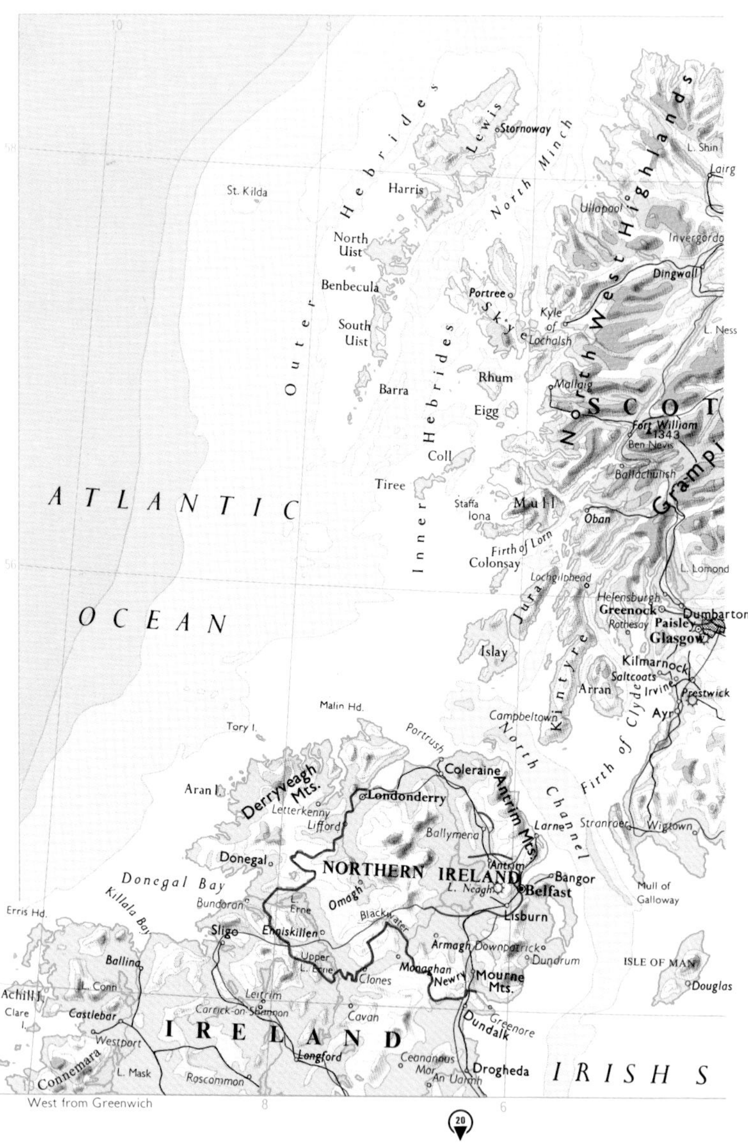
ATLANTIC
OCEAN
Outer Hebrides
Inner Hebrides
Lewis
Stornoway
North Minch
Harris
St. Kilda
North Uist
Benbecula
South Uist
Barra
Skye
Portree
Kyle of Lochalsh
Rhum
Eigg
Coll
Tiree
Staffa
Iona
Mull
Oban
Firth of Lorn
Colonsay
Jura
Islay
Lochgilphead
Kintyre
Arran
Campbeltown
North West Highlands
L. Shin
Lairg
Ullapool
Invergordo
Dingwall
L. Ness
Mallaig
Fort William
1343
Ben Nevis
Ballachulish
SCOT
Grampi
L. Lomond
Helensburgh
Greenock
Dumbarton
Rothesay
Paisley
Glasgow
Kilmarnock
Saltcoats
Irvine
Prestwick
Ayr
Firth of Clyde
North Channel
Stranraer
Wigtown
Mull of Galloway
ISLE OF MAN
Douglas
Malin Hd.
Tory I.
Portrush
Coleraine
Antrim Mts.
Aran I.
Derryveagh Mts.
Letterkenny
Lifford
Londonderry
Ballymena
Larne
Donegal
NORTHERN IRELAND
Antrim
L. Neagh
Bangor
Belfast
Lisburn
Donegal Bay
Killala Bay
Bundoran
Omagh
L. Erne
Blackwater
Erris Hd.
Sligo
Enniskillen
Armagh
Downpatrick
Dundrum
Ballina
Upper L. Erne
Monaghan
Clones
Newry
Mourne Mts.
Achill I.
L. Conn
Leitrim
Clare I.
Castlebar
Carrick-on-Shannon
Cavan
Dundalk
Greenore
Westport
IRELAND
Connemara
L. Mask
Roscommon
Longford
Ceanannus Mor
An Uaimh
Drogheda
IRISH S
West from Greenwich
10
9
8
6
58
56
20

1 : 4 000 000

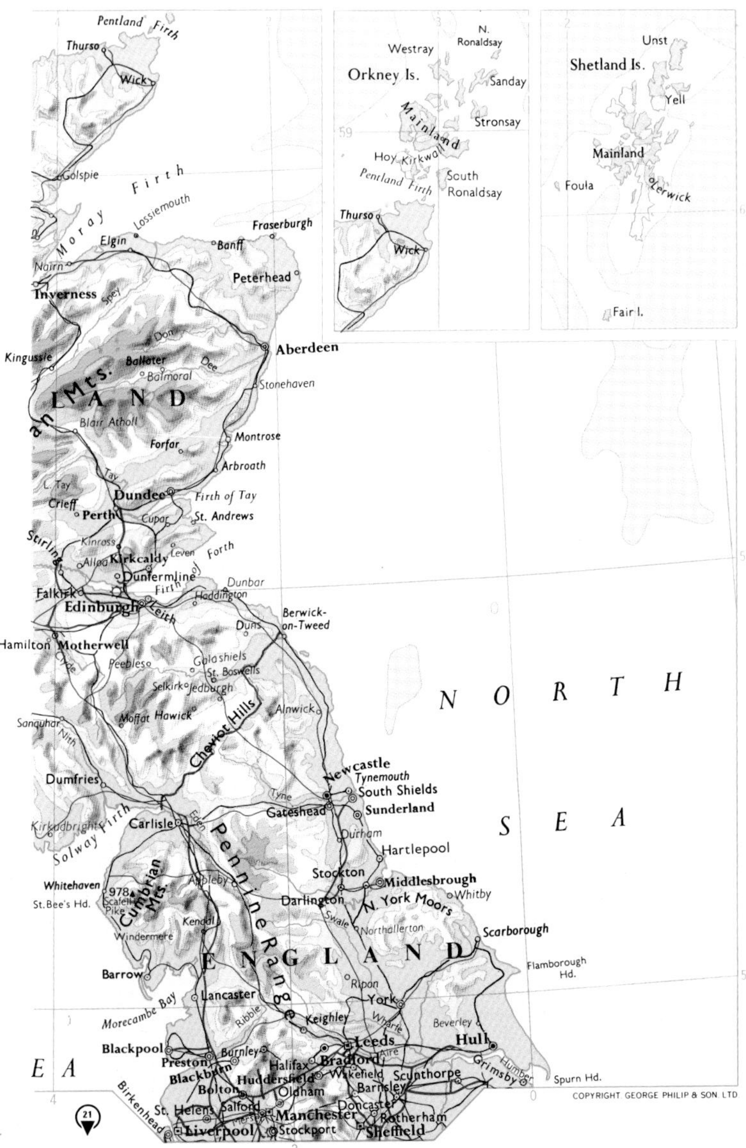

Pentland Firth
Thurso
Wick
Golspie
Moray Firth
Lossiemouth
Fraserburgh
Elgin
Banff
Nairn
Peterhead
Inverness
Spey
Don
Aberdeen
Kingussie
Ballater
Balmoral
Dee
Stonehaven
Blair Atholl
Montrose
Forfar
Arbroath
Tay
L. Tay
Dundee
Firth of Tay
Crieff
Perth
Cupar
St. Andrews
Kinross
Leven
Forth
Alloa
Kirkcaldy
Dunfermline
Firth of
Dunbar
Falkirk
Edinburgh
Leith
Haddington
Berwick-
on-Tweed
Duns
Hamilton
Motherwell
Clyde
Galashiels
Peebles
St. Boswells
Selkirk
Jedburgh
Moffat
Hawick
Cheviot Hills
Alnwick
Sanquhar
Nith
Newcastle
Tynemouth
South Shields
Dumfries
Tyne
Gateshead
Sunderland
Kirkcudbright
Carlisle
Eden
Solway Firth
Pennine Range
Durham
Hartlepool
Cumbrian Mts.
Stockton
Middlesbrough
Whitehaven
978
Scafell Pike
Appleby
Whitby
St. Bee's Hd.
Darlington
N. York Moors
Swale
Northallerton
Kendal
Scarborough
Windermere
ENGLAND
Flamborough
Hd.
Barrow
Ripon
Lancaster
York
Morecambe Bay
Ribble
Keighley
Wharfe
Beverley
Hull
Blackpool
Leeds
Preston
Burnley
Halifax
Bradford
Aire
Grimsby
Humber
Blackburn
Huddersfield
Wakefield
Scunthorpe
Spurn Hd.
Bolton
Oldham
Barnsley
Birkenhead
St. Helens
Salford
Doncaster
Manchester
Rotherham
Liverpool
Stockport
Sheffield
NORTH
SEA
EA
Orkney Is.
Westray
N.
Ronaldsay
Sanday
Mainland
Stronsay
Hoy
Kirkwall
South
Ronaldsay
Pentland Firth
Thurso
Wick
Shetland Is.
Unst
Yell
Mainland
Foula
Lerwick
Fair I.
59
60
56
54
4
3
2
0
21

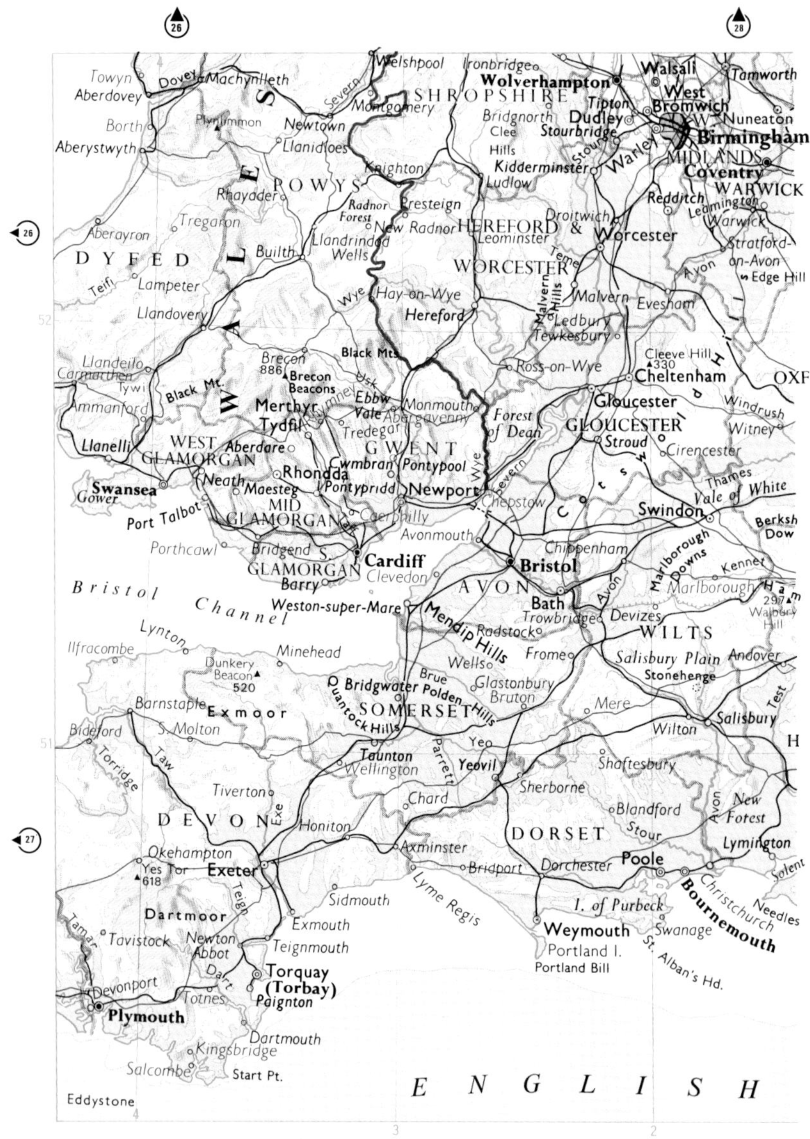

26
28
26
27
Towyn
Aberdovey
Machynlleth
Dovey
Borth
Aberystwyth
Plynlimmon
Newtown
Llanidloes
Welshpool
Severn
Montgomery
Ironbridge
Wolverhampton
SHROPSHIRE
Walsall
Tamworth
West Bromwich
Tipton
Dudley
Bridgnorth
Clee Hills
Stourbridge
Nuneaton
Birmingham
W. MIDLANDS
Coventry
Warley
Stour
Kidderminster
Ludlow
Knighton
POWYS
Rhayader
Radnor Forest
Presteign
New Radnor
WARWICK
Redditch
Leamington
Warwick
Droitwich
HEREFORD &
Worcester
Leominster
WORCESTER
Teme
Stratford-on-Avon
Avon
Edge Hill
Tregaron
Aberayron
DYFED
Builth
Llandrindod Wells
Teifi
Lampeter
Llandovery
Wye
Hay-on-Wye
Hereford
Malvern Hills
Malvern
Evesham
Ledbury
Tewkesbury
52
Llandeilo
Carmarthen
Tywi
Ammanford
Brecon
886
Brecon Beacons
Black Mt.
Black Mts
Usk
Ross-on-Wye
Cleeve Hill
330
Cheltenham
OXF
Merthyr Tydfil
Ebbw Vale
Monmouth
Abergavenny
Tredegar
Forest of Dean
Gloucester
GLOUCESTER
Windrush
Witney
Stroud
Cirencester
Llanelli
WEST GLAMORGAN
Aberdare
GWENT
Cwmbran
Pontypool
Wye
Rhondda
Neath
Swansea
Gower
Maesteg
Pontypridd
Newport
Severn
Chepstow
Thames
Vale of White
Swindon
Port Talbot
MID GLAMORGAN
Caerphilly
Avonmouth
Berksh Dow
Porthcawl
Bridgend
S. GLAMORGAN
Cardiff
Chippenham
Bristol
Marlborough Downs
Kennet
Barry
Clevedon
AVON
Bath
Avon
Marlborough
Ham
297
Walbury Hill
Bristol Channel
Weston-super-Mare
Mendip Hills
Trowbridge
Devizes
Lynton
Radstock
WILTS
Ilfracombe
Minehead
Wells
Frome
Salisbury Plain
Andover
Dunkery Beacon
520
Brue
Glastonbury
Stonehenge
Bridgwater
Polden Hills
Bruton
Test
Barnstaple
Exmoor
Quantock Hills
SOMERSET
Mere
Salisbury
Bideford
S. Molton
Wilton
H
51
Torridge
Taw
Taunton
Wellington
Parrett
Yeo
Yeovil
Shaftesbury
Sherborne
Tiverton
Chard
Blandford
New Forest
DEVON
Exe
Honiton
DORSET
Stour
Avon
Lymington
Okehampton
Axminster
Yes Tor
618
Exeter
Bridport
Dorchester
Poole
Solent
Teign
Sidmouth
Lyme Regis
I. of Purbeck
Christchurch
Needles
Bournemouth
Dartmoor
Exmouth
Weymouth
Swanage
Tamar
Tavistock
Newton Abbot
Teignmouth
Portland I.
Portland Bill
St. Alban's Hd.
Dart
Torquay (Torbay)
Devonport
Totnes
Paignton
Plymouth
Dartmouth
Kingsbridge
Salcombe
Start Pt.
ENGLISH
Eddystone
4
3
2

1 : 2 000 000

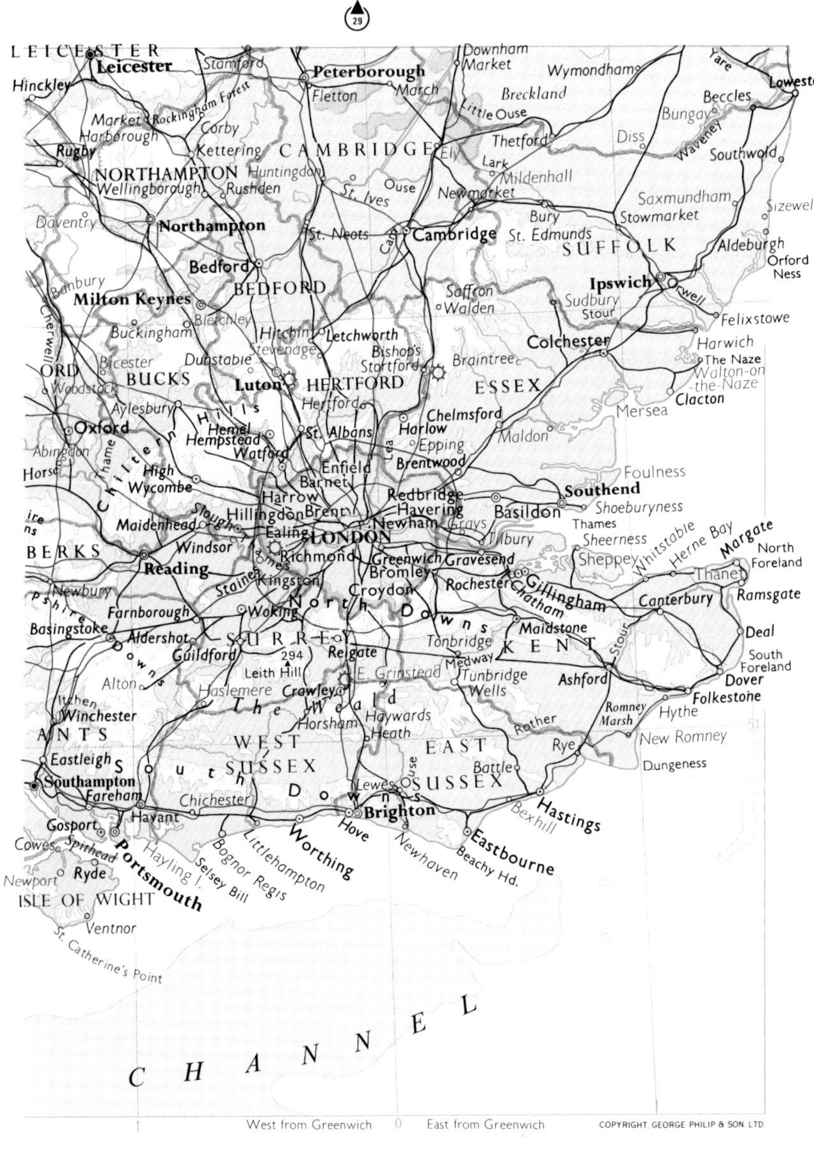

LEICESTER Leicester Stamford Peterborough Downham Market Wymondham Yare Lowestoft
Hinckley March Little Ouse Beccles
Market Rockingham Forest Corby Fletton Breckland Bungay Waveney Southwold
Harborough Kettering CAMBRIDGE Ely Thetford Diss
Rugby NORTHAMPTON Huntingdon Lark Mildenhall Saxmundham Sizewell
Wellingborough Rushden St. Ives Ouse Newmarket Stowmarket
Daventry Northampton St. Neots Cambridge Bury SUFFOLK Aldeburgh
St. Edmunds Orford Ness
Bedford Ipswich Orwell
Milton Keynes BEDFORD Saffron Sudbury Felixstowe
Buckingham Bletchley Walden Stour
ORD Bicester Dunstable Hitchin Stevenage Letchworth Bishop's Braintree Colchester Harwich
Woodstock BUCKS Luton HERTFORD Stortford ESSEX The Naze
Aylesbury Hertford St. Albans Chelmsford Walton-on-the-Naze
Oxford Hemel Harlow Maldon Mersea Clacton
Abingdon Hempstead Watford Epping
Horse High Enfield Brentwood Foulness
Wycombe Barnet Redbridge Southend
BERKS Harrow Brent Havering Basildon Shoeburyness
Maidenhead Hillingdon Newham Grays Thames
Slough Ealing LONDON Tilbury Sheerness Sheppey Whitstable Herne Bay Margate
Newbury Windsor Richmond Greenwich Gravesend North Foreland
Reading Staines Kingston Bromley Rochester Gillingham Thanet
Farnborough Woking Croydon Chatham Canterbury Ramsgate
Basingstoke Aldershot North Downs Maidstone Deal
Guildford SURREY 294 Reigate KENT South Foreland
Alton Leith Hill E. Grinstead Tonbridge Ashford Dover
Winchester Haslemere Crawley Tunbridge Wells Folkestone
ANTS The Weald Haywards Rother Romney Marsh Hythe
Horsham Heath New Romney
Eastleigh WEST EAST Rye 31
Southampton SUSSEX SUSSEX Battle Dungeness
Fareham Chichester South Downs Lewes Hastings
Gosport Havant Brighton Bexhill
Cowes Spithead Hove Eastbourne
Newport Ryde Littlehampton Worthing Newhaven Beachy Hd.
ISLE OF WIGHT Portsmouth Bognor Regis Selsey Bill
Ventnor Hayling I.
St. Catherine's Point

C H A N N E L

28

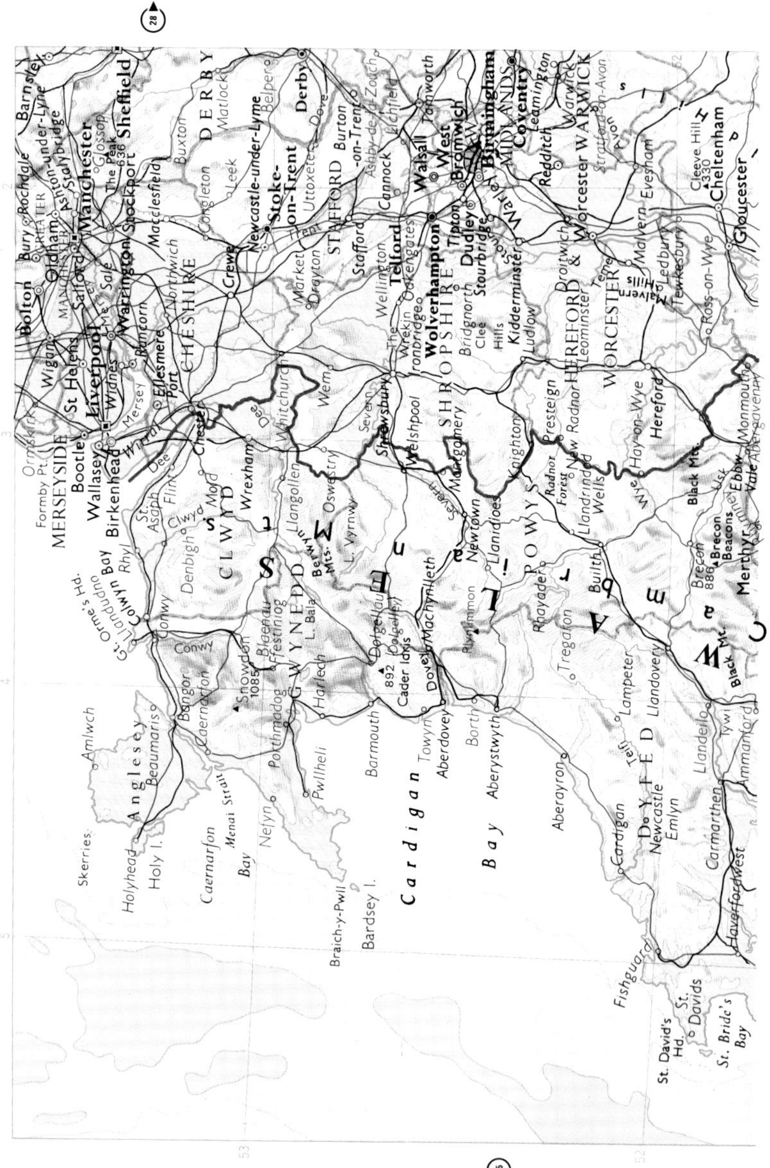
MERSEYSIDE
Formby Pt.
Ormskirk
Bootle
Wallasey
Birkenhead
Liverpool
St Helens
Wigan
Bolton
Bury
Rochdale
Oldham
Manchester
Salford
Stockport
Ashton-under-Lyne
Stalybridge
Barnsley
Sheffield
The Peak
636
Glossop
Warrington
Widnes
Runcorn
Ellesmere Port
Wirral
Mersey
Dee
Chester
CHESHIRE
Northwich
Macclesfield
Buxton
DERBY
Matlock
Belper
Derby
Congleton
Leek
Crewe
Newcastle-under-Lyme
Stoke-on-Trent
Uttoxeter
Burton-on-Trent
Ashby-de-la-Zouch
Lichfield
Tamworth
STAFFORD
Stafford
Market Drayton
Trent
Cannock
Walsall
West Bromwich
Birmingham
Coventry
WEST MIDLANDS
Wolverhampton
Telford
Wellington
Oakengates
The Wrekin
Ironbridge
Tipton
Dudley
Stourbridge
Kidderminster
Bridgnorth
Clee Hills
Ludlow
SHROPSHIRE
Shrewsbury
Whitchurch
Wem
Severn
Oswestry
Welshpool
Montgomery
HEREFORD & WORCESTER
Leominster
Droitwich
Worcester
Redditch
Leamington
Warwick
WARWICK
Stratford-on-Avon
Avon
Evesham
Malvern
Malvern Hills
Ledbury
Tewkesbury
Cleeve Hill
330
Cheltenham
Gloucester
Ross-on-Wye
Hereford
Hay-on-Wye
Presteign
New Radnor
Radnor Forest
Knighton
Llandrindod Wells
Wye
Builth
Monmouth
Abergavenny
Black Mts.
Usk
Ebbw Vale
Brecon
Brecon Beacons
886
Merthyr
Llandovery
Llandeilo
Tywi
Ammanford
Black Mt.
POWYS
Newtown
Llanidloes
Rhayader
Plynlimmon
Machynlleth
Dovey
Aberdovey
Towyn
Borth
Aberystwyth
Tregaron
Lampeter
Teifi
Aberayron
DYFED
Cardigan
Newcastle Emlyn
Carmarthen
Haverfordwest
Fishguard
St. Davids
St. David's Hd.
St. Bride's Bay
Cardigan Bay
CLWYD
Rhyl
Colwyn Bay
St. Asaph
Flint
Mold
Denbigh
Clwyd
Wrexham
Llangollen
Berwyn Mts.
L. Vyrnwy
GWYNEDD
L. Bala
Blaenau Ffestiniog
Dolgellau (Dolgelley)
Cader Idris
892
Barmouth
Harlech
Porthmadog
Snowdon
1085
Conwy
Llandudno
Great Orme's Hd.
Bangor
Caernarfon
Beaumaris
Anglesey
Amlwch
Holyhead
Holy I.
Skerries
Menai Strait
Caernarfon Bay
Nefyn
Pwllheli
Braich-y-Pwll
Bardsey I.
WALES

1 : 2 000 000

35

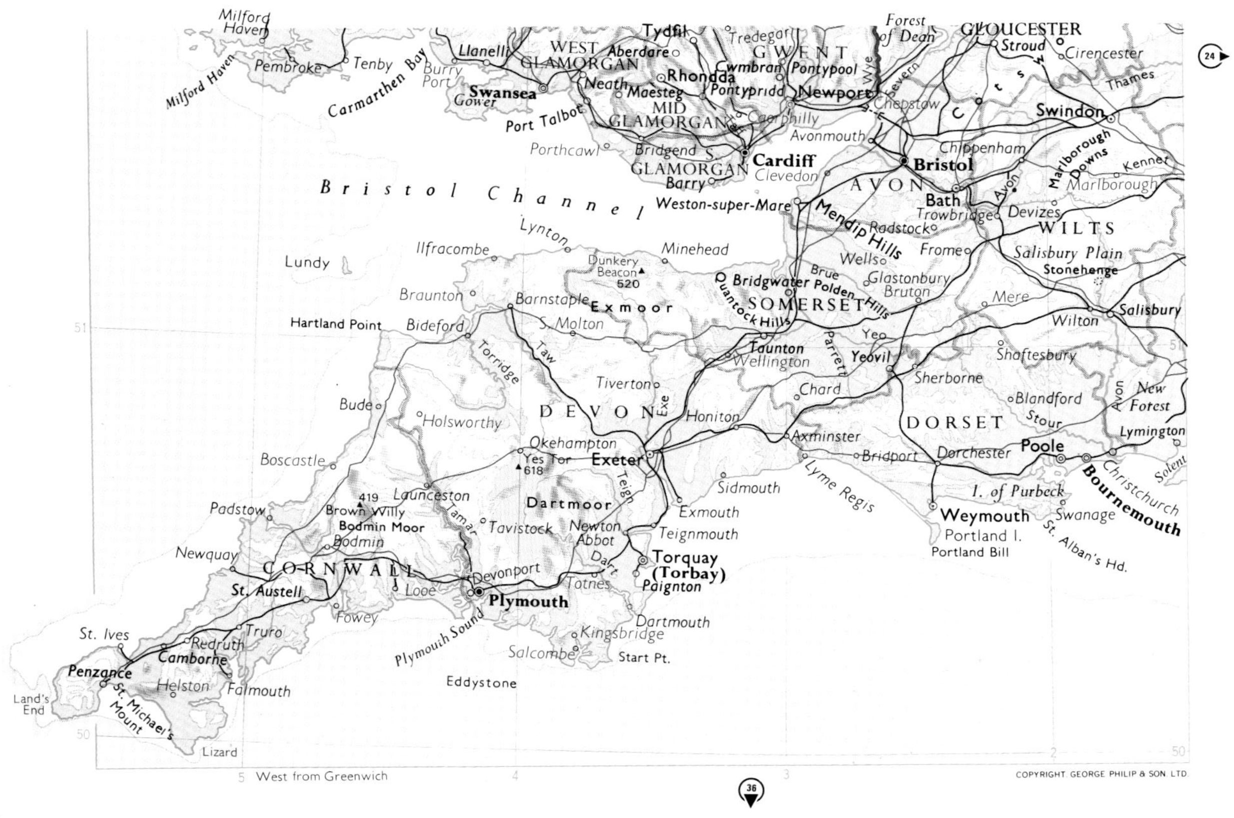
Milford Haven
Milford Haven
Pembroke
Tenby
Carmarthen Bay
Burry Port
Llanelli
Swansea
Gower
Port Talbot
Porthcawl
WEST GLAMORGAN
Neath
Aberdare
Merthyr Tydfil
Maesteg
MID GLAMORGAN
Bridgend
S. GLAMORGAN
Barry
Rhondda
Pontypridd
Caerphilly
Cardiff
Tredegar
GWENT
Cwmbran
Pontypool
Newport
Wye
Severn
Chepstow
Forest of Dean
Avonmouth
Clevedon
GLOUCESTER
Stroud
Cirencester
Thames
Swindon
Chippenham
Bristol
AVON
Bath
Marlborough Downs
Kennet
Marlborough
Devizes
WILTS
Trowbridge
Radstock
Frome
Salisbury Plain
Stonehenge
Salisbury
Wilton
Mere
Bristol Channel
Weston-super-Mare
Mendip Hills
Wells
Glastonbury
Bruton
Brue
Bridgwater
Polden Hills
Quantock Hills
SOMERSET
Lundy
Ilfracombe
Lynton
Minehead
Dunkery Beacon
520
Exmoor
Braunton
Barnstaple
S. Molton
Hartland Point
Bideford
Torridge
Taw
Taunton
Wellington
Parrett
Yeo
Yeovil
Sherborne
Shaftesbury
Blandford
Stour
Avon
New Forest
Lymington
Solent
Christchurch
Bournemouth
Poole
DORSET
Dorchester
Bridport
Chard
Tiverton
Exe
DEVON
Honiton
Axminster
Lyme Regis
Bude
Holsworthy
Okehampton
Yes Tor
618
Exeter
Teign
Sidmouth
Exmouth
Teignmouth
Boscastle
419
Brown Willy
Bodmin Moor
Launceston
Tamar
Tavistock
Dartmoor
Newton Abbot
Padstow
Bodmin
Newquay
CORNWALL
St. Austell
Looe
Devonport
Plymouth
Dart
Totnes
Torquay (Torbay)
Paignton
Dartmouth
Kingsbridge
Salcombe
Start Pt.
Fowey
Plymouth Sound
Eddystone
I. of Purbeck
Swanage
St. Alban's Hd.
Weymouth
Portland I.
Portland Bill
St. Ives
Truro
Redruth
Camborne
Penzance
Helston
Falmouth
St. Michael's Mount
Land's End
Lizard
51
50
5
4
3
2
West from Greenwich
24
36

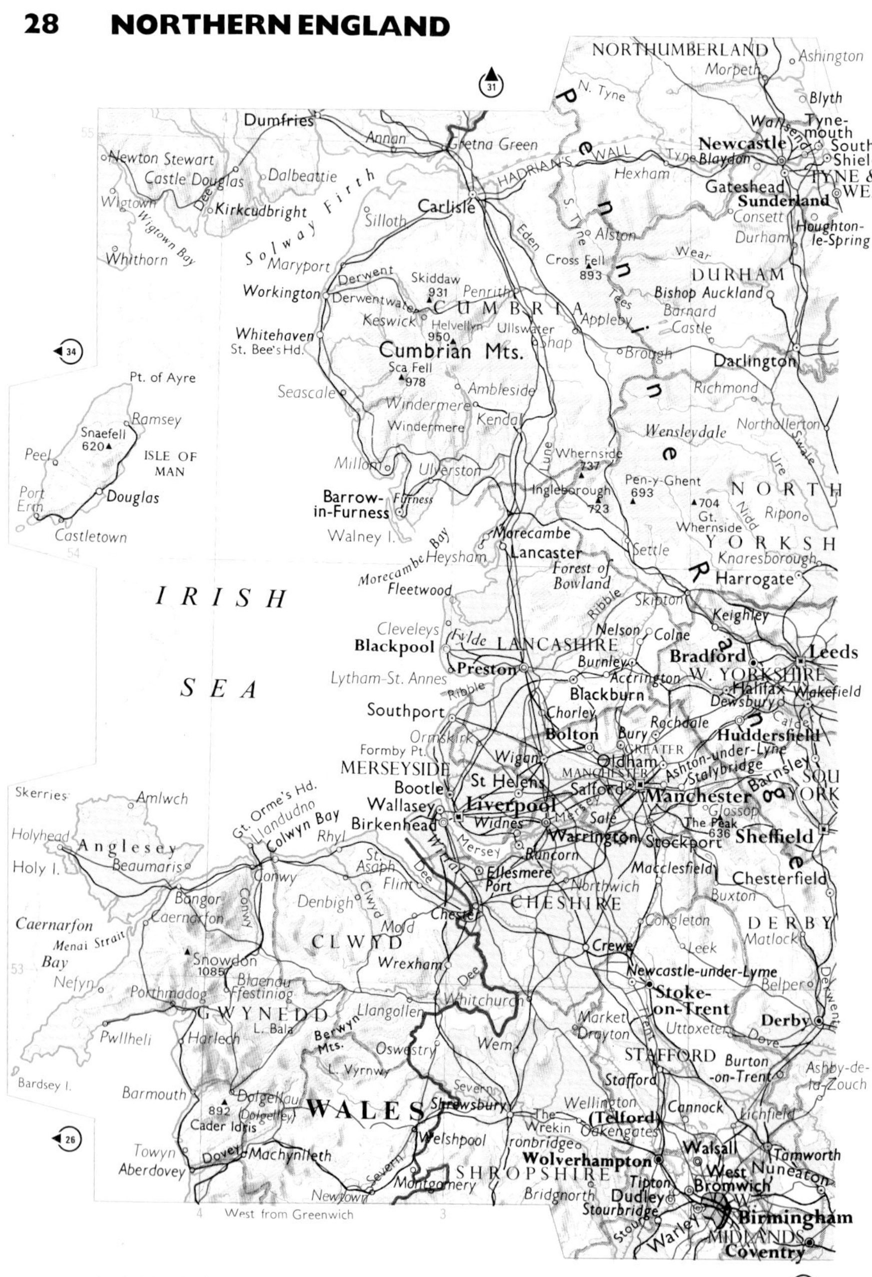
NORTHUMBERLAND
Ashington
Morpeth
Blyth
N. Tyne
Pennine Range
Dumfries
Annan
Gretna Green
Wallsend
Tynemouth
Newcastle
South Shields
TYNE & WEAR
Blaydon
Hexham
HADRIAN'S WALL
Gateshead
Sunderland
Newton Stewart
Castle Douglas
Dalbeattie
Dee
Kirkcudbright
Solway Firth
Carlisle
Silloth
Wigtown
Wigtown Bay
Whithorn
Maryport
Eden
S. Tyne
Alston
Consett
Durham
Houghton-le-Spring
Cross Fell 893
Wear
DURHAM
Derwent
Skiddaw 931
Penrith
Workington
Derwentwater
CUMBRIA
Tees
Bishop Auckland
Keswick
Helvellyn 950
Ullswater
Appleby
Barnard Castle
Whitehaven
St. Bee's Hd.
Shap
Cumbrian Mts.
Brough
Darlington
Sca Fell 978
Richmond
Pt. of Ayre
Seascale
Ambleside
Windermere
Kendal
Ramsey
Snaefell 620
ISLE OF MAN
Peel
Wensleydale
Northallerton
Swale
Ure
Millom
Ulverston
Lune
Whernside 737
Port Erin
Douglas
Barrow-in-Furness
Furness
Ingleborough 723
Pen-y-Ghent 693
704 Gt. Whernside
NORTH YORKSHIRE
Nidd
Ripon
Castletown
Walney I.
Morecambe Bay
Morecambe
Lancaster
Heysham
Settle
Knaresborough
Forest of Bowland
Harrogate
Fleetwood
IRISH SEA
Ribble
Skipton
Keighley
Cleveleys
Fylde
Nelson
Colne
Blackpool
LANCASHIRE
Bradford
Leeds
Preston
Burnley
W. YORKSHIRE
Lytham-St. Annes
Accrington
Halifax
Wakefield
Blackburn
Dewsbury
Southport
Chorley
Calder
Rochdale
Huddersfield
Ormskirk
Bolton
Bury
Formby Pt.
GREATER MANCHESTER
Oldham
Ashton-under-Lyne
MERSEYSIDE
Wigan
Stalybridge
Barnsley
SOUTH YORKSHIRE
Bootle
St Helens
Salford
Manchester
Skerries
Amlwch
Gt. Orme's Hd.
Wallasey
Liverpool
Llandudno
Colwyn Bay
Birkenhead
Widnes
Mersey
Sale
Glossop
The Peak 636
Sheffield
Holyhead
Anglesey
Rhyl
Wirral
Warrington
Stockport
Holy I.
Beaumaris
St. Asaph
Runcorn
Conwy
Flint
Dee
Ellesmere Port
Macclesfield
Chesterfield
Bangor
Denbigh
Clwyd
Northwich
CHESHIRE
Buxton
Caernarfon
Chester
Congleton
DERBY
Menai Strait
Mold
Matlock
Caernarfon Bay
CLWYD
Leek
Snowdon 1085
Wrexham
Crewe
Nefyn
Blaenau Ffestiniog
Newcastle-under-Lyme
Belper
Derwent
Porthmadog
Stoke-on-Trent
GWYNEDD
Llangollen
Whitchurch
Market Drayton
Trent
Derby
L. Bala
Uttoxeter
Dove
Pwllheli
Harlech
Berwyn Mts.
Oswestry
Wem
STAFFORD
Burton-on-Trent
Ashby-de-la-Zouch
L. Vyrnwy
Stafford
Bardsey I.
Barmouth
Severn
Dolgellau (Dolgelley)
892
Cader Idris
WALES
Shrewsbury
Wellington
The Wrekin
(Telford)
Cannock
Lichfield
Oakengates
Towyn
Dovey
Machynlleth
Welshpool
Ironbridge
Walsall
Tamworth
Aberdovey
Wolverhampton
West Bromwich
Nuneaton
Montgomery
SHROPSHIRE
Tipton
Newtown
Bridgnorth
Dudley
Birmingham
Stourbridge
Warley
Stour
W. MIDLANDS
Coventry
West from Greenwich
31
34
26
24

1 : 2 000 000

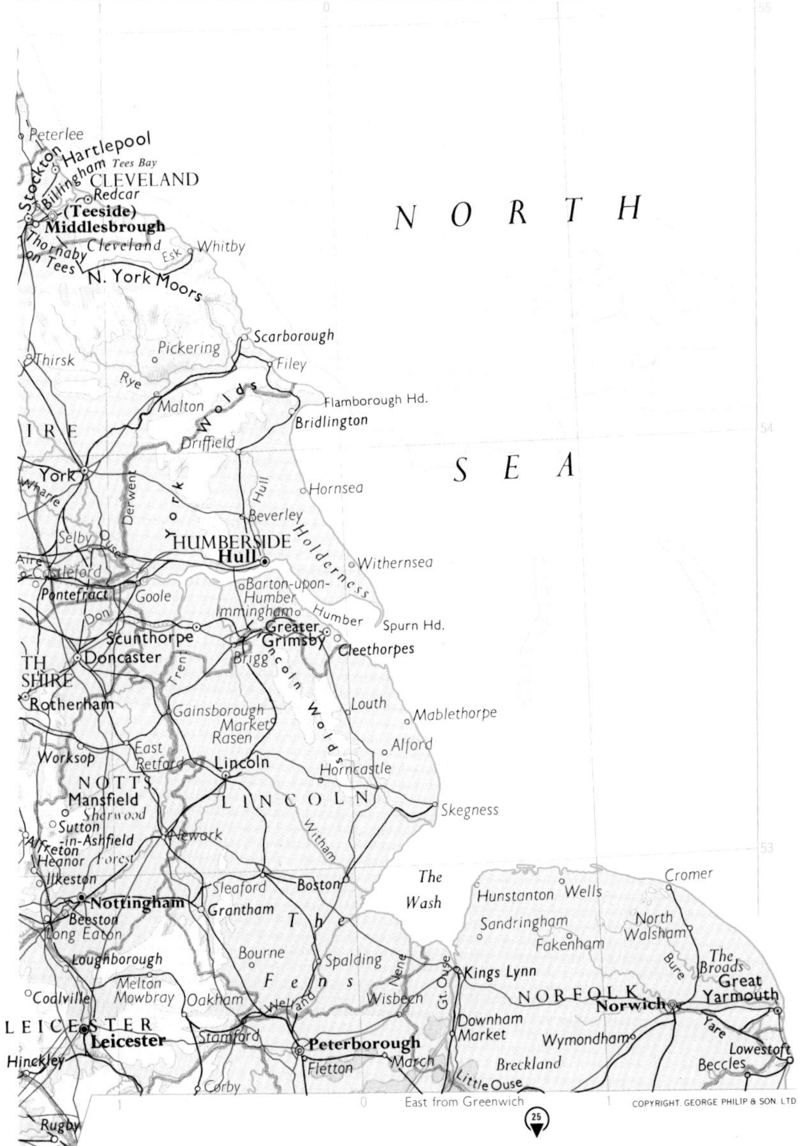

Peterlee
Hartlepool
Stockton
Billingham *Tees Bay*
CLEVELAND
Redcar
(Teeside)
Middlesbrough
Thornaby
on Tees
Cleveland *Esk* Whitby
N. York Moors

Thirsk
Pickering
Scarborough
Rye
Filey
Malton *Wolds*
Flamborough Hd.
IRE
Driffield
Bridlington

York
Wharfe
Derwent
Hull
Hornsea
SEA
Beverley
Selby
Ouse
HUMBERSIDE
Holderness
Aire
Castleford
Hull
Withernsea
Pontefract
Don
Goole
Barton-upon-
Humber
Immingham
Humber
Spurn Hd.
Scunthorpe
Greater
Grimsby
TH
Doncaster
Brigg
Cleethorpes
SHIRE
Trent
Lincoln
Rotherham
Gainsborough
Louth
Market
Mablethorpe
Rasen
Worksop
East
Wolds
Alford
Retford
Lincoln
NOTTS
Horncastle
Mansfield
LINCOLN
Skegness
Sherwood
Sutton
-in-Ashfield
Witham
Kirkby
Alfreton
Newark
Heanor *Forest*
Ilkeston
The
Sleaford
Boston
Cromer
Nottingham
Grantham
Wash
Hunstanton Wells
Beeston
The
North
Long Eaton
Sandringham
Walsham
Bourne
Loughborough
Spalding
Fakenham
*The
Broads*
Melton
Fens
Nene
Kings Lynn
Great
Coalville
Mowbray
Oakham
Gt. Ouse
Yarmouth
Welland
Wisbech
NORFOLK
Norwich
LEICESTER
Downham
Yare
Leicester
Stamford
Market
Wymondham
Lowestoft
Hinckley
Peterborough
March
Breckland
Beccles
Fletton
Little Ouse
Corby

Rugby

East from Greenwich

COPYRIGHT GEORGE PHILIP & SON. LTD

N O R T H

S E A

Y
o
r
k

L
i
n
c
o
l
n
  W
  o
  l
  d
  s

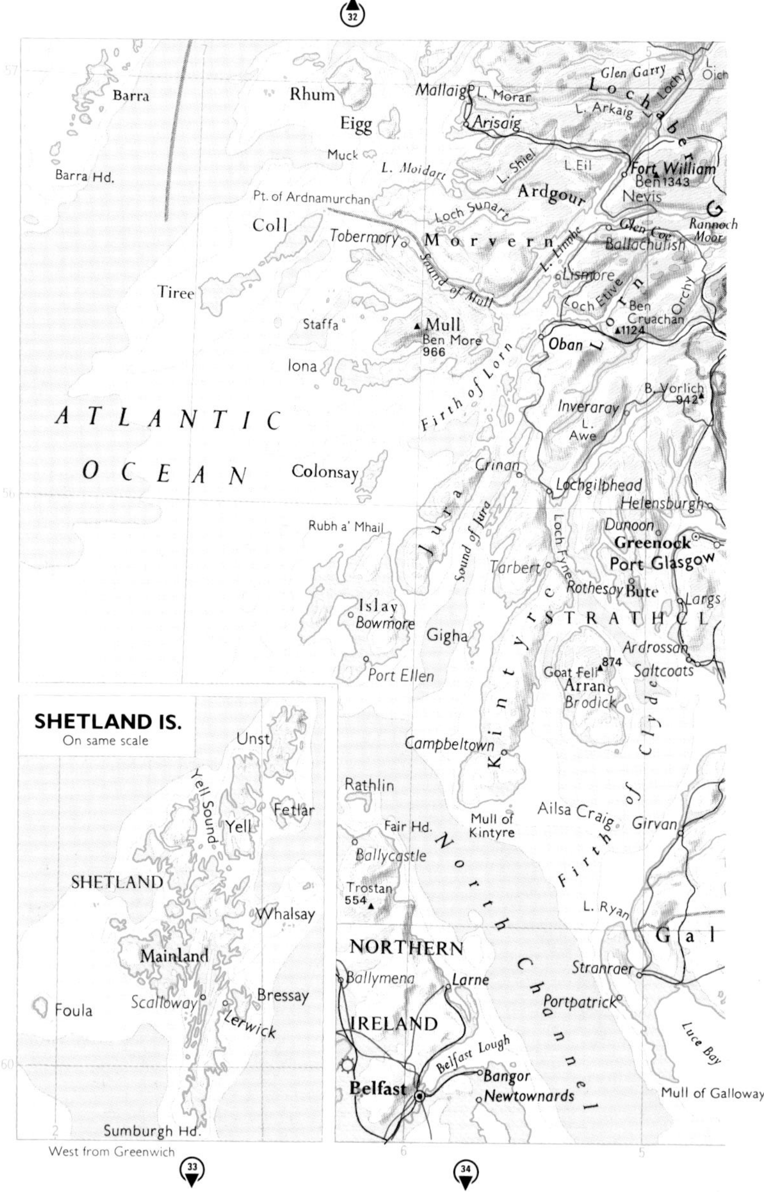
32
Barra
Barra Hd.
Rhum
Eigg
Muck
Mallaig
L. Morar
Arisaig
L. Arkaig
Glen Garry
Lochaber
Lochy
L. Moidart
L. Shiel
L. Eil
Fort William
Ben Nevis 1343
Pt. of Ardnamurchan
Ardgour
Loch Sunart
Coll
Tobermory
Morvern
Sound of Mull
L. Linnhe
Glen Coe
Ballachulish
Rannoch Moor
Lismore
Loch Etive
Lorn
Ben Cruachan 1124
Orchy
Tiree
Staffa
Mull
Ben More 966
Iona
Oban
Firth of Lorn
B. Vorlich 942
Inveraray
L. Awe
ATLANTIC OCEAN
Colonsay
Crinan
Jura
Lochgilphead
Helensburgh
Rubh a' Mhail
Sound of Jura
Loch Fyne
Dunoon
Greenock
Port Glasgow
Tarbert
Rothesay
Bute
Largs
Islay
Bowmore
Gigha
STRATHCL
Kintyre
Ardrossan
Goat Fell 874
Saltcoats
Port Ellen
Arran
Brodick
Firth of Clyde
SHETLAND IS.
On same scale
Unst
Yell Sound
Fetlar
Yell
SHETLAND
Whalsay
Mainland
Foula
Scalloway
Bressay
Lerwick
Sumburgh Hd.
West from Greenwich
Campbeltown
Rathlin
Fair Hd.
Mull of Kintyre
Ailsa Craig
Girvan
Ballycastle
North Channel
Trostan 554
L. Ryan
Gal
NORTHERN IRELAND
Ballymena
Larne
Stranraer
Portpatrick
Luce Bay
Belfast Lough
Bangor
Belfast
Newtownards
Mull of Galloway
33
34

1 : 2 000 000

33

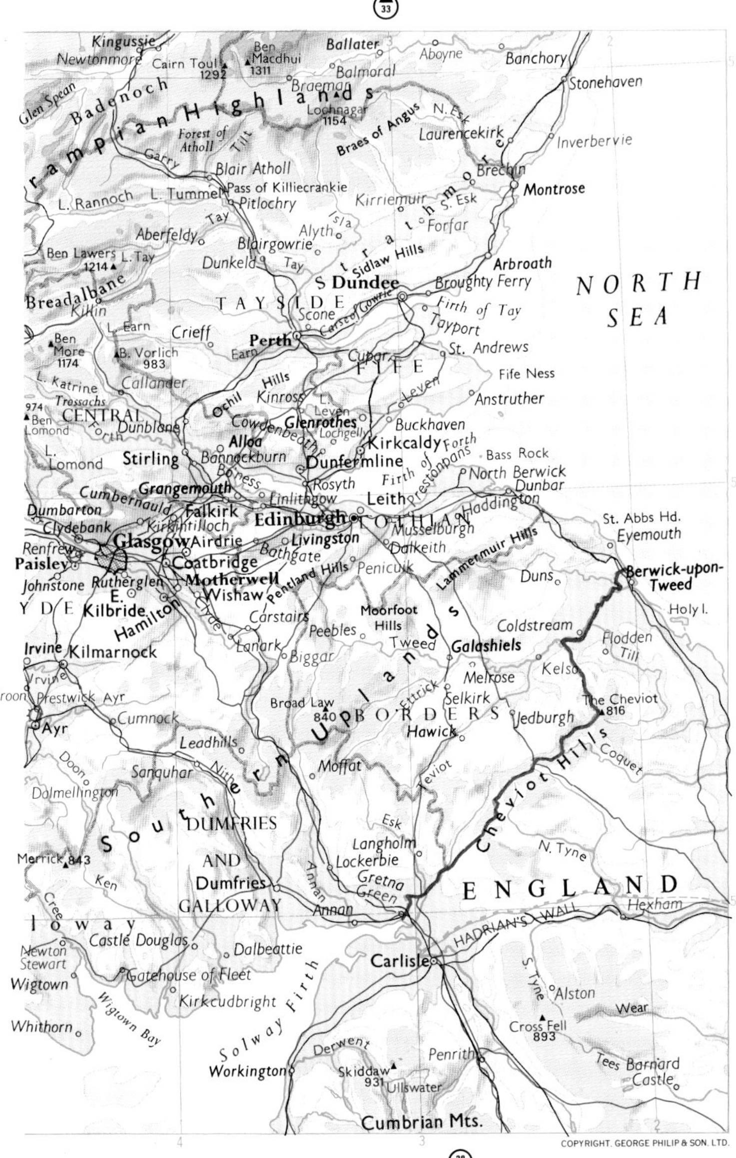
Kingussie
Newtonmore
Cairn Toul
1292
Ben
Macdhui
1311
Ballater
Aboyne
Banchory
Stonehaven
Balmoral
Braemar
Glen Spean
Badenoch
Grampian Highlands
Lochnagar
1154
N. Esk
Braes of Angus
Laurencekirk
Inverbervie
Forest of
Atholl
Tilt
Garry
Blair Atholl
Brechin
Montrose
L. Rannoch
L. Tummel
Pass of Killiecrankie
Pitlochry
Kirriemuir
S. Esk
Strathmore
Isla
Forfar
Alyth
Tay
Aberfeldy
Blairgowrie
Ben Lawers
1214
L. Tay
Dunkeld
Tay
Sidlaw Hills
Arbroath
Dundee
Broughty Ferry
NORTH
SEA
Breadalbane
Killin
TAYSIDE
Carse of Gowrie
Scone
Firth of Tay
Tayport
L. Earn
Crieff
Perth
St. Andrews
Ben
More
1174
B. Vorlich
983
Earn
Cupar
FIFE
Fife Ness
L. Katrine
Callander
Hills
Leven
Trossachs
Ochil
Kinross
Anstruther
974
Ben
Lomond
CENTRAL
Forth
Dunblane
L.
Leven
Cowdenbeath
Glenrothes
Lochgelly
Buckhaven
Alloa
Kirkcaldy
Forth
L.
Lomond
Stirling
Bannockburn
Dunfermline
Firth of
Prestonpans
Bass Rock
Bo'ness
Rosyth
North Berwick
Cumbernauld
Grangemouth
Linlithgow
Leith
Dunbar
Dumbarton
Falkirk
Haddington
St. Abbs Hd.
Clydebank
Kirkintilloch
Edinburgh
LOTHIAN
Musselburgh
Eyemouth
Renfrew
Glasgow
Airdrie
Livingston
Lammermuir Hills
Paisley
Bathgate
Dalkeith
Coatbridge
Penicuik
Berwick-upon-
Tweed
Johnstone
Rutherglen
Motherwell
Pentland Hills
Duns
E.
Wishaw
Kilbride
Moorfoot
Holy I.
CLYDE
Hamilton
Carstairs
Hills
Coldstream
Clyde
Peebles
Irvine
Kilmarnock
Lanark
Tweed
Galashiels
Flodden
Biggar
Till
Irvine
Melrose
Kelso
Troon
Prestwick
Ayr
Ettrick
Selkirk
The Cheviot
816
Broad Law
840
BORDERS
Jedburgh
Ayr
Cumnock
Hawick
Southern Uplands
Leadhills
Coquet
Doon
Nith
Moffat
Teviot
Cheviot Hills
Sanquhar
Dalmellington
Esk
DUMFRIES
AND
GALLOWAY
Langholm
N. Tyne
Merrick
843
Lockerbie
Ken
Annan
Gretna
Green
ENGLAND
Dumfries
Cree
Annan
Hexham
Galloway
HADRIAN'S WALL
Newton
Stewart
Castle Douglas
Dalbeattie
Carlisle
Wigtown
Gatehouse of Fleet
S. Tyne
Alston
Kirkcudbright
Wear
Wigtown Bay
Solway Firth
Whithorn
Cross Fell
893
Derwent
Penrith
Tees
Barnard
Castle
Workington
Skiddaw
931
Ullswater
Cumbrian Mts.
57
56
55
4
3
2

28

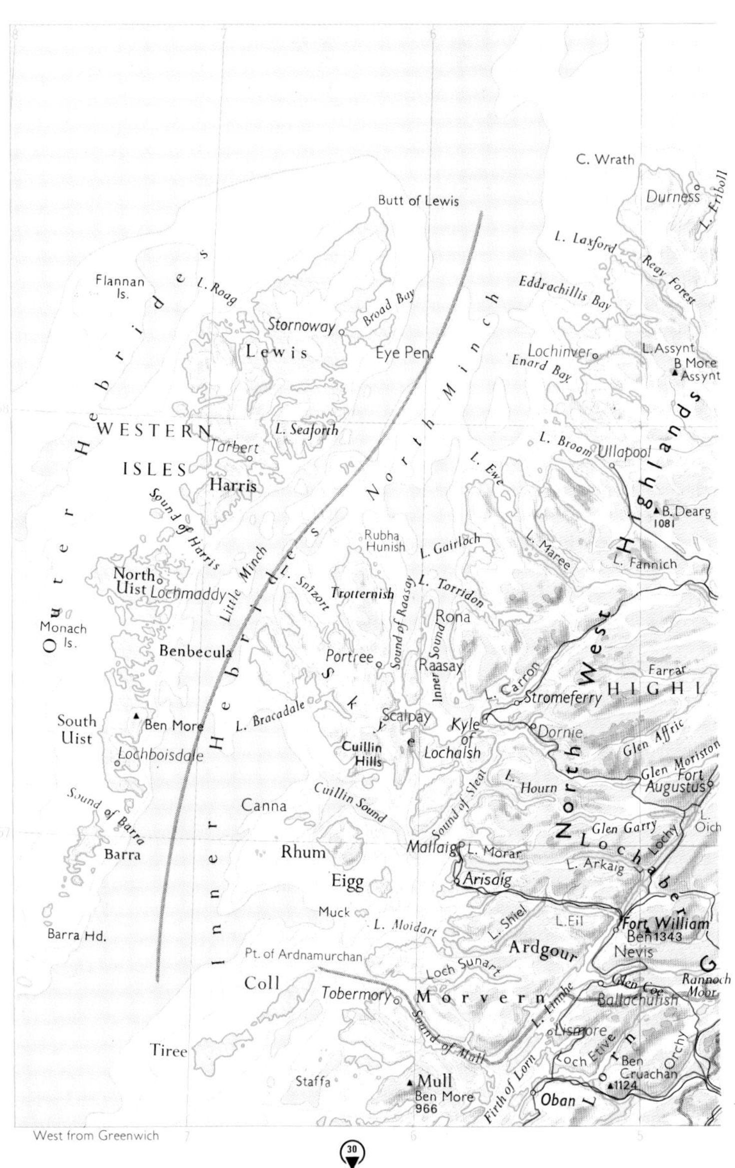

C. Wrath

Durness

L. Eriboll

Butt of Lewis

L. Laxford

Reay Forest

Flannan Is.

L. Roag

Eddrachillis Bay

Broad Bay

Lochinver

L. Assynt

Stornoway

Enard Bay

B More

Assynt

L e w i s

Eye Pen.

WESTERN

L. Seaforth

L. Broom Ullapool

ISLES

Tarbert

Harris

L. Ewe

B. Dearg
1081

Sound of Harris

Rubha
Hunish

L. Gairloch

L. Maree

L. Fannich

North
Uist Lochmaddy

Little Minch

L. Snizort

Trotternish

L. Torridon

Monach
Is.

Benbecula

Portree

Rona

L. Carron Stromeferry

HIGHL

South
Uist

Ben More

L. Bracadale

Raasay

Farrar

Lochboisdale

Scalpay

Kyle
of
Lochalsh

Dornie

Glen Affric

Cuillin
Hills

Glen Moriston

Cuillin Sound

L. Hourn

Fort
Augustus

Canna

Glen Garry

Oich

Barra

Rhum

Mallaig L. Morar

L. Arkaig

Sound of Barra

Eigg

Arisaig

Barra Hd.

Muck

L. Moidart

L. Shiel

L.Eil

Fort William
Ben 1343
Nevis

Pt. of Ardnamurchan

Ardgour

Rannoch
Moor

Coll

Tobermory M o r v e r n

Ballachulish

Lysmore

Tiree

Sound of Mull

Ben
Cruachan
1124

Staffa

Mull
Ben More
966

Firth of Lorn

Oban

Outer Hebrides

North Minch

Inner Hebrides

Sound of Raasay

Inner Sound

S k y e

Sound of Sleat

West Highlands

North Lochaber

Loch Sunart

Loch Etive

Loch Creran

Oban

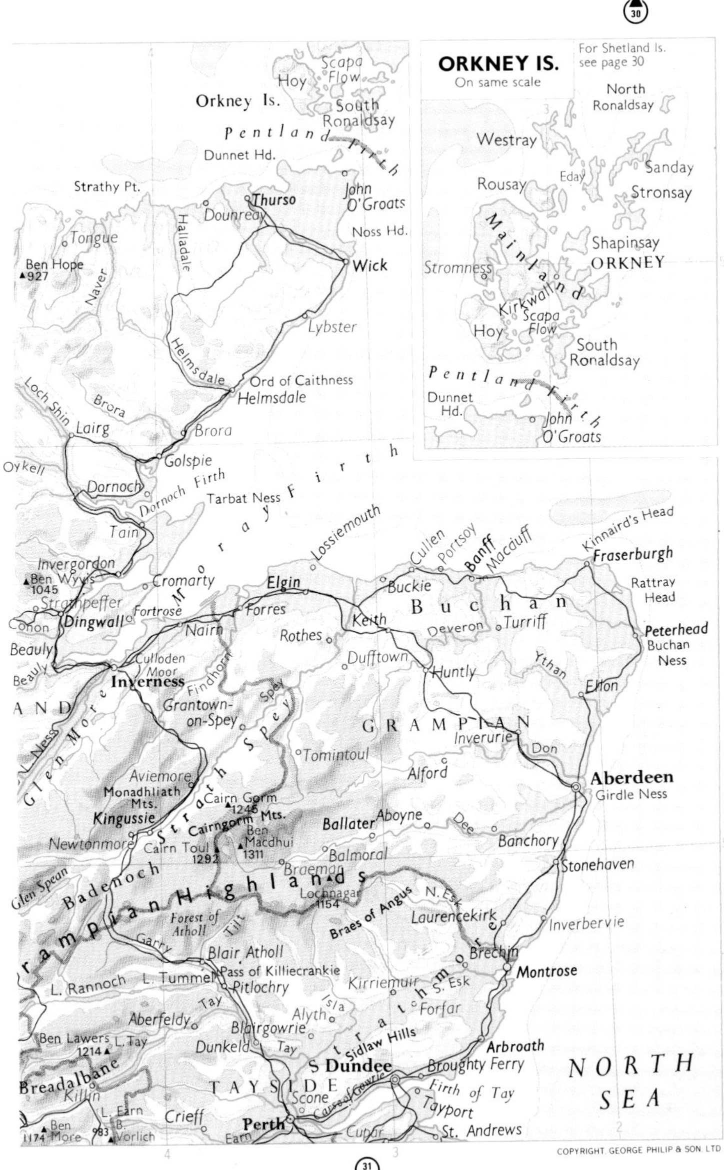

ORKNEY IS.
On same scale

For Shetland Is.
see page 30

Scapa Flow
Orkney Is.
Hoy
South Ronaldsay

Pentland Firth
Dunnet Hd.

Strathy Pt.
Thurso
John O'Groats

Tongue
Dounreay
Noss Hd.

Ben Hope
▲927
Naver
Halladale

Wick

Loch Shin
Brora
Lairg
Helmsdale
Ord of Caithness
Helmsdale
Lybster

Oykell
Dornoch
Golspie
Brora

Dornoch Firth
Tarbat Ness
Tain

North Ronaldsay

Westray
Eday
Rousay
Stronsay
Sanday

Shapinsay
Stromness
ORKNEY
Mainland
Kirkwall
Scapa Flow
Hoy
South Ronaldsay

Pentland Firth
Dunnet Hd.
John O'Groats

Moray Firth
Lossiemouth
Cullen
Portsoy
Banff
Macduff
Kinnaird's Head

Invergordon
Ben Wyvis
▲1045
Cromarty
Strathpeffer
Fortrose
Nairn
Forres
Elgin
Buckie
Keith
Fraserburgh
Rattray Head

Conon
Dingwall
Rothes
Deveron
Turriff
Peterhead
Buchan Ness

Beauly
B U C H A N

Beauly
Culloden Moor
Inverness
Dufftown
Huntly
Ythan
Ellon

Findhorn
Spey
Grantown-on-Spey

Glen More
Loch Ness
Strath Spey
Tomintoul
G R A M P I A N
Inverurie
Don

Aviemore
Monadhliath Mts.
Cairn Gorm
1245
Alford
Aberdeen
Girdle Ness

Kingussie
Cairngorm Mts.
Ben Macdhui
1311
Ballater
Aboyne
Dee
Banchory

Newtonmore
Cairn Toul
1292
Balmoral
Braemar

Glen Spean
Badenoch
Lochnagar
1154
Stonehaven

Grampian Highlands
Garry
Forest of Atholl
Till
Braes of Angus
Laurencekirk
Inverbervie

Blair Atholl
Pass of Killiecrankie
N. Esk
Brechin

L. Rannoch
L. Tummel
Pitlochry
Kirriemuir
S. Esk
Montrose

Isla
Forfar

Aberfeldy
Blairgowrie
Strathmore

Ben Lawers
1214▲
L. Tay
Dunkeld
Tay
Alyth
Sidlaw Hills
Arbroath

Breadalbane
Killin
Tay
S **Dundee**
Broughty Ferry
N O R T H

Ben More
1174
L. Earn
983
Vorlich
Crieff
Scone
Firth of Tay
Tayport
S E A

Perth
Earn
Cupar
St. Andrews

30

31

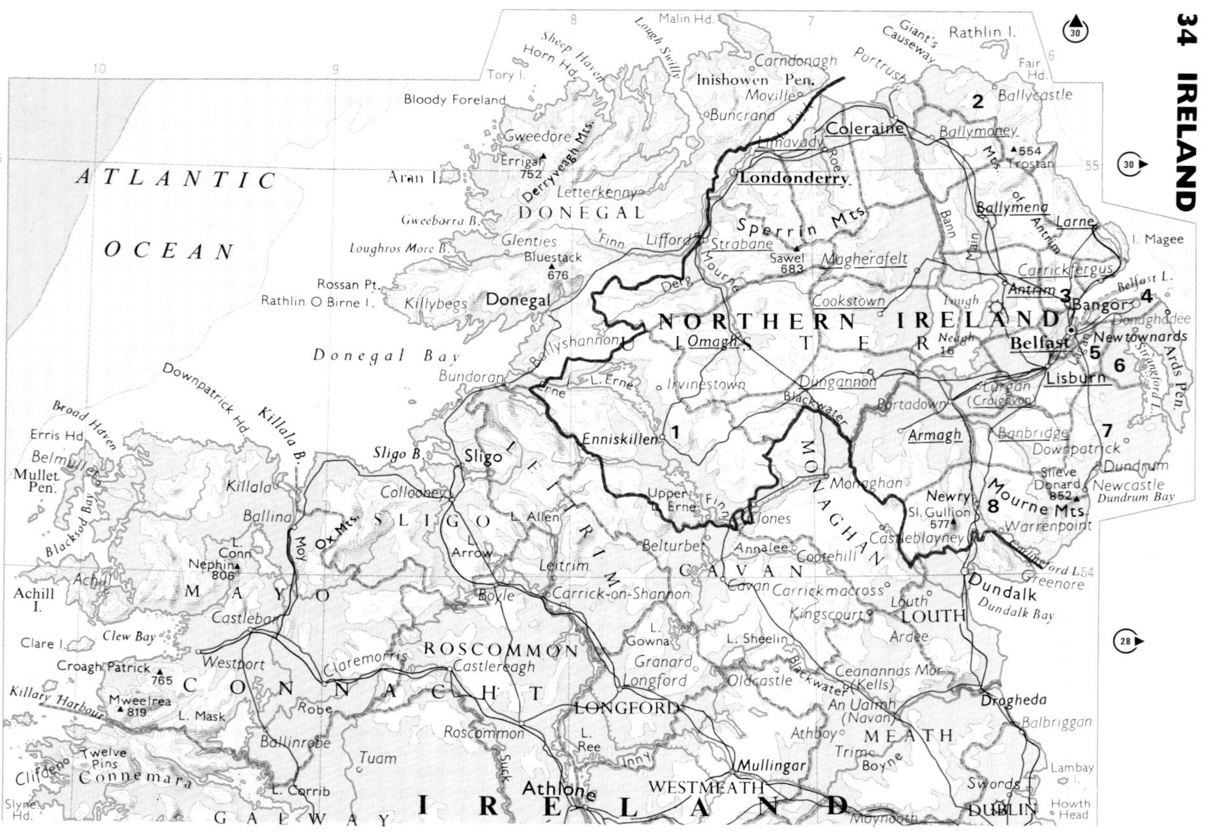

ATLANTIC
OCEAN
NORTHERN IRELAND
ULSTER
IRELAND
DONEGAL
MONAGHAN
CAVAN
LOUTH
MEATH
WESTMEATH
LONGFORD
LEITRIM
SLIGO
ROSCOMMON
MAYO
GALWAY
CONNACHT
Rathlin I.
Fair Hd.
Giant's Causeway
Portrush
Coleraine
Ballycastle
Ballymoney
Ballymena
Mts. of Antrim
554 Trostan
Larne
I. Magee
Antrim
Carrickfergus
Bangor
Belfast
Belfast L.
Newtownards
Ards Pen.
Strangford L.
Donaghadee
Lisburn
Lurgan (Craigavon)
Banbridge
Downpatrick
Dundrum
Dundrum Bay
Newcastle
Slieve Donard 852
Mourne Mts.
Warrenpoint
Carlingford L.
Newry
Sl. Gullion 577
Dundalk
Dundalk Bay
Greenore
Armagh
Portadown
Lough Neagh 16
Bann
Main
Dungannon
Cookstown
Magherafelt
Sperrin Mts.
Sawel 683
Londonderry
Limavady
Roe
Foyle
Strabane
Lifford
Omagh
Mourne
Derg
Enniskillen
L. Erne
Upper L. Erne
Irvinestown
Blackwater
Monaghan
Castleblayney
Clones
Cootehill
Carrickmacross
Kingscourt
Louth
Ardee
Drogheda
Balbriggan
Lambay I.
Howth Head
Swords
DUBLIN
Maynooth
Trim
Boyne
An Uaimh (Navan)
Ceanannas Mor (Kells)
Athboy
Mullingar
Oldcastle
L. Sheelin
Cavan
Annalee
Belturbet
L. Gowna
Granard
Longford
Inny
L. Ree
Athlone
Carrick-on-Shannon
Leitrim
Boyle
L. Allen
L. Arrow
Sligo
Sligo B.
Collooney
Ox Mts.
Castlerea
Roscommon
Suck
Tuam
Claremorris
Ballinrobe
Robe
L. Corrib
L. Mask
Westport
Castlebar
Ballina
Killala
Killala B.
Moy
L. Conn
Nephin 806
Croagh Patrick 765
Mweelrea 819
Clew Bay
Clare I.
Achill
Achill I.
Killary Harbour
Twelve Pins
Connemara
Clifden
Slyne Hd.
Belmullet
Mullet Pen.
Erris Hd.
Broad Haven
Blacksod Bay
Downpatrick Hd.
Donegal Bay
Donegal
Bundoran
Ballyshannon
Erne
Killybegs
Rossan Pt.
Rathlin O Birne I.
Loughros More B.
Gweebarra B.
Aran I.
Bluestack 676
Glenties
Finn
Letterkenny
Derryveagh Mts.
Errigal 752
Gweedore
Bloody Foreland
Tory I.
Horn Hd.
Sheep Haven
Lough Swilly
Malin Hd.
Inishowen Pen.
Buncrana
Moville
Carndonagh

1 : 2 000 000

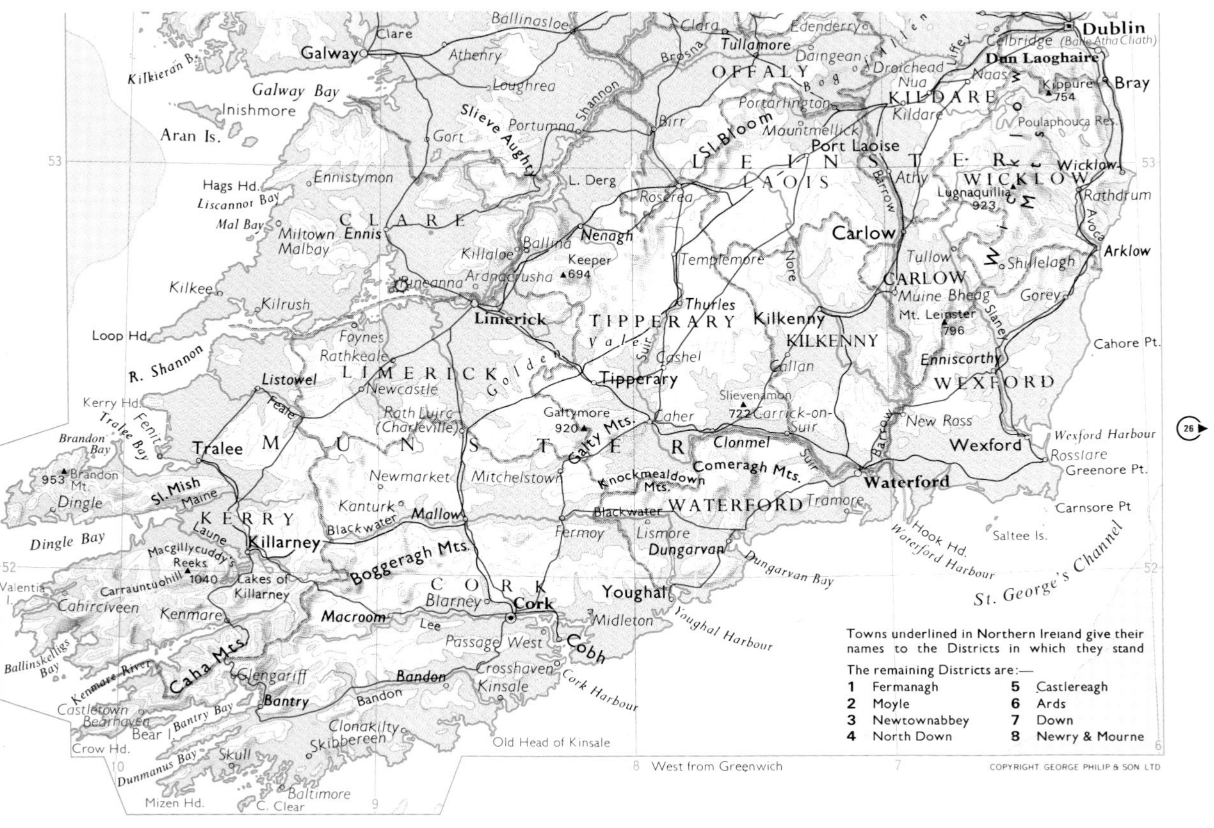

Towns underlined in Northern Ireland give their
names to the Districts in which they stand

The remaining Districts are:—

1	Fermanagh	**5**	Castlereagh
2	Moyle	**6**	Ards
3	Newtownabbey	**7**	Down
4	North Down	**8**	Newry & Mourne

St. George's Channel

West from Greenwich

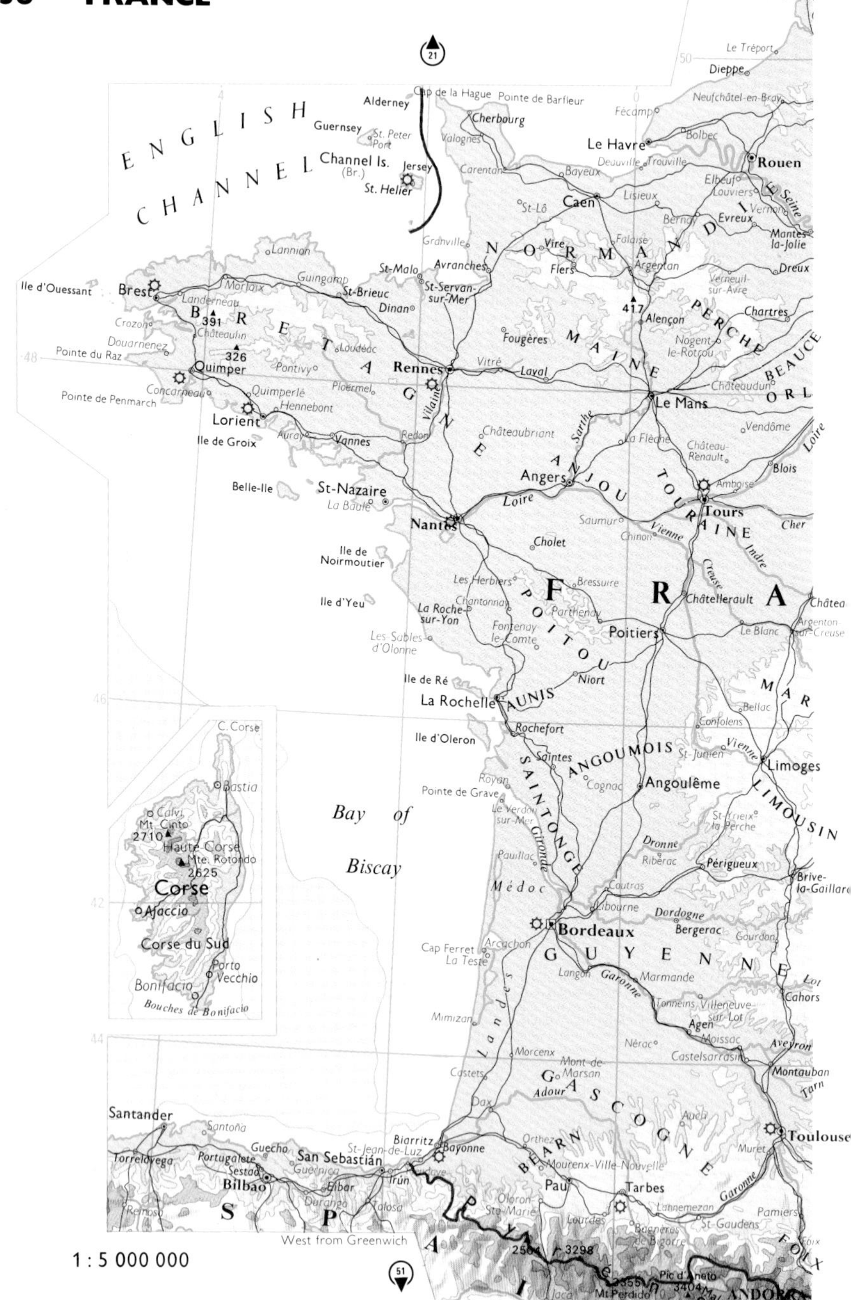

21
ENGLISH CHANNEL
Alderney
Guernsey
St. Peter Port
Channel Is. (Br.)
Jersey
St. Helier
Cap de la Hague
Pointe de Barfleur
Cap Gris-Nez
Boulogne-sur-Mer
Étaples
Berck-Plage
Le Tréport
Dieppe
Neufchâtel-en-Bray
Fécamp
Bolbec
Le Havre
Rouen
Deauville
Trouville
Elbeuf
Louviers
Seine
Cherbourg
Valognes
Carentan
Bayeux
Caen
Lisieux
St-Lô
Bernay
Evreux
Vernon
Mantes-la-Jolie
Granville
NORMANDIE
Vire
Falaise
Flers
Argentan
Dreux
Verneuil-sur-Avre
Avranches
St-Malo
St-Servan-sur-Mer
Dinan
Lannion
Guingamp
St-Brieuc
Morlaix
Ile d'Ouessant
Brest
Landerneau
391
BRETAGNE
Crozon
Châteaulin
326
Douarnenez
Pointe du Raz
Quimper
Loudéac
Pontivy
Rennes
Vitré
Laval
Fougères
MAINE
417
Alençon
PERCHE
Chartres
Nogent-le-Rotrou
BEAUCE
Châteaudun
ORL
Le Mans
Concarneau
Pointe de Penmarch
Quimperlé
Hennebont
Ploërmel
Vilaine
Lorient
Ile de Groix
Auray
Vannes
Redon
Châteaubriant
Sarthe
La Flèche
Vendôme
Château-Renault
Loire
Blois
Belle-Ile
St-Nazaire
La Baule
Nantes
ANJOU
Angers
TOURAINE
Ambolse
Tours
Cher
Saumur
Chinon
Vienne
Indre
Cholet
Ile de Noirmoutier
Les Herbiers
Bressuire
FRA
Ile d'Yeu
Chantonnay
POITOU
Parthenay
Creuse
Châtellerault
Château
La Roche-sur-Yon
Fontenay-le-Comte
Poitiers
Le Blanc
Argenton-sur-Creuse
Les Sables-d'Olonne
Niort
Ile de Ré
La Rochelle
AUNIS
MAR
Bellac
Rochefort
Confolens
Ile d'Oleron
Saintes
ANGOUMOIS
St-Junien
Limoges
SAINTONGE
Royan
Cognac
Angoulême
LIMOUSIN
Pointe de Grave
Le Verdon-sur-Mer
St-Yrieix-la-Perche
Bay of Biscay
Gironde
Dronne
Pauillac
Ribérac
Périgueux
Brive-la-Gaillarde
Médoc
Coutras
Libourne
Dordogne
Bordeaux
Bergerac
Gourdon
Arcachon
Cap Ferret
La Teste
GUYENNE
Langon
Garonne
Marmande
Lot
Cahors
Tonneins
Villeneuve-sur-Lot
Mimizan
Landes
Agen
Moissac
Nérac
Morcenx
Castelsarrasin
Aveyron
Montauban
Mont-de-Marsan
GASCOGNE
Castets
Adour
Tarn
Dax
Auch
Toulouse
Muret
Orthez
BEARN
Mourenx-Ville-Nouvelle
Pau
Tarbes
Oloron-Ste-Marie
Lourdes
Lannemezan
Pamiers
Bagnères-de-Bigorre
St-Gaudens
FOIX
Biarritz
Bayonne
St-Jean-de-Luz
Irún
San Sebastián
Guernica
Eibar
Durango
Tolosa
Santander
Santoña
Torrelavega
Guecho
Portugalete
Sestao
Bilbao
Reinosa
SPAIN
PYRÉNÉES
2504
3298
3355
Mt Perdido
Pic d'Aneto
3404
Maladeta
ANDORRA
Jaca
West from Greenwich
51
C. Corse
Bastia
Calvi
Mt. Cinto
2710
Haute-Corse
Mte. Rotondo
2625
Corse
Ajaccio
Corse du Sud
Porto Vecchio
Bonifacio
Bouches de Bonifacio
50
48
46
44
42
4
0

1 : 5 000 000

BELGIUM
BRUSSEL
LUXEM-BOURG
GERMANY
FRANCE
PARIS
FRANCHE-COMTÉ
SWITZERLAND
ITALY
TORINO
LYON
MARSEILLE
MONACO Nice

Kortrijk Ronse Liège Aachen
Lille Roubaix Verviers
Bruay Béthune Mons Namur Marche-en-Famenne 697
en-Artois Bully-les-Mines Valenciennes Charleroi Dinant
Douai Lens Denain Maubeuge 816 Idar-Oberstein
Arras Cambrai Coudry Fourmies Luxembourg Esch Kaiserslautern
Abbeville Le Cateau Hirson Bastogne Neunkirchen Homburg Zweibrücken
Somme Amiens Péronne Charleville-Mézières Villerupt Thionville Pirmasens
Beauvais Compiègne St-Quentin Hayange Völklingen Saarbrücken
Noyon Chauny Laon Verdun Metz Hombur Saargemünd Rastatt
Creil Soissons Reims Menehould Pont-à-Mousson Baden-Baden
Pontoise Meaux Châlons-sur-Marne Commercy Sarrebourg Haguenau Offenburg
Corbeil Coulommiers Château-Thierry Toul Nancy Strasbourg Lahr
Essonnes Melun Vitry-le-François Bar-le-Duc Lunéville St-Dié Sélestat Emmendingen
Étampes Provins Romilly-sur-Seine St-Dizier Neufchâteau Vittel Épinal Colmar Freiburg 1493
Fontainebleau Montereau-Fault-Yonne Troyes Chaumont Remiremont Guebwiller 1423
Orléans Montargis Sens Tonnerre Langres Vesoul Mulhouse Lörrach Rheinfelden
Gien Auxerre St-Florentin Plateau de Langres Belfort Basel Liestal
Salbris Vézelay 598 Dijon Besançon Montbéliard Olten
Vierzon Quincerey Côte-d'Or Dole Solothurn Langenthal
Bourges Nevers Autun Beaune La Chaux-de-Fonds Biel Bern
Issoudun St-Amand-Mont-Rond Moulins Le Creusot Chalon-sur-Saône Lons-le-Saunier Neuchâtel Fribourg Thun Interlaken
Montluçon Commentry Montceau-les-Mines Paray-le-Monial St-Claude 1718 Yverdon Jungfrau 4158
Guéret Vichy Cusset Mâcon Oyonnax LAUSANNE Montreux Berner Alpen
Aubusson Sarnat Roanne Bourg-en-Bresse Bellegarde-sur-Valserine Genève Aigle Sierre Pennine
Montluçon Thiers Villefranche-sur-Saône Nantua Belley Annecy Chamonix Alp Mt Cervin
Puy de Dôme 1463 Riom Tarare Bourgoin Aix-les-Bains Mont Blanc Aosta
Clermont Ferrand St-Étienne 1634 Rive-de-Gier Vienne Voiron Chambéry
Ussel Firminy Annonay Romans-sur-Isère Grenoble Pinerolo TORINO
1885 Puy de Sancy Le Puy Tournon Valence Massif du Pelvoux Carmagnola
Massif 1855 St-Flour Aubenas Montélimar Gap Saluzzo Fassano
Central 1469 Decazeville Pierrelatte Valréas 3051 Mt Viso L'Argentera Cune
Rodez Villefranche-de-Rouergue 1699 Orange Mt Ventoux 1909 3297
Millau 1565 Bagnols-sur-Cèze Alès Carpentras Digne Maritime Alps
Albi Graulhet 1267 Avignon Gorges Manosque Grasse
Castres Mazamet Nîmes Cavaillon Salon-de-Provence Draguignan Cannes Antibes
Castelnaudary Béziers Frontignan Aigues-Mortes Istres Aix-en-Provence Fréjus St-Raphael
Carcassonne Narbonne Agde Sète Port-St-Louis-du-Rhône Gardanne La Ciotat Toulon Hyères
Limoux Rhône Delta MARSEILLE La Seyne Îles d'Hyères
Rivesaltes Golfe du Lion
Perpignan Elne Port-Vendres
ROUSSILLON

East from Greenwich 6

COPYRIGHT GEORGE PHILIP & SON LTD

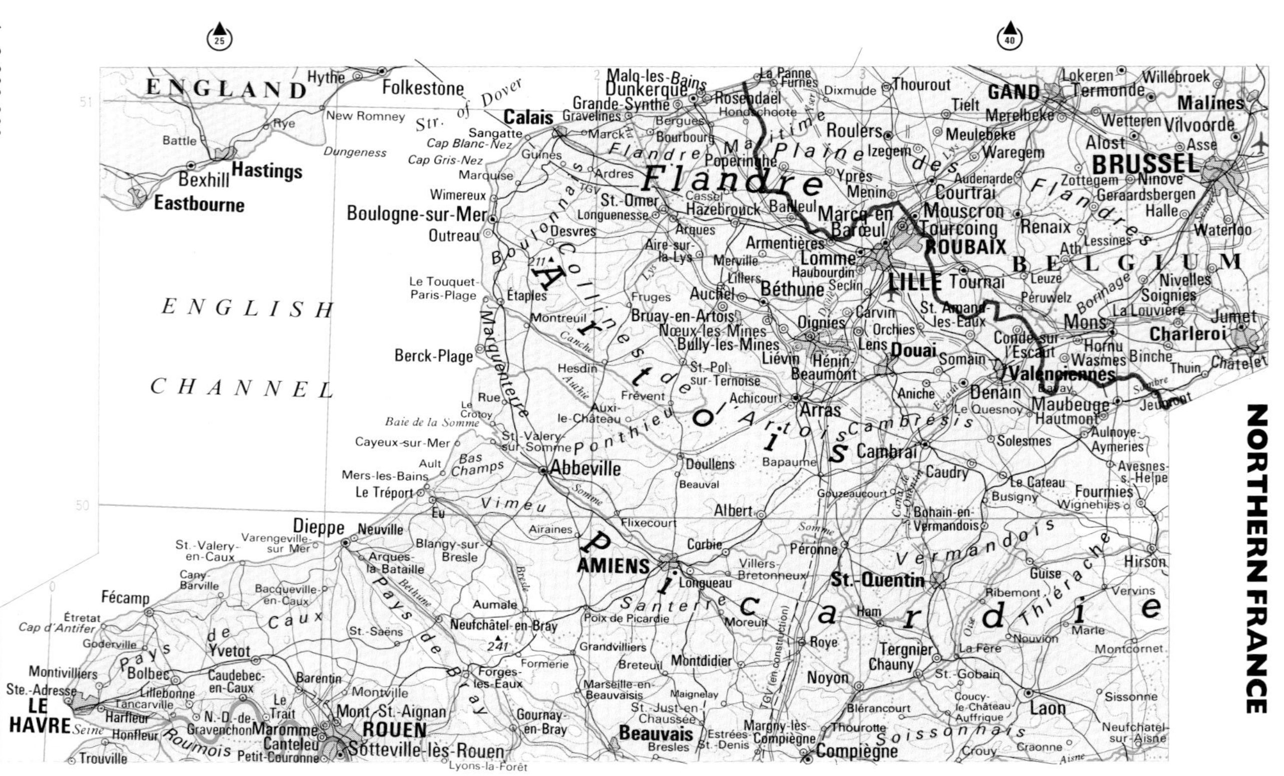

1 : 2 000 000

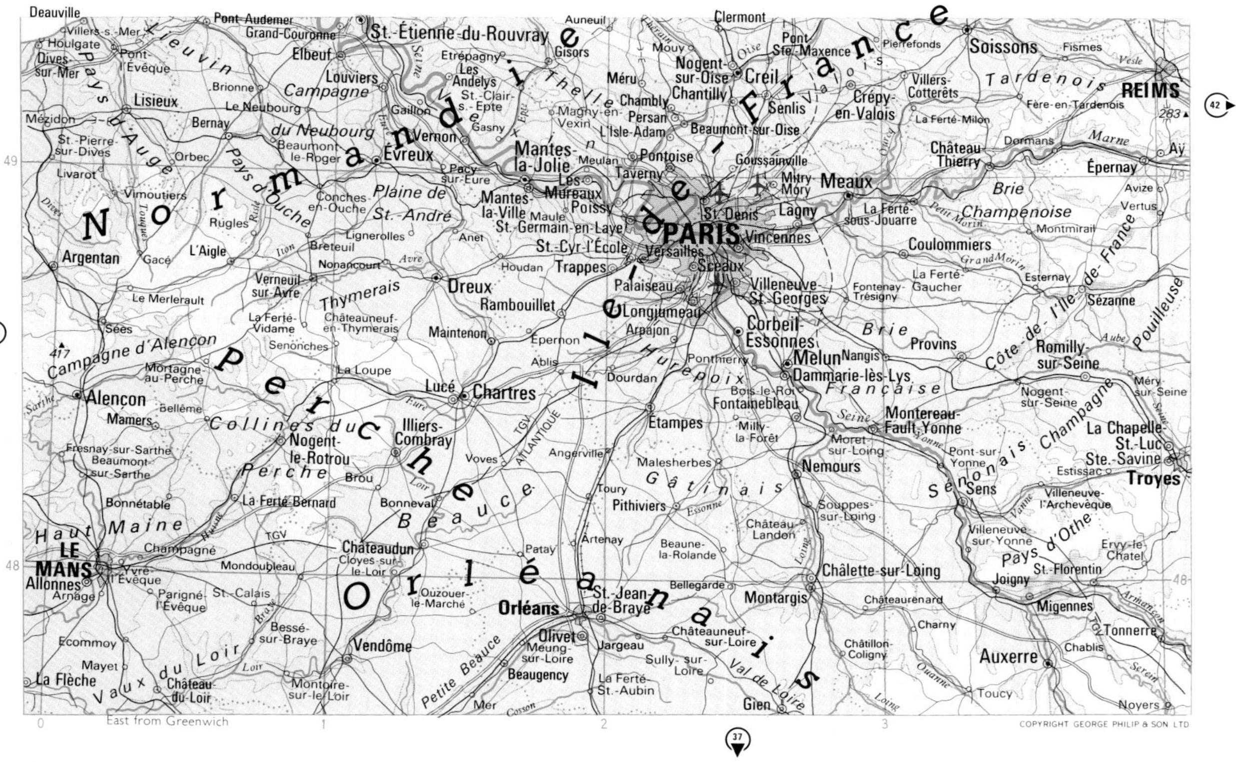

COPYRIGHT GEORGE PHILIP & SON LTD

42
Normandie
Île-de-France
Perche
Orléanais
Soissons
REIMS
Épernay
Château-Thierry
Meaux
PARIS
Versailles
St.-Denis
Vincennes
Pontoise
Creil
Senlis
Chantilly
Gisors
Mantes-la-Jolie
Évreux
Louviers
Elbeuf
Lisieux
Deauville
Pont-Audemer
Bernay
L'Aigle
Argentan
Alençon
Mamers
LE MANS
La Flèche
Vendôme
Châteaudun
Chartres
Dreux
Rambouillet
Étampes
Orléans
Pithiviers
Montargis
Gien
Nemours
Fontainebleau
Melun
Corbeil-Essonnes
Provins
Coulommiers
Sézanne
Nogent-sur-Seine
Romilly-sur-Seine
Troyes
Sens
Joigny
Auxerre
Tonnerre
Montereau-Fault-Yonne
Nogent-le-Rotrou
Beauce
Brie
Gâtinais
Hurepoix
Sénonais
East from Greenwich
36
37

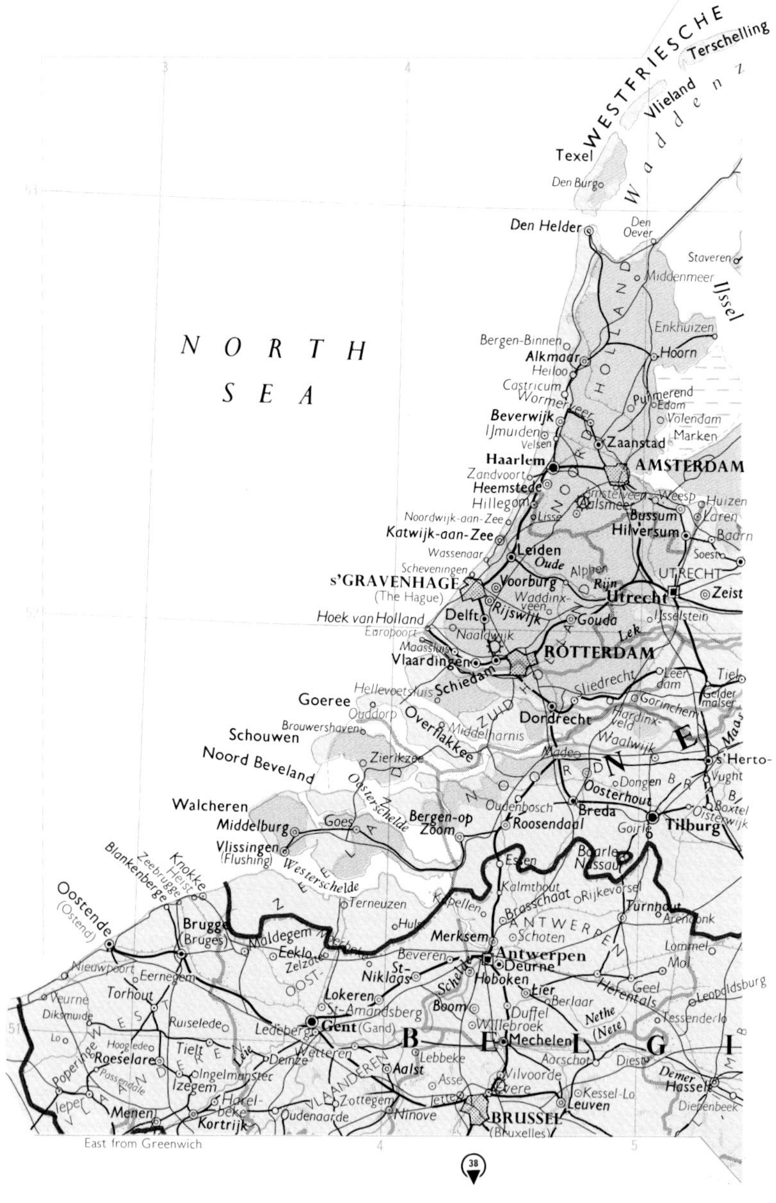
NORTH SEA
WESTFRIESCHE
Texel
Vlieland
Terschelling
Waddenz
Den Burg
Den Helder
Den Oever
Middenmeer
Staveren
IJssel
NOORD HOLLAND
Enkhuizen
Bergen-Binnen
Alkmaar
Hoorn
Heiloo
Castricum
Wormerveer
Purmerend
Edam
Volendam
Beverwijk
IJmuiden
Velsen
Zaanstad
Marken
Haarlem
AMSTERDAM
Zandvoort
Heemstede
Amstelveen
Weesp
Huizen
Hillegom
Aalsmeer
Bussum
Laren
Noordwijk-aan-Zee
Lisse
Hilversum
Baarn
Katwijk-aan-Zee
Leiden
Soest
Wassenaar
Oude Rijn
Alphen
Scheveningen
UTRECHT
s'GRAVENHAGE
(The Hague)
Voorburg
Utrecht
Zeist
Waddinxveen
Rijswijk
Delft
Gouda
IJsselstein
Hoek van Holland
Europoort
Naaldwijk
Lek
Maassluis
Vlaardingen
ROTTERDAM
Schiedam
Leerdam
Tiel
Hellevoetsluis
Sliedrecht
Geldermalsen
Goeree
Ouddorp
ZUID HOLLAND
Gorinchem
Dordrecht
Hardinxveld
Brouwershaven
Overflakkee
Middelharnis
Schouwen
Waalwijk
Maas
Made
Noord Beveland
Zierikzee
's Hertogenbosch
Vught
Dongen
Oosterhout
Oosterschelde
Walcheren
Oudenbosch
Breda
Boxtel
Oisterwijk
Bergen-op Zoom
Middelburg
Goes
Roosendaal
Goirle
Tilburg
ZEELAND
Vlissingen
(Flushing)
Baarle Nassau
Westerschelde
Essen
Knokke
Heist
Zeebrugge
Blankenberge
Oostende
(Ostend)
Kalmthout
Terneuzen
Kapellen
Brasschaat
Rijkevorsel
Turnhout
Arendonk
Brugge
(Bruges)
Hulst
Maldegem
Merksem
ANTWERPEN
Schoten
Eeklo
Zelzate
Beveren
Antwerpen
Deurne
Lommel
Mol
Nieuwpoort
Eernegem
St-Niklaas
Schelde
Hoboken
Lier
Geel
OOST-VLAANDEREN
Herentals
Leopoldsburg
Veurne
Torhout
Lokeren
Berlaar
Nethe
(Nete)
Diksmuide
WEST-VLAANDEREN
St-Amandsberg
Boom
Duffel
Tessenderlo
Ruiselede
Ledeberg
Gent (Gand)
Willebroek
Lo
Hooglede
Tielt
Leie
Wetteren
Mechelen
BELGIË
Roeselare
Deinze
Lebbeke
Aarschot
Diest
Poperinge
Passendale
Ingelmunster
Aalst
Demer
Hasselt
Izegem
Asse
Vilvoorde
Ieper
Harelbeke
Zottegem
Jette
Evere
Kessel-Lo
Diepenbeek
Menen
Kortrijk
Oudenaarde
Ninove
BRUSSEL
(Bruxelles)
Leuven
East from Greenwich
3
4
5
53
52
51

38

1 : 2 000 000

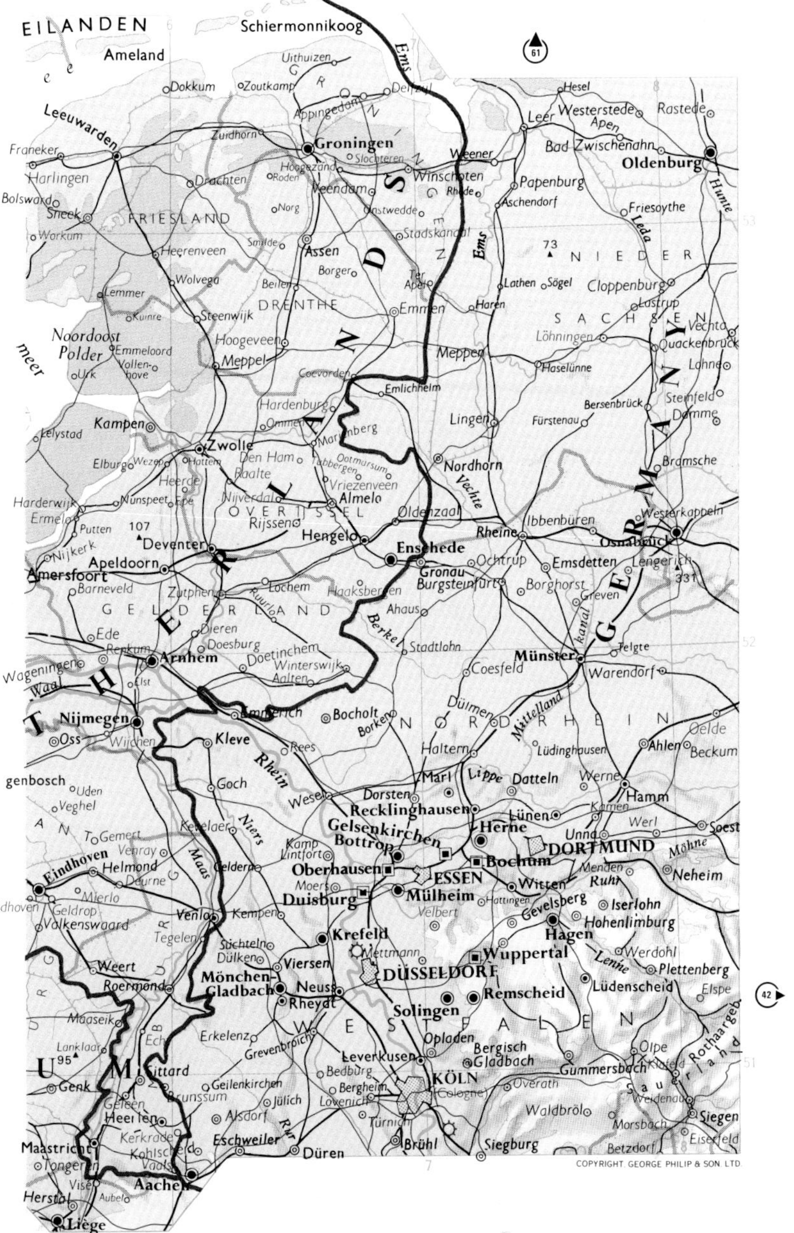

41

EILANDEN   Schiermonnikoog
Ameland

Dokkum   Zoutkamp   Uithuizen   Hesel
Leeuwarden   Zuidhorn   Appingedam   Delfzijl   Leer   Westerstede   Rastede
Franeker   Groningen   Slochteren   Apen   Bad Zwischenahn
Harlingen   Hoogezand   Weener   Oldenburg
Bolsward   Drachten   Roden   Winschoten   Papenburg   Hunte
Sneek   FRIESLAND   Norg   Veendam   Rhede   Aschendorf   Friesoythe
Workum   Heerenveen   Smilde   Onstwedde   Stadskanaal   NIEDER   Leda
Wolvega   Assen   73   SACHSEN   Cloppenburg   Lastrup
Lemmer   Borger   Lathen   Sögel   Vechta
Noordoost   Kuinre   Beilen   DRENTHE   Haren   Löhningen   Quackenbrück
Polder   Emmeloord   Steenwijk   Emmen   Haselünne   Lohne   Damme
Urk   Vollen-   Hoogeveen   Meppen   Bersenbrück   Steinfeld
meer   hove   Meppel   Emlichheim   Lingen   Fürstenau
Kampen   Hardenberg   Ommen   Coevorden   Nordhorn   Bramsche
Lelystad   Zwolle   Emlichheim   Vechte   Westerkappeln
Elburg   Wezep   Hatten   Den Ham   Oetmarsum   Ibbenbüren   Osnabrück
Harderwijk   Heerde   Raalte   Nijverdal   Vriezenveen   Almelo   Oldenzaal   Rheine   331
Ermelo   Nunspeet   Epe   OVERIJSSEL   Ochtrup   Emsdetten   Lengerich
Putten   107   Rijssen   Hengelo   Enschede   Gronau   Borghorst   Greven   Telgte
Nijkerk   Deventer   Lochem   Haaksbergen   Burgsteinfurt
Amersfoort   Apeldoorn   Zutphen   Ahaus   Coesfeld   Münster   Warendorf
Barneveld   GELDERLAND   Doesburg   Winterswijk   Stadtlohn   Berkel   52
Wageningen   Ede   Dieren   Doetinchem   Aalten   Dülmen   MITTELLAND   Gelde
Renkum   Arnhem   Elst   Emmerich   Bocholt   NORD   RHEIN   Ahlen   Beckum
Waal   Nijmegen   Wijchen   Kleve   Rees   Borken   Halterne   Lüdinghausen   Hamm
Oss   Uden   Goch   Wesel   Marl   Lippe   Dattein   Werne   Kamen   Soest
genbosch   Veghel   Kevelaer   Dorsten   Lünen   Werl
Gemert   Kamp   Recklinghausen   Herne   Unna   Menden   Neheim
Eindhoven   Venray   Lintfort   Gelsenkirchen   Bochum   DORTMUND   Mühne
Helmond   Deurne   Gelderne   Bottrop   ESSEN   Witten   Ruhr   Iserlohn
Mierlo   Moers   Oberhausen   Mülheim   Hattingen   Gevelsberg   Hohenlimburg
eldhoven   Geldrop   Venlo   Kempen   Duisburg   Velbert   Hagen
Valkenswaard   Tegelen   Krefeld   Mettmann   Werdohl
Weert   Stichteln   Viersen   DÜSSELDORF   Wuppertal   Lenne   Plettenberg
Roermond   Dülken   Mönchen-   Neuss   Remscheid   Lüdenscheid   Elspe   42
Maaseik   Gladbach   Rheydt   Solingen   WESTFALEN
Lanklaar   Erkelenz   Grevenbroich   Leverkusen   Opladen   Bergisch   Olpe   Rothaarge
Genk   Sittard   Geilenkirchen   Bedburg   Gladbach   Gummersbach   Siegen
Geleen   Brunssum   Jülich   Bergheim   KÖLN   Overath   Waldbröl   Eiserfeld
Heerlen   Alsdorf   Löwenich   Cologne   Morsbach   Betzdorf
Maastricht   Kerkrade   Eschweiler   Düren   Türnich   Brühl   Siegburg
Tongeren   Kohlscheid   Vaals   Aachen   COPYRIGHT GEORGE PHILIP & SON LTD
Vise   Aubel
Herstal
Liège

NORTH SEA
SCHLES
Helgoland
Deutsche Bucht
Ost-friesische Inseln
Norderney
Wangerooge
Borkum
Schiermonnikoog
Ameland
Terschelling
Texel
Cuxhaven
Elbe
Brunsbüttelkoog
Glückstadt
Weser
Wilhelmshaven
Bremerhaven
Emden
Leeuwarden
Sneek
Groningen
Den Helder
Oldenburg
Bremen
Assen
Alkmaar
Hoorn
IJsselmeer
Meppel
Ems
Verden
Aller
NETHERLANDS
Haarlem
Zaandam
Kampen
Zwolle
NIEDERSACHSEN
Nienburg
Amsterdam
Almelo
Lingen
Leine
's-Gravenhage (The Hague)
Leiden
Hilversum
Deventer
Rheine
Hoek van Holland
Gouda
Utrecht
Apeldoorn
Enschede
Osnabrück
Schiedam
Rotterdam
Arnhem
Minden
Hannover
Dordrecht
Waal
Nijmegen
Münster
Teutoburger Wald
Herford
Bielefeld
Maas
NORDRHEIN-WESTFALEN
Vlissingen
Breda
's-Hertogenbosch
Bocholt
Lippe
Hameln
Zeebrugge
Oostende
Tilburg
Detmold
Brugge
Antwerpen
Turnhout
Eindhoven
Oberhausen
Mülheim
Gelsenkirchen
Hamm
Paderborn
Duisburg
Dortmund
Gent (Gand)
Schelde
Krefeld
Bochum
Essen
G E
Göttingen
Mönchengladbach
Hagen
Ruhr
Kortrijk
Leie
Aalst
Brussel (Bruxelles)
Mechelen
Wuppertal
Kassel
Tourcoing
Roubaix
Leuven
Düsseldorf
Remscheid
Lille
BELGIUM
Maastricht
Heerlen
840
Münden
Tournai
Köln (Cologne)
Rothaargeb.
Eder
Liège
Aachen
Douai
Mons
Namur
Eupen
Bonn
Siegen
Marburg
Fulda
Valenciennes
Charleroi
Meuse
Verviers
Sieg
Cambrai
Malmedy
Rhein (Rhine)
Westerwald
Wetzlar
Giessen
Ardennes
Eifel
Koblenz
Limburg
Lahn
HESSEN
Vogelsberg 772
950
Rhön
St. Quentin
Hirson
RHEINLAND
Taunus
Charleville-Mézières
Mosel
Wiesbaden
Frankfurt
Hanau
Laon
Sedan
LUX.
Hunsrück
Mainz
Offenbach
Spessart
Soissons
Aisne
Luxembourg
Trier
Aschaffenburg
Longwy
Main
Darmstadt
Reims
Meuse
Saar
PFALZ
Worms
Würzburg
Château Thierry
Thionville
Kaiserslautern
SAARLAND
Neunkirchen
Ludwigshafen
Mannheim
Épernay
Saarbrücken
Speyer
Heidelberg
Châlons-sur-Marne
Verdun
Metz
CHAMPAGNE
LORRAINE
Neckar
Vitry-le-François
Karlsruhe
Aube
St. Dizier
Bar-le-Duc
Haguenau
Pforzheim
Heilbronn
FRANCE
Toul
Nancy
BADEN-WÜRTTEMBERG
Troyes
Marne
Lunéville
Stuttgart
Ludwigsburg
Baden-Baden
Esslingen
Strasbourg
Seine
Schwarzwald
Tübingen
St. Dié
Vosges
ALSACE
Chaumont
Épinal
Reutlingen
Ulm
Rottweil
Schwäbische Alb
Iller
Langres
Plateau de Langres
Colmar
1424
Rhein (Rhine)
Freiburg
Biberach
Avallon
(Danube)
Donau
Tuttlingen
Mulhouse
Memmingen
Belfort
Schaffhausen
Ravensburg
Basel
Konstanz
Friedrichshafen
Kempten
Winterthur
Bodensee
St. Gallen
Bregenz
Aarau
Zürich
VORARLBERG
Biel
Aare
Solothurn

4 6 8 10 52 50 48

East from Greenwich

1 : 5 000 000

38

44

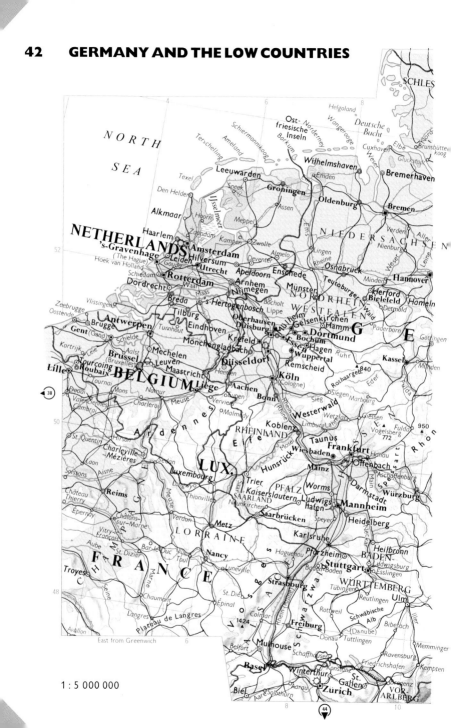

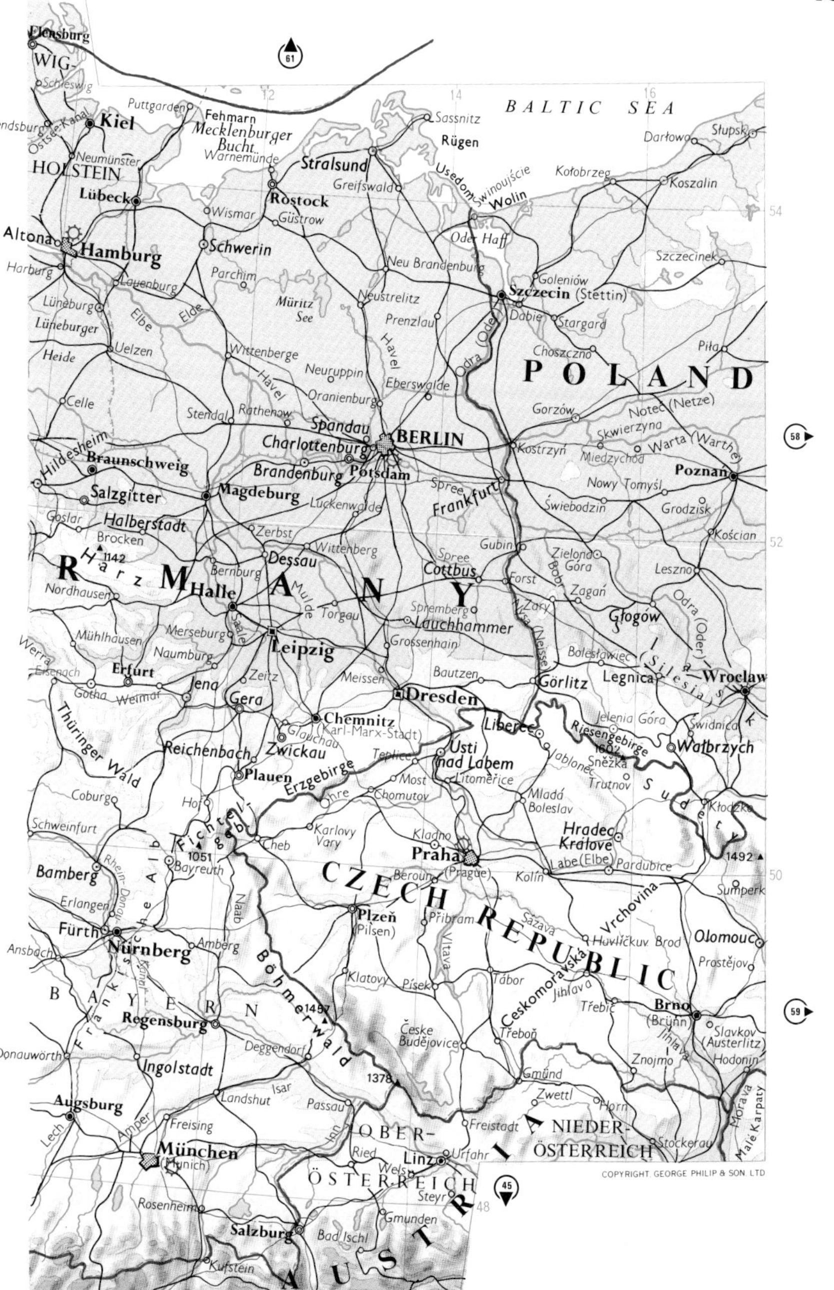

Flensburg
WIG-
Schleswig
Puttgarden
Fehmarn
Mecklenburger
Rendsburg
Ostsee Kanal
Kiel
Warnemünde Bucht
Neumünster
HOLSTEIN
Lübeck
Altona Hamburg
Harburg
Lüneburg
Lauenburg
Lüneburger
Heide
Uelzen
Celle
Hildesheim
Braunschweig
Salzgitter
Goslar Halberstadt
Brocken 1142
Harz Mts.
Nordhausen
Mühlhausen
Werra
Eisenach Erfurt
Gotha Weimar
Thüringer Wald
Coburg
Schweinfurt
Bamberg
Erlangen
Fürth
Ansbach
Nürnberg
B A Y E R N
Regensburg
Donauwörth
Ingolstadt
Augsburg
Freising
München (Munich)
Rosenheim

Wismar
Schwerin
Parchim
Müritz See
Neustrelitz
Prenzlau
Wittenberge
Neuruppin
Neubrandenburg

Rostock
Güstrow

Stralsund
Greifswald
Warnemünde

Sassnitz
Rügen
Usedom
Swinoujście
Wolin

BALTIC SEA
Darłowo Słupsko
Kołobrzeg
Koszalin
Szczecinek

Oder Haff
Goleniów
Szczecin (Stettin)
Dąbie Stargard
Oder
Choszczno
Piła
POLAND

Oranienburg
Eberswalde
Havel
Spandau
Charlottenburg BERLIN
Brandenburg Potsdam
Magdeburg
Lückenwalde
Zerbst
Bernburg Dessau
Wittenberg
Halle
Mulde
Torgau
Merseburg
Naumburg
Zeitz
Leipzig
Jena
Gera
Grossenhain
Meissen
Dresden
Chemnitz (Karl-Marx-Stadt)
Reichenbach
Zwickau
Plauen
Erzgebirge
Hof
Fichtel gebirge
1051
Bayreuth
Rhein-Main-Donau
Naab
Amberg
Böhmerwald 1457
Deggendorf
Landshut
Isar
Passau
Lech
Inn
OBER-
Linz
Wels
Steyr
ÖSTERREICH
Ried
Urfahr
Salzburg
Bad Ischl
Gmunden
Kufstein
AUSTRIA

Rathenow
Stendal
Spree
Frankfurt
Spree
Cottbus
Forst
Spremberg
Lauchhammer
Bautzen
Görlitz
Liberec
Ústí nad Labem
Litoměřice
Most
Chomutov
Teplice
Ohře
Cheb
Karlovy Vary
Kladno
Praha (Prague)
Beroun
Plzeň (Pilsen)
Klatovy
Písek
Most
Mladá Boleslav
Labe (Elbe)
Kolín
Příbram
Sázava
Tábor
Jihlava
Třeboň
České Budějovice
Gmünd
Zwettl
Horn
Freistadt
NIEDER-
ÖSTERREICH
Stockerau

Kostrzyn
Miedzychód
Skwierzyna
Warta Warthe
Nowy Tomyśl
Świebodzin
Poznań
Grodzisk
Kościan
Leszno
Głogów
Odra (Oder)
Bolesławiec
Legnica
Wrocław
Silesia
Jelenia Góra
Riesengebirge 1602
Jablonec
Trutnov
Śnieżka
Hradec Králové
Pardubice
Świdnica
Wałbrzych
Kłodzko
Sudety Mts.
1492
Šumperk
Vrchovina
Olomouc
Prostějov
Brno (Brünn)
Jihlava
Morava
Slavkov (Austerlitz)
Hodonín
Znojmo
Malé Karpaty

GORZÓW
Notec (Netze)
Zielona Góra
Zagań
Żary
Gubin

Klobuck
Beroun
Vltava
Českomoravská
Třebíč
Humlíčkuv Brod
CZECH REPUBLIC

Gorzów

COPYRIGHT GEORGE PHILIP & SON LTD

14
16
54
58
52
50
59
45
48
12
14
61
12
81

N 142
1051
1457
1378
1492

42

37

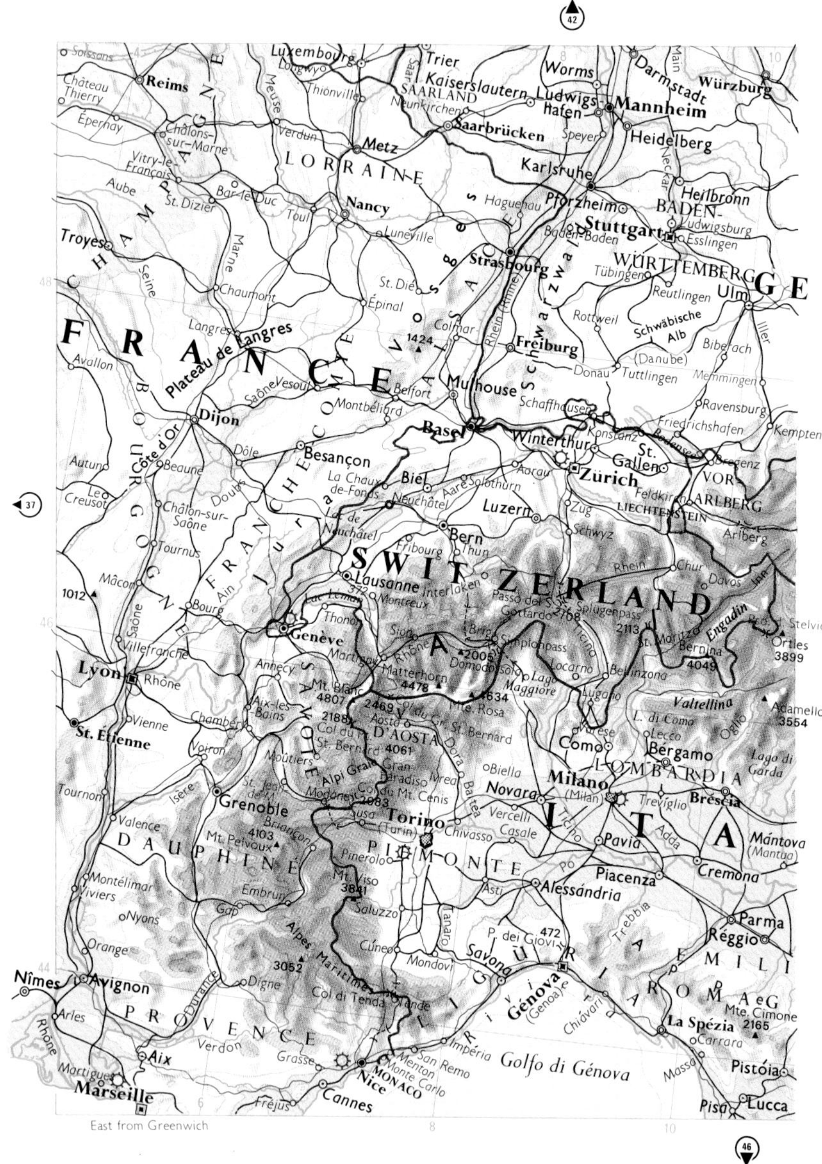
FRANCE
SWITZERLAND
ITALIA
GERMANY
LORRAINE
CHAMPAGNE
BOURGOGNE
FRANCHE-COMTÉ
SAVOIE
DAUPHINÉ
PROVENCE
PIEMONTE
LOMBARDIA
LIGURIA
EMILIA-ROMAGNA
BADEN-WÜRTTEMBERG
SAARLAND
VORARLBERG
LIECHTENSTEIN
MONACO
Luxembourg
Trier
Kaiserslautern
Worms
Darmstadt
Würzburg
Mannheim
Ludwigshafen
Heidelberg
Saarbrücken
Metz
Nancy
Reims
Karlsruhe
Pforzheim
Stuttgart
Heilbronn
Strasbourg
Freiburg
Mulhouse
Basel
Dijon
Besançon
Zürich
Bern
Luzern
Lausanne
Genève
Lyon
St. Étienne
Grenoble
Torino
Milano
Novara
Como
Bergamo
Brescia
Alessándria
Piacenza
Génova
Savona
Nice
Cannes
Marseille
Avignon
Nîmes
Aix
La Spézia
Parma
Réggio
Lucca
Pistóia
Cremona
Mántova
Golfo di Génova
Mt. Blanc 4807
Matterhorn 4478
Mte. Rosa 4634
Mt. Pelvoux 4103
Mt. Viso 3841
Ortles 3899
Adamello 3554
Bernina 4049
Mte. Cimone 2165
Rhein
Rhône
Donau
Po
Lac Léman
Lago Maggiore
Lago di Garda
Schwarzwald
Vosges
Jura
Alpi Graie
Alpes Maritimes
Plateau de Langres
Schwäbische Alb
East from Greenwich

46

1 : 5 000 000

43

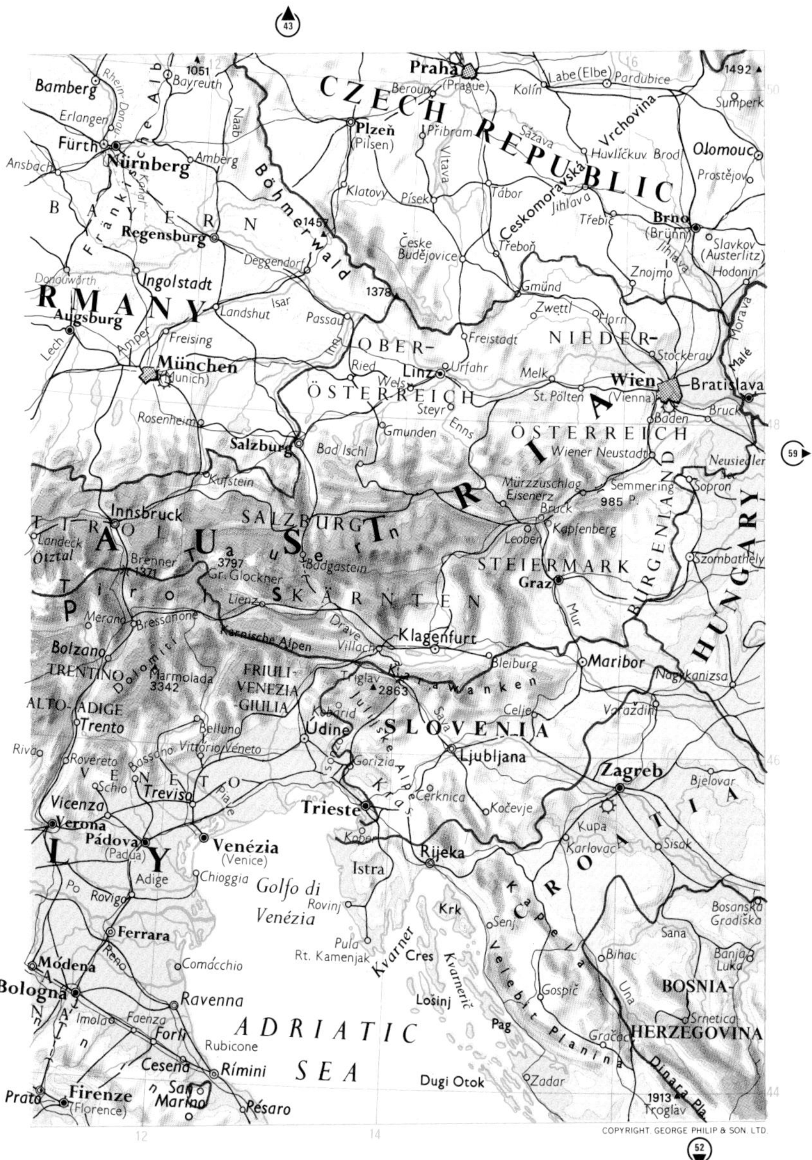
CZECH REPUBLIC
AUSTRIA
SLOVENIA
CROATIA
HUNGARY
BOSNIA-HERZEGOVINA
Praha (Prague)
Plzeň (Pilsen)
Brno (Brünn)
Olomouc
Nürnberg
Regensburg
Ingolstadt
Augsburg
München (Munich)
Salzburg
Innsbruck
Linz
Wien (Vienna)
Bratislava
Graz
Klagenfurt
Maribor
Ljubljana
Zagreb
Trieste
Rijeka
Venézia (Venice)
Pádova (Padua)
Verona
Vicenza
Treviso
Údine
Bolzano
Trento
Ferrara
Bologna
Modena
Ravenna
Rímini
Firenze (Florence)
San Marino
Golfo di Venézia
ADRIATIC SEA
Böhmerwald
ÖSTERREICH
STEIERMARK
KÄRNTEN
SALZBURG
BURGENLAND
FRIULI-VENEZIA-GIULIA
TRENTINO-ALTO-ADIGE
VENETO
Gr. Glockner 3797
Marmolada 3342
Triglav 2863
Istra
Krk
Cres
Velebit Planina
Dinara Pla.
Troglav 1913
Zadar
Dugi Otok

59
52

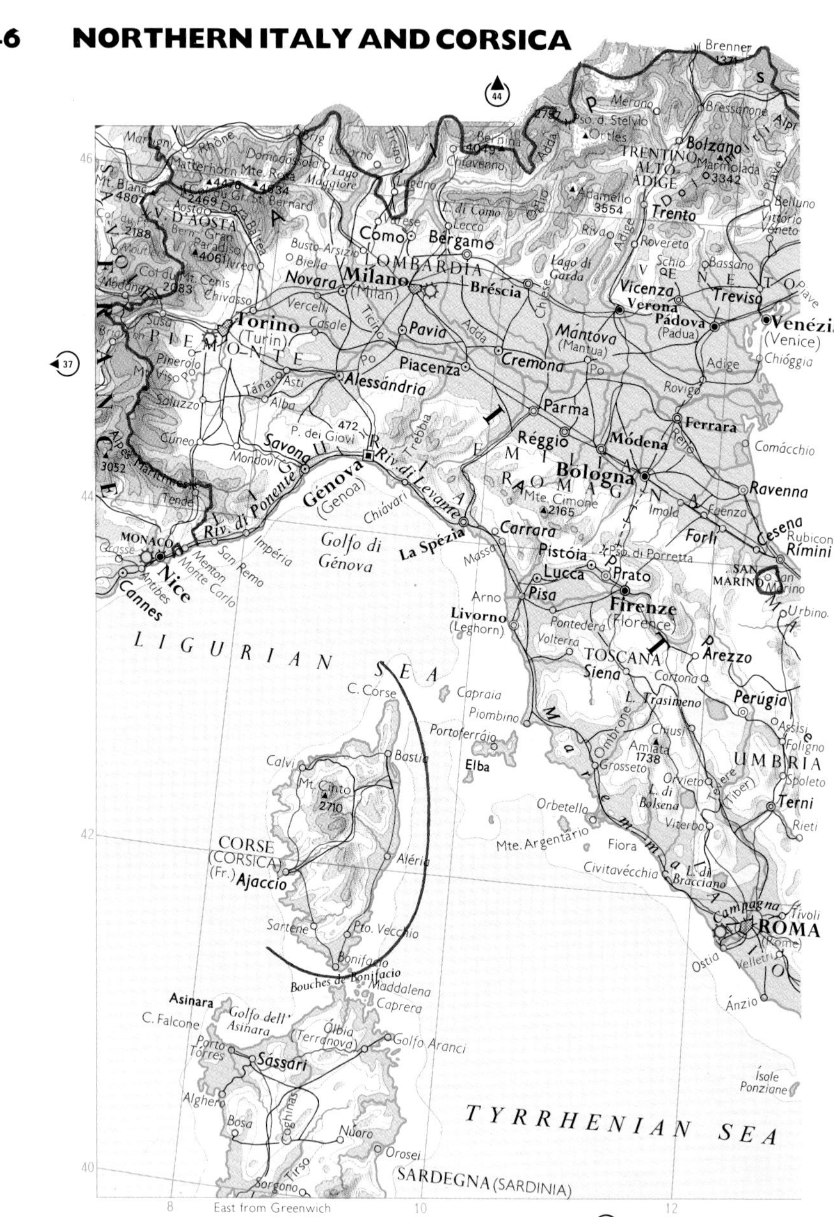
44
37
48
Brenner
Merano
Bressanone
Pso. d. Stelvio
Ortles
TRENTINO
ALTO
ADIGE
Bolzano
Marmolada
3342
Belluno
Vittorio Véneto
Bernina
4049
Chiavenna
Adda
Adamello
3554
Trento
Rovereto
Riva
L. di Como
Lecco
Como
Bergamo
Lugano
Varese
Locarno
Lago Maggiore
Domodossola
Brig
Martigny
Rhône
Matterhorn
Mte. Rosa
4634
4478
Mt. Blanc
4807
Gr. St. Bernard
2469
Aosta
Dora Baltea
V. D'AOSTA
Gran Paradiso
4061
Ivrea
Biella
Busto-Arsizio
LOMBARDIA
Novara
Milano
(Milan)
Bréscia
Lago di Garda
Chiese
Schio
Bassano
Vicenza
Verona
Pádova
(Padua)
Treviso
Piave
Venézia
(Venice)
Chióggia
VENETO
Col du Mt. Cenis
2083
Modane
Chivasso
Susa
Vercelli
Casale
Torino
(Turin)
Ticino
Pavia
Adda
Po
Mántova
(Mantua)
Cremona
Piacenza
PIEMONTE
Pinerolo
Mt. Viso
Tánaro
Asti
Alessándria
Saluzzo
Alba
Adige
Rovigo
Parma
Ferrara
Réggio
Módena
Bologna
Comácchio
EMILIA ROMAGNA
Mte. Cimone
2165
Imola
Faenza
Ravenna
Forlì
Cesena
Rubicone
Rímini
SAN MARINO
P. dei Giovi
472
Trebbia
Cúneo
Mondovì
Savona
Génova
(Genoa)
Riv. di Ponente
Riv. di Levante
Chiávari
Alpes Maritimes
3052
Tende
MONACO
Grasse
Nice
Antibes
Cannes
Menton
Monte Carlo
San Remo
Impéria
Golfo di Génova
La Spézia
Carrara
Massa
Pistóia
Pso. di Porretta
Lucca
Prato
Pisa
Arno
Firenze
(Florence)
Urbino
Livorno
(Leghorn)
Pontedera
Volterra
TOSCANA
Siena
Arezzo
Cortona
L. Trasimeno
Perúgia
LIGURIAN SEA
C. Corse
Capraia
Piombino
Portoferráio
Elba
Assisi
Foligno
UMBRIA
Spoleto
Chiusi
Amiata
1738
Ombrone
Grosseto
Orvieto
L. di Bolsena
Tevere
(Tiber)
Terni
Orbetello
Viterbo
Rieti
Mte. Argentario
Fiora
Civitavécchia
L. di Bracciano
Campagna
Tivoli
ROMA
(Rome)
Ostia
Velletri
LAZIO
Ánzio
Calvi
Bastia
Mt. Cinto
2710
CORSE
(CORSICA)
(Fr.)
Ajaccio
Aléria
Sartène
Pto. Vecchio
Bonifacio
Bouches de Bonifacio
Maddalena
Caprera
Asinara
C. Falcone
Golfo dell' Asinara
Porto Torres
Ólbia
(Terranova)
Golfo Aranci
Sássari
Alghero
Coghinas
Bosa
Nùoro
Orosei
Tirso
Sorgono
Ísole Ponziane
TYRRHENIAN SEA
SARDEGNA (SARDINIA)
Mare Tirreno
ITALIA
46
44
42
40
8
10
12
East from Greenwich

1 : 5 000 000

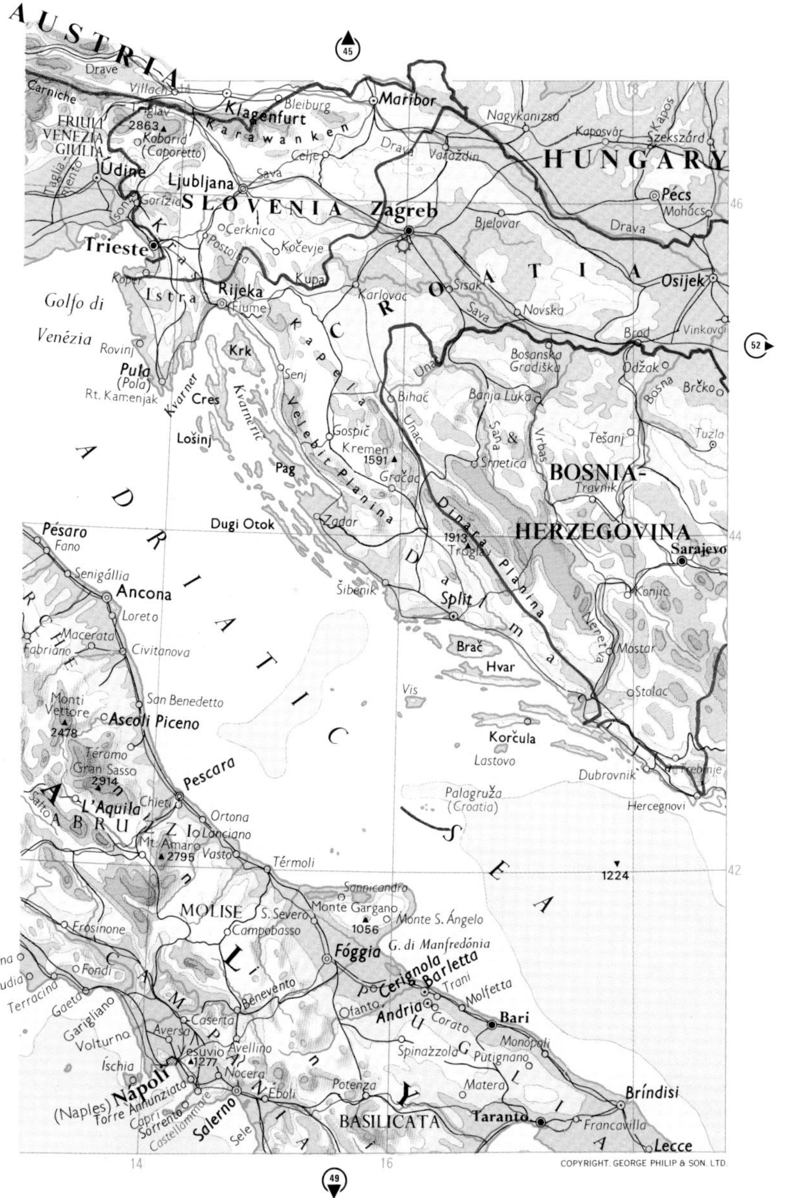
AUSTRIA
HUNGARY
SLOVENIA
CROATIA
BOSNIA-HERZEGOVINA
ADRIATIC SEA
FRIULI VENEZIA GIULIA
ABRUZZI
MOLISE
CAMPANIA
PUGLIA
BASILICATA
Golfo di Venézia
Klagenfurt
Ljubljana
Zagreb
Maribor
Trieste
Rijeka
(Fiume)
Údine
Sarajevo
Split
Pécs
Osijek
Ancona
Pescara
L'Aquila
Fóggia
Bari
Nápoli
(Naples)
Salerno
Taranto
Bríndisi
Lecce
Barletta
Andria
Cerignola
Ascoli Piceno
Pula
(Pola)
Krk
Cres
Lošinj
Pag
Dugi Otok
Brač
Hvar
Korčula
Karawanken
Kapela
Velebit Planina
Dinara Planina
Dalmacija
Istra
Kras
Kvarner
Kvarnerić
Drave
Drava
Sava
Kupa
Una
Unac
Sana
Vrbas
Bosna
Neretva
Kapos
Villach
Bleiburg
Celje
Varaždin
Nagykanizsa
Kaposvár
Szekszárd
Mohács
Bjelovar
Sisak
Novska
Karlovac
Brod
Vinkovci
Bosanska Gradiška
Odžak
Brčko
Banja Luka
Tešanj
Tuzla
Bihać
Gospič
Kremen
1591
Gračac
Srnetica
Travnik
Senj
Zadar
Šibenik
1913
Troglav
Kanjic
Mostar
Stolac
Vis
Lastovo
Dubrovnik
Trebinje
Palagruža
(Croatia)
Hercegnovi
1224
Carniche
Triglav
2863
Kobarid
(Caporetto)
Gorizia
Isonzo
Tagliamento
Cerknica
Postojna
Kočevje
Koper
Rovinj
Rt. Kamenjak
Pésaro
Fano
Senigállia
Loreto
Macerata
Fabriano
Civitanova
San Benedetto
Monti Vettore
2478
Teramo
Gran Sasso
2914
Chieti
Ortona
Lanciano
Mt. Amaro
2795
Vasto
Términi
Salto
Sannicandro
S. Severo
Monte Gargano
1056
Monte S. Ángelo
G. di Manfredónia
Campobasso
Frosinone
Fondi
Terracina
Gaeta
Garigliano
Volturno
Benevento
Caserta
Aversa
Vesuvio
1277
Avellino
Nocera
Íschia
Torre Annunziata
Capri
Sorrento
Castellammare
Éboli
Sele
Potenza
Ofanto
Trani
Molfetta
Corato
Monópoli
Putignano
Spinazzola
Matera
Francavilla
14
16
18
46
44
42
45
52
49

46

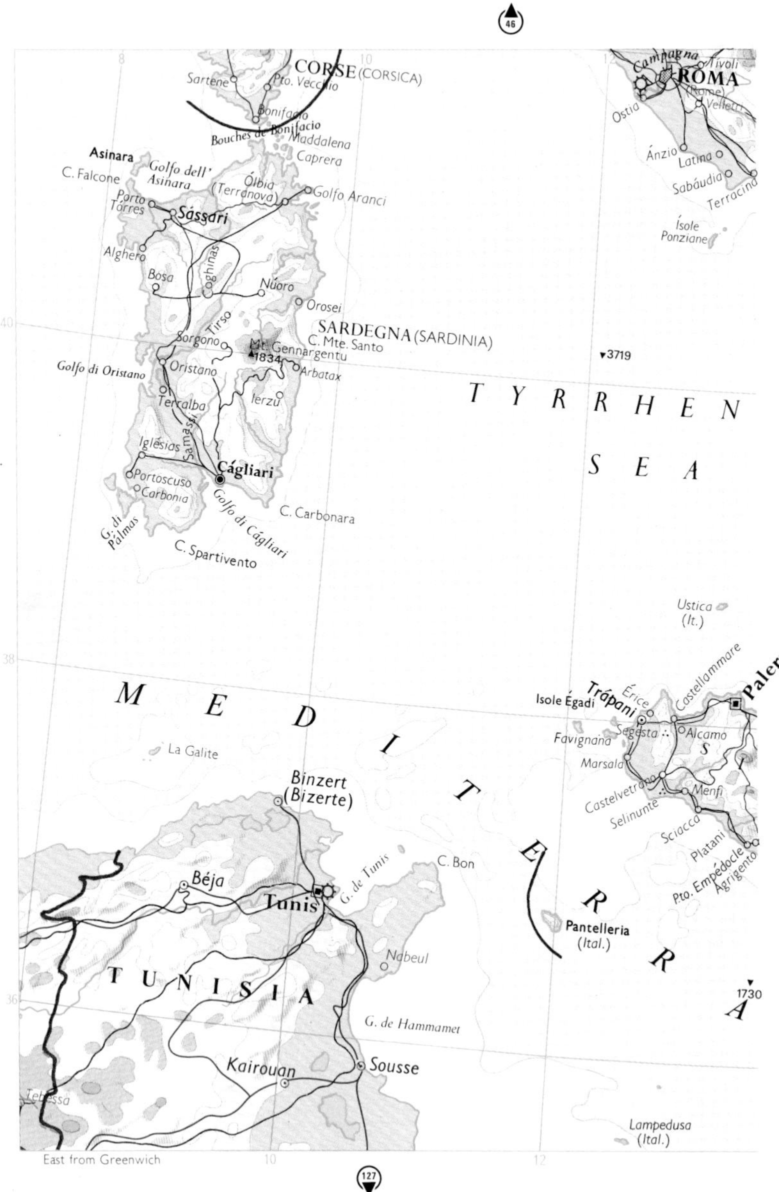
CORSE (CORSICA)
Sartene
Pto. Vecchio
Bonifacio
Bouches de Bonifacio
Maddalena
Caprera
Asinara
C. Falcone
Golfo dell' Asinara
Ólbia (Terranova)
Golfo Aranci
Porto Tórres
Sássari
Alghero
Bosa
Coghinas
Núoro
Orosei
Tirso
SARDEGNA (SARDINIA)
Sorgono
Mt. Gennargentu
1834
C. Mte. Santo
Golfo di Oristano
Oristano
Arbatax
Terralba
Ierzu
Iglésias
Samassi
Cágliari
Portoscuso
Carbonia
G. di Pálmas
Golfo di Cágliari
C. Carbonara
C. Spartivento
Campagna
Tivoli
ROMA (Rome)
Ostia
Velletri
Ánzio
Latina
Sabáudia
Terracina
Ísole Ponziane
3719
TYRRHEN SEA
Ustica (It.)
MEDITERRA
Isole Égadi
Trápani
Érice
Castellammare
Palerm
Segesta
Alcamo
Favignana
Marsala
Castelvetrano
Menfi
Selinunte
Sciacca
Platani
Pto. Empédocle
Agrigento
La Galite
Binzert (Bizerte)
C. Bon
G. de Tunis
Béja
Tunis
Pantelleria (Ital.)
Nabeul
TUNISIA
1730
G. de Hammamet
Kairouan
Sousse
Tebessa
Lampedusa (Ital.)
East from Greenwich

127

1 : 5 000 000

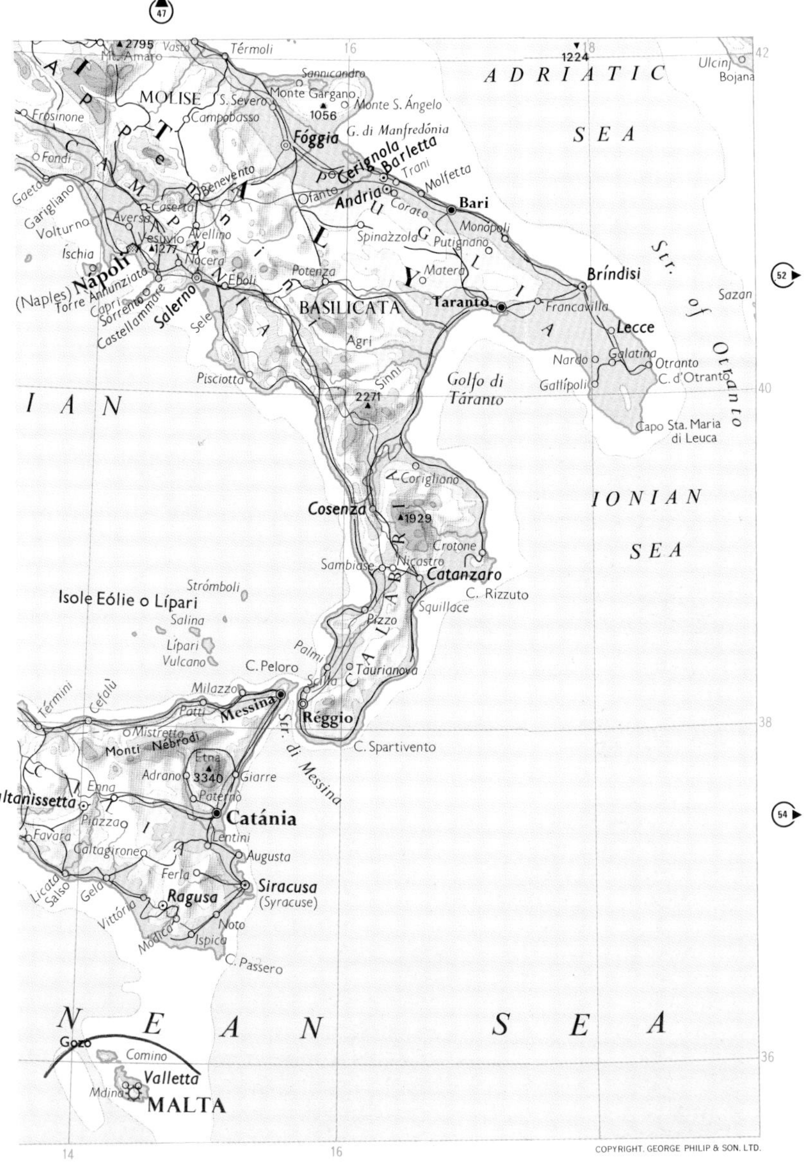

A D R I A T I C

S E A

MOLISE

Monte Gargano

G. di Manfredónia

Fóggia

Cerignola
Barletta

Andria
Corato

Trani
Molfetta

Bari

Spinazzola
Putignano
Monópoli

Caserta
Avellino

Potenza

Matera

Bríndisi

Sazan

(Naples) **Nápoli**

Salerno

BASILICATA

Taranto

Francavilla

Lecce

I T A L Y

Nardo
Galatina
Otranto

Pisciotta

Agri

Sinni
2271

Golfo di
Táranto

Gallípoli
C. d'Otranto

Capo Sta. Maria
di Leuca

I A N

Corigliano

I O N I A N

Cosenza

1929

Crotone

S E A

Sambiase
Nicastro
Catanzaro

Isole Eólie o Lípari

Strómboli

C. Rizzuto

Salina

Pizzo
Squillace

Lípari
Vulcano

C. Peloro

Palmi
Tauriánova

Milazzo

C A L A B R I A

Tếrmini
Cefalú

Patti

Messina

Sicilia

Monti Nebrodi
Mistretta

Réggio

C. Spartivento

Etna
Adrano 3340

Giarre

Caltanissetta

Enna

Paternò

Pizzo

Catánia

Favara
Caltagirone

Lentini

Augusta

Licata
Salso
Gela

Ferla

Vittória

Ragusa

Siracusa
(Syracuse)

Módica

Noto

Íspica

C. Passero

N E A N

S E A

Gozo
Comino

Valletta

Mdina

MALTA

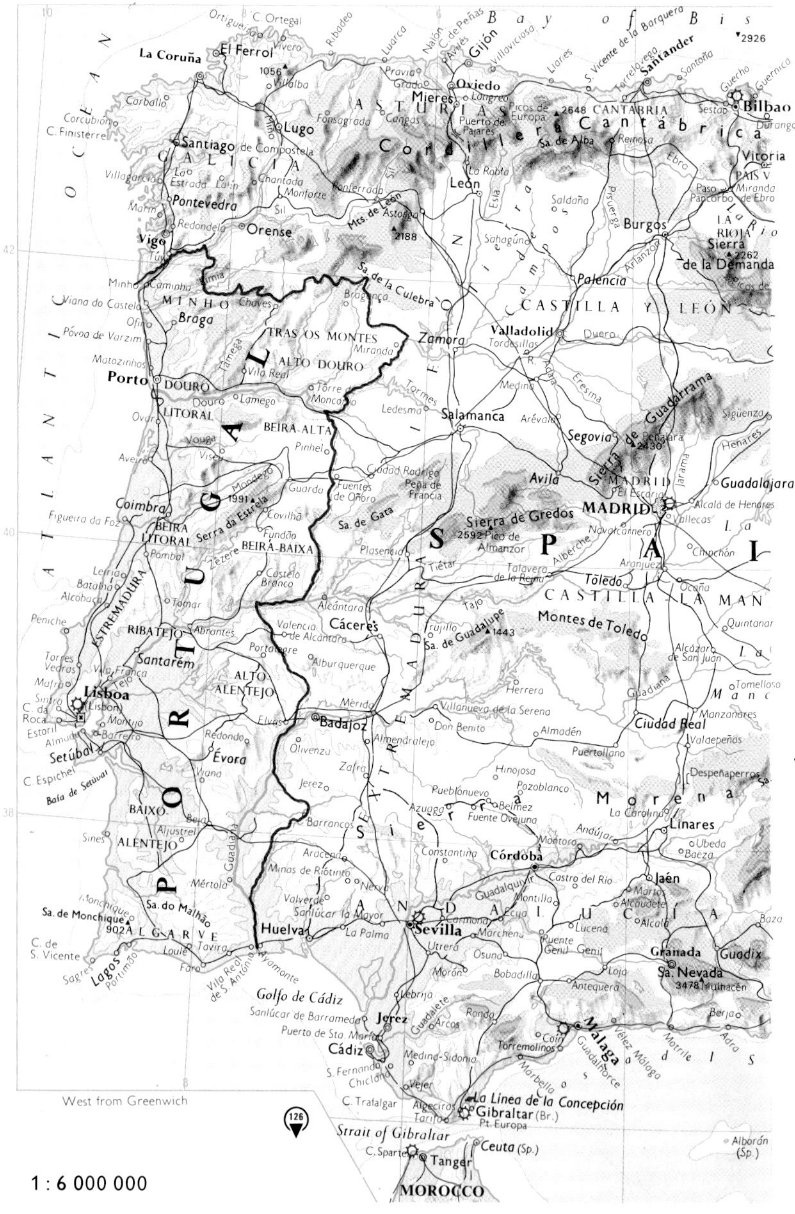

Bay of Biscay
ATLANTIC OCEAN
La Coruña
El Ferrol
C. Ortegal
Ortigueira
Vivero
Ribadeo
Luarca
Navia
C. de Peñas
Avilés
Gijón
Villaviciosa
Llanes
S. Vicente de la Barquera
Torrelavega
Santander
Santoña
2926
Guecho
Guernica
Bilbao
Durango
Sestao
1056
Villalba
Pravia
Grado
Oviedo
Mieres
Langreo
ASTURIAS
Picos de Europa
Puerto de Pajares
2648
CANTABRIA
Cordillera Cantábrica
Sa. de Alba
Reinosa
Carballo
Corcubión
C. Finisterre
Lugo
Fonsagrada
Cangas
Miño
Santiago de Compostela
GALICIA
Lalín
La Estrada
Chantada
Villagarcía
Monforte
Ponferrada
Sil
La Robla
León
Esla
Ebro
Vitoria
PAÍS V
Paso Pancorbo
Miranda de Ebro
Pontevedra
Marín
Redondela
Orense
Mts. de León
Astorga
2188
Saldaña
Sahagún
Pisuerga
Burgos
LA RIOJA
Sierra de la Demanda
2262
Vigo
Tuy
Minho
Caminha
Viana do Castelo
MINHO
Chaves
Braga
Ofir
Póvoa de Varzim
Bragança
Sa. de la Culebra
Palencia
Arlanzón
Picos de
CASTILLA Y LEÓN
TRÁS OS MONTES
Miranda
ALTO DOURO
Vila Real
Tâmega
Matozinhos
Porto
DOURO
Douro
Lamego
Tôrre de Moncorvo
Zamora
Valladolid
Tordesillas
Duero
Tormes
Medina
Eresma
Sierra de Guadarrama
Sigüenza
Ovar
LITORAL
Ledesma
Salamanca
Arévalo
Segovia
Peñalara
2430
Henares
Vouga
BEIRA-ALTA
Aveiro
Viseu
Pinhel
Ciudad Rodrigo
Peña de Francia
Ávila
Sierra de Guadarrama
MADRID
El Escorial
Jarama
Guadalajara
Alcalá de Henares
Vallecas
Mondego
1991
Guarda
Fuentes de Oñoro
Coimbra
Covilhã
Sa. de Gata
Sierra de Gredos
2592 Pico de Almanzor
Navalcarnero
Figueira da Foz
BEIRA LITORAL
Serra da Estrela
Fundão
BEIRA-BAIXA
Plasencia
Tiétar
Alberche
Chinchón
Pombal
Zêzere
Castelo Branco
Talavera de la Reina
Aranjuez
Toledo
Ocaña
Leiria
Batalha
Alcobaça
ESTREMADURA
Tomar
Alcántara
Tajo
CASTILLA-LA MAN
Peniche
RIBATEJO
Abrantes
Valencia de Alcántara
Cáceres
Trujillo
Sa. de Guadalupe
1443
Montes de Toledo
Quintanar
Santarém
Portalegre
Torres Vedras
Vila Franca
ALTO ALENTEJO
Alburquerque
Alcázar de San Juan
Mafra
Tejo
Lisboa (Lisbon)
Herrera
Guadiana
Tomelloso
Sintra
C. da Roca
Estoril
Almada
Montijo
Barreiro
Elvas
Mérida
Badajoz
Villanueva de la Serena
Don Benito
Almadén
Ciudad Real
Manzanares
Setúbal
Redondo
Évora
Olivenza
Almendralejo
Puertollano
Valdepeñas
C. Espichel
Baía de Setúbal
Viana
Zafra
Hinojosa
Despeñaperros
Jerez
Pueblonuevo
Pozoblanco
Sierra Morena
BAIXO ALENTEJO
Beja
Azuaga
Belmez
Fuente Ovejuna
La Carolina
Linares
Sines
Aljustrel
Barrancos
Andújar
Montoro
Úbeda
Baeza
Guadiana
Aracena
Constantina
Córdoba
Minas de Ríotinto
Mértola
Nerva
Castro del Río
Jaén
Valverde
Guadalquivir
Montilla
Martos
Alcaudete
Sa. do Malhão
Monchique
Sa. de Monchique
902
ALGARVE
Sanlúcar la Mayor
ANDALUCÍA
Écija
Lucena
Alcalá
Baza
Huelva
La Palma
Sevilla
Carmona
Marchena
Tavira
Loulé
Puente Genil
Genil
Granada
Guadix
C. de S. Vicente
Sagres
Lagos
Portimão
Faro
Vila Real de S. António
Ayamonte
Utrera
Osuna
Morón
Bobadilla
Loja
Sa. Nevada
3478 Mulhacén
Antequera
Golfo de Cádiz
Lebrija
Ronda
Sanlúcar de Barrameda
Jerez
Guadalete
Arcos
Berja
Puerto de Sta. María
Coín
Málaga
Vélez Málaga
Motril
Adra
Cádiz
Torremolinos
Guadalhorce
S. Fernando
Chiclana
Medina-Sidonia
Marbella
Vejer
C. Trafalgar
Algeciras
Tarifa
La Línea de la Concepción
Gibraltar (Br.)
Pt. Europa
Strait of Gibraltar
C. Spartel
Tanger
Ceuta (Sp.)
MOROCCO
Alborán (Sp.)
SPAIN
PORTUGAL
West from Greenwich
126

1 : 6 000 000

36

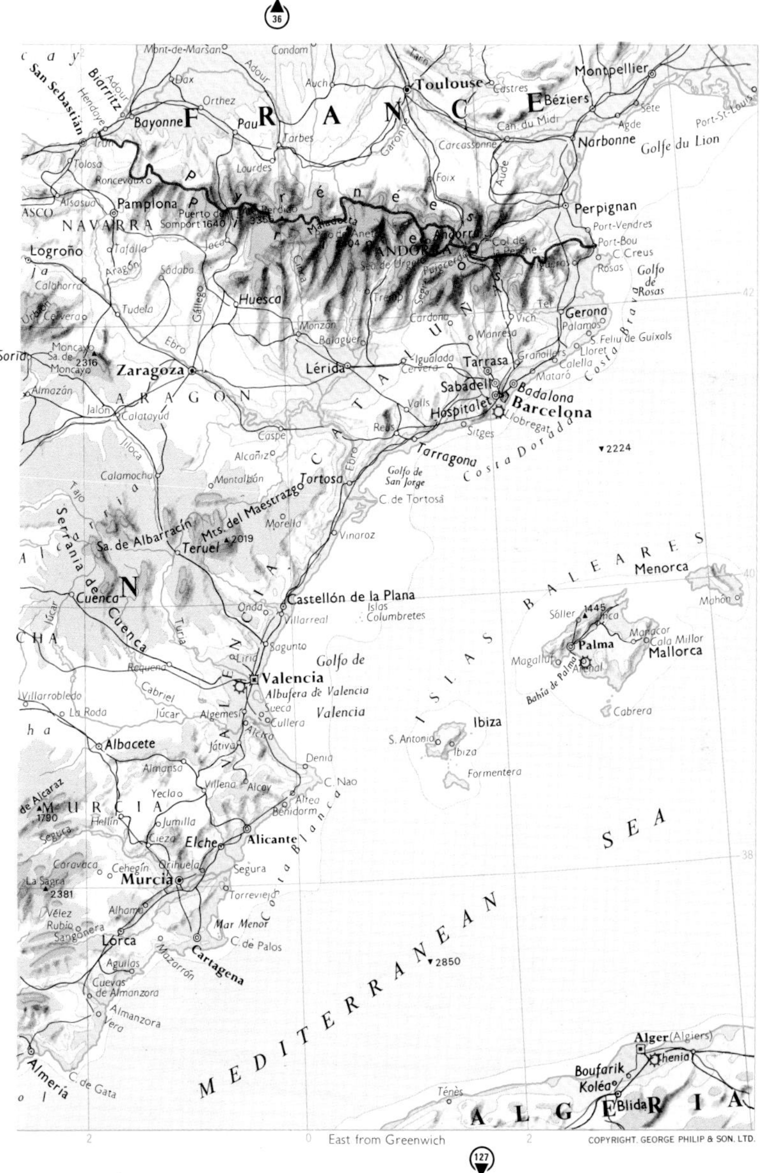
FRANCE
Toulouse
Montpellier
Béziers
Sète
Agde
Port-St-Louis
Narbonne
Golfe du Lion
Castres
Can. du Midi
Carcassonne
Mont-de-Marsan
Condom
Adour
Dax
Auch
Tarn
Garonne
Aude
Foix
Orthez
Bayonne
Biarritz
Hendaye
San Sebastián
Irún
Pau
Tarbes
Lourdes
Tolosa
Roncevaux
Pyrénées
Pamplona
Alsasua
NAVARRA
Puerto de Somport 1640
Jaca
Perpignan
Port-Vendres
Port-Bou
C. Creus
Rosas
Golfo de Rosas
ANDORRA
Andorra
Col de la Perche
Seo de Urgel
Puigcerdá
Tremp
Segre
Logroño
Tafalla
Aragón
Sádaba
Calahorra
Tudela
Gállego
Huesca
Cinca
Cervera
Urbión
Moncayo
Sa. de Moncayo
2316
Soria
Zaragoza
Ebro
Monzón
Balaguer
Lérida
Cardona
Vich
Manresa
Igualada
Cervera
Tarrasa
Granollers
Gerona
Palamós
S. Feliu de Guíxols
Lloret
Calella
Mataró
Costa Brava
Ter
CATALUÑA
Sabadell
Badalona
Hospitalet
Barcelona
Llobregat
Sitges
Valls
Reus
Tarragona
Costa Dorada
2224
Almazán
ARAGON
Jalón
Calatayud
Jiloca
Caspe
Alcañiz
Calamocha
Montalbán
Tortosa
Golfo de San Jorge
C. de Tortosa
Tajo
Morella
Vinaroz
Mts. del Maestrazgo
2019
Sa. de Albarracín
Teruel
Serranía de Cuenca
Cuenca
Júcar
Turia
VALENCIA
Castellón de la Plana
Onda
Villarreal
Islas Columbretes
ISLAS BALEARES
Menorca
Mahón
Sóller
1445
Inca
Manacor
Cala Millor
Palma
Mallorca
Magalluf
Arenal
Bahía de Palma
Cabrera
Sagunto
Liria
Golfo de Valencia
Valencia
Requena
Cabriel
Albufera de Valencia
Sueca
Cullera
Villarrobledo
La Roda
Júcar
Algemesí
Alcira
Játiva
Ibiza
S. Antonio
Formentera
Albacete
Almansa
Denia
C. Nao
Villena
Alcoy
Altea
Benidorm
Costa Blanca
Yecla
MURCIA
1790
Hellín
Jumilla
Segura
Cieza
Elche
Alicante
SEA
Caravaca
Cehegín
Orihuela
Murcia
La Sagra
2381
Torrevieja
Vélez Rubio
Sangonera
Alhama
Mar Menor
C. de Palos
Lorca
Cartagena
Mazarrón
Águilas
2850
Cuevas de Almanzora
Almanzora
Vera
MEDITERRANEAN
Almería
C. de Gata
Alger (Algiers)
Thenia
Boufarik
Koléa
Blida
Ténès
ALGERIA
42
40
38
2
0
2
East from Greenwich

127

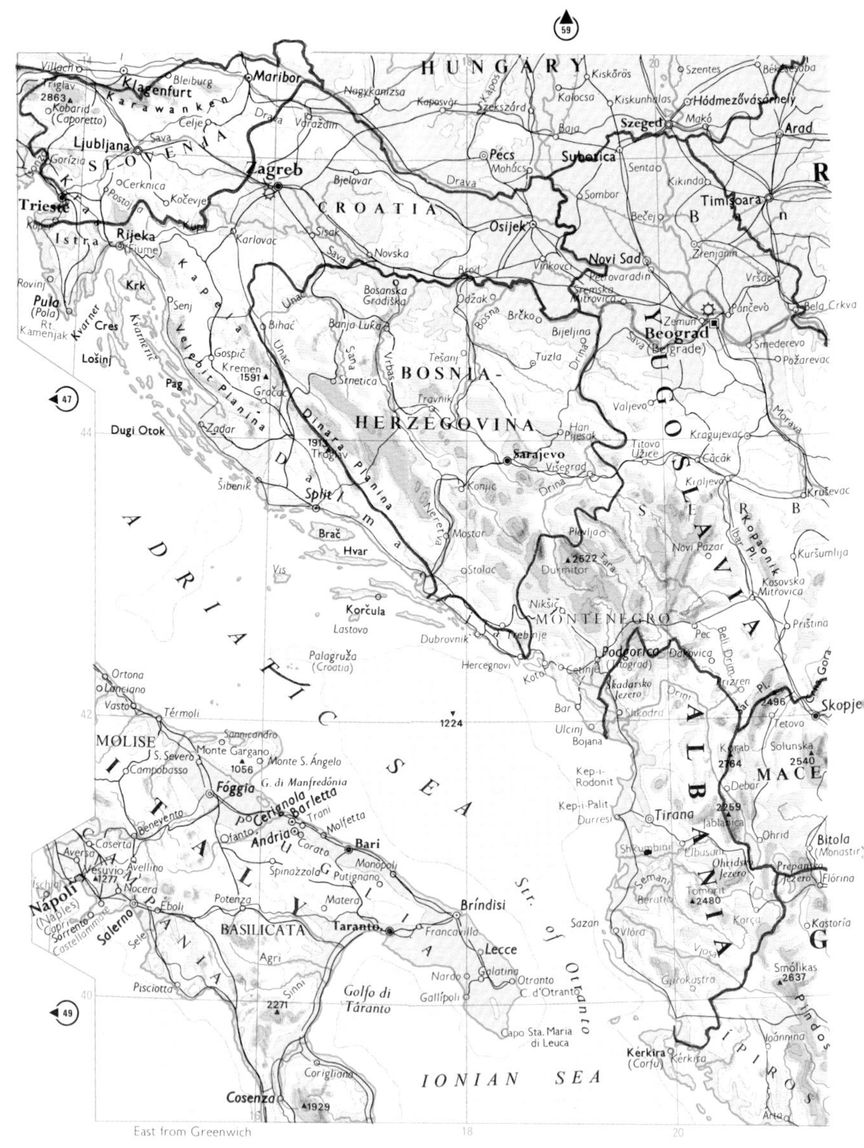
59
47
49
HUNGARY
SLOVENIA
CROATIA
BOSNIA-HERZEGOVINA
YUGOSLAVIA
SERBIA
MONTENEGRO
ALBANIA
ITALIA
MOLISE
CAMPANIA
BASILICATA
PUGLIA
CALABRIA
MACE
R
G
ADRIATIC SEA
IONIAN SEA
Str. of Otranto
Golfo di Táranto
G. di Manfredónia
Villach
Triglav
2863
Kobarid
(Caporetto)
Klagenfurt
Bleiburg
Karawanken
Maribor
Celje
Ljubljana
Sava
Gorizia
Cerknica
Postojna
Kočevje
Trieste
Koper
Kras
Istra
Rijeka
(Fiume)
Kupa
Zagreb
Karlovac
Varaždin
Drava
Nagykanizsa
Kaposvár
Kapos
Szekszárd
Kiskőrös
Kalocsa
Kiskunhalas
Szentes
Békéscsaba
Hódmezővásárhely
Makó
Szeged
Arad
Baja
Pécs
Mohács
Subotica
Senta
Kikinda
Sombor
Timişoara
Bečej
Banat
Zrenjanin
Novi Sad
Petrovaradin
Vršac
Bjelovar
Sisak
Novska
Osijek
Vinkovci
Brod
Sremska Mitrovica
Pančevo
Bela Crkva
Zemun
Beograd
(Belgrade)
Smederevo
Požarevac
Rovinj
Pula
(Pola)
Rt. Kamenjak
Kvarner
Cres
Lošinj
Krk
Kapela
Senj
Kvarnerić
Velebit Planina
Gospić
Kremen
1591
Pag
Gračac
Zadar
Dugi Otok
Una
Unac
Bihać
Bosanska Gradiška
Banja Luka
Sana
Vrbas
Srnetica
Odžak
Bosna
Brčko
Bijeljina
Tešanj
Tuzla
Drina
Travnik
Valjevo
Morava
Han Pijesak
Kragujevac
Sarajevo
Višegrad
Titovo Užice
Čačak
Dinara Planina
1913
Troglav
Dalmacija
Šibenik
Split
Konjic
Kraljevo
Kruševac
Brač
Hvar
Vis
Neretva
Mostar
Stolac
Pljevlja
Tara
2522
Durmitor
Novi Pazar
Ibar
Kopaonik
Kuršumlija
Kosovska Mitrovica
Priština
Korčula
Lastovo
Dubrovnik
Trebinje
Nikšić
Pec
Beli Drim
Ðakovica
Palagruža
(Croatia)
Hercegnovi
Kotor
Cetinje
Podgorica
(Titograd)
Prizren
Skadarsko Jezero
Drini
Šar Pl.
2496
Skopje
Tetovo
Bar
Shkodra
Ulcinj
Bojana
1224
Korab
2764
Solunska
2540
Debar
Kep-i-Rodonit
Kep-i-Palit
Durrësi
Tirana
2259
Jablanica
Ohrid
Bitola
(Monastir)
Shkumbini
Elbasani
Ohridsko Jezero
Prespansko Jezero
Flórina
Semani
Berati
Tomorit
2480
Korça
Kastoría
Sazan
Vlóra
Vjosa
Smólikas
2637
Gjirokastra
Pindos
Ioánnina
Ipiros
Kérkira
(Corfu)
Árta
Ortona
Lanciano
Vasto
Térmoli
Sannicandro
Monte Gargano
1056
Monte S. Ángelo
S. Severo
Campobasso
Fóggia
Cerignola
Barletta
Trani
Molfetta
Ofanto
Andria
Corato
Bari
Benevento
Caserta
Aversa
Avellino
Vesuvio
1277
Napoli
(Naples)
Ischia
Capri
Sorrento
Castellammare
Nocera
Salerno
Éboli
Sele
Potenza
Spinazzola
Putignano
Monopoli
Matera
Bríndisi
Taranto
Francavilla
Lecce
Agri
Sinni
Nardò
Galatina
Otranto
C. d'Otranto
Gallípoli
Capo Sta. Maria di Leuca
Pisciotta
2271
Corigliano
Cosenza
1929
14
16
18
20
44
42
40
East from Greenwich

1 : 6 000 000

57

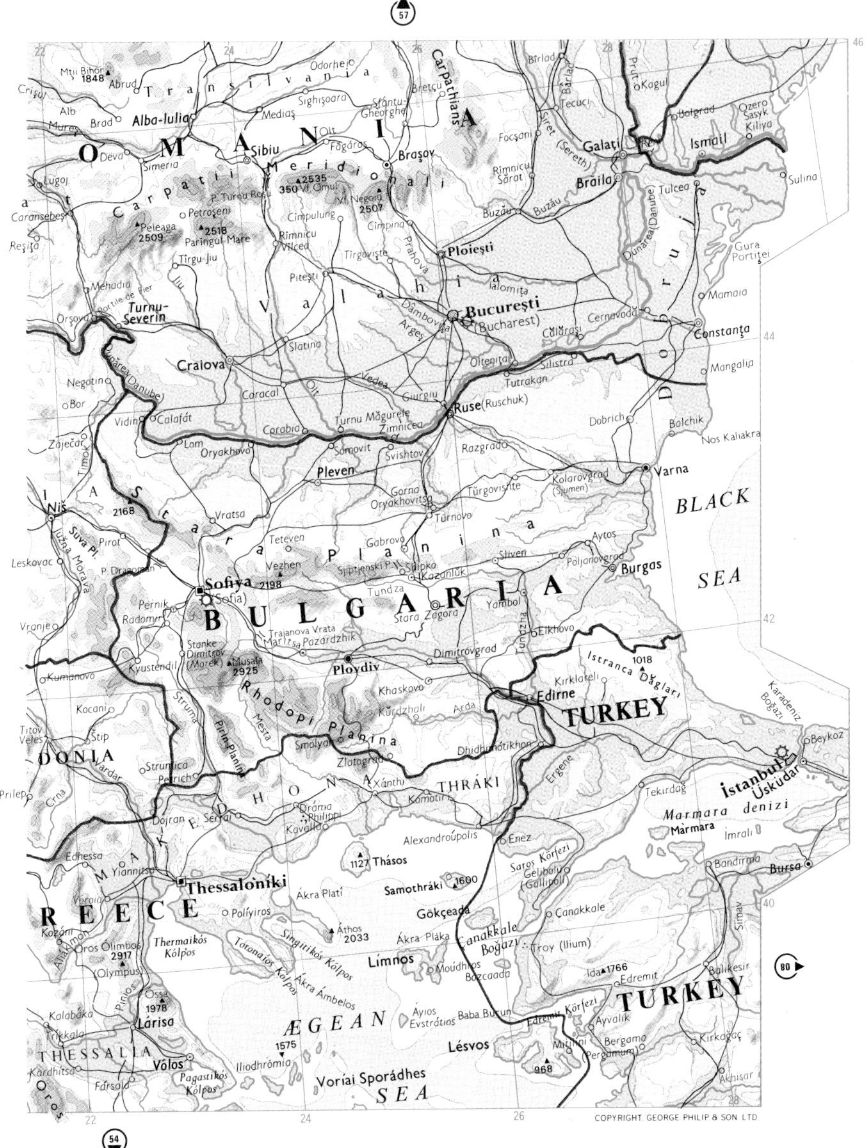

Transilvania
ROMANIA
Carpatii Meridionali
Carpathians
Valahia
Dobrogea
Stara Planina
BULGARIA
Rhodopi Planina
MAKEDHONIA
THRÁKI
GREECE
THESSALIA
TURKEY
BLACK SEA
ÆGEAN SEA
Marmara denizi
Alba-Iulia
Sibiu
Braşov
Bucureşti
(Bucharest)
Ploieşti
Craiova
Galaţi
Brăila
Constanţa
Ruse (Ruschuk)
Pleven
Varna
Burgas
Sofiya
(Sofia)
Plovdiv
Edirne
İstanbul
Üsküdar
Thessaloníki
Lárisa
Vólos
Bursa
Niš
Vidin
Calafat
Turnu-Severin
Tîrgu-Jiu
Piteşti
Sighişoara
Mediaş
Deva
Lugoj
Caransebeş
Reşiţa
Tulcea
Ismail
Sulina
Focşani
Buzău
Rîmnicu Sărat
Rîmnicu Vîlcea
Cîmpina
Cîmpulung
Tîrgovişte
Slatina
Caracal
Corabia
Giurgiu
Olteniţa
Călăraşi
Cernavodă
Mamaia
Mangalia
Silistra
Tutrakan
Dobrich
Balchik
Razgrad
Kolarovgrad
(Shumen)
Tŭrgovishte
Tŭrnovo
Gabrovo
Shipka
Kazanlŭk
Sliven
Yambol
Aytos
Elkhovo
Stara Zagora
Pazardzhik
Dimitrovgrad
Khaskovo
Kŭrdzhali
Smolyan
Zlatograd
Xánthi
Komotiní
Alexandroúpolis
Dráma
Kavála
Sérrai
Kyustendil
Pernik
Radomir
Vratsa
Lom
Oryakhovo
Svishtov
Pirot
Leskovac
Vranje
Kumanovo
Kocani
Štip
Strumica
Petrich
Prilep
Edhessa
Véroia
Kozáni
Tríkkala
Kardhítsa
Fársala
Kalabáka
Tekirdağ
Gelibolu
(Gallipoli)
Çanakkale
Çanakkale Boğazı
Troy (Ilium)
Edremit
Balıkesir
Ayvalık
Bergama
(Pergamum)
Kırkağaç
Akhisar
Bandırma
İmralı
Marmara
Enez
Saros Körfezi
Gökçeada
Bozcaada
Límnos
Samothráki 1600
Thásos 1127
Áthos 2033
Lésvos
Mitilíni
Voríai Sporádhes
Iliodhrómia
Ayios Evstrátios
Baba Burun
Edremit Körfezi
Ida 1766
Istranca Dağları 1018
Karadeniz Boğazı
Beykoz
Musala 2925
Vezhen 2198
Oros Ólimbos 2917
(Olympus)
Óssa 1978
Thermaikós Kólpos
Toronaíos Kólpos
Singitikós Kólpos
Pagastikós Kólpos
Ákra Platí
Ákra Pláka
Ákra Ámbelos
Peleaga 2509
Parîngul Mare 2518
Vf. Omul 2535
Vf. Negoiu 2507
Mţii Bihor 1848
Dunărea (Danube)
Iskŭr
Struma
Mesta
Arda
Maritsa
Tundzha
Vardar
Olt
Jiu
Mureş
Prut
Siret (Sereth)
Ialomiţa
Argeş
Vedea
Ergene
Timok
Južna Morava
Pinios
COPYRIGHT GEORGE PHILIP & SON LTD

80

54

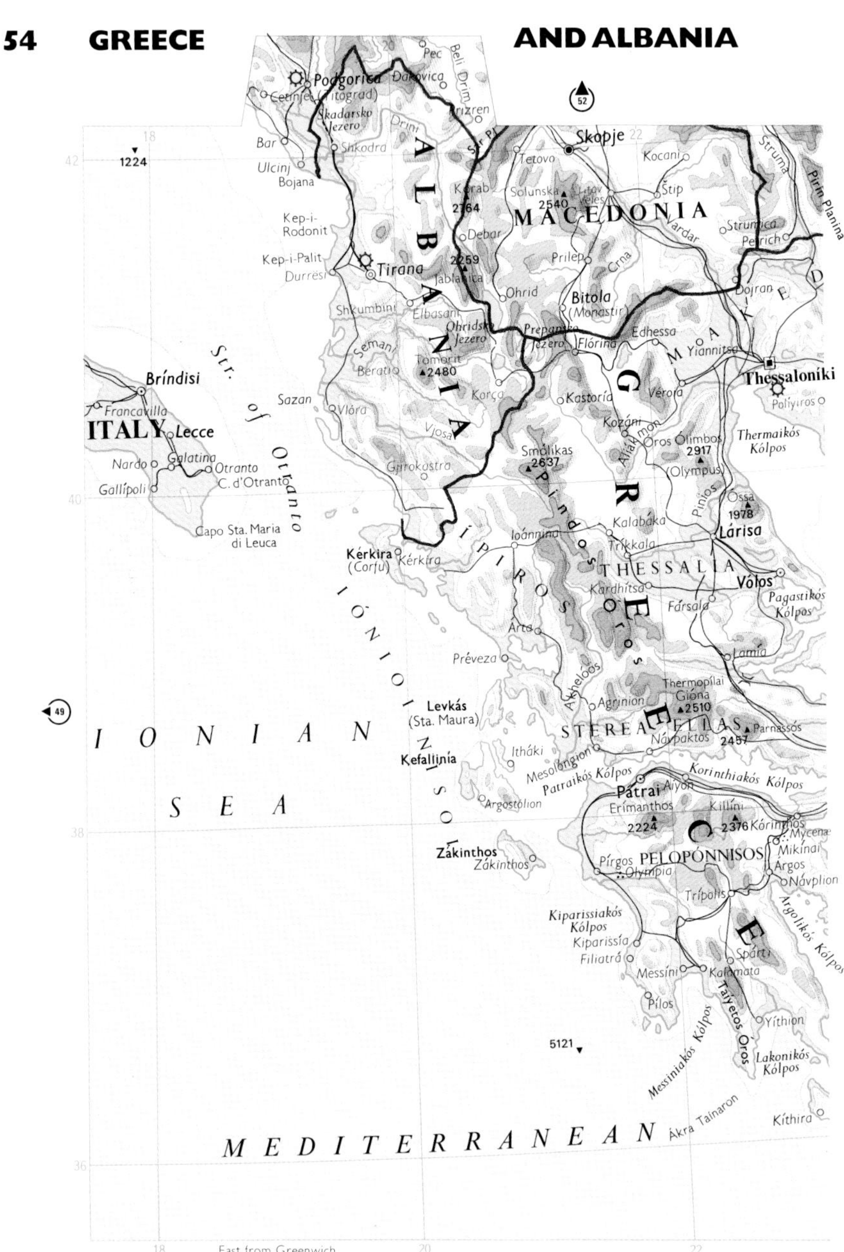
Podgorica
(Titograd)
Cetinje
Đakovica
Pec
Beli Drim
Prizren
Skadarsko Jezero
Drini
Bar
Shkodra
Ulcinj
Bojana
ALBANIA
Skopje
Tetovo
Kocani
Struma
Pirin Planina
Korab
2764
Solunska
2540
Veles
Štip
MACEDONIA
Kep-i-Rodonit
Debar
Vardar
Strumica
Petrich
Kep-i-Palit
Durrësi
Tirana
2259
Jablanica
Prilep
Crna
Ohrid
Bitola
(Monastir)
Dojran
Shkumbini
Elbasani
Ohridsko Jezero
Prespansko Jezero
Edhessa
Flórina
Yiannitsa
Semani
Berati
Tomorit
2480
Thessaloníki
Bríndisi
Korça
Kastoría
Véroia
Políyiros
Francavilla
Sazan
Vlóra
Kozáni
Aliákmon
Óros Ólimbos
2917
(Olympus)
Thermaikós Kólpos
ITALY
Lecce
Vjosa
Smólikas
2637
Nardò
Galatina
Otranto
C. d'Otranto
Gjirokastra
Gallípoli
Str. of Otranto
Píndos Óros
Piniós
Óssa
1978
Kalabáka
Lárisa
Capo Sta. Maria di Leuca
Ioánnina
Tríkkala
Kérkira
(Corfu)
Kérkira
ÍPIROS
THESSALIA
Vólos
Kardhítsa
Fársala
Pagastikós Kólpos
IÓNIOI NÍSOI
Árta
GREECE
Lamía
Préveza
Ákhelóos
Thermopílai
Gióna
2510
Agrínion
Levkás
(Sta. Maura)
STEREA ELLAS
Parnassós
2457
IONIAN SEA
Náfpaktos
Itháki
Kefallinía
Mesolóngion
Patraikós Kólpos
Pátrai
Aíyon
Korinthiakós Kólpos
Argostólion
Erímanthos
2224
Killíni
2376
Kórinthos
Mycenae
Mikínai
Zákinthos
Zákinthos
Pírgos
PELOPÓNNISOS
Olympia
Argos
Návplion
Trípolis
Argolikós Kólpos
Kiparissiakós Kólpos
Kiparissía
Filiatrá
Spárti
Messíni
Kalámata
Pílos
Taíyetos Óros
Messiniakós Kólpos
Yíthion
5121
Lakonikós Kólpos
Ákra Taínaron
Kíthira
MEDITERRANEAN
1224
East from Greenwich
18
20
22
42
40
38
36

52

49

1 : 5 000 000

53

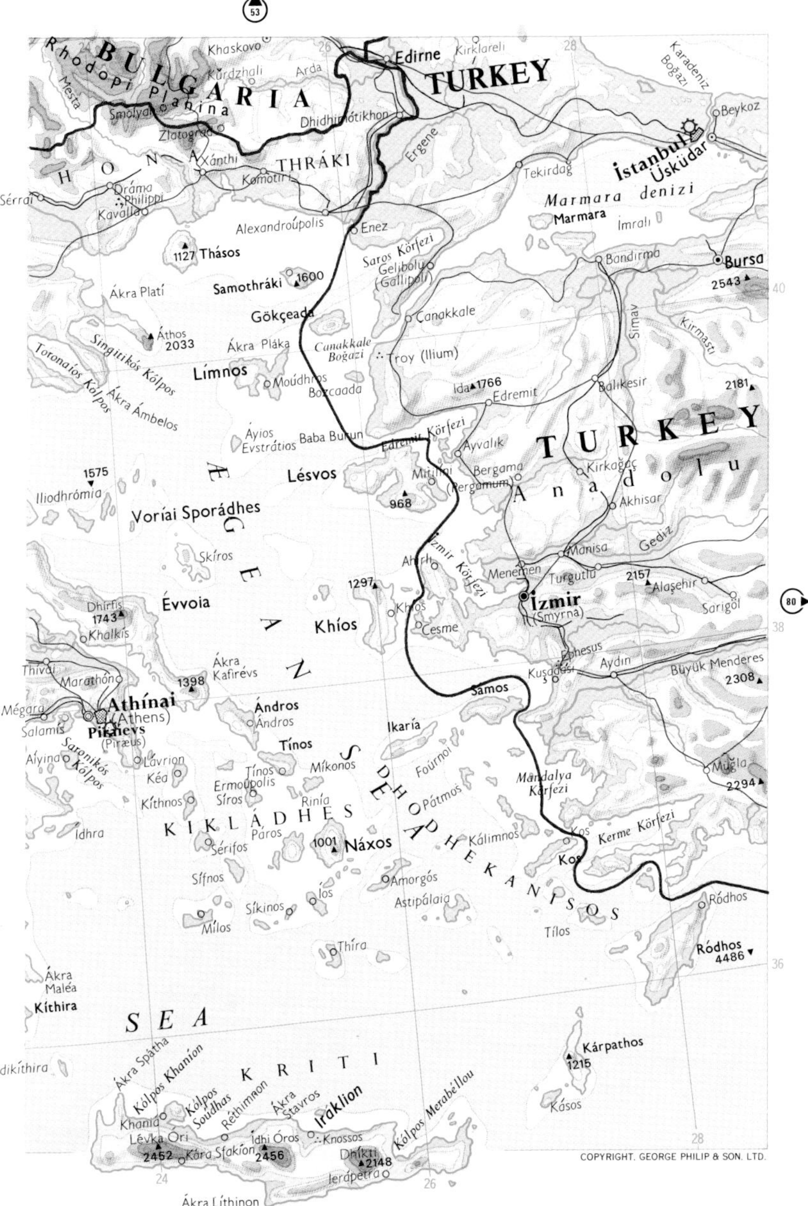

BULGARIA
TURKEY
Rhodópi Planina
Khaskovo
Kŭrdzhali
Edirne
Kirklareli
Karadeniz Boğazi
Smolyan
Zlatograd
Dhidhimótikhon
Beykoz
Xánthi
THRÁKI
Ergene
İstanbul
Üsküdar
Tekirdağ
Sérrai
Dráma
Philippi
Kavalla
Komotiní
Marmara denizi
Marmara
İmralı
Alexandroúpolis
Enez
Thásos
1127
Saros Körfezi
Gelibolu (Gallipoli)
Bandırma
Bursa
2543
Samothráki
1600
Ákra Platí
Gökçeada
Çanakkale
Simav
Kirmastı
Áthos 2033
Ákra Pláka
Canakkale Boğazi
Troy (Ilium)
Límnos
Moúdhros
Bozcaada
Ida 1766
Edremit
Balıkesir
2181
Singitikós Kólpos
Toronaíos Kólpos
Ákra Ámbelos
TURKEY
Áyios Evstrátios
Baba Burun
Edremit Körfezi
Ayvalık
Bergama (Pergamum)
Kirkağaç
Anadolu
1575
Lésvos
Mitilíni
968
Akhisar
Iliodhrómia
Voríai Sporádhes
AEGEAN
Gediz
Manisa
Skíros
Ahırlı
İzmir Körfezi
Menemen
Turgutlu
2157
Alaşehir
1297
İzmir (Smyrna)
Sarigöl
80
Dhírfis 1743
Évvoia
Khíos
Khalkís
Khíos
Cesme
Ephesus
Aydın
Büyük Menderes
Thívai
Marathón
1398
Ákra Kafirévs
Kuşadası
2308
Athínai (Athens)
Mégara
Ándros
Ándros
Samos
Salamís
Piraievs (Piræus)
Ikaría
Saronikós Kólpos
Tínos
Aíyina
Lávrion
Kéa
Tínos
Míkonos
Foúrnoi
Mandalya Körfezi
Muğla
2294
Ermoúpolis
Síros
Pátmos
Kíthnos
Riniá
DHODHEKÁNISOS
KIKLÁDHES
Kerme Körfezi
Ídhra
Páros
Kos
Sérifos
1001
Náxos
Kálimnos
Kos
Sífnos
Amorgós
Íos
Astipálaia
Síkinos
Ródhos
Mílos
Tílos
Thíra
Ródhos
4486
Ákra Maléa
Kíthira
SEA
Kárpathos
1215
Andikíthira
Ákra Spátha
Kólpos Khaníon
KRITI
Kólpos Soúdhas
Réthimnon
Ákra Stavros
Iráklion
Kólpos Merabéllou
Kásos
Khaniá
Lévka Óri
Ídhi Óros
Knossos
2452
Khóra Sfakíon
2456
Dhíkti
2148
Ierápetra
Ákra Líthinon

58

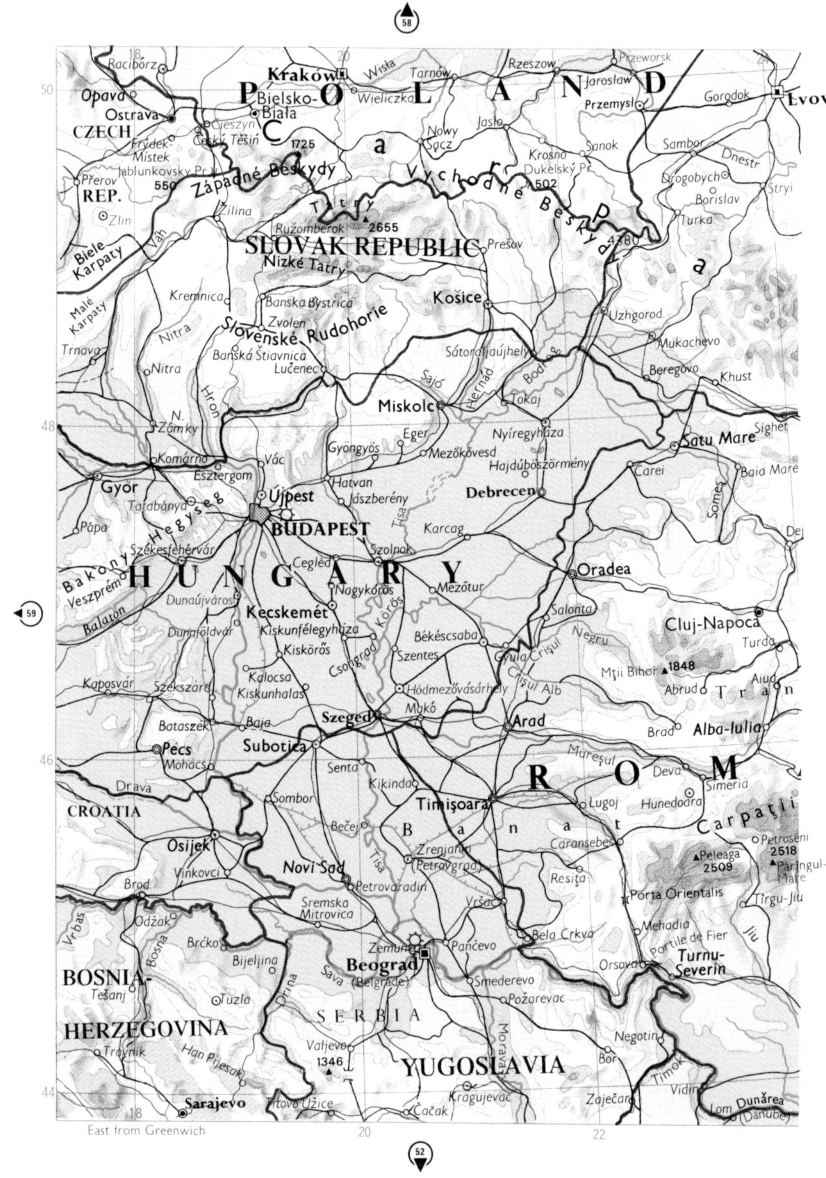
POLAND
CZECH REP.
SLOVAK REPUBLIC
HUNGARY
CROATIA
BOSNIA-HERZEGOVINA
SERBIA
YUGOSLAVIA
ROM
Kraków
Bielsko-Biała
Racibórz
Opava
Ostrava
Cieszyn
Český Těšín
Frýdek-Místek
Jablunkovský Pr.
Přerov
Zlín
Wisła
Tarnów
Wieliczka
Rzeszów
Przeworsk
Jarosław
Przemyśl
Gorodok
Lvov
Nowy Sącz
Jasło
Krosno
Sanok
Dukelský Pr.
Sambor
Dnestr
Drogobych
Borislav
Stryi
Turka
Západné Beskydy
Vychodné Beskydy
Karpaty
Tatry
2655
1725
550
502
1380
Žilina
Ružomberok
Prešov
Nizké Tatry
Biele Karpaty
Váh
Malé Karpaty
Kremnica
Banska Bystrica
Zvolen
Slovenské Rudohorie
Banská Štiavnica
Lučenec
Košice
Uzhgorod
Mukachevo
Sátoraljaújhely
Beregovo
Khust
Trnava
Nitra
Hron
Sajó
Hernád
Bodrog
Tokaj
Miskolc
N. Zámky
Eger
Nyíregyháza
Satu Mare
Sighet
Komárno
Vác
Gyöngyös
Mezőkövesd
Hajdúböszörmény
Carei
Baia Mare
Esztergom
Győr
Hatvan
Jászberény
Debrecen
Someş
Tatabánya
Újpest
BUDAPEST
Tisza
Karcag
Dej
Pápa
Bakony Hegység
Székesfehérvár
Szolnok
Cegléd
Oradea
Veszprém
Balaton
Dunaújváros
Nagykőrös
Mezőtúr
Kecskemét
Kőrös
Salonta
Cluj-Napoca
Dunaföldvár
Kiskunfélegyháza
Békéscsaba
Negru
Turda
Kiskőrös
Csongrád
Szentes
Gyula
Crişul
Mţii Bihor
1848
Kaposvár
Szekszárd
Kalocsa
Kiskunhalas
Hódmezővásárhely
Crişul Alb
Abrud
Aiud
Makó
Baja
Szeged
Arad
Brad
Alba-Iulia
Bataszék
Pecs
Subotica
Mureşul
Mohács
Senta
Deva
Simeria
Drava
Kikinda
Sombor
Timişoara
Lugoj
Hunedoara
Bečej
Banat
Carpaţii
Osijek
Zrenjanin (Petrovgrad)
Caransebeş
Petroşeni
Peleaga 2509
2518
Parîngul-Mare
Vinkovci
Novi Sad
Reşiţa
Brod
Petrovaradin
Porta Orientalis
Tîrgu-Jiu
Vrbas
Sremska Mitrovica
Vršac
Odžak
Mehadia
Portile de Fier
Jiu
Bosna
Brčko
Bela Crkva
Zemun
Pančevo
Bijeljina
Beograd (Belgrade)
Orsova
Turnu-Severin
Sava
Drina
Smederevo
Tešanj
Tuzla
Požarevac
Morava
Negotin
Travnik
Han Pijesak
Valjevo
1346
Bor
Timok
Kragujevac
Zaječar
Vidin
Sarajevo
Titovo Užice
Čačak
Lom
Dunărea (Danube)
East from Greenwich
18
20
22
24
44
46
48
50

59

52

1 : 5 000 000

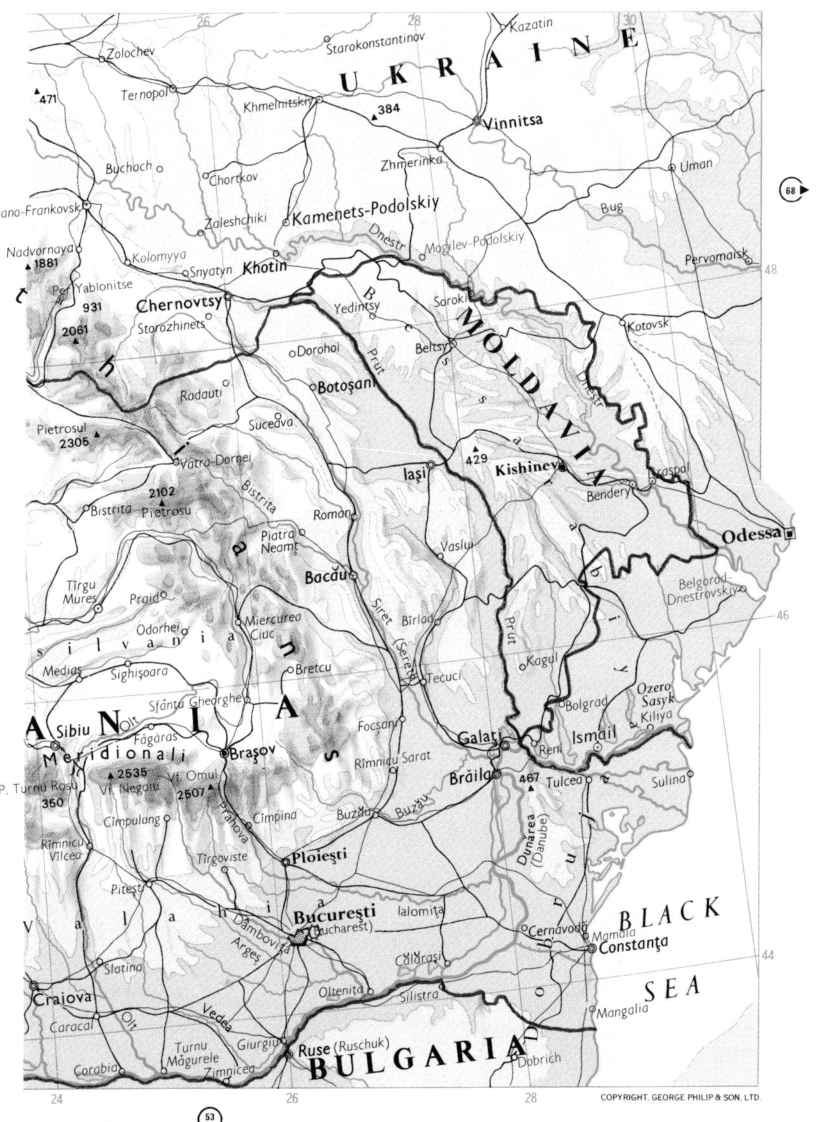
UKRAINE
MOLDAVIA
BULGARIA
BLACK SEA
Kazatin
Starokonstantinov
Zolochev
Ternopol
Khmelnitskiy
384
Vinnitsa
471
Zhmerinka
Uman
Buchach
Chortkov
Ivano-Frankovsk
Kamenets-Podolskiy
Bug
Zaleshchiki
Dnestr
Mogilev-Podolskiy
Nadvornaya
1881
Kolomyya
Snyatyn
Khotin
Pervomaisk
Per. Yablonitse
931
Chernovtsy
Yedintsy
Soroki
Storozhinets
2061
Kotovsk
Dorohoi
Beltsy
Prut
Botoşani
Radauti
Pietrosul
2305
Suceava
Vatra-Dornei
429
Iaşi
Kishinev
Bendery
2102
Pietrosu
Bistrita
Roman
Odessa
Piatra Neamţ
Vaslui
Bacău
Tîrgu Mureş
Praid
Belgorod-Dnestrovskiy
Siret
Bîrlad
Miercurea Ciuc
Odorhei
Prut
Mediaş
Sighişoara
Bretcu
Kagul
Tecuci
Ozero Sasyk
Sfântu Gheorghe
Bolgrad
Kiliya
Focşani
Galaţi
Ismail
Sibiu
Olt
Făgăras
Reni
Meridionali
Braşov
Rîmnicu Sarat
Brăila
2535
Vf. Omul
Vf. Negoiu
467
Tulcea
Sulina
P. Turnu Roşu
350
2507
Prahova
Cîmpina
Buzău
Dunărea (Danube)
Cîmpulung
Rîmnicu Vîlcea
Tîrgoviste
Ploieşti
Piteşti
Ialomiţa
Bucureşti (Bucharest)
Dâmboviţa
Argeş
Cernavodă
Mamaia
Constanţa
Călăraşi
Slatina
Craiova
Olteniţa
Silistra
Mangalia
Caracal
Olt
Vedea
Turnu Măgurele
Giurgiu
Ruse (Ruschuk)
Dobrich
Corabia
Zimnicea
24
26
28
30
48
46
44

68
53

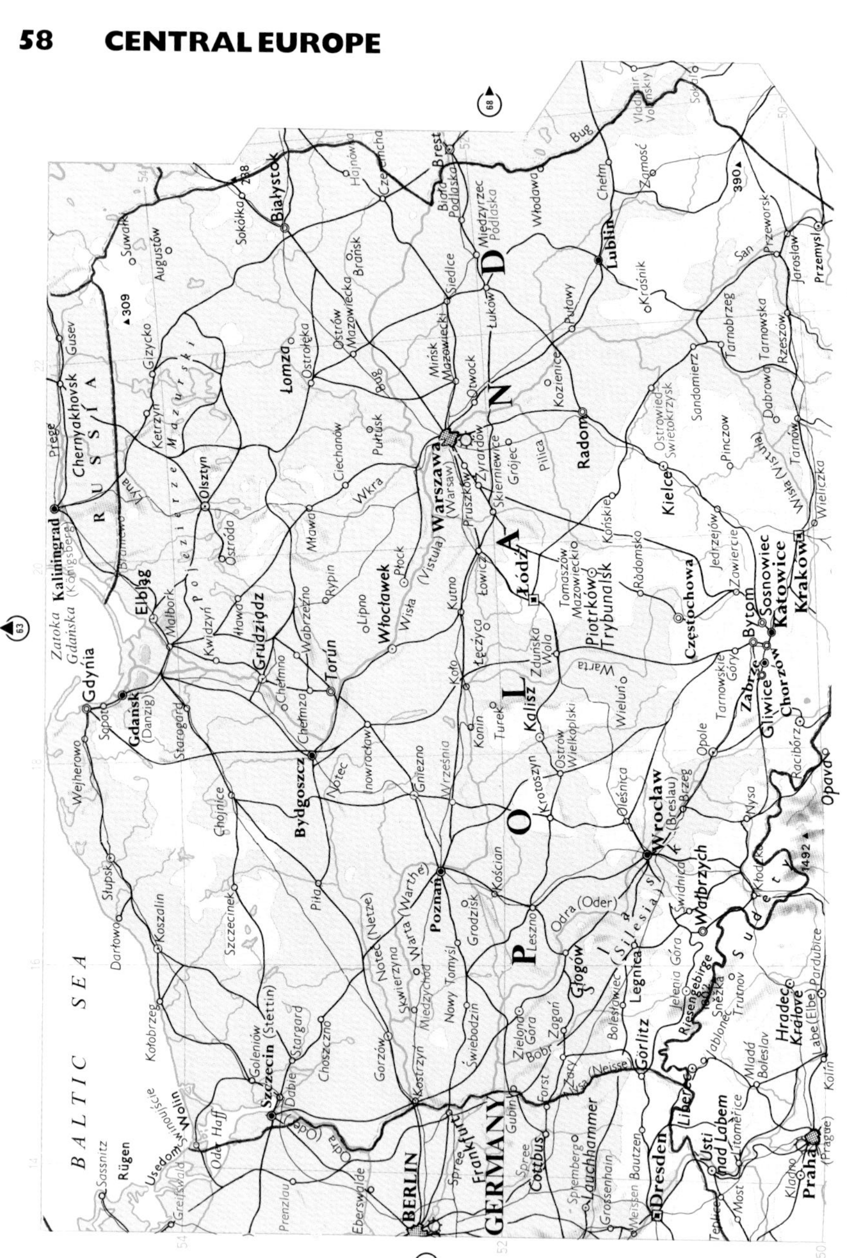
BALTIC SEA
RUSSIA
POLAND
GERMANY
Kaliningrad
Zatoka Gdańska
Gdynia
Gdańsk (Danzig)
Elbląg
Olsztyn
Białystok
Brest
Bydgoszcz
Toruń
Grudziądz
Włocławek
Warszawa (Warsaw)
Łódź
Lublin
Radom
Kielce
Częstochowa
Katowice
Kraków
Poznań
Wrocław (Breslau)
Szczecin (Stettin)
BERLIN
Dresden
Praha (Prague)
Opava
Wisła (Vistula)
Odra (Oder)
63
68
43

1 : 5 000 000

59

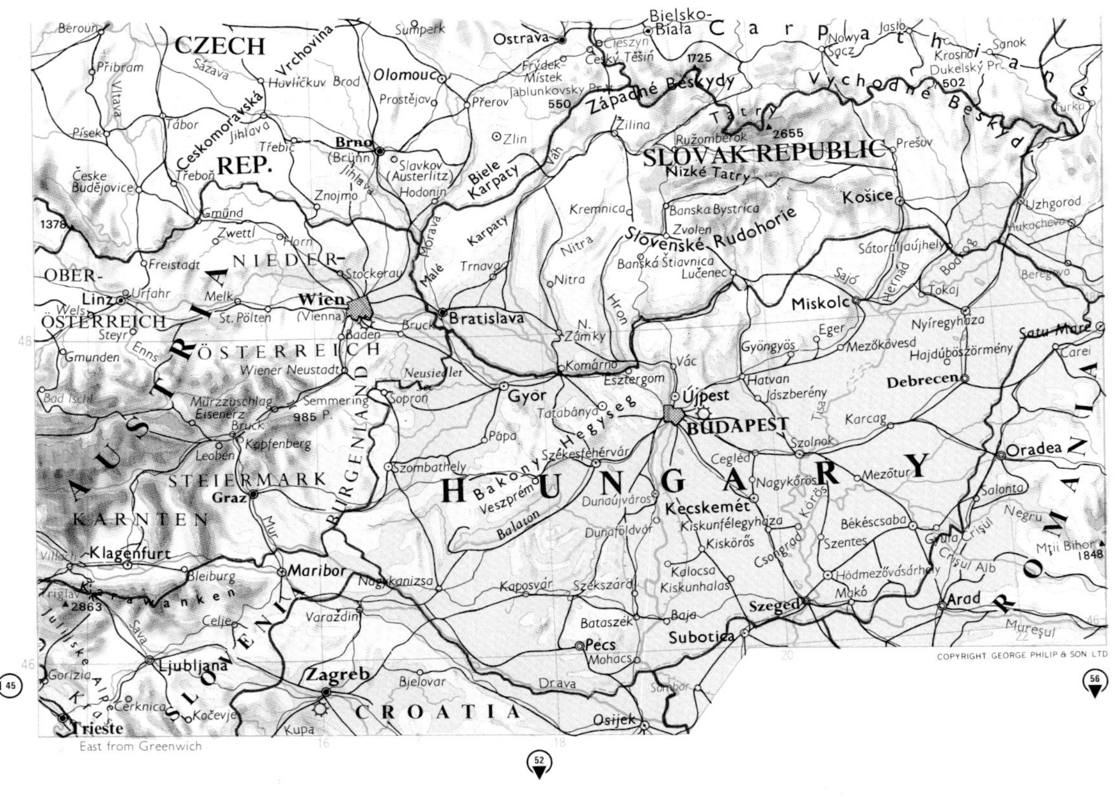

COPYRIGHT GEORGE PHILIP & SON LTD

East from Greenwich

SOUTHERN SCANDINAVIA

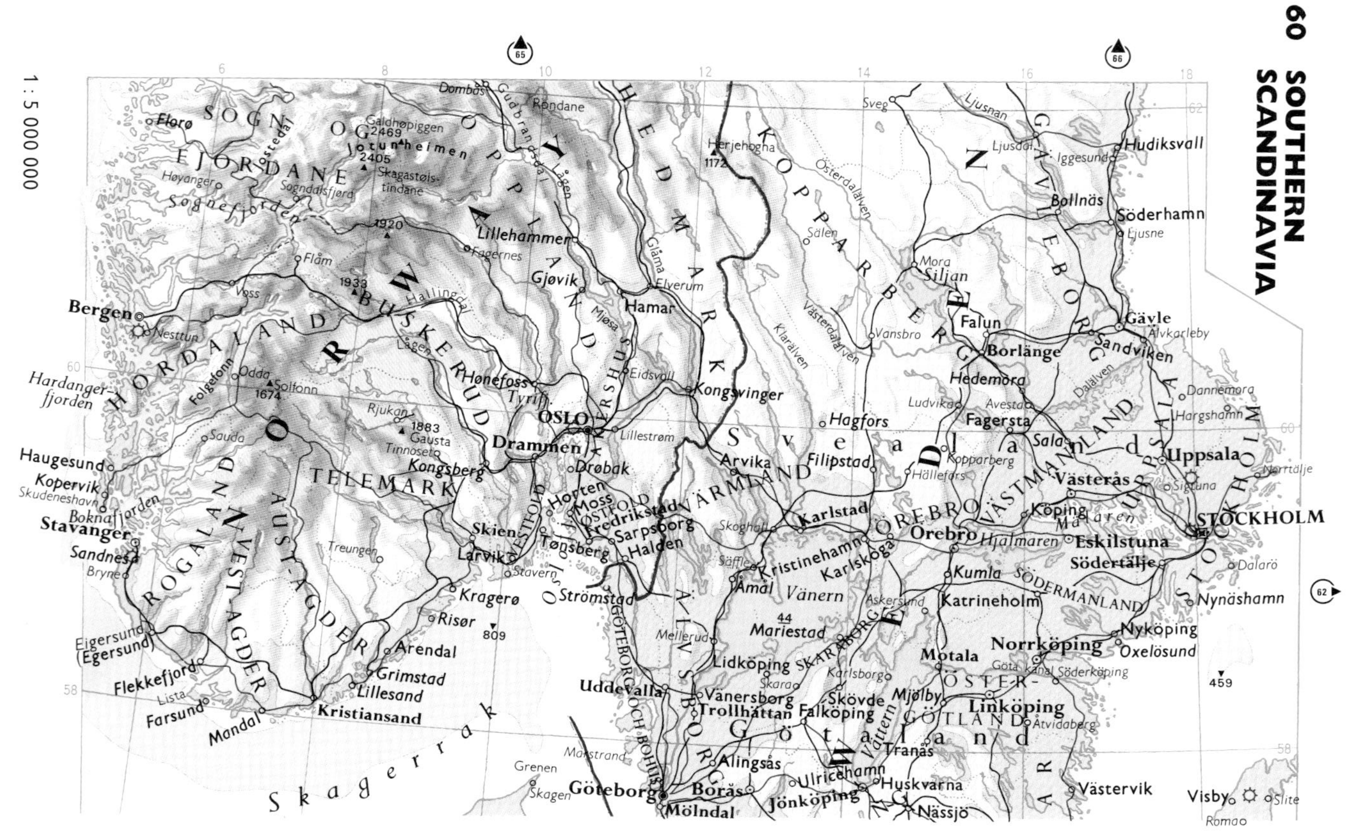

Hudiksvall
Söderhamn
Gävle
Sandviken
Bollnäs
Falun
Borlänge
Hedemora
Fagersta
Uppsala
Västerås
Sala
Eskilstuna
Södertälje
STOCKHOLM
Nynäshamn
Nyköping
Oxelösund
Norrköping
Linköping
Motala
Katrineholm
Kumla
Örebro
Karlskoga
Kristinehamn
Karlstad
Filipstad
Hagfors
Arvika
Kongsvinger
Hamar
Elverum
Lillehammer
Gjøvik
OSLO
Drammen
Drøbak
Moss
Fredrikstad
Sarpsborg
Halden
Horten
Tønsberg
Skien
Larvik
Kragerø
Risør
Arendal
Grimstad
Lillesand
Kristiansand
Mandal
Farsund
Flekkefjord
Egersund
Sandnes
Stavanger
Kopervik
Haugesund
Bergen
Florø
Voss
Odda
Kongsberg
Hønefoss
Strömstad
Uddevalla
Göteborg
Mölndal
Borås
Alingsås
Trollhättan
Vänersborg
Lidköping
Mariestad
Åmål
Skövde
Falköping
Jönköping
Huskvarna
Nässjö
Tranås
Mjölby
Västervik
Visby
Mora
Ludvika
Köping
HEDMARK
KOPPARBERG
GÄVLEBORG
BUSKERUD
TELEMARK
AUST-AGDER
VEST-AGDER
ROGALAND
HORDALAND
SOGN OG FJORDANE
OPPLAND
VÄRMLAND
ÄLVSBORG
GÖTEBORG OCH BOHUS
SÖDERMANLAND
Skagerrak

1 : 5 000 000

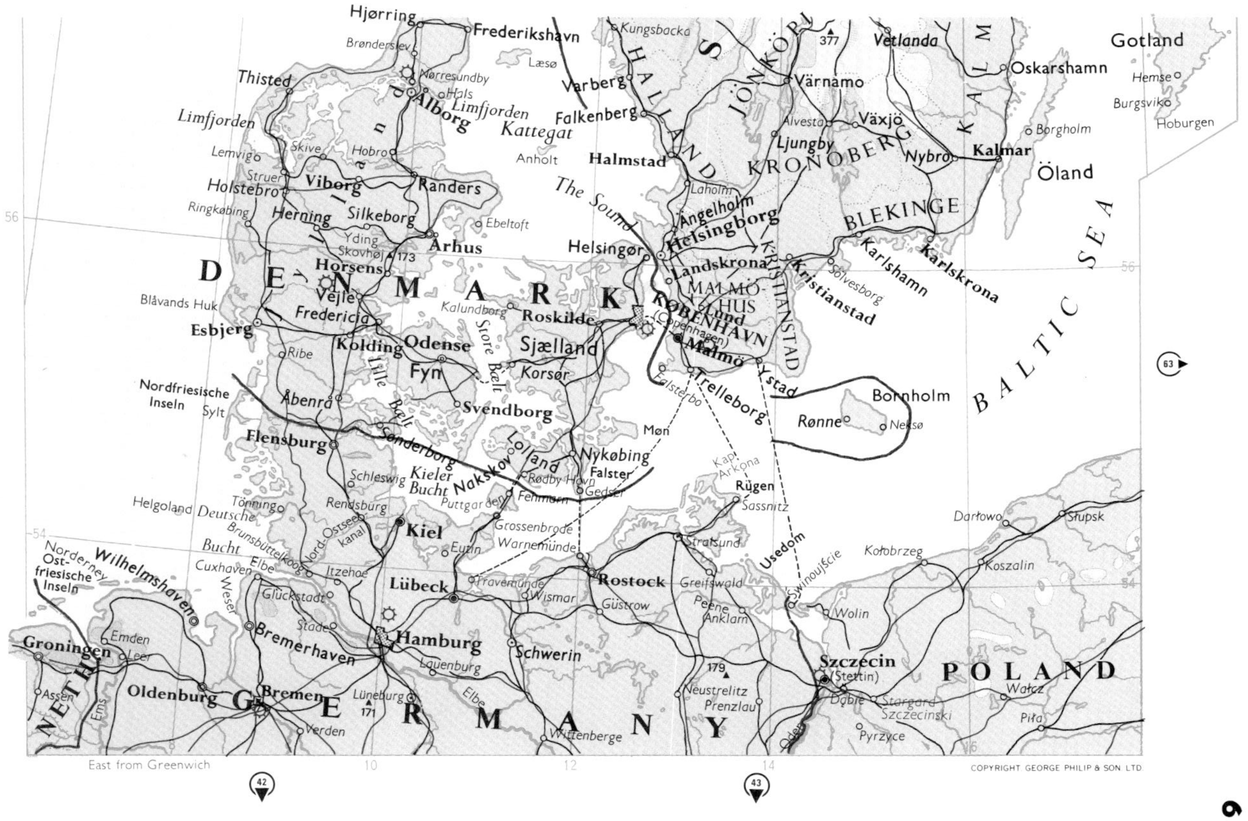
DENMARK
Jylland
Hjørring
Frederikshavn
Brønderslev
Læsø
Nørresundby
Hals
Ålborg
Limfjorden
Kattegat
Thisted
Limfjorden
Skive
Hobro
Lemvig
Struer
Viborg
Randers
Holstebro
Ringkøbing
Herning
Silkeborg
Ebeltoft
Anholt
Yding Skovhøj 173
Århus
Horsens
Vejle
Fredericia
Blåvands Huk
Esbjerg
Kolding
Odense
Fyn
Lille Bælt
Store Bælt
Kalundborg
Roskilde
Sjælland
Korsør
Ribe
Åbenrå
Svendborg
Nordfriesische Inseln
Sylt
Flensburg
Sønderborg
Lolland
Nakskov
Nykøbing
Falster
Møn
Rødby Havn
Gedser
Helsingør
KØBENHAVN (Copenhagen)
The Sound
SWEDEN
Kungsbacka
HALLAND
JÖNKÖPING
Varberg
Falkenberg
Halmstad
Laholm
Ängelholm
Helsingborg
Landskrona
MALMÖHUS
Lund
Malmö
Falsterbo
Trelleborg
Ystad
KRISTIANSTAD
Kristianstad
Sölvesborg
Karlshamn
Karlskrona
BLEKINGE
KRONOBERG
KALMAR
Värnamo
377
Vetlanda
Alvesta
Växjö
Ljungby
Nybro
Kalmar
Oskarshamn
Borgholm
Öland
Gotland
Hemse
Burgsvik
Hoburgen
BALTIC SEA
Bornholm
Rønne
Neksø
GERMANY
Schleswig
Kieler Bucht
Kiel
Rendsburg
Nord-Ostsee-kanal
Tönning
Helgoland
Deutsche Bucht
Brunsbüttelkoog
Cuxhaven
Elbe
Weser
Itzehoe
Glückstadt
Stade
Bremerhaven
Wilhelmshaven
Norderney
Ostfriesische Inseln
Groningen
Emden
Leer
Ems
Assen
NETH
Oldenburg
Bremen
Verden
Hamburg
Lüneburg
171
Lauenburg
Elbe
Lübeck
Eutin
Travemünde
Wismar
Puttgarden
Fehmarn
Grossenbrode
Warnemünde
Rostock
Güstrow
Schwerin
Wittenberge
Stralsund
Greifswald
Peene
Anklam
Rügen
Kap Arkona
Sassnitz
Usedom
Świnoujście
179
Neustrelitz
Prenzlau
Oder
POLAND
Szczecin (Stettin)
Dąbie
Stargard Szczeciński
Pyrzyce
Wolin
Kołobrzeg
Koszalin
Darłowo
Słupsk
Wałcz
Piła
56
54
10
12
14
16
East from Greenwich
42
43
63

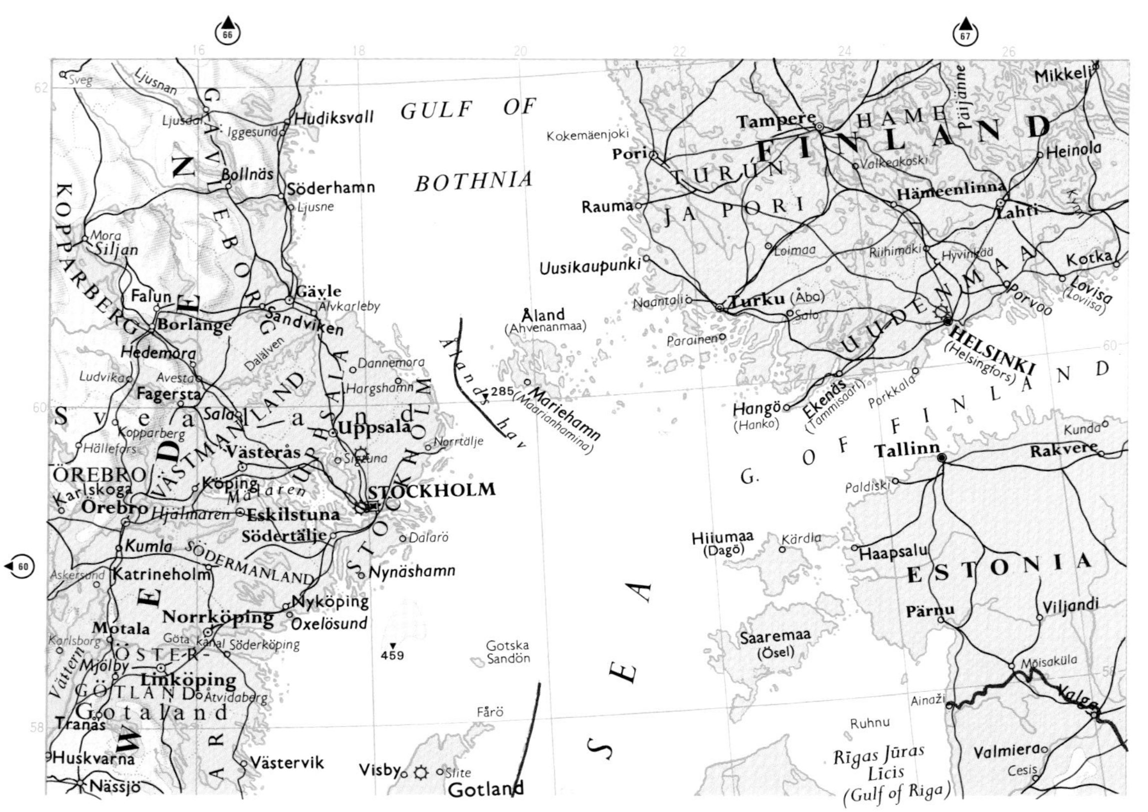
66
67
60
GULF OF BOTHNIA
FINLAND
ESTONIA
G. OF FINLAND
SEA
SWEDEN
Svealand
Götaland
Rīgas Jūras Licis
(Gulf of Riga)
Åland (Ahvenanmaa)
Mariehamn (Maarianhamina)
Ålands hav
285
459
HELSINKI (Helsingfors)
STOCKHOLM
Tallinn
Tampere
Turku (Åbo)
Pori
Rauma
Uusikaupunki
Naantali
Parainen
Salo
Loimaa
Hangö (Hanko)
Ekenäs (Tammisaari)
Porkkala
Hämeenlinna
Riihimäki
Hyvinkää
Lahti
Porvoo
Lovisa (Loviisa)
Kotka
Kymi
Heinola
Mikkeli
Päijänne
Valkeakoski
Kokemäenjoki
HÄME
TURUN JA PORI
UUDENMAA
Rakvere
Kunda
Paldiski
Haapsalu
Pärnu
Viljandi
Mõisaküla
Valga
Valmiera
Cesis
Ainaži
Ruhnu
Hiiumaa (Dagö)
Kärdla
Saaremaa (Ösel)
Gotska Sandön
Fårö
Gotland
Slite
Visby
Sveg
Ljusnan
Ljusdal
Iggesund
Hudiksvall
Bollnäs
Söderhamn
Ljusne
GÄVLEBORG
KOPPARBERG
Mora
Siljan
Falun
Borlänge
Hedemora
Gävle
Älvkarleby
Sandviken
Dalälven
Ludvika
Avesta
Fagersta
Sala
Kopparberg
Hällefors
ÖREBRO
Karlskoga
Örebro
VÄSTMANLAND
UPPSALA
STOCKHOLM
Dannemora
Hargshamn
Uppsala
Västerås
Sigtuna
Norrtälje
Köping
Mälaren
Hjälmaren
Eskilstuna
Södertälje
Dalarö
Kumla
SÖDERMANLAND
Nynäshamn
Askersund
Katrineholm
Nyköping
Oxelösund
Norrköping
Motala
Göta kanal
Söderköping
Karlsborg
Vättern
Mjölby
ÖSTERGÖTLAND
Linköping
Åtvidaberg
Tranås
Huskvarna
Nässjö
Västervik
16
18
20
22
24
26
62
60
58

1 : 5 000 000

63

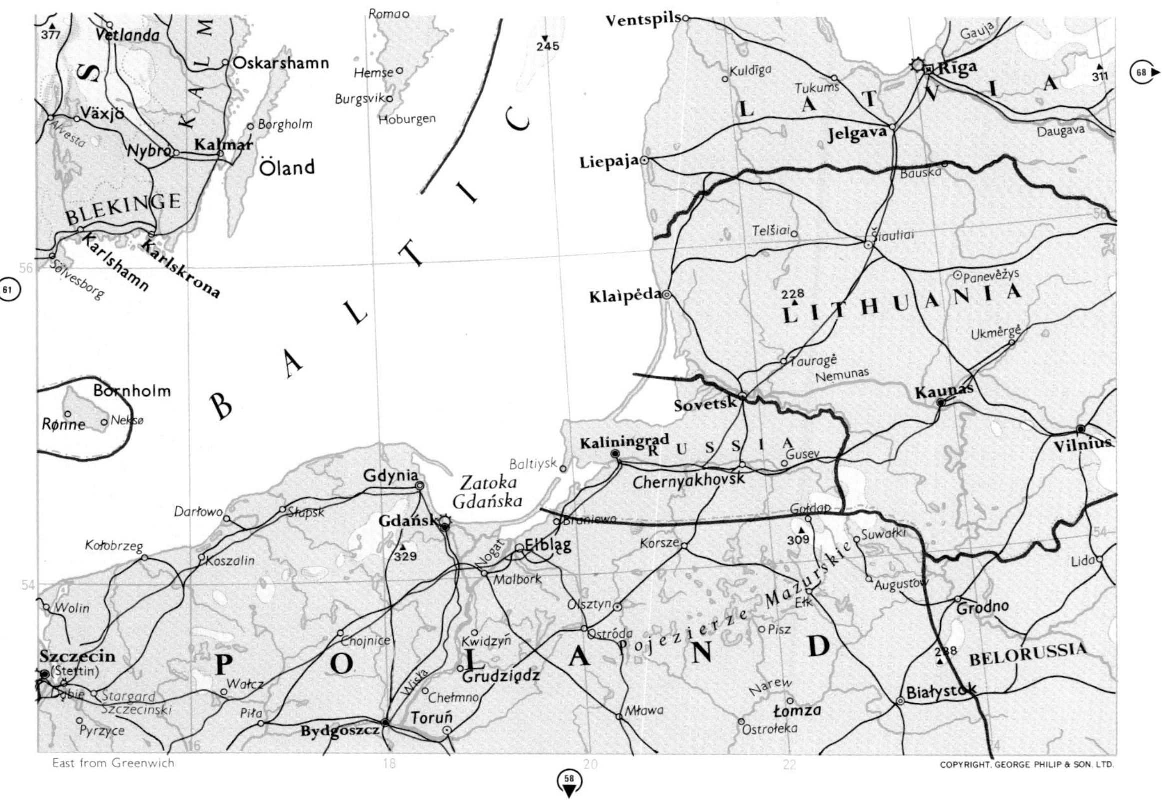

East from Greenwich

COPYRIGHT GEORGE PHILIP & SON LTD

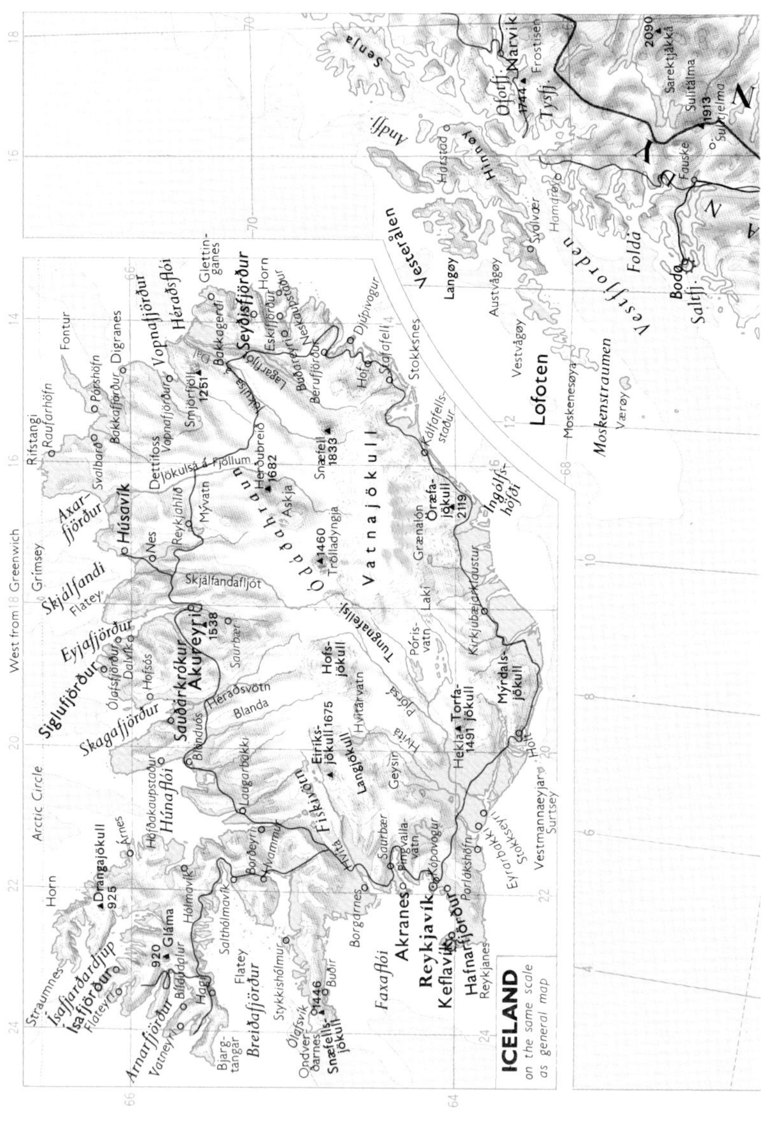

ICELAND
on the same scale
as general map

1 : 5 000 000

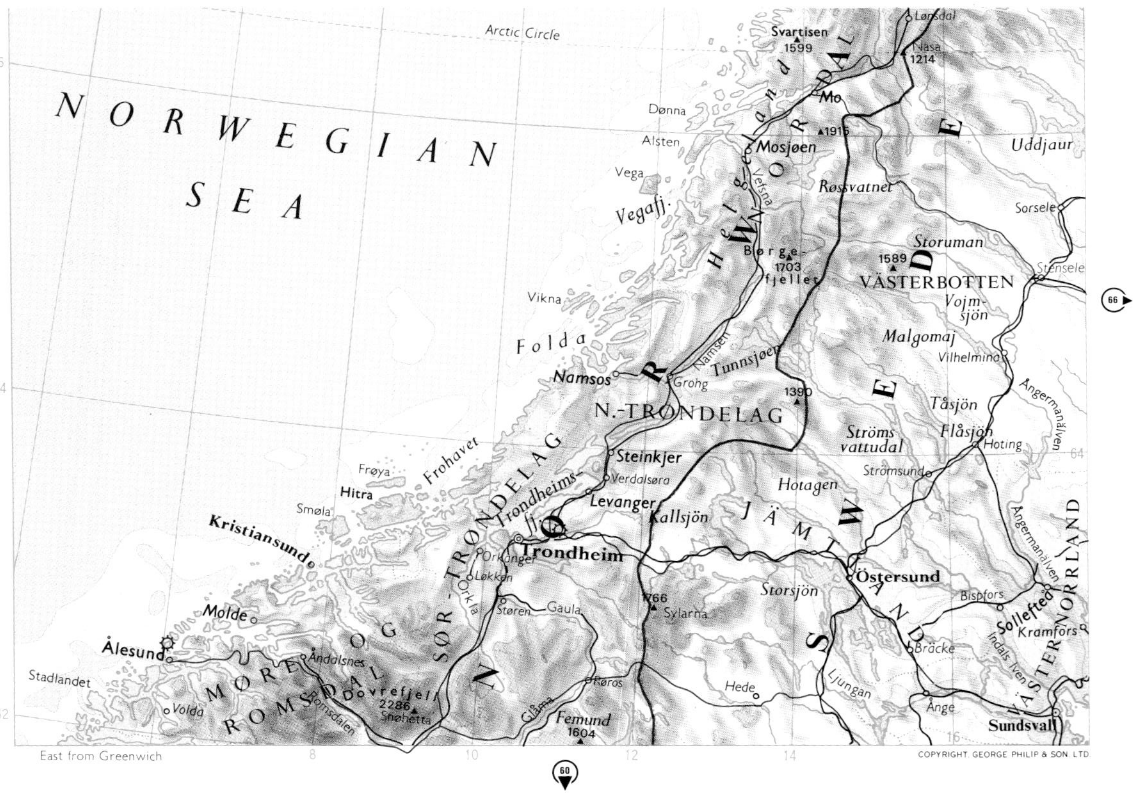

NORWEGIAN SEA

Arctic Circle

Stadlandet

Ålesund
Volda
Molde
Kristiansund
Smøla
Hitra
Frøya
Froya
Frohavet

MØRE OG ROMSDAL
Åndalsnes
Dovrefjell
2286
Snøhetta
Romsdalen

SØR-TRØNDELAG
Trondheim
Orkla
Gaula
Støren
Orkanger
Melhus

N-TRØNDELAG
Namsos
Steinkjer
Verdalsøra
Levanger
Trondheim
Vikna
Folda
Vega
Vegøli
Alsten
Donna
Vega

HELGELAND
Mosjøen
Vefsna
Mo
Svartisen
1599
Saltfjell
Lønsdal
Nasa
1214
1916
Børge-
1703
fjellet
Grong
Namsen
Tunnsjøen
1390

VÄSTERBOTTEN
Storuman
1589
Sorsele
Uddjaur
Sorsele
Sorsele

Malgoma
Vojm-
sjön
Vilhelmina
Ångermanälven
Ströms
vattudal
Strömsund

JÄMT-
LAND
Hotagen
Kallsjön
Storsjön
Hede
Sjarna
766
Tåsjön
Flåsjön
Hoting
Östersund
Bispfors
Brācke
Ljungan
Ange
Storsjön
Femund
1604
Røros

VÄSTERNORRLAND
Ångermanälven
Kramfors
Sollefteå
Indals älven
Sundsvall

East from Greenwich

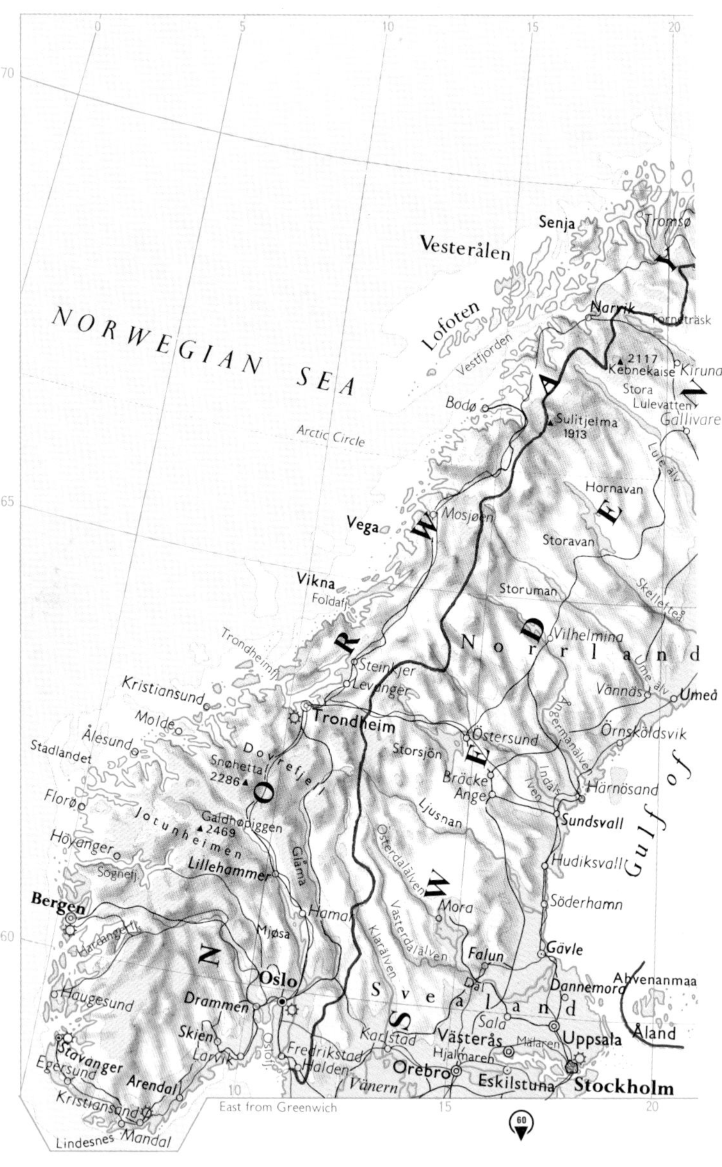

Tromsø

Senja

Vesterålen

Narvik　Torneträsk

Lofoten

Vestfjorden

2117
Kebnekaise　Kiruna
Stora
Lulevatten
Gällivare

Bodø

Sulitjelma
1913

Arctic Circle

Lule älv

NORWEGIAN SEA

Hornavan

Vega　Mosjøen

Storavan

Vikna

Storuman

Foldal

Skellefte

Trondheimf

Vilhelmina

Steinkjer
Levanger

Nor r l a n d

Vännäs　Umeå

Kristiansund

Molde

Trondheim

Östersund

Örnsköldsvik

Ålesund

Storsjön

Stadlandet

Dovrefjell

Snøhetta
2286

Bräcke
Ange

Härnösand

Florø

Galdhøpiggen
2469

Ljusnan

Sundsvall

Høyanger

Jotunheimen

Hudiksvall

Sognef

Lillehammer

Glåma

Mora

Söderhamn

Bergen

Hamar

Hardangerf

Mjøsa

Falun

Gävle

Ahvenanmaa

Haugesund

Drammen

Oslo

Dannemora

Svealand

Skien

Karlstad

Sala

Stavanger

Larvik

Fredrikstad

Västerås

Mälaren

Uppsala

Åland

Egersund

Arendal

Halden

Örebro

Hjalmaren

Eskilstuna

Stockholm

Kristiansand

Vänern

Lindesnes　Mandal

East from Greenwich

Gulf of

1 : 10 000 000

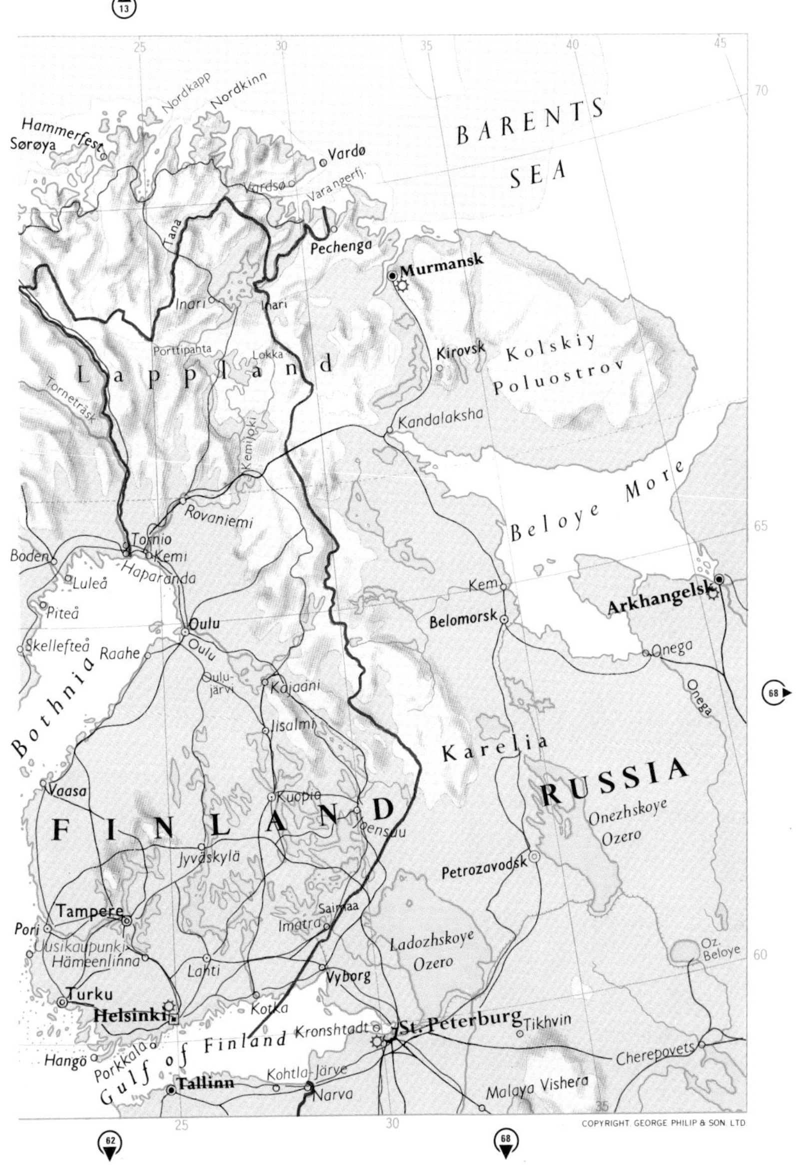

13
BARENTS SEA
Nordkapp
Nordkinn
Hammerfest
Sørøya
Vardø
Vardsø
Varangerfj.
Tana
Pechenga
Murmansk
Inari
Inari
Porttipahta
Lokka
Kirovsk
Kolskiy Poluostrov
Lappland
Torneträsk
Kemijoki
Kandalaksha
Beloye More
Rovaniemi
Tornio
Kemi
Haparanda
Boden
Luleå
Piteå
Kem
Arkhangelsk
Belomorsk
Oulu
Oulu
Skellefteå
Raahe
Onega
Onega
Oulu-järvi
Kajaani
Bothnia
Iisalmi
Karelia
RUSSIA
Vaasa
Kuopio
FINLAND
Joensuu
Onezhskoye Ozero
Jyväskylä
Petrozavodsk
Tampere
Saimaa
Pori
Imatra
Ladozhskoye Ozero
Uusikaupunki
Hämeenlinna
Lahti
Vyborg
Oz. Beloye
Turku
Helsinki
Kotka
St. Peterburg
Tikhvin
Kronshtadt
Gulf of Finland
Hangö
Porkkala
Kohtla-Järve
Cherepovets
Tallinn
Narva
Malaya Vishera
68
62
68

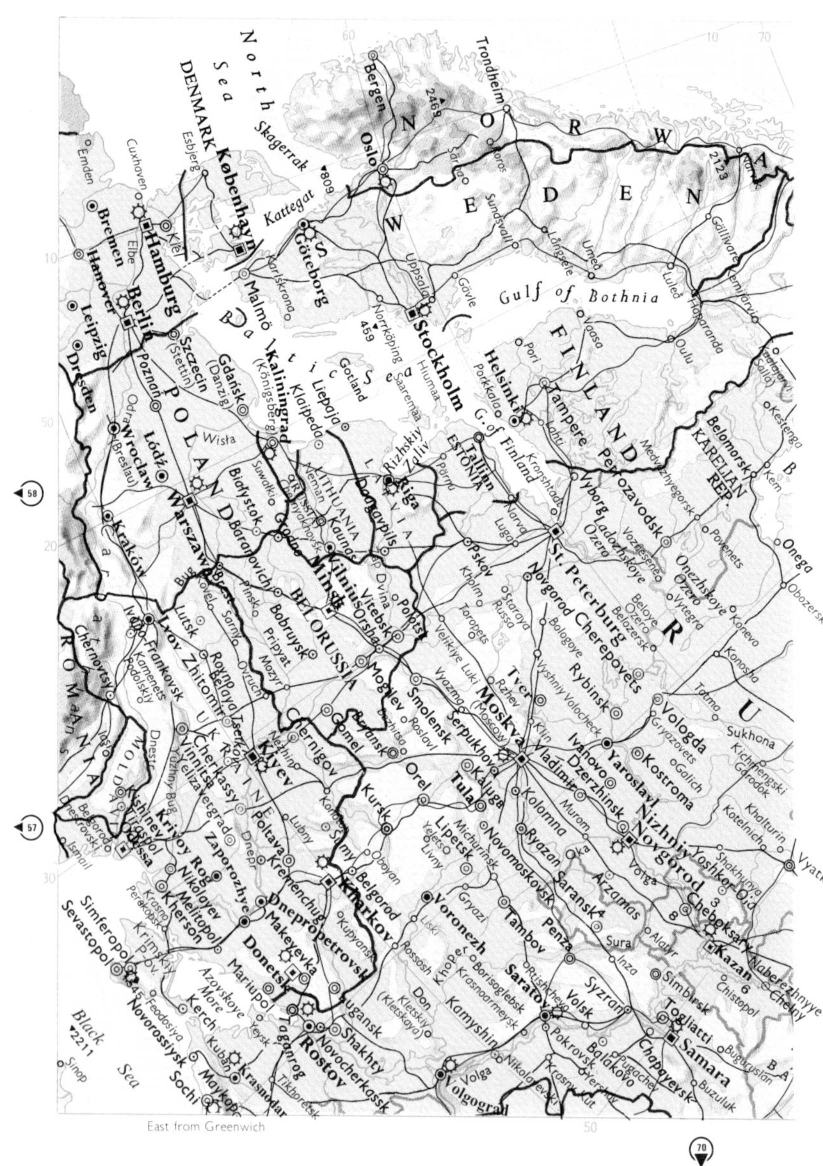
North Sea
Skagerrak
Kattegat
DENMARK
København
Esbjerg
Cuxhaven
Emden
Bremen
Hamburg
Kiel
Elbe
Hanover
Berlin
Leipzig
Dresden
Szczecin (Stettin)
Poznań
Odra
Wrocław (Breslau)
Łódź
POLAND
Warszawa
Kraków
Wisła
Gdańsk (Danzig)
Kaliningrad (Königsberg)
Suwałki
Białystok
Baltic Sea
Malmö
Karlskrona
Göteborg
Oslo
Bergen
Trondheim
2469
609
NORWAY
SWEDEN
Stockholm
Uppsala
Gävle
Norrköping
459
Gotland
Sundsvall
Särna
Røros
Umeå
Luleå
Gällivare
Gulf of Bothnia
Vaasa
Oulu
Pori
Tampere
Helsinki
Porkkala
FINLAND
Lahti
Haparanda
Kemijärvi
Kestenga
Belomorsk
KARELIAN REP.
Kem
Onega
Obozersky
Hiiumaa
Saaremaa
Rizhskiy Zaliv
Pärnu
Tallinn
ESTONIA
G. of Finland
Kronshtadt
Vyborg
Narva
Luga
St. Peterburg
Ladozhskoye Ozero
Petrozavodsk
Medvezhyegorsk
Onezhskoye Ozero
Voznesenye
Vytegra
Povenets
Konevo
Konosha
Liepāja
Klaipėda
LITHUANIA
Neman
Kaunas
Vilnius
LATVIA
Rīga
Daugavpils
Dvina
Pskov
Kholm
Novgorod
Staraya Russa
Toropets
Velikiye Luki
Polotsk
Vitebsk
Orsha
Minsk
BELORUSSIA
Baranovichi
Pinsk
Bobruysk
Pripyat
Mozyr
Mogilev
Gomel
Chernigov
Smolensk
Vyazma
Rzhev
Tver
Bologoye
Vyshniy Volochek
Cherepovets
Beloye Ozero
Belozersk
Rybinsk
Vologda
Totma
Sukhona
Gryazovets
Galich
Kostroma
Yaroslavl
Ivanovo
Vladimir
Dzerzhinsk
Nizhniy Novgorod
Murom
Kolomna
Moskva (Moscow)
Klin
Serpukhov
Kaluga
Tula
Roslavl
Bryansk
Orel
Kursk
Belgorod
Oboyan
Kharkov
Lipetsk
Yelets
Livny
Michurinsk
Novomoskovsk
Ryazan
Oka
Arzamas
Saransk
Penza
Tambov
Voronezh
Gryazi
Liski
Rossosh
Borisoglebsk
Khoper
Krasnoarmeysk
Kamyshin
Saratov
Rtishchevo
Volsk
Syzran
Balakovo
Pokrovsk
Pugachev
Chapayevsk
Samara
Togliatti
Simbirsk
Inza
Sura
Alatyr
Cheboksary
Yoshkar-Ola
Kazan
Chistopol
Naberezhnyye Chelny
Bugulma
Buguruslan
Buzuluk
Volga
Volgograd
Nikolayevsk
Don
Kletskiy (Kletskaya)
Shakhty
Novocherkassk
Rostov
Taganrog
Lugansk
Donetsk
Makeyevka
Dnepropetrovsk
Kupyansk
Kremenchug
Poltava
Lubny
Sumy
Konotop
Nezhin
Kiyev
Cherkassy
Kirovograd
Dnepr
Zaporozhye
Melitopol
Krivoy Rog
Nikolayev
Kherson
Odessa
Tiraspol
Kishinev
MOLDAVIA
Ismail
Belgorod-Dnestrovskiy
Dnestr
Vinnitsa
Yuzhnyy Bug
Zhitomir
Rovno
Lutsk
Kovel
Lvov
Ivano-Frankovsk
Chernovtsy
Kamenets-Podolskiy
UKRAINE
ROMANIA
Krasnoperekopsk
Krimskiy P-ov.
Simferopol
Sevastopol
Feodosiya
Kerch
Azovskoye More
Yeysk
Mariupol
Kuban
Krasnodar
Tikhoretsk
Novorossiysk
Maykop
Sochi
Black Sea
2211
Sinop
Kotelnich
Kirov
Khalturin
Vyatka
Shakhunya
Kichmengskiy Gorodok
East from Greenwich
50
60
70
10
20
30

58
57
70

1 : 20 000 000

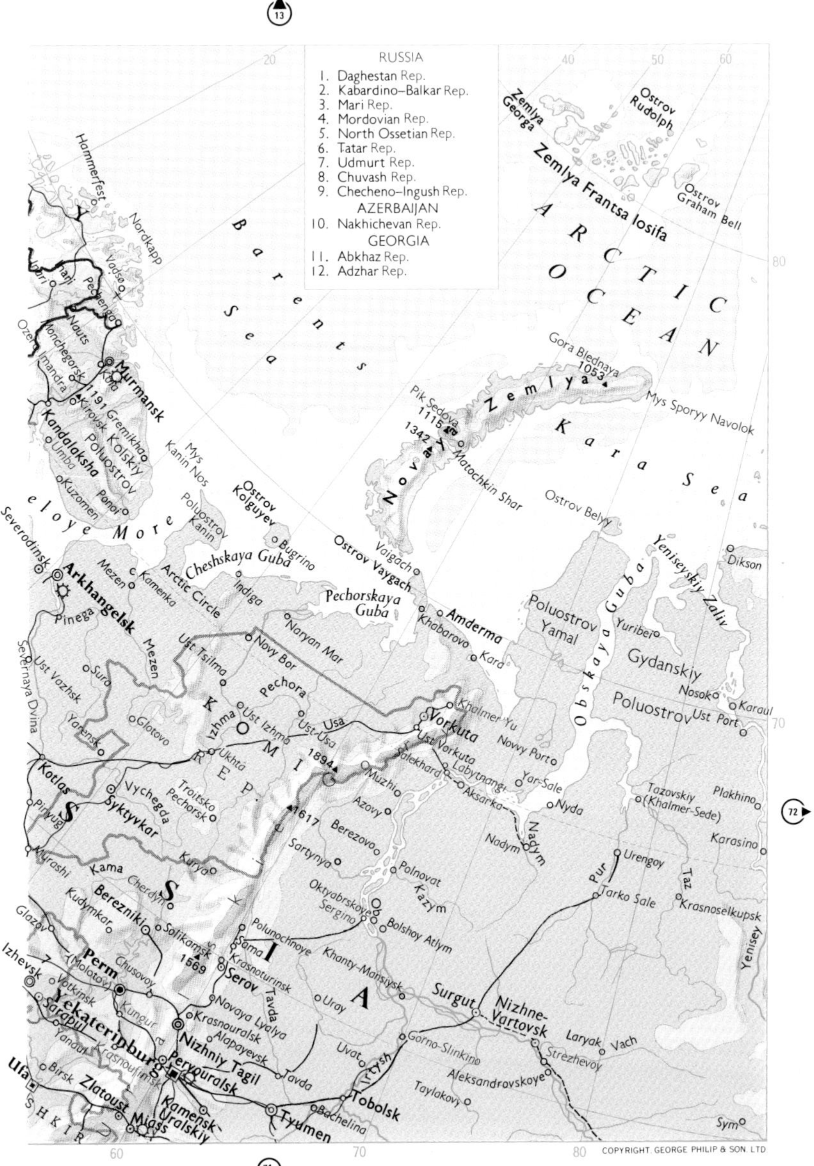

RUSSIA
1. Daghestan Rep.
2. Kabardino–Balkar Rep.
3. Mari Rep.
4. Mordovian Rep.
5. North Ossetian Rep.
6. Tatar Rep.
7. Udmurt Rep.
8. Chuvash Rep.
9. Checheno–Ingush Rep.
AZERBAIJAN
10. Nakhichevan Rep.
GEORGIA
11. Abkhaz Rep.
12. Adzhar Rep.

ARCTIC OCEAN

Zemlya Georga
Zemlya Frantsa Iosifa
Ostrov Rudolph
Ostrov Graham Bell

Hammerfest
Nordkapp
Vadsø
Kirkenes
Pechenga
Ozero Imandra
Monchegorsk
Olenegorsk
Gremikha
Kola
Murmansk
Kolskiy
Poluostrov
Umba
Kuzomen
Ponoy
Kandalaksha

Barents Sea

Mys Kanin Nos
Kanin
Nos
Poluostrov Kanin
Ostrov Kolguyev

Gora Blednaya 1053
Pik Sedova 1115
1342
Novaya Zemlya
Matochkin Shar
Mys Sporyy Navolok

Kara Sea

Ostrov Belyy

Beloye More

Severodvinsk
Arkhangelsk
Pinega
Mezen
Severnaya Dvina
Ust Vazhsk
Yarensk
Glotovo
Kotlas
Pinyug
Syktyvkar
Vychegda
Pechorsk

Arctic Circle
Indiga
c. Kamenka
Ostrov Vaygach
Bugrino
Volgoch
Cheshskaya Guba
Naryan Mar
Pechorskaya Guba
Khabarovo
Kara
Amderma
Poluostrov Yamal
Yuribey

Obskaya Guba
Yeniseyskiy Zaliv
Dikson

Novy Bor
Ust Tsilma
Izhma
Ukhta
Troitsko
Pechorsk
K O M I
A.S.S.R.
Ust Izhma
Ust Usa
Usa
1894
Vorkuta
Ust Vorkuta
Usa
Labytnangi
Salekhard
Aksarka
Azovy
Muzhio
Nowyy Port
Yar-Sale
Nyda

Khalmer-Yu
Gydanskiy
Nosok
Poluostrov
Ust Port
Karaul

Tazovskiy (Khalmer-Sede)
Plakhino
Karasino

Vychegda
Kirov
Sartynya
1617
Berezovo
Polnovat
Kazym
Nadym
Nadym
Pur
Urengoy
Tarko Sale
Taz
Krasnoselkupsk
Yenisey

Glazov
Izhevsk
Votkinsk
Cherdyn
Kudymkar
Berezniki
Solikamsk
Poluochnoye
Polunochnoye
Sosva
Krasnouralsk
Serov
Sosva
Khanty-Mansiysk
Oktyabrskoye
Serginq
Bolshoy Atlym

S I B E R I A

Perm
Kungur
Molotovo
Chusovoy
Chusovoy
1569
Kama

Ekaterinburg
Kasli
Sysert
Yalutorovsk
Birsk
Zlatoust
Miass
Kamensk-Uralskiy
Tyumen
Tobolsk
Bachelina
Irtysh
Tavda
Tavda
Uvat
Gorno-Slinkino
Taylakovy
Aleksandrovskoye
Sym
Strezhevoy
Laryak
Vach

Nizhnly Tagil
Verkhouralsk
Alapayevsk
Novaya Lyalya
Uray
Surgut
Nizhne-Vartovsk

B A S H K I R

COPYRIGHT. GEORGE PHILIP & SON. LTD

KAZAKHSTAN AND CENTRAL ASIA

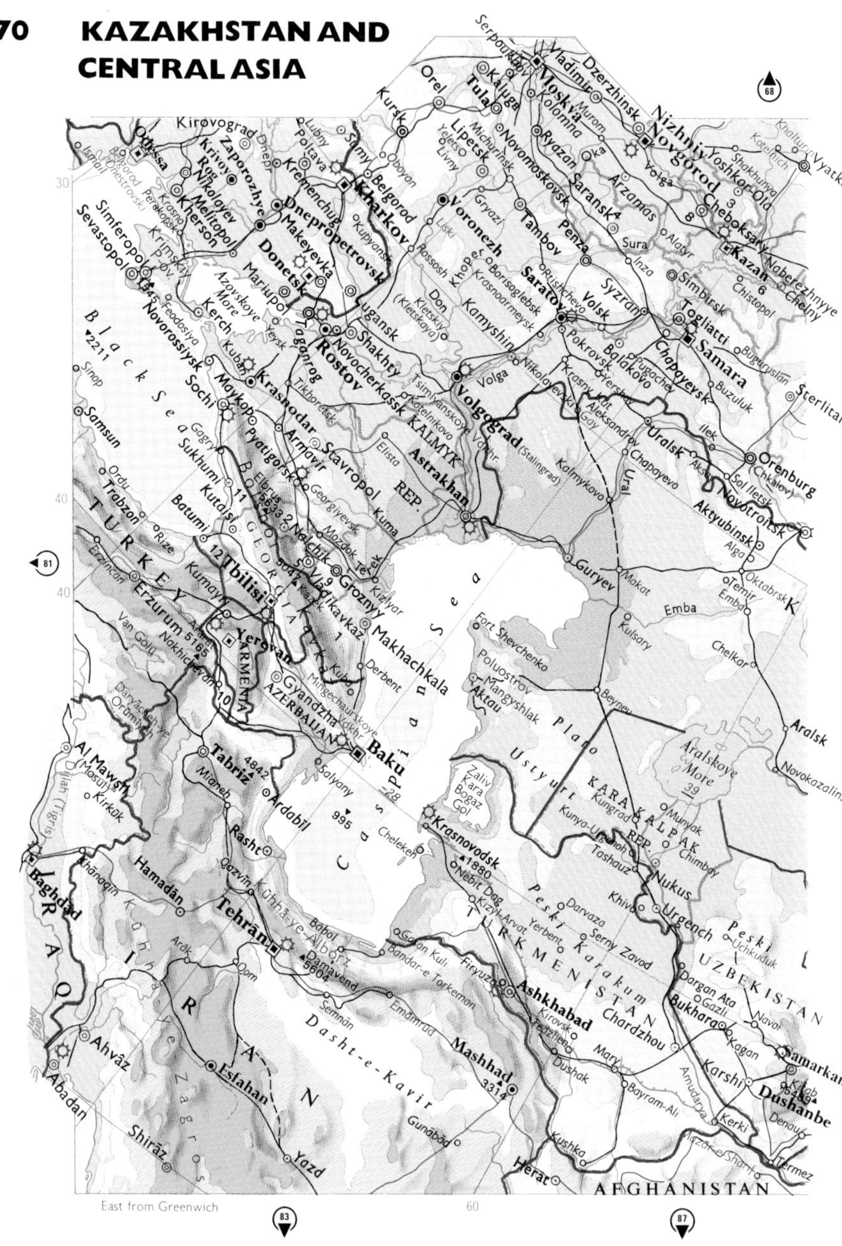
Black Sea
Caspian Sea
Aral'skoye More
TURKEY
GEORGIA
ARMENIA
AZERBAIJAN
IRAN
IRAQ
TURKMENISTAN
UZBEKISTAN
AFGHANISTAN
KALMYK REP.
KARAKALPAK REP.
Moskva
Volgograd
Astrakhan
Tbilisi
Yerevan
Baku
Tehrān
Ashkhabad
Dushanbe
Samarkand
Tashauz
Nukus
Urgench
Bukhara
Mashhad
Esfahan
Baghdād
Dasht-e-Kavir
Peski Karakum
Plato Ustyurt
East from Greenwich

1 : 20 000 000

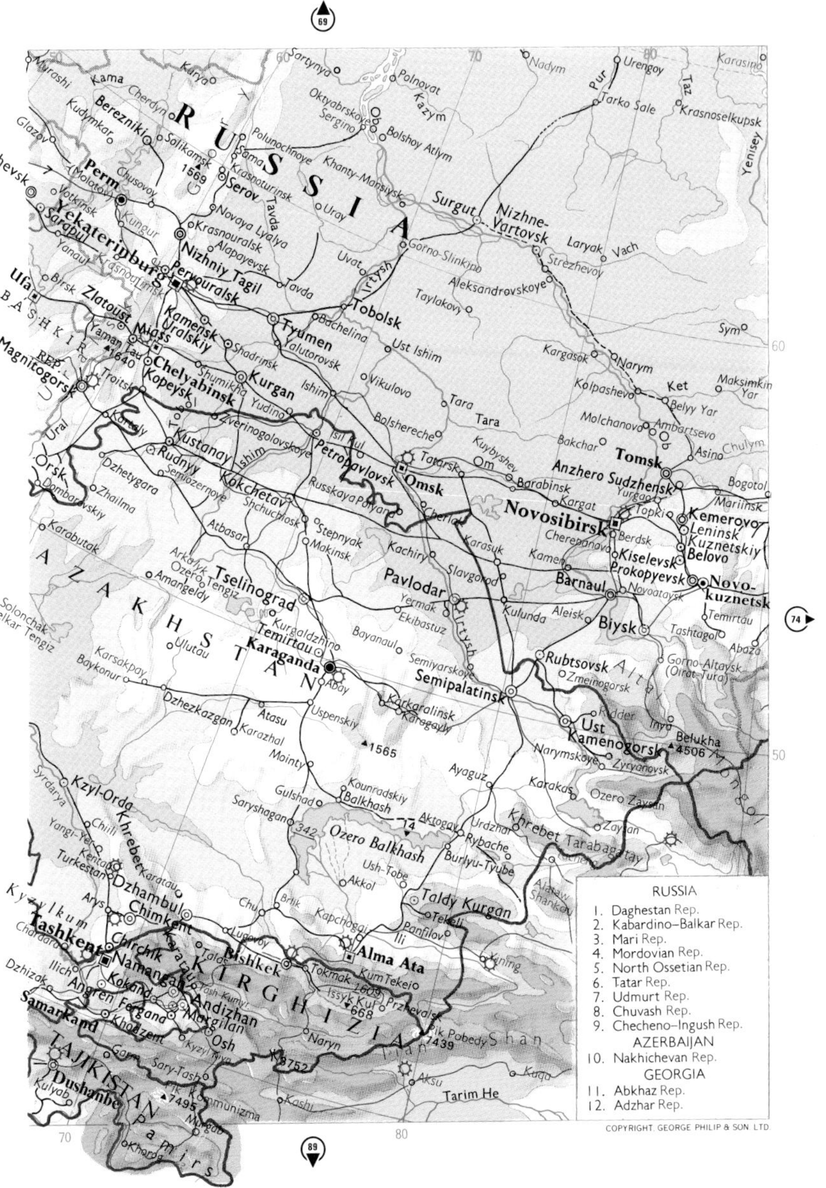

RUSSIA
1. Daghestan Rep.
2. Kabardino–Balkar Rep.
3. Mari Rep.
4. Mordovian Rep.
5. North Ossetian Rep.
6. Tatar Rep.
7. Udmurt Rep.
8. Chuvash Rep.
9. Checheno–Ingush Rep.
AZERBAIJAN
10. Nakhichevan Rep.
GEORGIA
11. Abkhaz Rep.
12. Adzhar Rep.

COPYRIGHT GEORGE PHILIP & SON LTD.

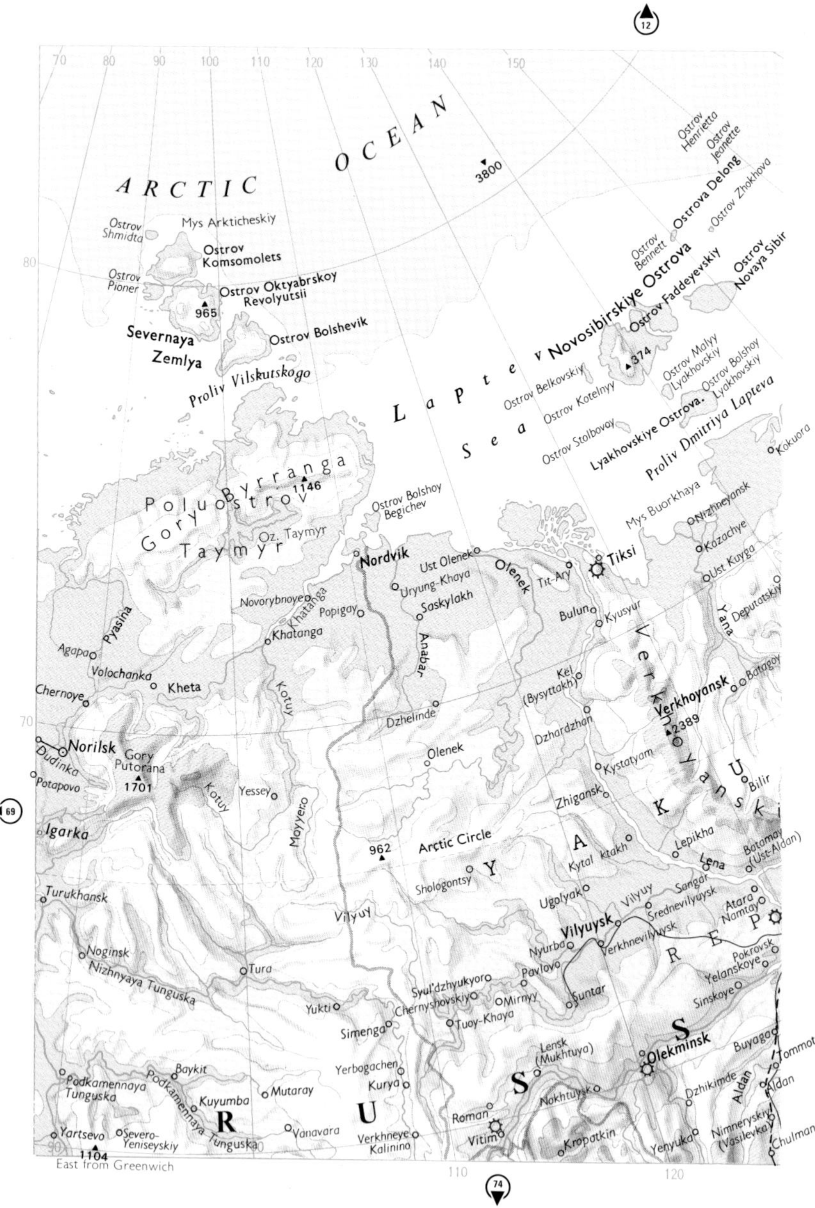

ARCTIC OCEAN

A R C T I C

Ostrov Henrietta
Ostrov Jeanette
Ostrova Delong
Ostrov Zhokhova

3800

Mys Arkticheskiy
Ostrov Shmidta
Ostrov Pioner
Ostrov Komsomolets
Ostrov Oktyabrskoy Revolyutsii
965
Ostrov Bennett
Ostrov Faddeyevskiy
Ostrov Novaya Sibir
Ostrov Malyy Lyakhovskiy
Ostrov Bolshoy Lyakhovskiy

Severnaya Zemlya
Ostrov Bolshevik

Novosibirskiye Ostrova

Proliv Vilkitskogo

L a p t e v

Ostrov Belkovskiy
Ostrov Kotelnyy
374
Ostrov Stolbovoy

S e a

Lyakhovskiye Ostrova

Proliv Dmitriya Lapteva

Kolura

P o l u o s t r o v
B y r r a n g a
G o r y
146
T a y m y r

Oz. Taymyr

Mys Buorkhaya

Nizhneyansk

Ostrov Bolshoy Begichev

Nordvik

Novorybnoye
Khatanga
Popigay
Ust Olenek
Uryung-Khaya
Saskylakh

Olenek
Tit-Ary
Bulun
Kyusyur

☼ **Tiksi**

Kazachye

Ust Kuyga

Agapa
Pyasina
Volochanka
Kheta
Khatanga

Anabar
Kotuy

Kel (Bysyttakh)

Yana

Deputatskiy

V
e
r
k
h
o
y
a
n
s
k

Chernoye

Dzhelinde

Dzhardzhan

Billir

Verkhoyansk
2389

☼ **Norilsk**
Dudinka
Gory Putorana
1701
Potapovo

Olenek

Kystatyam

U

◄ 69

Kotuy

Yessey

Zhigansk

Lepikha
Lena
Botomoy (Ust-Aldan)

Sangar

Igarka

962

Arctic Circle

Y

Kytal ktakh

A

Atara
Namtsy

Turukhansk

Vilyuy

Shologontsy
Ugolyak

Vilyuy
Srednevilyuysk

☼ **Vilyuysk**

R

Pokrovsk

Noginsk
Nizhnyaya Tunguska
Tura

Yukti

Nyurba
Verkhnevilyuysk

Yelanskoye

Pavlovo

Sinskoye

E

Simenga
Syul'dzhyukyoro
Chernyshevskiy
Tuoy-Khaya
Omirnyy
Suntar

P

S

Baykit
Podkamennaya Tunguska
Podkamennaya
Kuyumba
Mutaray
Tunguska

Yerbogachen
Kurya

Lensk (Mukhtuya)

☼ **Olekminsk**

Buyaga

Tommot

Aldan

Dzhikimde

Yartsevo
Severo-Yeniseyskiy
Vanavara

Roman

R   U   S
Verkhneye-Kalinina

Vitim

Nakhtuysk

Yenyuka
Nimnyrskiy (Vasilevka)

Kropatkin

Chulman

Nimnyrskiy

1104
East from Greenwich

1 : 20 000 000

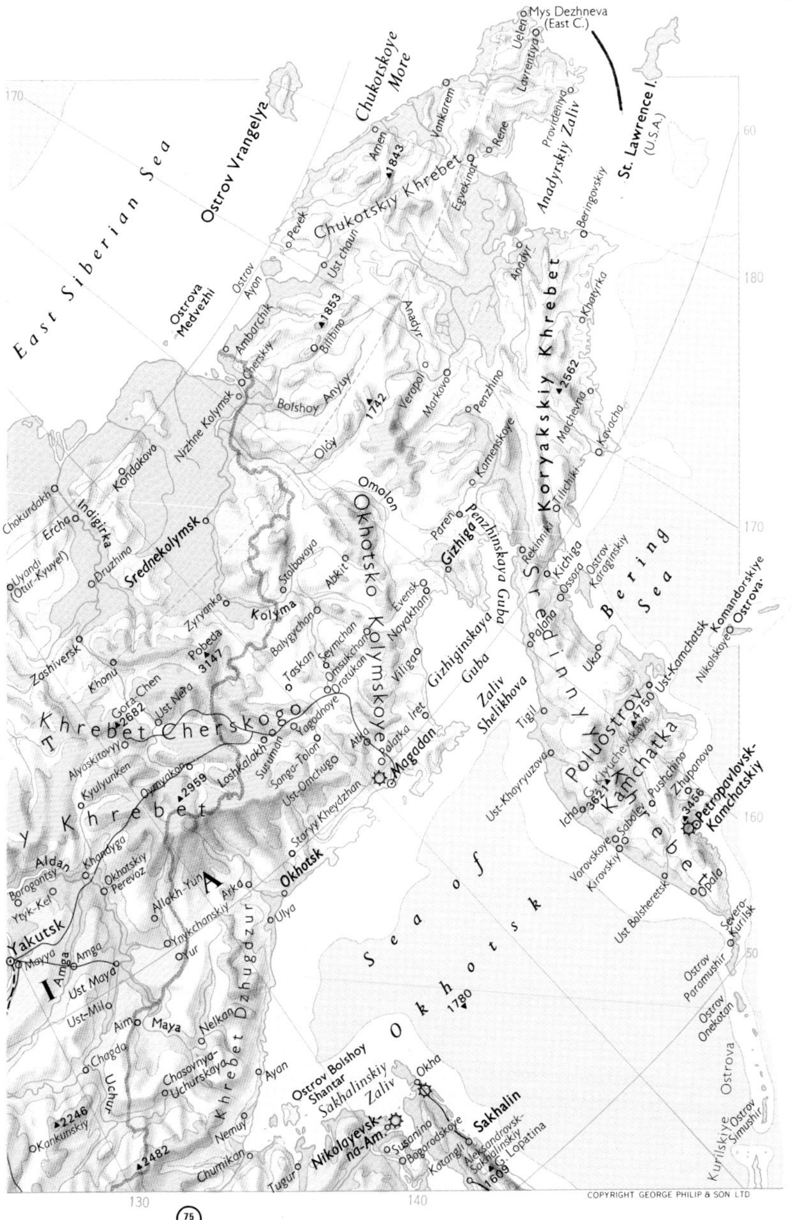

East Siberian Sea

Chukotskoye More

Ostrov Vrangelya

Mys Dezhneva
(East C.)

Uelen

Lawrentiya

St. Lawrence I.
(U.S.A.)

Provideniya

Beringovskiy

Anadyrskiy Zaliv

Chukotskiy Khrebet

▲1843

Vankarem

Enmelen

Egvekinot

Nete

Peek

Ust Chaun

Ostrova
Medvezhi

Ostrov
Ayon

Ambarchik

Chersky

▲1853

Anadyr

Bilibino

Markovo

Ugolnyy

Chapligino

Koryakskiy Khrebet

▲2562

Khatyrka

Kamchatskiy Khrebet

Vyvenka

Koryaksky

Kichiga

Karaga

Ostrov
Karaginskiy

Bering
Sea

Nizhne Kolymsk

Koldakovo

Chukurdakh

Erchoa

Indigirka

Uyandi
(Otur-Kyuyel)

Druzhina

Srednekolymsk

Olgy

Bolshoy Anyuy

Anyuy

▲1742

Vetvgol

Penzhino

Poren

Penzhinskaya Guba

Rekinniki

Slobodskoye

Abkit

Kolyma

Omolon

Gizhiga

Sredinnyy

Polana

Ukoo

Ossora

Komandorskiye
Ostrova

Nizhne-Kamchatsk

Zashiversk

Khonu

Gora Chen
▲2682

Poseda
▲3147

Zyryanka

Bolyaerhona

Taskan

Seymchan

Omsukchan

Yevensk

Naydzhano

Khatunka

Okhotsko Kolymskoye

Gizhiginskaya
Guba

Vliigoa

Zaliv
Shelikhova

Tigil

Kozyrevskoye

Ust-Kamchatsk

Klyuchi
▲4750

Pushchino

Zhupanova

▲3456

Petropavlovsk-
Kamchatskiy

Khrebet Cherskogo

T

Y Khrebet

Alyaskitovyy

▲2959

Kyulyunken

Oymyakon

Logikolakh

Susuman

Sanga-Talon

Yagodnoye

Palatka

Iret

Ola

Magadan

Ust-Omchug

Starry Kheydzhan

Ust-Khoyryuzovo

Ichosa

▲3621

Sobolev

Kirovskiy

Vorovskoye

Ust Bolsheretsk

Ozerno

▲160

Aldan

Khandyga

Okhotskiy
Perevoz

Okhotsk

Okho

Poluostrov

Kamchatka

Ostrov
Kurilsk

Yakutsk

Berogontsy

Ytyc-Kel

Okhotsk

Olekm-

Mayya

Amga

Ust Maya

Ust-Milo

Maya

Aimo

Nelkan

Aldoma

Ulya

Sea
of
Okhotsk

▲1780

Ostrov
Paromushir

Ostrova
Onekotan

Kurilskiy Ostrov
Simushir

Ostrova

Chasoryu-

Uchurskaya

Khrebet Dzhugdzur

Ayan

Chogdo

Uchur

▲2246

Kankumskiy

Nemuy

Chumikan

Tuguro

▲1482

Ostrov Bolshoy
Shantar

Bolshoy
Sakhalinskiy
Zaliv

Nikolayevsk-
na-Am.

Susunino

Okha

Okha

Bogorodskoye

Katangli

Aleksandrovsk-
Sakhalinskiy

Sakhalin

▲1609

Mys
Lobatina

Kurilskiye Ostrova

COPYRIGHT GEORGE PHILIP & SON LTD

170

180

170

160

50

60

130

140

72

71

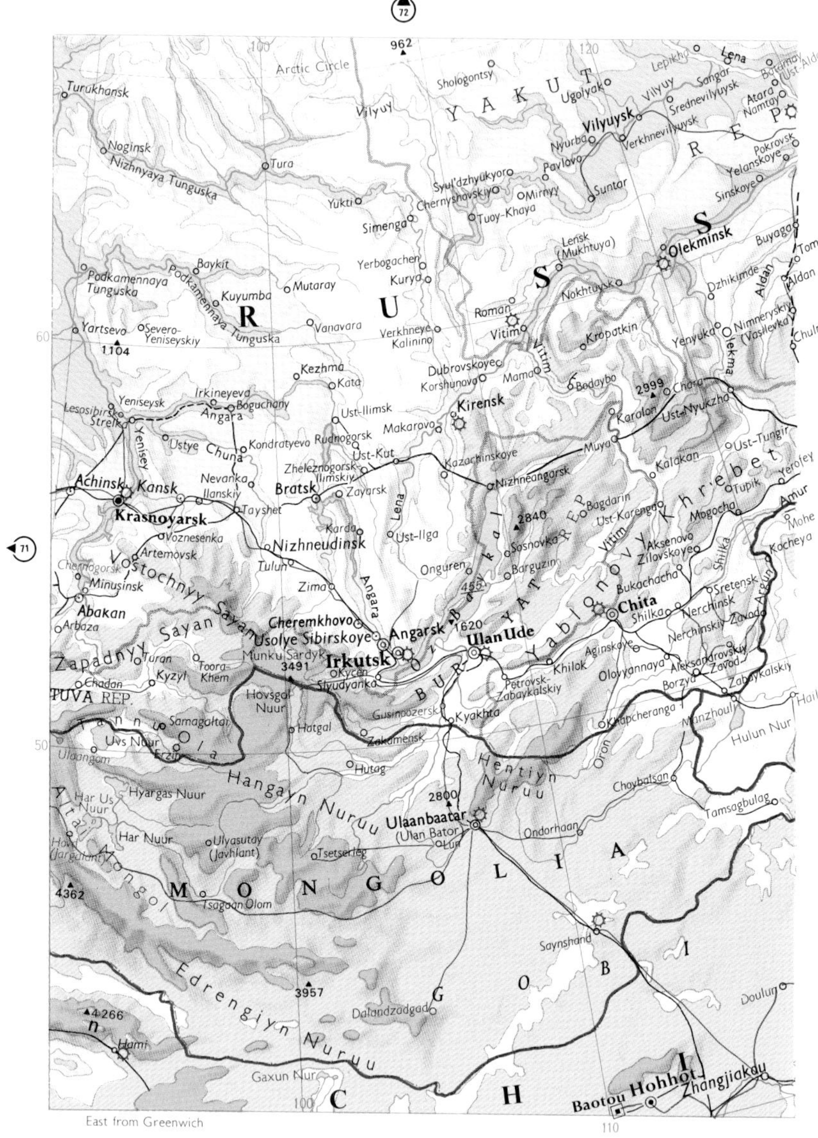

100
962
120
Arctic Circle
Turukhansk
Sholongontsy
Y A K U T
Lepikha
Lena
Batamay (Ust-Aldan)
Ugolyak
Vilyuy
Sangar
Srednevilyuysk
Atara
Namtay
Vilyuysk
Verkhnevilyuysk
R E P
Noginsk
Nizhnyaya Tunguska
Tura
Nyurba
Pavlovo
Syul'dzhyukyor
Chernyshovskiy
Mirnyy
Suntar
Pokrovsk
Yelanskoye
Sinskoye
Yukti
Tuoy-Khaya
Simenga
S
Olekminsk
Buyaga
Tommot
Lensk (Mukhtuya)
Yerbogachen
Kuryd
Baykit
Podkamennaya Tunguska
Kuyumba
Mutaray
U
S
Nokhtuysk
Dzhikimde
Aldan
R
Roman
Vitim
Kropotkin
Yartsevo
Severo-Yeniseyskiy
Vanavara
Verkhneye Kalinino
Yenyuka
Nimnervskiy (Vasilevka)
Iekma
Chulman
60
1104
Kezhma
Dubrovskoye
Korshunovo
Mama
Vitim
Bodaybo
2999
Chara
Kata
Kirensk
Karalon
Ust-Nyukzha
Irkineyeva
Yeniseysk
Boguchany
Lesosibirsk
Strelka
Angara
Ust-Ilimsk
Makarovo
Muya
Ust-Tungir
Yenisey
Ustye
Chuna
Kondratyevo
Rudnogorsk
Ust-Kut
Kazachinskoye
Kalakan
Zheleznogorsk-Ilimskiy
Nizhneangarsk
Tupik
Yerofey
Achinsk
Kansk
Nevanka
Ilanskiy
Bratsk
Zayarsk
Lena
Bagdarin
Krasnoyarsk
Tayshet
Karda
2840
Ust-Karenga
Mogocha
Amur
Voznesenka
Ust-Ilga
Sosnovka
Mohe
Artemovsk
Nizhneudinsk
Vitim
Aksenovo
Zilovskoye
Kocheya
Chernogorsk
Tulun
Onguren
Barguzin
Minusinsk
Vostochnyy Sayan
Zima
Angara
455
Bukachacha
Shilka
Sretensk
Abakan
Chita
Shilka
Nerchinsk
Arbaza
Sayan
Cheremkhovo
Angarsk
1620
Nerchinskiy Zavod
Usolye Sibirskoye
Ulan Ude
Yablonovyy
Argun
Zapadnyy
Turan
Toora-Khem
Munku Sardyk
Irkutsk
Aginskoye
Kyzyl
3491
Kycen
Khilok
Olovyannaya
Aleksandrovskiy Zavod
Chadan
Slyudyanka
Petrovsk-Zabaykalskiy
Borzya
Zabaykalskiy
TUVA REP.
Hovsgol Nuur
BURYAT REP.
Hailar
Gusinoozersk
Kyakhta
Khapcheranga
Manzhouli
Samagaltai
Hatgal
Hulun Nur
Uvs Nuur
Zakamensk
50
Erzin
Oron
Ulaangom
Hutag
Hentiyn Nuruu
Har Us Nuur
Hyargas Nuur
Hangayn Nuruu
Choybalsan
2800
Tamsagbulag
Ulaanbaatar (Ulan Bator)
Har Nuur
Ulyasutay (Javhlant)
Lun
Ondorhaan
Hovd (Jargalant)
Tsetserleg
A
Altai
L I
4362
M O N G O L I A
Tsagaan Olom
Mongol
Saynshand
I
B
O
G
3957
Edrengiyn Nuruu
Dalandzadgad
Doulun
4266
Hami
Gaxun Nur
I
C H
Baotou
Hohhot
Zhangjiakou
100
110

East from Greenwich

1 : 20 000 000

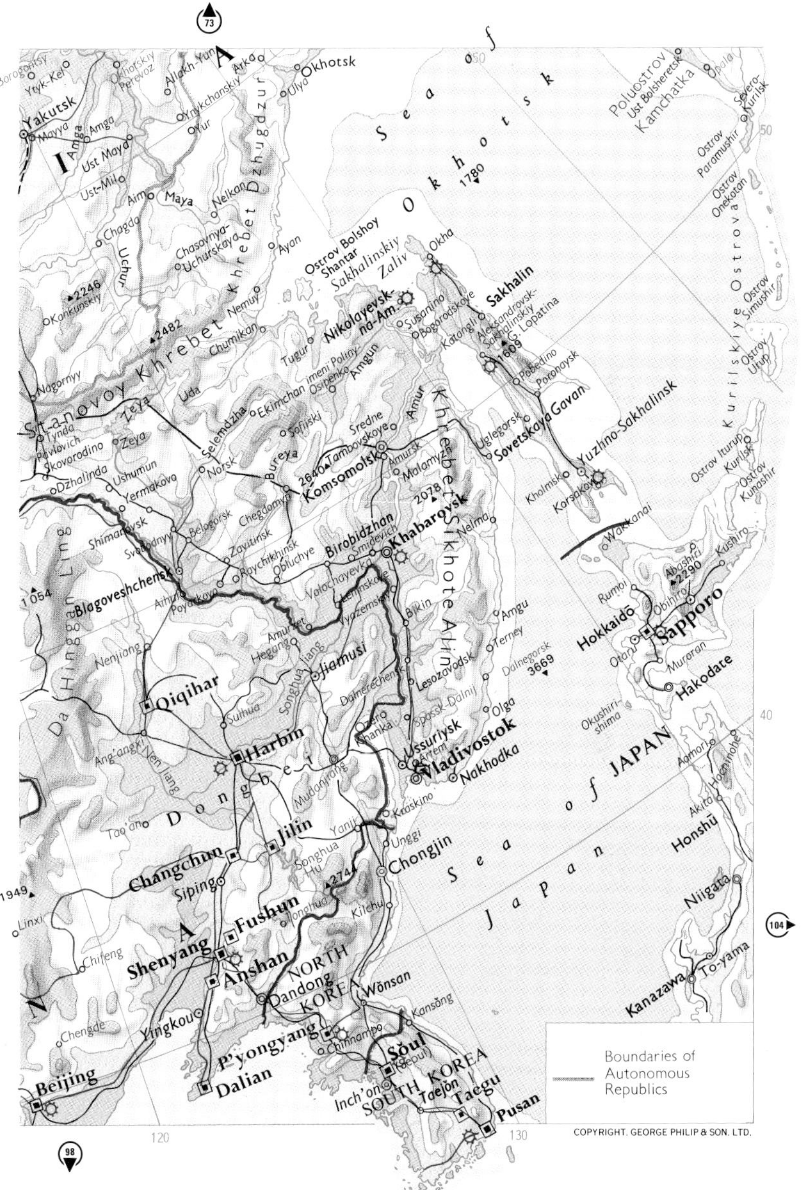
Sea of Okhotsk
Sea of JAPAN
Sea of Japan
Boundaries of Autonomous Republics
NORTH KOREA
SOUTH KOREA
Sakhalin
Hokkaido
Honshū
Yakutsk
Okhotsk
Khabarovsk
Vladivostok
Harbin
Beijing
Shenyang
P'yongyang
Sŏul
Pusan
Sapporo

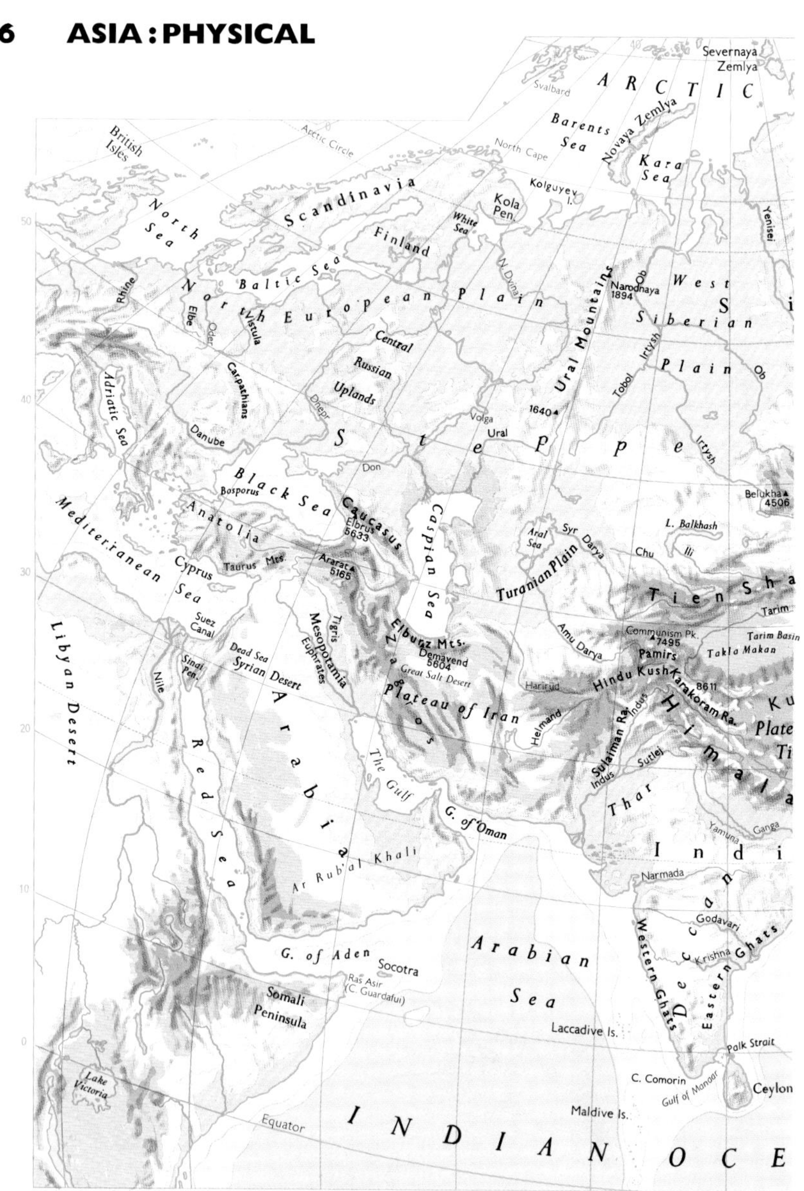
Severnaya Zemlya
ARCTIC
Svalbard
Barents Sea
Novaya Zemlya
Kara Sea
British Isles
Arctic Circle
North Cape
Kolguyev I.
Kola Pen.
White Sea
North Sea
Scandinavia
Finland
Yenisei
Baltic Sea
N. Dvina
Rhine
North European Plain
Ural Mountains
Narodnaya 1894
Ob
West Siberian Plain
Elbe
Oder
Vistula
Central Russian Uplands
Irtysh
Tobol
Carpathians
Dnepr
Adriatic Sea
Danube
Volga
Ural
1640
Steppe
Don
Black Sea
Bosporus
Caucasus
Elbrus 5633
Caspian Sea
Belukha 4506
Mediterranean Sea
Anatolia
Aral Sea
Syr Darya
L. Balkhash
Ili
Chu
Turanian Plain
Cyprus
Taurus Mts.
Ararat 5165
Tien Shan
Tarim
Suez Canal
Tigris
Mesopotamia
Euphrates
Elburz Mts.
Demavend 5604
Amu Darya
Communism Pk. 7495
Pamirs
Tarim Basin
Takla Makan
Libyan Desert
Dead Sea
Syrian Desert
Sinai Pen.
Nile
Zagros
Great Salt Desert
Plateau of Iran
Harirud
Hindu Kush
Karakoram Ra.
8611
Himalaya
Helmand
Indus
Sulaiman Ra.
Sutlej
Arabia
Red Sea
The Gulf
G. of Oman
Thar
Yamuna
Ganga
India
Ar Rub'al Khali
Narmada
Deccan
Godavari
Krishna
Western Ghats
Eastern Ghats
Arabian Sea
G. of Aden
Socotra
Ras Asir (C. Guardafui)
Somali Peninsula
Laccadive Is.
Palk Strait
Lake Victoria
C. Comorin
Gulf of Manaar
Ceylon
Maldive Is.
Equator
INDIAN OCE
East from Greenwich
40
50
60
70
80

1 : 60 000 000

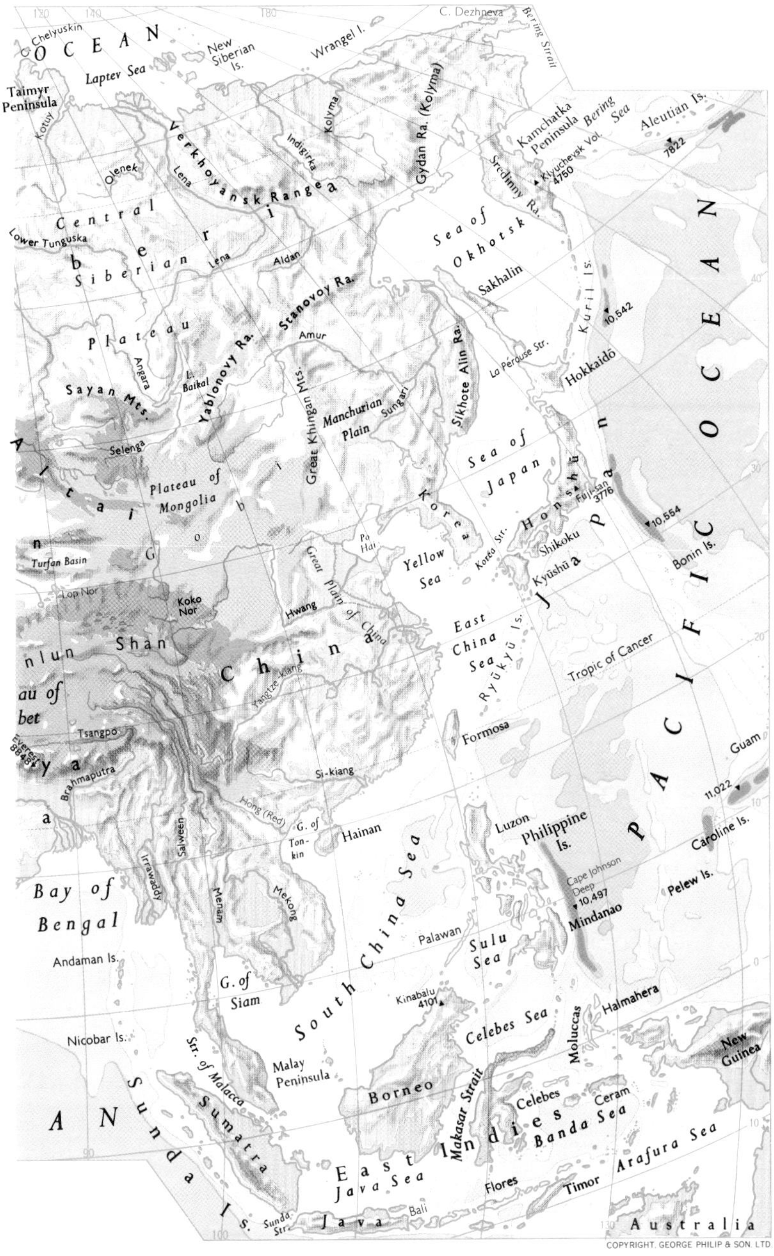

O C E A N

Chelyuskin

Taimyr
Peninsula

Laptev Sea

New
Siberian
Is.

Wrangel I.

C. Dezhneva

Bering Strait

Kotuy

Olenek

Lena

Verkhoyansk Range

Indigirka

Kolyma

Gydan Ra. (Kolyma)

Kamchatka
Peninsula

Bering Sea

Aleutian Is.

7822

Lower Tunguska

C e n t r a l

S i b e r i a n

Lena

Aldan

Srednny Ra.

Kyuchevsk Vol.
4750

b

Plateau

Angara

Baikal

Selenga

Sayan Mts.

Yablonoy Ra.

Stanovoy Ra.

Amur

Sea of
Okhotsk

Sakhalin

Kurils

10,542

Hokkaido

10,854

A l t a i

Plateau of
Mongolia

G o b i

Great Khingan Mts.

Manchurian
Plain

Sungari

Sikhote Alin Ra.

La Pérouse Str.

Sea of
Japan

Honshu

Fuji
3776

Turfan Basin

Lop Nor

Koko
Nor

Korea

Korea Str.

Shikoku

Kyushu

Bonin Is.

nlun   Shan

C h i n a

Hwang

Yangtze

Si-kiang

Po
Hai

Yellow
Sea

East
China
Sea

Ryukyu Is.

Tropic of Cancer

aū of
bet

Tsangpo

Brahmaputra

Salween

Hong (Red)

Si-kiang

Formosa

a

y a

Mekong

Meinam

Irrawaddy

G. of
Ton-
kin

Hainan

Luzon

Philippine
Is.

Guam

11,022

Caroline Is.

Bay of
Bengal

Andaman Is.

G. of
Siam

Palawan

Sulu
Sea

Cape Johnson
Deep
10,497

Mindanao

Pelew Is.

P A C I F I C   O C E A N

J a p a n

Nicobar Is.

Str. of Malacca

Sumatra

Malay
Peninsula

South China Sea

Kinabalu
4101

Borneo

Celebes Sea

Makasar Strait

Celebes

Moluccas

Ceram

Halmahera

New
Guinea

A N

S u n d a   I s.

Sunda
Str.

Java

Bali

East

Java Sea

Flores

Timor

Banda Sea

Arafura Sea

Australia

I n d i e s

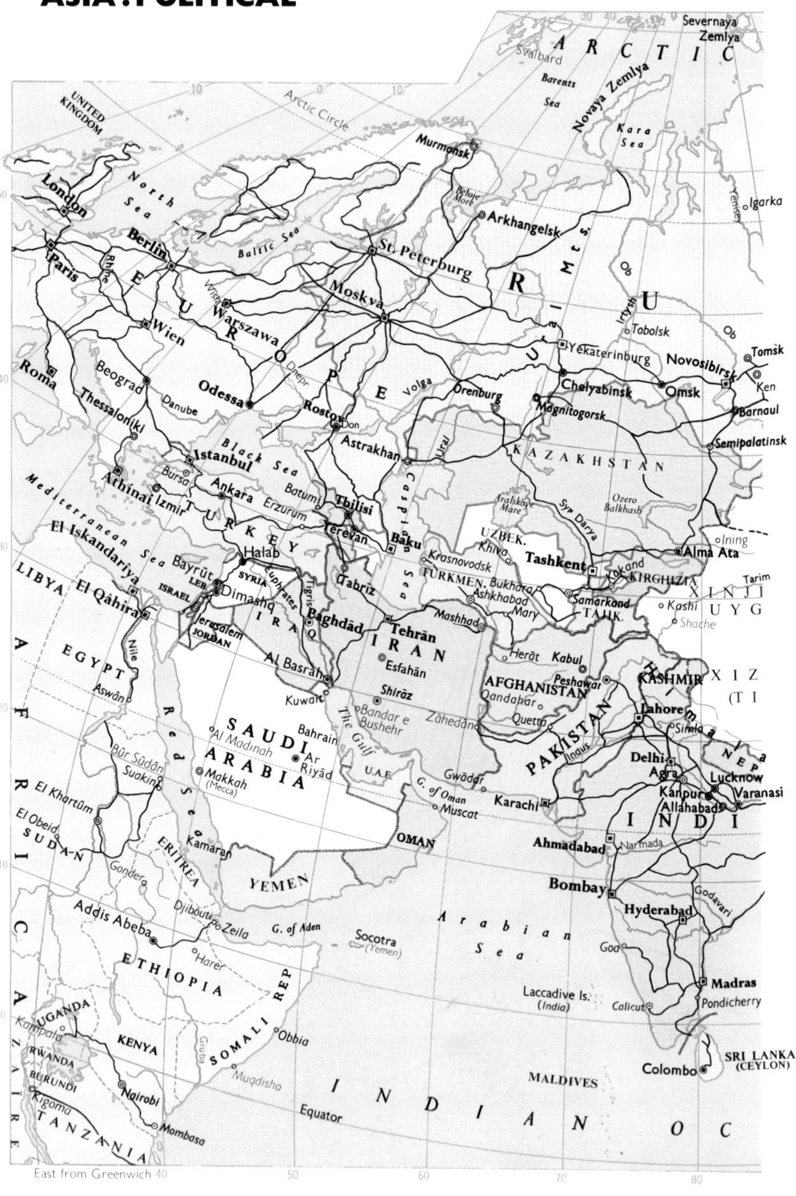

ARCTIC
Severnaya Zemlya
Svalbard
Barents Sea
Novaya Zemlya
Kara Sea
Arctic Circle
UNITED KINGDOM
North Sea
Baltic Sea
London
Paris
Berlin
Rhine
Wien
Roma
Beograd
Danube
Thessaloniki
Athínai
Istanbul
Bursa
Izmir
Ankara
Erzurum
Batumi
Tbilisi
Yerevan
Baku
Black Sea
Mediterranean Sea
TURKEY
EUROPE
Warszawa
Wisła
Odessa
Dnepr
Moskva
St. Peterburg
Murmansk
Beloje More
Arkhangelsk
Rostov
Don
Volga
Astrakhan
Orenburg
Ural
Caspian Sea
Ural Mts
Yekaterinburg
Chelyabinsk
Magnitogorsk
Tobolsk
Irtysh
Ob
Omsk
Novosibirsk
Tomsk
Barnaul
Semipalatinsk
Igarka
Yenisey
KAZAKHSTAN
Aralskoye More
Ozero Balkhash
Syr Darya
UZBEK.
Khiva
Tashkent
Kokand
KIRGHIZIA
Alma Ata
Ining
Tarim
XINJIANG UYG
Kashi
Shache
Samarkand
TAJIK.
Bukhara
Ashkhabad
Mary
TURKMEN.
Krasnovodsk
Mashhad
Tehrān
IRAN
Esfahān
Shirāz
Bandar e Bushehr
Zāhedān
Tabriz
Halab
SYRIA
LEB.
Bayrūt
Dimashq
ISRAEL
Jerusalem
JORDAN
Euphrates
Tigris
IRAQ
Baghdād
Al Basrah
Kuwait
Bahrain
The Gulf
SAUDI ARABIA
Al Madinah
Ar Riyād
Makkah (Mecca)
U.A.E.
G. of Oman
Muscat
OMAN
YEMEN
Kamaran
G. of Aden
Socotra (Yemen)
Herāt
Kabul
AFGHANISTAN
Qandahar
Quetta
Peshawar
KASHMIR
XIZ (TI
Lahore
Simla
Himalaya
NEP
PAKISTAN
Indus
Gwādar
Karachi
Delhi
Agra
Lucknow
Kanpur
Allahabad
Varanasi
INDIA
Ahmadabad
Narmada
Bombay
Hyderabad
Godavari
Goa
Madras
Pondicherry
Calicut
Laccadive Is. (India)
SRI LANKA (CEYLON)
Colombo
MALDIVES
Arabian Sea
INDIAN OCEAN
El Iskandarîya
El Qâhira
LIBYA
EGYPT
Nile
Aswân
Red Sea
Bûr Sûdân
Suakin
El Khartûm
El Obeid
SUDAN
ERITREA
Gondera
Djibouti
Zeila
Addis Abeba
Harer
ETHIOPIA
SOMALI REP
Obbia
Giuba
Muqdisho
UGANDA
Kampala
KENYA
RWANDA
BURUNDI
Kigoma
Nairobi
Mombasa
TANZANIA
ZAÏRE
AFRICA
Equator
East from Greenwich

1 : 60 000 000

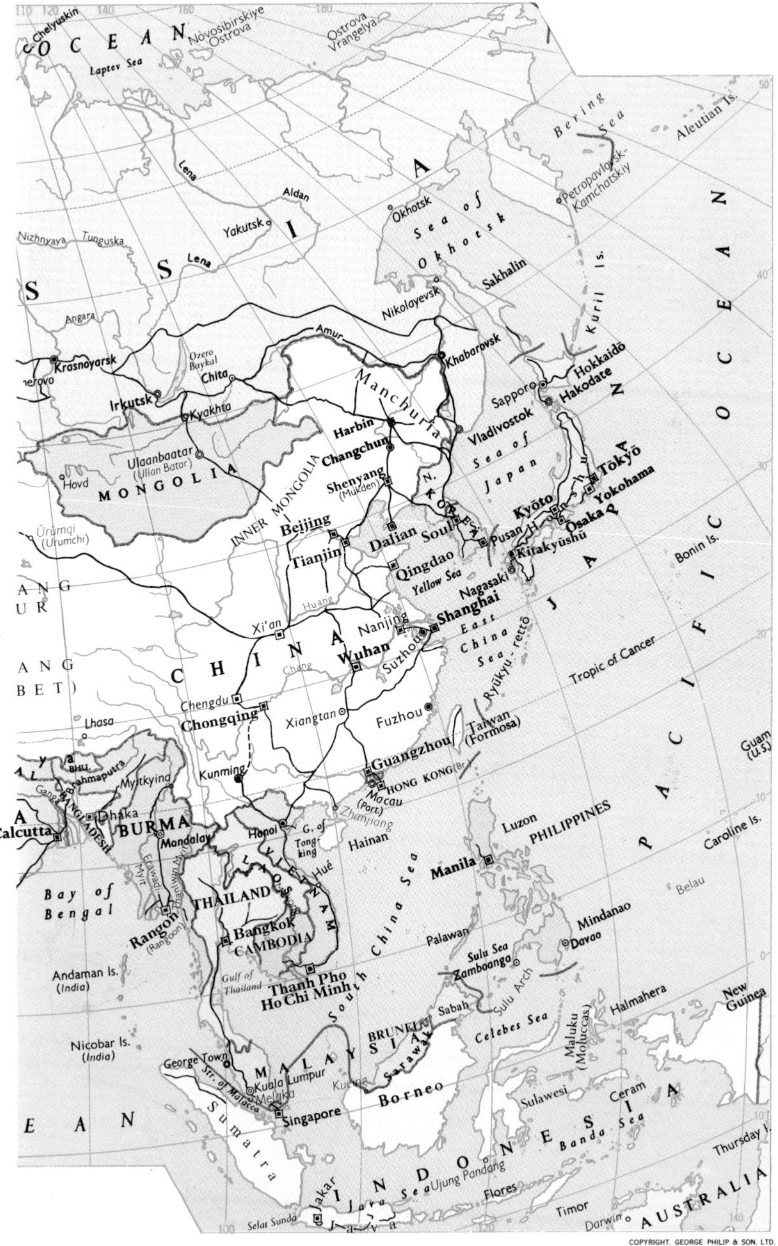

C. Chelyuskin
O C E A N
Novosibirskiye Ostrova
Ostrova Vrangelya
Laptev Sea
Bering Sea
Aleutian Is.
Lena
Aldan
A
Petropavlovsk-Kamchatskiy
Okhotsk
Sea of Okhotsk
Yakutsk
I
Nizhnyaya Tunguska
S
Lena
S
Sakhalin
Kuril Is.
Nikolayevsk
Angara
Amur
Ozero Baykal
Krasnoyarsk
Khabarovsk
Hokkaido
Hakodate
Sapporo
Chita
Irkutsk
Kyakhta
Manchuria
Harbin
Vladivostok
Changchun
Sea of Japan
Ulaanbaatar (Ulan Bator)
Hovd
MONGOLIA
INNER MONGOLIA
Shenyang (Mukden)
N. KOREA
Tōkyō
Yokohama
Kyōto
Ōsaka
Honshu
Ürümqi (Urumchi)
Beijing
Dalian
Soul
Pusan
Kitakyūshū
Tianjin
Qingdao
Yellow Sea
Nagasaki
Bonin Is.
Huang
Shanghai
Xi'an
Nanjing
East China Sea
Wuhan
Suzhou
CHINA
Chang
Ryūkyū-rettō
Tropic of Cancer
PACIFIC OCEAN
JAPAN
Chengdu
Chongqing
Xiangtan
Fuzhou
Taiwan (Formosa)
Lhasa
Brahmaputra
BHU.
Myitkying
Ganges
BANGLADESH
Dhaka
Calcutta
Kunming
Guangzhou
HONG KONG (Br.)
Macau (Port.)
Zhanjiang
Guam (U.S.)
BURMA
Mandalay
Hanoi
G. of Tong-king
Hainan
Luzon
PHILIPPINES
Caroline Is.
Bay of Bengal
Erawadi
Thanlwin
LAOS
VIETNAM
Hué
South China Sea
Manila
THAILAND
Rangon (Rangoon)
Bangkok
CAMBODIA
Belau
Palawan
Mindanao
Davao
Sulu Sea
Zamboanga
Andaman Is. (India)
Gulf of Thailand
Thanh Pho Ho Chi Minh
Sulu Arch
Sabah
Halmahera
New Guinea
Nicobar Is. (India)
BRUNEI
MALAYSIA
Sarawak
Celebes Sea
Maluku (Moluccas)
George Town
Kuala Lumpur
Str. of Malacca
Melaka
Kuching
Borneo
Sulawesi
Ceram
Singapore
Sumatra
INDONESIA
Banda Sea
E A N
Ujung Pandang
Java Sea
Flores
Jakarta
Thursday I.
Java
Timor
Selat Sunda
Darwin
AUSTRALIA

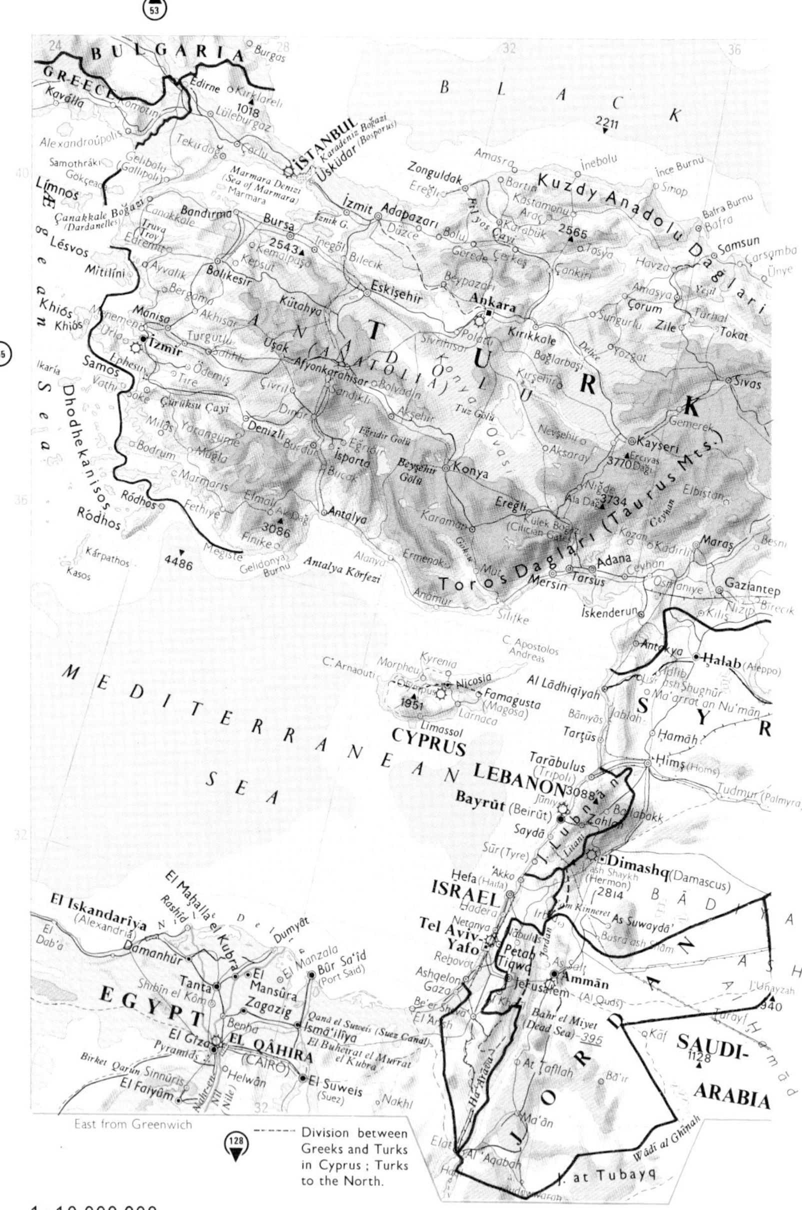

1 : 10 000 000

East from Greenwich

Division between
Greeks and Turks
in Cyprus ; Turks
to the North.

70

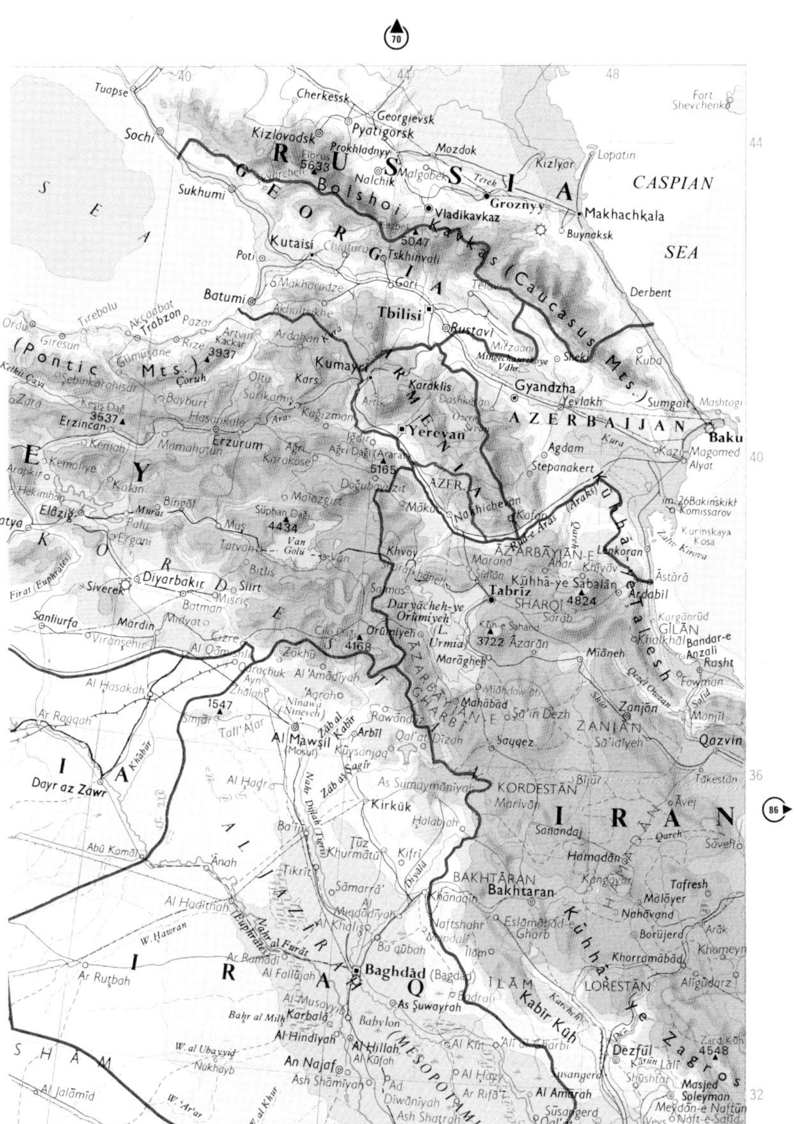
RUSSIA
GEORGIA
ARMENIA
AZERBAIJAN
IRAN
IRAQ
CASPIAN SEA
Bolshoi Kavkas (Caucasus Mts.)
(Pontic Mts.)
Tbilisi
Yerevan
Baku
Baghdād
Tabrīz
Groznyy
Makhachkala
Vladikavkaz
Kutaisi
Batumi
Sukhumi
Sochi
Tuapse
Rustavi
Gyandzha
Kumayri
Erzurum
Trabzon
Diyarbakır
Al Mawşil
Kirkūk
Arbīl
Hamadān
Bakhtaran
Qazvin
Rasht
Ardabil
Dezfūl
Ahvāz
Karbalā
An Najaf
Al Ḩillah
Al 'Amārah
Dayr az Zawr
Darvācheh-ye Orūmiyeh (L. Urmia)
Van Golü
Kūhhā-ye Zagros
(MESOPOTAMIA)
AL JAZIRAH
Kūhhā-ye Talesh
KORDESTĀN
LORESTĀN
GĪLĀN
ZANJĀN
BAKHTĀRAN
ĪLĀM
ĀZARBĀYJĀN-E SHARQĪ
ĀZARBĀYJĀN-E GHARBĪ
AZER.
Elbrus 5633
5047
3937
3537
5165
4434
4168
4824
3722
1547
4548
40
44
48
36
32

86

82

80
81

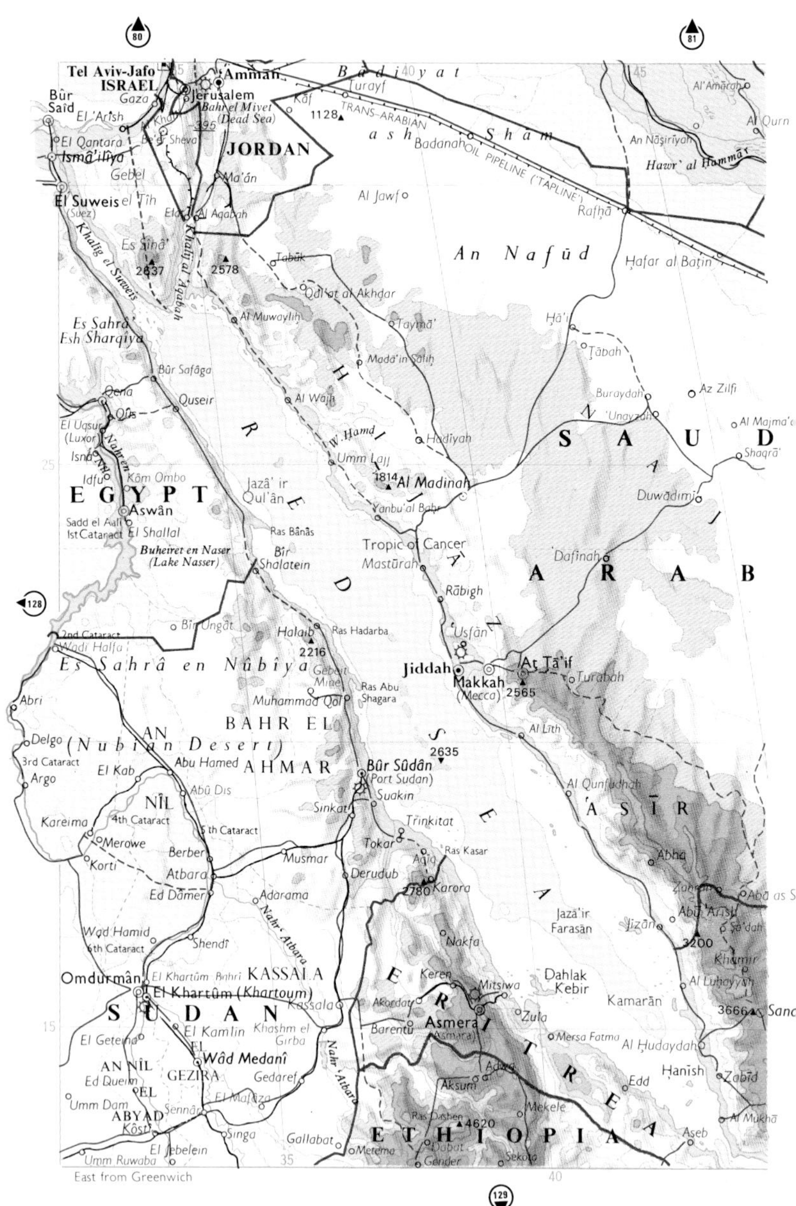
Tel Aviv-Jafo
ISRAEL
Ammān
Jerusalem
Bahr el Miyet (Dead Sea)
JORDAN
Bûr Saîd
Gaza
El 'Arîsh
El Qantara
Ismâ'ilîya
El Suweis (Suez)
Ma'ān
Al 'Aqabah
Khalîg el Suweis
Khalîj al 'Aqabah
Es Sînâ'
2637
2578
Badiyat ash Sham
Turayf
Kāf
1128
TRANS-ARABIAN OIL PIPELINE ('TAPLINE')
Badanah
Al Jawf
Rafḩā
Al 'Amārah
Al Qurn
An Nāṣirīyah
Hawr' al Hammār
An Nafūd
Ḩafar al Bāţin
Tabūk
Qal'at al Akhḍar
Al Muwaylih
Taymā'
Es Sahrâ Esh Sharqîya
Bûr Safâga
Qena
Quseir
Qûs
El Uqsur (Luxor)
Isna
Idfu
Kôm Ombo
EGYPT
Aswân
Sadd el Aali
1st Cataract
El Shallal
Buheiret en Naser (Lake Nasser)
Mada'in Şāliḩ
Al Wajh
W. Hamḍ
Umm Lajj
1814
Al Madīnah
Hadīyah
Yanbu' al Baḩr
Jazâ' ir Qul'ân
Ras Bânâs
Bîr Shalatein
Tropic of Cancer
Mastūrah
Rābigh
HIJAZ
RED SEA
Ḩā'il
Ţābah
Buraydah
'Unayzah
Az Zilfī
Al Majma'ah
Shaqrā'
Duwādimī
NAJD
SAUDI ARABIA
Dafīnah
Bîr Ungât
Halaib
2216
Ras Hadarba
2nd Cataract
Wadi Halfa
Es Sahrâ en Nûbîya
Gebeit Mine
Ras Abu Shagara
Muhammad Qol
BAHR EL AHMAR
'Usfān
Jiddah
Makkah (Mecca)
At Tā'if
2565
Turabah
Al Līth
2635
Abri
Delgo
3rd Cataract
Argo
El Kab
AN NÎL
(Nubian Desert)
Abu Hamed
Abû Dis
Bûr Sûdân (Port Sudan)
Suakin
Sinkat
Trinkitat
Kareima
4th Cataract
5th Cataract
Merowe
Korti
Berber
Atbara
Musmar
Tokar
Ras Kasar
Aqiq
Derudub
Karora
2780
Ed Damer
Adarama
Nahr 'Atbara
Al Qunfudhah
'ASIR
Abhā
Zahran
Abā as Sa'ūd
Abū 'Arīsh
Jīzān
Şa'dah
3200
Khamir
Jazā'ir Farasān
Nakfa
Wad Hamid
6th Cataract
Shendi
Omdurmân
El Khartûm Bahri
KASSALA
El Khartûm (Khartoum)
SUDAN
Kassala
Keren
Mitsiwa
Dahlak Kebir
Akordat
Asmera (Asmara)
Zula
ERITREA
Kamarān
Al Luhayyah
3666
Sanc
El Geteina
El Kamlin
Khashm el Girba
Barentu
Mersa Fatma
Al Ḩudaydah
AN NÎL
Ed Dueim
Wâd Medanî
GEZIRA
Gedaref
Adwa
Aksum
Ḩanīsh
Zabīd
Edd
Umm Dam
EL ABYAD
Sennâr
El Mafâza
Mekele
Al Mukhā
Kôsti
Ras Dashen
4620
ETHIOPIA
Aseb
Singa
El Jebelein
Gallabat
Metema
Dabat
Gonder
Sekota
Umm Ruwaba
25
15
35
40
45
East from Greenwich

128
129

1 : 15 000 000

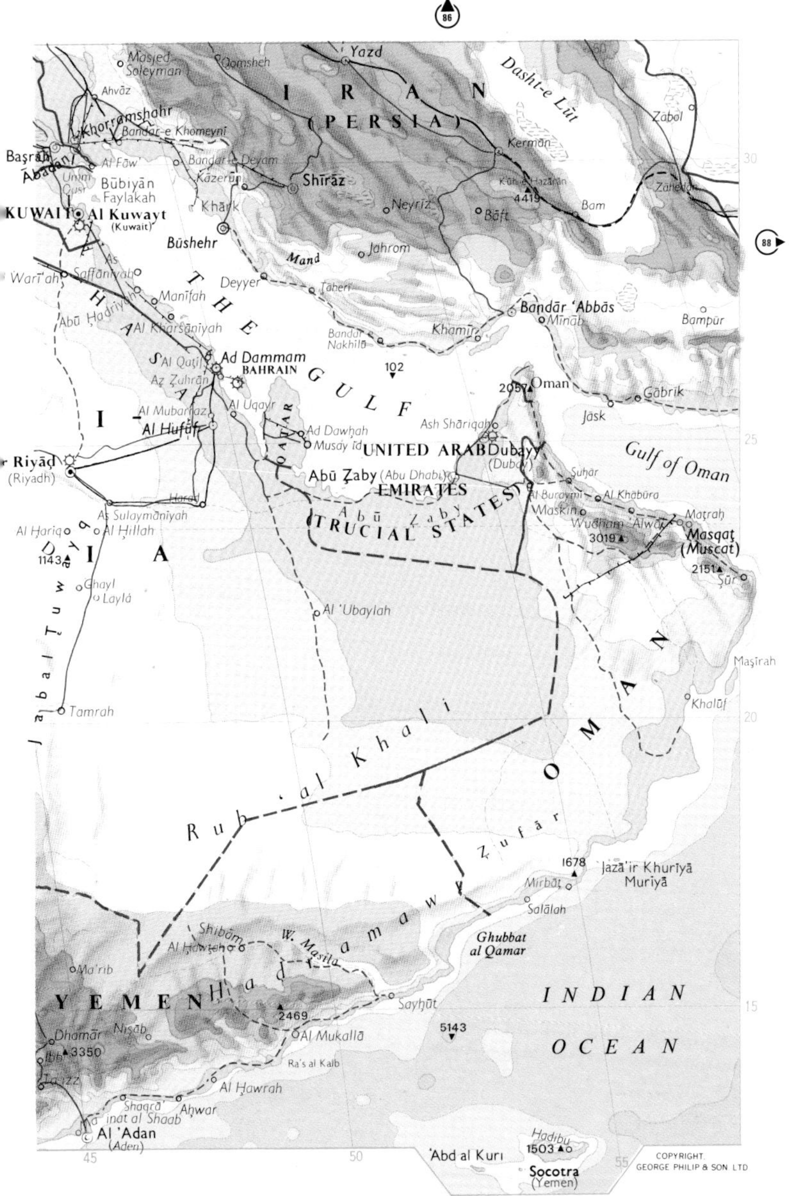
86
88
IRAN
(PERSIA)
Yazd
Qomsheh
Masjed Soleyman
Ahvāz
Khorramshahr
Bandar-e Khomeyni
Başrah
Ābādān
Al Fāw
Bandar-e Deyam
Kāzerūn
Shīrāz
Kermān
Zābol
Zāhedān
Bam
Bāft
Neyrīz
Kūh-e Hazārān
4419
Dasht-e Lūt
Būbiyān
Faylakah
KUWAIT
Al Kuwayt
(Kuwait)
Khārk
Būshehr
Mand
Jahrom
Deyyer
Tāheri
Bandar 'Abbās
Mīnāb
Bampūr
Khamīr
Bandar Nakhīlū
As Saffānīyah
Warī'ah
Manīfah
Abū Ḩadrīyah
Al Kharsānīyah
THE GULF
Ad Dammam
BAHRAIN
Al Qaţīf
Az Zuhrān
102
2057
Oman
Gābrīk
Jāsk
Al Mubarraz
Al Hufūf
Al Uqayr
QATAR
Ad Dawḩah
Musay'īd
Ash Shāriqah
UNITED ARAB
EMIRATES
Dubayy
(Dubai)
Gulf of Oman
Abū Ẓaby
(Abu Dhabi)
Riyāḑ
(Riyadh)
Şuḩār
Al Buraymī
Al Khābūra
Maskin
Wudham 'Alwā
3019
Maţraḩ
Masqaţ
(Muscat)
Abū Ẓaby
TRUCIAL STATES
Ḩaraḑ
As Sulaymānīyah
Al Ḩarīq
Al Ḩillah
1143
2151
Şūr
Ghayl
Laylā
Al 'Ubaylah
Maşīrah
Jabal Tuwayq
Tamrah
Khalūf
Rub' al Khālī
OMAN
Ẓufār
1678
Jazā'ir Khurīyā Murīyā
Mirbāţ
Şalālah
Ghubbat al Qamar
Shibām
Al Ḩawţah
W. Masīla
Ḩadramawt
Ma'rib
YEMEN
Nisāb
2469
Sayḩūt
INDIAN OCEAN
5143
Dhamār
3350
Ibb
Ta'izz
Al Mukallā
Ra's al Kalb
Al Ḩawrah
Shaqrā'
Aḩwar
Madīnat al Shaab
Al 'Adan
(Aden)
Ḩadibū
1503
'Abd al Kūrī
Socotra
(Yemen)
30
25
20
15
45
50
55

81

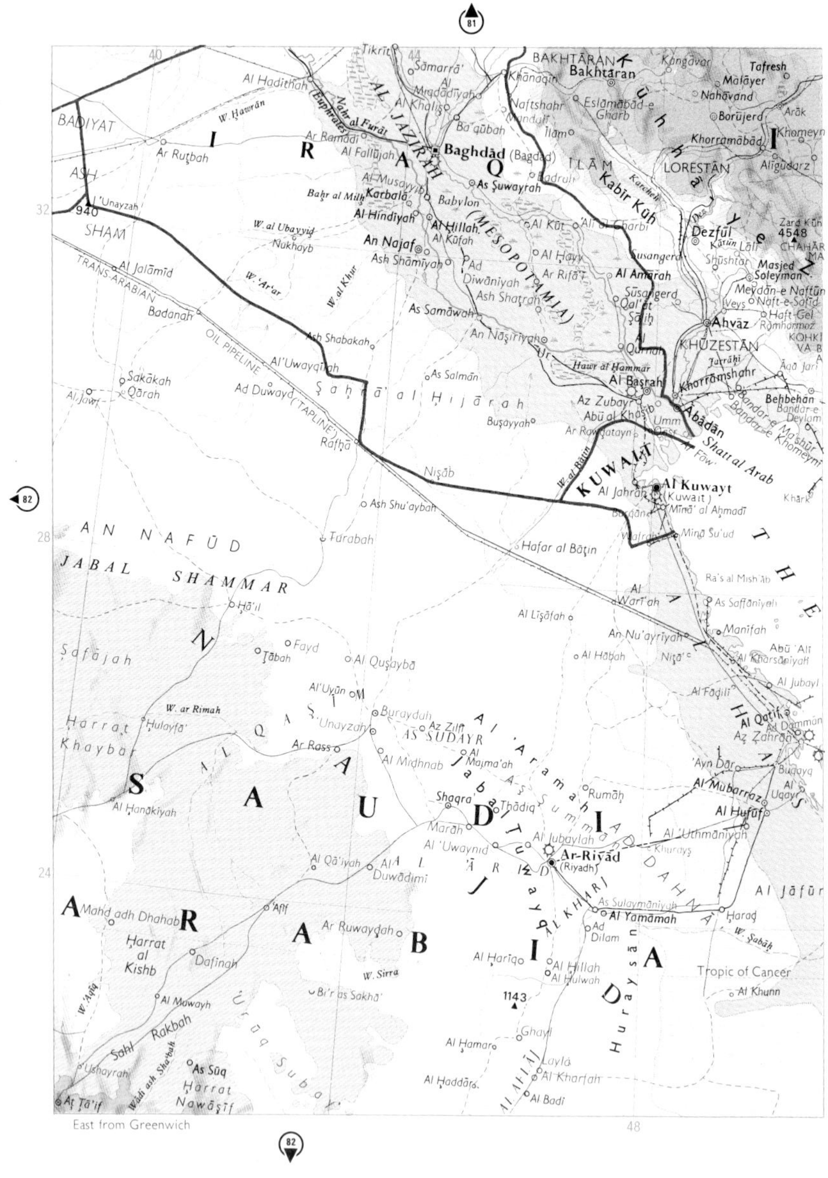

IRAQ
SAUDI ARABIA
KUWAIT
Baghdād (Bagdad)
Al Baṣrah
Al Kuwayt (Kuwait)
Ar-Riyāḍ (Riyadh)
AL JAZIRAH
(MESOPOTAMIA)
Ṣaḥrā' al Ḥijārah
AN NAFŪD
JABAL SHAMMAR
AL QAṢĪM
AS SUDAYR
AD DAHNĀ'
Tropic of Cancer
Shatt al Arab
East from Greenwich

82

82

1 : 10 000 000

Qom ○ Daryācheh-ye Namak

KHORASAN
Nagineh ○ Gonābād 60
Boshrūyeh ○ Ferdows ○ Qāyen Daryācheh-i-Namaksar
Kāshān Jandaq ○ Khvor ○ Tabas ○ Deyhūk Yazdān Shindand
Mahallāt ○ Qāyen

I R A N
Naţanz Zāvāreh Ardestān ○ Anārak Deyhūk ○ Khūr ○ Bīrjand Tabas 2886 AFGHANISTAN
ESFAHĀN Nā'īn Mazhān ○ Sarbīsheh Harī Rūd
Tīrān Esfahan Nāy Band DASHT-E LŪT (Great Sand Desert) Shūsf
Najafābād Kūhpāyeh Ardakān Kharānaq Nehbandān Daryācheh-ye Seistan
Shahr Kord Varzaneh YAZD Nadūshan Shīr Kūh Shūsf Zābol
HĀLĪ VA BAKHTĪĀRĪ Qomsheh Bāţlāq-e Gavkhūni ○ Yazd Bāfq Seistan
Kūh-e Alījūq 4075 Rāvar ○ Shāh Rūd Numakzār-e Shahdād Zāhedān (Duzdab)
3723 Izad Khvāst Zarand Shahdād Kūh-e Seh Konj Nosratābād
Abādeh ○ Kūh-e Bol 3660 Deh Bīd Rafsanjān Kermān 3992 KERMĀN Ladīz 4042 Kūh-e Taftān
Gāchsārān Ardakān Sa'ādatābād Lāvar Meydān Shahr-e Bābak Kūh-e Hazārān Tahrūd Bam Fahraj Bībābān-e Kermān Khāsh Sīāreh
Kāzerūn Persepolis Shīrāz Daryācheh-ye Tashk Sa'īdābād 4419 Kūh-e 3962 Bīābān-e Barez
Ganāveh Bandar-e Rīg FĀRS Sarvestān Neyrīz Meydān-e Gel Bāft Sabzvārān SISTĀN
Borāzjān Fasā Dārāb Dowlatābād
BŪSHEHR Farāshband Fīrūzābād Jahrom Shūr Tārom Kahnūi Halil Rūd Hāmūn-e Jāz Mūriān Bampūr Īrānshahr
Khvormūj Mand Deyyer 'Alāmarvdasht Lār Kūh-e Furgun 3280 Shamil HORMOZGAN BALŪCHESTĀN
Tāhert Nāy Band Bastak 2804 Kūh-e Hormoz Bandar Kūhhā-ye Bashākerd Remeshk
Bandar-e Nakhīlū Jazīreh-ye Lāvān Bandar-e Chārak Qeshm Jaz-ye Mināb Kūh-e Kūhrān 2163 Bent Nīkshahr
Al Muharraq Manāmah Qeys 102 Forūr Bandar-e Lengeh Bāsaīdū Qeshm Ras-e Kūhrān Strait of Hormuz Oman 2057 Jāsk Jāpūn Qayr-e Qānd
BAHRAIN Ra's Rakan Sirri Sirrī Bandar-e Lengeh Ra's al Khaymah Rāpsh Ra's-e Meydānī Ra's-e Tanq Chāh Bahār
'Awālī Dukhān Ad Dawhah Dalmā Abū al Musay'īd Ash Shāriqah (Sharjah) 'Ajmān Al Fujayrah Suhār Wadhām Alwaj Gulf of Oman
QATAR Al Wakrah Dās As Zarqā Umm al Qaywayn Dubayy (Dubay) Al Khabūra Masqaţ (Muscat)
Bū Hasa Abū Zaby (Abū Dhabi) AL BAŢINAH Al Quraynī
Sīr Banī Yās Habshān Murban Ţarīf Al Buraymi Al Wāhāt al Buraymī Mosking Ma'rūh
UNITED ARAB EMIRATES Abū Ţabī 1372 Jabal Al Mulaiddah Ibrā 2151 Sūr Ra's al Hadd
(TRUCIAL STATES) JIWĀ 3019 Izki Ibrā Tiwī As Suwayh
'Azīz Bunayyān ○ Arādah W. 'Ayn W. Aswad Ţash Shām OMAN W. Bacha
Al Quraynī W. 'Umayri Ādam W. Andām Al Kāmil Al Ashkharah
O M A N 60
52 56 COPYRIGHT GEORGE PHILIP & SON LTD

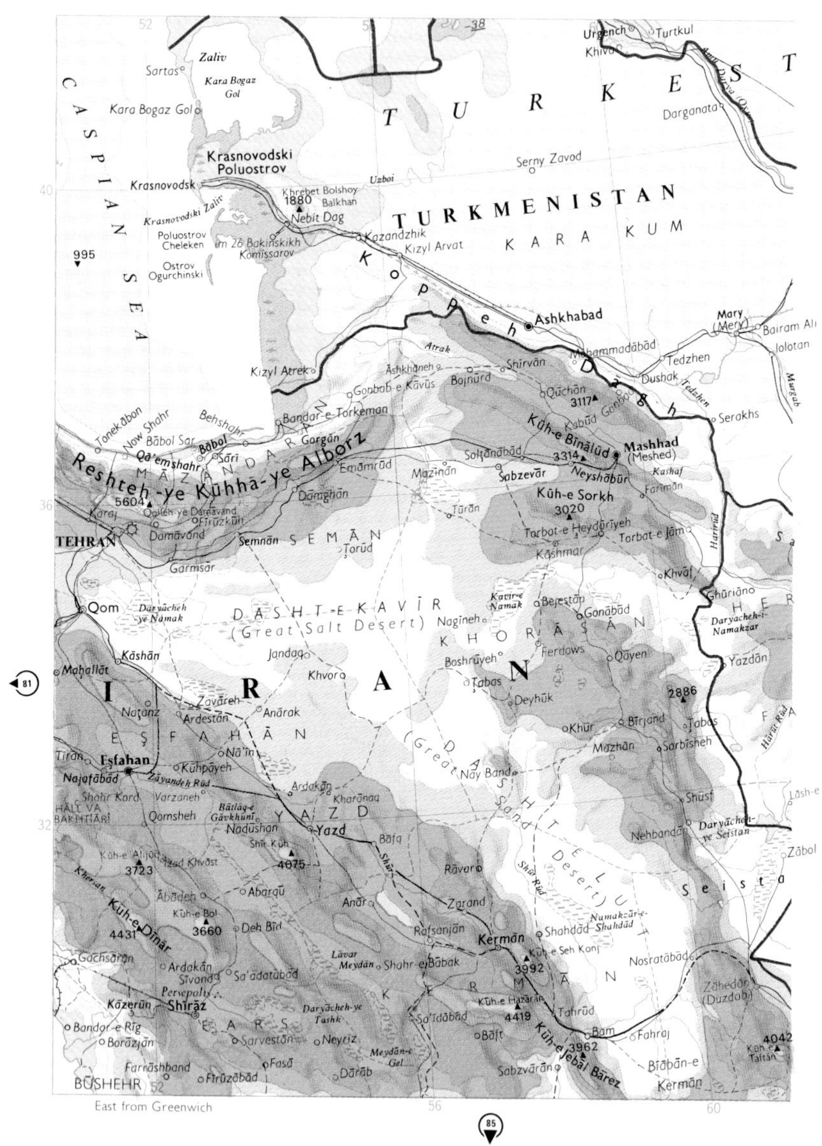

CASPIAN SEA
TURKESTAN
TURKMENISTAN
KARA KUM
Kopet Dāgh
IRAN
Zaliv Kara Bogaz Gol
Sartas
Kara Bogaz Gol
Krasnovodski Poluostrov
Krasnovodsk
Krasnovodski Zaliv
Poluostrov Cheleken
Ostrov Ogurchinski
995
Uzboi
Khrebet Bolshoy Balkhan
1880
Nebit Dag
im 26 Bakinskikh Komissarov
Kazandzhik
Kizyl Arvat
Ashkhabad
Urgench
Turtkul
Khiva
Darganata
Serny Zavod
Mary (Merv)
Bairam Ali
Iolotan
Murgab
Tedzhen
Dushak
Mohammadābād
Serakhs
Atrak
Kizyl Atrek
Āshkhāneh
Shirvān
Bojnūrd
Gonbad-e Kāvūs
Qūchān
3117
Bandar-e Torkeman
Behshahr
Tonekābon
Now Shahr
Bābol Sar
Bābol
Sārī
Gorgān
Qā'emshahr
MĀZANDARĀN
Reshteh-ye Kūhha-ye Alborz
Kūh-e Bīnālūd
3314
Mashhad (Meshed)
Kashaf
Neyshābūr
Soltānābād
Sabzevār
Emāmrūd
Mazīnān
Dāmghān
Kūh-e Sorkh
3020
Farīmān
5604
Qolleh-ye Damāvand
Karaj
Fīrūzkūh
Damāvand
TEHRAN
Semnān
SEMNĀN
Tūrān
Torūd
Torbat-e Heydārīyeh
Torbat-e Jām
Kāshmar
Harīrūd
Garmsār
Khvāf
Ghūriān
Qom
Daryācheh-ye Namak
DASHT-E KAVĪR (Great Salt Desert)
Kavīr-e Namak
Nagīneh
Bejestān
Gonābād
KHORĀSĀN
Daryācheh-i-Namakzar
Kāshān
Jandaq
Ferdows
Qāyen
Boshrūyeh
Yazdān
Mahallāt
Khvor
Tabas
Deyhūk
2886
Natanz
Zavāreh
Anārak
Ardestān
Khūr
Bīrjand
Tabas
Hārūt Rūd
EŞFAHĀN
Nā'īn
Mazhān
Sarbīsheh
Tirān
Eşfahān
Najafābād
Kūhpāyeh
Zāyandeh Rūd
Nay Band
DASHT-E LUT (Great Sand Desert)
Shahr Kord
Varzaneh
Ardakān
Kharānaq
Shusf
HALL VA BAKHTIARI
Qomsheh
Bātlāq-e Gāvkhūnī
YAZD
Nadūshan
Yazd
Bāfq
Nehbandān
Daryācheh-ye Seīstan
Zābol
Shīr Kūh
4075
Kūh-e Alījūq
3723
Izad Khvāst
Rāvar
Seistan
Ābādeh
Abarqū
Anār
Zarand
Kūh-e Bol
3660
Kūh-e Dīnār
4431
Deh Bīd
Rafsanjān
Kermān
Shahdād
Namakzār-e Shahdād
Gachsārān
Kūh-e Seh Konj
3992
Nosratābād
Ardakān
Sīvand
Sa'ādatābād
Lāvar Meydān
Shahr-e Bābak
KERMĀN
Persepolis
Zāhedān (Duzdab)
Kāzerūn
Shīrāz
Daryācheh-ye Tashk
Kūh-e Hazārān
4419
Tahrūd
FARS
Sa'īdābād
Bandar-e Rīg
Borāzjān
Sarvestān
Neyrīz
Bāft
Bam
Fahraj
Kūh-e Jebāl Bārez
3962
4042
Kūh-e Taftān
Farrāshband
Fasā
Meydān-e Gel
Dārāb
Sabzvārān
Bīābān-e Kermān
BŪSHEHR
Fīrūzābād
Lāsh-e Jo
52
56
60
36
32
40
38
East from Greenwich

81

85

1 : 10 000 000

70

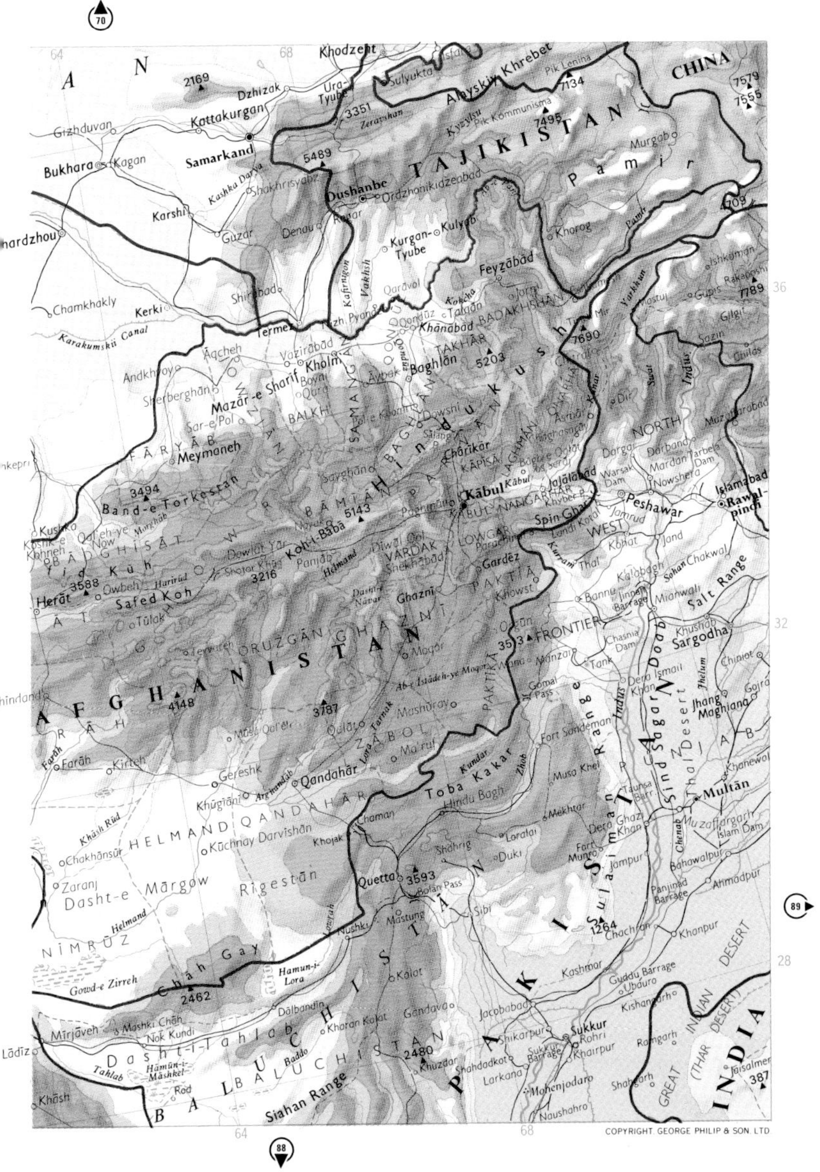

TAJIKISTAN
CHINA
AFGHANISTAN
PAKISTAN
INDIA
Khodzent
Dzhizak
Ura-Tyube
Kattakurgan
Gizhduvan
Bukhara
Kagan
Samarkand
Kashka Darya
Shakhrisyabz
Karshi
Guzar
Chardzhou
Denau
Dushanbe
Ordzhonikidzeabad
Kurgan-Tyube
Kulyab
Khorog
Murgab
Pamir
Pik Lenina
Pik Kommunisma
7134
7495
7579
7555
7709
5489
3351
2169
Alayskiy Khrebet
Zeravshan
Vakhsh
Kafirnigan
Sulyukta
Isfara
Kerki
Chamkhakly
Karakumskii Canal
Termez
Shirabad
Feyzābād
Qondūz
Tāloqān
Khānābād
Kholm
Baghlān
Āqcheh
Andkhvoy
Sherberghān
Mazār-e Sharif
Sar-e Pol
Meymaneh
BALKH
SAMANGĀN
BADAKHSHĀN
TAKHĀR
FĀRYĀB
5203
7690
Hindu Kush
Chārikār
Kābul
Jalālābād
KĀPĪSĀ
LAGHMĀN
NANGARHĀR
KUNAR
Band-e Torkestān
3494
Bāmiān
5143
Paghmān
Koh-i-Baba
Kushka
Qal'eh-ye Now
BĀDGHĪSĀT
Dowlat Yār
Shotor Khāl
Panjāb
Helmand
Harirud
Herāt
3588
Owbeh
Safed Koh
3216
Tūlak
Ghazni
Gardēz
VARDAK
LOWGAR
PAKTĪĀ
Khowst
ORUZGĀN
GHAZNĪ
Moqor
Ab-e Istādeh-ye Moqor
4148
3787
Shindand
Farāh
Qalāt
Mashūray
ZĀBOL
Ma'ruf
Mūsā Qal'eh
Kirteh
Gereshk
Qandahār
Arghandāb
Khūgiānī
Khāsh Rūd
HELMAND
QANDAHĀR
Chakhānsūr
Kūchnay Darvīshān
Zaranj
Dasht-e Mārgow
Rigestān
NĪMRŪZ
Gowd-e Zirreh
Chāh Gay
2462
Hamun-i-Lora
Chaman
Khojak
Quetta
3593
Bolān Pass
Mastung
Nushki
Kalat
Sibi
Dālbandin
Mirjāveh
Mashki Chāh
Nok Kundi
Dasht-i-Tahlab
Tahlab
Hāmūn-i-Māshkel
Rod
Lādīz
Khāsh
Kharan Kalat
Gandava
2480
Khuzdar
Siahan Range
BALUCHISTAN
Peshawar
Islamabad
Rawalpindi
Nowshera
Mardan
Tarbela Dam
Warsak Dam
Khyber P.
Landi Kotal
Jamrud
Spin Ghar
Kohat
Thal
Kurram
Bannu
Jinnah Barrage
Mianwali
Kalabagh
Sohan
Chakwal
Salt Range
Sargodha
Khushab
Chiniot
Jhang Maghiana
Gojra
Jhelum
Sind Sagar Doab
Thal Desert
Dera Ismail Khan
Chasma Dam
Tank
Wana
Manzai
Gomal Pass
Fort Sandeman
Zhob
Kundar
Toba Kakar
Hindu Bagh
Muso Khel
Mekhtar
Loralai
Duki
Shahrig
Sulaiman Range
Dera Ghazi Khan
Fort Munro
Taunsa Barr.
Multān
Khanewal
Muzaffargarh
Islam Dam
Chenab
Bahawalpur
Jampur
Ahmadpur
Panjnad Barrage
Chachran
Khanpur
1264
Kashmor
Guddu Barrage
Ubauro
Jacobabad
Shikarpur
Sukkur
Rohri
Sukkur Barrage
Khairpur
Shahdadkot
Larkana
Mohenjodaro
Naushahro
Kishangarh
Ramgarh
Shahgarh
Jaisalmer
387
GREAT INDIAN DESERT (THAR DESERT)
NORTH WEST FRONTIER
Gilgit
Chilas
Ishkoman
Gupis
Rakaposhi
7789
Mastuj
Yarkhun
Swat
Dir
Dargai
Muzaffarabad
Indus
Mir
3513
Ourgun
PUNJAB
SIND
64
68
36
32
28

89

88

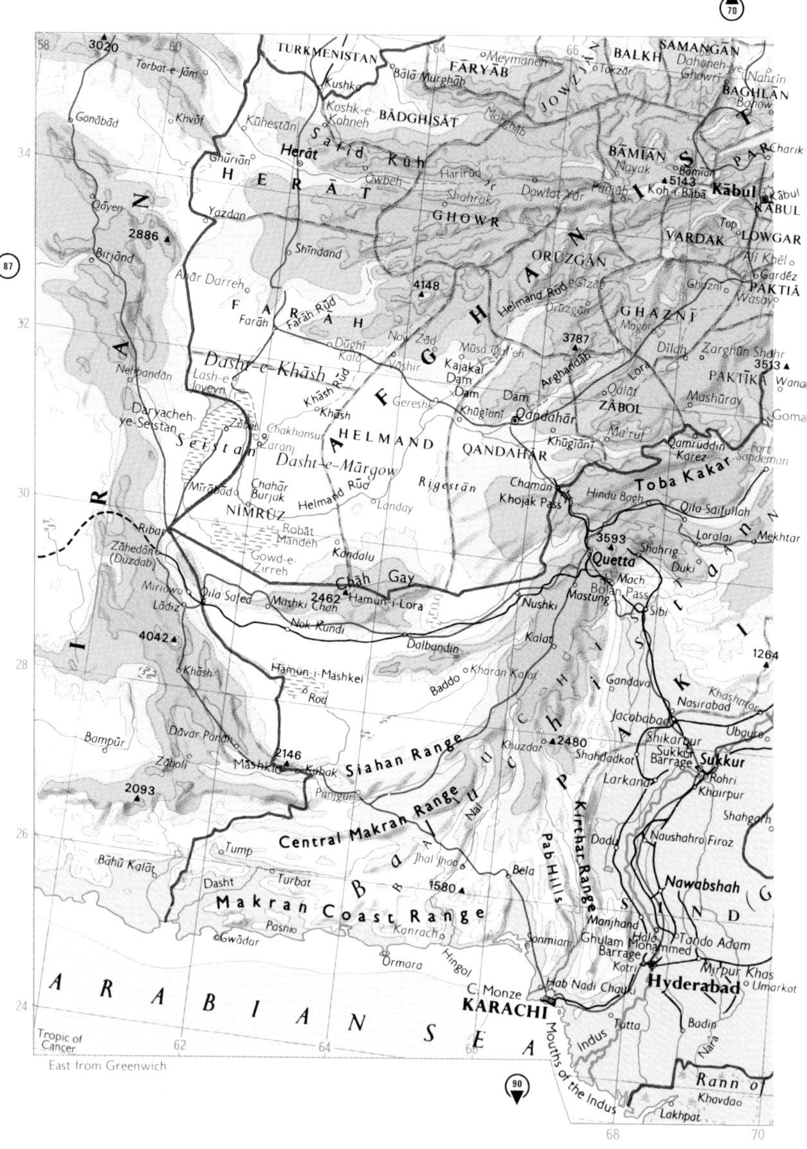
70
87
90
TURKMENISTAN
FĀRYĀB
JOWZJĀN
BALKH
SAMANGĀN
BAGHLĀN
BĀDGHĪSĀT
HERĀT
BĀMIĀN
PARWAN
Kabul
KĀBUL
GHOWR
VARDAK
LOWGAR
ORŪZGĀN
PAKTIĀ
GHAZNĪ
PAKTĪKA
ZĀBOL
FARĀH
HELMAND
QANDAHĀR
NĪMRŪZ
AFGHANISTAN
IRAN
PAKISTAN
BALUCHISTAN
SIND
ARABIAN SEA
Torbat-e-Jām
Gonābād
Khvāf
Kūhestān
Kushk
Koshk-e-Kohneh
Bālā Murghāb
Meymaneh
Tokzār
Dahaneh-ye-Ghowri
Nahrin
Baghlān
Bahow
Charikh
Herāt
Safīd Kūh
Ghūriān
Owbeh
Harīrūd
Shahrak
Dowlat Yār
Panjāb
Bāmiān
Koh-i-Bābā
Top
Qāyen
Yazdan
Shīndand
Bīrjand
Anār Darreh
Farāh
Farāh Rūd
Helmand Rūd
Ali Khel
Gardēz
Ghazni
Wasay
Orūzgān
Mogor
Dilah
Zarghūn Shahr
Dūghi Kala
Now Zād
Mūsā Qal'eh
Kajakai Dam
Arghandāb
Washīr
Dasht-e-Khāsh
Lash-e Joveyn
Nehbandān
Khāsh Rūd
Khāsh
Gereshk
Khūgiānī
Qandahār
Qalāt
Mashūray
Wana
Goma
Daryācheh-ye-Seīstan
Seistan
Zābol
Zaranj
Chakhansur
Dasht-e-Mārgow
Ma'ruf
Qamruddin Karez
Fort Sandeman
Toba Kakar
Mīrābād
Chahār Burjak
Rigestān
Chaman
Khojak Pass
Hindu Bagh
Qila Saifullah
Landay
Robāt Mandeh
Loralai
Mekhtar
Ribat
Zāhedān (Duzdab)
Gowd-e-Zirreh
Kandalu
Chāh Gay
3593
Quetta
Shahrig
Duki
Mirjawa
Qila Safed
Mashki Chah
Hamun-i-Lora
Nushki
Mastung
Mach
Bolan Pass
Sibi
Lādiz
Nok Kundi
Dalbandin
Kalat
Khāsh
Hamun-i-Mashkel
Rod
Baddo
Kharan Kalat
Gandava
Nasirabad
Khashmor
Jacobabad
Ubauro
Bampūr
Dāvar Panāh
Khuzdar
Shikarpur
Sukkur Barrage
Sukkur
Shahdadkot
Zāboli
Mashkid
Kuhak
Siahan Range
Rohri
Khairpur
Larkana
Panjgur
Central Makran Range
Nal
Kirthar Range
Shahgarh
Dadu
Naushahro Firoz
Tump
Jhal Jhao
Pab Hills
Bāhū Kalāt
Dasht
Turbat
Bela
Nawabshah
Makran Coast Range
Manjhand
Hala
Tando Adam
Pasni
Kanrach
Sonmiani
Ghulam Mohammed Barrage
Gwādar
Ormara
Hingol
Kotri
Hyderabad
Mirpur Khas
Umarkot
C. Monze
Hab Nadi Chauki
KARACHI
Tatta
Indus
Badin
Nara
Mouths of the Indus
Rann of
Khavda
Lakhpat
3020
2886
4148
3787
3513
5143
2462
4042
1264
2480
2146
2093
1580
58
60
62
64
66
68
70
34
32
30
28
26
24
Tropic of Cancer
East from Greenwich

1 : 10 000 000

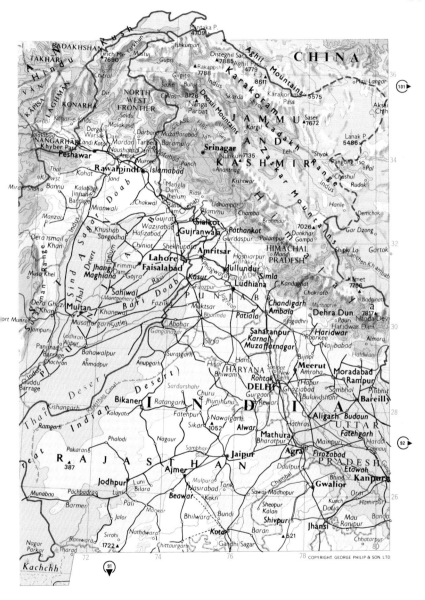

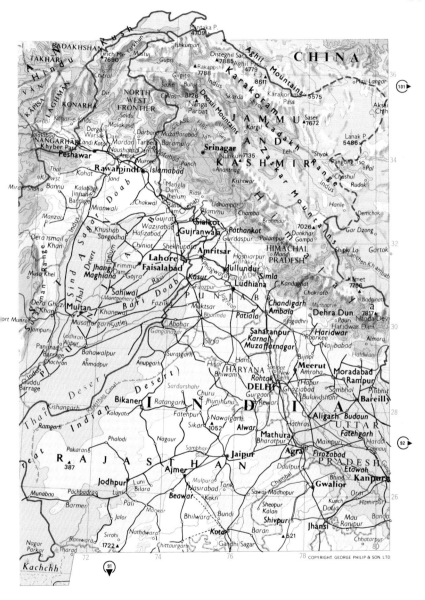

COPYRIGHT GEORGE PHILIP & SON LTD.

CHINA
Mintaka P.
4709
Ishkuman
BADAKHSHAN
TAKHAR
Hindu Kush
Tirich Mir
7690
Yarkhun
Mastuj
Gupis
Disteghil Sar
7885
Aghil Pass
4779
Aghil Mountains
Rakaposhi
7788
Gilgit
Karakoram
K 2
8611
Chitral
Bunji
Indus
Sazin
Chilas
8126
Nanga Parbat
Deosai Mountains
Skardu
Shyok
Karakoram Pass
5575
Haji Langar
Aksai Chih
Dir
NORTH WEST FRONTIER
KONARHA
LAGHMAN
KAPISA
Saidu
Malakand
Konar-e Khas
Dargai
Warsak Dam
Mardan
Tarbela Dam
Darband
Muzaffarabad
CEASE FIRE LINE
1st Jan 1949
JAMMU AND KASHMIR
Kargil
Ladakh Range
Saser
7672
Lanak P.
5486
Jalalabad
NANGARHAR
Landi Kotal
Khyber Pass
Peshawar
Naushahra
Attock
Baramula
Abbotabad
Murree
Srinagar
Nunkun 7135
Leh
Shyok
Zaskar Mountains
Pangong Tso
Pal
Thal
Kohat
Rawalpindi
Islamabad
Punch
Anantnag
Khowst
Jand
Kishtwar
Chushul
Rudok
Miram Shah
Bannu
Kalabagh
Jinnah Barrage
Mangla Dam
Jhelum
Riasi
Chakwal
Rasul Dam
Chenab
Udhampur
Jammu
Hanle
Mianwali
Chamba
Brahmaur
Demchok
Manzai
Indus
Gujrat
Wazirabad
Sialkot
Himalaya
7026
Dankhar Gompa
Gar Dzong
Khushab
Sargodha
Hafizabad
Gujranwala
Pathankot
Gurdaspur
Palampur
Dera Ismail Khan
Chiniot
Shekhupura
Amritsar
HIMACHAL PRADESH
Mandi
Shipki La
Gartok
Lahore
Hoshiarpur
Bhakra Dam
Nangal Dam
Lanchen Khambab
Jhang Maghiana
Trimmu Dam
Faisalabad
Jullundur
Phagwara
Gojra
Kasur
Ravi
Simla
Ludhiana
Kandaghat
Kamet
7756
Musa Khel
Sahiwal
(Montgomery)
Firozpur
Chakrata
Badrinath
Sind Sagar Doab
Thal Desert
Bari Doab
Jagraon
PUNJAB
Dera Ghazi Khan
Multan
Fazilka
Muktsar
Chandigarh
Mussoorie
Khanewal
Bhatinda
Patiala
Ambala
Dehra Dun
7817
Nanda Devi
Pauri
Haridwar Dam
Sulaiman Range
Fort Munro
Jampur
Musaffargarh
Sutlej
Abohar
Jagadhri
Ganganagar
Saharanpur
Haridwar
Roorkee
Almora
Lodhran
Alipur
Sirsa
Karnal
Muzaffarnagar
Najibabad
Panjnad Barrage
Bahawalpur
Suratgarh
Bijnor
Haldwani
Chachran
Ahmadpur
Anupgarh
Hisar
Hansi
HARYANA
Sonipat
Meerut
Moradabad
Amroha
Guddu Barrage
Bhiwani
Rohtak
New Delhi
DELHI
Hapur
Rampur
Sardarshahr
Churu
Ghaziabad
Sambhal
Pilibhit
Jhunjhunu
Gurgaon
Rewari
Bulandshahr
Bareilly
Rajasthan Canal
Bikaner
Ratangarh
INDIA
Kishangarh
Kolayat
Fatehpur
Nawalgarh
Aligarh
Budaun
Thar
Great Indian Desert
Ramgarh
Sikar
1052
Alwar
Hathras
UTTAR PRADESH
Fatehgarh
Mathura
Bharatpur
Phalodi
Nagaur
Mainpuri
Hardoi
Kannauj
Pokaran
Sambhar
Jaipur
Agra
Firozabad
RAJASTHAN
387
Ajmer
Etawah
Daulpur
Ganga
Jodhpur
Luni
Bilara
Malpura
Chambal
Bhind
Kanpur
Nasirabad
Tonk
Gwalior
Munabao
Pachpadra
Beawar
Kekri
Sawai Madhopur
Orai
Barmer
Pali
Sheopur Kalan
Kunch
Hamirpur
Marwar
Datia
Jalor
Bhilwara
Bundi
Shivpuri
Mau Ranipur
Banda
Sirohi
Nathdwara
Kota
Baran
Jhansi
Raniwara
521
Chhatarpur
Nagar Parkar
Tharad
1722
Chittaurgarh
Gandhi Sagar
Kachchh
72
74
76
78
80
36
34
32
30
28
26
101
92
91

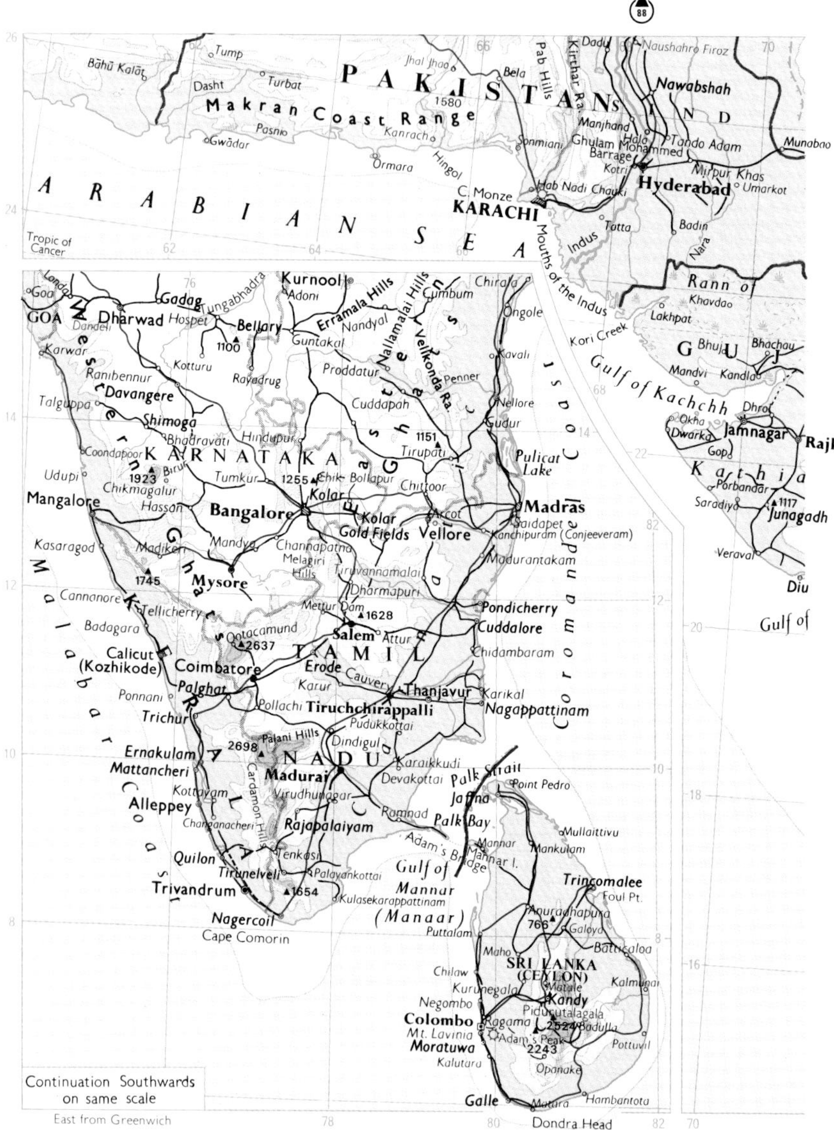
PAKISTAN
Makran Coast Range
ARABIAN SEA
Karachi
Hyderabad
Nawabshah
KARNATAKA
Bangalore
Mysore
Mangalore
Madras
Coimbatore
Madurai
Tiruchchirappalli
Salem
Pondicherry
Cuddalore
Trivandrum
Quilon
Alleppey
Ernakulam
Calicut (Kozhikode)
Palk Strait
Palk Bay
Gulf of Mannar (Manaar)
Jaffna
Trincomalee
SRI LANKA (CEYLON)
Kandy
Colombo
Galle
Dondra Head
Cape Comorin
Continuation Southwards on same scale
East from Greenwich

1 : 10 000 000

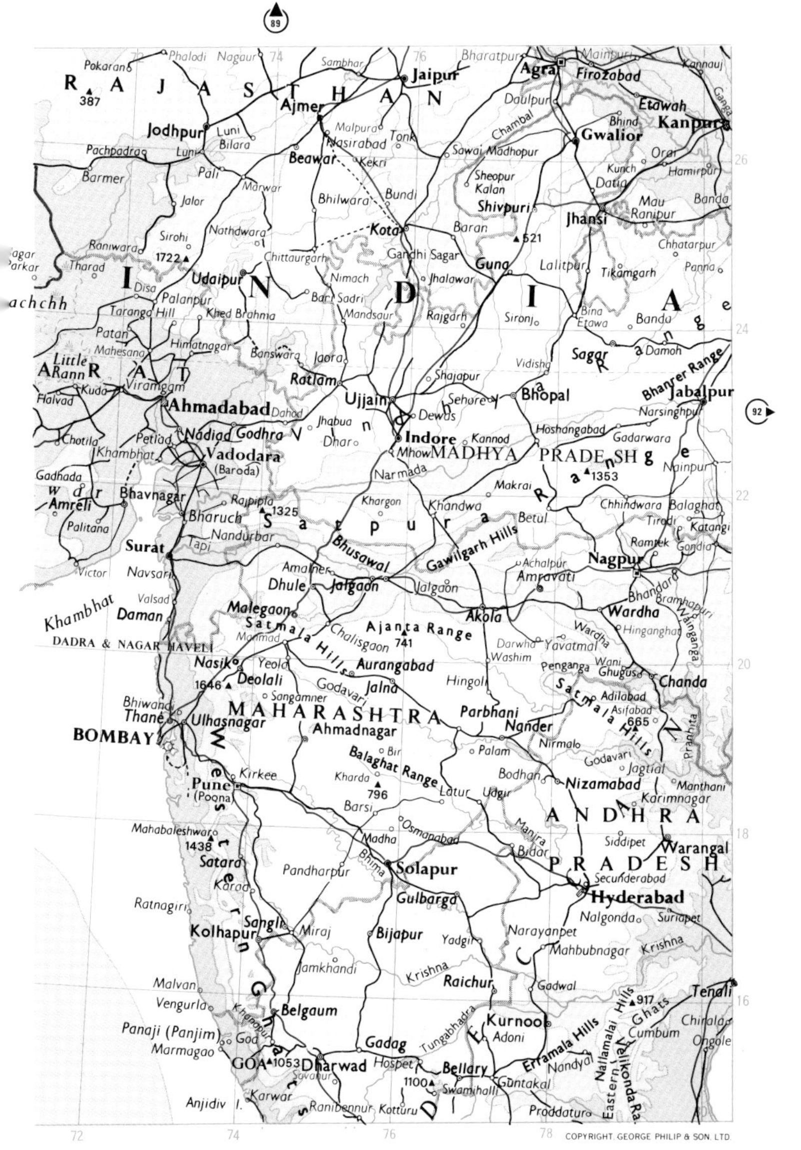
89
92
RAJASTHAN
INDIA
MADHYA PRADESH
MAHARASHTRA
ANDHRA PRADESH
Jaipur
Agra
Firozabad
Ajmer
Jodhpur
Gwalior
Kanpur
Etawah
Beawar
Bhilwara
Bundi
Kota
Shivpuri
Jhansi
Udaipur
Chittaurgarh
Guna
Lalitpur
Palanpur
Disa
Ratlam
Ujjain
Bhopal
Sagar
Jabalpur
Ahmadabad
Nadiad
Godhra
Vadodara
(Baroda)
Indore
Dewas
Mhow
Bhavnagar
Amreli
Bharuch
Surat
Navsari
Daman
DADRA & NAGAR HAVELI
Nasik
Deolali
Malegaon
Dhule
Jalgaon
Bhusawal
Akola
Amravati
Nagpur
Wardha
Chanda
Aurangabad
Jalna
Parbhani
Nander
Nizamabad
Warangal
BOMBAY
Thane
Ulhasnagar
Ahmadnagar
Pune
(Poona)
Kirkee
Latur
Solapur
Gulbarga
Bidar
Secunderabad
Hyderabad
Satara
Sangli
Kolhapur
Miraj
Bijapur
Raichur
Kurnool
Belgaum
Gadag
Dharwad
Bellary
GOA
Panaji (Panjim)
Marmagao
Karwar
Satpura Range
Ajanta Range
Balaghat Range
Western Ghats
Eastern Ghats
Narmada
Tapi
Godavari
Krishna
Bhima
Tungabhadra
72
74
76
78
26
24
22
20
18
16

EASTERN INDIA, BANGLADESH AND BURMA

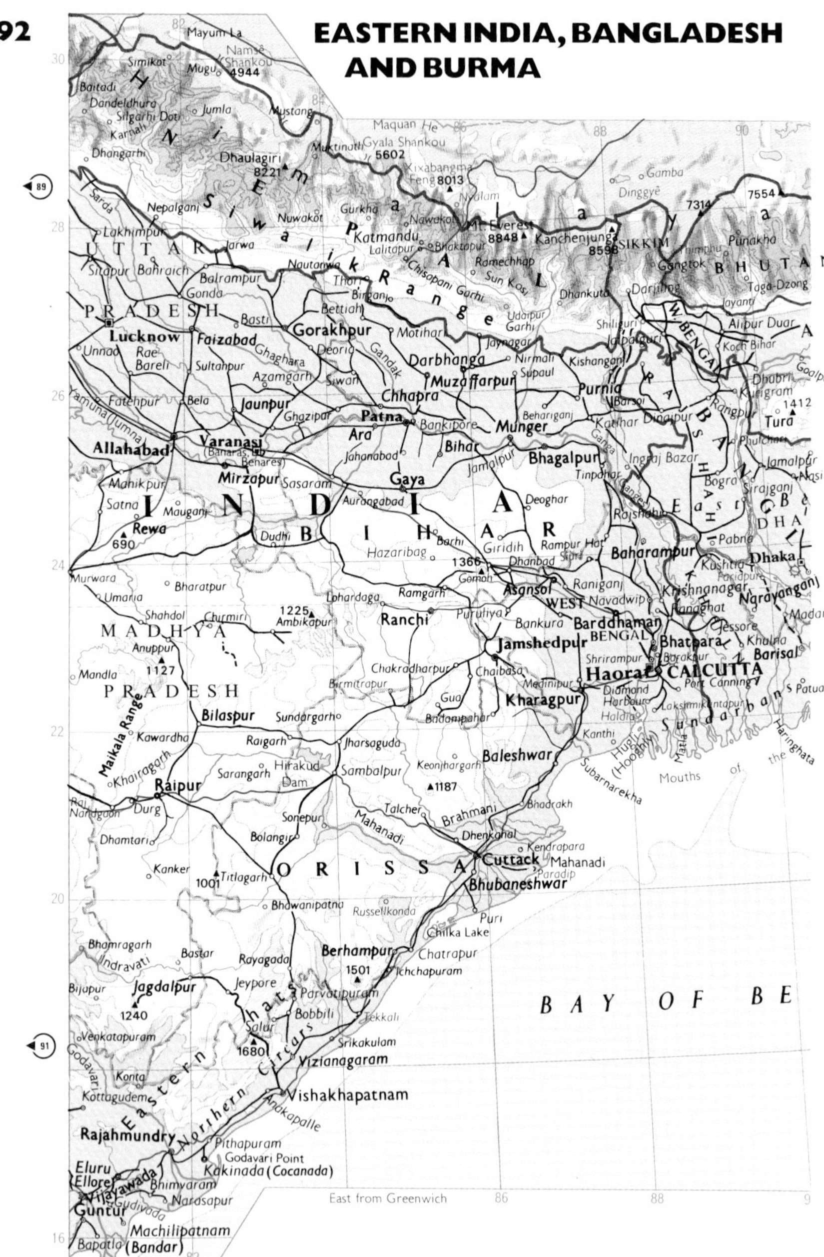

NEPAL
Himalaya
Siwalik Range
UTTAR PRADESH
INDIA
BIHAR
MADHYA PRADESH
ORISSA
WEST BENGAL
BANGLADESH
BHUTAN
SIKKIM
Lucknow
Faizabad
Gorakhpur
Allahabad
Varanasi (Banaras, Benares)
Mirzapur
Patna
Gaya
Ranchi
Jamshedpur
Kharagpur
CALCUTTA
Haora
Dhaka
Bilaspur
Raipur
Cuttack
Bhubaneshwar
Berhampur
Jagdalpur
Vizianagaram
Vishakhapatnam
Rajahmundry
Kakinada (Cocanada)
Machilipatnam (Bandar)
Eastern Ghats
Northern Circars
Mt. Everest 8848
Kanchenjunga 8598
Katmandu
BAY OF BE
Mouths of the
Sundarbans
East from Greenwich

1 : 10 000 000

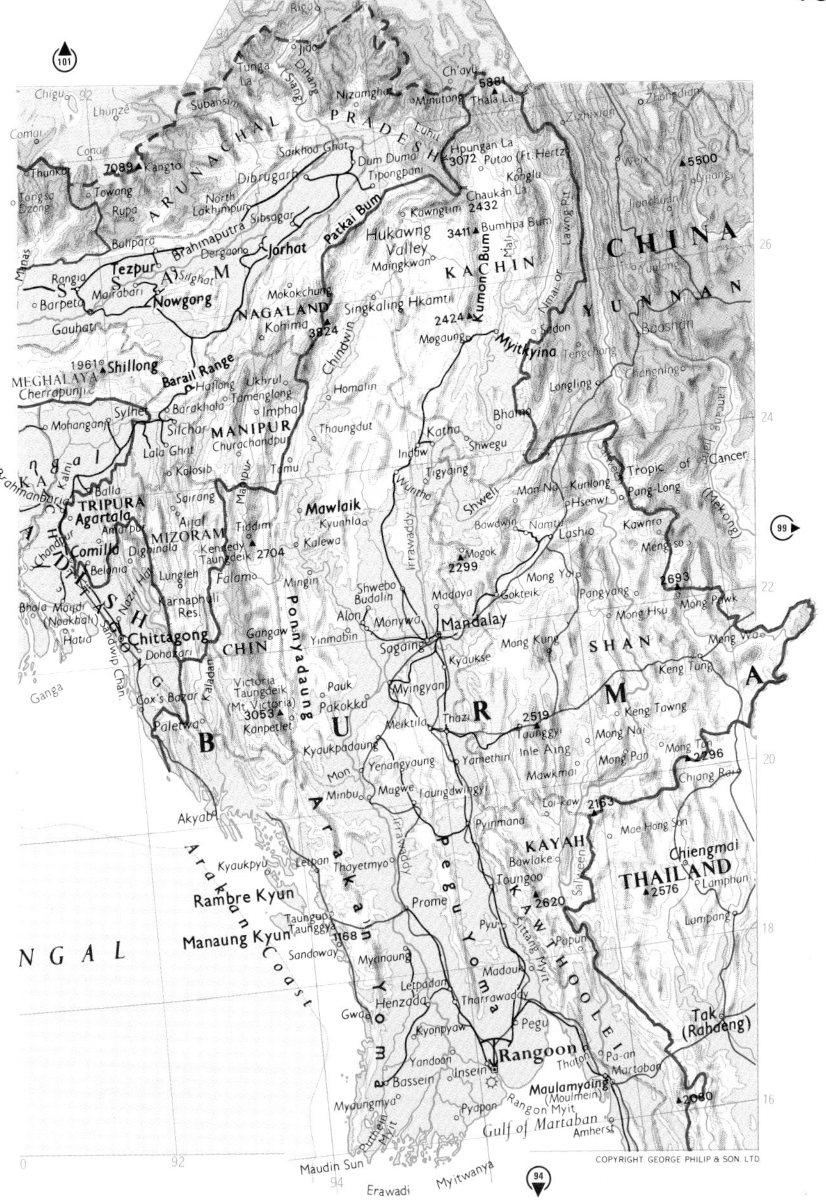

BURMA
CHINA
YUNNAN
ASSAM
BANGLADESH
THAILAND
ARUNACHAL PRADESH
NAGALAND
MANIPUR
MIZORAM
TRIPURA
MEGHALAYA
KACHIN
CHIN
SHAN
KAYAH
KAWTHOOLEI
Bay of Bengal
Mandalay
Rangoon
Chittagong
Shillong
Myitkyina
Maulamyaing (Moulmein)
Gulf of Martaban
Arakan Coast
Arakan Yoma
Pegu Yoma
Rambre Kyun
Manaung Kyun
Tropic of Cancer
Irrawaddy
Chindwin
Salween
Hukawng Valley
Patkai Bum
Barail Range
Ponnyadaung
Lashio
Bhamo
Akyab
Prome
Pegu
Bassein
Tezpur
Jorhat
Nowgong
Dibrugarh
Imphal
Kohima
Agartala
Comilla
Chiengmai
Tak (Rahaeng)

93

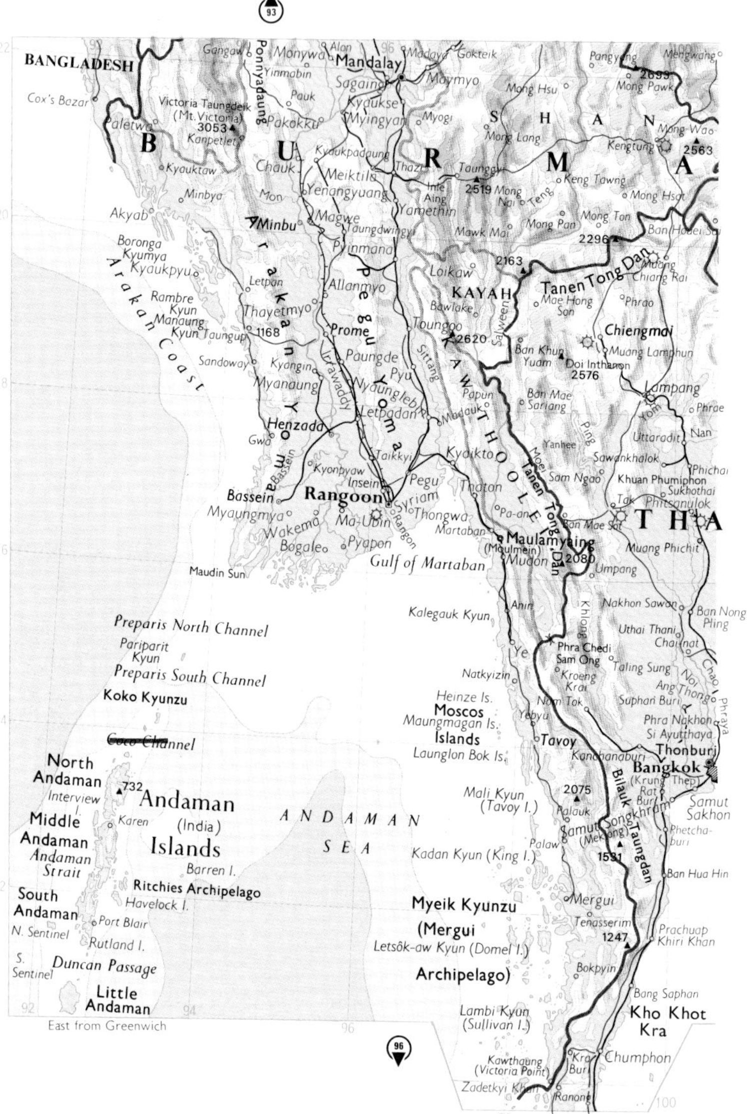

BANGLADESH
Cox's Bazar
Gangaw
Monywa
Alon
Mandalay
Madaya
Gokteik
Pangyang
Mengwang
Ponnyadaung
Yinmabin
Sagaing
Maymyo
Mong Hsu
2693
Mong Pawk
Pauk
Kyaukse
Victoria Taungdeik
(Mt. Victoria)
3053
Pakokku
Myingyan
Myogi
S H A N
Mong Wa
Paletwa
Kanpetlet
Mong Lang
Kengtung
2563
B U R M A
Chauk
Kyaukpadaung
Thazi
Taunggyi
Keng Tawng
Kyauktaw
Meiktila
Inle
2519
Mong Nai
Teng
Mong Hsat
Minbya
Mon
Yenangyuang
Aing
Yamethin
Akyab
Minbu
Magwe
Taungdwingyi
Mawk Mai
Mong Pan
Mong Ton
Ban Houei Sai
2296
Boronga Kyumya
Pyinmana
2163
Arakan Coast
Kyaukpyu
Letpan
Loikaw
Tanen Tong Dan
Muang Chiang Rai
Allanmyo
KAYAH
Rambre Kyun
Thayetmyo
Pegu
Bawlake
Mae Hong Son
Phrao
Manaung Kyun
Taungup
1168
Prome
Toungoo
Salween
Chiengmai
2620
Ban Khun Yuam
Muang Lamphun
Sandoway
Kyangin
Paungde
Sittang
Doi Inthanon
2576
Irrawaddy
Pyu
Myanaung
Nyaunglebin
Papun
Ban Mae Sariang
Lampang
Phrae
Yoma
Letpadan
Madauk
Henzada
Ping
Yom
Gwa
KAWTHOOLEI
Yanhee
Uttaradit
Nan
Arakan Yoma
Taikkyi
Kyaikto
Moei
Sawankhalok
Bassein
Kyonpyaw
Phichai
Insein
Pegu
Sam Ngao
Khuan Phumiphon
Sukhothai
Bassein
Rangoon
Syriam
Thaton
Tak
Phitsanulok
Myaungmya
Thongwa
Pa-an
Ban Mae Sot
THA
Wakema
Ma-Ubin
Rangoon
Martaban
Maulamyaing
(Moulmein)
Bogale
Pyapon
Mudon
2080
Muang Phichit
Gulf of Martaban
Maudin Sun
Umpang
Kalegauk Kyun
Anin
Nakhon Sawan
Ban Nong Pling
Khlong
Preparis North Channel
Uthai Thani
Chai Nat
Pariparit Kyun
Ye
Phra Chedi
Sam Ong
Preparis South Channel
Natkyizin
Taling Sung
Kroeng Krai
Noi
Chao Phraya
Koko Kyunzu
Heinze Is.
Nam Tok
Ang Thong
Moscos
Yebyu
Suphan Buri
Maungmagan Is.
Phra Nakhon Si Ayutthaya
Islands
Tavoy
Coco Channel
Launglon Bok Is.
Kanchanaburi
Thonburi
North Andaman
Bangkok
(Krung Thep)
Rat Buri
732
Mali Kyun
(Tavoy I.)
2075
Interview I.
Andaman
Samut Sakhon
Palauk
Middle Andaman
Karen
(India)
ANDAMAN
Samut Songkhram
Phetchaburi
Islands
SEA
Palaw
(Mekong)
Andaman Strait
Kadan Kyun (King I.)
1531
Bilauk Taungdan
Barren I.
Ban Hua Hin
South Andaman
Ritchies Archipelago
Myeik Kyunzu
Mergui
Havelock I.
N. Sentinel
Port Blair
(Mergui
Tenasserim
Prachuap Khiri Khan
Rutland I.
1247
Letsôk-aw Kyun (Domel I.)
S. Sentinel
Duncan Passage
Archipelago)
Bokpyin
Little Andaman
Bang Saphan
Kho Khot Kra
Lambi Kyun
(Sullivan I.)
Kra Buri
Chumphon
Kawthaung
(Victoria Point)
Zadetkyi Kyun
Ranong
East from Greenwich
22
20
18
16
14
12
92
94
96
98
100

96

1 : 10 000 000

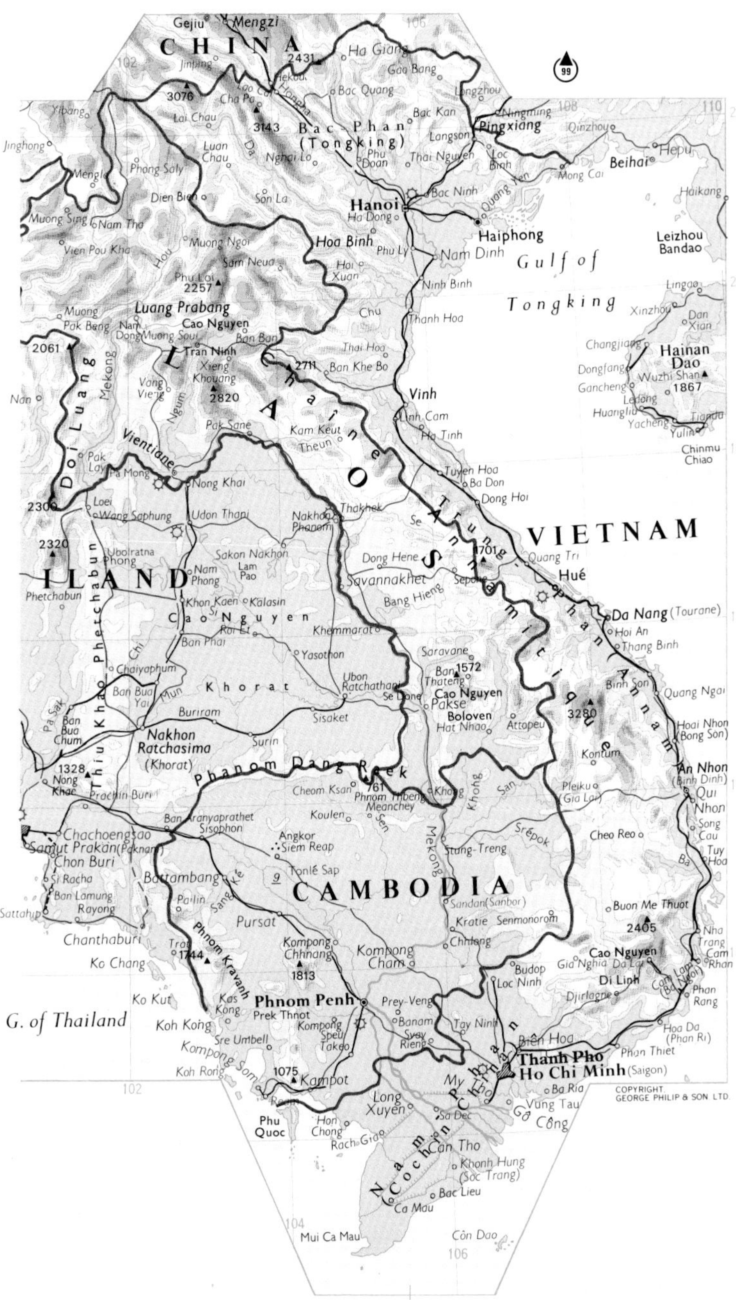
CHINA
VIETNAM
LAOS
CAMBODIA
Gulf of Tongking
G. of Thailand
Hanoi
Haiphong
Vientiane
Phnom Penh
Thanh Pho Ho Chi Minh (Saigon)
Hué
Da Nang (Tourane)
Luang Prabang
Hainan Dao
Leizhou Bandao
Beihai
Vinh
Savannakhet
Pakse
Nakhon Ratchasima (Khorat)
Battambang
Kampot
Can Tho
Phu Quoc
Mekong
COPYRIGHT. GEORGE PHILIP & SON LTD.

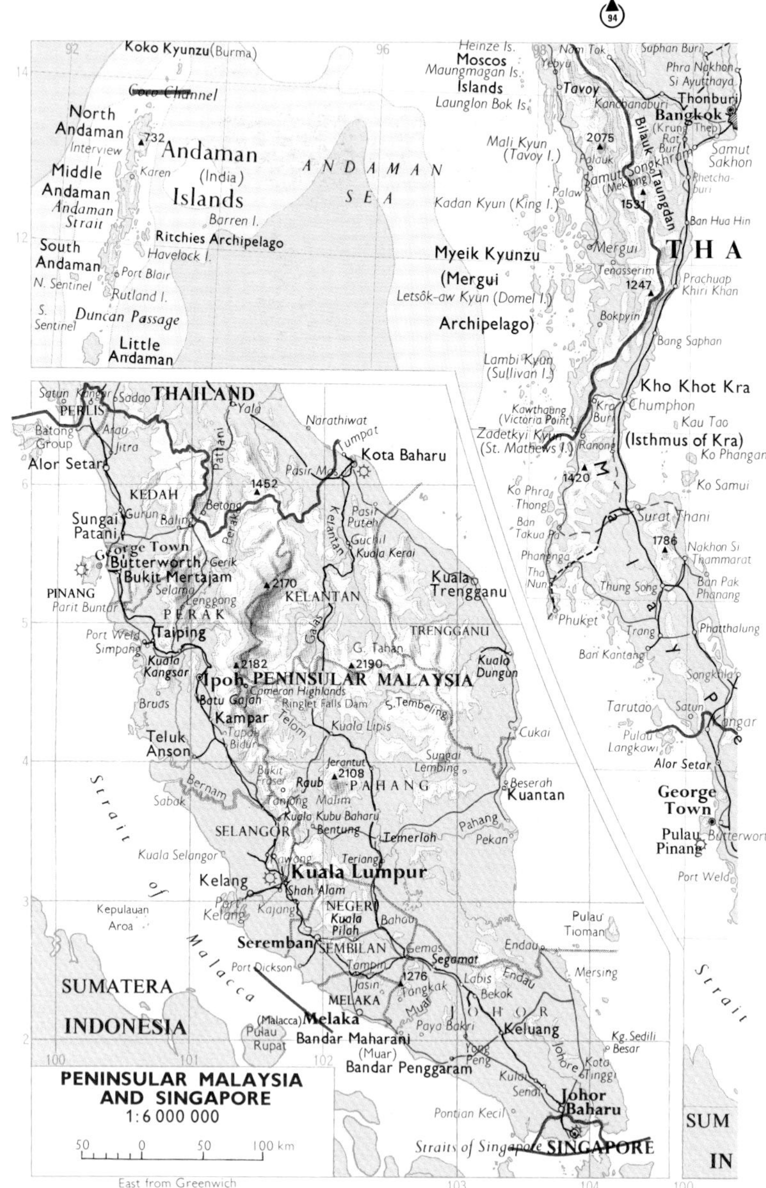

**PENINSULAR MALAYSIA
AND SINGAPORE**
1:6 000 000

50   0   50   100 km

East from Greenwich

1 : 10 000 000

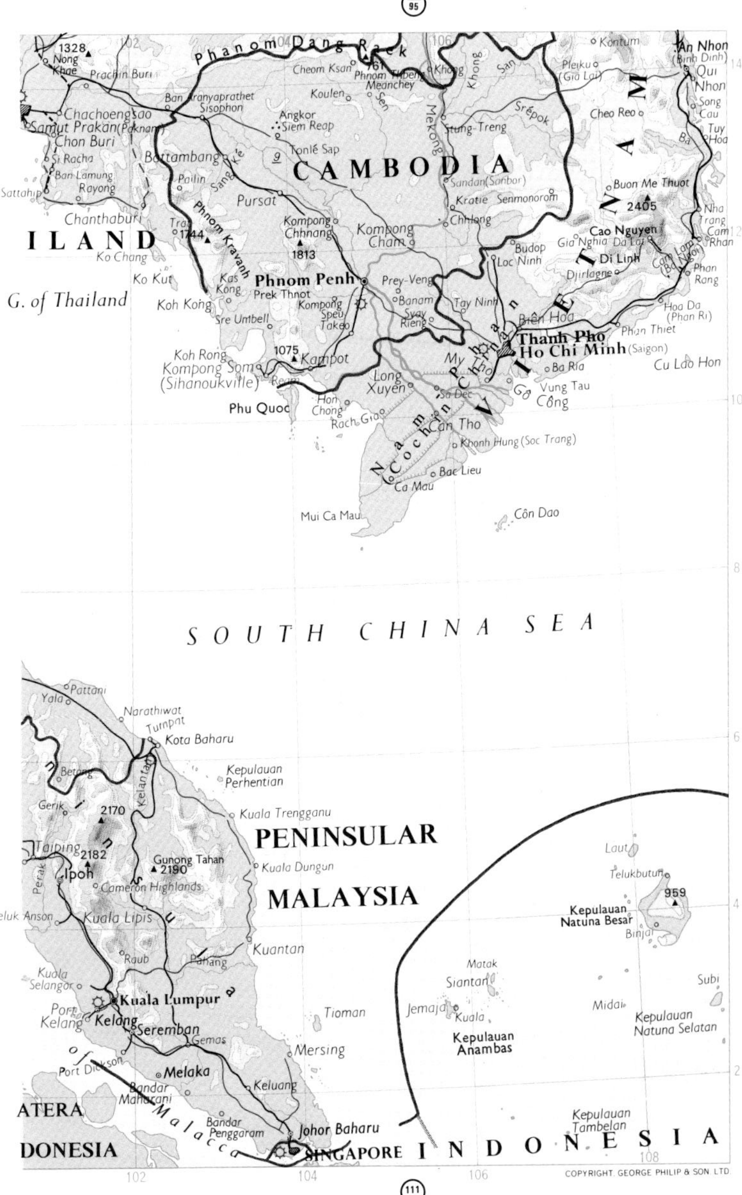

95

1328
Nong
Khae
Prachin Buri
Ban Aranyaprathet
Sisophon
Chachoengsao
Samut Prakan
Paknam
Chon Buri
Si Racha
Ban Lamung
Rayong
Sattahip

Phanom Dang Rek
Cheom Ksan
Khong
Khong San
Kontum
Pleiku
(Gia Lai)
An Nhon
Binh Dinh
Qui
Nhon
Song
Cau
Tuy
Hoa

CAMBODIA

Phnom
Meanchey
Angkor
Siem Reap
Tonlé Sap
Battambang
Pailin
Pursat
Kompong
Chhnang
1813
Srépok
Cheo Reo
Sandan (Sanban)
Senmonorom
Kompong
Cham
Kratie
Chhlong

THAI LAND
Chanthaburi
Trat
1744
Ko Chang
Ko Kut
Phnom Kravanh
Phnom Penh
Prek Thnot
Kas
Kong
Sre Umbell
Kompong
Speu
Takeo
Prey Veng
Banam
Svay
Rieng
Tay Ninh
Buon Me Thuot
2405
Cao Nguyen
Gia Nghia
Da Lat
Di Linh
Djiriagne
Nha
Trang
Cam Ranh
Phan
Rang
Hoa Da
(Phan Ri)
Phan Thiet

G. of Thailand
Koh Kong
1075
Kampot
Kompong Som
(Sihanoukville)
Koh Rong
Phu Quoc
Hon
Chong
Rach Gia
Long
Xuyen
Can Tho
Soc Trang
Khonh Hung (Soc Trang)
Bac Lieu
My Tho
Go Cong
Thanh Pho
Ho Chi Minh (Saigon)
Bien Hoa
Ba Ria
Vung Tau
Cu Lao Hon

VIETNAM

Nam   Bo   Cochin China

Mui Ca Mau
Ca Mau
Côn Dao

SOUTH CHINA SEA

Pattani
Yala
Narathiwat
Tumpat
Kota Baharu
Betong
Gerik
2170
Taiping
2182
Ipoh
Gunong Tahan
2190
Cameron Highlands
Teluk Anson
Kuala Lipis
Kelantan
Kuala Perhentian
Kuala Trengganu
Kuala Dungun

PENINSULAR
MALAYSIA

Laut
Telukbutum
959
Kepulauan
Natuna Besar
Binjai
Subi

Kuala
Selangor
Kuala Lumpur
Port
Kelang
Kelang
Seremban
Gemas
Port Dickson
Bandar
Maharani
Melaka
Bandar
Penggaram
Keluang
Johor Baharu
SINGAPORE

Raub
Pahang
Kuantan
Tioman
Mersing

Matak
Siantan
Jemaja
Kuala
Midai
Kepulauan
Anambas
Kepulauan
Natuna Selatan

Str. of Malacca

ATERA
DONESIA

Kepulauan
Tambelan

INDONESIA

Kepulauan
Tembelan

COPYRIGHT GEORGE PHILIP & SON LTD.

111

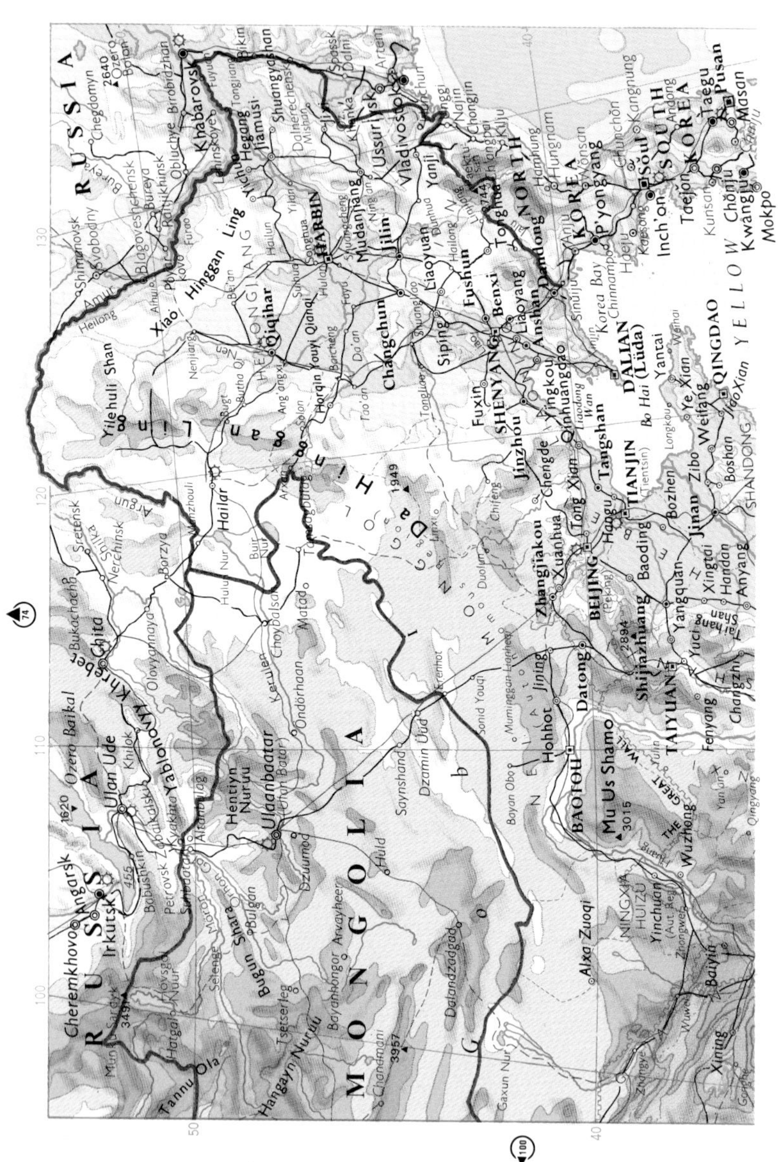
RUSSIA
MONGOLIA
NORTH KOREA
SOUTH KOREA
YELLOW
Ulaanbaatar
Irkutsk
Chita
Ulan Ude
Khabarovsk
Vladivostok
HARBIN
Qiqihar
Changchun
Jilin
SHENYANG
Fushun
Anshan
Benxi
DALIAN (Lüda)
BEIJING (Peking)
TIANJIN (Tientsin)
Tangshan
QINGDAO
Jinan
Zibo
Shijiazhuang
TAIYUAN
Datong
Hohhot
BAOTOU
Zhangjiakou
P'yongyang
Sŏul
Pusan
Taegu
Mu Us Shamo
Xiao Hinggan Ling
Da Hinggan Ling
Yilehuli Shan
Hentiyn Nuruu
Hangayn Nuruu
Tannu Ola
Ozero Baikal
Bo Hai
Korea Bay
Xining
Yinchuan

1 : 20 000 000

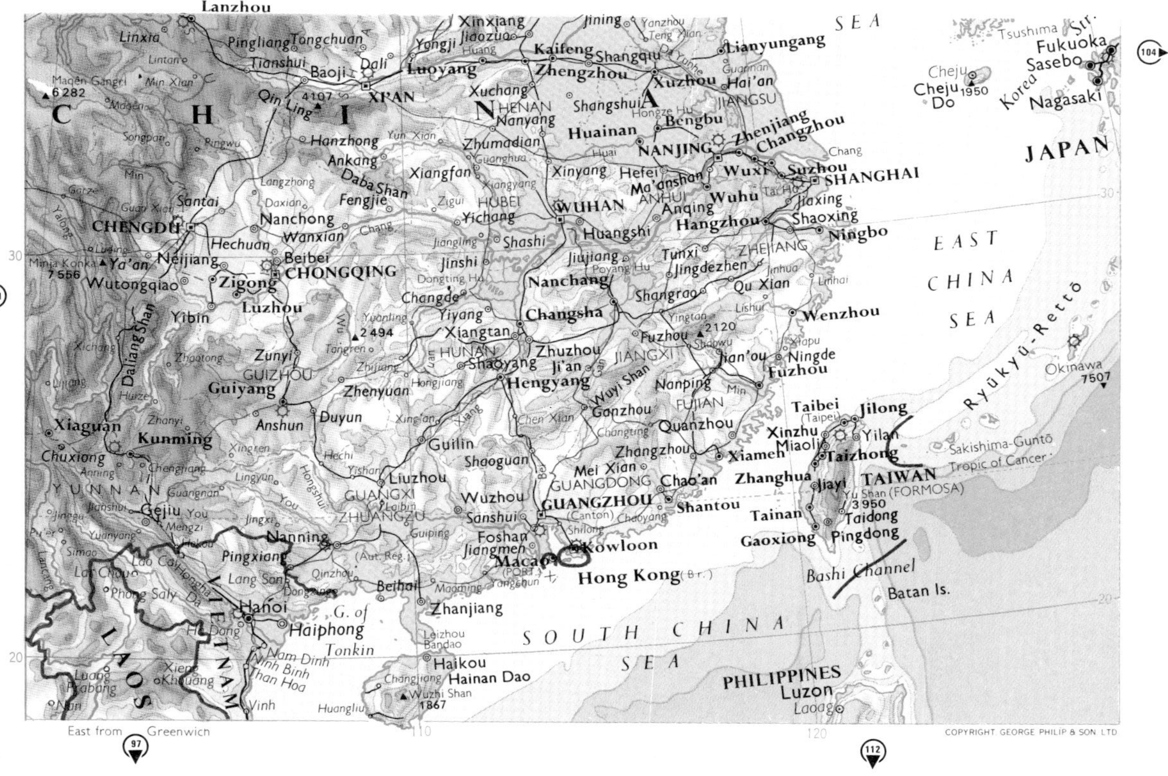

Lanzhou
C H I N A
JAPAN
EAST CHINA SEA
SOUTH CHINA SEA
SEA
Ryūkyū-Rettō
Okinawa
7507
Sakishima-Guntō
Tropic of Cancer
Tsushima Str.
Fukuoka
Sasebo
Nagasaki
Korea
Cheju Do
Cheju
1950
Lianyungang
Hai'an
Xuzhou
Shangqiu
Kaifeng
Zhengzhou
Jining
Yanzhou
Teng Xian
Xinxiang
Jiaozuo
Yongji
Luoyang
Xuchang
Dali
Baoji
Tianshui
Pingliang
Tongchuan
XI'AN
Qin Ling
4107
Linxia
Lintan
Maqên Gangri
6282
Min Xian
Songpan
Hanzhong
Ankang
Daba Shan
Fengjie
Xiangfan
Zhumadian
Nanyang
HENAN
Shangshui
Huainan
Bengbu
JIANGSU
NANJING
Zhenjiang
Changzhou
Wuxi
Suzhou
SHANGHAI
Chang
Hefei
Ma'anshan
ANHUI
Wuhu
Anqing
Hangzhou
Jiaxing
Shaoxing
Ningbo
Xinyang
WUHAN
Huangshi
HUBEI
Yichang
Shashi
Zigui
Jiangling
Jinshi
Dongting Hu
Changde
Yiyang
Xiangtan
Changsha
Nanchang
Jiujiang
Poyang Hu
Jingdezhen
Tunxi
ZHEJIANG
Jinhua
Qu Xian
Shangrao
Wenzhou
Linhai
Yingtan
Fuzhou
2120
Jian'ou
Ningde
Fuzhou
Nanping
FUJIAN
Min
Zhuzhou
Ji'an
JIANGXI
HUNAN
Shaoyang
Hengyang
Wuyi Shan
Ganzhou
Quanzhou
Xiamen
Zhangzhou
Mei Xian
GUANGDONG
Chao'an
Shantou
GUANGZHOU
(Canton)
Foshan
Jiangmen
Macao
(PORT.)
Kowloon
Hong Kong (Br.)
Shaoguan
Guilin
Liuzhou
Wuzhou
Sanshui
GUANGXI
ZHUANGZU
(Aut. Reg.)
Nanning
Pingxiang
Beihai
Zhanjiang
Leizhou Bandao
Haikou
Hainan Dao
Wuzhi Shan
1867
Huangliu
Changjiang
G. of Tonkin
Haiphong
Hanoi
Nam Dinh
Ninh Binh
Than Hoa
Vinh
VIETNAM
LAOS
Luang Prabang
Xieng Khouang
Phong Saly
Lao Cai
Lang Son
CHENGDU
Santai
Nanchong
Wanxian
Hechuan
Beibei
CHONGQING
Neijiang
Zigong
Luzhou
Yibin
Ya'an
Minya Konka
7556
Wutongqiao
Daliang Shan
Xichang
Zhaotong
Zunyi
GUIZHOU
Guiyang
Anshun
Duyun
Zhenyuan
2494
Tongren
Xiaguan
Kunming
Chuxiong
YUNNAN
Gejiu
Mengzi
Taibei
(Taipei)
Jilong
Yilan
Xinzhu
Miaoli
Taizhong
Zhanghua
Jiayi
TAIWAN
(FORMOSA)
Yu Shan
3950
Tainan
Taidong
Gaoxiong
Pingdong
Bashi Channel
Batan Is.
PHILIPPINES
Luzon
Laoag
30
20
110
120
East from Greenwich
97
101
104
112
COPYRIGHT GEORGE PHILIP & SON LTD

71

98

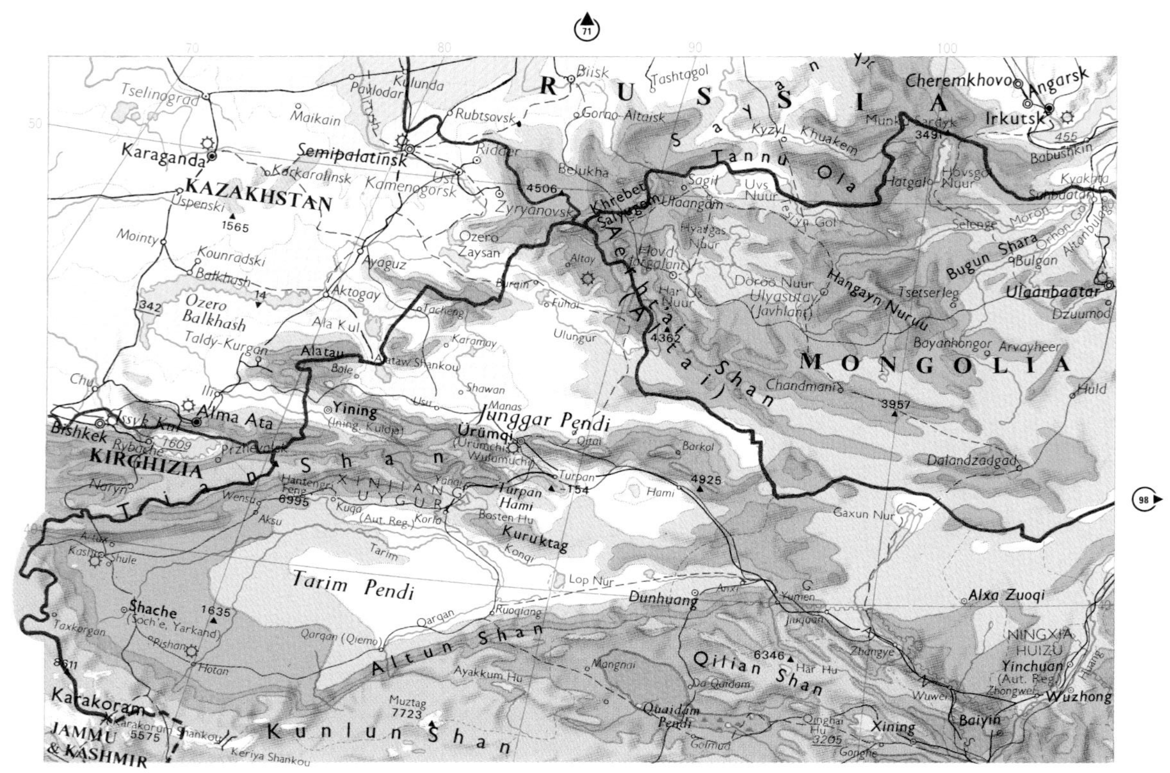
RUSSIA
MONGOLIA
KAZAKHSTAN
KIRGHIZIA
JAMMU & KASHMIR
NINGXIA HUIZU (Aut. Reg.)
XINJIANG UYGUR (Aut. Reg.)
Sayan
Tannu Ola
Hangayn Nuruu
Altai Shan
Tian Shan
Altun Shan
Kunlun Shan
Qilian Shan
Karakoram
Junggar Pendi
Tarim Pendi
Qaidam Pendi
Kuruktag
Ozero Balkhash
Ozero Zaysan
Lop Nur
Irkutsk
Angarsk
Cheremkhovo
Ulaanbaatar
Kyzyl
Biisk
Gorno-Altaisk
Rubtsovsk
Semipalatinsk
Ust-Kamenogorsk
Zyryanovsk
Pavlodar
Tselinograd
Karaganda
Alma Ata
Bishkek
Yining
Ürümqi
Turpan
Hami
Dunhuang
Alxa Zuoqi
Yinchuan
Wuzhong
Baiyin
Xining
Aksu
Shache
Hotan
Muztag 7723

1 : 20 000 000

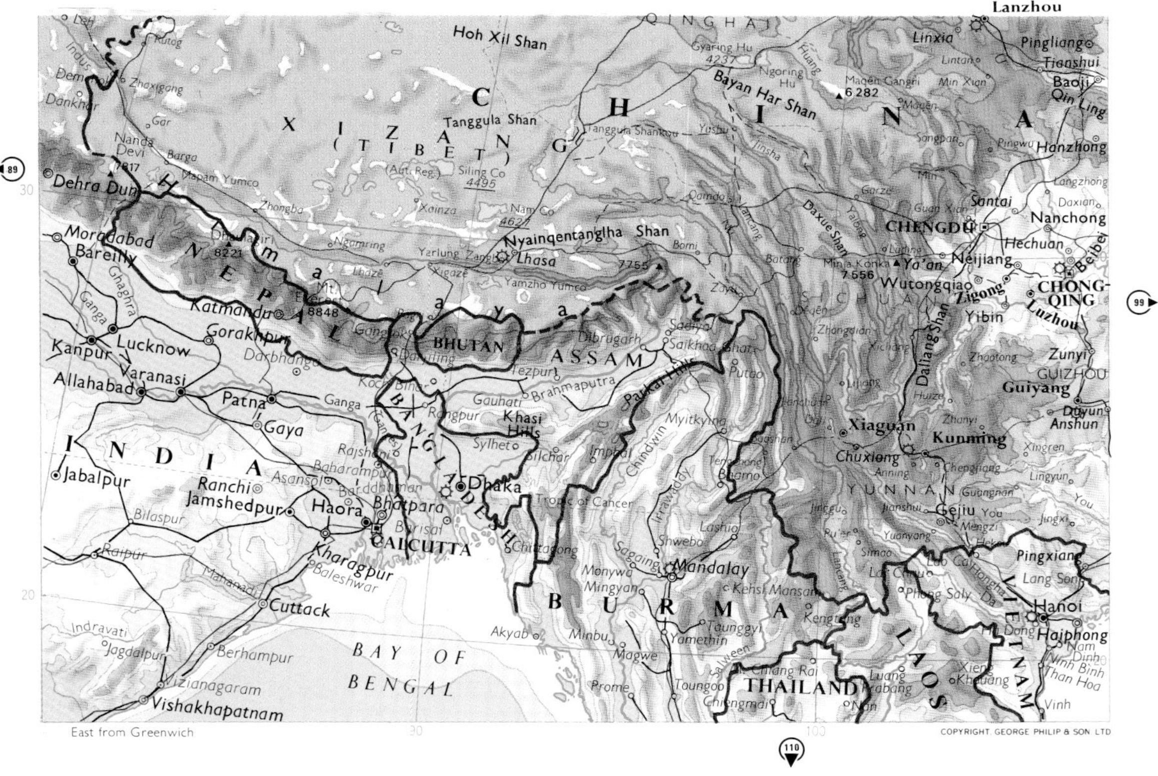

Lanzhou

COPYRIGHT GEORGE PHILIP & SON LTD

Hoh Xil Shan
CHINA
XIZANG (TIBET) (Aut. Reg.)
Tanggula Shan
Siling Co 4495
Nam Co 4627
Nyainqentanglha Shan
Lhasa
Bayan Har Shan
Gyaring Hu 4237
Ngoring Hu
Maqên Gangri 6282
Linxia
Pingliang
Tianshui
Baoji
Qin Ling
Hanzhong
Nanchong
Santai
CHENGDU
Hechuan
Neijiang
Ya'an
Minya Konka 7556
Wutongqiao
Zigong
CHONG-QING
Luzhou
Yibin
Zunyi
GUIZHOU
Guiyang
Duyun
Anshun
Kunming
Xiaguan
Chuxiong
YUNNAN
Gejiu
Daliang Shan
Daxue Shan
SICHUAN
Dehra Dun
Moradabad
Bareilly
Nanda Devi 7817
NEPAL
Himalaya
Katmandu
Mt. Everest 8848
8221
BHUTAN
ASSAM
Dibrugarh
Brahmaputra
Khasi Hills
Sylhet
Dhaka
BANGLADESH
CALCUTTA
Haora
Bhatpara
Kharagpur
Cuttack
Gorakhpur
Lucknow
Kanpur
Varanasi
Allahabad
Patna
Gaya
INDIA
Jabalpur
Ranchi
Jamshedpur
Asansol
Berhampur
Vizianagaram
Vishakhapatnam
BAY OF BENGAL
Akyab
BURMA
Mandalay
Monywa
Mingyan
Sagaing
Shwebo
Lashio
Myitkyina
Chindwin
Irrawaddy
Imphal
Tropic of Cancer
Chittagong
Minbu
Magwe
Prome
Toungoo
Yamethin
Taunggyi
Kengtung
THAILAND
Chiang Rai
Chiengmai
LAOS
Luang Prabang
VIETNAM
Hanoi
Haiphong
Lang Son
Pingxiang
Nam Dinh
Ninh Binh
Thanh Hoa
Vinh
Ganga
Ghaghra
Indus
Leh
East from Greenwich
30
20
100
89
99
110

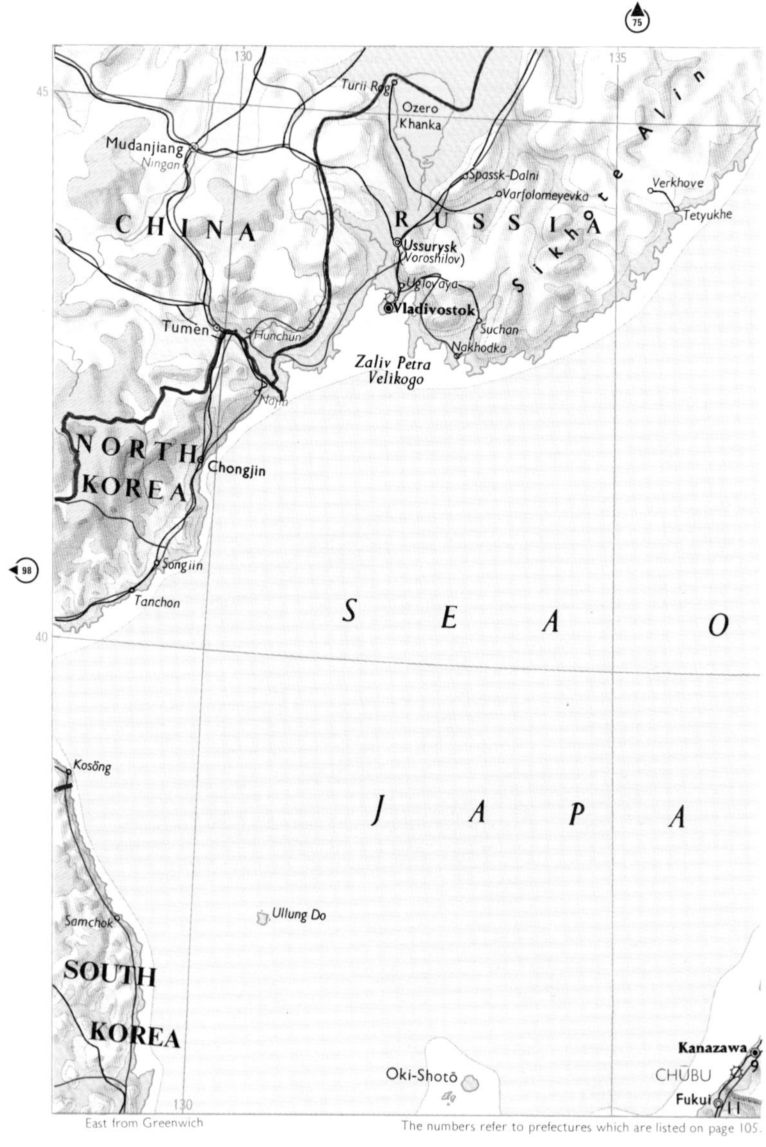

75

45

130

135

Turii Rog

Ozero
Khanka

Mudanjiang
Ningan

Spassk-Dalni
Varfolomeyevka

Verkhove
Tetyukhe

CHINA

RUSSIA

Sikhote Alin

Ussurysk
(Voroshilov)

Ugloyaya

Vladivostok

Tumen

Hunchun

Suchan
Nakhodka

Najin

Zaliv Petra
Velikogo

NORTH
KOREA

Chongjin

98

Songjin

Tanchon

40

S E A

O

Kosŏng

J A P A

Samchok

Ullung Do

SOUTH

KOREA

Kanazawa

CHŪBU

Oki-Shotō

Fukui

11

130

East from Greenwich

The numbers refer to prefectures which are listed on page 105.

1 : 7 500 000

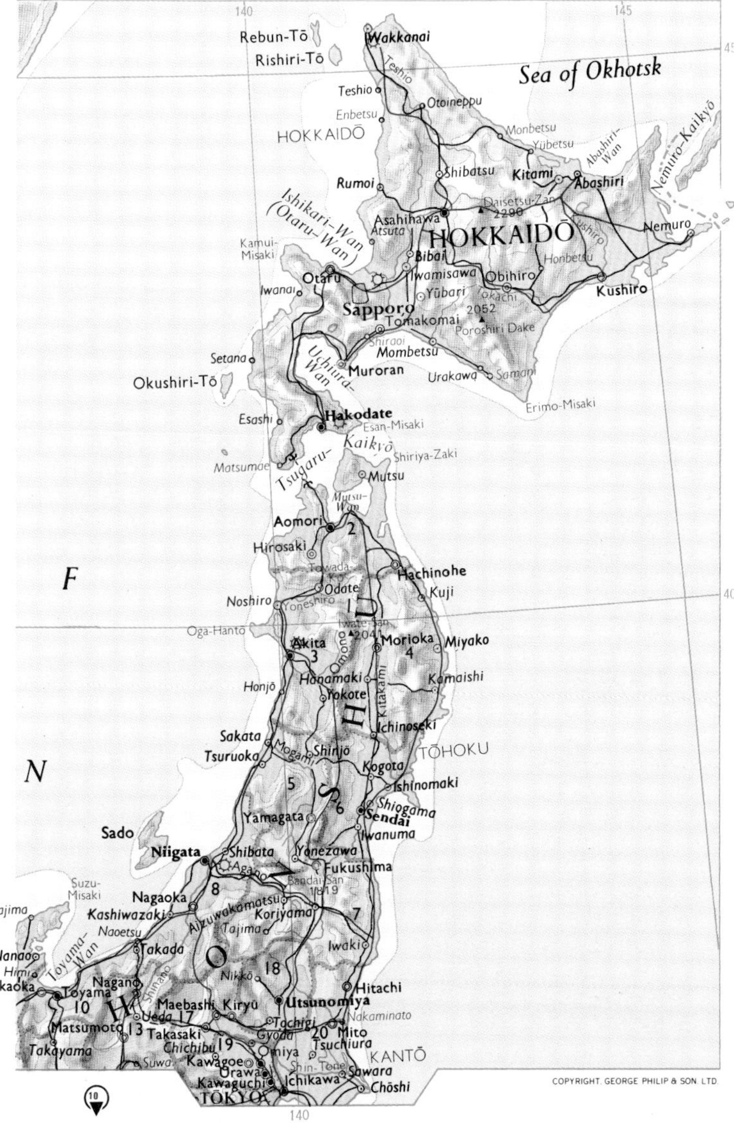

Rebun-Tō
Rishiri-Tō
Wakkanai
Teshio
Sea of Okhotsk
Teshio
Otoineppu
Enbetsu
Monbetsu
Yubetsu
HOKKAIDŌ
Rumoi
Shibatsu
Kitami
Abashiri
Abashiri-Wan
Nemuro-Kaikyō
Asahikawa
Daisetsu-Zan
2290
Kamui-
Misaki
Atsuta
HOKKAIDŌ
Nemuro
Iwanai
Otaru
Bibai
Iwamisawa
Honbetsu
Kushiro
Sapporo
Yūbari
Obihiro
Tokachi
Tomakomai
2052
Setana
Shiraoi
Mombetsu
Poroshiri Dake
Okushiri-Tō
Murotan
Urakawa
Samani
Uchiura-Wan
Erimo-Misaki
Esashi
Hakodate
Esan-Misaki
Matsumae
Kaikyō
Shiriya-Zaki
Tsugaru-
Mutsu
Mutsu-
Wan
Aomori
Hirosaki
2
Hachinohe
Odate
Kuji
Noshiro
Yoneshiro
Oga-Hantō
Akita
Morioka
Miyako
3
Honjō
Hanamaki
Kamaishi
Yokote
Ichinoseki
Sakata
Shinjo
TŌHOKU
Tsuruoka
Kogota
5
Ishinomaki
Yamagata
Shiogama
Sendai
Iwanuma
Sado
Niigata
Shibata
Yonezawa
Fukushima
Suzu-
Misaki
Nagaoka
Bandai-San
Wajima
Kashiwazaki
Koriyama
Naoetsu
Tajimi
Iwaki
Nanao
Takada
Himi
Nikkō
18
Hitachi
Takaoka
Toyama
Nagano
Maebashi Kiryū
Utsunomiya
Nakaminato
Matsumoto
Ueda 17
Takasaki
Tochigi
Mito
Takayama
Chichibu 19
Ōmiya
Tsuchiura
Suwa
Kawagoe
Urawa
KANTŌ
Kawaguchi
Ichikawa
Chōshi
TOKYO
140

COPYRIGHT GEORGE PHILIP & SON LTD.

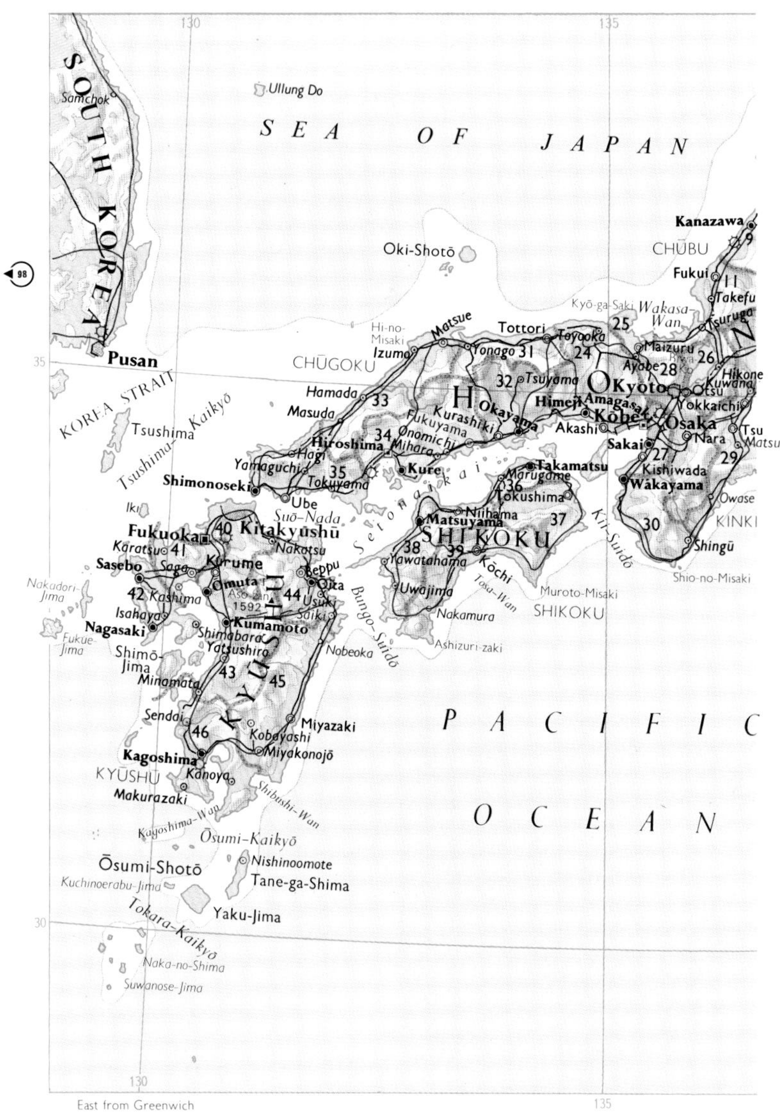

SOUTH KOREA

SEA OF JAPAN

Samchŏk

Ullung Do

Oki-Shotō

Kanazawa
CHŪBU
Fukui
Takefu
Tsuruga
Maizuru
Kyō-ga-Saki Wakasa-Wan
Ayabe
Hikone
Kusatsu
Tottori
Toyooka
25
26
Matsue
Hi-no-Misaki
Izumo
Yonago 31
24
Tsuyama
Kyōto
Amaga-
Yokkaichi
Pusan
CHŪGOKU
Hamada 33
Masuda
HO...a
Okā...a
Himeji
Kōbe
Osaka
Tsu
Matsus...
Fukuyama
Kurashiki
Akashi
Nara
Korea Strait
Tsushima
Hagi
Onomichi
Mihara
Sakai
Kishiwada
29
Tsushima-Kaikyō
Hiroshima 34
Kure
Marugame
Wakayama
Yamaguchi
Tokuyama 35
Owase
Shimonoseki
Tokushima
KINKI
Ikí
Suō-Nada
36
30
Shingū
Ube
Takamatsu
37
Fukuoka 40 Kitakyūshū
Karatsu 41
Nakatsu
Matsuyama
SHIKOKU
Nihama 39
Kōchi
Shio-no-Misaki
Sasebo
Saga
Kurume
Beppu
38
Yawatahama
Muroto-Misaki
Nakadori-Jima
42 Kashima
Ōmuta
44 Ōita
Usuki
Uwajima
SHIKOKU
Isahaya
1592
Saiki
Nakamura
Nagasaki
Shimabara
Kumamoto
Yatsushiro
Nobeoka
Ashizuri-zaki
Fukue-Jima
Shimo-Jima
43 45
Minamata
PACIFIC
Sendai 46
Miyazaki
Kobayashi
Kagoshima
Kanoya
Miyakonojō
OCEAN
KYŪSHŪ
Makurazaki
Shibushi-Wan
Kagoshima-Wan
Ōsumi-Kaikyō
Ōsumi-Shotō
Nishinoomote
Kuchinoerabu-Jima
Tane-ga-Shima
Tokara-Kaikyō
Yaku-Jima

Naka-no-Shima

Suwanose-Jima

98

130 135

1 : 7 500 000

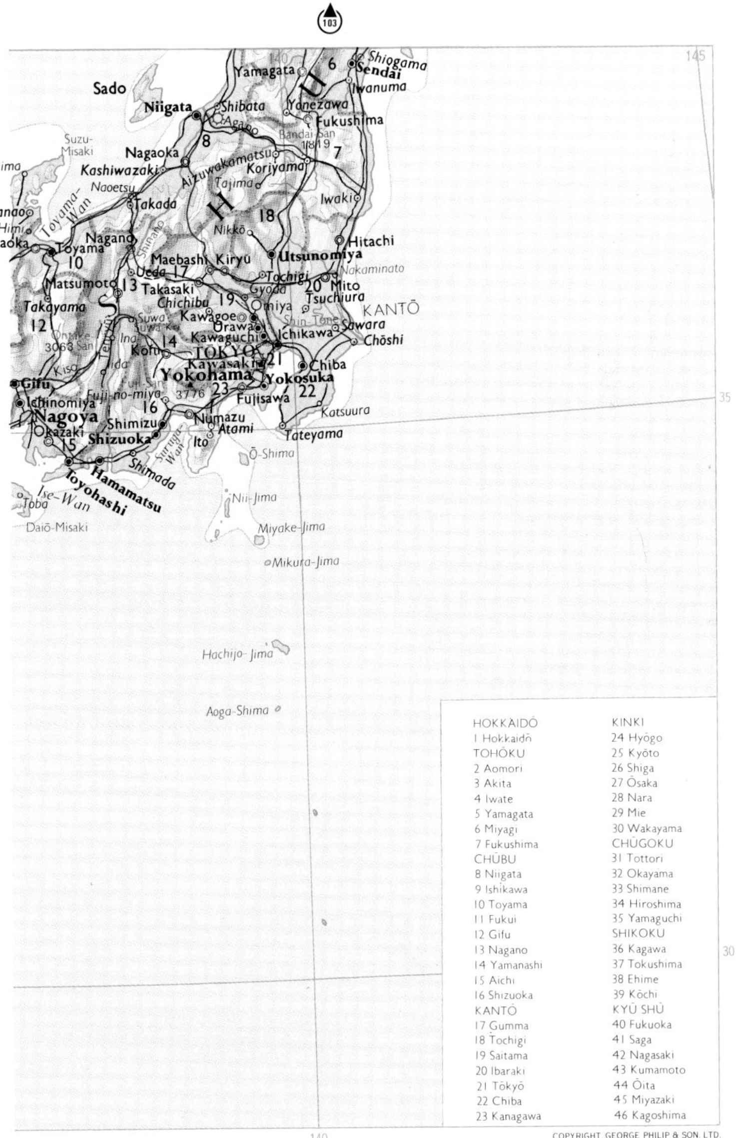

HOKKAIDŌ	KINKI
1 Hokkaidō	24 Hyōgo
TOHŌKU	25 Kyōto
2 Aomori	26 Shiga
3 Akita	27 Osaka
4 Iwate	28 Nara
5 Yamagata	29 Mie
6 Miyagi	30 Wakayama
7 Fukushima	CHŪGOKU
CHŪBU	31 Tottori
8 Niigata	32 Okayama
9 Ishikawa	33 Shimane
10 Toyama	34 Hiroshima
11 Fukui	35 Yamaguchi
12 Gifu	SHIKOKU
13 Nagano	36 Kagawa
14 Yamanashi	37 Tokushima
15 Aichi	38 Ehime
16 Shizuoka	39 Kōchi
KANTŌ	KYŪ SHŪ
17 Gumma	40 Fukuoka
18 Tochigi	41 Saga
19 Saitama	42 Nagasaki
20 Ibaraki	43 Kumamoto
21 Tōkyō	44 Ōita
22 Chiba	45 Miyazaki
23 Kanagawa	46 Kagoshima

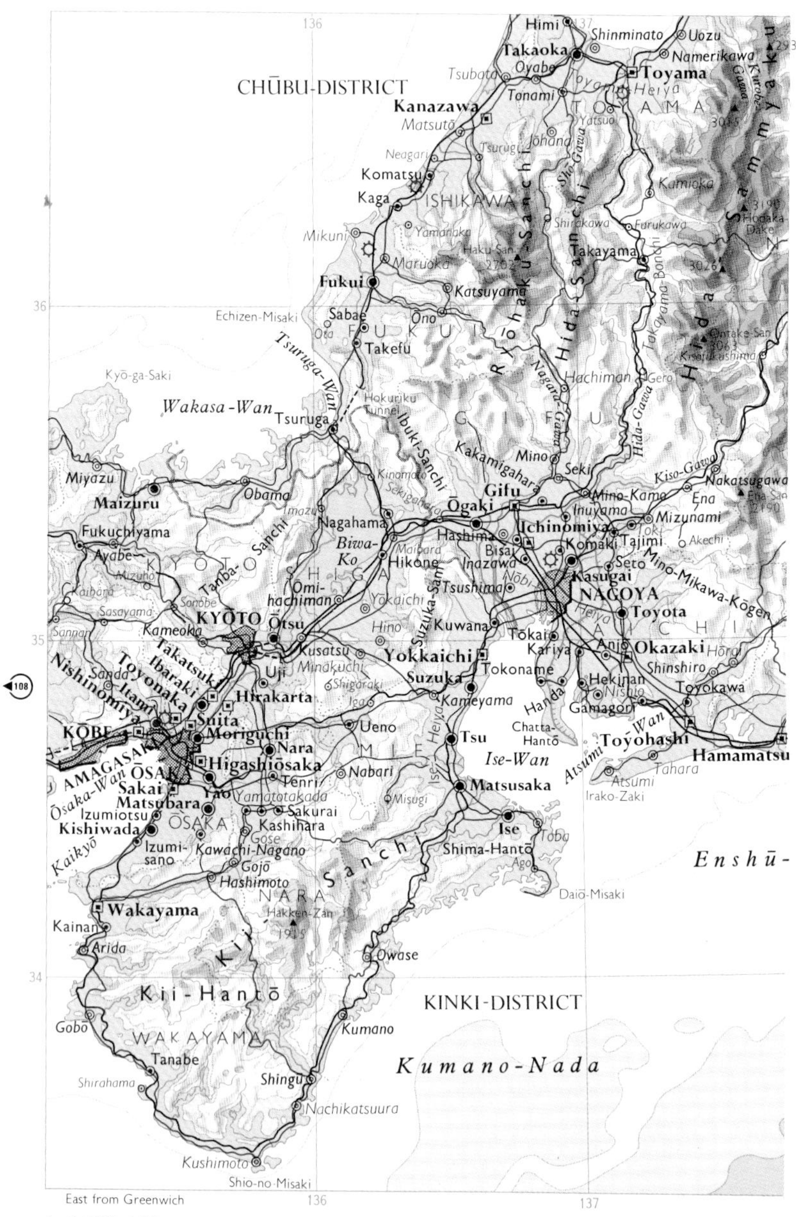
CHŪBU-DISTRICT
KINKI-DISTRICT
Himi
Shinminato
Uozu
Takaoka
Namerikawa
Toyama
Kanazawa
Komatsu
Kaga
Mikuni
Fukui
Katsuyama
Sabae
Ōno
Takefu
Echizen-Misaki
Tsuruga-Wan
Tsuruga
Wakasa-Wan
Kyō-ga-Saki
Hokuriku Tunnel
Ibuki-Sanchi
Ryōhaku-Sanchi
Hida-Sanchi
Hida-Sammyaku
Takayama
Hachiman
Gero
Ontake-San 3063
Hodaka-Dake
Miyazu
Maizuru
Fukuchiyama
Ayabe
Obama
Nagahama
Biwa-Ko
Hikone
Ōmi-hachiman
Tamba-Sanchi
KYŌTO
Ōtsu
Kameoka
Takatsuki
Ibaraki
Toyonaka
Nishinomiya
Itami
KŌBE
AMAGASAKI
ŌSAKA
Suita
Moriguchi
Hirakata
Higashiōsaka
Nara
Sakai
Yao
Tenri
Matsubara
Izumiotsu
Kishiwada
Izumi-sano
Kawachi-Nagano
Kashihara
Sakurai
Gojō
Hashimoto
Wakayama
Kainan
Arida
Gobō
Tanabe
Shirahama
Kushimoto
Shio-no-Misaki
Kii-Hantō
Kii-Sanchi
Nara
Hakken-Zan 1915
Owase
Kumano
Shingu
Nachikatsuura
Kumano-Nada
Gifu
Ōgaki
Mino
Seki
Ichinomiya
Kasugai
NAGOYA
Toyota
Okazaki
Tajimi
Mizunami
Nakatsugawa
Ena
Kiso-Gawa
Seto
Mino-Mikawa-Kōgen
Tsushima
Kuwana
Yokkaichi
Suzuka
Kameyama
Tsu
Matsusaka
Ise
Toba
Shima-Hantō
Daiō-Misaki
Ise-Wan
Chatta-Hantō
Handa
Tōkai
Kariya
Anjō
Hekinan
Gamagōri
Toyohashi
Toyokawa
Shinshiro
Hamamatsu
Atsumi
Irako-Zaki
Enshū-
Ueno
Nabari
Uji
Ōsaka-Wan
Kii-Kaikyō
East from Greenwich

1 : 2 500 000

105

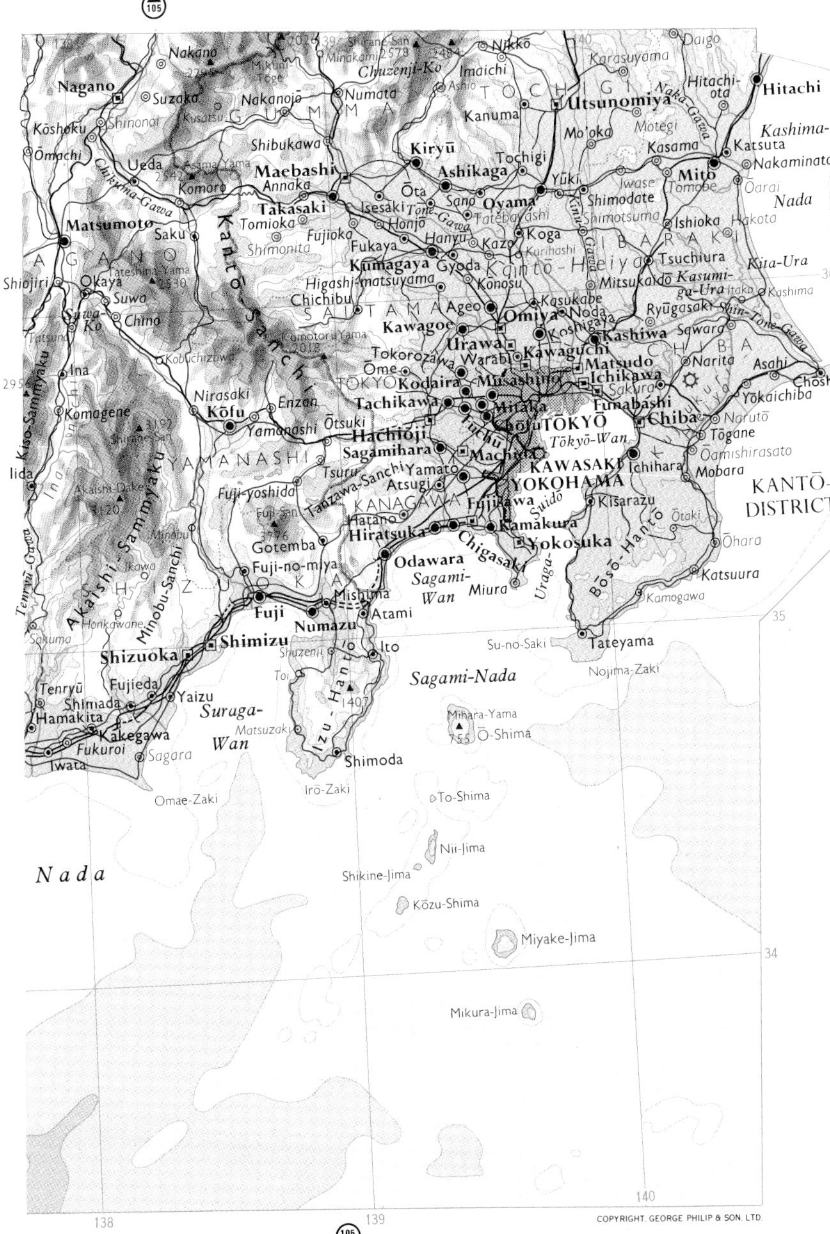
Nagano
Suzaka
Nakano
Kōshoku
Ōmachi
Shinonoi
Kusatsu
Mikuni Tōge
Nakanojō
Numata
Shirane-San
Minakami
Chuzenji-Ko
Nikkō
Imaichi
Ashio
Karasuyama
Daigo
Hitachi-ota
Hitachi
T O C H I G I
Utsunomiya
Naka-Gawa
Kanuma
Mo'oka
Motegi
Kashima-
Katsuta
Kasama
Nakaminato
Mito
Tomobe
Ōarai
Nada
G U N M A
Shibukawa
Kiryū
Tochigi
Ashikaga
Ueda
Asama Yama
Komoro
Maebashi
Annaka
Takasaki
Ōta
Isesaki
Sano
Oyama
Yūki
Iwase
Shimodate
Shimotsuma
Ishioka
Hokota
Chikuma-Gawa
Tomioka
Tone-Gawa
Honjō
Tatebayashi
Kinu-Gawa
Matsumoto
Saku
Fujioka
Fukaya
Hanyu
Kazo
Koga
Kurihashi
I B A R A K I
Kita-Ura
Shimonita
Kantō-Sanchi
Kumagaya
Gyoda
Kantō-Heiya
Tsuchiura
N A G A N O
Tateshina-Yama
Shiojiri
Okaya
Suwa
Suwa-Ko
Chino
Higashi-matsuyama
Chichibu
Kōnosu
Mitsukaidō
Kasumi-ga-Ura
Itaka
Kashima
S A I T A M A
Ageo
Kasukabe
Noda
Omiya
Kawagoe
Ryūgasaki
Shin-Tone-Gawa
Koshigaya
Kashiwa
Sawara
Kumotori Yama
Urawa
Warabi
Kawaguchi
Matsudo
C H I B A
Tatsuno
Kobuchizawa
Tokorozawa
Narita
Ōme
Ichikawa
Asahi
Ina
Kiso-Sammyaku
TŌKYŌ
Kodaira
Musashino
Sakura
Chōshi
Nirasaki
Enzan
Tachikawa
Mitaka
Funabashi
Yōkaichiba
Komagene
Kōfu
Chōfu
TŌKYŌ
Chiba
Narutō
Shirane-San
Yamanashi
Ōtsuki
Fuchu
Tōgane
Hachiōji
Tōkyō-Wan
Kujukuri-hama
Ina-Sanchi
Sagamihara
Machida
Ōamishirasato
Iida
YAMANASHI
KAWASAKI
Ichihara
Mobara
Tsuru
Tanzawa-Sanchi
Yamato
Atsugi
YOKOHAMA
KANTŌ-DISTRICT
Akaishi-Dake
Fuji-yoshida
KANAGAWA
Fujisawa
Uraga-Suidō
Kisarazu
Fuji-San
Hatano
Ōtaki
Minobu
Hiratsuka
Kamakura
Ōhara
Gotemba
Chigasaki
Yokosuka
Akaishi-Sammyaku
Ikawa
Fuji-no-miya
Odawara
Bōsō-Hantō
Minobu-Sanchi
Tenryū-Gawa
Sagami-Wan
Miura
Katsuura
S H I Z U O K A
Mishima
Fuji
Atami
Kamogawa
Honkawane
Numazu
Sakuma
Shimizu
Ito
Su-no-Saki
Tateyama
Shizuoka
Shuzenji
Toi
Sagami-Nada
Nojima-Zaki
Izu-Hantō
Tenryū
Fujieda
Shimada
Yaizu
Hamakita
Suruga-Wan
Mihara-Yama
Ō-Shima
Kakegawa
Matsuzaki
Fukuroi
Iwata
Sagara
Shimoda
Omae-Zaki
Irō-Zaki
To-Shima
Nii-Jima
Nada
Shikine-Jima
Kōzu-Shima
Miyake-Jima
Mikura-Jima
138
139
140
36
35
34

105

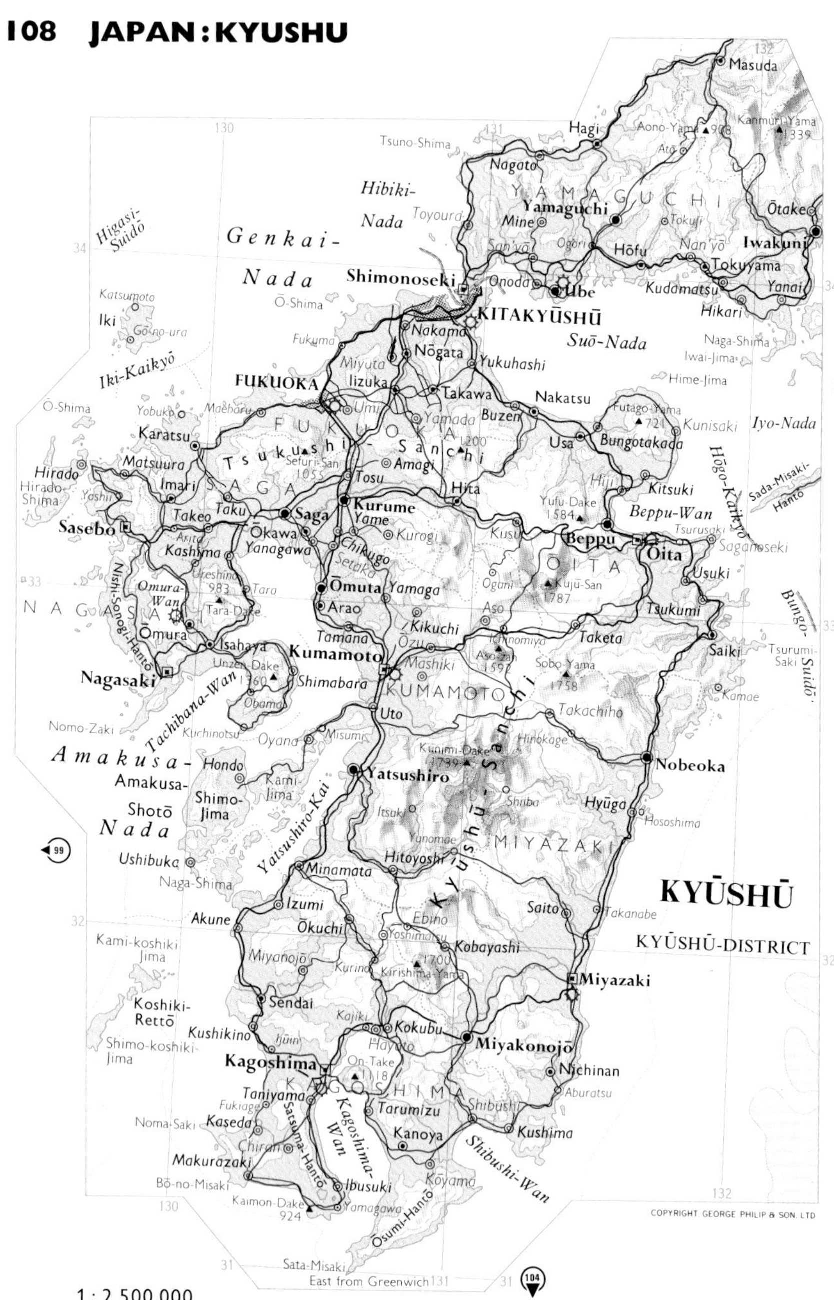

Masuda
Hagi
Aono-Yama 908
Kanmuri-Yama 1339
Tsuno-Shima
Ato
Nagato
YAMAGUCHI
Yamaguchi
Hibiki-
Nada
Toyoura
Mine
Tokuji
Ōtake
Iwakuni
Higasi-Suidō
Genkai-
Nada
San'yō
Ogōri
Hōfu
Nan'yō
Tokuyama
Shimonoseki
Onoda
Ube
Kudamatsu
Yanai
Hikari
Katsumoto
Iki
Gō-no-ura
Ō-Shima
KITAKYŪSHŪ
Nakama
Suō-Nada
Fukuma
Nōgata
Naga-Shima
Iwai-Jima
Miyuta
Yukuhashi
Iki-Kaikyō
FUKUOKA
Iizuka
Hime-Jima
Takawa
Nakatsu
Ō-Shima
Yobuko
Maebaru
Umi
Yamada
Buzen
Futago-Yama 721
Kunisaki
Iyo-Nada
FUKUOKA
Karatsu
Tsukushi-Sanchi
1200
Usa
Bungotakada
Hōgo-Kaikyō
Hirado
Hirado-Shima
Matsuura
Sefuri-San 1055
Amagi
Hiji
Sada-Misaki-Hantō
Imari
SAGA
Tosu
Hita
Kitsuki
Yoshii
Kurume
Yufu-Dake 1584
Beppu-Wan
Takeo
Taku
Saga
Yame
Tsurusaki
Sasebo
Ōkawa
Kurogi
Kusu
Beppu
Saganoseki
Kashima
Yanagawa
Chikugo
Ōita
Arita
Setaka
ŌITA
Usuki
Nishi-Sonogi-Hantō
Ureshino 983
Ōmuta
Yamaga
Oguni
Kujū-San 1787
Bungo-Suidō
Omura-Wan
Tara
NAGASAKI
Tara-Dake
Arao
Aso
Tsukumi
Kikuchi
Ōmura
Tamana
Ichinomiya
Taketa
Isahaya
Kumamoto
Ōzu
Aso-zan 1592
Saiki
Tsurumi-Saki
Unzen-Dake 1360
Mashiki
Sobo-Yama 1758
Nagasaki
Shimabara
KUMAMOTO
Tachibana-Wan
Obama
Kamae
Uto
Takachiho
Nomo-Zaki
Kuchinotsu
Misumi
Hinokage
Oyano
Amakusa-
Hondo
Kunimi-Dake 1739
Nobeoka
Amakusa-Shotō
Kami-Jima
Yatsushiro
Kyūshū-Sanchi
Shimo-Jima
Yatsushiro-Kai
Shiiba
Hyūga
Nada
Itsuki
Hososhima
Yunomae
MIYAZAKI
Ushibuka
Hitoyoshi
Naga-Shima
Minamata
KYŪSHŪ
Izumi
Saito
Takanabe
Akune
Ebino
Ōkuchi
Yoshimatsu
Kami-koshiki-Jima
Kobayashi
KYŪSHŪ-DISTRICT
Miyanojō
Kurino
1700
Kirishima-Yama
Miyazaki
Sendai
Koshiki-Rettō
Kajiki
Kushikino
Kokubu
Miyakonojō
Ijūin
Hayato
Shimo-koshiki-Jima
Kagoshima
On-Take 1118
Nichinan
KAGOSHIMA
Aburatsu
Taniyama
Fukiage
Satsuma-Hantō
Kagoshima-Wan
Tarumizu
Shibushi
Noma-Saki
Kaseda
Kushima
Chiran
Kanoya
Shibushi-Wan
Makurazaki
Bō-no-Misaki
Ibusuki
Kōyama
Kaimon-Dake 924
Yamagawa
Ōsumi-Hantō
Sata-Misaki
East from Greenwich
130
131
132
31
32
33
34
99
104
109
COPYRIGHT GEORGE PHILIP & SON LTD

1 : 2 500 000

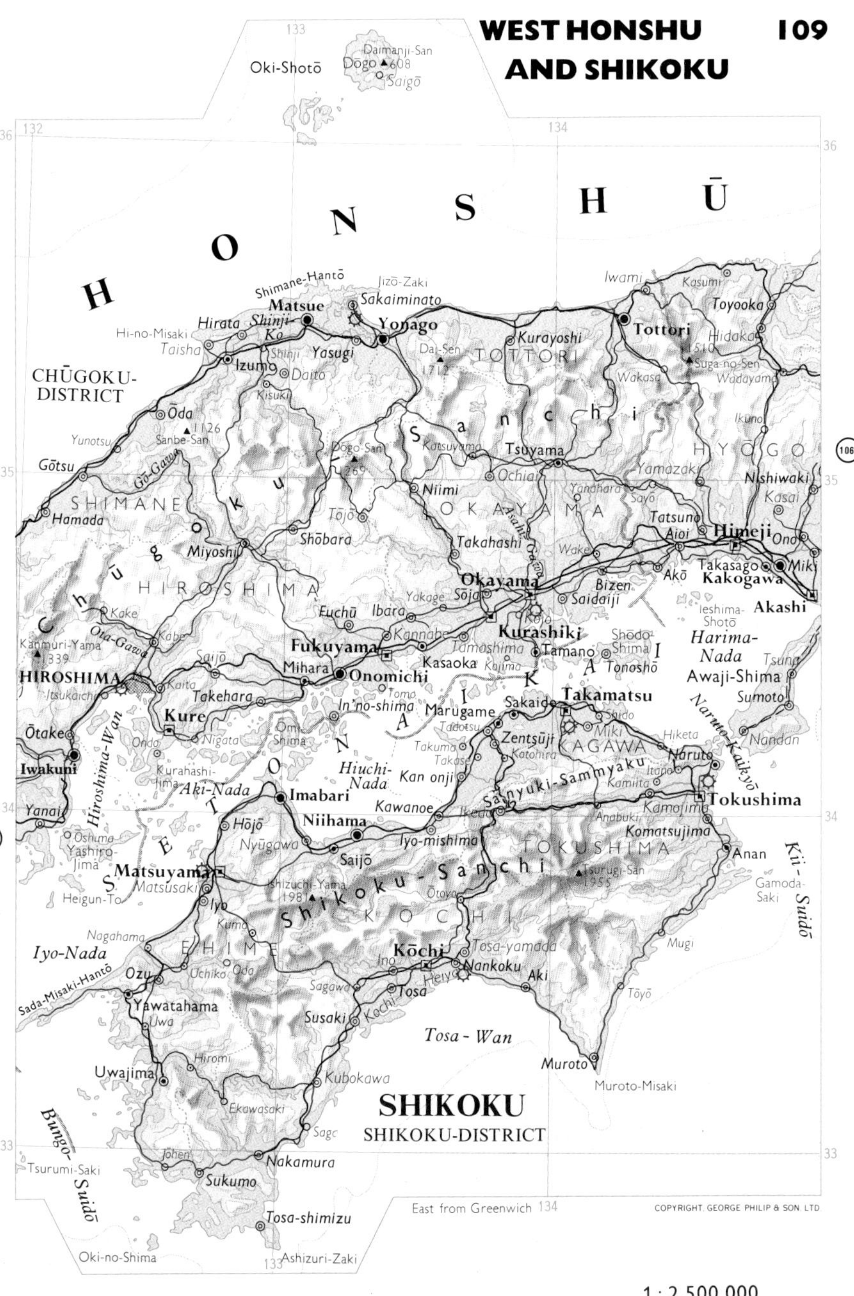

133

Oki-Shotō

Daimanji-San
Dogo ▲608
● Saigō

132

36   134   36

H O N S H Ū

H   O   N   S   O   N   S   H   Ū

Shimane-Hantō   Jizō-Zaki   Iwami   Kasumi   Toyooka
Hino-Misaki   Hirata   Shinji   Matsue   Sakaiminato   Tottori
Taisha   Kō   Yonago   Kurayoshi   Hidaka
          Izumo   Yasugi   Dai-Sen   Wakasa   Suga-no-Sen   Wadayama
CHŪGOKU-   Daito   Kisuki   1712   TOTTORI   510   Ikuno
DISTRICT   Yamazaki   HYOGO
          Ōda   1126   Ochiai   Yanahara   Sayō   Tatsuno   Nishiwaki
Yunotsu   Sanbe-San   Dōgo-San   Katsuyama   Tsuyama   Aioi   Himeji   Ono   Kasai
Gōtsu   1266   Niimi   Wak   Akō   Takasago   Miki
SHIMANE   Tōjō   OKAYAMA   Bizen   Saidaiji   Ieshima-   Kagogawa   Akashi
Hamada   Shōbara   Takahashi   Okayama   Shotō   Harima-
          Miyoshi   CHŪGOKU-SANCHI   Sōja   Kurashiki   Shōdo-   Nada   Tsun
Kake   Ota-Gawa   Euchū   Ibara   Kannab   Tamashima   Tamano   Shima   I   Tonoshō   Awaji-Shima
Kanmuri-Yama   Kabe   Saijō   Kasaoka   Kojima   A   Sumoto
1339   HIROSHIMA   Mihara   Onomichi   Tomo   Sakaide   Takamatsu   Nandan
Itsukaichi   Takehara   In'no-shima   Marugame   Tadotsu   Zentsūji   Miki   Hiketa   Naruto-Kaikyo
HIROSHIMA   Ōta-ke   Oda   Nigata   Ōmi-Shima   Takuma   Takasu   Kotohira   KAGAWA   Itano
Iwakuni   Yanai   Kurahashi-   Aki-Nada   Hiuchi-   Kan onji   Sanuki-Sammyaku   Kamiita   Tokushima
          jima   Nada   Kawanoe   Anabuki   Kamojima
Yashiro-   Imabari   Niihama   Iyo-mishima   TOKUSHIMA   Anan
Jima   Hōjō   Nyūgawa   Saijō   Shikoku-Sanchi   Gamoda-
Matsuyama   Matsusaki   Ishizuchi-Yama   Ōtoyo   KOCHI   Tsurugi-San   Saki
          Iyo   1982   1955
Nagahama   Kuma   EHIME   Tōyō
Iyo-Nada   Ōzu   Uchiko   Oda   Sagawa   Ing   Kōchi   Nankoku   Aki
Sada-Misaki-Hantō   Yawatahama   Susaki   Kōchi   Heiya   Tosa   Mugi
Uwa   Hiromi   Kubokawa   Tosa - Wan   Muroto
Uwajima   Muroto-Misaki
Bungo-Suidō   Ekawasaki   Sagc   # SHIKOKU
Tsurumi-Saki   Sukumo   Jōhen   Nakamura   SHIKOKU-DISTRICT
Oki-no-Shima   Tosa-shimizu   Ashizuri-Zaki

East from Greenwich 134   COPYRIGHT GEORGE PHILIP & SON LTD

1 : 2 500 000

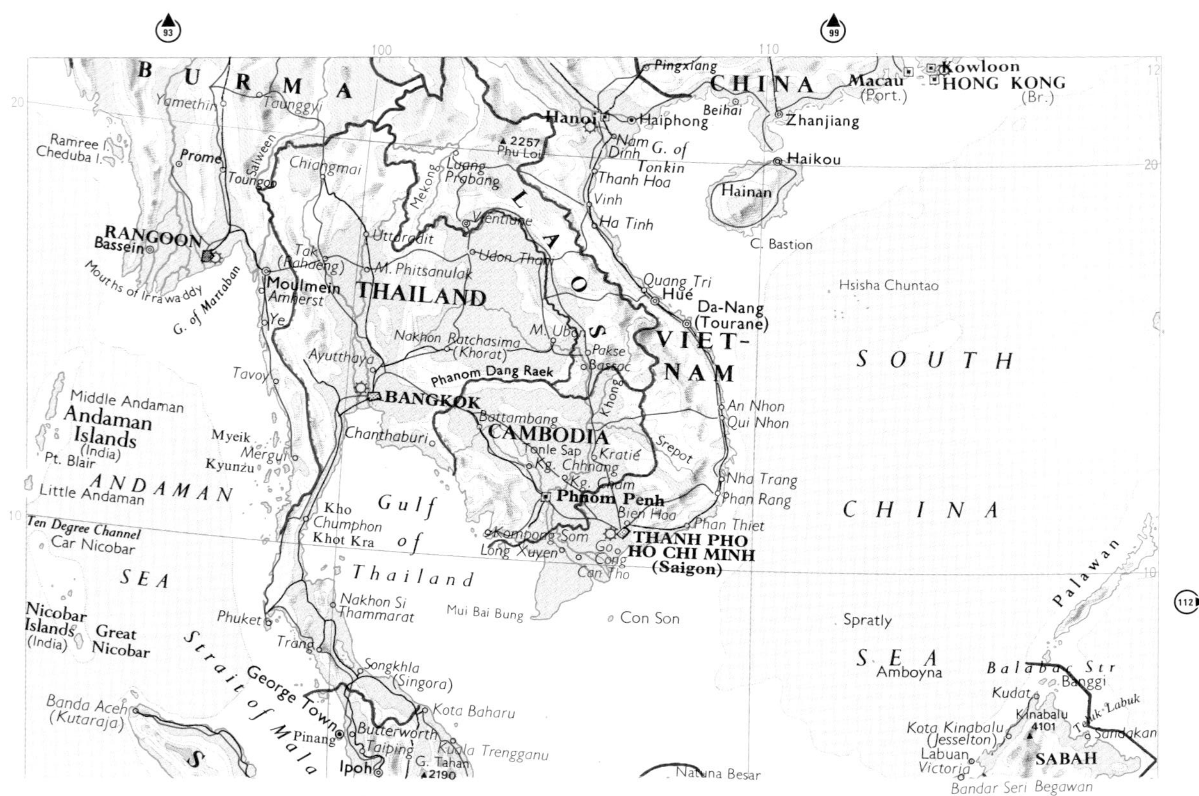

BURMA
CHINA
HONG KONG (Br.)
Kowloon
Macau (Port.)
Zhanjiang
Haikou
Hainan
Beihai
Pingxiang
Haiphong
Hanoi
Nam Dinh
G. of Tonkin
Thanh Hoa
Vinh
Ha Tinh
Quang Tri
Hué
Da-Nang (Tourane)
VIET-NAM
LAOS
Luang Prabang
Phu Loi
2257
Vientiane
Udon Thani
M. Ubon
Pakse
Bassac
Khong
THAILAND
CAMBODIA
Phnom Penh
Tonle Sap
Kg. Chhnang
Kratié
Srepot
An Nhon
Qui Nhon
Nha Trang
Phan Rang
Phan Thiet
THANH PHO HO CHI MINH (Saigon)
Bien Hoa
Go Cong
Can Tho
Con Son
Long Xuyen
Kompong Som
Battambang
Phanom Dang Raek
Nakhon Ratchasima (Khorat)
BANGKOK
Chanthaburi
Ayutthaya
M. Phitsanulok
Uttaradit
Mekong
Chiangmai
Taunggyi
Salween
Toungoo
Tak (Rahaeng)
Moulmein
Amherst
Ye
Tavoy
Mergui
Myeik
Kyunzu
G. of Martaban
Yamethin
Prome
RANGOON
Bassein
Mouths of Irrawaddy
Ramree I.
Cheduba I.
Middle Andaman
Andaman Islands (India)
Pt. Blair
Little Andaman
ANDAMAN SEA
Ten Degree Channel
Car Nicobar
Nicobar Islands (India)
Great Nicobar
Banda Aceh (Kutaraja)
Strait of Mala
George Town
Pinang
Phuket
Trang
Butterworth
Taiping
Ipoh
G. Tahan
2190
Kuala Trengganu
Kota Baharu
Songkhla (Singora)
Nakhon Si Thammarat
Kho Chumphon
Khot Kra
Gulf of Thailand
Mui Bai Bung
SOUTH CHINA SEA
Hsisha Chuntao
C. Bastion
Spratly
Amboyna
Natuna Besar
Palawan
Balabac Str
Banggi
Kudat
Kinabalu
4101
Kota Kinabalu (Jesselton)
Labuan
Victoria
Bandar Seri Begawan
SABAH
Sandakan
Teluk Labuk
93
99
112
10
20
100
110

1 : 20 000 000

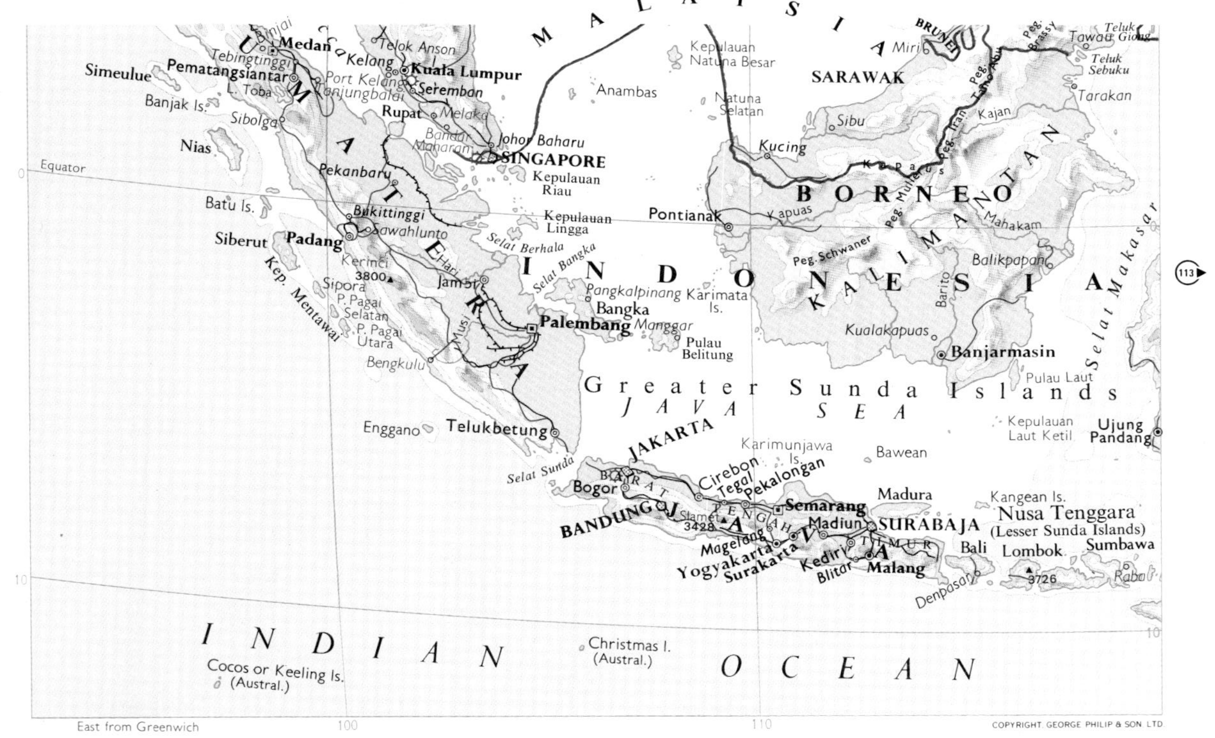
MALAYSIA
INDONESIA
SUMATERA
BORNEO
KALIMANTAN
JAVA
SARAWAK
BRUNEI
Greater Sunda Islands
JAVA SEA
INDIAN OCEAN
Nusa Tenggara
(Lesser Sunda Islands)
Medan
Binjai
Tebingtinggi
Pematangsiantar
Simeulue
L. Toba
Banjak Is.
Sibolga
Nias
Telok Anson
Kelang
Kuala Lumpur
Port Kelang
Tanjungbalai
Seremban
Rupat
Melaka
Bandar Maharani
Johor Baharu
SINGAPORE
Kepulauan Riau
Kepulauan Lingga
Anambas
Kepulauan Natuna Besar
Natuna Selatan
Equator
Pekanbaru
Batu Is.
Bukittinggi
Sawahlunto
Siberut
Padang
Kerinci
3800
Sipora
P. Pagai Selatan
P. Pagai Utara
Kep. Mentawai
Selat Berhala
Selat Bangka
Hari
Jambi
Pangkalpinang
Bangka
Karimata Is.
Palembang
Manggar
Pulau Belitung
Musi
Bengkulu
Enggano
Telukbetung
Selat Sunda
Pontianak
Kapuas
Kucing
Sibu
Miri
Kajan
Peg. Iran
Peg. Muller
Peg. Tama Abu
Peg. Brassy
Tawau
Teluk Giong
Teluk Sebuku
Tarakan
Mahakam
Peg. Schwaner
Balikpapan
Barito
Kualakapuas
Banjarmasin
Pulau Laut
Selat Makasar
Kepulauan Laut Ketil
Ujung Pandang
JAKARTA
Bogor
BARAT
BANDUNG
Cirebon
Tegal
Pekalongan
Karimunjawa Is.
Slamet
3428
TENGAH
Semarang
Magelang
Yogyakarta
Surakarta
Madiun
Kediri
Blitar
Malang
TIMUR
SURABAJA
Madura
Bawean
Kangean Is.
Bali
Denpasar
Lombok
Sumbawa
3726
Raba
Christmas I. (Austral.)
Cocos or Keeling Is. (Austral.)
0
10
100
110
East from Greenwich
113

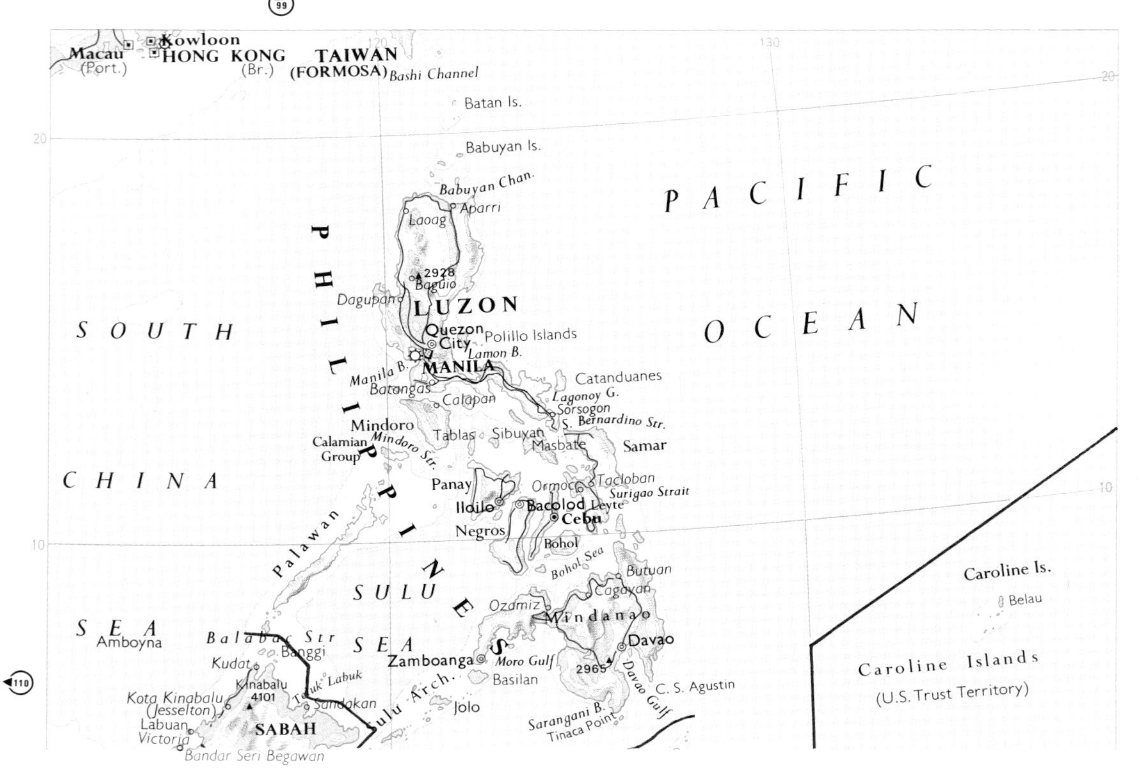
Macau
(Port.)
Kowloon
HONG KONG
(Br.)
TAIWAN
(FORMOSA)
Bashi Channel
Batan Is.
Babuyan Is.
Babuyan Chan.
Aparri
Laoag
2928
Baguio
Dagupan
LUZON
Quezon City
Polillo Islands
Lamon B.
MANILA
Manila B.
Batangas
Calapan
Catanduanes
Lagonoy G.
Sorsogon
S. Bernardino Str.
Mindoro
Tablas
Sibuyan
Masbate
Samar
Calamian Group
Mindoro Str.
Panay
Ormoc
Tacloban
Surigao Strait
Iloilo
Bacolod
Leyte
Cebu
Negros
Bohol
Bohol Sea
Butuan
Cagayan
Ozamiz
Mindanao
Davao
2965
Davao Gulf
C. S. Agustin
Sarangani B.
Tinaca Point
Zamboanga
Moro Gulf
Basilan
Jolo
Sulu Arch.
PHILIPPINES
Palawan
SULU SEA
SOUTH CHINA SEA
PACIFIC OCEAN
Amboyna
Balabac Str
Banggi
Kudat
Kinabalu
4101
Teluk Labuk
Sandakan
Kota Kinabalu
(Jesselton)
Labuan
Victoria
SABAH
Bandar Seri Begawan
Caroline Is.
Belau
Caroline Islands
(U.S. Trust Territory)
120
130
20
10
99
110

1 : 20 000 000

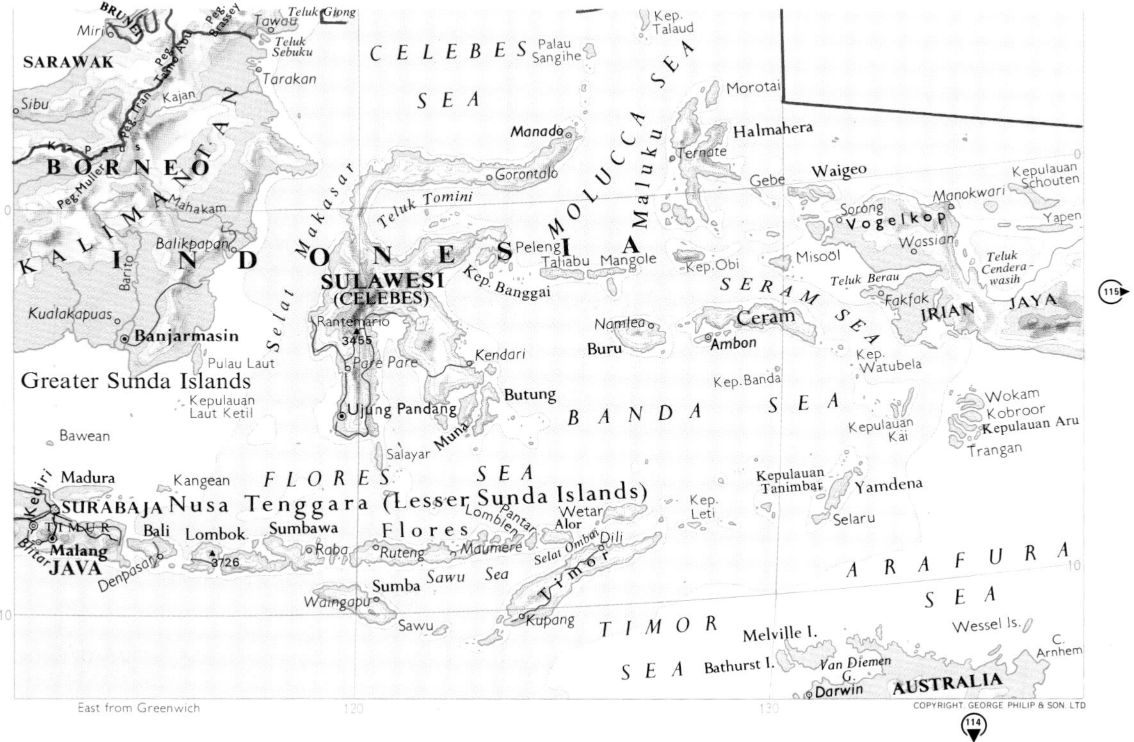

113

Kepulauan
Schouten
Yapen
IRIAN
Vogelkop JAYA
Manokwari
Wossian
Teluk
Cendera-
wasih
Waigeo
Sorong
Faktok
Kep.
Misool
Teluk Berau
Watubela
Wokam
Kobroor
Kepulauan Aru
Trangan
Halmahera
Gebe
Kep. Obi
SERAM SEA
Ceram Sea
Kep. Banda
Ambon
A R A F U R A
Morotai
Kep.
Talaud
Ternate
Kep. Leti
BANDA SEA
Kepulauan
Tanimbar
Yamdena
Selaru
S E A
Wessel Is.
C.
Arnhem
Namlea
Buru
Kep.
Leti
Van Diemen
G.
Darwin
AUSTRALIA
MOLUCCA SEA
Pulau
Sanghe
Manado
Gorontalo
Kep. Banggai
Peleng
Talabu Mangole
Butung
Wetar
Alor
Pantar
Lomblen
Dili
TIMOR
Melville I.
Bathurst I.
SEA
CELEBES
SEA
Teluk Tomini
SULAWESI
(CELEBES)
Kendari
FLORES SEA
Ndumere
Maumere
Selat Ombai
Kupang
T I M O R
East from Greenwich

Teluk Ciong
Tawau
Teluk
Sebuku
Tarakan
Selat Makasar
Pare Pare
3455
Rantekario
Ujung Pandang
Salayar
Nusa Tenggara (Lesser Sunda Islands)
Flores
Ruteng
Sumba Sawu Sea
Sawu
COPYRIGHT GEORGE PHILIP & SON LTD

SARAWAK
BRUNEI
Miri
Sibu
Peg. Kapuas
Kajan
Peg. Iran
Mahakam
Balikpapan
Barito
Kudakapuas
BORNEO
KALIMANTAN
Banjarmasin
Pulau Laut
Kepulauan
Laut Ketil
Greater Sunda Islands
Bawean
Kangean
Madura
SURABAJA
Kediri
Malang
Blitar
JAVA
Denpasar
Bali
Lombok
3726
Sumbawa
Wangapu
East from Greenwich

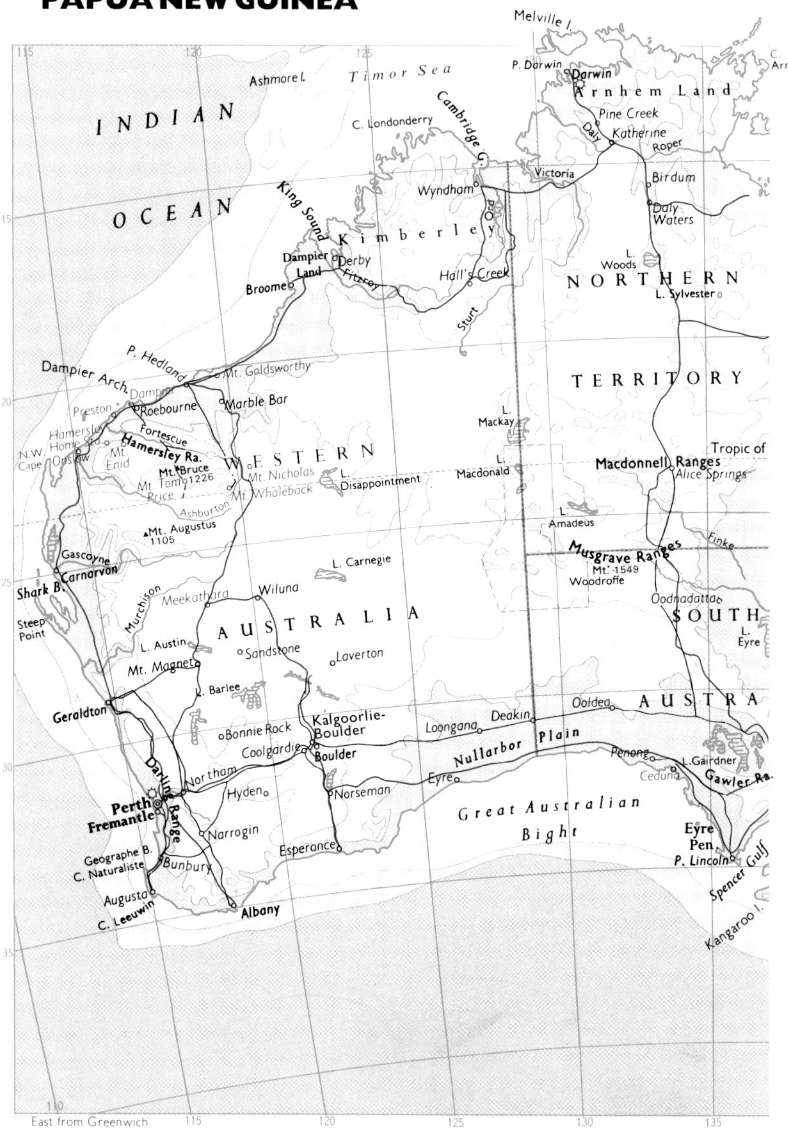

1 : 24 000 000

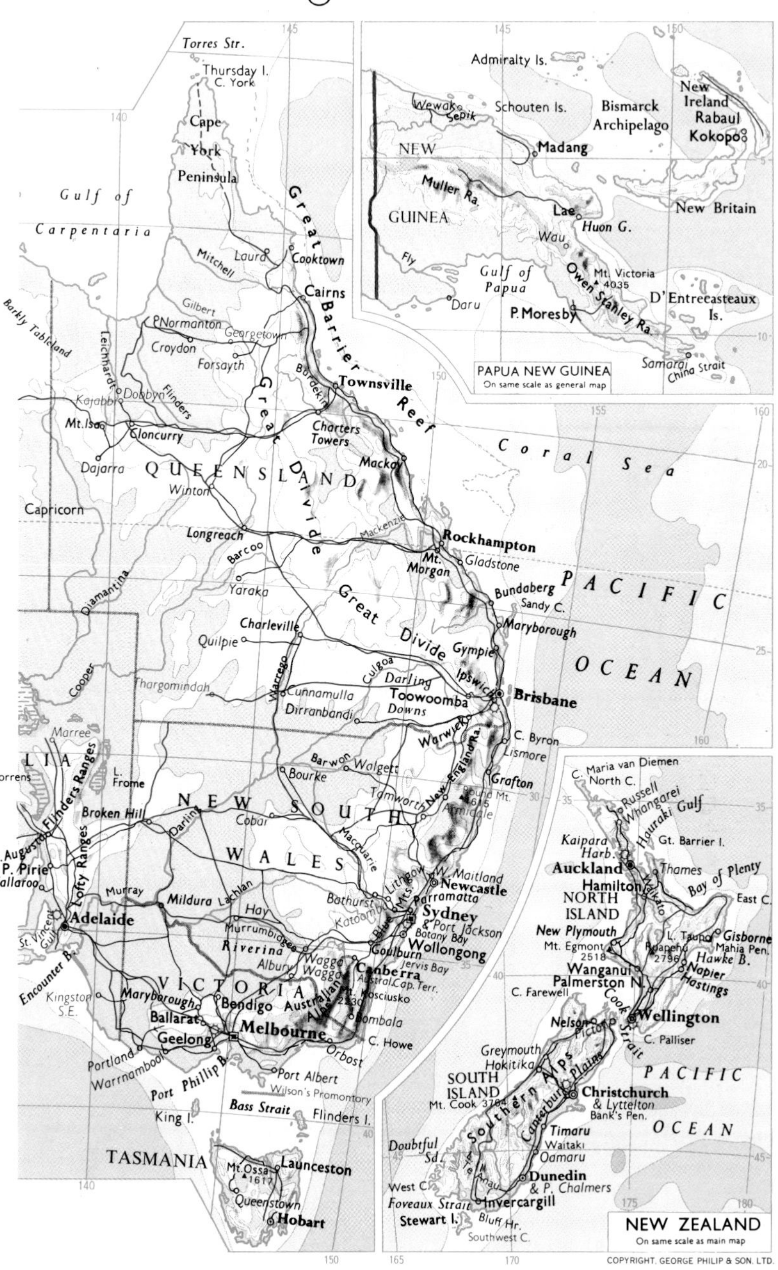

Torres Str.

Thursday I.
C. York

Cape
York
Peninsula

Gulf of
Carpentaria

Admiralty Is.

Wewak
Sepik
Schouten Is.
Bismarck
Archipelago
New
Ireland
Rabaul
Kokopo

NEW

GUINEA

Madang

Muller Ra.

Lae
Huon G.
Wau

New Britain

Fly

Gulf of
Papua

Daru

Mt. Victoria
4035

Owen Stanley Ra.

D'Entrecasteaux
Is.

P. Moresby

Samarai
China Strait

PAPUA NEW GUINEA
On same scale as general map

Mitchell

Cooktown

Laura

Cairns

Gilbert

P. Normanton
Georgetown

Croydon
Forsayth

Croydon

Great Barrier Reef

Townsville

Barkly Tableland

Leichhardt

Kajabbi
Dobbyn

Mt. Isa

Cloncurry

Flinders

Charters
Towers

Mackay

Dajarra

QUEENSLAND

Great Divide

Coral Sea

Capricorn

Winton

Longreach

Barcoo

Diamantina

Yaraka

Mackenzie

Rockhampton

Mt.
Morgan
Gladstone

PACIFIC

Cooper

Thargomindah

Charleville

Quilpie

Great Divide

Bundaberg
Sandy C.
Maryborough

Gympie

OCEAN

Marree

Warrego

Cunnamulla
Dirranbandi

Culgoa

Darling

Toowoomba
Downs

Ipswich

Brisbane

LIA

Torrens

L.
Frome

Flinders Ranges

Broken Hill

Thargomindah

Warrego

Balonne

Warwick

C. Byron
Lismore

New England Ra.

Bourke

Walgett

Tamworth

Inverell Mt.

Grafton

NEW SOUTH

Cobar

Darling

Macquarie

Armidale

P. Augusta
P. Pirie
Wallaroo

Flinders Ranges

WALES

L. Torrens

Lithgow

Mt. Maitland

Newcastle

Parramatta

St. V. Gulf

Murray

Mildura

Lachlan

Bathurst

Katoomba

Sydney
Port Jackson
Botany Bay

Adelaide

Riverina

Hay

Murrumbidgee

Wagga
Wagga

Goulburn

Wollongong

Jervis Bay

Encounter
B.

Kingston
S.E.

VICTORIA

Albury

Canberra

Fed. Cap. Terr.

Maryborough

Bendigo

Australian Alps

Kosciusko 2230

Bombala

Ballarat

Melbourne

Murray

C. Howe

Portland

Geelong

Orbost

Warrnambool

Port Albert

Wilson's Promontory

Port Phillip B.

Bass Strait
Flinders I.

King I.

TASMANIA

Mt. Ossa
1617

Launceston

Queenstown

Hobart

C. Maria van Diemen
North C.

Russell
Whangarei

Kaipara
Harb.

Hauraki Gulf

Gt. Barrier I.

Auckland

Thames

Bay of Plenty

Hamilton

NORTH
ISLAND

East C.

New Plymouth

Mt. Egmont
2518

L. Taupo
2796

Hawke B.

Mahia Pen.

Gisborne

Wanganui

Napier
Hastings

Palmerston N.

C. Farewell

Nelson

Cook Strait

Wellington

C. Palliser

Greymouth

Hokitika

SOUTH
ISLAND

Southern Alps

Mt. Cook 3764

Canterbury Plains

PACIFIC

Christchurch
& Lyttelton

Bank's Pen.

Timaru

OCEAN

Doubtful
Sd.

Waitaki
Oamaru

West C.

Foveaux Strait

Stewart I.

Dunedin
& P. Chalmers

Invercargill

Bluff Hr.

Southwest C.

NEW ZEALAND
On same scale as main map

121

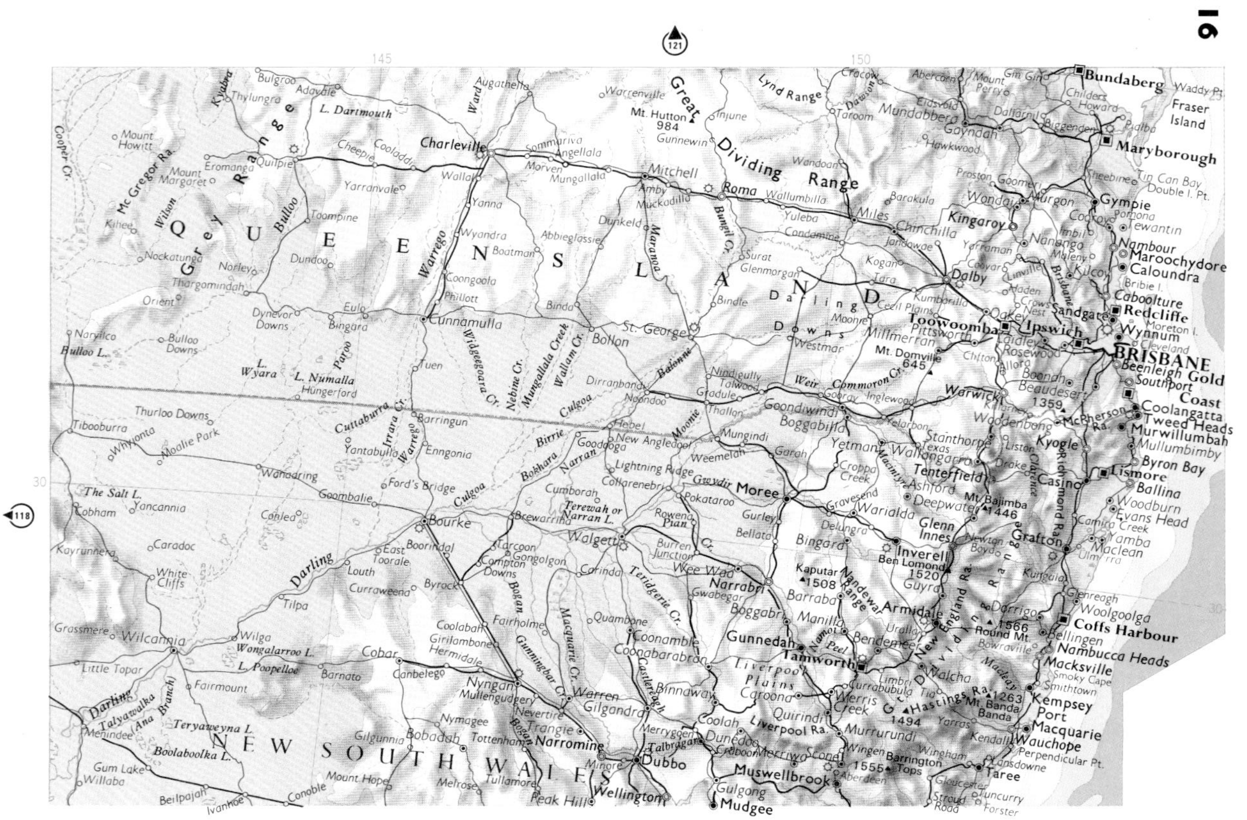

Q U E E N S L A N D
N E W S O U T H W A L E S
Great Dividing Range
Darling Downs
Grey Range
Bundaberg
Maryborough
Fraser Island
Gympie
Maroochydore
Caloundra
Nambour
Caboolture
Redcliffe
Wynnum
BRISBANE
Ipswich
Toowoomba
Beenleigh
Gold Coast
Southport
Coolangatta
Tweed Heads
Murwillumbah
Byron Bay
Lismore
Ballina
Casino
Grafton
Coffs Harbour
Nambucca Heads
Macksville
Kempsey
Port Macquarie
Wauchope
Taree
Kingaroy
Dalby
Warwick
Tenterfield
Glenn Innes
Inverell
Armidale
Tamworth
Gunnedah
Narrabri
Moree
Goondiwindi
Roma
Mitchell
Charleville
Cunnamulla
St. George
Walgett
Bourke
Dubbo
Wellington
Narromine
Muswellbrook
Mudgee
Coonabarabran
Nyngan
Cobar
Wilcannia
Tibooburra
Quilpie
Mt. Hutton 984
Kaputar 1508
Barrington Tops 1555
Darling
Warrego
Maranoa
Paroo
Bulloo
Cooper Cr.
Macquarie Cr.
Castlereagh
Liverpool Ra.
Liverpool Plains
Nandewar Range
New England Ra.
Richmond Ra.
McPherson Ra.
Macintyre
Gwydir
Balonne
Culgoa
Narran
Bogan

118

1 : 8 000 000

122

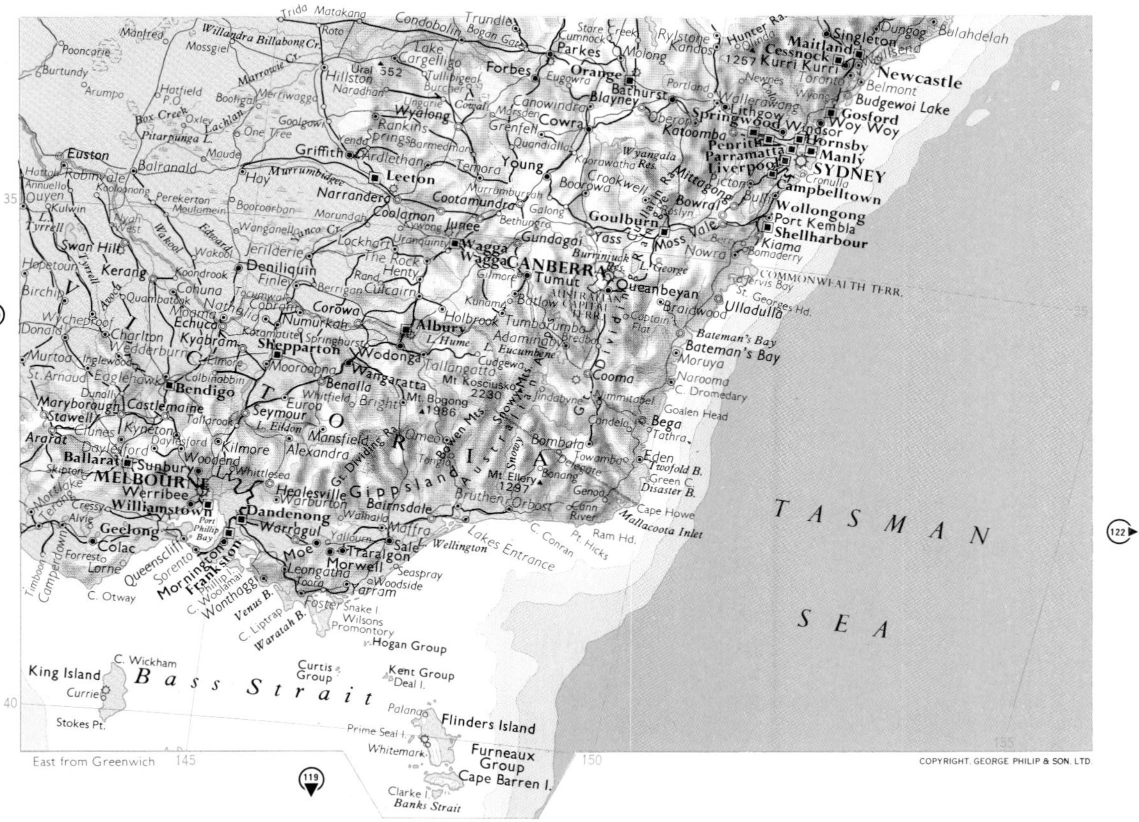
T A S M A N
S E A
B a s s   S t r a i t
Newcastle
SYDNEY
Wollongong
CANBERRA
MELBOURNE
Geelong
Ballarat
Bendigo
Albury
Wagga Wagga
Goulburn
Bathurst
Orange
Parkes
Forbes
Cowra
Young
Griffith
Leeton
Hay
Deniliquin
Shepparton
Wangaratta
Wodonga
Cooma
Bega
Eden
Queanbeyan
Bateman's Bay
Ulladulla
Kiama
Shellharbour
Port Kembla
Campbelltown
Liverpool
Parramatta
Penrith
Manly
Hornsby
Gosford
Woy Woy
Maitland
Cessnock
Singleton
Katoomba
Lithgow
Dandenong
Frankston
Mornington
Moe
Morwell
Traralgon
Sale
Bairnsdale
Lakes Entrance
Wilsons Promontory
Flinders Island
Furneaux Group
Cape Barren I.
Banks Strait
King Island
Currie
C. Wickham
C. Otway
Kent Group
Hogan Group
Curtis Group
Mt. Kosciusko 2230
Snowy Mts.
Murrumbidgee
Swan Hill
Kerang
Echuca
Euston
Balranald
COMMONWEALTH TERR.
East from Greenwich

119

119

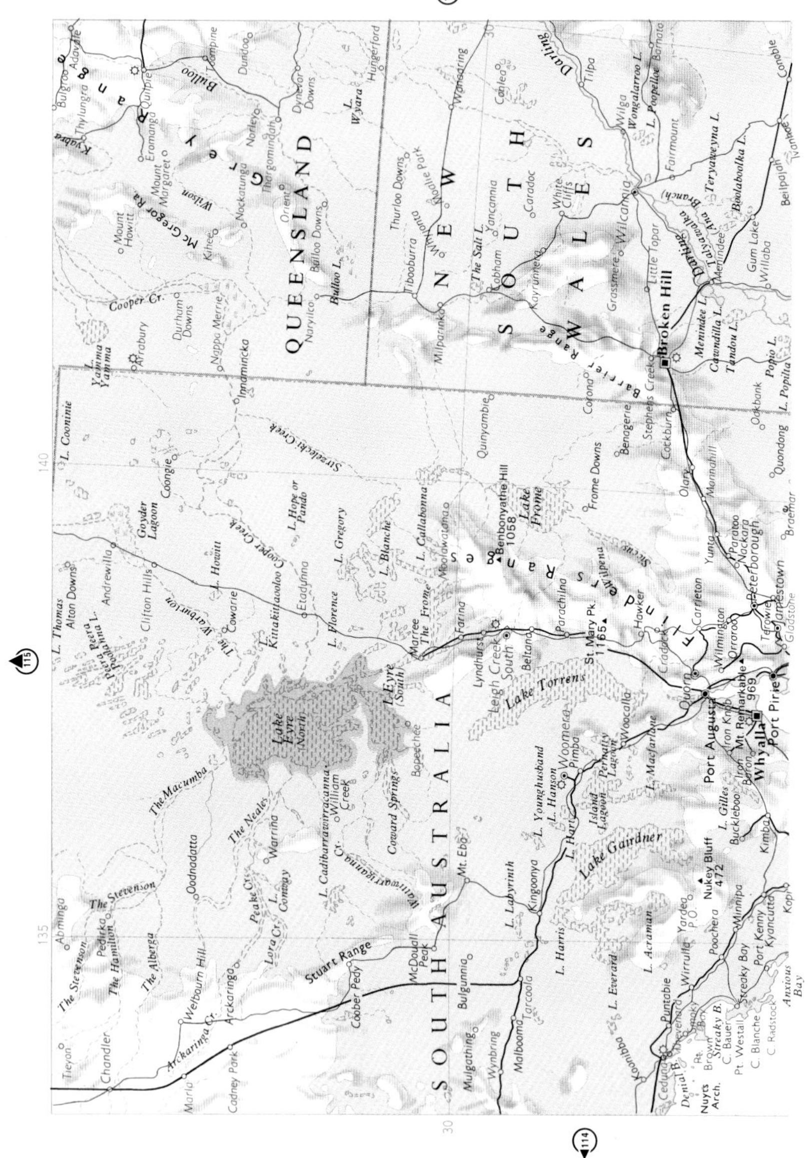

1 : 8 000 000

119

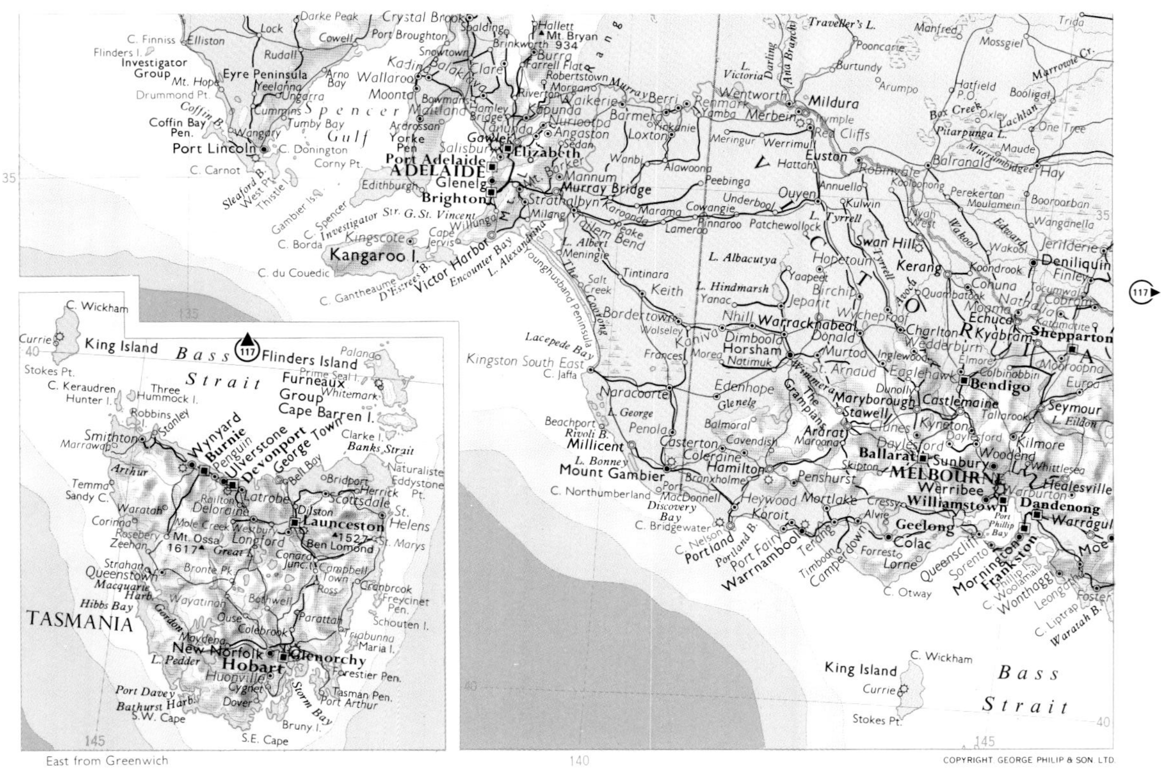

East from Greenwich

COPYRIGHT GEORGE PHILIP & SON LTD.

114

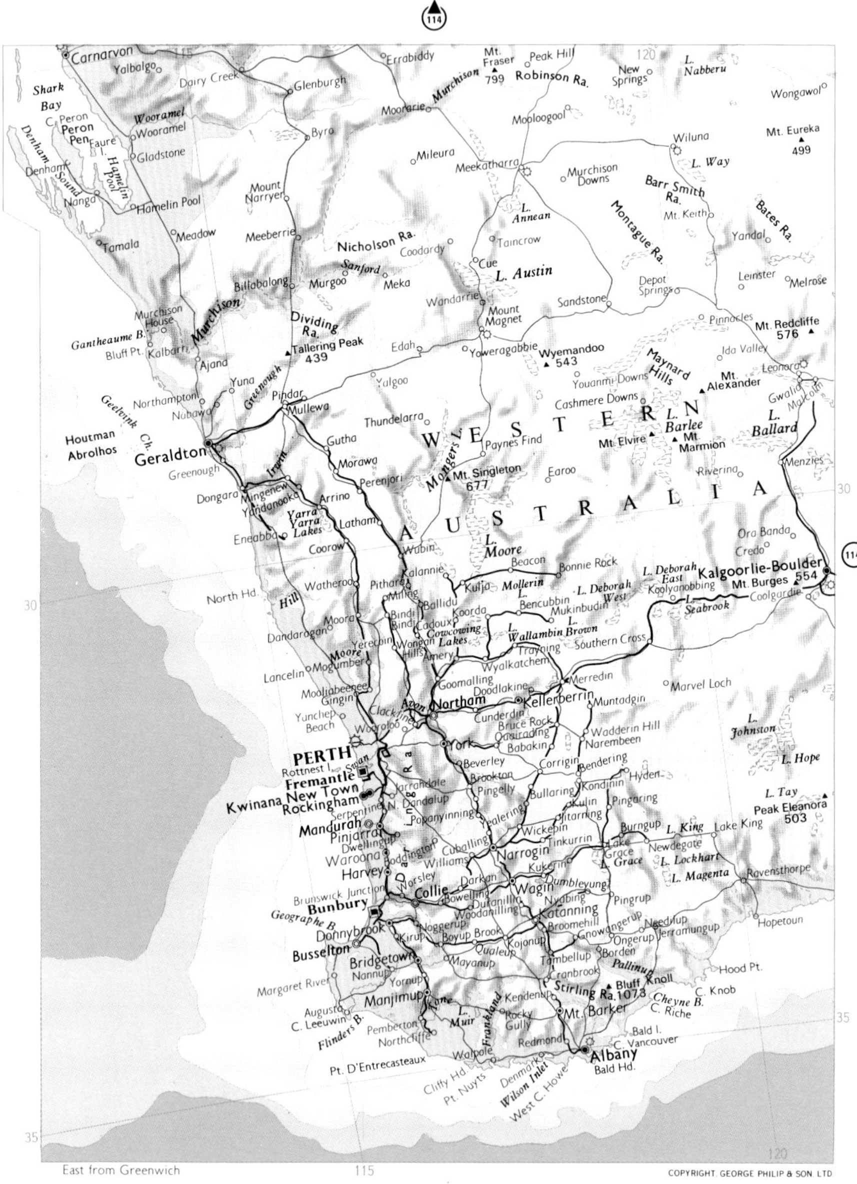
Carnarvon
Yalbalgo
Dairy Creek
Shark Bay
C. Peron
Peron Pen
Faure I.
Denham Sound
Denham
Nanga
Wooramel
Gladstone
Hamelin Pool
Tamala
Meadow
Errabiddy
Glenburgh
Byro
Moorarie
Murchison
Mt. Fraser 799
Peak Hill
Robinson Ra.
New Springs
L. Nabberu
Wongawol
Mooloogool
Wiluna
L. Way
Mt. Eureka 499
Mileura
Meekatharra
Murchison Downs
Barr Smith Ra.
Mt. Keith
Bates Ra.
Montague Ra.
L. Annean
Mount Narryer
Meeberrie
Nicholson Ra.
Coodardy
Taincrow
Cue
L. Austin
Yandal
Leinster
Melrose
Sanford
Murgoo
Meka
Billabalong
Wandarrie
Mount Magnet
Sandstone
Depot Springs
Murchison House
Gantheaume B.
Bluff Pt.
Kalbarri
Ajana
Dividing Ra.
Tallering Peak 439
Edah
Yoweragabbie
Wyemandoo 543
Pinnacles
Mt. Redcliffe 576
Ida Valley
Maynard Hills
Leonora
Mt. Alexander
Youanmi Downs
Gwalia
Malcolm
Yuna
Greenough
Northampton
Nabawa
Geelvink Ch.
Pindar
Mullewa
Yalgoo
Cashmere Downs
Houtman Abrolhos
Geraldton
Greenough
Thundelarra
Gutha
Morawa
W E S T E R N
L. Barlee
L. Ballard
Paynes Find
Mt. Elvire
Mt. Marmion
Mongers L.
Mt. Singleton 677
Menzies
Eraoo
Riverina
Perenjori
Irwin
Dongara
Mingenew
Yandanooka
Arrino
A U S T R A L I A
Yarra Yarra Lakes
Latham
Eneabba
Coorow
L. Moore
Ora Banda
Credo
Wubin
Beacon
Bonnie Rock
L. Deborah East
Kalgoorlie-Boulder
Kalannie
Mollerin
Kulja
L. Deborah West
Koolyanobbing
Mt. Burges 554
Watheroo
Pithara
Dalwallinu
Ballidu
Bencubbin
Mukinbudin
Coolgardie
L. Seabrook
North Hd.
Hill
Moora
Bindi Bindi
Cadoux
Koorda
L. Wallambin
L. Brown
Dandaragan
Cowcowing Lakes
Yerecoin
Wongan Hills
Trayning
Southern Cross
Moore
Mogumber
Lancelin
Amery
Wyalkatchem
Merredin
Marvel Loch
Goomalling
Dowerin
Doodlakine
Mooliabeenee
Gingin
Avon
Northam
Kellerberrin
Muntadgin
Yanchep Beach
Clackline
Cunderdin
Bruce Rock
L. Johnston
Wooroloo
Quairading
Wadderin Hill
Narembeen
PERTH
Swan
York
Babakin
Rottnest I.
Beverley
Corrigin
Bendering
L. Hope
Fremantle
Kwinana New Town
Rockingham
Jarrahdale
Brookton
Kondinin
Hyden
N. Dandalup
Pingelly
Bullaring
Kulin
Pingaring
L. Tay
Peak Eleanora 503
Serpentine
Darling Ra.
Popanyinning
Yealering
Jitarning
Mandurah
Pinjarra
Wickepin
Burngup
L. King
Lake King
Dwellingup
Cuballing
Narrogin
Tinkurrin
Waroona
Boddington
Williams
Lake Grace
Newdegate
Harvey
L. Grace
L. Lockhart
Kukerin
Darkan
Norsley
L. Magenta
Ravensthorpe
Brunswick Junction
Collie
Wagin
Dumbleyung
Bowelling
Dulanillin
Nyabing
Pingrup
Bunbury
Woodanilling
Katanning
Geographe B.
Noggerup
Broomehill
Needilup
Donnybrook
Kirup
Boyup Brook
Gnowangerup
Jerramungup
Hopetoun
Busselton
Qualeup
Kojonup
Ongerup
Bridgetown
Mayanup
Tambellup
Borden
Nannup
Yornup
Pallinup
Hood Pt.
Margaret River
Cranbrook
Bluff Knoll
Stirling Ra. 1073
C. Knob
Manjimup
Tone
Kendenup
Cheyne B.
Augusta
C. Leeuwin
L. Muir
Frankland
Rocky Gully
Mt. Barker
C. Riche
Flinders B.
Pemberton
Northcliffe
Redmond
Bald I.
C. Vancouver
Walpole
Albany
Bald Hd.
Pt. D'Entrecasteaux
Cliffy Hd.
Pt. Nuyts
Denmark
Wilson Inlet
West C. Howe
25
30
35
115
120
East from Greenwich
COPYRIGHT GEORGE PHILIP & SON LTD

114

1 : 8 000 000

115

CORAL SEA
Great Barrier Reef
QUEENSLAND
Great Dividing Range
Bougainville Reef
Moore Reefs
Holmes Reefs
Willis Group
Magdelaine Cays
Herald Cays
Coringa Is.
Flinders Reefs
Diamond Is.
Lihou Reefs & Cays
Abington Reef
Tregrosse Is.
Palmer
Lakeland
Rossville
1148
Bloomfield
C. Tribulation
Daintree
Mossman
Miallo
Rumula
Port Douglas
Walsh P.O.
Walsh
Mount Molloy
Clifton Beach
Mt. Mulligan
Biboohra
Kuranda
Mungana
Mareeba
Cairns
Lynd
Chillagoe
Dimbulah
Tolga
Edmonton
Gordonvale
Almaden
Atherton
1612
Deeral
Petford
Herberton
Babinda
Bullock Creek
Fossilbrook
Mount Garnet
Ravenshoe
South Johnstone
Innisfail
Mourilyan
El Arish
Tully
Dunk I.
Herbert
Mount Surprise
Bilyana
Rockingham Bay
Cardwell
C. Sandwich
Einasleigh
Hinchinbrook I.
Conjuboy
Halifax
Kidston
Carpentaria Downs
Palm Is.
The Lynd
Ingham
Gt. Palm I.
Greenvale Mine
Bambaroo
Greenvale
Seaview Ra.
Halifax Bay
Rollingstone
Burdekin
C. Cleveland
Clarke River P.O.
Townsville
Giru
C. Bowling Green
Brandon
Toonpan
Woodstock
Reid River
Ayr
Home Hill
Mingela
C. Upstart
Charters Towers
Gumlu
Guthalungra
Ravenswood
Bowen
Gloucester I.
Balfe's Creek
Homestead
Leichhardt Ra.
Binbee
Hook I.
Pentland
Dalbeg
Collinsville
Whitsunday I.
Airlie Beach
Hughenden
Shaw I.
Prairie
Torrens Creek
Clarke Ra.
Proserpine
Longton
Cape
Burdekin River Project
Yalboroo
Cumberland Islands
Torrens Cr.
1259
Kungurri
Towerhill Cr.
Yarrowmere
Kuttabul
Mackay
Mount Coolon
Netherdale
L. Buchanan
Mirani
Uanda
Mount Douglas
Suttor
Denham Ra.
Prudhoe I.
Landsborough Cr.
Connors Ra.
Sarina
Northumberland Islands
Koumala
Goonyella
Ilbilbie
Percy Is.
Nebo
L. Galilee
Moranbah
Carmila
Isaac
Broad Sd.
Long I.
Peak Downs Mine
Arthur Pt.
Muttaburra
St. Lawrence
Belyando
Miclere
Dysart
Townshend I.
Blair Athol
May Downs
Aramac
Peak Ra.
Darr
Clermont
Ogmore
C. Clinton
Cramsie
Longreach
Peak Downs
Mackenzie
C. Manifold
Ilfracombe
Marlborough
Brixton
Barcaldine
Capella
Fitzroy
Kunwarara
Water Park Pt.
Dartmouth
Lochnagar
Mt. Tabletop 823
Rubyvale
Yaamba
Yeppoon
Jericho
Emerald
Blackwater
Ridgelands
Emu Park
Anakie
Alpha
Willows
Comet
Bluff
Dingo
Rockhampton
Alice
Pinehill
Bogantungan
Gogango
Mount Morgan
Tropic of Capricorn
Yalleroi
Drummond Range
Gindie
Duaringa
Pt. Alma
Curtis I.
Nogoa
Fernlees
Dululu
Bajool
Raglan
Isisford
Blackall
Dawson Range
Mt. Larcom
Gladstone
Benlidi
Northampton Downs
Laleham
Calliope
P. Curtis
Emmet
Barcoo
Springsure
Baralaba
Callide
Castlevale
Expedition Range
Boyne
Gowan Range
Terrick Terrick
Rolleston
Biloela
Miriam Vale
Yaraka
Tambo
Carnarvon
Banana
Thangool
Nagoorin
Warrego Range
Bauhinia Downs
Moura
Dawes Ra.
1312
Barngo
Mt. King 868
Theodore
Rosedale
Bulloo
Blackwater Cr.
Langlo
Carnarvon Ra.
Cannondale Mt.
734
Monto
Bargara
150
20
25
145
150
East from Greenwich

115
116

1 : 8 000 000

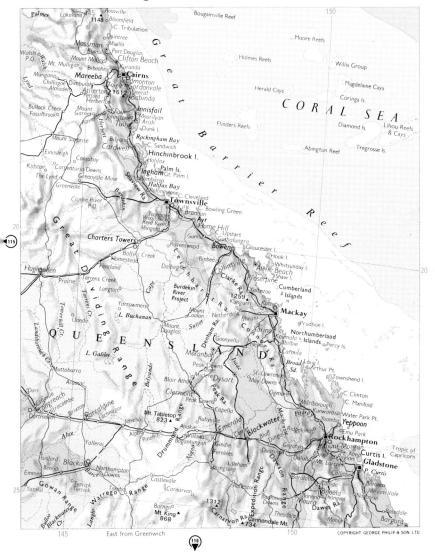

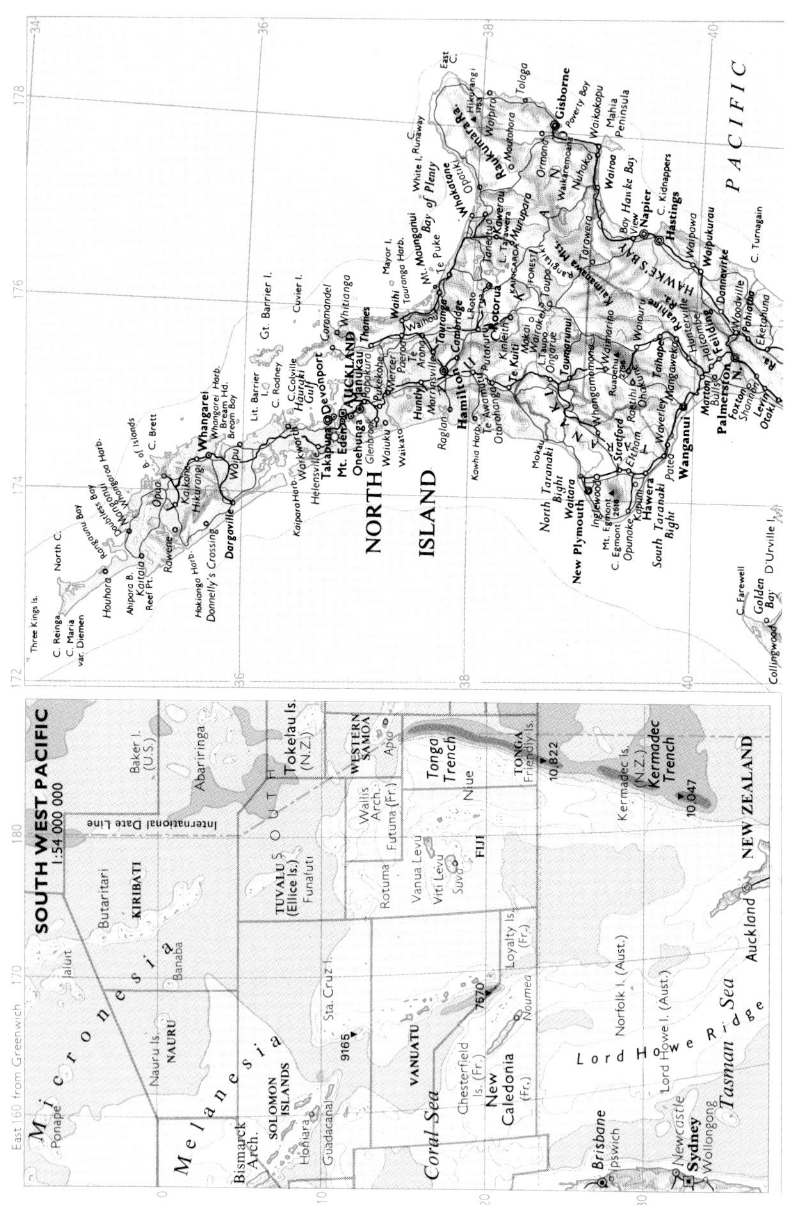

NORTH ISLAND

C. Reinga, C. Maria van Diemen, Three Kings Is., North C., Houhora, Ahipara B., Kaitaia, Reef Pt., Rawene, Opua, B. of Islands, C. Brett, Kaikohe, Hikurangi, Whangarei, Whangarei Harb., Bream Hd., Bream Bay, Whangaroa Harb., Hokianga Harb., Donnelly's Crossing, Dargaville, Wairoa, Ruawai, Kaipara Harb., Helensville, Waiuku, Waikato, Lt. Barrier I., Gt. Barrier I., Cuvier I., C. Colville, C. Rodney, Takapuna, Devonport, AUCKLAND, Mt. Eden, Onehunga, Manukau, Glenbrook, Pukekohe, Coromandel, Whitianga, Hauraki Gulf, Thames, Waihi, Paeroa, Morrinsville, Te Aroha, Tauranga, Mt. Maunganui, Te Puke, Bay of Plenty, White I., Whakatane, Opotiki, Raukumara, East C., Hicks Bay, Te Araroa, Tolaga, Tologa, Gisborne, Poverty Bay, Waikokopu, Mahia Peninsula, Nuhaka, Wairoa, Bay, Hawke Bay, C. Kidnappers, Napier, Hastings, Waipawa, Waipukurau, C. Turnagain, HAWKE'S BAY, Dannevirke, Pahiatua, Eketahuna, Masterton, Carterton, Featherston, Martinborough, Palmerston N., Feilding, Bulls, Foxton, Levin, Otaki, Wanganui, Waverley, Patea, Hawera, Eltham, Stratford, Inglewood, Waitara, New Plymouth, North Taranaki Bight, South Taranaki Bight, Mt. Egmont 2518, C. Egmont, Opunake, Kapuni, Mokau, Kawhia Harb., Raglan, Ngaruawahia, Hamilton, Cambridge, Te Awamutu, Otorohanga, Te Kuiti, Taumarunui, Ohakune, Raetihi, Waiouru, Ruapehu, Ngauruhoe, Tongariro, L. Taupo, Taupo, Wairakei, Putaruru, Tokoroa, Rotorua, L. Rotorua, L. Rotoiti, Kawerau, Murupara, Te Anau, Whakatane

PACIFIC · Collingwood, Golden Bay, Farewell, D'Urville I.

SOUTH WEST PACIFIC
1:54 000 000

East 160 from Greenwich · International Date Line

Micronesia · Melanesia

Ponape, Jaluit, Butaritari, Tarawa, KIRIBATI, Banaba, Nauru Is., NAURU, Bismarck Arch., SOLOMON ISLANDS, Hoihara, Guadalcanal, 9165, Sta. Cruz Is., VANUATU, 7570, New Caledonia (Fr.), Chesterfield Is. (Fr.), Noumea, Loyalty Is. (Fr.), Coral Sea, Brisbane, Ipswich, Newcastle, Sydney, Wollongong, Lord Howe I. (Aust.), Lord Howe Ridge, Norfolk I. (Aust.), Tasman Sea

Baker I. (U.S.), Abariringa, Tokelau Is. (N.Z.), WESTERN SAMOA, Apia, Wallis Arch., Futuna (Fr.), Rotuma, Vanua Levu, Viti Levu, Suva, FIJI, Niue, Tonga Trench, TONGA (Friendly) Is., 10,822, Kermadec Is. (N.Z.), Kermadec Trench, 10,047, Auckland, NEW ZEALAND, Tuvalu (Ellice Is.), Funafuti

115

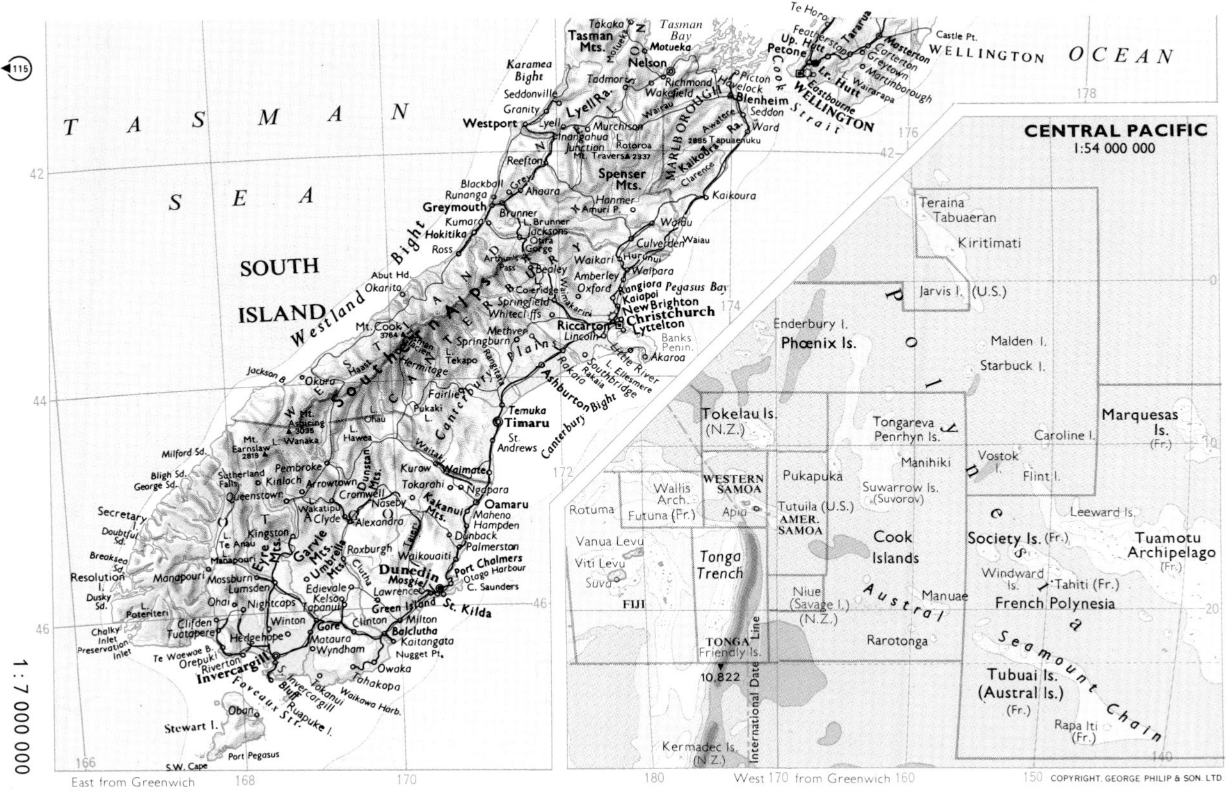

TASMAN SEA
WELLINGTON OCEAN
SOUTH ISLAND
Westland Bight
Southern Alps
Canterbury Plains
Canterbury Bight
Cook Strait
Foveaux Str.
Tasman Bay
Karamea Bight
Pegasus Bay
Takaka
Tasman Mts.
Motueka
Nelson
Tadmor
Richmond
Wakefield
Seddonville
Granity
Westport
Lyell
Lyell Ra.
Murchison
Inangahua Junction
L. Rotoroa
Mt. Travers 2337
Reefton
Spenser Mts.
MARLBOROUGH
Kaikoura Ra.
Tapuaenuku 2885
Awatere
Clarence
Kaikoura
Picton
Havelock
Blenheim
Seddon
Ward
Te Horo
Featherston
Up. Hutt
Petone
Lr. Hutt
Eastbourne
WELLINGTON
Tararua
Masterton
Carterton
Greytown
Martinborough
Wairarapa
Castle Pt.
Blackball
Runanga
Greymouth
Ahaura
Brunner
L. Brunner
Jacksons
Otira Gorge
Kumara
Hokitika
Ross
Arthur's Pass
Bealey
Hanmer
Amuri P.
Waiau
Culverden
Hurunui
Waikari
Waipara
Amberley
Oxford
Rangiora
Kaiapoi
New Brighton
Christchurch
Lyttelton
Riccarton
Lincoln
Banks Penin.
Akaroa
Little River
L. Ellesmere
Southbridge
Rakaia
Ashburton
Coleridge
Springfield
Whitecliffs
Waimakariri
Methven
Springburn
Abut Hd.
Okarito
Mt. Cook 3764
Tasman Glacier
Hermitage
L. Tekapo
Rangitata
Fairlie
L. Pukaki
Temuka
Timaru
St. Andrews
Jackson B.
Okuru
Haast
Mt. Aspiring 3035
L. Wanaka
L. Ohau
L. Hawea
Mt. Earnslaw 2819
Milford Sd.
Bligh Sd.
George Sd.
Sutherland Falls
Kinloch
Pembroke
Arrowtown
Queenstown
Dunstan Mts.
Cromwell
Kurow
Waitaki
Waimate
Tokarahi
Ngapara
Kakanui Mts.
Oamaru
Maheno
Hampden
Naseby
Wakatipu
Clyde
Alexandra
Secretary I.
Doubtful Sd.
Breaksea Sd.
Resolution I.
Dusky Sd.
L. Te Anau
Kingston
Eyre Mts.
Garvie Mts.
Umbrella Mts.
Roxburgh
Taieri
Dunback
Palmerston
Waikouaiti
Port Chalmers
Otago Harbour
C. Saunders
Dunedin
Mosgiel
St. Kilda
Manapouri
L. Manapouri
Mossburn
Lumsden
Clutha
Edievale
Kelso
Tapanui
Lawrence
Green Island
Milton
L. Poteriteri
Ohai
Nightcaps
Winton
Gore
Clinton
Balclutha
Kaitangata
Clifden
Tuatapere
Hedgehope
Mataura
Wyndham
Nugget Pt.
Owaka
Tahakopa
Chalky Inlet
Preservation Inlet
Te Waewae B.
Orepuki
Riverton
Invercargill
Bluff
Tokanui
Waikawa Harb.
Ruapuke I.
Oban
Stewart I.
Port Pegasus
S.W. Cape
East from Greenwich
1 : 7 000 000
CENTRAL PACIFIC
1:54 000 000
Teraina
Tabuaeran
Kiritimati
Jarvis I. (U.S.)
Enderbury I.
Phœnix Is.
Malden I.
Starbuck I.
Polynesia
Tokelau Is. (N.Z.)
Tongareva Penrhyn Is.
Manihiki
Caroline I.
Marquesas Is. (Fr.)
Vostok I.
Flint I.
WESTERN SAMOA
Apia
Wallis Arch.
Futuna (Fr.)
Rotuma
Pukapuka
Suwarrow Is. (Suvorov)
Tutuila (U.S.)
AMER. SAMOA
Leeward Is.
Society Is. (Fr.)
Tuamotu Archipelago (Fr.)
Vanua Levu
Viti Levu
Suva
FIJI
Tonga Trench
Cook Islands
Windward Is.
Tahiti (Fr.)
French Polynesia
Niue (Savage I.) (N.Z.)
Austral
Manuae
Rarotonga
Seamount Chain
TONGA Friendly Is.
10,822
International Date Line
Tubuai Is. (Austral Is.) (Fr.)
Rapa Iti (Fr.)
Kermadec Is. (N.Z.)
West 170 from Greenwich 160
COPYRIGHT, GEORGE PHILIP & SON, LTD.

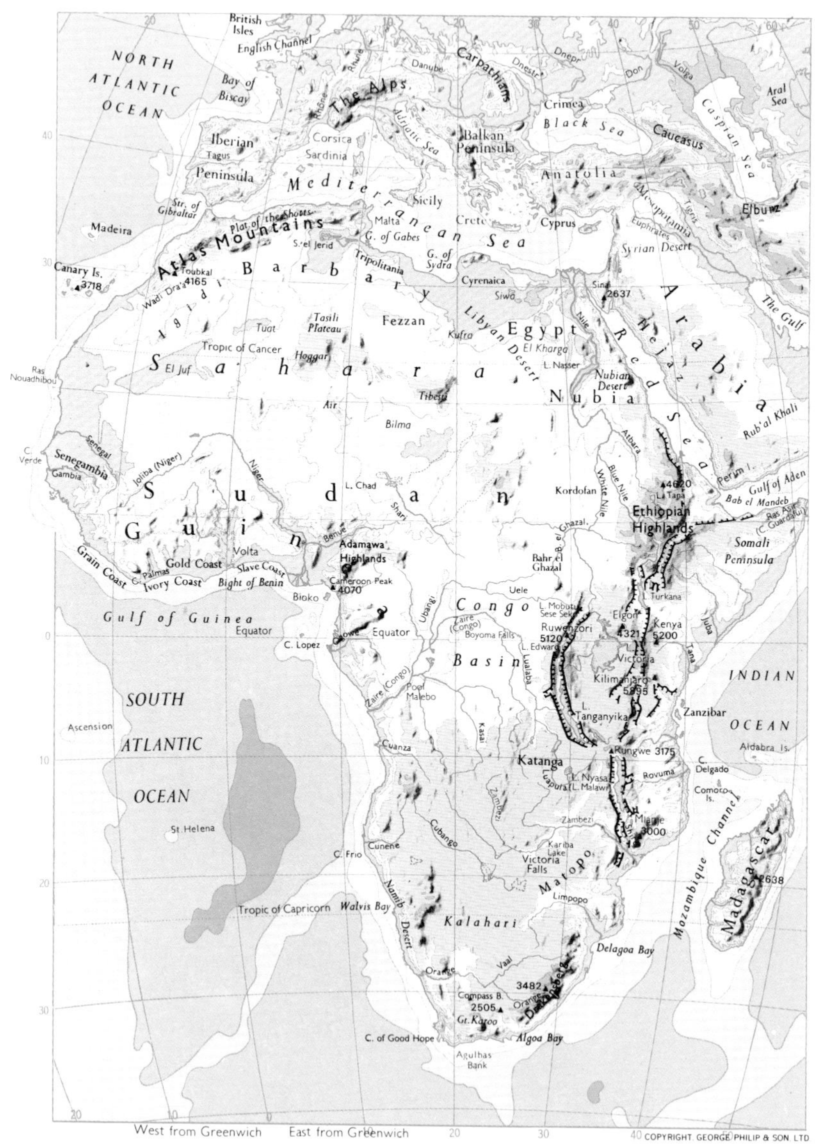
British Isles
English Channel
NORTH ATLANTIC OCEAN
Bay of Biscay
Rhine
Danube
Carpathians
Dnestr
Dnepr
Don
Volga
Aral Sea
Rhône
The Alps
Crimea
Black Sea
Caspian Sea
Caucasus
Iberian Peninsula
Tagus
Corsica
Sardinia
Adriatic Sea
Balkan Peninsula
Anatolia
Mediterranean Sea
Sicily
Str. of Gibraltar
Madeira
Plat. of the Shotts
Atlas Mountains
Malta
G. of Gabes
Crete
Cyprus
Tigris
Mesopotamia
Euphrates
Elburz
S. el Jerid
G. of Sydra
Syrian Desert
Canary Is.
3718
Toubkal 4165
Wadi Dra'a
Barbary
Tripolitania
Cyrenaica
Siwa
Sinai
2637
Arabia
The Gulf
Igidi
Tuat
Tasili Plateau
Fezzan
Kufra
Egypt
El Kharga
Libyan Desert
Nile
Hejaz
Red Sea
Tropic of Cancer
Hoggar
L. Nasser
Nubian Desert
Ras Nouadhibou
Sahara
El Juf
Tibesti
Nubia
Air
Bilma
Rub'al Khali
C. Verde
Senegal
Senegambia
Gambia
Joliba (Niger)
Niger
Atbara
Perim I.
Gulf of Aden
Sudan
L. Chad
Kordofan
Blue Nile
White Nile
4620
Ras Dashan
Bab el Mandeb
Ras Asir (C. Guardafui)
Shari
Ethiopian Highlands
Guinea
Benue
B. el Ghazal
Somali Peninsula
Volta
Adamawa Highlands
Grain Coast
C. Palmas
Gold Coast
Slave Coast
Ivory Coast
Bight of Benin
Bahr el Ghazal
Cameroon Peak
4070
Bioko
Uele
L. Turkana
Ubangi
Congo Basin
L. Mobutu Sese Seko
Elgon
Kenya
Gulf of Guinea
Equator
Zaire (Congo)
Boyoma Falls
Ruwenzori 5120
4321
5200
Juba
C. Lopez
Ogowe
L. Edward
Lualaba
Victoria
Tana
INDIAN OCEAN
SOUTH ATLANTIC OCEAN
Zaire (Congo)
Pool Malebo
Kilimanjaro
5895
Ascension
L. Tanganyika
Zanzibar
Kasai
Aldabra Is.
Cuanza
Katanga
Rungwe 3175
C. Delgado
Luapula
L. Nyasa (L. Malawi)
Rovuma
Zambezi
Comoro Is.
St. Helena
Mlanje 3000
Shire
Cubango
Cunene
Kariba Lake
C. Frio
Victoria Falls
Mozambique Channel
Madagascar
2638
Matopo
Namib Desert
Limpopo
Tropic of Capricorn
Walvis Bay
Kalahari
Delagoa Bay
Orange
Vaal
3482
Drakensberg
Compass B. 2505
Gt. Karoo
C. of Good Hope
Algoa Bay
Agulhas Bank
West from Greenwich
East from Greenwich

1 : 70 000 000

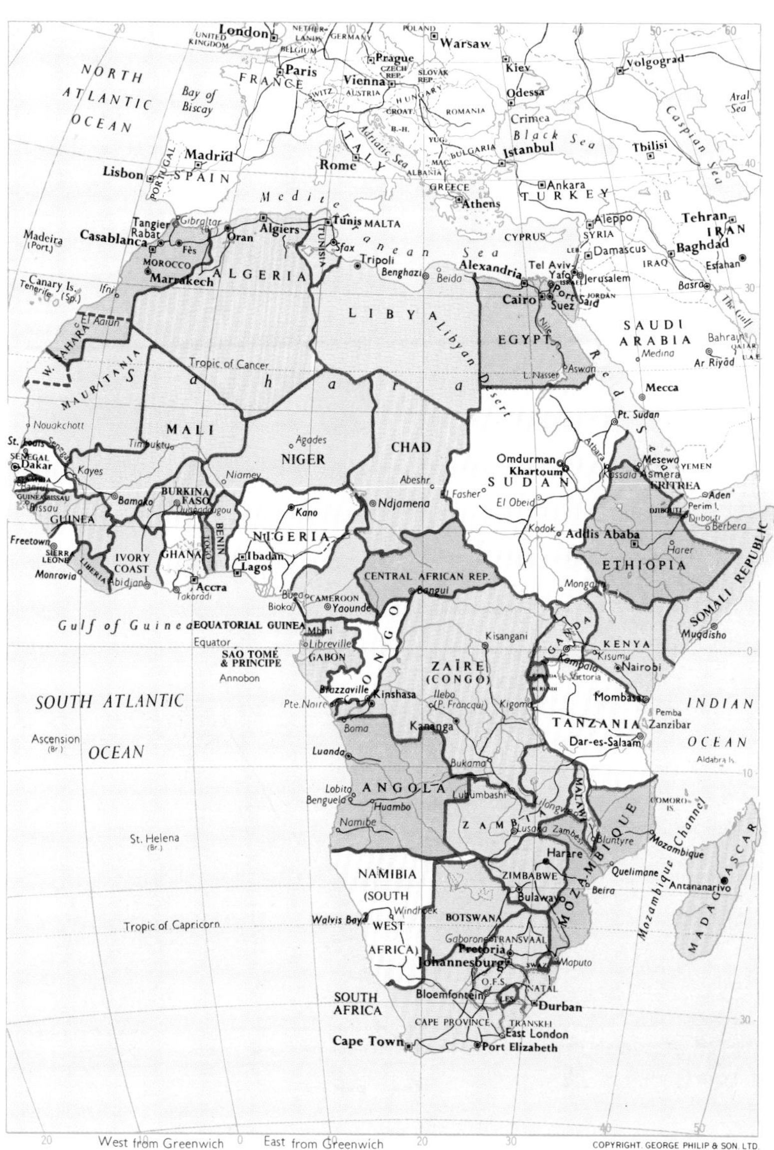

1 : 70 000 000

50

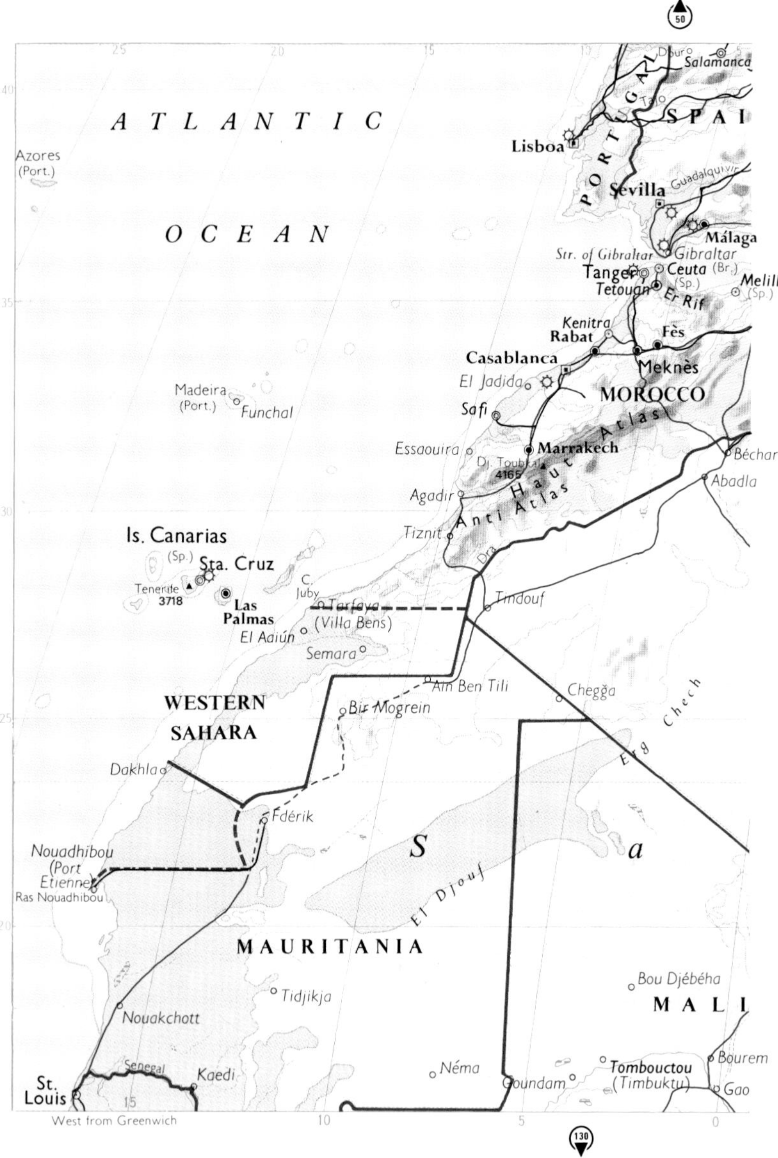
ATLANTIC
OCEAN
Azores
(Port.)
PORTUGAL
SPAI
Lisboa
Salamanca
Sevilla
Guadalquivir
Málaga
Str. of Gibraltar
Gibraltar
Tanger
Ceuta (Br.)
(Sp.)
Tetouan
Er Rif
Melill
(Sp.)
Kenitra
Rabat
Fès
Casablanca
Meknès
El Jadida
MOROCCO
Madeira
(Port.)
Funchal
Safi
Essaouira
Marrakech
Dj. Toubkal
4165
Haut Atlas
Béchar
Abadla
Agadir
Anti Atlas
Tiznit
Dra
Is. Canarias
(Sp.)
Sta. Cruz
Tenerife
3718
Las
Palmas
C.
Juby
Tarfaya
(Villa Bens)
Tindouf
El Aaiún
Semara
Aïn Ben Tili
Chegga
WESTERN
SAHARA
Bir Mogrein
Erg Chech
Dakhla
Fdérik
Nouadhibou
(Port
Etienne)
Ras Nouadhibou
S
a
El Djouf
MAURITANIA
Bou Djébéha
Tidjikja
MALI
Nouakchott
Senegal
Néma
Tombouctou
(Timbuktu)
Bourem
St.
Louis
Kaedi
Goundam
Gao
West from Greenwich

130

1 : 20 000 000

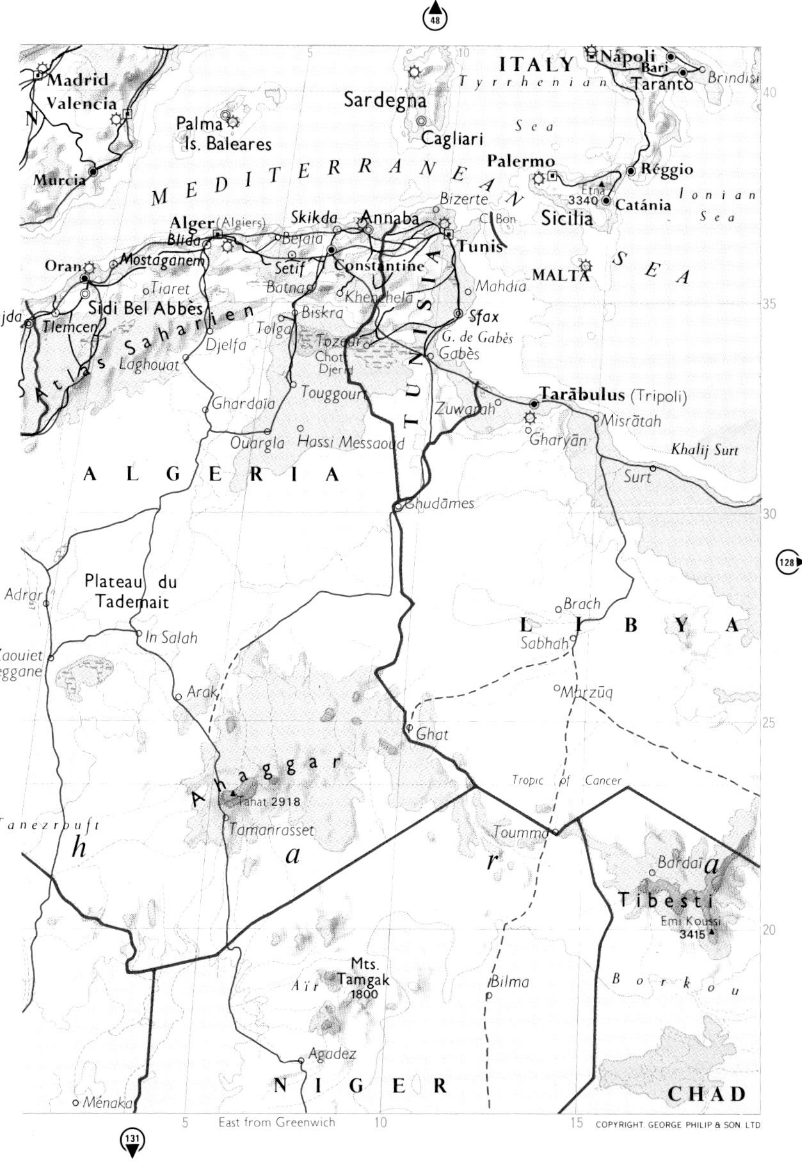

48

ITALY **Nápoli**
Bari
Taranto Brindisi

Tyrrhenian

Sardegna

Cagliari

Sea

Palermo

Etna
3340 **Catánia** **Réggio**

Sicilia *Ionian*

Sea

MEDITERRANEAN

Madrid
Valencia

Palma
Is. Baleares

Murcia

Bizerte
C. Bon

MALTA

S E A

Alger (Algiers)   Skikda   **Annaba**
Blida   Bejaia
Tunis

Oran **Mostaganem**
Setif   **Constantine**

ujda   **Sidi Bel Abbès**   *Tiaret*
Batna   Khenchela   *Mahdia*

Tlemcen   Biskra   **Sfax**
Tolga
Djelfa   Tozeur   G. de Gabès
Chott   **Gabès**
Laghouat   Djerid

Ghardaïa   Touggourt   Zuwárah   **Tarābulus** (Tripoli)
Gharyān   Misrātah

Ouargla   Hassi Messaoud   Surt   Khalij Surt

A L G E R I A   Ghudāmes

Plateau du
Tademaīt   Brach   **L   I   B   Y   A**

Adrar   Sabhah

Zaouiet
eggane   In Salah
Arak   Marzūq

Ghat

A h a g g a r   Tropic of Cancer

Tanezrouft   Tahat 2918
h   Tamanrasset   Toumma   *r*   *a*

a   Bardaï

T i b e s t i
Emi Koussi
3415 ▲

Mts.
Tamgak   Bilma   *B o r k o u*
Aïr   1800

Agadez

N   I   G   E   R   **C H A D**

Ménaka

128

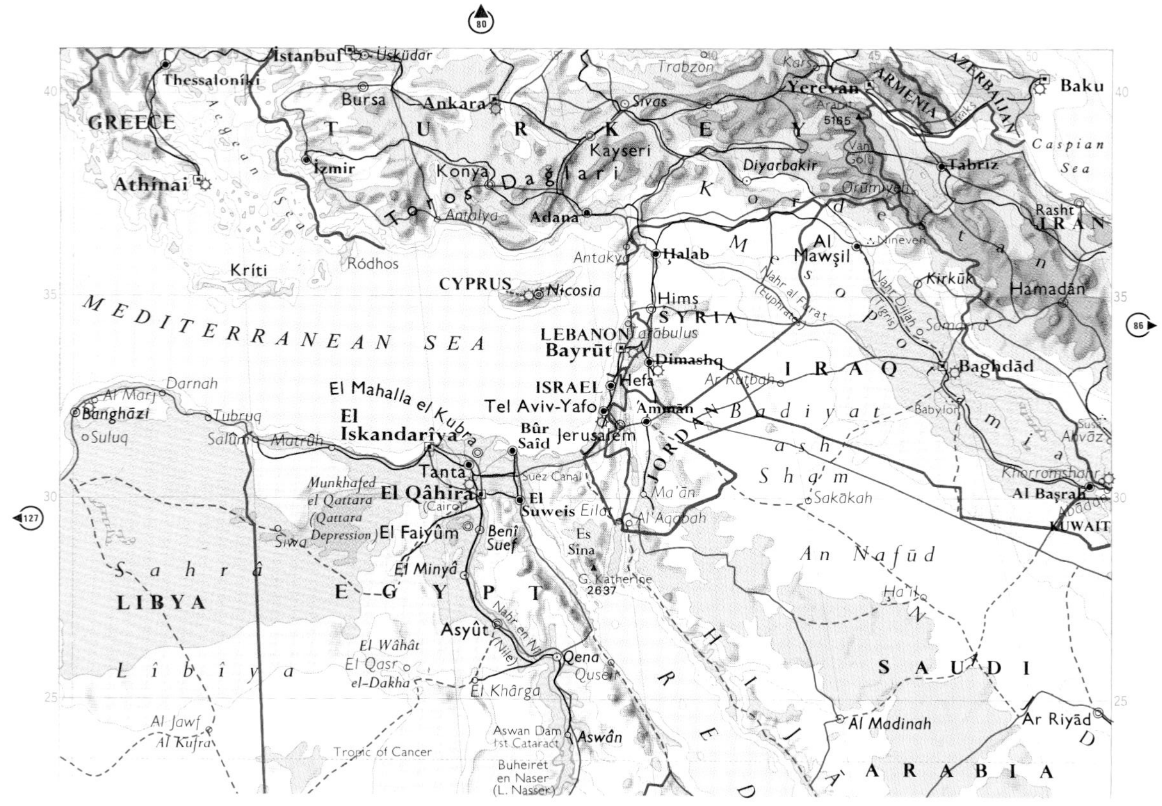
MEDITERRANEAN SEA
TURKEY
SYRIA
LEBANON
ISRAEL
JORDAN
IRAQ
IRAN
CYPRUS
EGYPT
LIBYA
SAUDI ARABIA
KUWAIT
GREECE
ARMENIA
AZERBAIJAN
Istanbul
Üsküdar
Ankara
Izmir
Bursa
Konya
Adana
Antalya
Kayseri
Sivas
Trabzon
Kars
Diyarbakir
Toros Dağlari
Kordestan
Mesopotamia
Antakya
Halab
Hims
Tarabulus
Dimashq
Bayrūt
Hefa
Tel Aviv-Yafo
Jerusalem
'Ammān
Ma'ān
Al 'Aqabah
Eilat
Ar Rutbah
Badiyat ash Sham
Baghdād
Babylon
Samarra
Al Başrah
Khorramshahr
Ahvāz
Susa
Abadan
Kirkūk
Al Mawşil
Nineveh
Nahr Dijlah (Tigris)
Nahr al Furat (Euphrates)
Tabrīz
Orūmīyeh
Van Gölü
Ararat
5165
Hamadān
Rasht
Baku
Yerevan
Thessaloníki
Athínai
Kríti
Ródhos
Aegean Sea
Nicosia
Darnah
Al Marj
Banghāzi
Suluq
Tubruq
Salûm
Matrûh
El Mahalla el Kubra
El Iskandarîya
Tanta
Bûr Saîd
Suez Canal
El Qâhira (Cairo)
El Suweis
El Faiyûm
Benî Suef
El Minyâ
Asyût
Qena
Quseir
Aswân
Aswan Dam
1st Cataract
Buheiret en Naser (L. Nasser)
Munkhafed el Qattara (Qattara Depression)
Siwa
El Wâhât
El Qasr
el-Dakha
El Khârga
Es Sina
G. Katherine
2637
Nahr en Nil (Nile)
Sahrâ Lîbîya
Al Jawf
Al Kufra
Tropic of Cancer
An Nafūd
Sakākah
Ha'il
Al Madinah
Ar Riyād
Hijaz
Red Sea
Caspian Sea

1 : 20 000 000

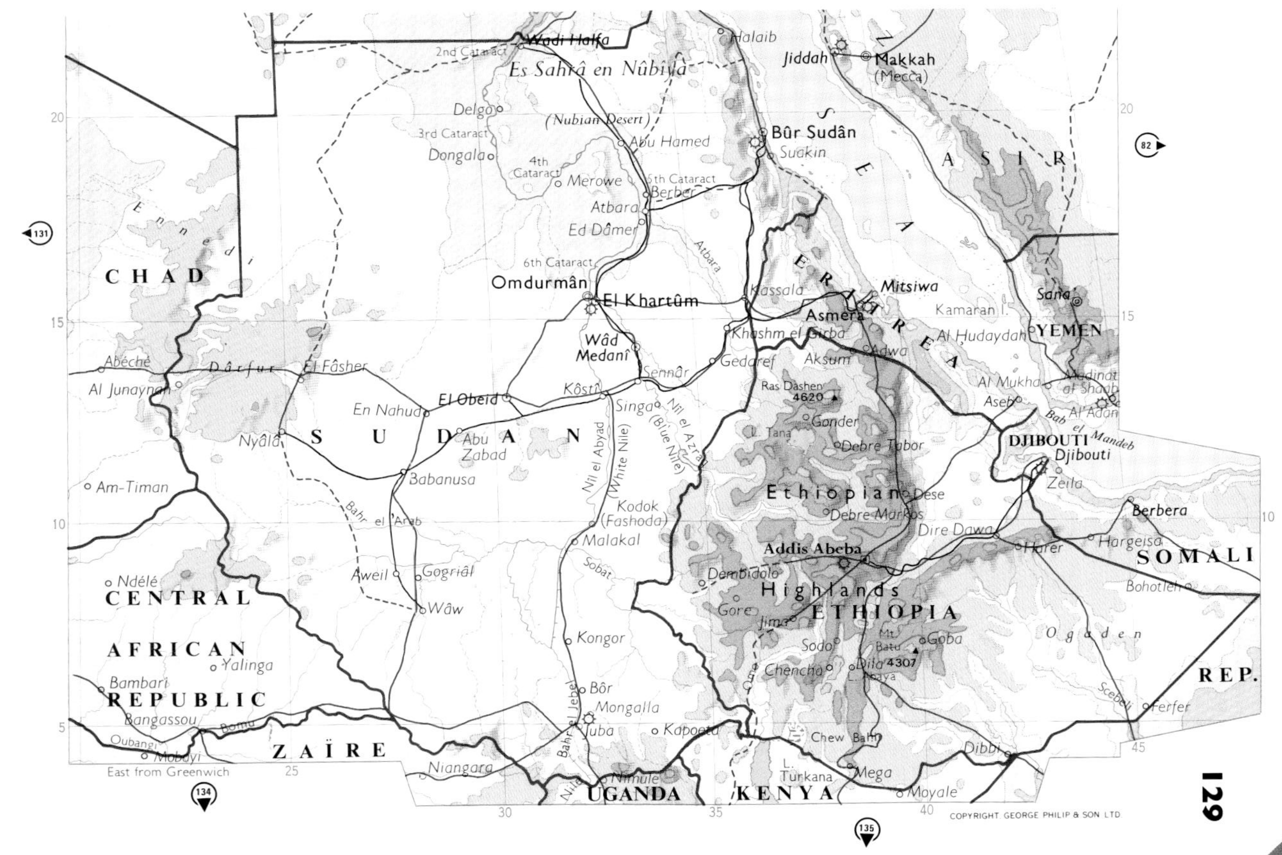

SOMALI
REP.

Berbera

SOMALI

Bohotleh

O g a d e n

Scebi Scerfer

Jiddah

Makkah
(Mecca)

N A S I R

S E A

R E D

Sana

YEMEN

Kamaran I.

Al Hudaydah
Al Mukhao

Al Luhayyah

Bab el Mandeb

Al Mukha

DJIBOUTI

Djibouti

Zeila

Asel

Harqeisa

Hargeisa

Dibba

Berbera

Būr Sudân

Suakin

Halaib

Mitsiwa

E R I T R E A

Asmera

Dire Dawa

ETHIOPIA

Gaba

Mt.
1d 4307

E t h i o p i a n

Highlands

Moyale

Es Sahrâ en Nûbiva

Kassala

Khashm el Girba

Gedaref

Aksum

Ras Dashen
4620

Debre Tabor

Debre Markos

Addis Abeba

Dembidolo

Gore

Jima

Sodo

Chencha

Soddo

Chew Bahir

L.
Turkana

Mega

KENYA

Wadi Halfa

Abū Hamed

(Nubian Desert)

4th
Cataract

Merowe

Atbara

Atbara

Ed Dâmer

Berber

5th Cataract

6th Cataract

El Khartûm

Omdurmân

Wâd
Medanî

Nîl el Azraq
(Blue Nile)

Sennar

Kôsti

Singa

Nîl el Abyad
(White Nile)

Kodok
(Fashoda)

Malakal

Sobat

Kongor

Bôr

Bahr el Jebel

Mongalla

Juba

UGANDA

Nile

Delgo

3rd Cataract

Dongola

2nd Cataract

Dongola

S U D A N

El Obeid

Abu
Zabad

En Nahud

Babanusa

Gogrial

Wâw

Bahr el Arab

Aweil

Niangara

ZAIRE

Darfur

El Fâsher

Nyala

CENTRAL

AFRICAN

REPUBLIC

Ndélé

Ydinga

Bambari

Bangassou

Am-Timan

Abéché

Al Junaynah

C H A D

E n n e d i

126

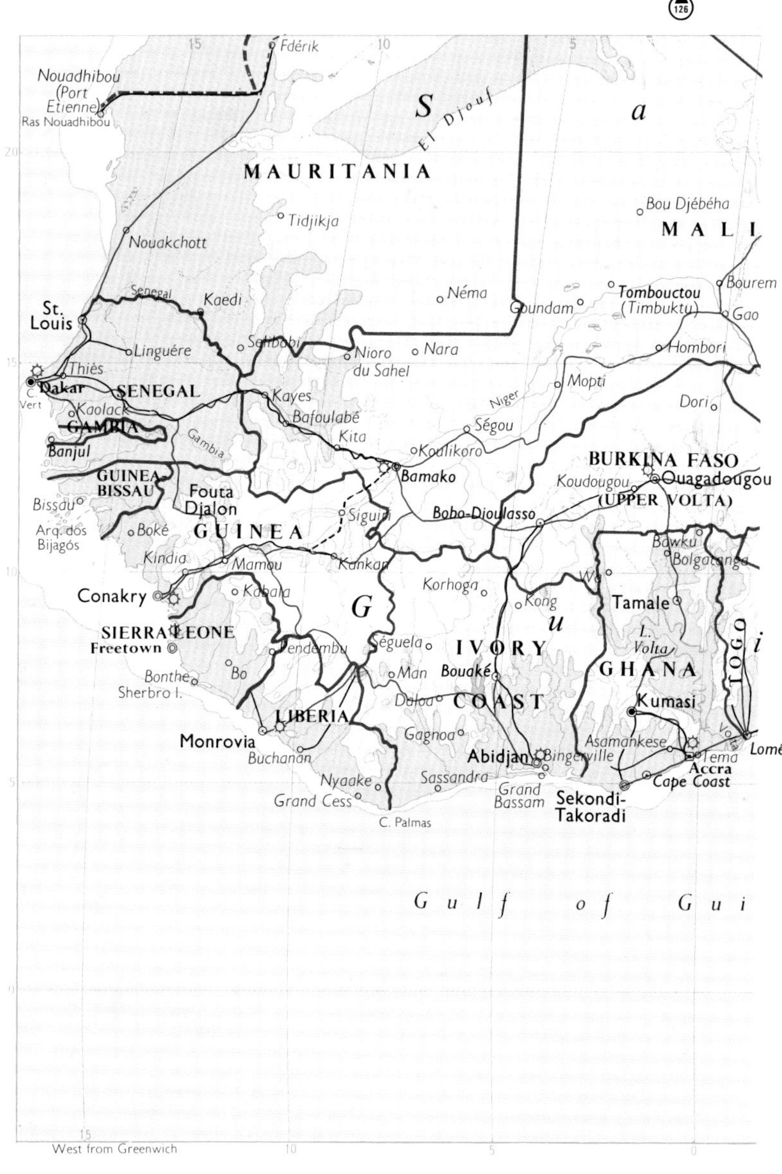

Fdérik
Nouadhibou (Port Etienne)
Ras Nouadhibou
S a
El Djouf
MAURITANIA
Bou Djébéha
MALI
Tidjikja
Nouakchott
Bourem
Senegal
Néma
Tombouctou (Timbuktu)
St. Louis
Kaedi
Goundam
Gao
Linguére
Selibabi
Nioro du Sahel
Nara
Hombori
Thiès
Dakar
C. Vert
SENEGAL
Mopti
Kayes
Niger
Dori
Kaolack
GAMBIA
Bafoulabé
Ségou
Gambia
Kita
Banjul
Koulikoro
BURKINA FASO
GUINEA-BISSAU
Bamako
Koudougou
Ouagadougou
Fouta Djalon
(UPPER VOLTA)
Bissau
Siguiri
Bobo-Dioulasso
Arq. dos Bijagós
Boké
GUINEA
Bawku
Kindia
Bolgatanga
Mamou
Kankan
Wa
Conakry
Kabala
Korhogo
Tamale
Kong
G u i
SIERRA LEONE
Freetown
L. Volta
Pendembu
Séguela
IVORY COAST
GHANA
TOGO
Bonthe
Bo
Man
Bouaké
Sherbro I.
Daloa
Kumasi
LIBERIA
Gagnoa
Asamankese
Volta
Monrovia
Abidjan
Bingerville
Tema
Lomé
Buchanan
Accra
Sassandra
Cape Coast
Nyaake
Grand Bassam
Grand Cess
Sekondi-Takoradi
C. Palmas
Gulf of Gui
West from Greenwich

1 : 20 000 000

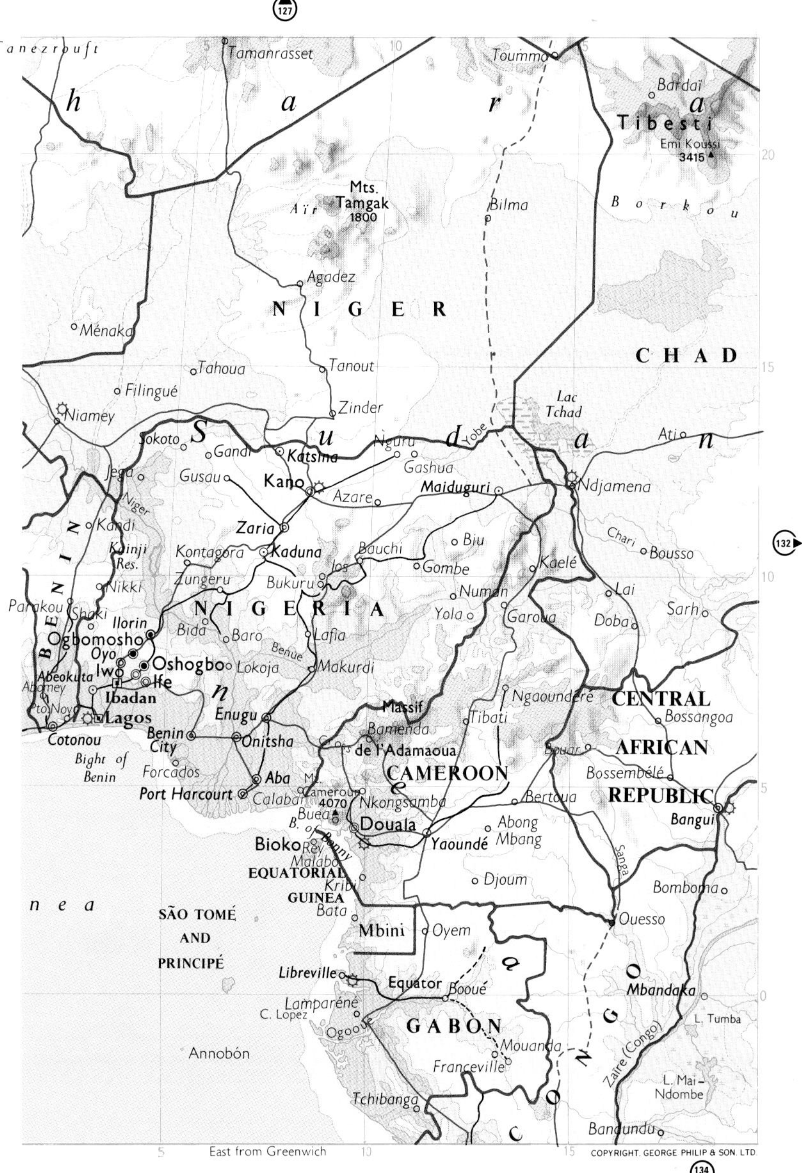

anezrouft

Tamanrasset

Toummo

Bardaï

Tibesti
Emi Koussi
3415 ▲

h   *a*   *r*   *a*

Mts.
Tamgak
1800

Aïr

Bilma

B o r k o u

20

Agadez

N I G E R

C H A D

Ménaka

15

Tahoua   Tanout

Niamey   Filingué   Zinder   Lac
Tchad   Atï

Sokoto   *S*   *u*   Ngaru   *d*   *a*   *n*
Gandi   Katsina   Yobe

Jega   Gusau   **Kano**   Ndjamena

Kcontagora   **Zaria** Azare   Gashua
Kaduna   Maiduguri

Niger   Kainji   Kaduna   Bauchi   Biu   Chari   Bousso
Res.   Zungeru   Jos   Bukuru Gombe   Kaélé
Nikki   Numan   Lai
Parakou   Shaki   Ilorin   Bida   Baro   Benue   Yola   Garoua   Doba   Sarh

B Ogbomosho Oyo   Lafia
E Abeokuta Iwo   Oshogbo Lokoja Makurdi
N Adamey   Ife   *n*   Ngaoundéré   **CENTRAL**
I Lagos   Ibadan   Enugu   Massif   Tibati   Bossangoa
Cotonou   Benin   Onitsha   Bamenda   **AFRICAN**
Bight of   City   de l'Adamaoua   Sanaga   Bossembélé
Benin   Forcados   Aba   **CAMEROON**   Bertoua   **REPUBLIC**
Port Harcourt Calabar Cameroun   Abong   Djoum   Bangui
Bioko Buea 4070 **Douala** Yaoundé Mbang

n e a   SÃO TOMÉ   Malabo
AND   **EQUATORIAL**   Kribi   Bomba
PRINCIPE   **GUINEA**   Bata   Ouesso

Libreville   Mbini   Oyem
Equator   Booué
Lamparéné   *a*   Mbandaka   0
C. Lopez   Ogooué   **GABON**   L. Tumba
Annobón   Mouanda
Franceville   L. Mai-
Ndombe
Tchibanga   Bandundu

5   East from Greenwich   10   15   COPYRIGHT GEORGE PHILIP & SON LTD

Bight of Benin

128

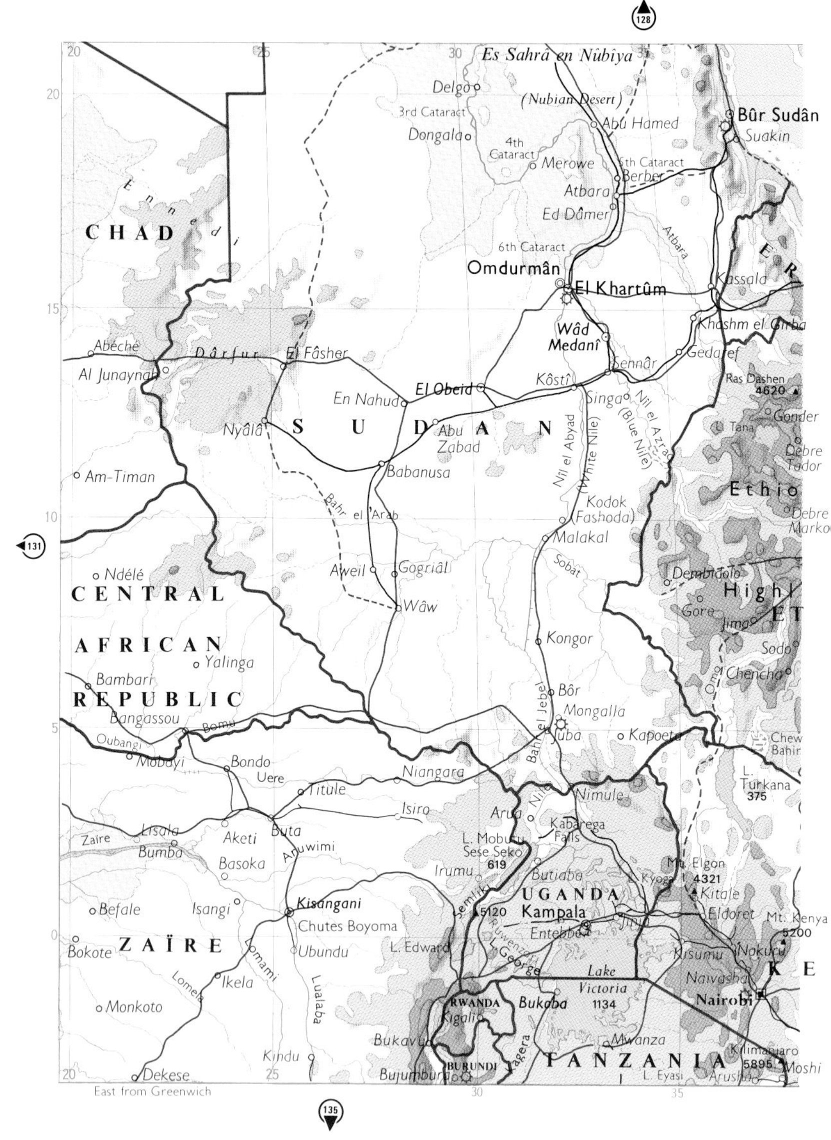

Es Sahrâ en Nûbîya
(Nubian Desert)
Delgo
3rd Cataract
Dongala
4th Cataract
Merowe
Abû Hamed
Bûr Sudân
Suakin
5th Cataract
Berber
Atbara
Ed Dâmer
6th Cataract
Omdurmân
El Khartûm
Kassala
Khashm el Girba
Wâd Medanî
Gedaref
Sennâr
Kôstî
Singa
El Obeid
En Nahud
El Fâsher
Dârfur
Abéché
Al Junaynah
Nyâlâ
SUDAN
Abu Zabad
Babanusa
Nil el Abyad (White Nile)
Nil el Azraq (Blue Nile)
Kodok (Fashoda)
Malakal
Sobat
Bahr el 'Arab
Aweil
Gogriâl
Wâw
Kongor
Bôr
Mongalla
Juba
Kapoeta
Bahr el Jebel
CHAD
Ennedi
Am-Timan
Ndélé
CENTRAL AFRICAN REPUBLIC
Yalinga
Bambari
Bangassou
Bomu
Oubangi
Mobayi
Bondo
Uere
Niangara
Titule
Isiro
Buta
Aketi
Lisala
Zaïre
Bumba
Basoka
Aruwimi
Kisangani
Chutes Boyoma
Isangi
Befale
Bokote
ZAÏRE
Ubundu
Lomami
Lomela
Ikela
Monkoto
Lualaba
Kindu
Dekese
Ras Dashen 4620
Gonder
Tana
Debre Tabor
Ethio
Debre Marko
Dembidolo
Gore
Jima
High
Sodo
Chencha
Omo
Chew Bahir
L. Turkana 375
Nimule
Nile
Arua
Kabarega Falls
L. Mobutu Sese Seko 619
Irumu
Butiaba
Kyoga
Mt. Elgon 4321
Kitale
UGANDA
Kampala
Entebbe
Jinja
Semliki
5120
Ruwenzori
L. George
L. Edward
Eldoret
Mt. Kenya 5200
Kisumu
Nakuru
Naivasha
Nairobi
Lake Victoria 1134
RWANDA
Kigali
Bukoba
Bukavu
Kagera
Mwanza
BURUNDI
Bujumbura
TANZANIA
L. Eyasi
Kilimanjaro 5895
Arusha
Moshi
20
25
30
35
15
10
5
0
East from Greenwich

131

135

1 : 20 000 000

82

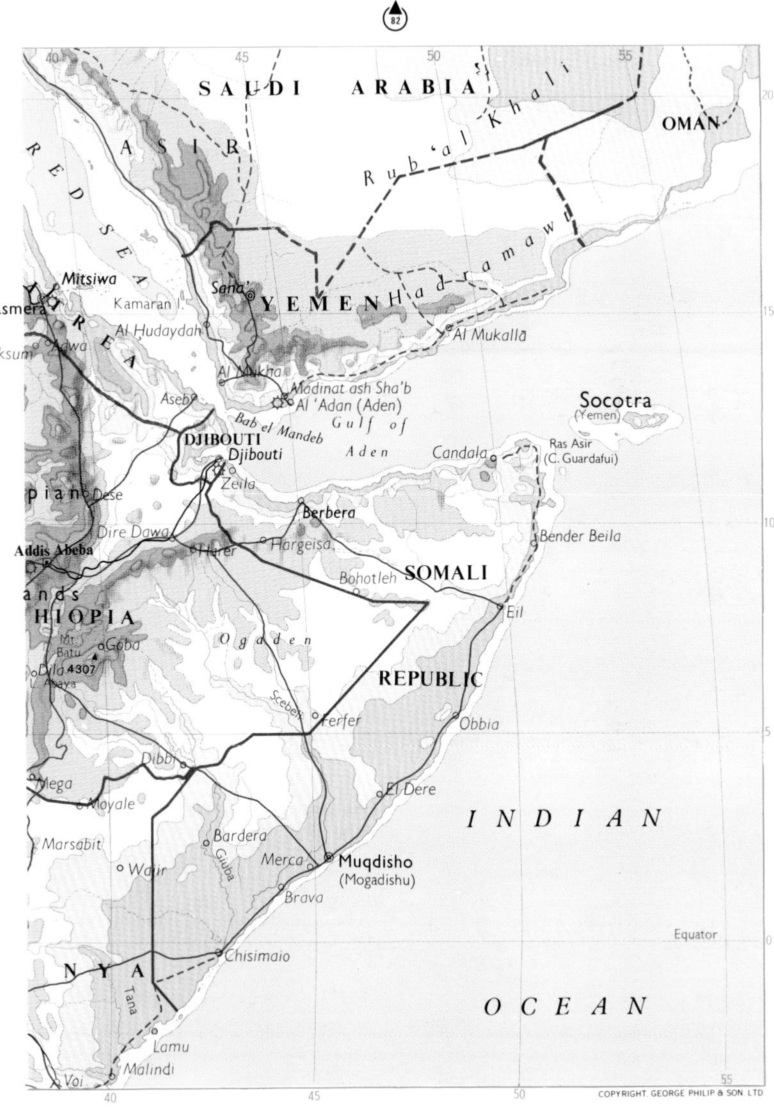
SAUDI ARABIA
OMAN
Rub 'al Khali
ASIR
RED SEA
YEMEN
Hadramawt
Sana'
Mitsiwa
Asmera
Kamaran I.
Al Hudaydah
Al Mukalla
Aksum
Adwa
Al Mukha
Madinat ash Sha'b
Al 'Adan (Aden)
Aseb
Socotra
(Yemen)
Bab el Mandeb
Gulf of Aden
DJIBOUTI
Djibouti
Candala
Ras Asir
(C. Guardafui)
Zeila
Dese
Berbera
Dire Dawa
Harer
Hargeisa
Bender Beila
Addis Abeba
Bohotleh
SOMALI
REPUBLIC
Eil
Ogaden
Goba
Mt. Batu
4307
Dila
L. Abaya
Scebeli
Ferfer
Obbia
Dibbi
Mega
Moyale
El Dere
INDIAN
OCEAN
Marsabit
Bardera
Giuba
Merca
Muqdisho
(Mogadishu)
Wajir
Brava
Equator
Chisimaio
Tana
Lamu
Malindi
Voi
COPYRIGHT GEORGE PHILIP & SON LTD

131

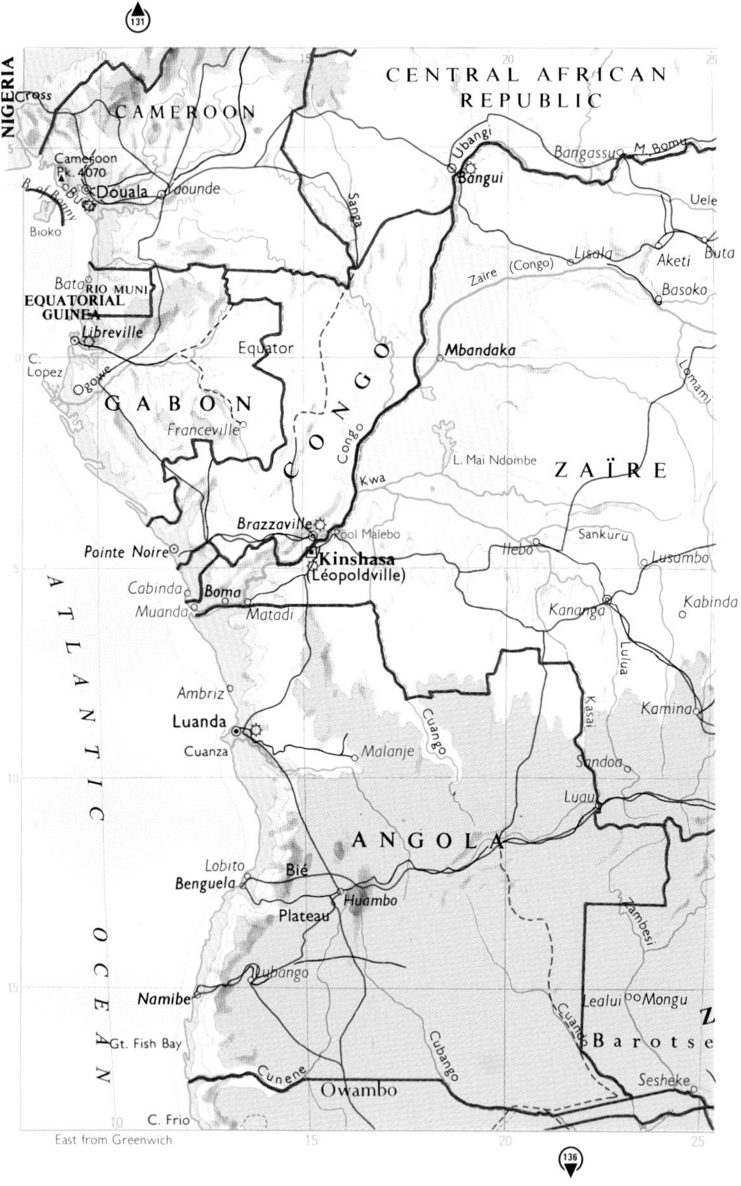
NIGERIA
Cross
CAMEROON
CENTRAL AFRICAN REPUBLIC
Ubangi
Bangui
Bangassu
M. Bomu
Uele
Cameroon Pk. 4070
Douala
Yaounde
B. of Bonny
Bioko
Sanga
Lisala
Aketi
Buta
Zaïre (Congo)
Basoko
Bata
RIO MUNI
EQUATORIAL GUINEA
Libreville
Equator
C. Lopez
Ogowe
Mbandaka
Lomami
GABON
CONGO
Franceville
Congo
L. Mai Ndombe
ZAÏRE
Kwa
Brazzaville
Pool Malebo
Kinshasa (Léopoldville)
Sankuru
Ilebo
Lusambo
Pointe Noire
Cabinda
Boma
Muanda
Matadi
Kananga
Kabinda
ATLANTIC OCEAN
Lulua
Ambriz
Kasai
Kamina
Luanda
Cuango
Cuanza
Malanje
Sandoa
Luau
ANGOLA
Lobito
Benguela
Bié
Huambo
Plateau
Zambesi
Lubango
Namibe
Lealui
Mongu
Cuando
Barotse
Gt. Fish Bay
Cubango
Cunene
Owambo
Sesheke
C. Frio
East from Greenwich
10
15
20
25
0
5

136

1 : 20 000 000

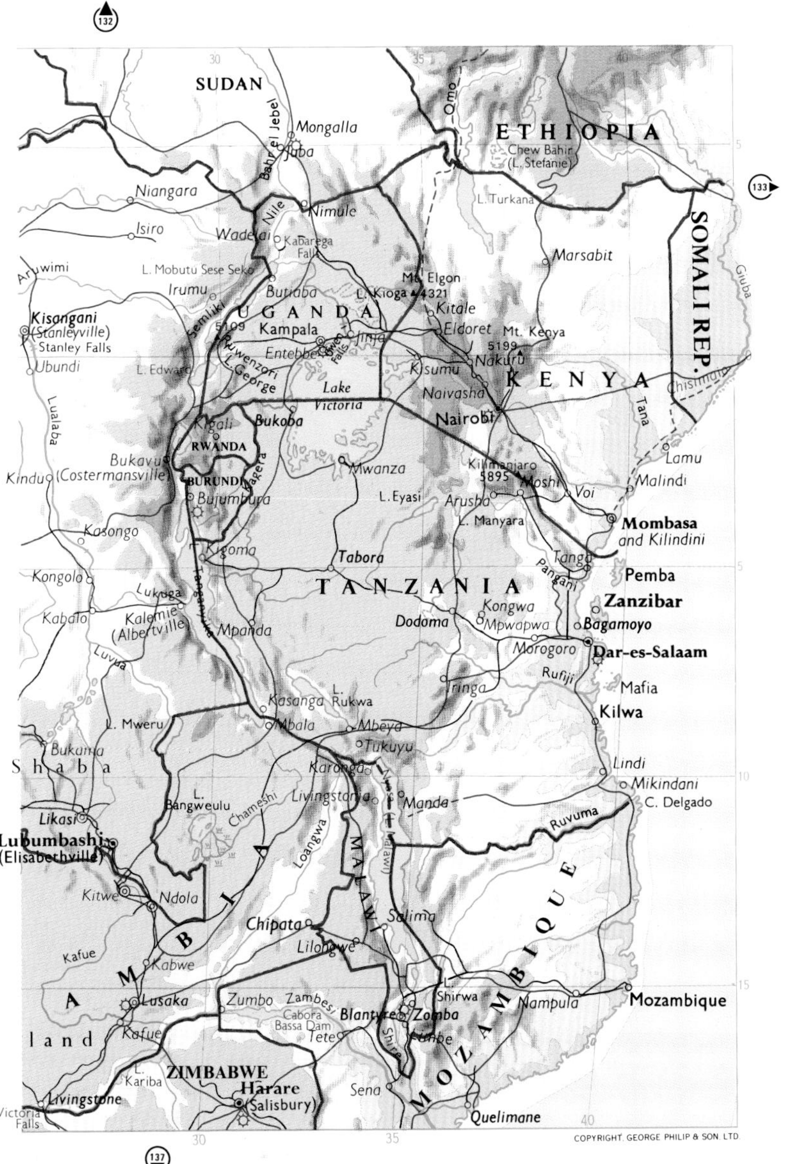

COPYRIGHT GEORGE PHILIP & SON LTD

132
SUDAN
ETHIOPIA
Mongalla
Juba
Bahr el Jebel
Omo
Chew Bahir
(L. Stefanie)
Niangara
Isiro
Nimule
Nile
L. Turkana
Wadelai
Kabarega Falls
SOMALI REP.
Marsabit
Aruwimi
L. Mobutu Sese Seko
Giuba
Irumu
Butiaba
Mt. Elgon
L. Kioga
4321
Kitale
UGANDA
Kisangani
(Stanleyville)
Stanley Falls
Semliki
5109
Kampala
Jinja
Eldoret
Mt. Kenya
5199
Ruwenzori
Owen Falls
Entebbe
Nakuru
Ubundi
L. Edward
L. George
Kisumu
KENYA
Lake Victoria
Naivasha
Chisimaio
Tana
Lualaba
Nairobi
Kigali
Bukoba
RWANDA
Lamu
Bukavu
(Costermansville)
Kagera
Mwanza
Kilimanjaro
5895
Malindi
Kindu
BURUNDI
Moshi
Voi
Bujumbura
L. Eyasi
Arusha
Mombasa
and Kilindini
Kasongo
L. Manyara
Kigoma
Tabora
Tanga
Pangani
Pemba
Kongolo
TANZANIA
Zanzibar
Lukuga
Tanganyika
Kongwa
Kabalo
Kalemie
(Albertville)
Mpanda
Dodoma
Mpwapwa
Bagamoyo
Morogoro
Dar-es-Salaam
Luvua
Rufiji
Iringa
Mafia
L. Rukwa
Kasanga
Kilwa
L. Mweru
Mbala
Mbeya
Tukuyu
Bukama
Shaba
Karonga
Lindi
Nyasa (L. Malawi)
Mikindani
Livingstonia
Manda
C. Delgado
L. Bangweulu
Chambeshi
Ruvuma
Likasi
Lubumbashi
(Elisabethville)
Loangwa
MALAWI
Kitwe
Ndola
ZAMBIA
MOZAMBIQUE
Salima
Chipata
Lilongwe
Kafue
Kabwe
Shirwa
Mozambique
Lusaka
Zumbo
Zambesi
Blantyre
Zomba
Nampula
Cabora Bassa Dam
Tete
Shire
Lumbe
Kafue
L. Kariba
ZIMBABWE
Harare
(Salisbury)
Sena
Livingstone
Victoria Falls
Quelimane
30
35
40
5
10
15
133
137

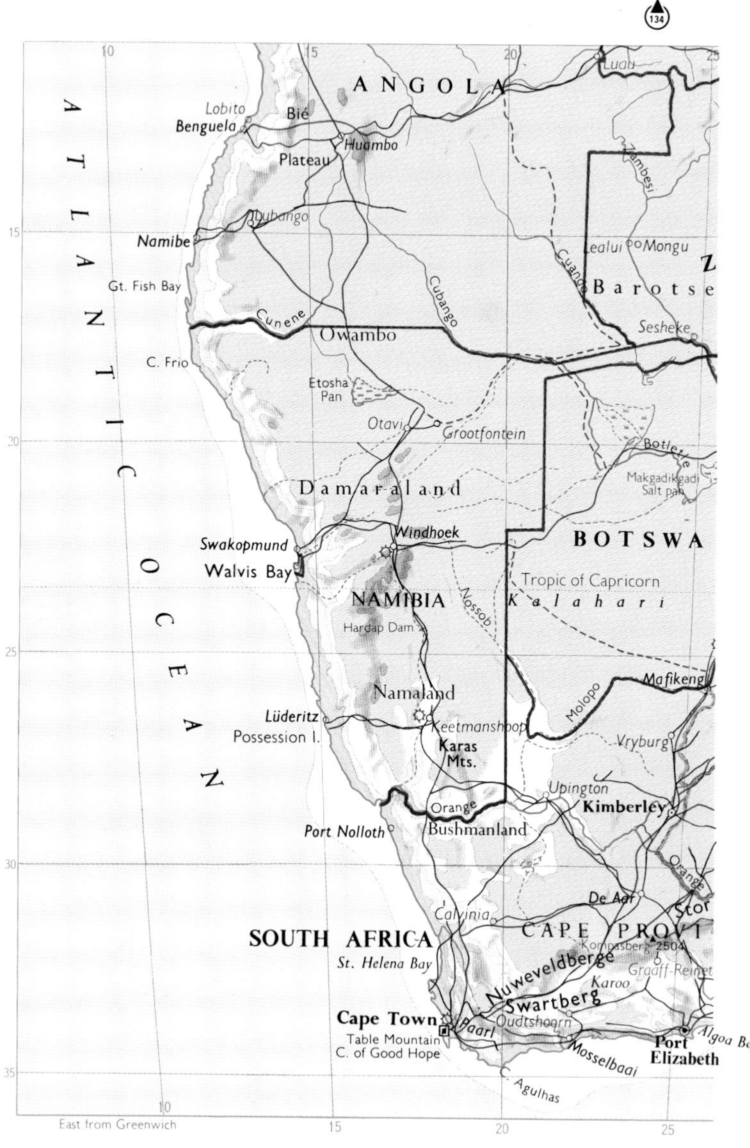
134
ANGOLA
Lobito
Benguela
Bié
Huambo
Plateau
Lubango
Namibe
Gt. Fish Bay
Cunene
Owambo
Cubango
C. Frio
Etosha Pan
Otavi
Grootfontein
Damaraland
Swakopmund
Walvis Bay
Windhoek
NAMIBIA
Hardap Dam
Nossob
Namaland
Lüderitz
Possession I.
Keetmanshoop
Karas Mts.
Orange
Port Nolloth
Bushmanland
ATLANTIC OCEAN
SOUTH AFRICA
St. Helena Bay
Calvinia
CAPE PROV
Kompasberg 2504
Nuweveldberge
Graaff-Reinet
Karoo
Swartberg
Oudtshoorn
Cape Town
Paarl
Table Mountain
C. of Good Hope
Mosselbaai
C. Agulhas
Port Elizabeth
Algoa B
De Aar
Kimberley
Upington
Vryburg
Molopo
Mafikeng
Tropic of Capricorn
Kalahari
BOTSWA
Makgadikgadi Salt pan
Botletle
Sesheke
Barotse
Lealui
Mongu
Cuando
Zambesi
Luau
East from Greenwich

1 : 20 000 000

135

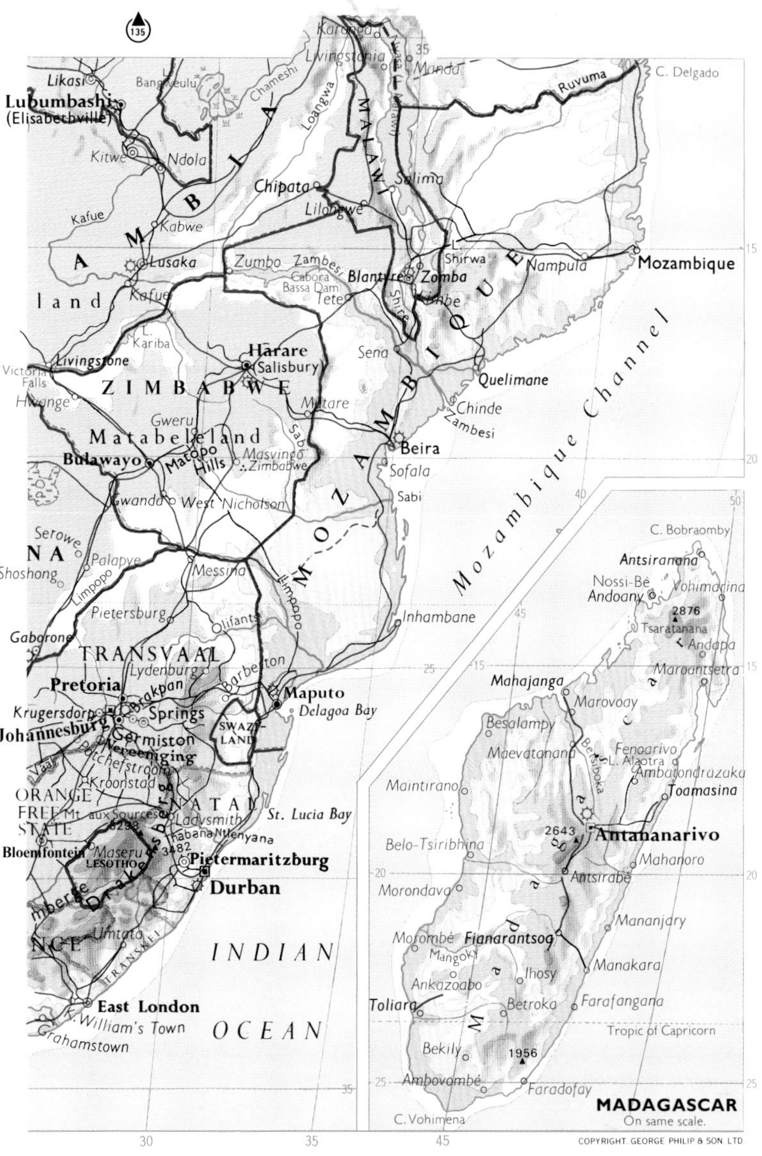

Likasi
Lubumbashi
(Elisabethville)
Bangweulu
Chameshi
Kitwe
Ndola
Kafue
Kabwe
Lusaka
Kafue
land
Karonga
Livingstonia
Loangwa
Manda
Ruvuma
C. Delgado
MALAWI
Chipata
Salima
Lilongwe
Zumbo
Zambesi
Cabora Bassa Dam
Tete
Blantyre
Zomba
Shirwa
Nampula
Mozambique
L. Kariba
Livingstone
Victoria Falls
Hwange
Harare
(Salisbury)
ZIMBABWE
Sena
Quelimane
Chinde
Zambesi
Mutare
Gweru
Matabeleland
Bulawayo
Matopo Hills
Masvingo
Zimbabwe
Beira
Sofala
Sabi
Gwanda
West Nicholson
MOZAMBIQUE
Mozambique Channel
Serowe
NA
Palapye
Shoshong
Messina
Limpopo
Pietersburg
Olifants
Inhambane
Gaborone
TRANSVAAL
Lydenburg
Barberton
Pretoria
Maputo
Delagoa Bay
Krugersdorp
Brakpan
Springs
Johannesburg
Germiston
SWAZILAND
Vereeniging
Vaal
Potchefstroom
Kroonstad
ORANGE FREE STATE
Mt aux Sources
3299
NATAL
Ladysmith
St. Lucia Bay
Bloemfontein
Thabana Ntlenyana
3482
Maseru
LESOTHO
Pietermaritzburg
Durban
Drakensberg
Umtata
TRANSKEI
INDIAN
OCEAN
East London
K. William's Town
Grahamstown
C. Bobraomby
Antsiranana
Nossi-Bé
Andoany
Vohimarina
2876
Tsaratanana
Andapa
Maroantsetra
Mahajanga
Marovoay
Besalampy
Maevatanana
Betsiboka
Fenoarivo
L. Alaotra
Ambatondrazaka
Maintirano
Toamasina
2643
Antananarivo
Belo-Tsiribihina
Mahanoro
Antsirabe
Morondava
Mananjary
Morombé
Fianarantsoa
Mangoky
Manakara
Ihosy
Ankazoabo
Toliara
Betroka
Farafangana
Tropic of Capricorn
Bekily
1956
Ambovombé
Faradofay
C. Vohimena
MADAGASCAR
On same scale.

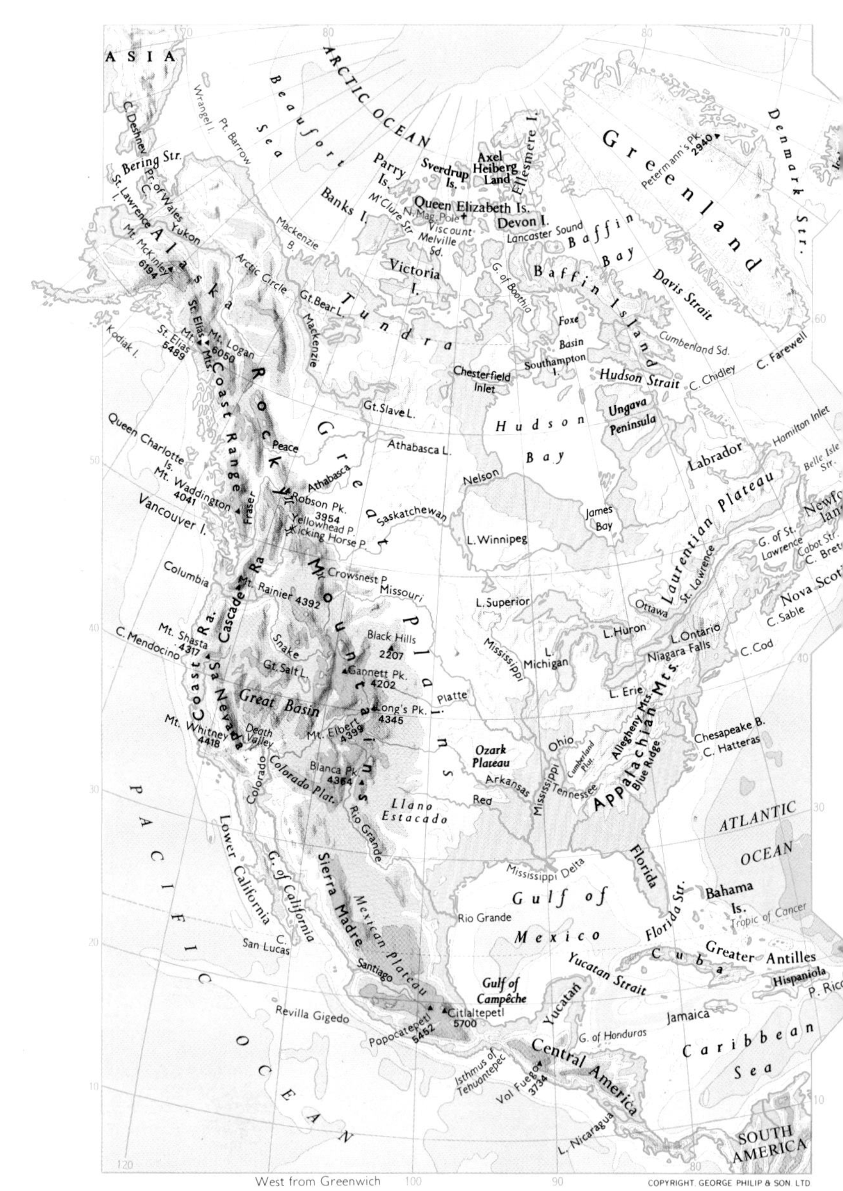
ASIA
ARCTIC OCEAN
Beaufort Sea
Wrangel I.
Pt. Barrow
C. Deshnev
Bering Str.
Pr. of Wales C.
St. Lawrence I.
Yukon
Alaska
Mt. McKinley 6194
Mackenzie B.
Arctic Circle
Parry Is.
Sverdrup Is.
Axel Heiberg Land
Ellesmere I.
Banks I.
M'Clure Str.
N. Mag. Pole
Queen Elizabeth Is.
Viscount Melville Sd.
Devon I.
Lancaster Sound
Greenland
Petermann's Pk. 2940
Denmark Str.
Baffin Bay
Victoria I.
G. of Boothia
Baffin Island
Davis Strait
Gt. Bear L.
Tundra
Mackenzie
St. Elias Mts.
Mt. Logan 6050
Mt. St. Elias 5489
Kodiak I.
Foxe Basin
Southampton I.
Cumberland Sd.
C. Farewell
C. Chidley
Hudson Strait
Chesterfield Inlet
Coast Range
Rocky Mountains
Gt. Slave L.
Ungava Peninsula
Hudson Bay
Hamilton Inlet
Queen Charlotte Is.
Peace
Great Plains
Athabasca L.
Labrador
Belle Isle Str.
Mt. Waddington 4041
Fraser
Athabasca
Robson Pk. 3954
Yellowhead P.
Kicking Horse P.
Saskatchewan
Nelson
James Bay
Laurentian plateau
Vancouver I.
L. Winnipeg
G. of St. Lawrence
Cabot Str.
C. Breton
Newfoundland
Columbia
Cascade Ra.
Crowsnest P.
Missouri
Mt. Rainier 4392
L. Superior
St. Lawrence
Ottawa
Nova Scotia
C. Sable
Coast Ra.
Mt. Shasta 4317
C. Mendocino
Snake
Black Hills 2207
Mississippi
L. Michigan
L. Huron
L. Ontario
Niagara Falls
C. Cod
Gt. Salt L.
Gannett Pk. 4202
Sierra Nevada
Great Basin
Platte
L. Erie
Appalachian Mts.
Allegheny Mts.
Long's Pk. 4345
Mt. Whitney 4418
Death Valley
Mt. Elbert 4399
Ozark Plateau
Ohio
Cumberland Plat.
Blue Ridge
Chesapeake B.
C. Hatteras
Colorado
Colorado Plat.
Blanca Pk. 4364
Arkansas
Tennessee
Red
Llano Estacado
Rio Grande
PACIFIC OCEAN
Lower California
G. of California
Sierra Madre
ATLANTIC OCEAN
Mississippi Delta
Florida
Gulf of Mexico
Bahama Is.
Florida Str.
Tropic of Cancer
Mexican Plateau
Rio Grande
C. San Lucas
Cuba
Greater Antilles
Hispaniola
P. Rico
Yucatan Strait
Santiago
Gulf of Campêche
Yucatan
Citlaltepetl 5700
Popocatepetl 5452
Revilla Gigedo
Jamaica
G. of Honduras
Caribbean Sea
Central America
Isthmus of Tehuantepec
Vol Fuego 3734
L. Nicaragua
SOUTH AMERICA
West from Greenwich

1 : 60 000 000

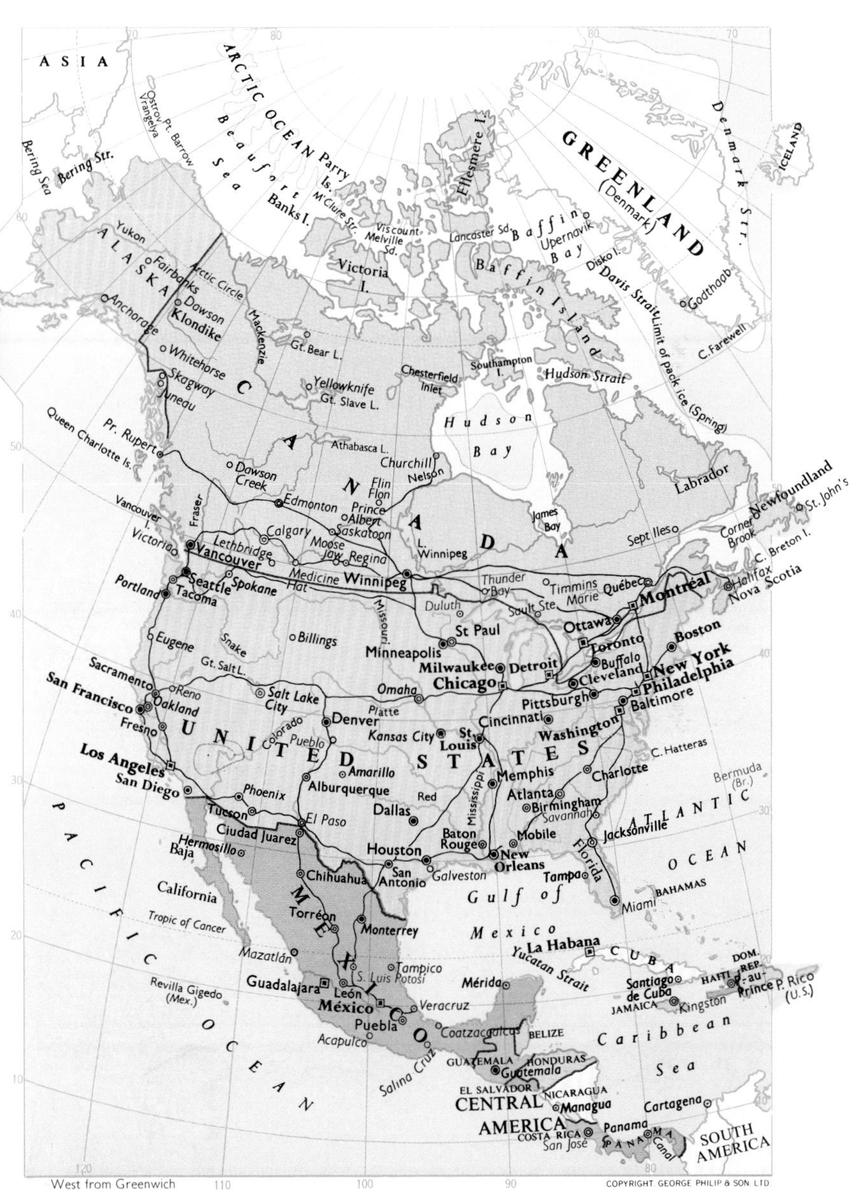

ASIA

ARCTIC OCEAN

Ostrov Vrangelya
Pt. Barrow

Bering Sea
Bering Str.

Parry Is.
M'Clure Str.
Banks I.

Beaufort Sea

Ellesmere I.

GREENLAND
(Denmark)

ICELAND

Denmark Str.

Viscount Melville Sd.

Victoria I.

Lancaster Sd.

Baffin Bay

Upernavik

Disko I.

Godthaab

Davis Strait Limit of pack ice (Spring)

C. Farewell

ALASKA
Yukon
Fairbanks
Anchorage
Klondike
Dawson
Whitehorse
Skagway
Juneau

Arctic Circle

Baffin Island

CANADA

Gt. Bear L.

Yellowknife
Gt. Slave L.

Mackenzie

Chesterfield Inlet

Southampton

Hudson Strait

Labrador

Queen Charlotte Is.
Pr. Rupert

Dawson Creek

Athabasca L.

Churchill
Nelson

Hudson Bay

James Bay

Sept Iles

Corner Brook
Newfoundland
St. John's

Vancouver
Victoria
Vancouver

Fraser
Edmonton
Prince Albert
Calgary
Lethbridge
Moose Jaw
Medicine Hat
Saskatoon
Regina

Winnipeg

Thunder Bay

Timmins
Sault Ste. Marie

Québec
Montréal

C. Breton I.
Halifax
Nova Scotia

Portland
Seattle
Tacoma
Spokane

Duluth

St Paul
Minneapolis
Milwaukee
Chicago

Ottawa
Toronto
Buffalo
Detroit
Cleveland
Boston
New York
Philadelphia
Baltimore

Eugene
Sacramento
San Francisco
Oakland
Reno
Fresno

Billings

Snake
Gt. Salt L.
Salt Lake City

Omaha
Platte
Denver
Colorado
Pueblo

Missouri

Kansas City

St Louis
Cincinnati
Pittsburgh
Washington

C. Hatteras

Bermuda (Br.)

UNITED STATES

Los Angeles
San Diego

Phoenix
Tucson

Amarillo
Alburquerque
El Paso

Red

Dallas

Memphis

Atlanta
Birmingham
Savannah

Charlotte

ATLANTIC

Ciudad Juarez
Hermosillo
Baja

California

Mississippi

Houston
San Antonio
Baton Rouge
New Orleans
Mobile

Jacksonville

Florida

OCEAN

PACIFIC OCEAN

Chihuahua

Galveston

Tampa

Gulf of Mexico

Miami

BAHAMAS

Tropic of Cancer

Revilla Gigedo (Mex.)

Torreón
Mazatlán

Monterrey

La Habana

CUBA

Guadalajara
León
México
Puebla
Acapulco

Tampico
S. Luis Potosí
Mérida
Veracruz
Coatzacualcos
Salina Cruz

Yucatan Strait

Santiago de Cuba

HAITI
DOM. REP.
Port-au-Prince

JAMAICA
Kingston

P. Rico (U.S.)

MEXICO

BELIZE

Caribbean Sea

GUATEMALA
Guatemala
EL SALVADOR
NICARAGUA
CENTRAL
AMERICA
COSTA RICA
San José

HONDURAS

Managua

Panama
PANAMA
Canal

Cartagena

SOUTH AMERICA

1 : 60 000 000

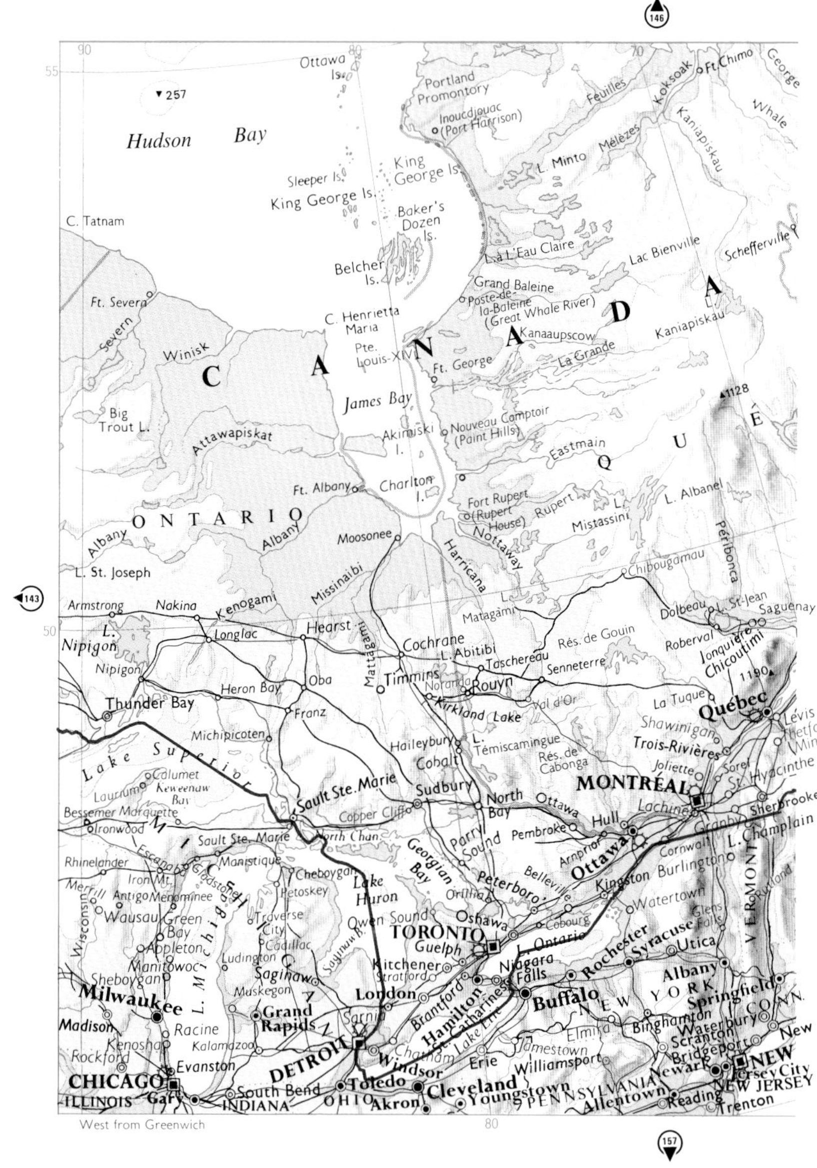

147

60
50
50
Nain
NEWFOUNDLAND
C. Harrison
Indian Harbour
Hopedale
Rigolet
Cartwright
L. Melville
Petitsikapau L.
COAST OF LABRADOR
Michikamau Lake
North West R.
Goose Bay
Battle Harb.
Belle Isle
Lobstick L.
Churchill Falls
Churchill
Str. of Belle Isle
Ashuanipi L.
QUEBEC
Natashquan
St-Augustin-Saguenay
Notre Dame B.
Twillingate
Lewisporte
Gander
Bonavista
Trinity B.
Carbonear
St. John's
Romaine
Natashquan
Grand Falls
Buchans
Corner Brook
814
NEWFOUNDLAND
Harbour Grace
Placentia B.
Placentia
Trepassey
C. Race
Moisie
Mingan
Î. d'Anticosti
Moisie
Sept Îles
Port-Cartier
Manicouagan
Gulf of St. Lawrence
C. Ray
P. aux Basques
ST.-PIERRE et MIQUELON (Fr.)
C. de Gaspé
Gaspé
R. St. Lawrence
Baie-Comeau
Betsiamites
Matane
Pén. de Gaspé
Campbellton
Rimouski
Dalhousie
Bathurst
Îs. de la Madeleine
Cabot Str.
C. North
Cape Breton I.
Glace Bay
Sydney
Port Hawkesbury
Mulgrave
Chatham
Tignish
PR. EDWARD I.
Summerside
Charlottetown
Rivière-du-Loup
Tadoussac
Newcastle
NEW BRUNSWICK
Northumberland Str.
Pictou
New Glasgow
NOVA SCOTIA
Edmundston
St. Leonard
Moncton
Amherst
Springhill
Truro
Windsor
Dartmouth
Halifax
Sable I. (Nova Scotia)
Woodstock
Fredericton
Saint John
Kentville
Digby
B. of Fundy
Bridgewater
Liverpool
Shelburne
C. Sable
Yarmouth
MAINE
Bangor
Augusta
Lewiston
1917
Portland
NEW HAMPSHIRE
Manchester
Concord
Lowell
MASS.
Boston
C. Cod
Worcester
Providence
RHODE I.
New Haven
NEW YORK
ATLANTIC OCEAN
6309
40
40
70
60

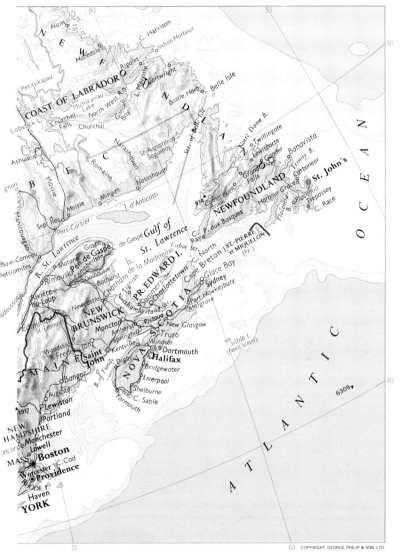

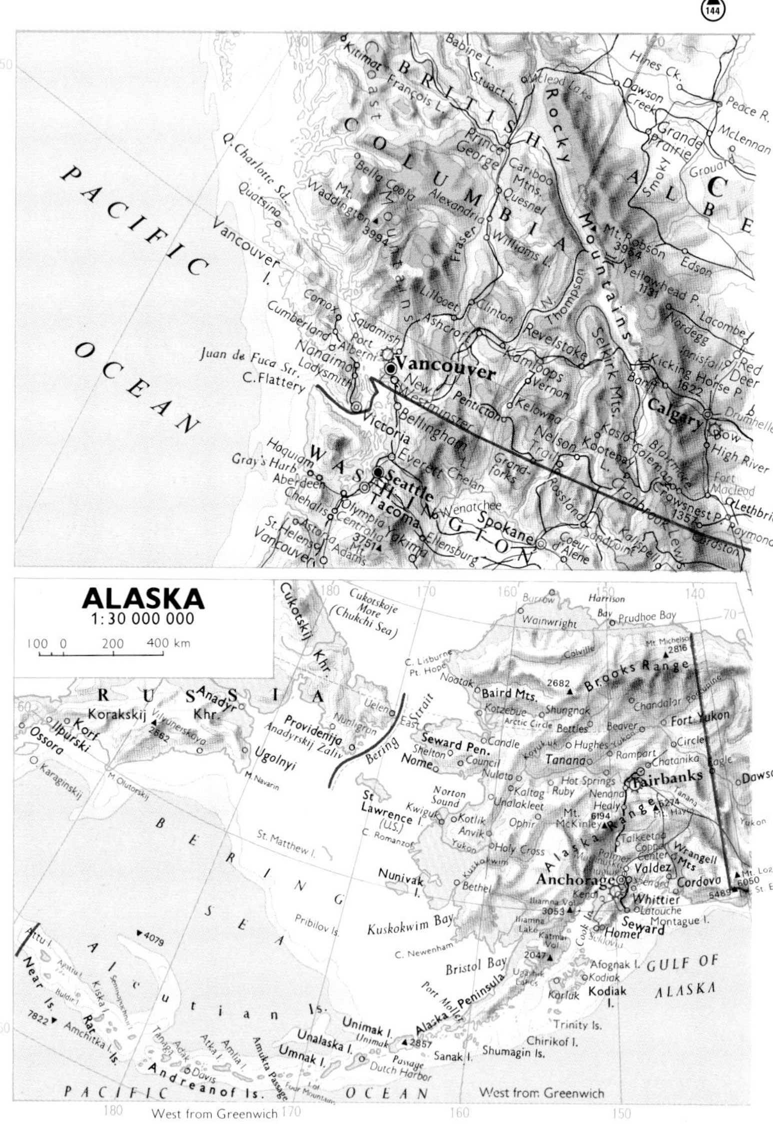

1 : 15 000 000

145

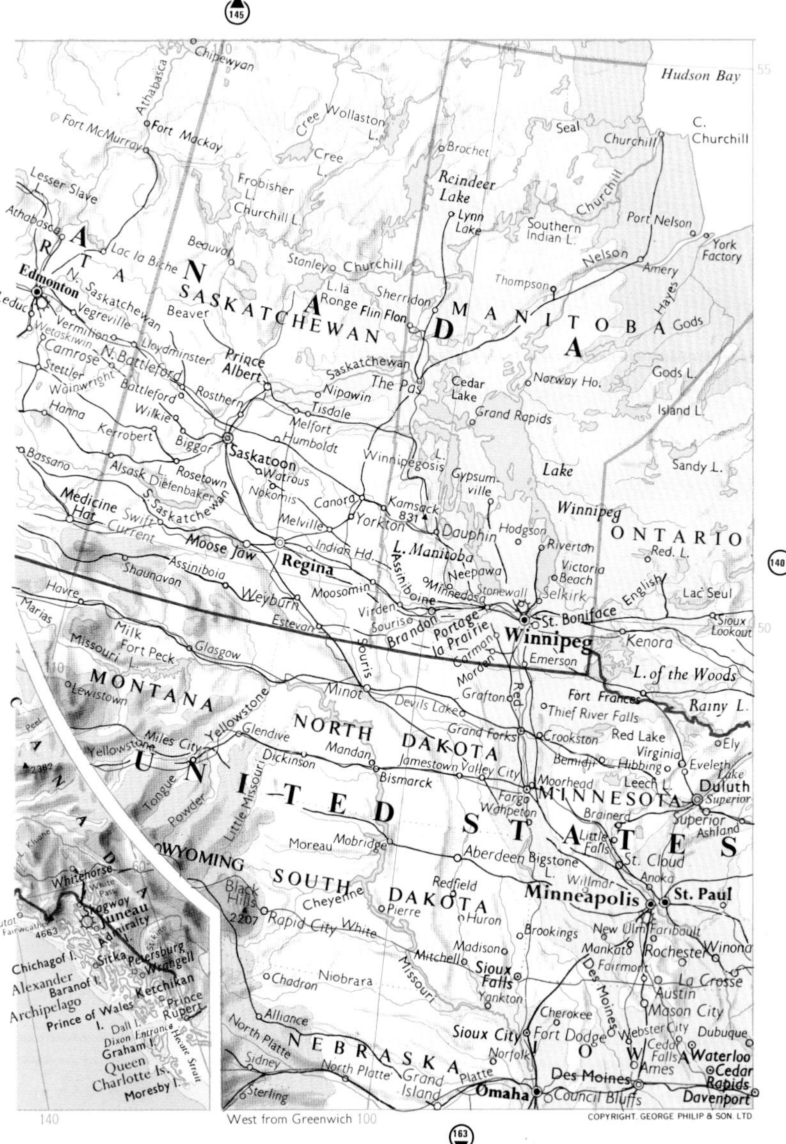
Hudson Bay
C. Churchill
Churchill
Seal
Chipewyan
Athabasca
Fort McMurray
Fort Mackay
Cree
Wollaston L.
Cree L.
Brochet
Reindeer Lake
Lynn Lake
Frobisher L.
Churchill L.
Lesser Slave L.
Athabasca
Southern Indian L.
Port Nelson
York Factory
Nelson
Amery
Hayes
Beauval
Stanley
Churchill
Lac la Biche
Edmonton
Leduc
Vegreville
Vermilion
Wetaskiwin
Camrose
Stettler
Wainwright
Hanna
Bassano
Medicine Hat
N. Saskatchewan
Lloydminster
N. Battleford
Battleford
Wilkie
Kerrobert
Biggar
Rosetown
Alsask
L. Diefenbaker
S. Saskatchewan
Swift Current
Moose Jaw
Regina
Shaunavon
Assiniboia
Weyburn
Estevan
Havre
Marias
Milk
Fort Peck
Glasgow
Missouri L.
MONTANA
Lewistown
Yellowstone
Miles City
Glendive
Tongue
Powder
Little Missouri
WYOMING
Beaver
SASKATCHEWAN
Prince Albert
Rosthern
Saskatoon
Watrous
Nokomis
Humboldt
Melfort
Tisdale
Nipawin
Saskatchewan
The Pas
L. la Ronge
Sherridon
Flin Flon
Thompson
MANITOBA
Gods
Gods L.
Island L.
Sandy L.
Norway Ho.
Cedar Lake
Grand Rapids
Winnipegosis L.
Gypsumville
Lake Winnipeg
ONTARIO
Red. L.
Lac Seul
Canora
Kamsack
831
Yorkton
Melville
Indian Hd.
Moosomin
Virden
Souris
Brandon
Assiniboine
Minnedosa
Neepawa
L. Manitoba
Dauphin
Hodgson
Riverton
Victoria Beach
Selkirk
Stonewall
Portage la Prairie
Carman
Morden
Winnipeg
St. Boniface
Emerson
English
Sioux Lookout
Kenora
L. of the Woods
Fort Frances
Rainy L.
Minot
Souris
Devils Lake
Grafton
Red
Thief River Falls
Grand Forks
Crookston
Red Lake
NORTH DAKOTA
Mandan
Dickinson
Bismarck
Jamestown
Valley City
Fargo
Moorhead
Wahpeton
Bemidji
Hibbing
Virginia
Eveleth
Ely
Leech L.
MINNESOTA
Duluth
Superior
Lake Superior
Ashland
Brainerd
Little Falls
St. Cloud
Anoka
Minneapolis
St. Paul
UNITED STATES
Moreau
Mobridge
Aberdeen
Bigstone L.
Willmar
SOUTH DAKOTA
Cheyenne
Redfield
Pierre
Huron
Black Hills
2207
Rapid City
White
Brookings
Madison
Mitchell
Sioux Falls
Yankton
Missouri
Niobrara
Chadron
Alliance
North Platte
NEBRASKA
Sidney
North Platte
Grand Island
Platte
Sterling
Omaha
Council Bluffs
Norfolk
Sioux City
Cherokee
Fort Dodge
IOWA
Des Moines
Ames
Webster City
Cedar Falls
Waterloo
Cedar Rapids
Davenport
Dubuque
Mason City
Austin
La Crosse
Rochester
Winona
Faribault
New Ulm
Mankato
Fairmont
Des Moines
CANADA
Peel
2382
Kluane
Whitehorse
White Pass
Skagway
Juneau
Admiralty I.
Yakutat
Mt. Fairweather
4663
Chichagof I.
Sitka
Petersburg
Wrangell
Alexander Archipelago
Baranof I.
Ketchikan
Prince of Wales I.
Dall I.
Prince Rupert
Dixon Entrance
Hecate Strait
Graham I.
Queen Charlotte Is.
Moresby I.
55
50
110
60
140
West from Greenwich 100
COPYRIGHT. GEORGE PHILIP & SON. LTD.

140

163

142

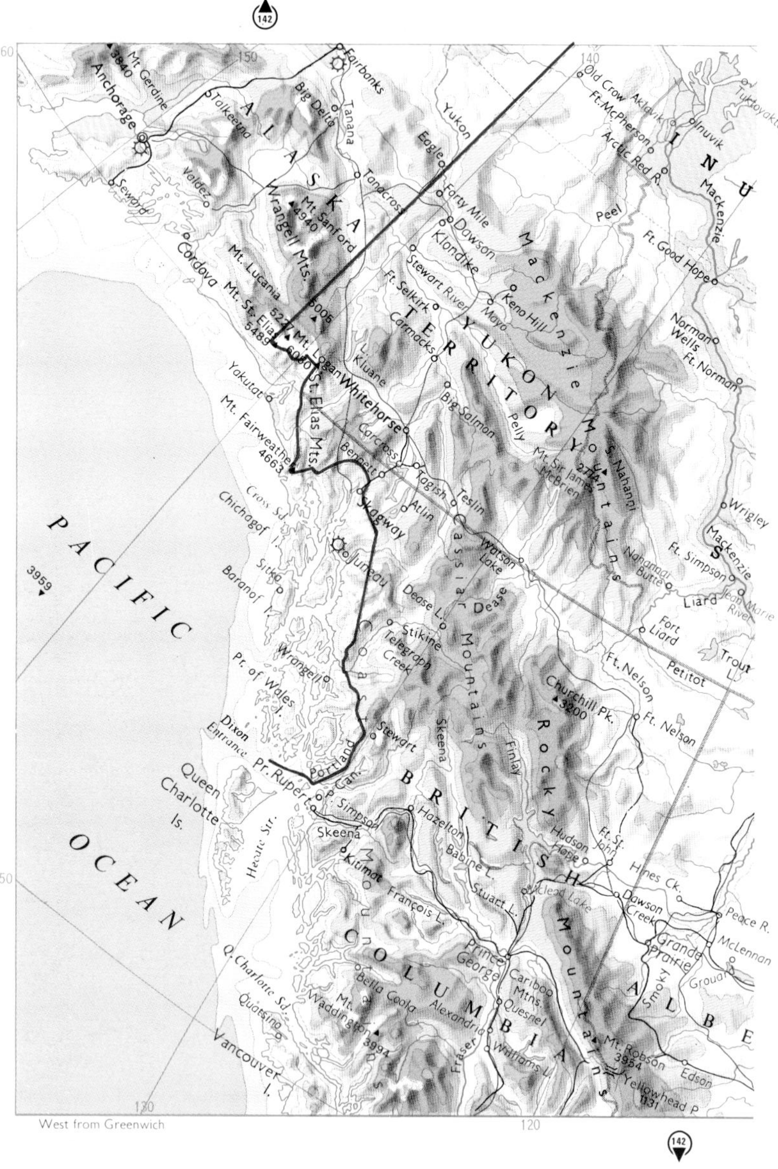
60
150
140
50
130
120
Mt Gerdine
3840
Anchorage
Talkeetna
Seward
Valdez
Cordova
Fairbanks
Big Delta
Tanana
Tanacross
ALASKA
Wrangell Mts.
Mt. Sanford
4940
Mt. Lucania
5227
5005
Mt. St. Elias
5489
Mt. Logan
6050
St. Elias Mts.
Yakutat
Mt. Fairweather
4663
Yukon
Eagle
Forty Mile
Dawson
Klondike
Stewart River
Ft. Selkirk
Mayo
Keno Hill
Carmacks
L. Kluane
Whitehorse
Carcross
Bennett
Tagish
Atlin
Teslin
Big Salmon
Pelly
Skagway
Juneau
Cross Sd.
Chichagof I.
Sitka
Baranof I.
Wrangell
Pr. of Wales I.
Dixon Entrance
Portland
Stewart
Pr. Rupert
P. Simpson
Queen Charlotte Is.
Hecate Str.
Skeena
Kitimat
Telegraph Creek
Stikine
Dease L.
Dease
Watson Lake
Cassiar Mountains
Coast Mts.
YUKON TERRITORY
Mackenzie Mountains
Mt. Sir James McBrien
2762
S. Nahanni
Nahanni Butte
Old Crow
Aklavik
Ft. McPherson
Inuvik
Tuktoyaktuk
Arctic Red R.
Peel
Mackenzie
Ft. Good Hope
Norman Wells
Ft. Norman
Wrigley
Mackenzie
Ft. Simpson
Liard
Jean Marie River
Fort Liard
Trout L.
Petitot
Ft. Nelson
Ft. Nelson
Churchill Pk.
3200
Rocky Mountains
Finlay
Skeena
Hazelton
Babine L.
Stuart L.
François L.
McLeod Lake
Hudson Hope
Ft. St. John
Hines Ck.
Dawson Creek
Peace R.
McLennan
Grande Prairie
Grouard
Smoky
Prince George
Cariboo Mtns.
Quesnel
Alexandria
Fraser
Williams L.
Bella Coola
Mt. Waddington
3994
Q. Charlotte Sd.
Quatsino
Vancouver I.
Mt. Robson
3954
Yellowhead P.
1131
Edson
BRITISH COLUMBIA
ALBERTA
PACIFIC OCEAN
3959
West from Greenwich

142

1 : 15 000 000

12

130
120
110
100
Banks Island
762
Viscount Melville Sound
Prince Albert Pen.
M'Clintock Channel
Prince of Wales Island
Somerset Island
C. Bathurst
Franklin B.
Stanton
Anderson
Amundsen Gulf
Holman Island
Darnley Bay
Prince Albert Sd.
Victoria Island
C. Baring
Dolphin & Union Str.
Horton
Franklin Str.
Wollaston Pen.
K I T I K M E O T
Boothia
573
Peninsula
70
Coppermine
Coronation Gulf
Cambridge Bay
Spence Bay
King William I.
Kent Pen.
Franklin Mts.
Smith Arm
Dease Arm
Fort Franklin
Gt. Bear Lake
157
Keith Arm
Gt. Bear
Echo Bay
Coppermine
Bathurst Inlet
Bathurst Inlet
Queen Maud Gulf
Gjoa Haven
Adelaide Pen.
Chantrey Inlet
Burnside
L. Pelly
L. Macdougall
Arctic Circle
L. de Gras
Back
L. Garry
N O R T H W E S T T E R R I T O R I E S
F O R T H
M I T H
Lac la Martre
Yellowknife
L. Aylmer
Rae
Clinton Colden L.
Baker L.
Chesterfield Inlet
Baker Lake
Yellowknife
Fort Providence
Fort Reliance
Dubawnt L.
K E E W A T I N
158
Great Slave L.
Snowdrift
Yathkyed L.
Chesterfield Inlet
Rankin Inlet
Hay River
Fort Resolution
Pine Point
Whale Cove
Dubawnt
Caribou Mts.
1036
Meander River
Ft. Smith
Ft. Vermilion
Slave
Wholdaia L.
Eskimo Pt.
Thlewiaza
Peace
Uranium City
Kasba L.
L. Claire
Fort Chipewyan
Lake Athabasca
Fond-du-Lac
Nueltin L.
Hudson Bay
60
Wabiskaw
Athabasca
Wollaston L.
Cree
Seal
C. Churchill
Churchill
Fort McMurray
Fort Mackay
Brochet
M A N I T O B A
Cree L.
S A S K A T C H E W A N
Reindeer Lake
Lesser Slave L.
Frobisher L.
Churchill
Churchill L.
Lynn Lake
Port Nelson
Southern Indian L.
York Factory
Athabasca
Lac la Biche
Beauval
Nelson
Amery
R T A
Stanley
Churchill
Thompson
Edmonton
L. la Ronge
Sherridon
110
100

146
143

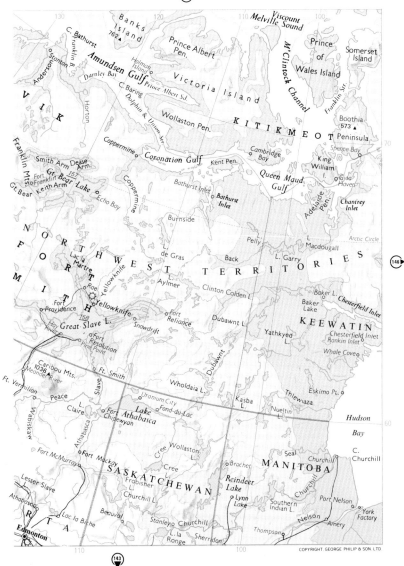

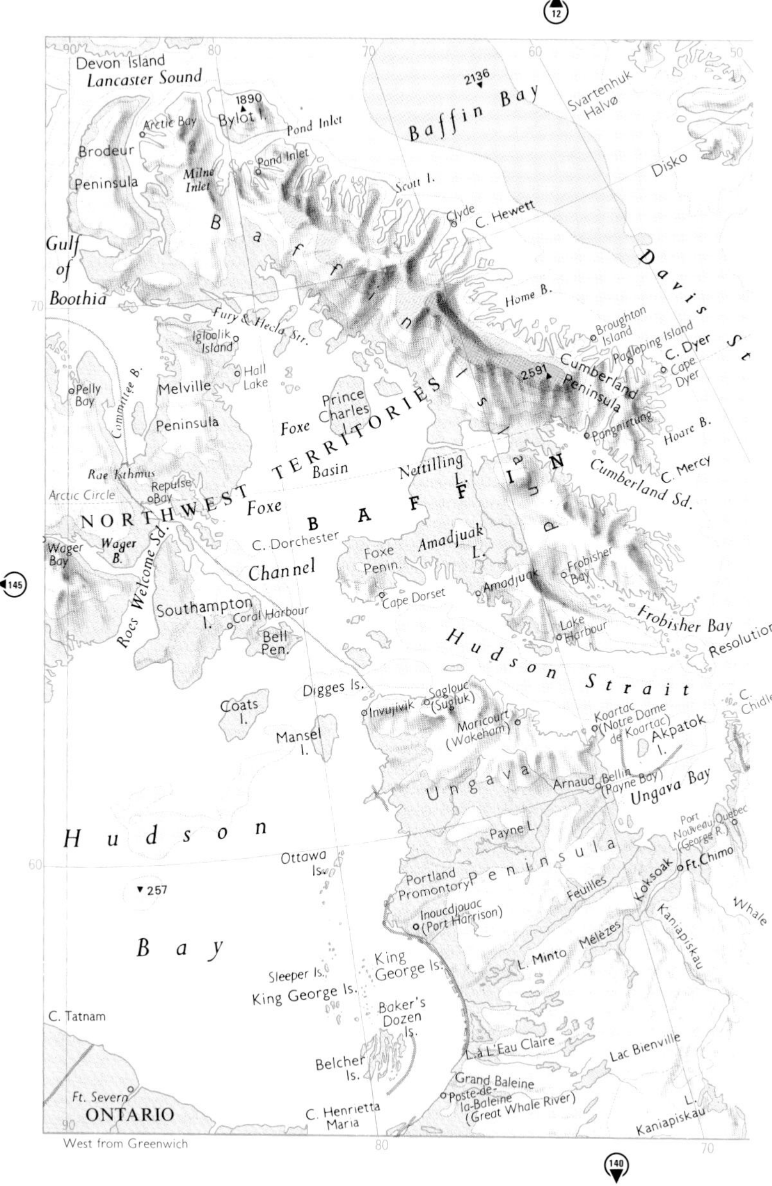

Devon Island
Lancaster Sound
Arctic Bay
Brodeur
Peninsula
Bylot I.
Pond Inlet
Pond Inlet
Milne Inlet
1890
Scott I.
Clyde
C. Hewett
Baffin Bay
2136
Svartenhuk Halvø
Disko
Gulf
of
Boothia
Fury & Hecla Str.
Igloolik Island
Hall Lake
B a f f i n
Home B.
Davis St
Melville
Committee B.
Pelly Bay
Peninsula
Prince Charles I.
Foxe
Basin
NORTH WEST T E R R I T O R I E S
2591
Cumberland Peninsula
Broughton Island
Padloping Island
C. Dyer
Cape Dyer
Pangnirtung
Houre B.
Rae Isthmus
Repulse Bay
Arctic Circle
Nettilling L.
Cumberland Sd.
C. Mercy
Wager Bay
Wager B.
Ross Welcome Sd.
Foxe
Channel
C. Dorchester
B A F F I N
Foxe Penin.
Amadjuak L.
Amadjuak
Cape Dorset
Frobisher Bay
Lake Harbour
Frobisher Bay
Resolution
Southampton I.
Coral Harbour
Bell Pen.
Digges Is.
Invujivik
Sagluoc (Sugluk)
H u d s o n   S t r a i t
C. Chidley
Coats I.
Mansel I.
Maricourt (Wakeham)
Koartac (Notre Dame de Koartac)
Akpatok I.
U n g a v a
Arnaud (Bellin (Payne Bay))
Ungava Bay
Payne L.
Port Nouveau-Quebec (George R.)
Ft. Chimo
H u d s o n
257
Ottawa Is.
Portland Promontory
P e n i n s u l a
Feuilles
Koksoak
Whale
Inoucdjouac (Port Harrison)
L. Minto
Mélezes
Kaniapiskau
B a y
Sleeper Is.
King George Is.
King George Is.
Baker's Dozen Is.
L. Minto
C. Tatnam
Belcher Is.
Lac Bienville
Ft. Severn
ONTARIO
C. Henrietta Maria
Grand Baleine
Poste-de-la-Baleine (Great Whale River)
La L'Eau Claire
L. Kaniapiskau

West from Greenwich

1 : 15 000 000

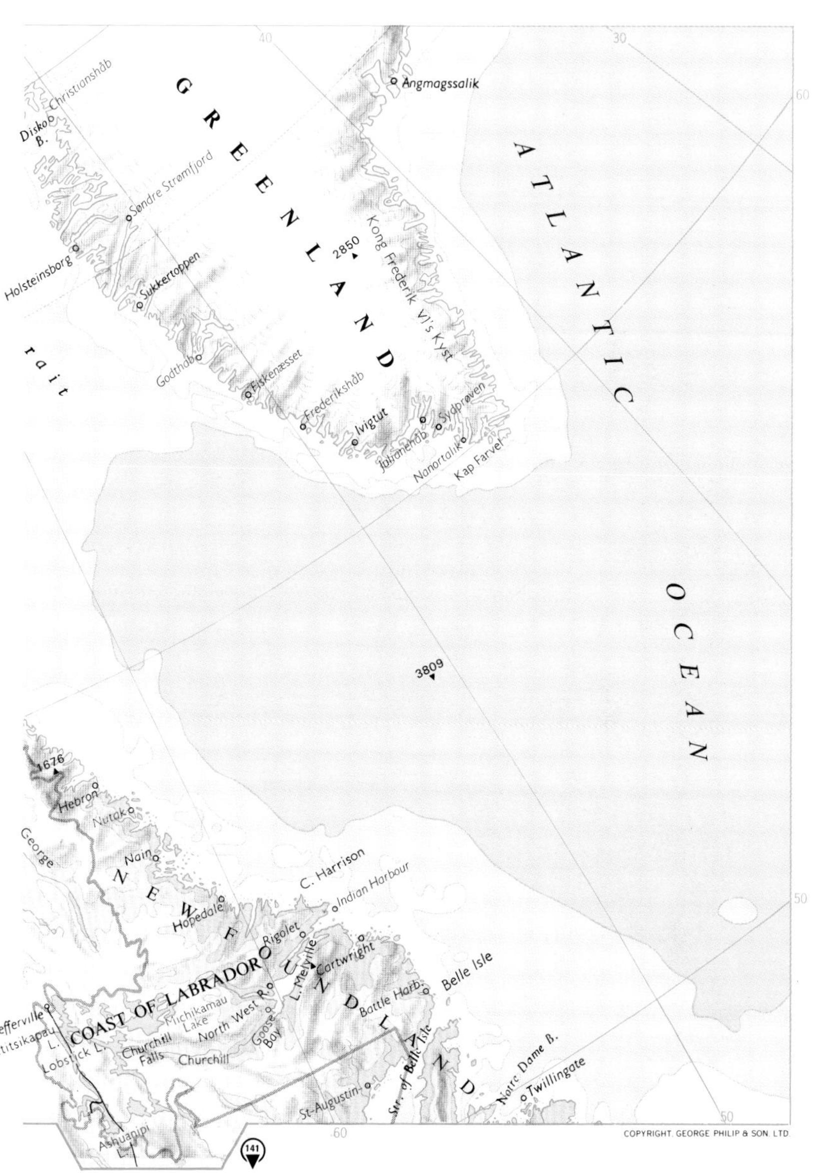
GREENLAND
ATLANTIC OCEAN
Ångmagssalik
Christianshåb
Disko B.
Søndre Strømfjord
Holsteinsborg
Sukkertoppen
Godthåb
Fiskenæsset
Frederikshåb
Ivigtut
Julianehåb
Sydprøven
Nanortalik
Kap Farvel
Kong Frederik VI's Kyst
2850
3809
1676
Hebron
Nutak
George
Nain
C. Harrison
Indian Harbour
Hopedale
Rigolet
Cartwright
L. Melville
COAST OF LABRADOR
NEWFOUNDLAND
Belle Isle
Battle Harb.
Schefferville
Petitsikapau L.
Lobstick L.
Michikamau Lake
Churchill Falls
Churchill
North West R.
Goose Bay
St-Augustin
Str. of Belle Isle
Notre Dame B.
Twillingate
Ashuanipi L.
40
30
60
50
141

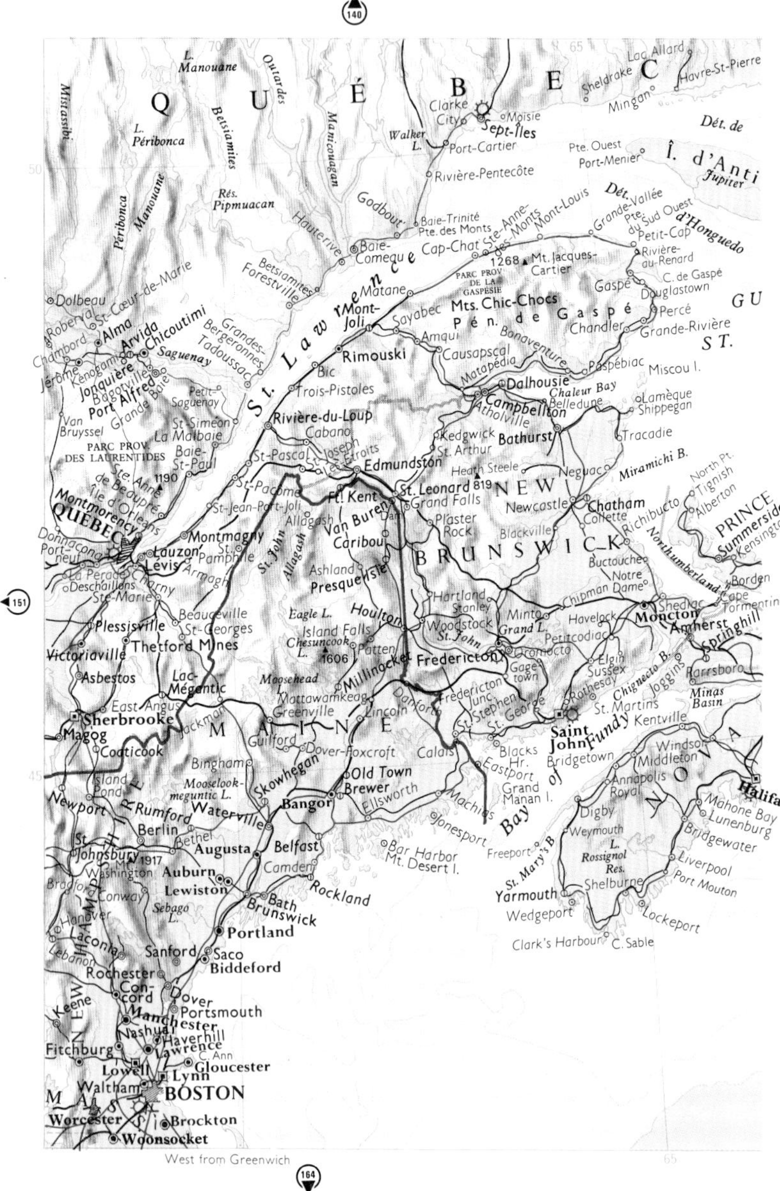
140
151
164
Q U É B E C
L. Manouane
Outardes
Mistassibi
L. Péribonca
Betsiamites
Manicouagan
Clarke City
Moisie
Sept-Îles
Walker L.
Port-Cartier
Rivière-Pentecôte
Sheldrake
Lac Allard
Havre-St-Pierre
Mingan
Dét. de
Pte. Ouest
Port-Menier
Î. d'Anticosti
Jupiter
Rés. Pipmuacan
Péribonca
Manouane
Godbout
Hauterive
Baie-Trinité
Pte. des Monts
Baie-Comeau
Cap-Chat
Ste-Anne-des-Monts
Mont-Louis
Grande-Vallée
Dét. d'Honguedo
Pte. du Sud Ouest
Petit-Cap
Rivière-au-Renard
C. de Gaspé
1268 Mt. Jacques-Cartier
PARC PROV. DE LA GASPÉSIE
Gaspé
Douglastown
Betsiamites
Forestville
Matane
St. Lawrence
Mont-Joli
Sayabec
Mts. Chic-Chocs
Pén. de Gaspé
Percé
Chandler
Grande-Rivière
GU
ST.
Dolbeau
St-Cœur-de-Marie
Roberval
Chambord
Alma
Arvida
Chicoutimi
Grandes-Bergeronnes
Tadoussac
Saguenay
Rimouski
Amqui
Causapscal
Bonaventure
Paspébiac
Miscou I.
Jérôme
Kénogami
Jonquière
Bagotville
Port Alfred
Grande Baie
Petit-Saguenay
Bic
Trois-Pistoles
Matapédia
Dalhousie
Chaleur Bay
Belledune
Campbellton
Atholville
Lamèque
Shippegan
Van Bruyssel
St-Siméon
La Malbaie
Rivière-du-Loup
Cabano
Kedgwick
Bathurst
Tracadie
PARC PROV. DES LAURENTIDES
Baie-St-Paul
St-Pascal
St-Joseph
Les Étroits
Edmundston
St. Arthur
Heath Steele
Neguac
Miramichi B.
North Pt.
Tignish
Alberton
1190
Ste. Anne de Beaupré
Île d'Orléans
Montmorency
QUEBEC
St-Pacôme
St-Jean-Port-Joli
Ft. Kent
St. Leonard
819
Grand Falls
NEW BRUNSWICK
Newcastle
Chatham
Collette
Richibucto
PRINCE
Summerside
Kensington
Allagash
Van Buren
Dam
Plaster Rock
Blackville
Northumberland
Donnacona
Port-neuf
Montmagny
St. Pamphile
Lauzon
Lévis
Armagh
La Pérade
Deschaillons
Charny
Ste-Marie
St. John
Caribou
Ashland
Presque Isle
Buctouche
Notre Dame
Borden
Cape Tormentine
Chipman
Shediac
Moncton
Beauceville
St-Georges
Plessisville
Eagle L.
Houlton
Hartland
Stanley
Woodstock
Minto
Grand L.
Havelock
Amherst
Springhill
Victoriaville
Thetford Mines
Island Falls
Chesuncook L.
1606
Patten
Fredericton
Oromocto
Petitcodiac
Elgin
Sussex
Gagetown
Asbestos
Lac-Mégantic
Moosehead L.
Millinocket
Chignecto B.
Joggins
Parrsboro
Minas Basin
East Angus
Mattawamkeag
Greenville
Lincoln
Danforth
Fredericton Junc.
St. Stephen
St. George
Rothesay
St. Martins
Kentville
Sherbrooke
Magog
Coaticook
Jackman
MAINE
Guilford
Dover-Foxcroft
Calais
Saint John
Bay of Fundy
Windsor
Middleton
NOVA
Blacks Hr.
Eastport
Grand Manan I.
Bridgetown
Annapolis Royal
Halifax
Bingham
Old Town
Brewer
Ellsworth
Machias
Island Pond
Newport
Mooselookmeguntic L.
Skowhegan
Bangor
Digby
Mahone Bay
Lunenburg
Rumford
Waterville
Jonesport
Weymouth
Bridgewater
Berlin
Bethel
Augusta
Belfast
Bar Harbor
Mt. Desert I.
Freeport
St. Mary's B.
L. Rossignol Res.
Liverpool
St Johnsbury
Mt. Washington 1917
Auburn
Lewiston
Camden
Rockland
Port Mouton
Bradford
Conway
Sebago L.
Bath
Brunswick
Yarmouth
Shelburne
Wedgeport
Lockeport
Hanover
Laconia
Portland
Lebanon
Sanford
Saco
Biddeford
Clark's Harbour
C. Sable
Rochester
Concord
Dover
Portsmouth
Keene
NEW HAMPSHIRE
Manchester
Nashua
Haverhill
Lawrence
C. Ann
Fitchburg
Lowell
Lynn
Gloucester
Waltham
BOSTON
MASS.
Worcester
Brockton
Woonsocket
70
65
50
45
West from Greenwich

1 : 7 000 000

141

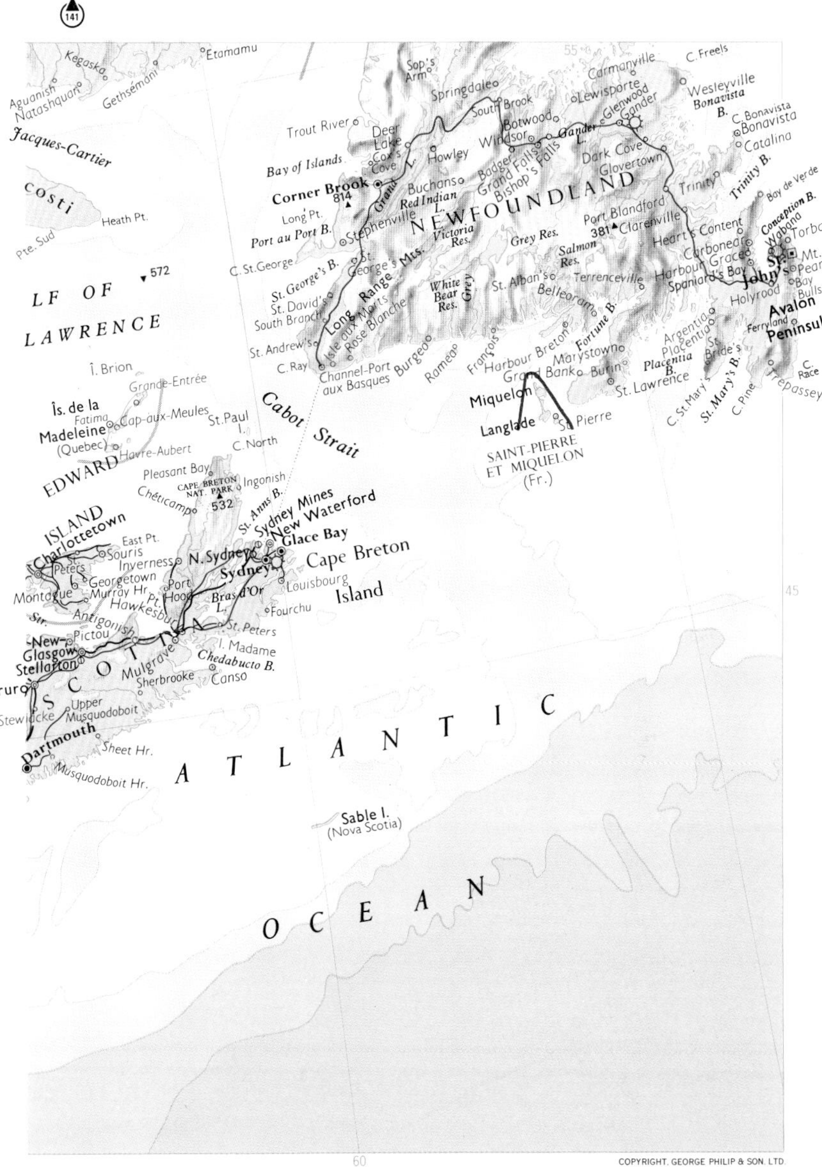
NEWFOUNDLAND
Corner Brook
Bay of Islands
Trout River
Deer Lake
Springdale
Lewisporte
Gander
Botwood
Grand Falls
Bishop's Falls
Glovertown
Clarenville
Trinity
Bonavista
C. Bonavista
Catalina
Wesleyville
C. Freels
Carmanville
Buchans
Stephenville
Port au Port B.
C. St. George
St. George's B.
Long Range Mts.
Channel-Port aux Basques
C. Ray
Burgeo
Ramea
Harbour Breton
Grand Bank
Marystown
Burin
St. Lawrence
Fortune B.
Placentia B.
Placentia
Argentia
St. John's
Torbay
Mt. Pearl
Bay Bulls
Holyrood
Ferryland
Avalon Peninsula
C. Race
Trepassey
C. Pine
St. Mary's B.
Carbonear
Harbour Grace
Heart's Content
Conception B.
Bay de Verde
Trinity B.
Miquelon
Langlade
St. Pierre
SAINT-PIERRE ET MIQUELON (Fr.)
Cabot Strait
C. North
St. Paul I.
Îs. de la Madeleine (Quebec)
Cap-aux-Meules
Havre-Aubert
Grande-Entrée
Î. Brion
LF OF LAWRENCE
Jacques-Cartier
costi
Heath Pt.
Pte. Sud
Etamamu
Kegaska
Natashquan
Aguanish
Gethsémani
EDWARD ISLAND
Charlottetown
Souris
East Pt.
Georgetown
Montague
Murray Hr.
Cape Breton Island
CAPE BRETON NAT. PARK
Ingonish
Pleasant Bay
Chéticamp
Inverness
Port Hood
Sydney Mines
New Waterford
Glace Bay
N. Sydney
Sydney
Louisbourg
Fourchu
Bras d'Or L.
St. Peters
I. Madame
Chedabucto B.
Canso
Pt. Hawkesbury
Antigonish
Pictou
New Glasgow
Stellarton
Truro
Mulgrave
Sherbrooke
Upper Musquodoboit
Stewiacke
Dartmouth
Sheet Hr.
Musquodoboit Hr.
ATLANTIC OCEAN
Sable I. (Nova Scotia)
55
45
60

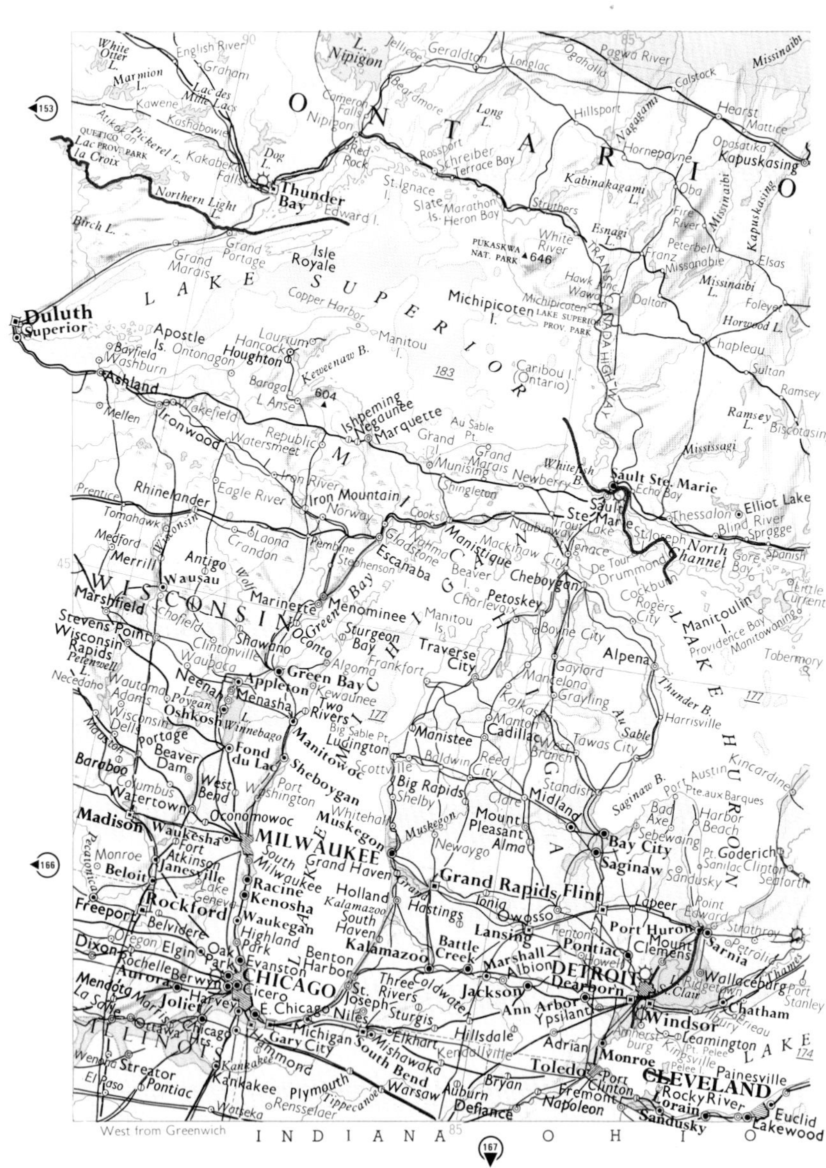
ONTARIO
LAKE SUPERIOR
MICHIGAN
WISCONSIN
ILLINOIS
INDIANA
OHIO
LAKE HURON
LAKE MICHIGAN
LAKE ERIE
L. Nipigon
Thunder Bay
Duluth
Superior
Isle Royale
Apostle Is.
Sault Ste. Marie
Marquette
Green Bay
Appleton
Oshkosh
Madison
MILWAUKEE
Racine
Kenosha
Rockford
CHICAGO
Gary
Hammond
South Bend
Grand Rapids
Lansing
Flint
Saginaw
Bay City
Kalamazoo
Battle Creek
Jackson
Ann Arbor
DETROIT
Dearborn
Windsor
Toledo
CLEVELAND
Lakewood
Euclid
Lorain
Sandusky
Sarnia
Port Huron
Chatham
Kapuskasing
Hearst
Chapleau
Wawa
Manitoulin I.
North Channel
Alpena
Traverse City
Petoskey
Cheboygan
Escanaba
Menominee
Iron Mountain
Ironwood
Ashland
Wausau
Stevens Point
Fond du Lac
Sheboygan
Manitowoc
Muskegon
Joliet
Aurora
Elgin
Waukegan
Evanston
Cicero
Kankakee
Elkhart
Mishawaka
Monroe
Pontiac
Port Clinton
Fremont
Napoleon
Defiance
Goderich
Wallaceburg
Leamington
West from Greenwich
153
166
167
174
177
183

1 : 7 000 000

140

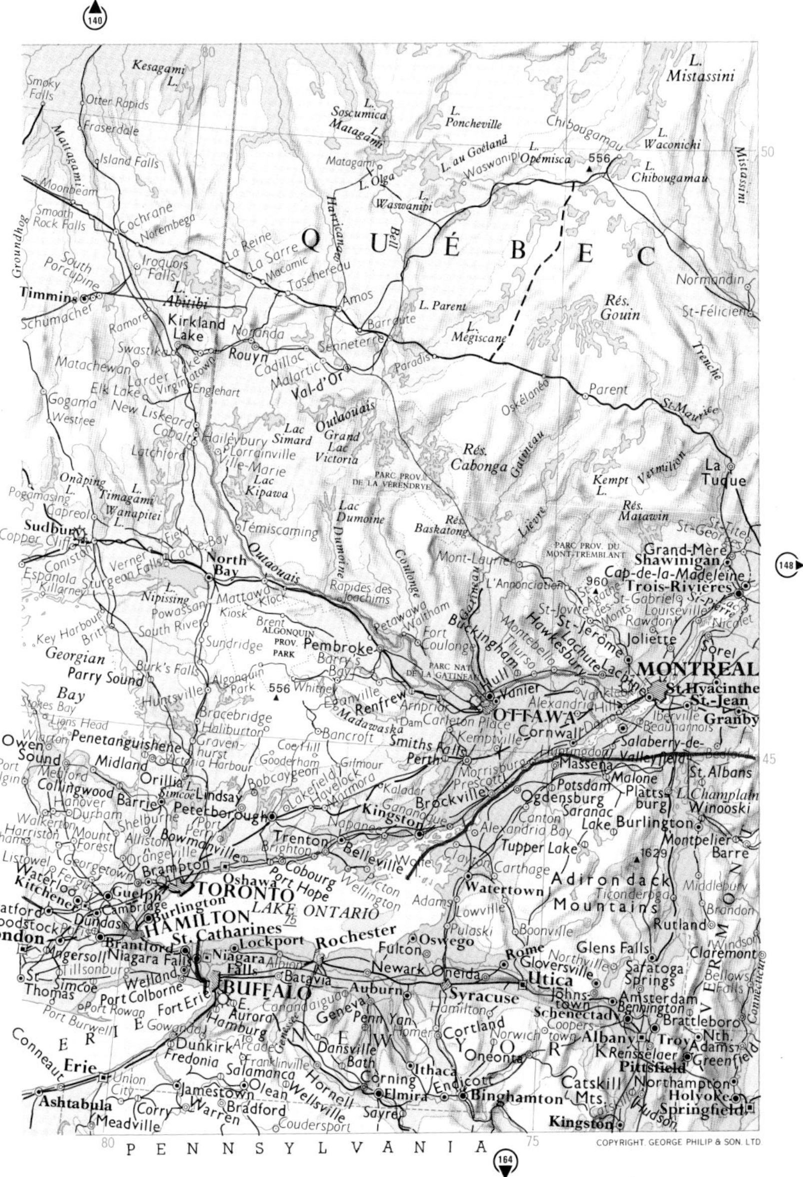

Q U É B E C
L. Mistassini
Kesagami L.
Smoky Falls
Otter Rapids
Fraserdale
Island Falls
Mattagami
Moonbeam
Smooth Rock Falls
Cochrane
Norembega
Groundhog
South Porcupine
Timmins
Schumacher
Iroquois Falls
L. Abitibi
La Reine
La Sarre
Macamic
Taschereau
Amos
Kirkland Lake
Ramore
Swastika
Matachewan
Larder Lake
Virginiatown
Englehart
Elk Lake
Gogama
Westree
New Liskeard
Cobalt
Haileybury
Latchford
Lorrainville
Ville-Marie
Noranda
Rouyn
Cadillac
Malartic
Val-d'Or
Senneterre
Barraute
L. Soscumica
Matagami
L. Matagami
L. Olga
L. Waswanipi
Harricana
Bell
L. Poncheville
L. au Goëland
Waswanipi
L. Opémisca
556
Chibougamau
L. Waconichi
L. Chibougamau
Mistassini
Normandin
St-Félicien
Rés. Gouin
L. Parent
L. Megiscane
Paradis
Trenche
Parent
Oskélanéo
St-Maurice
Outaouais
Lac Simard
Grand Lac Victoria
Lac Kipawa
PARC PROV. DE LA VÉRENDRYE
Rés. Cabonga
Gatineau
Vermilion
La Tuque
Kempt L.
Rés. Matawin
Onaping L.
Pogamasing
Timagami
Capreol
Wanapitei L.
Sudbury
Copper Cliff
Coniston
Verner
Sturgeon Falls
Field
Cache Bay
North Bay
Espanola
Killarney
L. Nipissing
Mattawa
Klock
Témiscaming
Lac Dumoine
Dumoine
Rés. Baskatong
Lièvre
Coulonge
Rapides des Joachims
Mont-Laurier
PARC PROV. DU MONT-TREMBLANT
L'Annonciation
960
St-Georges
Grand-Mère
Shawinigan
Cap-de-la-Madeleine
Trois-Rivières
St-Pierre
Louiseville
Rawdon
Nicolet
Joliette
Sorel
Ste-Agathe-des-Monts
St-Jovite
St-Gabriel
St-Jérôme
Lachute
Hawkesbury
Lachine
MONTREAL
St.Hyacinthe
St.-Jean
Granby
Iberville
Beauharnois
Powassan
Kiosk
Key Harbour
Britt
South River
Brent
ALGONQUIN PROV. PARK
Sundridge
Georgian Bay
Parry Sound
Burk's Falls
Algonquin Park
Huntsville
556
Petawawa
Waltham
Fort Coulonge
Buckingham
Thurso
Montebello
PARC NAT. DE LA GATINEAU
Pembroke
Barry's Bay
Whitney
Eganville
Renfrew
Arnprior
Madawaska
Dam
Carleton Place
Hull
Vanier
OTTAWA
Alexandria
Vankleek Hill
Cornwall
Kemptville
Salaberry-de-Valleyfield
Stokes Bay
Lions Head
Wiarton
Owen Sound
Port Elgin
Bracebridge
Haliburton
Bancroft
Coe Hill
Smiths Falls
Perth
Penetanguishene
Gravenhurst
Midland
Victoria Harbour
Gooderham
Gilmour
Meaford
Collingwood
Orillia
Lake Simcoe
Bobcaygeon
Lakefield
Havelock
Marmora
Kaladar
Morrisburg
Prescott
Brockville
Huntingdon
Massena
Malone
Potsdam
Ogdensburg
Bedford
St. Albans
L. Champlain
Plattsburg
Winooski
Hanover
Durham
Barrie
Lindsay
Peterborough
Gananoque
Kingston
Napanee
Canton
Saranac Lake
Burlington
Montpelier
Barre
Walkerton
Harriston
Mount Forest
Shelburne
Alliston
Orangeville
Port Perry
Bowmanville
Trenton
Brighton
Belleville
Alexandria Bay
Tupper Lake
1629
Listowel
Georgetown
Fergus
Brampton
Oshawa
Cobourg
Port Hope
Wellington
Picton
Wolfe I.
Clayton
Carthage
Watertown
Adirondack Mountains
Ticonderoga
Middlebury
Brandon
Waterloo
Kitchener
Guelph
Cambridge
TORONTO
Burlington
HAMILTON
Dundas
LAKE ONTARIO
75
Stratford
Woodstock
Paris
London
Brantford
St. Catharines
Ingersoll
Tillsonburg
Niagara Falls
Lockport
Rochester
Fulton
Oswego
Lowville
Pulaski
Boonville
Rutland
Windsor
Claremont
St. Thomas
Simcoe
Welland
Port Colborne
Fort Erie
Port Rowan
Port Burwell
BUFFALO
Batavia
Albion
Newark
Oneida
Rome
Utica
Northville
Gloversville
Glens Falls
Saratoga Springs
Johnstown
Amsterdam
Bellows Falls
Connecticut
E. Aurora
Hamburg
Gowanda
Canandaigua
Geneva
Auburn
Penn Yan
Syracuse
Hamilton
Homer
Cortland
Norwich
Cooperstown
Schenectady
Bennington
Brattleboro
Albany
Troy
Nth. Adams
Rensselaer
Greenfield
Pittsfield
E R I E
N E W Y O R K
V E R M O N T
Conneaut
Dunkirk
Fredonia
Arcade
Franklinville
Salamanca
Olean
Dansville
Bath
Ithaca
Oneonta
Erie
Union City
Jamestown
Wellsville
Hornell
Corning
Elmira
Endicott
Binghamton
Catskill Mts.
Northampton
Holyoke
Springfield
Hudson
Ashtabula
Corry
Warren
Bradford
Meadville
Coudersport
Sayre
Kingston
80
75
50
45
P E N N S Y L V A N I A

148

164

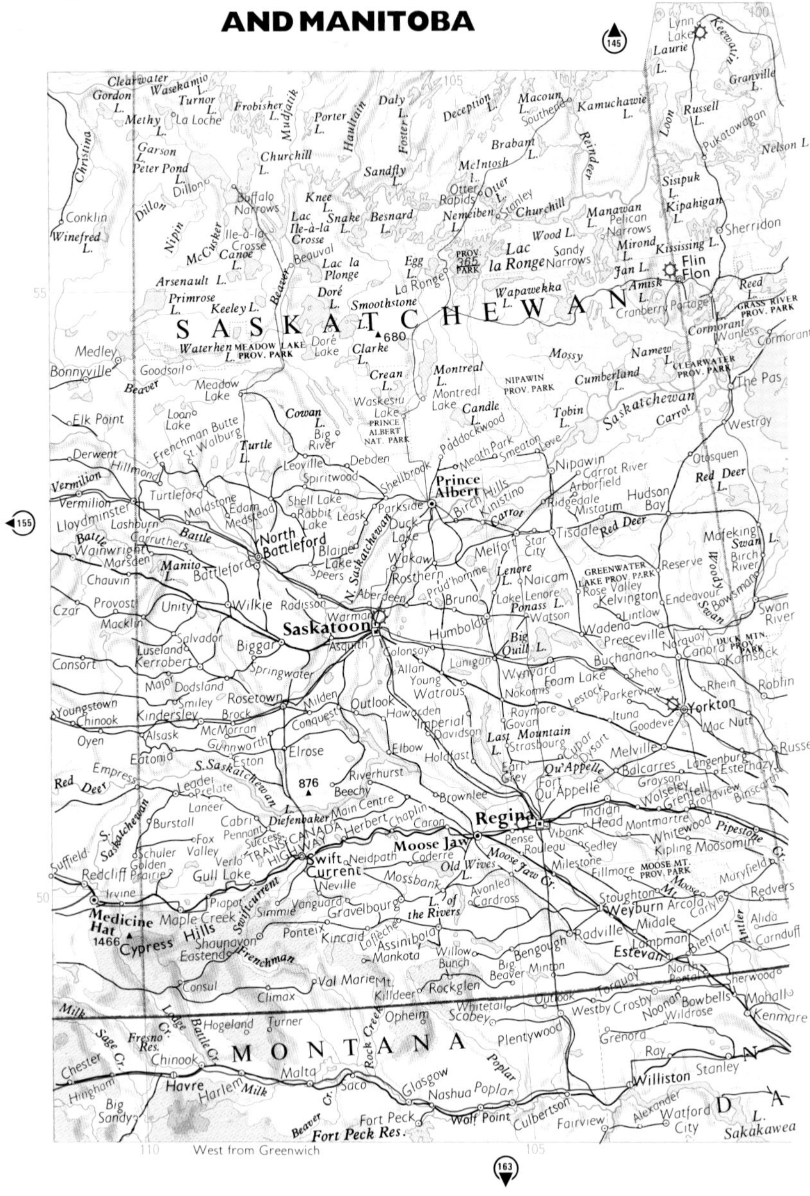
145
Lynn Lake
Laurie L.
Keewatin
Granville L.
Clearwater L.
Wasekamio L.
Gordon L.
Turnor L.
Methy L.
La Loche
Frobisher L.
Mudjatik
Porter L.
Haultain
Daly L.
Foster
Deception L.
Macoun L.
Southend
Kamuchawie L.
Reindeer
Loon
Russell L.
Pukatawagan
Nelson L.
Christina
Garson L.
Peter Pond L.
Dillon
Churchill L.
Sandfly L.
Brabant L.
McIntosh L.
Otter Rapids
Otter L.
Stanley
Churchill
Sisipuk L.
Kipahigan L.
Sherridon
Conklin
Winefred L.
Buffalo Narrows
Knee L.
Lac Ile-à-la Crosse
Snake L.
Besnard L.
Nemeiben L.
Manawan L.
Pelican Narrows
Wood L.
Kississing L.
Nipin
McCusker
Ile-à-la-Crosse
Canoe L.
Beauval
Lac la Plonge
Egg L.
PROV. PARK 365
Lac la Ronge
Sandy Narrows
Mirond L.
Jan L.
Flin Flon
Arsenault L.
Primrose L.
Keeley L.
Beaver
Doré L.
Smoothstone L.
La Ronge
Wapawekka L.
Amisk L.
Cranberry Portage
Reed L.
GRASS RIVER PROV. PARK
55
SASKATCHEWAN
680
Waterhen L.
MEADOW LAKE PROV. PARK
Doré Lake
Clarke L.
Cormorant L.
Wanless
Cormorant
Medley
Bonnyville
Goodsoil
Mossy
Namew L.
CLEARWATER PROV. PARK
Montreal L.
Montreal Lake
Crean L.
NIPAWIN PROV. PARK
Cumberland L.
The Pas
Meadow Lake
Beaver
Waskesiu Lake
Candle L.
Tobin L.
Saskatchewan
Carrot
Elk Point
Loon Lake
Frenchman Butte
St. Walburg
Cowan L.
Big River
PRINCE ALBERT NAT. PARK
Paddockwood
Westray
Turtle L.
Derwent
Hillmond
Leoville
Debden
Meath Park
Smeaton
Love
Nipawin
Otosquen
Vermilion
Spiritwood
Shellbrook
Prince Albert
Carrot River
Arborfield
Red Deer L.
Turtleford
Maidstone
Edam
Shell Lake
Birch Hills
Kinistino
Ridgedale
Mistatim
Hudson Bay
155
Lloydminster
Lashburn
Medstead
Rabbit Lake
Leask
Parkside
Duck Lake
Carrot
Tisdale
Red Deer
Mafeking
Battle
Wainwright
Carruthers
North Battleford
N. Saskatchewan
Star City
Melfort
Swan L.
Birch River
Marsden
Manito L.
Battleford
Blaine Lake
Wakaw
Reserve
Woody
Chauvin
Speers
Rosthern
Prud'homme
Lenore L.
Naicam
GREENWATER LAKE PROV. PARK
Rose Valley
Kelvington
Endeavour
Bowsman
Czar
Provost
Unity
Wilkie
Radisson
Aberdeen
Bruno
Lake Lenore
Ponass L.
Swan
Swan River
Macklin
Warman
Saskatoon
Humboldt
Watson
Lintlaw
Wadena
Preeceville
Salvador
Biggar
Asquith
Big Quill L.
Norquay
Canora
DUCK MTN. PROV. PARK
Kamsack
Luseland
Kerrobert
Colonsay
Lanigan
Wynyard
Buchanan
Sheho
Consort
Springwater
Allan
Young
Foam Lake
Rhein
Roblin
Major
Dodsland
Watrous
Nokomis
Lestock
Parkerview
Youngstown
Smiley
Rosetown
Milden
Outlook
Yorkton
Chinook
Kindersley
Brock
Conquest
Hawarden
Raymore
Ituna
Goodeve
Mac Nutt
Oyen
Alsask
McMorran
Imperial
Davidson
Govan
Last Mountain L.
Gunnworth
Elrose
Elbow
Strasbourg
Cupar
Dysart
Melville
Russell
Eatonia
Eston
Holdfast
Earl Grey
Empress
S. Saskatchewan
Riverhurst
Qu'Appelle
Balcarres
Langenburg
Esterhazy
Red Deer
Leader
Prelate
876
Beechy
Fort Qu'Appelle
Grayson
Wolseley
Grenfell
Broadview
Binscarth
Lancer
Diefenbaker L.
Main Centre
Brownlee
Burstall
Cabri
Pennant
Herbert
Chaplin
Caron
Regina
Indian Head
Montmartre
Success
TRANS-CANADA HIGHWAY
Moose Jaw
Pense
Vibank
Whitewood
Pipestone
Fox Valley
Rouleau
Sedley
Kipling
Moosomin
Suffield
Schuler
Verlo
Swift Current
Neidpath
Coderre
Moose Jaw Cr.
Golden Prairie
Old Wives L.
Milestone
Fillmore
MOOSE MT. PROV. PARK
Maryfield
Redcliff
Gull Lake
Mossbank
Irvine
Neville
Avonlea
Stoughton
Moose Mt.
Redvers
Medicine Hat
Piapot
Swiftcurrent
Vanguard
L. of the Rivers
Cardross
Weyburn
Arcola
Carlyle
50
Maple Creek
Simmie
Gravelbourg
Midale
Alida
1466
Cypress Hills
Shaunavon
Ponteix
Kincaid
Lafleche
Assiniboia
Radville
Lampman
Bienfait
Antler
Carnduff
Eastend
Frenchman
Mankota
Willow Bunch
Bengough
Estevan
Big Beaver
Minton
North Portal
Sherwood
Consul
Val Marie
Mt. Killdeer
Rockglen
Torquay
Outlook
Westby
Crosby
Noonan
Bowbells
Mohall
Climax
Whitetail
Scobey
Wildrose
Kenmare
Milk
Lodge Cr.
Battle Cr.
Hogeland
Turner
Rock Creek
Opheim
Sage Cr.
Fresno Res.
Chinook
MONTANA
Plentywood
Grenora
Chester
Malta
Poplar
Ray
Hingham
Havre
Harlem
Milk
Saco
Glasgow
Nashua
Poplar
Williston
Stanley
Big Sandy
Beaver Cr.
Fort Peck
Fort Peck Res.
Wolf Point
Culbertson
Fairview
Alexander
Watford City
Sakakawea L.
DAKOTA
110
West from Greenwich
105
163

1 : 7 000 000

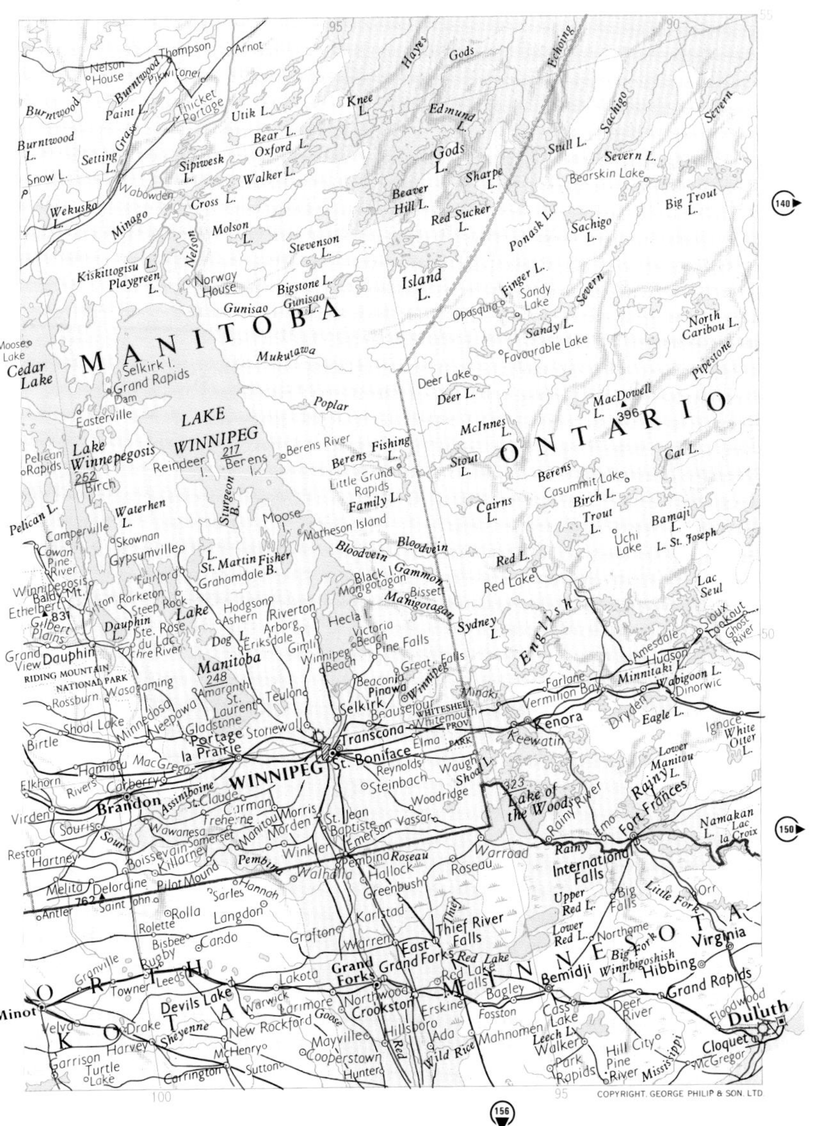

MANITOBA
ONTARIO
LAKE WINNIPEG
Lake Manitoba
Lake Winnipegosis
Cedar Lake
Thompson
Arnot
Nelson House
Burntwood
Pikwitonei
Thicket Portage
Paint L.
Utik L.
Knee L.
Hayes
Gods
Edmund L.
Echoing
Sachigo
Severn
Burntwood L.
Setting L.
Snow L.
Bear L.
Oxford L.
Sipiwesk L.
Walker L.
Gods L.
Stull L.
Severn L.
Bearskin Lake
Wabowden
Wekusko L.
Minago
Cross L.
Beaver Hill L.
Sharpe L.
Red Sucker L.
Big Trout L.
Molson L.
Stevenson L.
Ponask L.
Sachigo L.
Kiskittogisu L.
Playgreen L.
Nelson
Norway House
Bigstone L.
Island L.
Gunisao
Gunisao L.
Opasquia
Finger L.
Sandy Lake
Sandy L.
North Caribou L.
Moose Lake
Mukutawa
Favourable Lake
Pipestone
Selkirk I.
Grand Rapids Dam
Deer Lake
Deer L.
MacDowell L.
396
Easterville
Poplar
McInnes L.
Pelican Rapids
252
217
Reindeer I.
Berens I.
Berens River
Berens
Fishing L.
Stout L.
Cat L.
Birch I.
Little Grand Rapids
Family L.
Casummit Lake
Birch L.
Cairns L.
Pelican L.
Waterhen L.
Sturgeon B.
Moose I.
Matheson Island
Trout L.
Bamaji L.
Camperville
Skownan
Bloodvein
Uchi Lake
L. St. Joseph
Cowan
Pine River
Gypsumville
St. Martin L.
Fisher B.
Gammon
Red L.
Red Lake
Lac Seul
Winnipegosis
Baldy Mt.
831
Ethelbert
Gilbert Plains
Fairford
Grahamdale
Black I.
Manigotagan
Bissett
Sylton
Rorketon
Steep Rock
Hodgson
Ashern
Riverton
Dauphin L.
Ste. Rose du Lac
Ochre River
Dog L.
Arborg
Eriksdale
Hecla I.
Victoria Beach
Pine Falls
Sydney L.
English
Sioux Lookout
Ghost River
Amesdale
Hudson
Grand View
Dauphin
RIDING MOUNTAIN NATIONAL PARK
248
Gimli
Winnipeg Beach
Great Falls
Beaconia
Pinawa
Winnipeg
Farlane
Minnitaki L.
Wabigoon L.
Dinorwic
Wasagaming
Amaranth
St. Laurent
Teulon
Minaki
Vermilion Bay
Rossburn
Minnedosa
Neepawa
Gladstone
Selkirk
Beausejour
WHITESHELL PROV. PARK
Whitemouth
Kenora
Dryden
Eagle L.
Ignace
White Otter L.
Shoal Lake
Birtle
Portage la Prairie
Stonewall
Transcona
Elma
Keewatin
Lower Manitou L.
Hamiota
MacGregor
WINNIPEG
St. Boniface
Reynolds
Waugh
Shoal L.
Elkhorn
Rivers
Carberry
Steinbach
323
Lake of the Woods
Rainy L.
Fort Frances
Brandon
Assiniboine
St. Claude
Carman
Woodridge
Rainy River
Emo
Namakan L.
Lac la Croix
Virden
Souris
Treherne
Morris
St. Jean Baptiste
Vassar
Wawanesa
Manitou
Morden
Emerson
Reston
Hartney
Somerset
Boissevain
Killarney
Winkler
Pembina
Roseau
Warroad
Rainy
International Falls
Melita
Deloraine
Pilot Mound
Walhalla
Hallock
762
Saint John
Sarles
Hannah
Greenbush
Orr
Antler
Rolla
Langdon
Karlstad
Upper Red L.
Big Falls
Little Fork
Rolette
Thief
Thief River Falls
Lower Red L.
Northome
Bisbee
Cando
Grafton
Warren
East Grand Forks
Big Fork
Virginia
Rugby
Granville
Red Lake
Bemidji
Winnibigoshish L.
Hibbing
Towner
Leeds
Lakota
Grand Forks
Red Lake Falls
Bagley
Grand Rapids
Minot
Devils Lake
Warwick
Larimore
Northwood
Crookston
Erskine
Cass Lake
Deer River
Floodwood
Duluth
Velva
Drake
Sheyenne
New Rockford
Goose
Hillsboro
Fosston
Leech L.
Cloquet
Ada
Mahnomen
Walker
Hill City
Mayville
Harvey
McHenry
Cooperstown
Red
Wild Rice
Park Rapids
Pine River
Mississippi
McGregor
Garrison
Turtle Lake
Carrington
Sutton
Hunter
NORTH DAKOTA
MINNESOTA
95
90
55
50
100

140
150

156

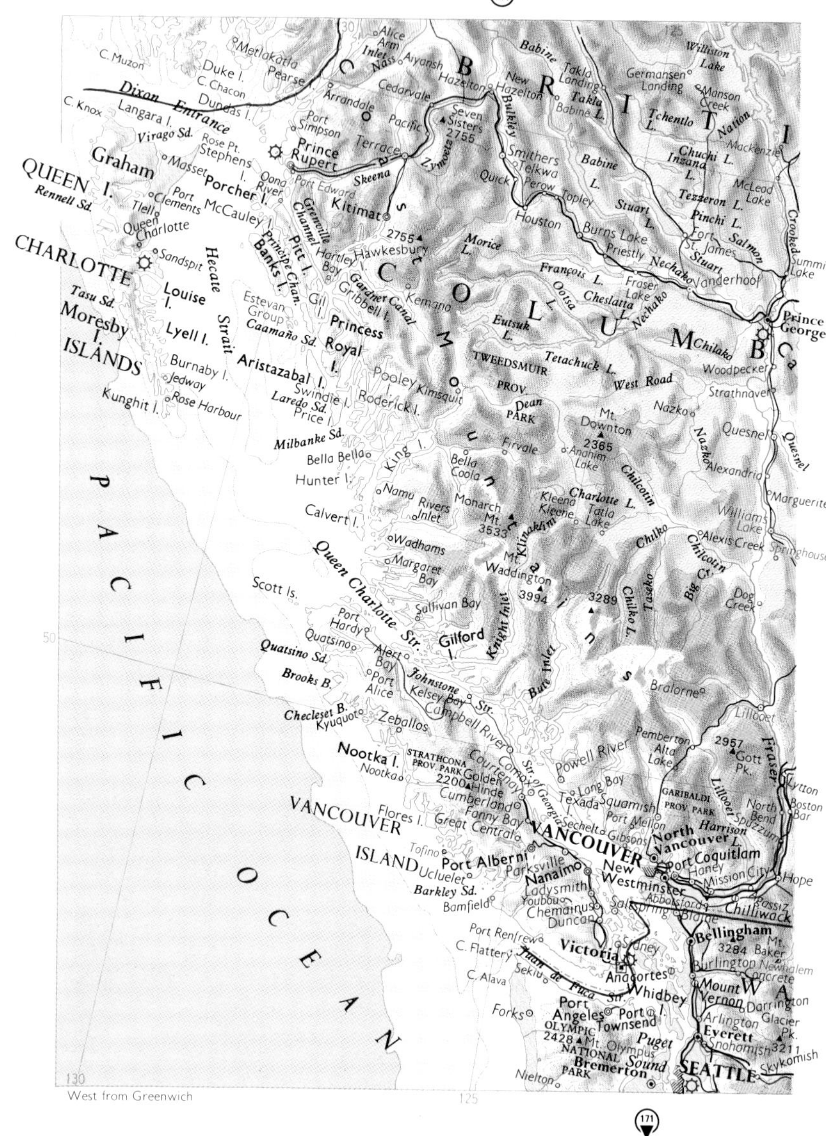

West from Greenwich

1 : 7 000 000

145

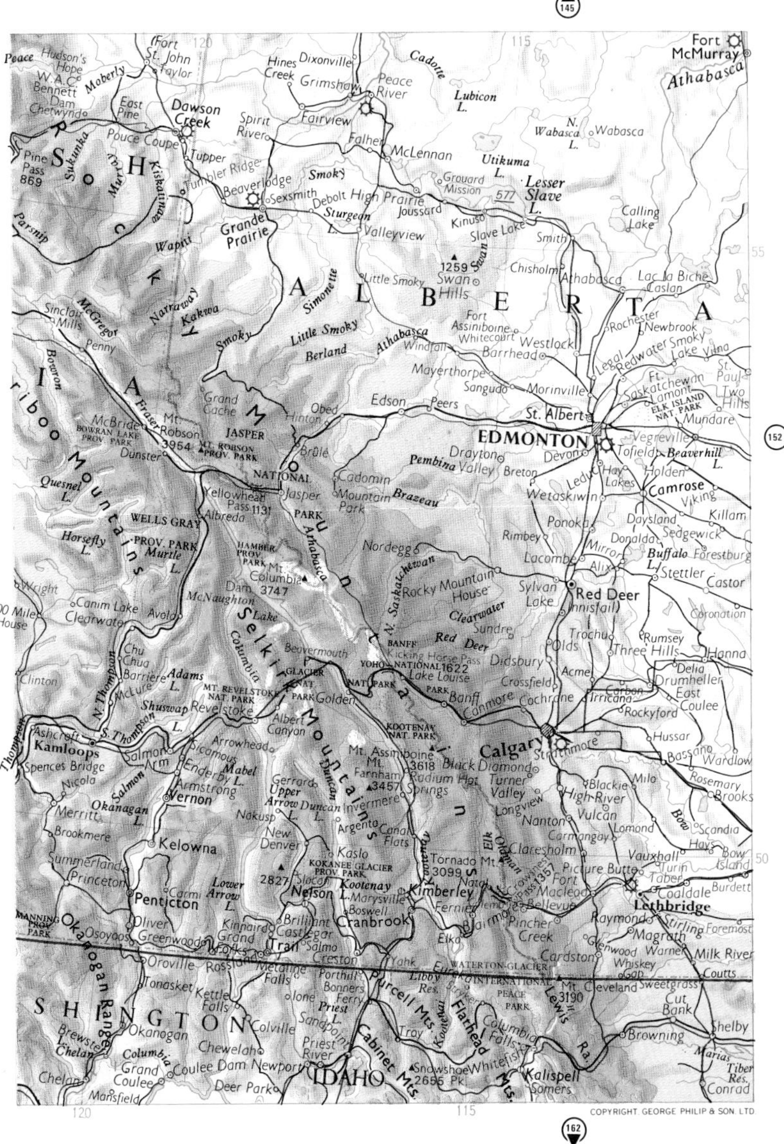

120
115
Fort McMurray
Athabasca
Peace
Hudson's Hope
W.A.C. Bennett Dam
Chetwynd
Moberly
Fort St. John
Taylor
Dawson Creek
East Pine
Pouce Coupe
Tupper
Tumbler Ridge
Pine Pass 869
Sukunka
Murray
Kiskatinaw
Hines Creek
Dixonville
Cadotte
Grimshaw
Peace River
Lubicon L.
Spirit River
Fairview
Falher
McLennan
N. Wabasca L.
Wabasca
Utikuma L.
Lesser Slave L.
Beaverlodge
Sexsmith
Smoky
Debolt
High Prairie
Grouard Mission
577
Joussard
Sturgeon L.
Grande Prairie
Valleyview
Kinuso
Slave Lake
Smith
Calling Lake
Parsnip
Wapiti
1259
Swan
Swan Hills
Chisholm
Athabasca
Lac la Biche
Caslan
55
Little Smoky
Simonette
ALBERTA
Sinclair Mills
McGregor
Narraway
Kakwa
Penny
Smoky
Little Smoky
Berland
Athabasca
Fort Assiniboine
Whitecourt
Windfall
Westlock
Barrhead
Rochester
Newbrook
Legal
Redwater
Smoky Lake
Vilna
St. Paul
Two Hills
Mayerthorpe
Sangudo
Morinville
Ft. Saskatchewan
Lamont
ELK ISLAND NAT. PARK
Mundare
Bowron
Grand Cache
Obed
Hinton
Edson
Peers
St. Albert
EDMONTON
Vegreville
Tofield
Beaverhill L.
McBride
BOWRAN LAKE PROV. PARK
Mt. Robson 3954
MT. ROBSON PROV. PARK
JASPER
Fraser
Dunster
Brûlé
Drayton Valley
Pembina
Devon
Breton
Leduc
Hay Lakes
Holden
Camrose
Viking
Quesnel L.
NATIONAL
Cadomin
Mountain Park
Brazeau
Yellowhead Pass 1131
Jasper
PARK
Wetaskiwin
Killam
WELLS GRAY PROV. PARK
Albreda
Ponoka
Daysland
Sedgewick
Horsefly L.
Murtle L.
HAMBER PROV. PARK
Mt. Columbia 3747
Athabasca
Rimbey
Donalda
Forestburg
Nordegg
Lacombe
Mirror
Buffalo L.
Alix
Stettler
Castor
N. Saskatchewan
Rocky Mountain House
Sylvan Lake
Red Deer
Wright
100 Mile House
Canim Lake
Clearwater
Avola
McNaughton Lake
Clearwater
Innisfail
Coronation
Sundre
Selkirk
Columbia
Red Deer
Trochu
Olds
Rumsey
Three Hills
Hanna
Chu Chua
Barriere
Beavermouth
BANFF
Kicking Horse Pass
Didsbury
Delia
Drumheller
East Coulee
Clinton
Adams L.
McLure
N. Thompson
GLACIER
YOHO NATIONAL 1622
Lake Louise
Crossfield
Acme
Carbon
MT. REVELSTOKE NAT. PARK
NAT. PARK
PARK
Golden
Banff
Canmore
Cochrane
Irricana
Rockyford
Shuswap L.
Revelstoke
S. Thompson
Thompson
Ashcroft
Kamloops
Albert Canyon
Arrowhead
KOOTENAY NAT. PARK
Calgary
Strathmore
Hussar
Salmon Arm
Sicamous
Mt. Assiniboine 3618
Mt. Farnham 3457
Black Diamond
Bassano
Wardlow
Spences Bridge
Nicola
Enderby
Mabel L.
Armstrong
Vernon
Duncan
Radium Hot Springs
Turner Valley
Blackie
Milo
High River
Rosemary
Brooks
Salmon
Gerrard
Upper Arrow L.
Duncan L.
Invermere
Longview
Vulcan
Merritt
Okanagan L.
Nakusp
Argenta
Canal Flats
Nanton
Lomond
Bow
Scandia
Brookmere
New Denver
Carmangay
Hays
Kelowna
Kaslo
Claresholm
Vauxhall
Bow Island
Summerland
KOKANEE GLACIER PROV. PARK
Tornado Mt. 3099
Elk
Oldman
Picture Butte
Turin
Taber
Burdett
50
Princeton
2827
Slocan
Natal
Crowsnest Pass 1357
Fort Macleod
Coaldale
Penticton
Carmi
Lower Arrow L.
Nelson
Kootenay L.
Marysville
Kimberley
Fernie
Bellevue
Lethbridge
Boswell
Blairmore
Pincher Creek
Raymond
Stirling
Foremost
MANNING PROV. PARK
Okanogan
Oliver
Osoyoos
Greenwood
Kinnaird
Grand Forks
Castlegar
Brilliant
Cranbrook
Elko
Magrath
Trail
Salmo
Creston
Glenwood
Warner
Milk River
Oroville
Rossland
Metaline Falls
Porthill
Bonners Ferry
Yahk
Libby Res.
Eureka
WATERTON-GLACIER INTERNATIONAL PEACE PARK
Cardston
Whiskey Gap
Coutts
Tonasket
Kettle Falls
Ione
Priest L.
Purcell Mts.
Kootenai
Mt. Cleveland 3190
Lewis
Sweetgrass
Cut Bank
SHINGTON
Okanogan Range
Okanogan
Colville
Sandpoint
Troy
Flathead
Columbia Falls
Browning
Shelby
Brewster
Chelan
Columbia
Chewelah
Priest River
Cabinet Mts.
Whitefish
Ra.
Marias
Tiber Res.
Grand Coulee
Coulee Dam
Newport
IDAHO
Snowshoe Pk. 2665
Kalispell
Somers
Mts.
Conrad
Deer Park
Mansfield

152

162

140

163

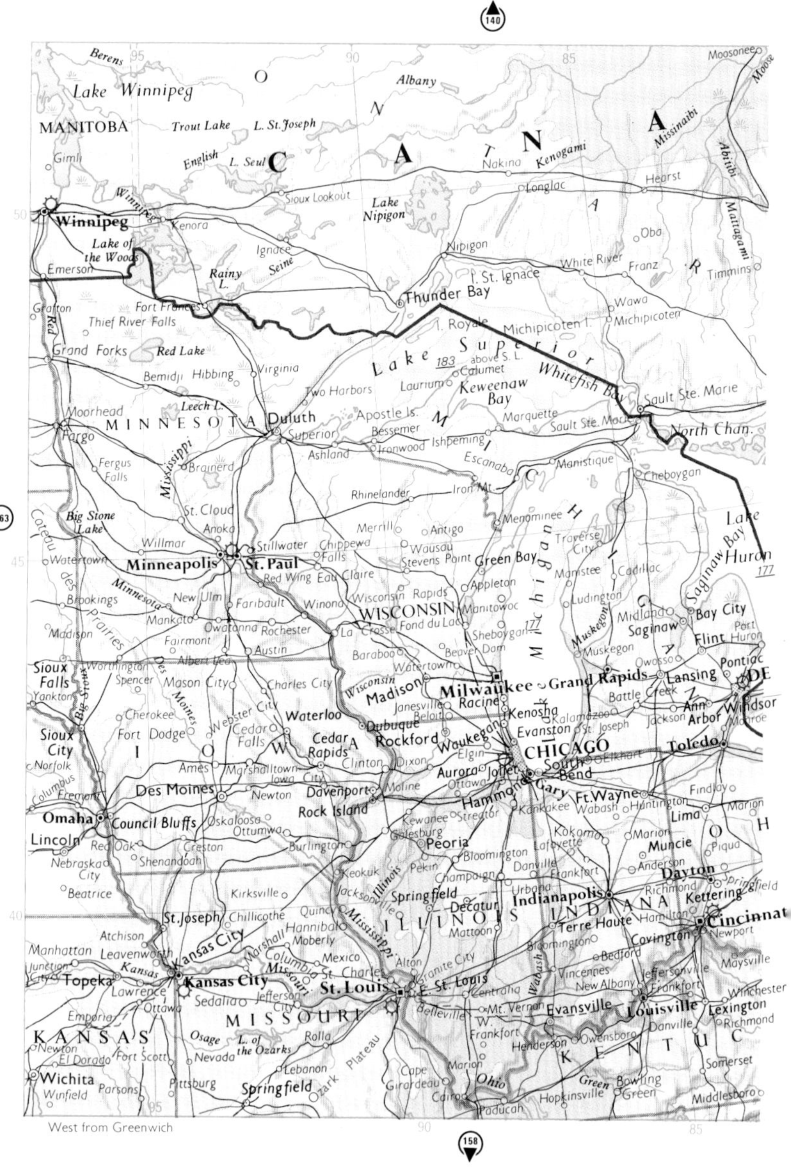

95
90
85
50
45
40
Berens
Lake Winnipeg
MANITOBA
Gimli
Winnipeg
Winnipeg
Lake of the Woods
Emerson
Kenora
Ignace
Seine
Rainy L.
Fort Frances
Trout Lake
L. St. Joseph
English
L. Seul
Sioux Lookout
Albany
O N T A R I O
C A N A D A
Lake Nipigon
Nakina
Kenogami
Longlac
Hearst
Missinaibi
Moose
Moosonee
Abitibi
Mattagami
Timmins
Oba
Franz
White River
Nipigon
I. St. Ignace
Thunder Bay
I. Royale
Wawa
Michipicoten
Michipicoten I.
Lake Superior
183 above S. L.
Calumet
Laurium
Keweenaw Bay
Whitefish Bay
Sault Ste. Marie
North Chan.
Grafton
Red
Thief River Falls
Grand Forks
Red Lake
Bemidji
Hibbing
Virginia
Two Harbors
Leech L.
Moorhead
Fargo
MINNESOTA
Duluth
Superior
Apostle Is.
Ashland
Bessemer
Ironwood
Ishpeming
Marquette
Sault Ste. Marie
Escanaba
Manistique
Cheboygan
Fergus Falls
Mississippi
Brainerd
Rhinelander
Iron Mt.
Menominee
M I C H I G A N
Lake Huron
177
Saginaw Bay
Big Stone Lake
St. Cloud
Anoka
Merrill
Antigo
Wausau
Stevens Point
Traverse City
Coteau des Prairies
Watertown
Willmar
Minneapolis
St. Paul
Stillwater
Chippewa Falls
Eau Claire
Green Bay
Manistee
Cadillac
Minnesota
Brookings
New Ulm
Faribault
Red Wing
Winona
Wisconsin Rapids
Appleton
Ludington
Midland
Bay City
Mankato
WISCONSIN
Manitowoc
Saginaw
Madison
Owatonna
Rochester
Fond du Lac
La Crosse
Sheboygan
177
Lake Michigan
Muskegon
Muskegon
Flint
Port Huron
Fairmont
Austin
Albert Lea
Baraboo
Beaver Dam
Owosso
Pontiac
Sioux Falls
Worthington
Des Moines
Spencer
Mason City
Charles City
Watertown
Wisconsin
Madison
Milwaukee
Grand Rapids
Lansing
Yankton
Big Sioux
Cherokee
Webster City
Waterloo
Janesville
Racine
Battle Creek
Ann Arbor
Windsor
Beloit
Kenosha
Kalamazoo
Jackson
Monroe
Sioux City
Fort Dodge
Cedar Falls
Cedar Rapids
Dubuque
Rockford
Waukegan
Evanston
St. Joseph
I O W A
Elgin
CHICAGO
Toledo
Norfolk
Ames
Marshalltown
Clinton
Dixon
Aurora
Joliet
South Bend
Elkhart
Iowa City
Ottawa
Hammond
Gary
Columbus
Fremont
Des Moines
Newton
Davenport
Moline
Ft. Wayne
Findlay
Huntington
Marion
Rock Island
Kewanee
Streator
Kankakee
Wabash
Lima
Omaha
Council Bluffs
Oskaloosa
Ottumwa
Galesburg
Lincoln
Red Oak
Creston
Burlington
Peoria
Kokomo
Marion
O H I O
Nebraska City
Shenandoah
Bloomington
Lafayette
Muncie
Piqua
Keokuk
Pekin
Illinois
Danville
Anderson
Beatrice
Kirksville
Champaign
Frankfort
Dayton
Springfield
Jacksonville
Springfield
Urbana
Richmond
Decatur
Indianapolis
Kettering
Quincy
ILLINOIS
INDIANA
Hamilton
St. Joseph
Chillicothe
Hannibal
Mississippi
Mattoon
Terre Haute
Cincinnati
Atchison
Moberly
Newport
Covington
Kansas City
Marshall
Bloomington
Manhattan
Leavenworth
Columbia
Mexico
Bedford
Maysville
Junction City
Kansas
Missouri
St. Charles
Alton
Granite City
Vincennes
Jeffersonville
Topeka
Kansas City
St. Louis
E. St. Louis
Wabash
New Albany
Frankfort
Winchester
Lawrence
Sedalia
Jefferson City
Centralia
Lexington
Ottawa
Belleville
Mt. Vernon
Evansville
Louisville
Emporia
MISSOURI
W. Frankfort
Danville
Richmond
KANSAS
Osage
L. of the Ozarks
Rolla
Henderson
Owensboro
K E N T U C K Y
Newton
El Dorado
Fort Scott
Nevada
Plateau
Marion
Somerset
Wichita
Parsons
Pittsburg
Lebanon
Ozark
Cape Girardeau
Ohio
Green
Bowling Green
Winfield
Springfield
Cairo
Paducah
Hopkinsville
Middlesboro
West from Greenwich

158

1 : 12 000 000

141

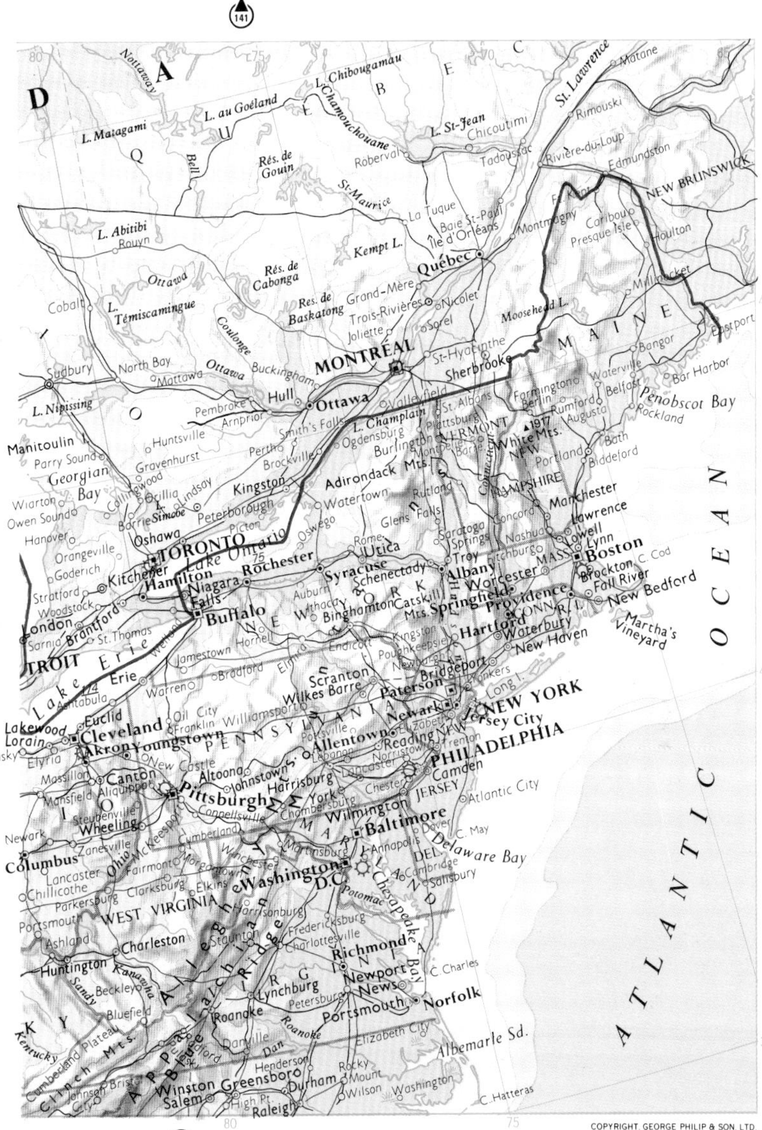

L. Chibougamau
Chamouchouane
L. au Goéland
L. Matagami
Rés. de Gouin
L. St-Jean
Chicoutimi
Roberval
Tadoussac
St. Lawrence
Matane
Rimouski
Rivière-du-Loup
Edmundston
NEW BRUNSWICK
St-Maurice
La Tuque
Baie St-Paul
Île d'Orléans
Montmagny
Caribou
Presque Isle
Houlton
L. Abitibi
Rouyn
Kempt L.
Québec
Rés. de Cabonga
Ottawa
L. Témiscamingue
Cobalt
Res. de Baskatong
Grand-Mère
Trois-Rivières
Nicolet
Sorel
Joliette
Coulonge
Moosehead L.
MAINE
Bangor
Eastport
North Bay
Mattawa
Sudbury
MONTREAL
St-Hyacinthe
Sherbrooke
Buckingham
Hull
Ottawa
L. Nipissing
Pembroke
Arnprior
Smith's Falls
L. Champlain
Valleyfield
St. Albans
Farmington
Waterville
Bar Harbor
Penobscot Bay
Rockland
Belfast
Augusta
Rumford
Berlin
Manitoulin I.
Parry Sound
Huntsville
Gravenhurst
Perth
Brockville
Ogdensburg
Plattsburg
Burlington
VERMONT
Montpelier
Barre
White Mts.
NEW HAMPSHIRE
Portland
Bath
Biddeford
Georgian Bay
Collingwood
Orillia
Lindsay
L. Simcoe
Kingston
Adirondack Mts.
Rutland
Connecticut
Wiarton
Owen Sound
Barrie
Peterborough
Picton
Watertown
Glens Falls
Concord
Manchester
Lawrence
Lowell
Lynn
Hanover
Oshawa
TORONTO
Lake Ontario
Oswego
Rome
Utica
Saratoga Springs
Nashua
Fitchburg
MASS.
Boston
Orangeville
Goderich
Kitchener
Hamilton
Rochester
Syracuse
Schenectady
Troy
Albany
Worcester
Brockton
C. Cod
Stratford
Woodstock
Niagara Falls
Auburn
Ithaca
NEW YORK
Catskill Mts.
Springfield
Providence
Fall River
New Bedford
London
Brantford
Buffalo
Binghamton
CONN.
R.I.
Sarnia
St. Thomas
Hornell
Hartford
Waterbury
Martha's Vineyard
DETROIT
Lake Erie
Welland
Jamestown
Elmira
Endicott
Kingston
Poughkeepsie
New Haven
Bradford
Newburgh
Bridgeport
Yonkers
Long I.
Warren
Erie
Scranton
Wilkes Barre
Paterson
NEW YORK
Ashtabula
Oil City
Franklin
Williamsport
Newark
Elizabeth
Jersey City
Lakewood
Euclid
Lorain
Cleveland
Youngstown
PENNSYLVANIA
Pottsville
Allentown
Reading
NEW JERSEY
Trenton
PHILADELPHIA
Elyria
Akron
New Castle
Lebanon
Norristown
Massillon
Canton
Altoona
Johnstown
Lancaster
Camden
Mansfield
Aliquippa
Pittsburgh
Harrisburg
York
Chester
Atlantic City
OHIO
Steubenville
Connellsville
Chambersburg
Wilmington
Baltimore
Dover
C. May
Newark
Wheeling
Cumberland
Delaware Bay
Columbus
Zanesville
Martinsburg
Annapolis
DEL.
Lancaster
Fairmont
Morgantown
Winchester
Cambridge
Salisbury
Chillicothe
Parkersburg
Clarksburg
Elkins
Washington D.C.
MARYLAND
Potomac
Chesapeake Bay
Portsmouth
WEST VIRGINIA
Harrisonburg
Fredericksburg
Ashland
Charleston
Staunton
Charlottesville
Richmond
VIRGINIA
Huntington
Kanawha
Sandy
Beckley
Newport News
C. Charles
Lynchburg
Petersburg
Norfolk
Portsmouth
KY.
Bluefield
Roanoke
Kentucky
Cumberland Plateau
Clinch Mts.
Danville
Dan
Elizabeth City
Albemarle Sd.
Appalachian Mts.
Blue Ridge
Allegheny Mts.
Henderson
Rocky Mount
Greensboro
Durham
Wilson
Washington
Johnson City
Bristol
Winston Salem
High Pt.
Raleigh
C. Hatteras
ATLANTIC OCEAN

159

156

161

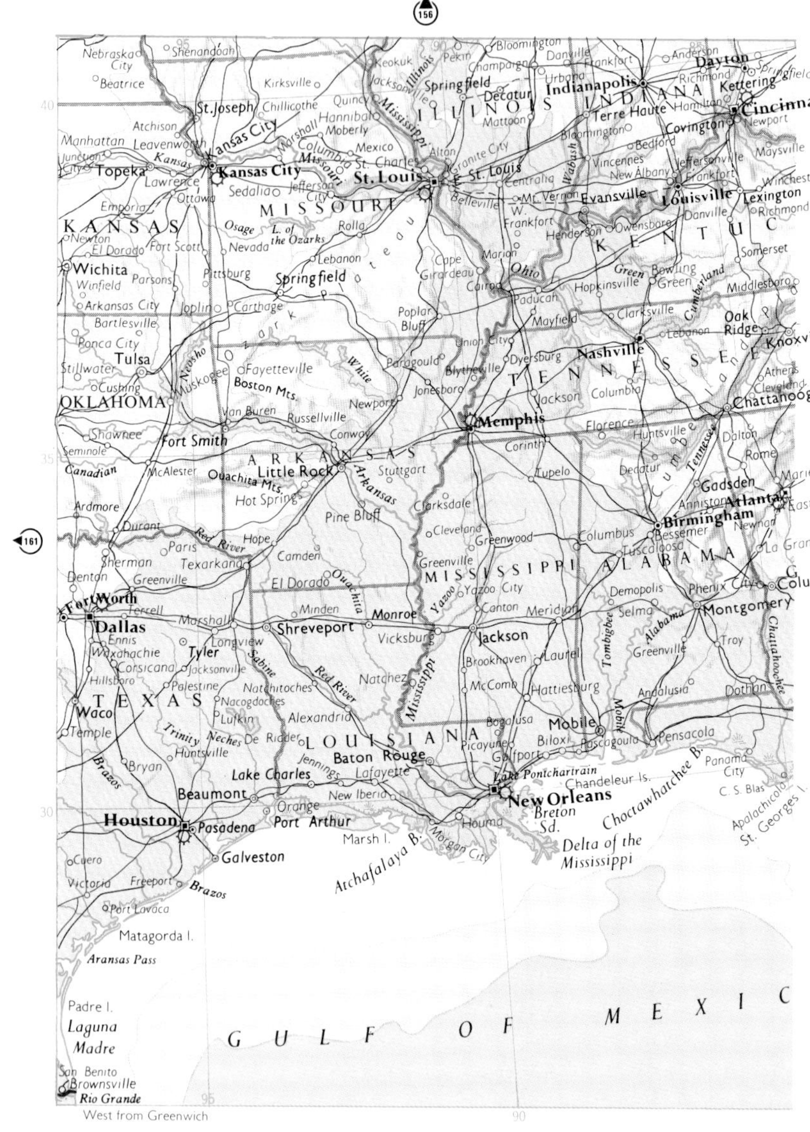
Nebraska City
Shenandoah
Bloomington
Pekin
Danville
Anderson
Dayton
Springfield
Beatrice
Kirksville
Keokuk
Jacksonville
Illinois
Champaign
Urbana
Frankfort
Richmond
Kettering
Springfield
Decatur
Indianapolis
INDIANA
Hamilton
Cincinna
40
St. Joseph
Chillicothe
Quincy
Mississippi
ILLINOIS
Mattoon
Terre Haute
Covington
Newport
Atchison
Hannibal
Moberly
Manhattan
Leavenworth
Kansas City
Marshall
Columbia
Missouri
Mexico
St. Charles
Alton
Granite City
Bloomington
Bedford
Maysville
Junction City
Kansas
Topeka
Kansas City
Lawrence
Sedalia
Jefferson City
St. Louis
E. St. Louis
Centralia
Wabash
Vincennes
New Albany
Jeffersonville
Frankfort
Winchester
Ottawa
Emporia
MISSOURI
Belleville
Mt. Vernon
Evansville
Louisville
Lexington
Richmond
KANSAS
Osage
L. of the Ozarks
Rolla
W. Frankfort
Henderson
Owensboro
Danville
Newton
El Dorado
Fort Scott
Nevada
Lebanon
Cape Girardeau
Marion
KENTUC
Somerset
Wichita
Winfield
Parsons
Pittsburg
Springfield
Ohio
Green
Bowling Green
Cairo
Hopkinsville
Cumberland
Middlesboro
Arkansas City
Joplin
Carthage
Paducah
Bartlesville
Poplar Bluff
Mayfield
Clarksville
Oak Ridge
Ponca City
Lebanon
Knoxvi
Tulsa
Union City
Paragould
Dyersburg
Nashville
Stillwater
Neosho
Fayetteville
White
Blytheville
TENNESSEE
Athens
Cushing
Muskogee
Boston Mts.
Jonesboro
Jackson
Columbia
Cleveland
OKLAHOMA
Newport
Chattanoog
Van Buren
Russellville
Memphis
Florence
Shawnee
Fort Smith
Conway
Huntsville
Dalton
Seminole
35
Corinth
Canadian
ARKANSAS
McAlester
Little Rock
Stuttgart
Tupelo
Decatur
Rome
Ouachita Mts.
Arkansas
Gadsden
Marie
Hot Springs
Anniston
Atlanta
East
Ardmore
Clarksdale
Pine Bluff
Birmingham
Durant
Cleveland
Bessemer
Newnan
Red River
Hope
Greenwood
Columbus
La Grang
Paris
Camden
Tuscaloosa
Sherman
Texarkana
Greenville
ALABAMA
Denton
Greenville
El Dorado
Ouachita
MISSISSIPPI
Yazoo
Yazoo City
Demopolis
Phenix City
Colum
Fort Worth
Minden
Canton
Meridian
Selma
Montgomery
Terrell
Marshall
Monroe
Dallas
Ennis
Longview
Shreveport
Vicksburg
Jackson
Tombigbee
Alabama
Chattahoochee
Tyler
Troy
Waxahachie
Sabine
Brookhaven
Laurel
Greenville
Corsicana
Jacksonville
Red River
Hillsboro
Palestine
Natchitoches
Natchez
McComb
Hattiesburg
Andalusia
Dothan
TEXAS
Nacogdoches
Mississippi
Waco
Lufkin
Alexandria
Bogalusa
Mobile
Temple
Trinity
Neches
De Ridder
LOUISIANA
Mobile
Pensacola
Huntsville
Picayune
Biloxi
Pascagoula
Baton Rouge
Gulfport
Brazos
Bryan
Jennings
Panama City
Lake Charles
Lafayette
Lake Pontchartrain
Chandeleur Is.
Choctawhatchee B.
C. S. Blas
Beaumont
New Iberia
Orange
New Orleans
30
Breton Sd.
Apalachicola
St. Georges I.
Houston
Pasadena
Port Arthur
Houma
Marsh I.
Morgan City
Delta of the Mississippi
Atchafalaya B.
Galveston
Cuero
Victoria
Freeport
Brazos
Port Lavaca
Matagorda I.
Aransas Pass
Padre I.
Laguna Madre
GULF OF MEXICO
San Benito
Brownsville
Rio Grande
95
90
West from Greenwich

1 : 12 000 000

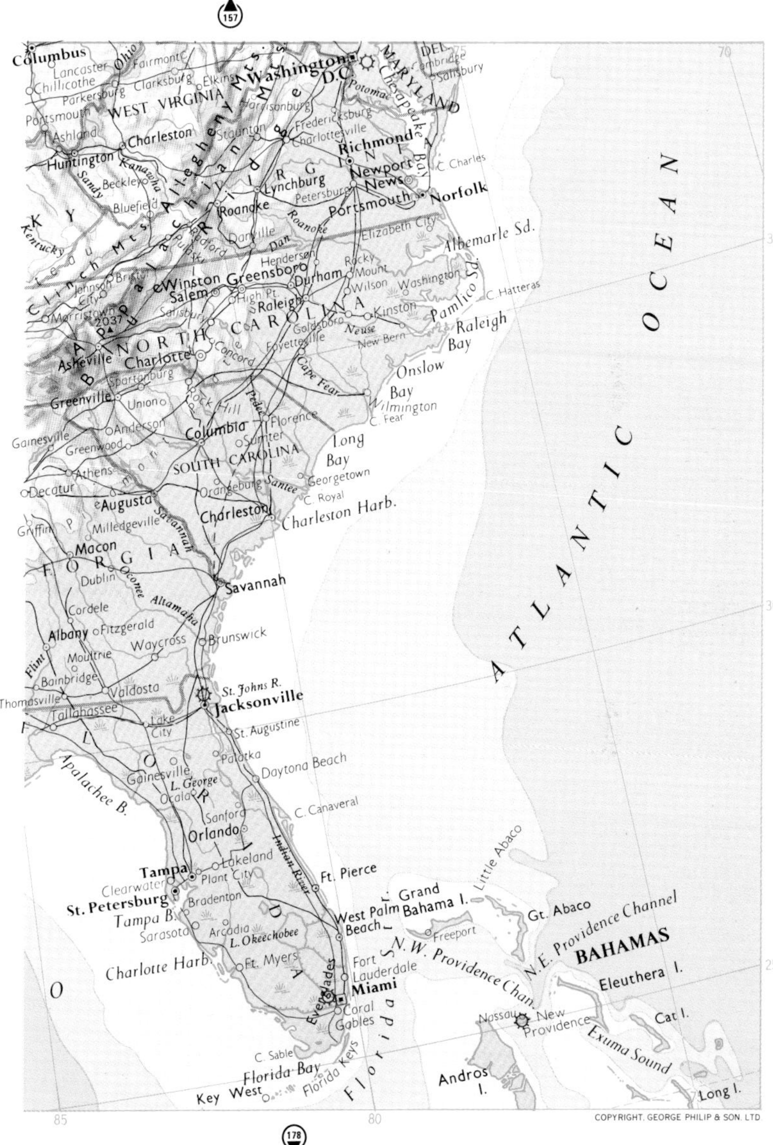

70

Columbus
Lancaster Ohio Fairmont
Chillicothe
Parkersburg Clarksburg Elkins
Portsmouth WEST VIRGINIA Washington, D.C. MARYLAND Cambridge Salisbury
Ashland Harrisonburg Potomac R.
Huntington Charleston Kanawha Fredericksburg
Kentucky Beckley Charlottesville Richmond
Bluefield Roanoke Lynchburg Newport News C. Charles
KY Kearny Johnson City Roanoke Petersburg Portsmouth Norfolk
Morristown 2037 Bristol Danville Dan Elizabeth City 35
Asheville Winston Greensboro Henderson Rocky Mount Albemarle Sd.
Salem Durham Wilson Washington C. Hatteras
NORTH CAROLINA Raleigh Goldsboro Kinston Pamlico Sd.
Charlotte Concord Fayetteville Neuse New Bern Raleigh
Greenville Spartanburg Cape Fear Onslow Bay
Union Rock Hill Bay Wilmington
Gainesville Anderson Columbia Florence C. Fear
Greenwood Sumter Long
Athens SOUTH CAROLINA Orangeburg Santee Bay
Decatur Georgetown
Augusta Savannah P. Royal
Griffin Milledgeville Charleston Charleston Harb.
Macon GEORGIA
Dublin Oconee Altamaha
Cordele Savannah
Albany Fitzgerald Brunswick
Moultrie Waycross
Flint Bainbridge Valdosta St. Johns R.
Thomasville Tallahassee Lake City Jacksonville
FLORIDA St. Augustine
Gainesville Palatka
Apalachee B. Ocala Daytona Beach
L. George
Sanford C. Canaveral
Orlando
Tampa Lakeland Ft. Pierce
Clearwater Plant City Indian River
St. Petersburg Bradenton West Palm Grand
Tampa B. Beach Bahama I. Little Abaco
Sarasota Arcadia Gt. Abaco
Charlotte Harb. L. Okeechobee N.W. Providence Chan. N.E. Providence Channel
Ft. Myers Freeport
Fort BAHAMAS
Lauderdale
Everglades Miami Eleuthera I.
Coral 25
Gables Nassau New
C. Sable Providence Cat I.
Florida Bay Exuma Sound
Key West Florida Keys Andros Long I.
Florida I.

A T L A N T I C   O C E A N

30

85 80 COPYRIGHT. GEORGE PHILIP & SON. LTD

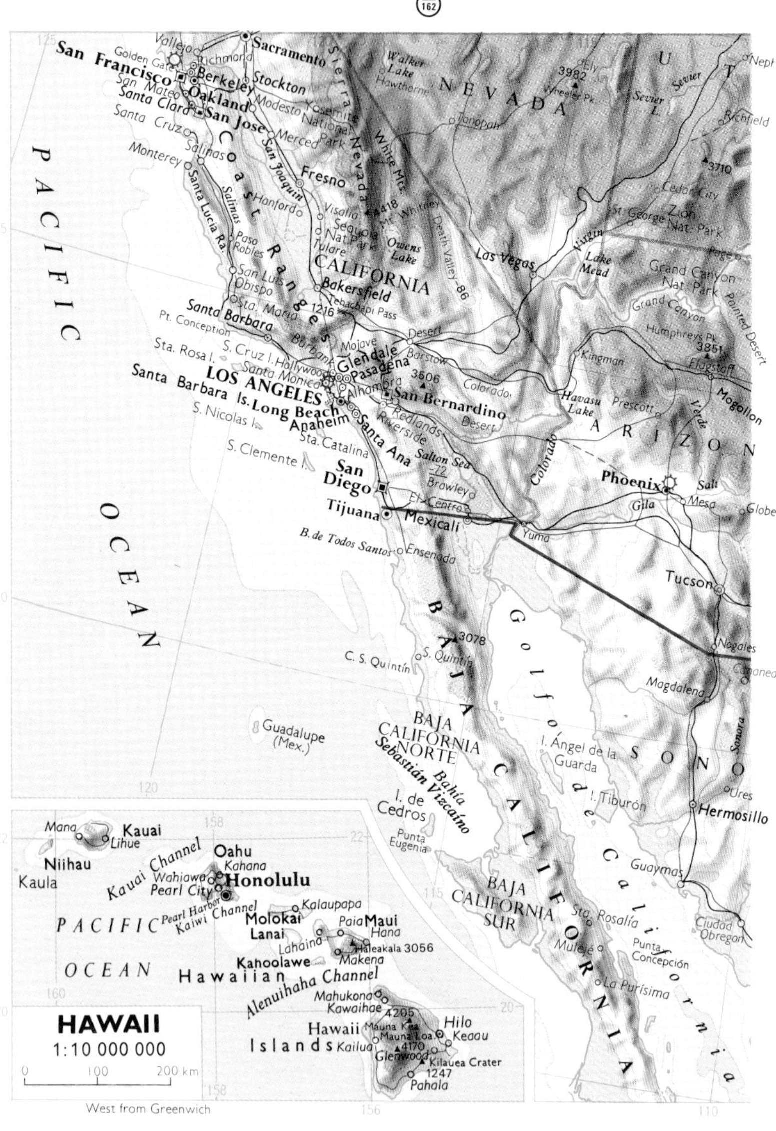

HAWAII
1:10 000 000
0   100   200 km

West from Greenwich

1 : 12 000 000

163

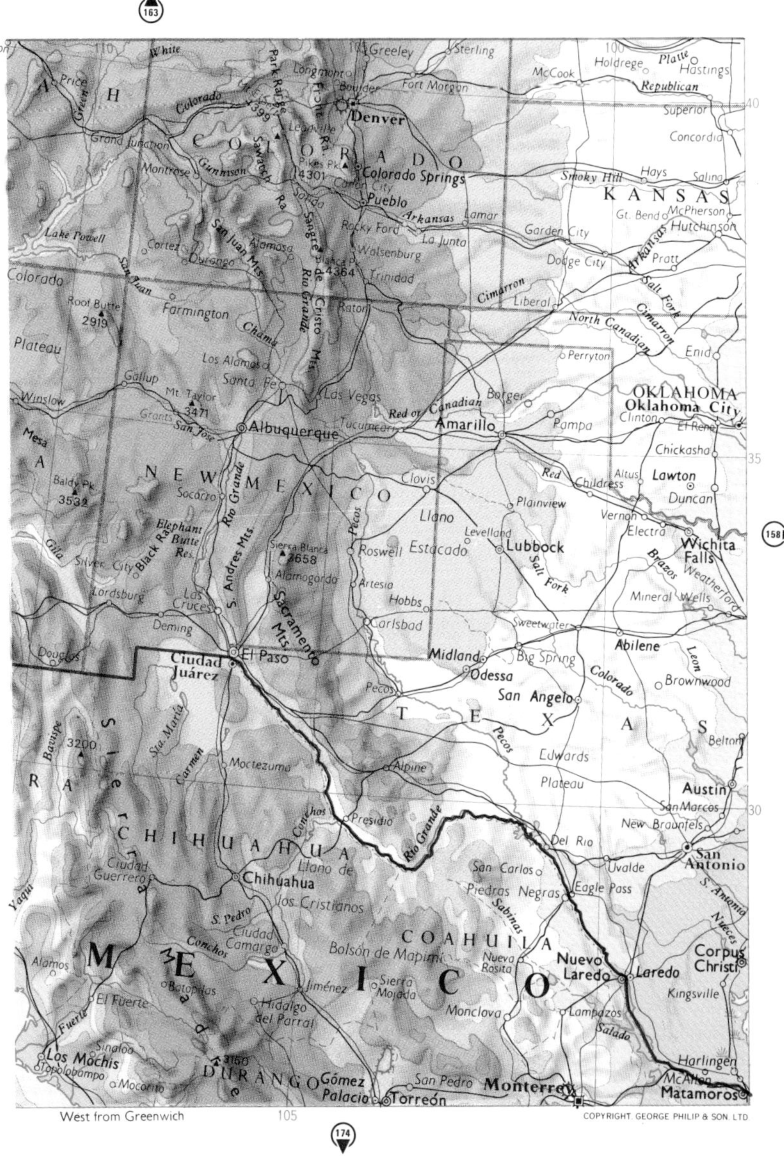

COLORADO
KANSAS
OKLAHOMA
NEW MEXICO
TEXAS
MEXICO
CHIHUAHUA
COAHUILA
DURANGO
Sierra Madre
Denver
Greeley
Sterling
Longmont
Boulder
Fort Morgan
McCook
Holdrege
Platte
Hastings
Republican
Superior
Concordia
Colorado Springs
Pikes Pk.
4301
Cañon City
Pueblo
Leadville
Park Range
Front Ra.
Sawatch Ra.
4399
Gunnison
Grand Junction
Montrose
Colorado
White
Green
Price
Lake Powell
Smoky Hill
Hays
Salina
Gt. Bend
McPherson
Hutchinson
Arkansas
Lamar
Rocky Ford
La Junta
Garden City
Dodge City
Pratt
Salida
Sangre de Cristo Mts.
Blanca Pk.
4364
Walsenburg
Trinidad
Alamosa
San Juan Mts.
Cortez
Durango
Rio Grande
San Juan
Colorado Plateau
Root Butte
2919
Farmington
Chama
Raton
Cimarron
Liberal
North Canadian
Salt Fork
Enid
Perryton
Los Alamos
Santa Fe
Las Vegas
Gallup
Mt. Taylor
3471
Winslow
Grants
San Jose
Albuquerque
Tucumcari
Red or Canadian
Borger
Amarillo
Pampa
Oklahoma City
Clinton
El Reno
Chickasha
Mesa
Baldy Pk.
3532
Socorro
Clovis
Red
Childress
Altus
Lawton
Duncan
Plainview
Vernon
Electra
Wichita Falls
Llano Estacado
Levelland
Lubbock
Pecos
Roswell
Sierra Blanca
3658
Alamogordo
Artesia
Hobbs
Carlsbad
Elephant Butte Res.
Black Ra.
S. Andres Mts.
Gila
Silver City
Lordsburg
Las Cruces
Deming
Douglas
Sacramento Mts.
Brazos
Weatherford
Mineral Wells
Sweetwater
Abilene
Big Spring
Midland
Odessa
Leon
Brownwood
San Angelo
Ciudad Juárez
El Paso
Colorado
Belton
Bavispe
3200
Sta. María
Carmen
Moctezuma
Alpine
Edwards Plateau
Austin
San Marcos
New Braunfels
Conchos
Presidio
Del Rio
San Antonio
Uvalde
Ciudad Guerrero
Chihuahua
Llano de los Cristianos
San Carlos
Piedras Negras
Eagle Pass
Sabinas
S. Antonio
Nueces
Yaqui
S. Pedro
Ciudad Camargo
Bolsón de Mapimí
Nueva Rosita
Nuevo Laredo
Laredo
Corpus Christi
Alamos
Batopilas
El Fuerte
Jiménez
Sierra Mojada
Kingsville
Hidalgo del Parral
Monclova
Lampazos
Salado
Fuerte
Sinaloa
3150
Los Mochis
Topolobampo
Mocorito
Gómez Palacio
Torreón
San Pedro
Monterrey
Harlingen
McAllen
Matamoros
110
105
100
40
35
30

158

West from Greenwich 105

174

142

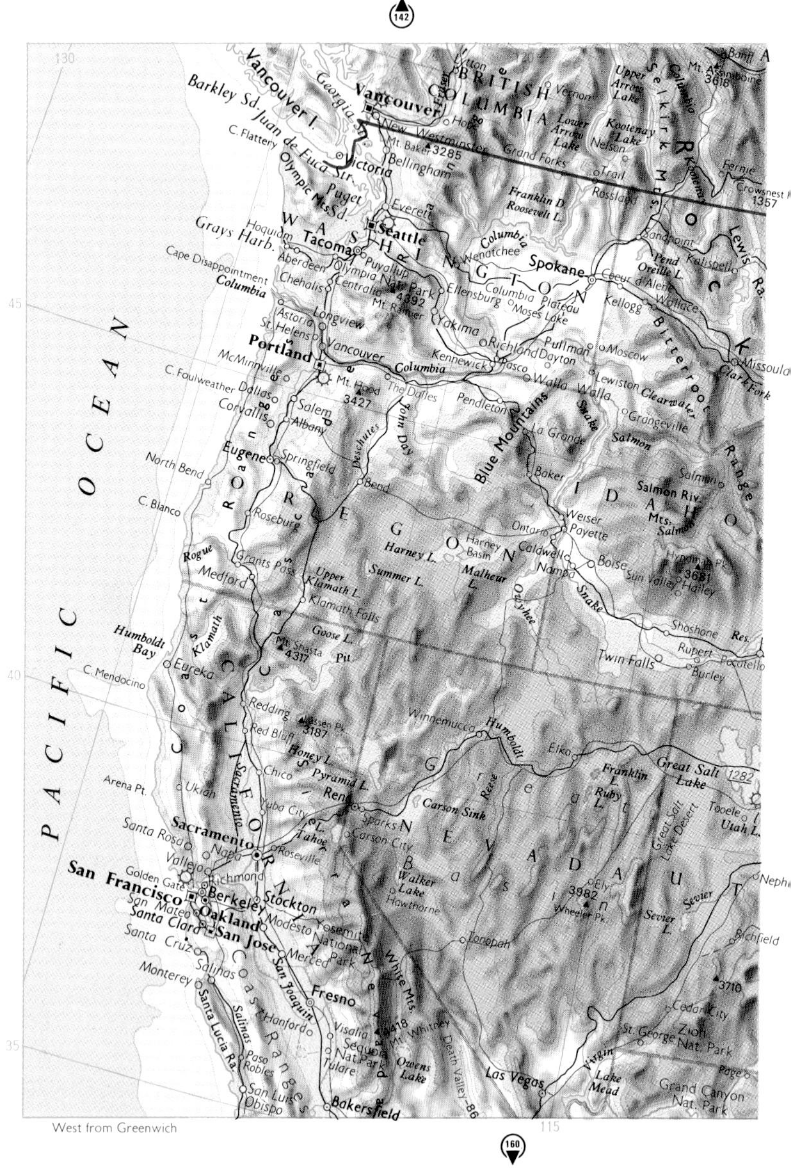
PACIFIC OCEAN
130
45
40
35
115
West from Greenwich
BRITISH COLUMBIA
WASHINGTON
OREGON
IDAHO
CALIFORNIA
NEVADA
UTAH
Vancouver I.
Barkley Sd.
Georgia Str.
Juan de Fuca Str.
Vancouver
Victoria
New Westminster
Mt. Baker 3285
Bellingham
Hope
Lytton
Vernon
C. Flattery
Olympic Mts.
Puget Sd.
Everett
Seattle
Tacoma
Hoquiam
Grays Harb.
Aberdeen
Olympia
Puyallup
Chehalis
Centralia
Cape Disappointment
Columbia
Mt. Rainier 4392
Wenatchee
Ellensburg
Yakima
Moses Lake
Columbia Plateau
Spokane
Coeur d'Alene
Kellogg
Wallace
Sandpoint
Pend Oreille L.
Kalispell
Lewis Ra.
Missoula
Clark Fork
Bitterroot Range
Selkirk Mts.
Upper Arrow Lake
Lower Arrow Lake
Kootenay Lake
Nelson
Trail
Rossland
Grand Forks
Franklin D. Roosevelt L.
Mt. Assiniboine 3618
Banff
Fernie
Crowsnest P. 1357
Astoria
St. Helens
Longview
Portland
Vancouver
Mt. Hood 3427
The Dalles
Richland
Kennewick
Pasco
Pullman
Moscow
Dayton
Walla Walla
Pendleton
Lewiston
Clearwater
Grangeville
Snake
Salmon
McMinnville
C. Foulweather
Dallas
Corvallis
Salem
Albany
John Day
Deschutes
Blue Mountains
La Grande
Baker
Eugene
Springfield
North Bend
C. Blanco
Bend
Roseburg
Cascade Range
Coast Range
Ontario
Weiser
Payette
Harney Basin
Harney L.
Malheur L.
Summer L.
Caldwell
Nampa
Boise
Sun Valley
Hailey
Hyndman Pk. 3681
Salmon Riv. Mts.
Salmon
Owyhee
Rogue
Grants Pass
Medford
Upper Klamath L.
Klamath Falls
Goose L.
Humboldt Bay
Klamath
Eureka
C. Mendocino
Mt. Shasta 4317
Pit
Shoshone
Rupert
Twin Falls
Burley
Pocatello
Res.
Redding
Lassen Pk. 3187
Red Bluff
Honey L.
Winnemucca
Humboldt
Elko
Great Salt Lake
1282
Franklin L.
Ruby L.
Chico
Pyramid L.
Reno
Carson Sink
Reese
Great Basin
Arena Pt.
Ukiah
Sacramento
Yuba City
L. Tahoe
Sparks
Carson City
Tooele
Utah L.
Great Salt Lake Desert
Santa Rosa
Napa
Roseville
Vallejo
Golden Gate
Richmond
San Francisco
Berkeley
Oakland
San Mateo
Santa Clara
San Jose
Santa Cruz
Stockton
Modesto
Walker Lake
Hawthorne
Ely
3982
Wheeler Pk.
Sevier
Sevier L.
Nephi
Richfield
Yosemite National Park
Merced
Tonopah
Sierra Nevada
White Mts.
Monterey
Salinas
San Joaquin
Fresno
Hanford
Visalia
Mt. Whitney 4418
Sequoia Nat. Park
Tulare
Owens Lake
Death Valley -86
3710
Cedar City
Zion Nat. Park
St. George
Santa Lucia Ra.
Coast Ranges
Paso Robles
San Luis Obispo
Bakersfield
Las Vegas
Virgin
Lake Mead
Grand Canyon Nat. Park
Page

160

1 : 12 000 000

143

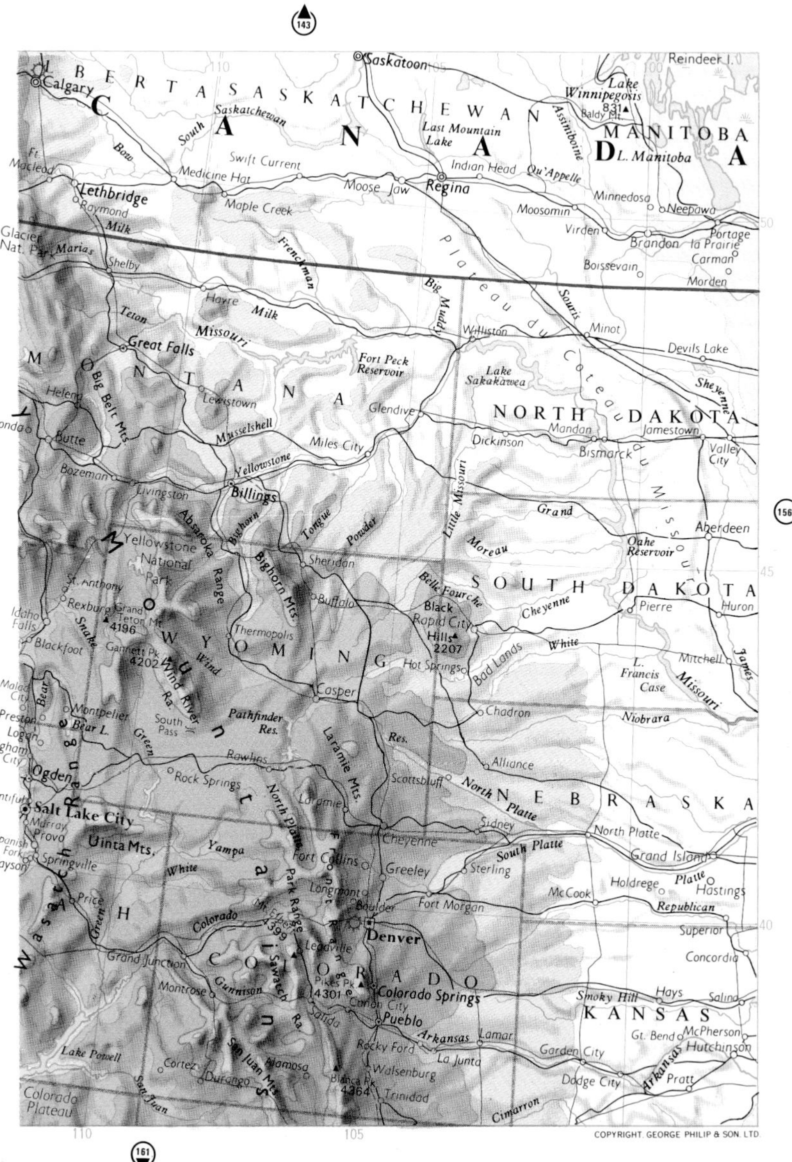

Saskatoon
Reindeer L.
Calgary
A L B E R T A
S A S K A T C H E W A N
C A N A D A
Lake Winnipegosis
831
Baldy Mt.
M A N I T O B A
South Saskatchewan
Bow
Last Mountain Lake
Assiniboine
L. Manitoba
Ft. Macleod
Medicine Hat
Swift Current
Indian Head
Qu'Appelle
Lethbridge
Moose Jaw
Regina
Minnedosa
Neepawa
Raymond
Maple Creek
Moosomin
Milk
Virden
Brandon
Portage la Prairie
Carman
Glacier Nat. Park
Marias
Frenchman
Plateau du Coteau du Missouri
Boissevain
Morden
Shelby
Big Muddy
Souris
Havre
Milk
Teton
Williston
Minot
Missouri
Great Falls
Devils Lake
Fort Peck Reservoir
Lake Sakakawea
Sheyenne
M O N T A N A
Big Belt Mts
Helena
Lewistown
Glendive
N O R T H   D A K O T A
Anaconda
Musselshell
Mandan
Jamestown
Butte
Miles City
Dickinson
Bismarck
Valley City
Yellowstone
Bozeman
Billings
Livingston
Little Missouri
Grand
Absaroka Range
Tongue
Powder
Aberdeen
Yellowstone National Park
Bighorn
Oahe Reservoir
Moreau
Sheridan
Bighorn Mts
St. Anthony
Belle Fourche
S O U T H   D A K O T A
Rexburg
Grand Teton Mt
4196
Buffalo
Black Hills
2207
Cheyenne
Pierre
Huron
Idaho Falls
Snake
Rapid City
Thermopolis
Blackfoot
Gannett Pk
4202
W Y O M I N G
Wind
Wind River Ra.
Hot Springs
Bad Lands
White
Mitchell
James
L. Francis Case
Missouri
Malad City
Bear
Casper
Chadron
Preston
Montpelier
Bear L.
Pathfinder Res.
Niobrara
Logan
South Pass
Green
Laramie Mts.
Res.
Brigham City
Rawlins
Alliance
Ogden
Rock Springs
Scottsbluff
North Platte
Bountiful
Salt Lake City
North Platte
Laramie
N E B R A S K A
Murray
Provo
Uinta Mts.
Sidney
North Platte
Spanish Fork
Cheyenne
Payson
Springville
Yampa
Fort Collins
South Platte
Grand Island
White
Greeley
Sterling
Platte
Holdrege
Hastings
Wasatch Range
Park Range
Longmont
McCook
Price
U T A H
Boulder
Fort Morgan
Republican
Green
Colorado
Mt Elbert
4399
Denver
Superior
R O C K Y   M O U N T A I N S
Leadville
Front Range
Grand Junction
Concordia
C O L O R A D O
Sawatch Ra.
Pikes Pk
4301
Montrose
Gunnison
Colorado Springs
Smoky Hill
Hays
Salina
Canon City
Salida
K A N S A S
Pueblo
Arkansas
Lamar
Gt. Bend
McPherson
Rocky Ford
Garden City
Hutchinson
Lake Powell
Alamosa
La Junta
Cortez
San Juan Mts
Walsenburg
Arkansas
Durango
Blanca Pk
4364
Dodge City
Pratt
Colorado Plateau
San Juan
Trinidad
Cimarron
110
105
100
50
45
40

156

161

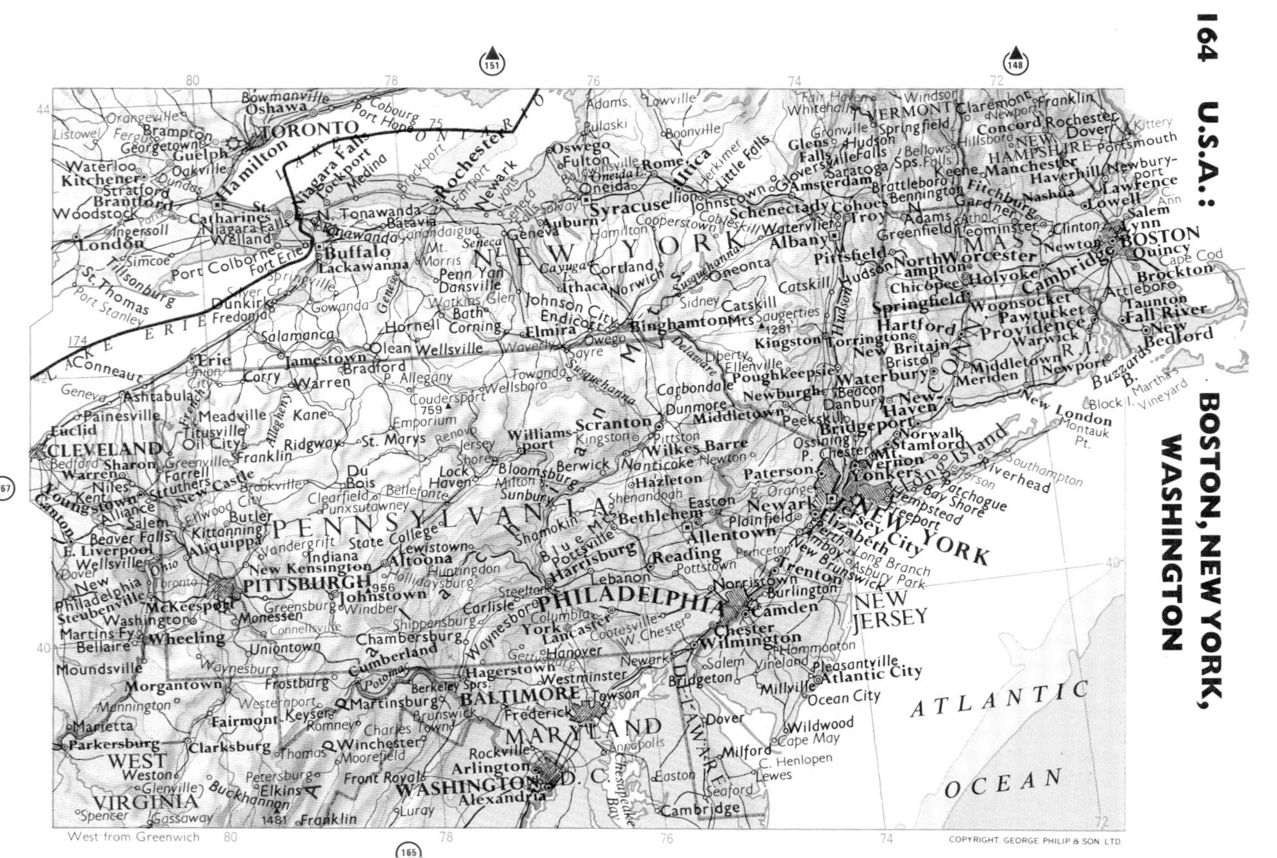

1 : 6 000 000

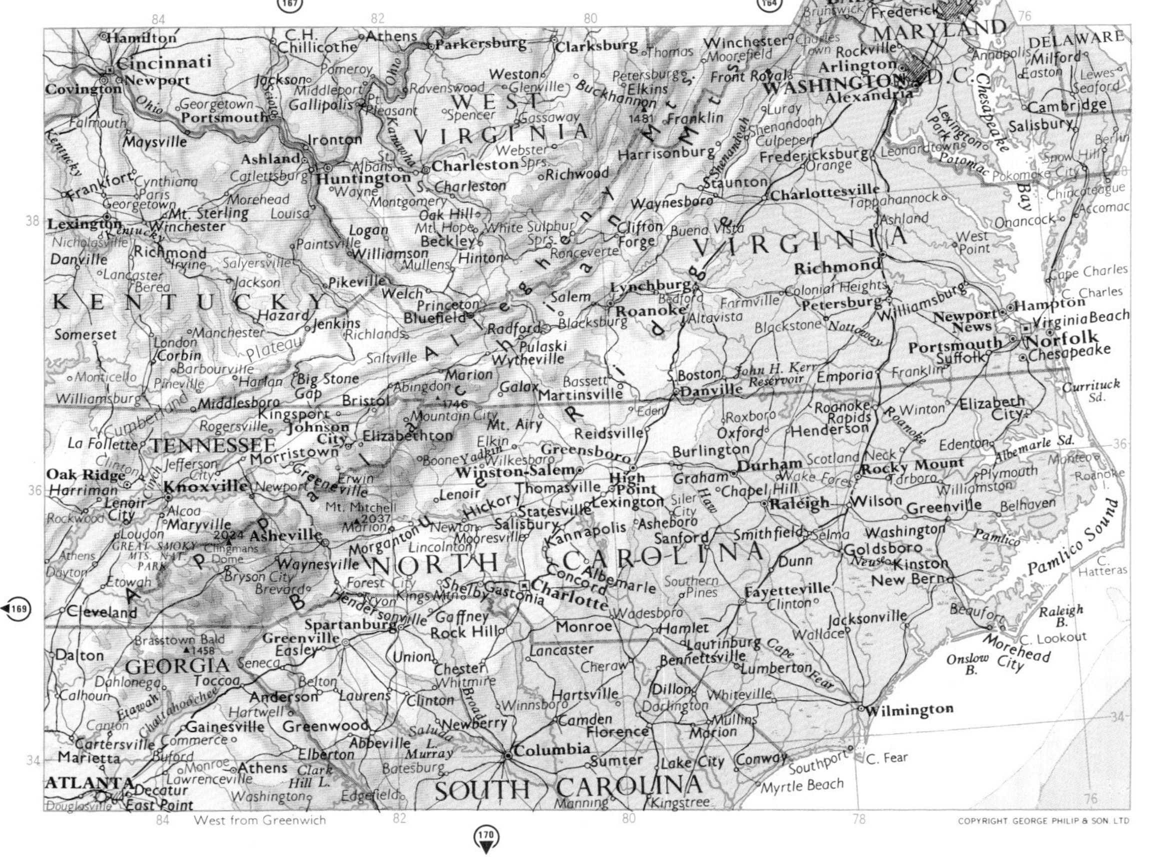
DELAWARE
MARYLAND
WASHINGTON D.C.
WEST VIRGINIA
VIRGINIA
KENTUCKY
TENNESSEE
NORTH CAROLINA
SOUTH CAROLINA
GEORGIA
Allegheny Mts.
Blue Ridge
Appalachian
Cumberland Plateau
Chesapeake Bay
Pamlico Sound
Albemarle Sd.
Currituck Sd.
Onslow B.
Raleigh B.
C. Hatteras
C. Lookout
C. Fear
C. Charles
Cape Charles
Virginia Beach
Norfolk
Chesapeake
Portsmouth
Hampton
Newport News
Richmond
Petersburg
Williamsburg
Charlottesville
Fredericksburg
Alexandria
Arlington
Rockville
Frederick
Annapolis
Cambridge
Salisbury
Winchester
Staunton
Lynchburg
Roanoke
Danville
Martinsville
Bristol
Kingsport
Johnson City
Knoxville
Oak Ridge
Asheville
Charlotte
Greensboro
Winston-Salem
High Point
Durham
Raleigh
Chapel Hill
Fayetteville
Wilmington
New Bern
Greenville
Rocky Mount
Elizabeth City
Columbia
Spartanburg
Anderson
Florence
Sumter
ATLANTA
Decatur
East Point
Marietta
Gainesville
Athens
Lexington
Frankfort
Cincinnati
Covington
Newport
Hamilton
Ashland
Huntington
Charleston
Parkersburg
Clarksburg
Beckley
Bluefield
Mt. Mitchell 2037
1746
GREAT SMOKY MTS. NAT. PARK
Clingmans Dome 2024
Brasstown Bald 1458
Ohio
Kentucky
Potomac
Shenandoah
Roanoke
Clark Hill L.
John H. Kerr Reservoir
167
164
169
170
38
36
34
76
78
80
82
84
West from Greenwich
COPYRIGHT GEORGE PHILIP & SON. LTD

1 : 6 000 000

156

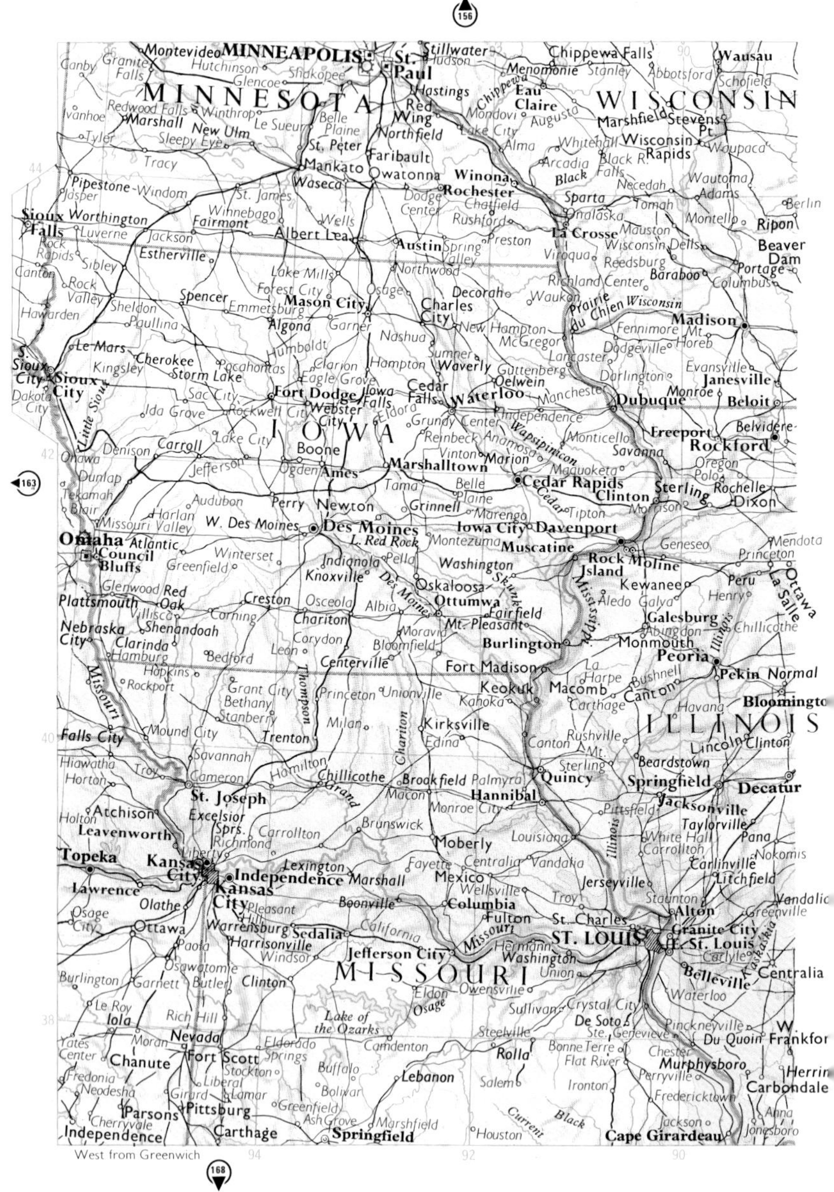

MINNESOTA
WISCONSIN
IOWA
ILLINOIS
MISSOURI
Montevideo
MINNEAPOLIS
St. Paul
Stillwater
Hudson
Chippewa Falls
Wausau
Canby
Granite Falls
Hutchinson
Shakopee
Glencoe
Hastings
Menomonie
Stanley
Abbotsford
Schofield
Redwood Falls
Winthrop
Red Wing
Eau Claire
Ivanhoe
Marshall
Le Sueur
Belle Plaine
Mondovi
Augusta
Marshfield
Stevens Pt.
Tyler
New Ulm
Sleepy Eye
St. Peter
Northfield
Lake City
Whitehall
Wisconsin Rapids
Waupaca
Tracy
Mankato
Faribault
Alma
Arcadia
Black R. Falls
Pipestone
Windom
Waseca
Owatonna
Winona
Black
Necedah
Wautoma
Jasper
St. James
Dodge Center
Rochester
Sparta
Tomah
Adams
Berlin
Sioux Falls
Worthington
Winnebago
Fairmont
Wells
Chatfield
Rushford
Onalaska
Montello
Ripon
Luverne
Jackson
Albert Lea
Austin
Preston
La Crosse
Mauston
Rock Rapids
Estherville
Spring Valley
Viroqua
Wisconsin Dells
Beaver Dam
Canton
Sibley
Lake Mills
Northwood
Reedsburg
Baraboo
Portage
Rock Valley
Forest City
Osage
Decorah
Richland Center
Columbus
Hawarden
Sheldon
Spencer
Emmetsburg
Mason City
Charles City
Waukon
Prairie du Chien
Wisconsin
Madison
Paullina
Algona
Garner
Nashua
New Hampton
McGregor
Fennimore
Mt. Horeb
Le Mars
Humboldt
Sumner
Lancaster
Dodgeville
S. Sioux City
Sioux City
Dakota City
Cherokee
Kingsley
Storm Lake
Pocahontas
Clarion
Eagle Grove
Hampton
Waverly
Guttenberg
Oelwein
Darlington
Evansville
Janesville
Little Sioux
Sac City
Fort Dodge
Webster City
Iowa Falls
Cedar Falls
Waterloo
Manchester
Dubuque
Monroe
Beloit
Ida Grove
Rockwell City
Eldora
Grundy Center
Independence
Belvidere
Lake City
Reinbeck
Anamosa
Wapsipinicon
Monticello
Freeport
Rockford
Onawa
Denison
Carroll
Boone
Vinton
Marion
Savanna
Oregon
Jefferson
Ogden
Ames
Marshalltown
Maquoketa
Polo
Dunlap
Tama
Belle Plaine
Cedar Rapids
Sterling
Rochelle
Tekamah
Audubon
Perry
Newton
Grinnell
Cedar
Clinton
Dixon
Blair
Harlan
Marengo
Tipton
Morrison
Missouri Valley
W. Des Moines
Des Moines
Iowa City
Davenport
Omaha
Atlantic
L. Red Rock
Montezuma
Muscatine
Mendota
Council Bluffs
Winterset
Rock Island
Moline
Geneseo
Princeton
Greenfield
Indianola
Pella
Washington
Ottawa
Knoxville
Des Moines
Oskaloosa
Skunk
Kewanee
Peru
La Salle
Glenwood
Red Oak
Creston
Osceola
Albia
Ottumwa
Mississippi
Aledo
Galva
Henry
Plattsmouth
Villisca
Corning
Chariton
Fairfield
Galesburg
Nebraska City
Shenandoah
Corydon
Moravia
Mt. Pleasant
Abingdon
Chillicothe
Clarinda
Hamburg
Leon
Bloomfield
Burlington
Monmouth
Peoria
Illinois
Bedford
Centerville
Fort Madison
La Harpe
Bushnell
Pekin
Normal
Hopkins
Rockport
Grant City
Thompson
Princeton
Unionville
Kahoka
Keokuk
Macomb
Canton
Havana
Bloomington
Bethany
Stanberry
Carthage
Missouri
Milan
Chariton
Kirksville
Rushville
Lincoln
Clinton
Falls City
Mound City
Trenton
Edina
Canton
Mt. Sterling
Savannah
Hiawatha
Troy
Hamilton
Beardstown
Horton
Cameron
Chillicothe
Brookfield
Palmyra
Quincy
Springfield
Decatur
St. Joseph
Grand
Macon
Hannibal
Jacksonville
Holton
Atchison
Excelsior Sprs.
Monroe City
Pittsfield
Taylorville
Leavenworth
Carrollton
Richmond
Brunswick
Louisiana
White Hall
Pana
Liberty
Moberly
Carrollton
Nokomis
Topeka
Kansas City
Lexington
Fayette
Centralia
Vandalia
Carlinville
Independence
Marshall
Mexico
Jerseyville
Litchfield
Lawrence
Kansas City
Wellsville
Troy
Staunton
Vandalia
Olathe
Pleasant Hill
Boonville
Columbia
Alton
Greenville
Osage City
Ottawa
Warrensburg
Sedalia
California
Fulton
St. Charles
Granite City
Paola
Harrisonville
Missouri
Hermann
ST. LOUIS
E. St. Louis
Kaskaskia
Jefferson City
Washington
Carlyle
Osawatomie
Windsor
Union
Centralia
Burlington
Garnett
Butler
Clinton
Belleville
Eldon
Owensville
Waterloo
Osage
Le Roy
Iola
Rich Hill
Lake of the Ozarks
Sullivan
Crystal City
De Soto
Pinckneyville
W. Frankfort
Ste. Genevieve
Yates Center
Moran
Nevada
Eldorado Springs
Camdenton
Steelville
Du Quoin
Chanute
Fort Scott
Stockton
Bonne Terre
Chester
Rolla
Flat River
Murphysboro
Buffalo
Herrin
Fredonia
Liberal
Lebanon
Salem
Ironton
Perryville
Carbondale
Neodesha
Girard
Lamar
Bolivar
Fredericktown
Parsons
Pittsburg
Greenfield
Current
Black
Anna
Cherryvale
Ash Grove
Marshfield
Jackson
Jonesboro
Independence
Carthage
Springfield
Houston
Cape Girardeau
44
42
40
38
96
94
92
90
West from Greenwich

163

168

1 : 6 000 000

150

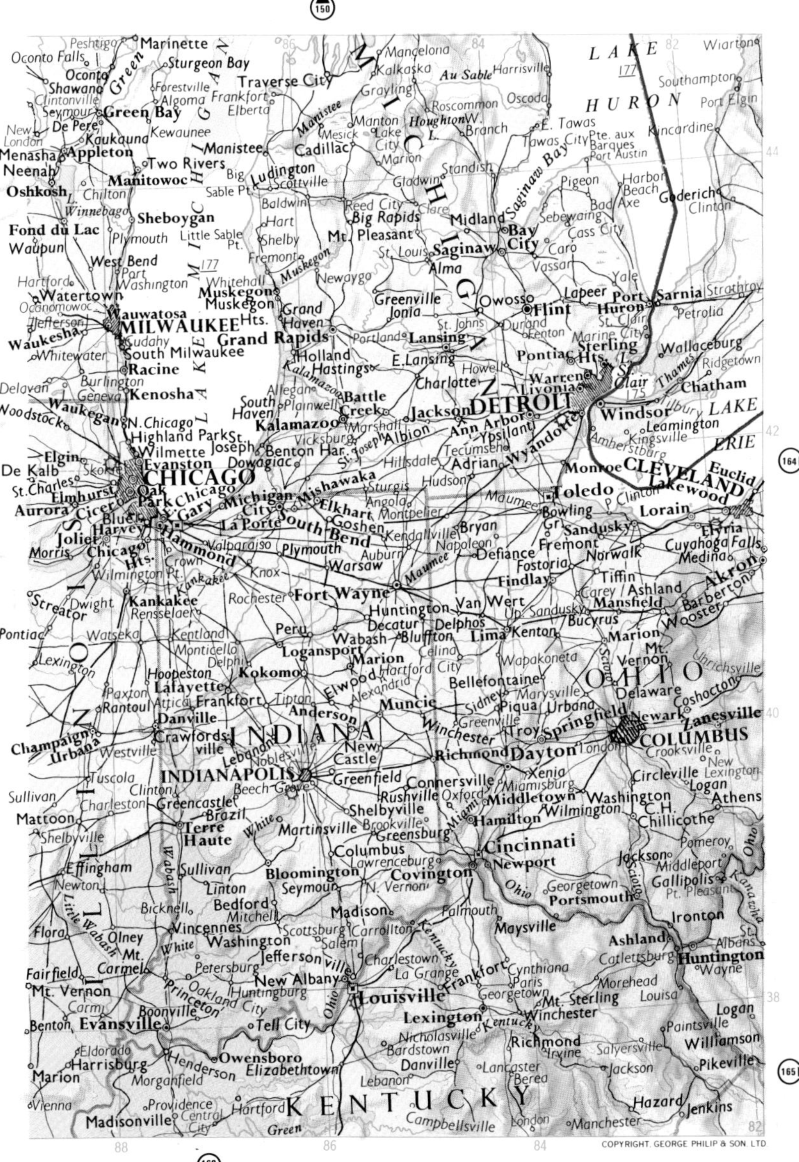

Peshtigo
Marinette
Oconto Falls
Sturgeon Bay
Oconto
Shawano
Green
Forestville
Algoma
Traverse City
Frankfort
Elberta
Mancelona
Kalkaska
Au Sable
Harrisville
LAKE
HURON
177
82
Wiarton
Southampton
Port Elgin
Clintonville
Seymour
Green Bay
De Pere
New London
Kaukauna
Kewaunee
Menasha
Appleton
Neenah
Manistee
Two Rivers
Manitowoc
Oshkosh
Chilton
L. Winnebago
Fond du Lac
Waupun
Sheboygan
Plymouth
West Bend
Port Washington
Hartford
Watertown
Oconomowoc
Jefferson
Wauwatosa
MILWAUKEE
Waukesha
Cudahy
South Milwaukee
Whitewater
Racine
Burlington
Delavan
Geneva
Kenosha
Woodstock
Waukegan
N. Chicago
Highland Park
Wilmette
Evanston
Elgin
De Kalb
Skokie
CHICAGO
St. Charles
Elmhurst
Oak Park
Aurora
Cicero
Blue I.
Harvey
Joliet
Chicago Hts.
Morris
Crown Pt.
Wilmington
Streator
Dwight
Pontiac
Lexington
Grayling
Roscommon
Oscoda
Manistee
Manton
Mesick
Lake City
Houghton L.
W. Branch
E. Tawas
Tawas City
Pte. aux Barques
Port Austin
Kincardine
Cadillac
Marion
Standish
Saginaw Bay
44
Big Sable Pt.
Ludington
Scottville
Gladwin
Clare
Pigeon
Harbor Beach
Bad Axe
Goderich
Clinton
Baldwin
Reed City
Big Rapids
Midland
Bay City
Sebewaing
Cass City
Caro
Hart
Little Sable Pt.
Shelby
Mt. Pleasant
St. Louis
Saginaw
Vassar
Fremont
Muskegon
Newaygo
Alma
Whitehall
Muskegon
Muskegon Hts.
Greenville
Ionia
Owosso
Flint
Lapeer
Port Huron
Sarnia
Strathroy
Yale
Petrolia
Grand Haven
St. Johns
Durand
St. Clair
Marine City
Grand Rapids
Portland
Lansing
Fenton
Sterling Hts.
Wallaceburg
Holland
E. Lansing
Howell
Pontiac
Ridgetown
Hastings
Kalamazoo
Charlotte
Warren
Livonia
Thames
Chatham
Allegan
Plainwell
Battle Creek
Jackson
DETROIT
L. St. Clair
175
South Haven
Marshall
Ann Arbor
Windsor
Tilbury
LAKE
Kalamazoo
Albion
Ypsilanti
Leamington
St. Joseph
Vicksburg
Kingsville
42
Benton Har.
Tecumseh
Amherstburg
ERIE
Dowagiac
Hillsdale
Adrian
Wyandotte
Monroe
CLEVELAND
Euclid
Michigan City
Mishawaka
Sturgis
Hudson
Toledo
Lakewood
Gary
Elkhart
Angola
Maumee
Bowling Gr.
P. Clinton
Lorain
La Porte
South Bend
Montpelier
Goshen
Bryan
Sandusky
Elyria
Hammond
Valparaiso
Plymouth
Kendallville
Napoleon
Fremont
Cuyahoga Falls
Auburn
Defiance
Fostoria
Norwalk
Medina
Knox
Warsaw
Maumee
Findlay
Tiffin
Akron
Kankakee
Rochester
Fort Wayne
Carey
Ashland
Barberton
Kankakee
Rensselaer
Huntington
Van Wert
Up. Sandusky
Mansfield
Wooster
Watseka
Kentland
Peru
Decatur
Delphos
Bucyrus
Monticello
Wabash
Bluffton
Lima
Kenton
Marion
Logansport
Marion
Celina
Mt. Vernon
Delphi
Hartford City
Wapakoneta
Uhrichsville
Hoopeston
Kokomo
OHIO
Paxton
Lafayette
Elwood
Alexandria
Bellefontaine
Marysville
Delaware
Coshocton
Rantoul
Attica
Frankfort
Tipton
Anderson
Muncie
Sidney
Piqua
Urbana
Danville
Winchester
Greenville
Springfield
Newark
Zanesville
40
Champaign
Urbana
Crawfordsville
INDIANA
New Castle
Troy
COLUMBUS
Westville
Lebanon
Noblesville
Richmond
Dayton
London
Crooksville
New Lexington
Tuscola
INDIANAPOLIS
Greenfield
Connersville
Xenia
Circleville
Sullivan
Clinton
Beech Grove
Rushville
Oxford
Miamisburg
Logan
Charleston
Greencastle
Shelbyville
Middletown
Washington C.H.
Athens
Mattoon
Brazil
Brookville
Wilmington
Terre Haute
White
Martinsville
Greensburg
Miami
Hamilton
Chillicothe
Shelbyville
Cincinnati
Pomeroy
Ohio
Wabash
Columbus
Newport
Effingham
Sullivan
Bloomington
Lawrenceburg
Covington
Jackson
Middleport
Newton
Linton
Seymour
N. Vernon
Ohio
Georgetown
Scioto
Gallipolis
Pt. Pleasant
Kanawha
Portsmouth
Bicknell
Bedford
Madison
Falmouth
Little Wabash
Mitchell
Ironton
Flora
Vincennes
Scottsburg
Carrollton
Maysville
Olney
White
Washington
Salem
Kentucky
Ashland
St. Albans
Mt. Carmel
Jeffersonville
Charlestown
Catlettsburg
Huntington
Fairfield
Petersburg
New Albany
La Grange
Frankfort
Cynthiana
Wayne
Mt. Vernon
Princeton
Oakland City
Huntingburg
Paris
Morehead
Carmi
Louisville
Georgetown
Mt. Sterling
Louisa
38
Boonville
Ohio
Winchester
Logan
Benton
Evansville
Tell City
Lexington
Kentucky
Paintsville
Eldorado
Nicholasville
Richmond
Williamson
Harrisburg
Henderson
Owensboro
Bardstown
Irvine
Salyersville
Pikeville
Morganfield
Elizabethtown
Danville
Lancaster
Jackson
Marion
Lebanon
Berea
Vienna
Providence
Hartford
KENTUCKY
Hazard
Jenkins
Madisonville
Central City
Green
Campbellsville
London
Manchester
82
88
86
84

164

165

169

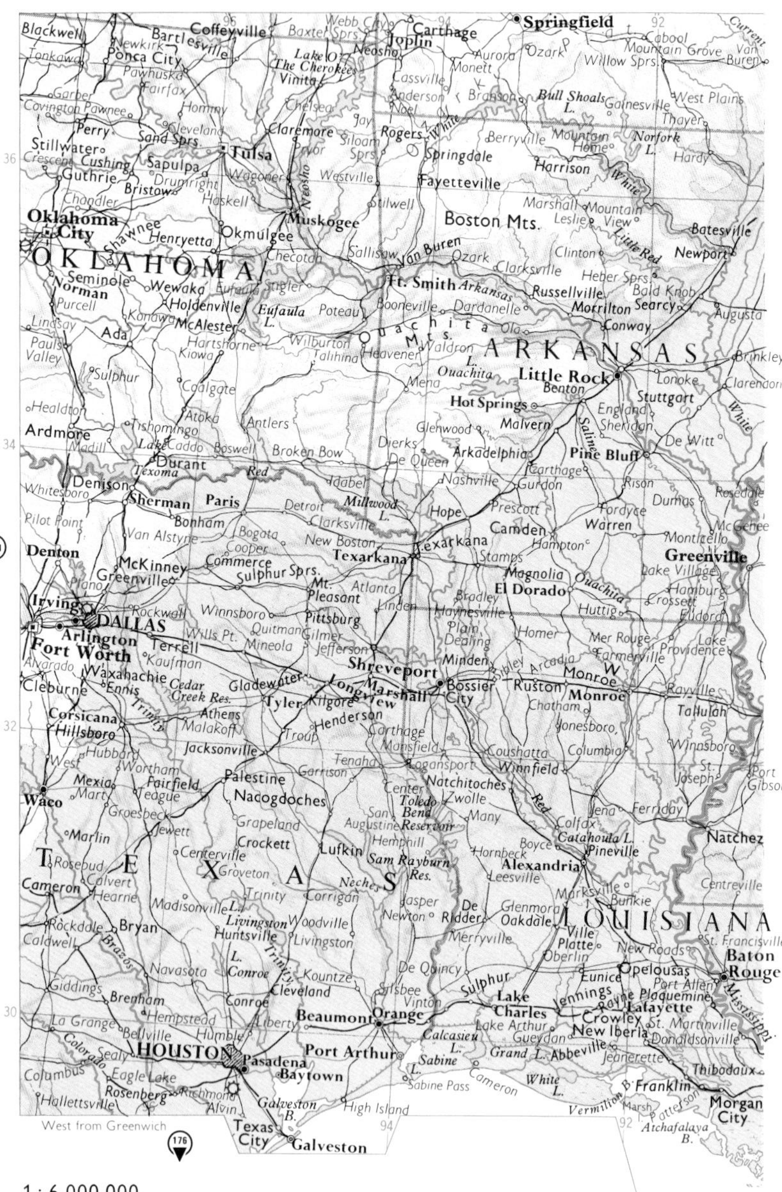

1 : 6 000 000

167

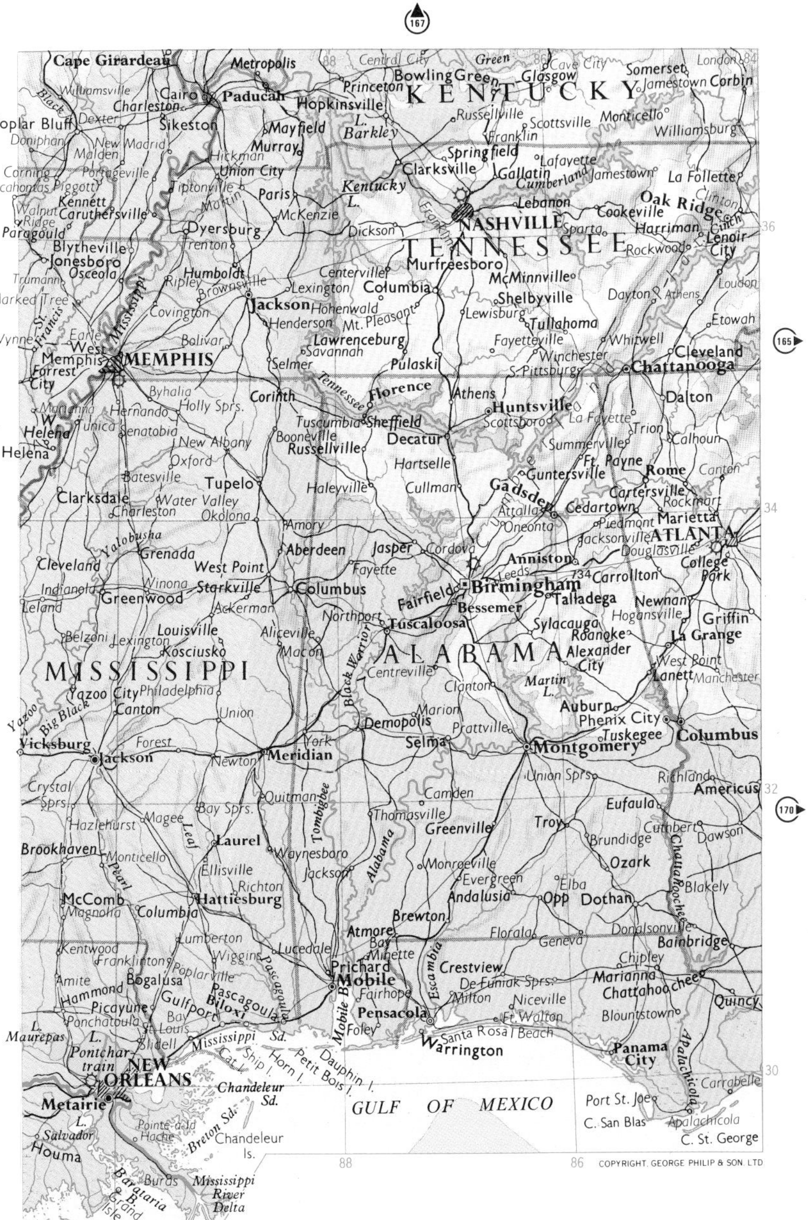
Cape Girardeau
Metropolis
Central City
Green
Cave City
Somerset
London
Corbin
Bowling Green
Glasgow
Jamestown
Princeton
KENTUCKY
Williamsville
Cairo
Paducah
Hopkinsville
Black
Charleston
Poplar Bluff
Dexter
Sikeston
Mayfield
L. Barkley
Russellville
Scottsville
Monticello
Williamsburg
Doniphan
New Madrid
Murray
Franklin
Malden
Hickman
Springfield
Lafayette
Corning
Portageville
Union City
Clarksville
Gallatin
Cumberland
Jamestown
La Follette
Pocahontas
Piggott
Tiptonville
Paris
Kentucky L.
Oak Ridge
Clinton
Kennett
Martin
Lebanon
Walnut Ridge
Caruthersville
McKenzie
Cookeville
Paragould
Dyersburg
Dickson
NASHVILLE
Sparta
Harriman
Clinch
Lenoir City
Blytheville
Trenton
TENNESSEE
Rockwood
Jonesboro
Murfreesboro
Trumann
Osceola
Humboldt
Centerville
McMinnville
Loudon
Ripley
Brownsville
Lexington
Columbia
Marked Tree
Jackson
Hohenwald
Shelbyville
Dayton
Athens
Covington
Lewisburg
St. Francis
Henderson
Mt. Pleasant
Tullahoma
Etowah
Wynne
Earle
Bolivar
Lawrenceburg
Fayetteville
Whitwell
West Memphis
MEMPHIS
Savannah
Winchester
Cleveland
Forrest City
Selmer
Pulaski
S. Pittsburg
Chattanooga
Byhalia
Tennessee
Florence
Athens
Dalton
Marianna
Hernando
Holly Sprs.
Corinth
Huntsville
W. Helena
Tunica
Senatobia
Tuscumbia
Sheffield
Scottsboro
La Fayette
Trion
Helena
New Albany
Booneville
Decatur
Calhoun
Russellville
Summerville
Oxford
Hartselle
Ft. Payne
Batesville
Rome
Canton
Tupelo
Guntersville
Clarksdale
Haleyville
Cullman
Gadsden
Cartersville
Water Valley
Charleston
Rockmart
Okolona
Attalla
Cedartown
Amory
Oneonta
Piedmont
Marietta
Yalobusha
Jacksonville
ATLANTA
Grenada
Aberdeen
Jasper
Cordova
Douglasville
Cleveland
Anniston
College Park
West Point
Fayette
Leeds
Carrollton
Winona
Indianola
Starkville
Columbus
Birmingham
Greenwood
Fairfield
Talladega
Leland
Ackerman
Bessemer
Newnan
Hogansville
Griffin
Northport
Tuscaloosa
Louisville
Aliceville
Sylacauga
Roanoke
Belzoni
Lexington
La Grange
Kosciusko
Macon
Black Warrior
ALABAMA
Alexander City
MISSISSIPPI
West Point
Centreville
Lanett
Manchester
Martin L.
Yazoo City
Philadelphia
Clanton
Canton
Yazoo
Big Black
Marion
Auburn
Union
Phenix City
Demopolis
Prattville
Columbus
Vicksburg
Forest
York
Selma
Tuskegee
Jackson
Meridian
Montgomery
Newton
Union Sprs.
Richland
Crystal Sprs.
Quitman
Camden
Americus
Tombigbee
Eufaula
Bay Sprs.
Thomasville
Hazlehurst
Magee
Leaf
Greenville
Troy
Cuthbert
Dawson
Laurel
Brundidge
Brookhaven
Monticello
Waynesboro
Alabama
Pearl
Ellisville
Monroeville
Ozark
Jackson
Evergreen
Elba
Blakely
Richton
McComb
Andalusia
Opp
Dothan
Magnolia
Columbia
Hattiesburg
Chattahoochee
Brewton
Atmore
Florala
Donalsonville
Lumberton
Geneva
Kentwood
Bay Minette
Bainbridge
Franklinton
Wiggins
Lucedale
Pascagoula
Chipley
Poplarville
Prichard
Crestview
Amite
Bogalusa
Mobile
Escambia
Marianna
Hammond
Gulfport
Pascagoula
Fairhope
De Funiak Sprs.
Chattahoochee
Biloxi
Milton
Niceville
Quincy
Picayune
Pensacola
Mobile B.
Bay St. Louis
Ponchatoula
Foley
Ft. Walton
Blountstown
L. Maurepas
L. Pontchartrain
Slidell
Mississippi Sd.
Santa Rosa I. Beach
Warrington
Panama City
Apalachicola
Cat I.
Ship I.
Horn I.
Petit Bois I.
Dauphin I.
NEW ORLEANS
Chandeleur Sd.
Carrabelle
Metairie
GULF OF MEXICO
Port St. Joe
L. Salvador
Pointe à la Hache
Breton Sd.
Chandeleur Is.
C. San Blas
Apalachicola
C. St. George
Houma
Burds
Mississippi River Delta
Barataria B.
Grand Isle
36
34
32
30
88
86
84
90
734

165

170

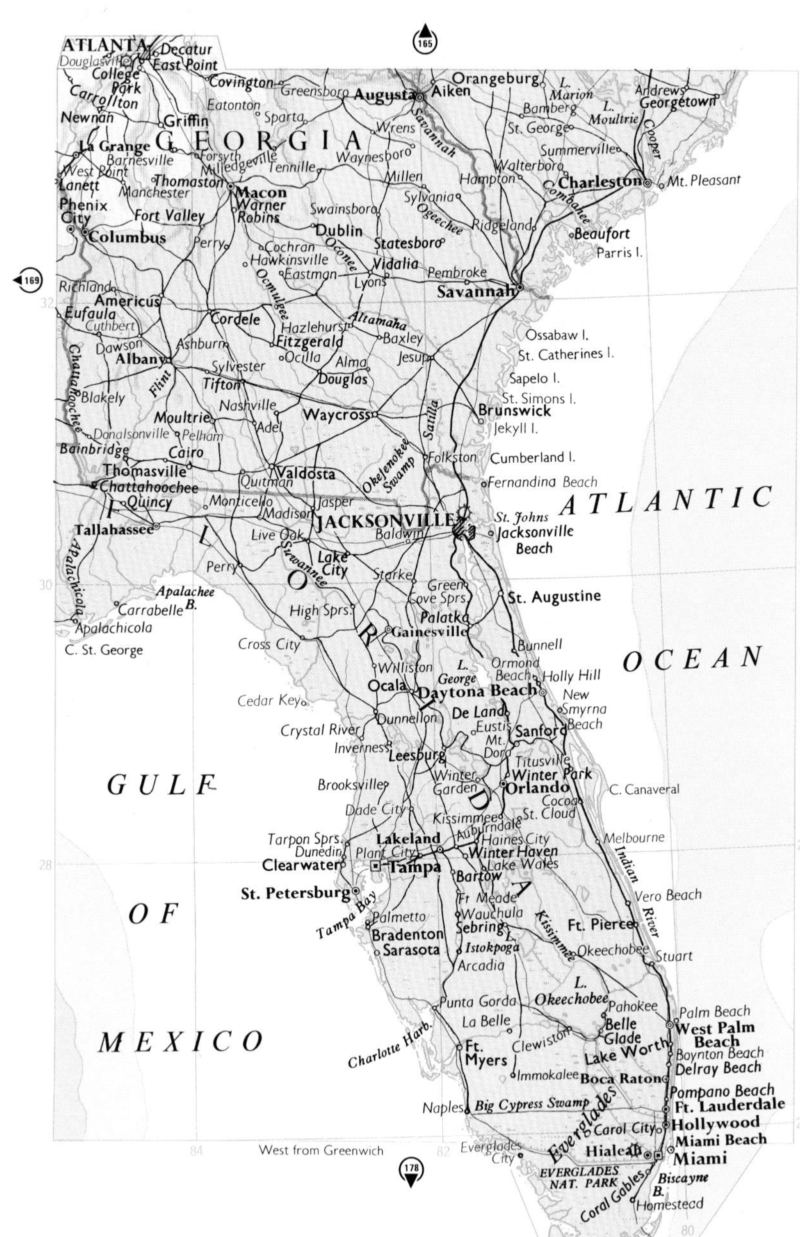
165
169
178
ATLANTA
Decatur
Douglasville
East Point
College Park
Carrollton
Covington
Greensboro
Augusta
Aiken
Orangeburg
L. Marion
Bamberg
L. Moultrie
Andrews
Georgetown
Newnan
Griffin
Eatonton
Sparta
Wrens
Savannah
St. George
Cooper
La Grange
GEORGIA
Barnesville
Forsyth
Milledgeville
Tennille
Waynesboro
Summerville
West Point
Lanett
Thomaston
Manchester
Macon
Warner Robins
Millen
Hampton
Walterboro
Charleston
Mt. Pleasant
Combahee
Phenix City
Columbus
Fort Valley
Swainsboro
Sylvania
Ogeechee
Ridgeland
Beaufort
Parris I.
Dublin
Perry
Cochran
Hawkinsville
Oconee
Statesboro
Vidalia
Eastman
Ocmulgee
Lyons
Pembroke
Savannah
Richland
Americus
Eufaula
Cuthbert
Cordele
Altamaha
Hazlehurst
Baxley
Fitzgerald
Ocilla
Dawson
Ashburn
Albany
Alma
Jesup
Ossabaw I.
St. Catherines I.
Sapelo I.
Chattahoochee
Flint
Sylvester
Tifton
Douglas
Blakely
Nashville
Waycross
St. Simons I.
Brunswick
Jekyll I.
Moultrie
Adel
Satilla
Okefenokee Swamp
Donalsonville
Pelham
Bainbridge
Cairo
Folkston
Cumberland I.
Thomasville
Valdosta
Quitman
Fernandina Beach
Chattahoochee
Quincy
Monticello
Jasper
Madison
JACKSONVILLE
St. Johns
Jacksonville Beach
ATLANTIC
Tallahassee
FLORIDA
Live Oak
Baldwin
Apalachicola
Perry
Suwannee
Lake City
Starke
Green Cove Sprs.
St. Augustine
Apalachee B.
Carrabelle
High Sprs.
Palatka
Gainesville
Apalachicola
C. St. George
Cross City
Bunnell
OCEAN
Williston
L. George
Ormond Beach
Holly Hill
Ocala
Daytona Beach
New Smyrna Beach
Cedar Key
De Land
Dunnellon
Eustis
Sanford
Crystal River
Mt. Dora
Inverness
Leesburg
Titusville
Winter Garden
Winter Park
Orlando
C. Canaveral
GULF
Brooksville
Cocoa
Dade City
Kissimmee
St. Cloud
Auburndale
Tarpon Sprs.
Dunedin
Lakeland
Haines City
Melbourne
Plant City
Winter Haven
Clearwater
Tampa
Lake Wales
Indian River
Bartow
St. Petersburg
Ft. Meade
Vero Beach
Tampa Bay
Wauchula
OF
Palmetto
Sebring
Ft. Pierce
Kissimmee
Bradenton
L. Istokpoga
Sarasota
Okeechobee
Stuart
Arcadia
L. Okeechobee
Punta Gorda
Pahokee
Palm Beach
La Belle
Belle Glade
West Palm Beach
MEXICO
Charlotte Harb.
Ft. Myers
Clewiston
Lake Worth
Boynton Beach
Immokalee
Delray Beach
Boca Raton
Pompano Beach
Ft. Lauderdale
Naples
Big Cypress Swamp
Everglades
Carol City
Hollywood
Miami Beach
Hialeah
Miami
Everglades City
EVERGLADES NAT. PARK
Biscayne B.
Coral Gables
Homestead
West from Greenwich
32
30
28
26
84
82
80

1 : 6 000 000

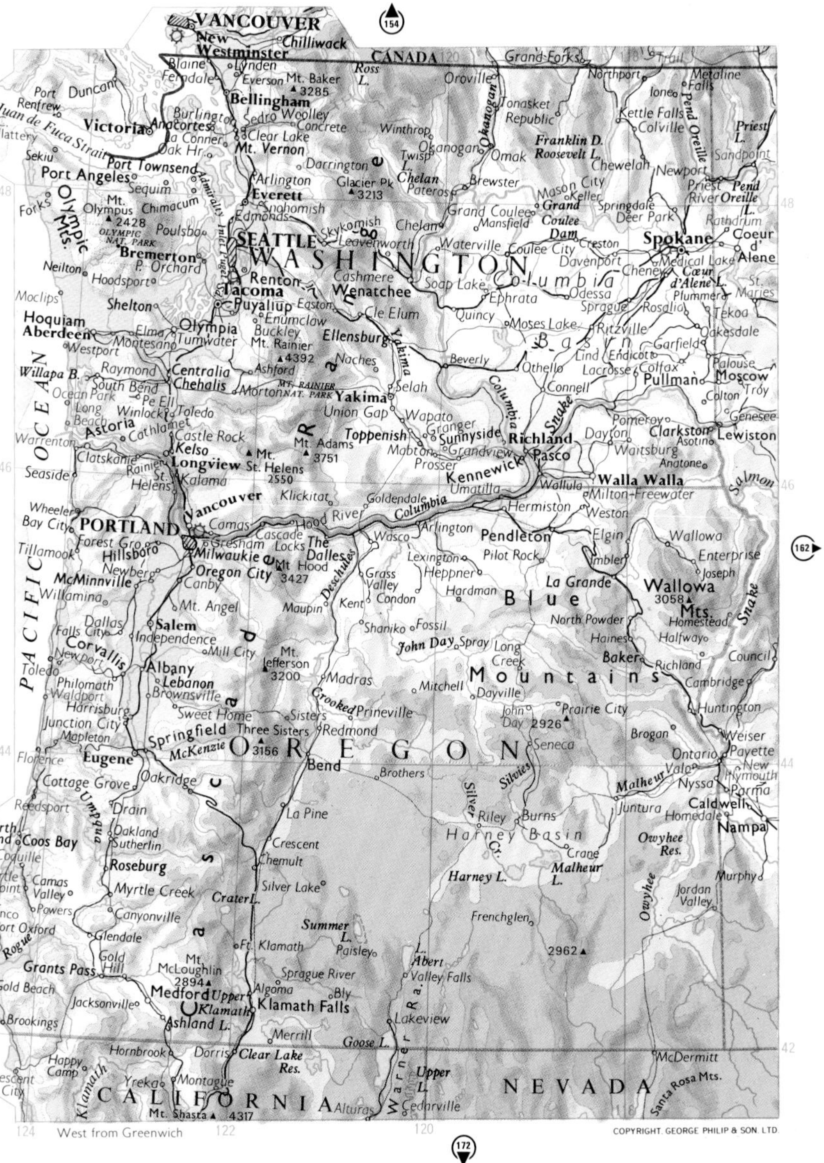
154
VANCOUVER
New Westminster
Chilliwack
CANADA
Grand Forks
Trail
Blaine
Lynden
Ferndale
Everson
Mt. Baker 3285
Ross L.
Oroville
Northport
Metaline Falls
Port Renfrew
Duncan
Victoria
Juan de Fuca Strait
C. Flattery
Bellingham
Burlington
Sedro Woolley
Anacortes
Concrete
La Conner
Clear Lake
Oak Hr.
Mt. Vernon
Winthrop
Okanogan
Tonasket
Republic
Ione
Kettle Falls
Colville
Pend Oreille
Priest L.
Franklin D. Roosevelt L.
Omak
Chewelah
Sandpoint
Sekiu
Port Angeles
Port Townsend
Sequim
Darrington
Arlington
Twisp
Chelan L.
Pateros
Brewster
Newport
Everett
Glacier Pk 3213
Mason City
Keller
Priest River
Pend Oreille L.
Forks
Olympic Mts.
Mt. Olympus 2428
OLYMPIC NAT. PARK
Chimacum
Poulsbo
Admiralty Inlet
Snohomish
Edmonds
Skykomish
Leavenworth
Chelan
Grand Coulee
Mansfield
Grand Coulee Dam
Springdale
Deer Park
Rathdrum
SEATTLE
WASHINGTON
Waterville
Coulee City
Creston
Spokane
Coeur d'Alene
Bremerton
P. Orchard
Nellton
Hoodsport
Renton
Cashmere
Davenport
Medical Lake
Cheney
Cœur d'Alene L.
St. Maries
Columbia Basin
Moclips
Tacoma
Wenatchee
Soap Lake
Ephrata
Odessa
Plummer
Shelton
Puyallup
Easton
Cle Elum
Sprague
Rosalia
Tekoa
Hoquiam
Aberdeen
Olympia
Tumwater
Elma
Montesano
Enumclaw
Buckley
Mt. Rainier
4392
Ellensburg
Quincy
Moses Lake
Ritzville
Oakesdale
Westport
Garfield
Lind
Endicott
Willapa B.
Raymond
Centralia
Chehalis
Ashford
Naches
Yakima
Beverly
Othello
Lacrosse
Colfax
Palouse
Pullman
Moscow
Ocean Park
South Bend
Morton
MT. RAINIER NAT. PARK
Selah
Connell
Colton
Troy
Long Beach
Pe Ell
Winlock
Toledo
Union Gap
Wapato
Granger
Columbia
Snake
Pomeroy
Genesee
Astoria
Cathlamet
Castle Rock
Mt. Adams 3751
Toppenish
Sunnyside
Richland
Dayton
Clarkston
Asotin
Lewiston
Warrenton
Kelso
Mabton
Grandview
Pasco
Waitsburg
Clatskanie
Longview
Mt. St. Helens 2550
Prosser
Kennewick
Anatone
Seaside
Rainier
St. Helens
Kalama
Umatilla
Walla Walla
Salmon
Wallula
Milton-Freewater
Vancouver
Klickitat
Goldendale
Hermiston
Weston
Wheeler
Bay City
PORTLAND
Camas
Hood River
Columbia
Arlington
Pendleton
Elgin
Wallowa
162
Tillamook
Forest Gro
Gresham
Cascade Locks
The Dalles
Wasco
Lexington
Pilot Rock
Imbler
Enterprise
Hillsboro
Milwaukie
Mt Hood 3427
Deschutes
Heppner
Joseph
Newberg
Oregon City
Grass Valley
La Grande
Wallowa 3058 Mts.
McMinnville
Willamina
Canby
Hardman
Blue
Condon
Kent
Maupin
Mt. Angel
North Powder
Homestead
Dallas
Salem
Shaniko
Fossil
Haines
Halfway
Falls City
Independence
John Day
Spray
Long Creek
Corvallis
Mill City
Newport
Mt. Jefferson 3200
Baker
Council
Toledo
Albany
Richland
Mountains
Madras
PACIFIC OCEAN
Philomath
Lebanon
Mitchell
Dayville
Cambridge
Waldport
Brownsville
Harrisburg
Sweet Home
Crooked
Prineville
John Day
Prairie City
Huntington
Junction City
2926
Sisters
Springfield
Three Sisters
Redmond
Brogan
Weiser
Mapleton
McKenzie
3156
OREGON
Seneca
Payette
Florence
Eugene
Bend
Ontario
New Plymouth
Vale
Brothers
Oakridge
Malheur
Nyssa
Cottage Grove
Silvies
Parma
Silver Cr.
Juntura
Caldwell
Reedsport
Drain
La Pine
Riley
Burns
Homedale
Umpqua
Nampa
North Bend
Coos Bay
Oakland
Sutherlin
Crescent
Harney Basin
Owyhee Res.
Coquille
Chemult
Crane
Roseburg
Myrtle Point
Harney L.
Malheur L.
Murphy
Camas Valley
Silver Lake
Myrtle Creek
Jordan Valley
Owyhee
Crater L.
Powers
Canyonville
Frenchglen
Port Orford
Summer L.
Glendale
Rogue
Ft. Klamath
Paisley
Abert L.
2962
Gold Hill
Grants Pass
Mt. McLoughlin 2894
Sprague River
Valley Falls
Gold Beach
Medford
Upper Klamath L.
Algoma
Bly
Klamath Falls
Jacksonville
Brookings
Ashland
Lakeview
Warner Ra.
Merrill
Goose L.
Hornbrook
Dorris
Clear Lake Res.
McDermitt
Happy Camp
Klamath
Upper L.
Crescent City
Yreka
Montague
Santa Rosa Mts.
NEVADA
CALIFORNIA
Alturas
Cedarville
Mt. Shasta 4317
124
122
120
118
48
46
44
42
West from Greenwich
COPYRIGHT GEORGE PHILIP & SON LTD.
172

1 : 6 000 000

163

171

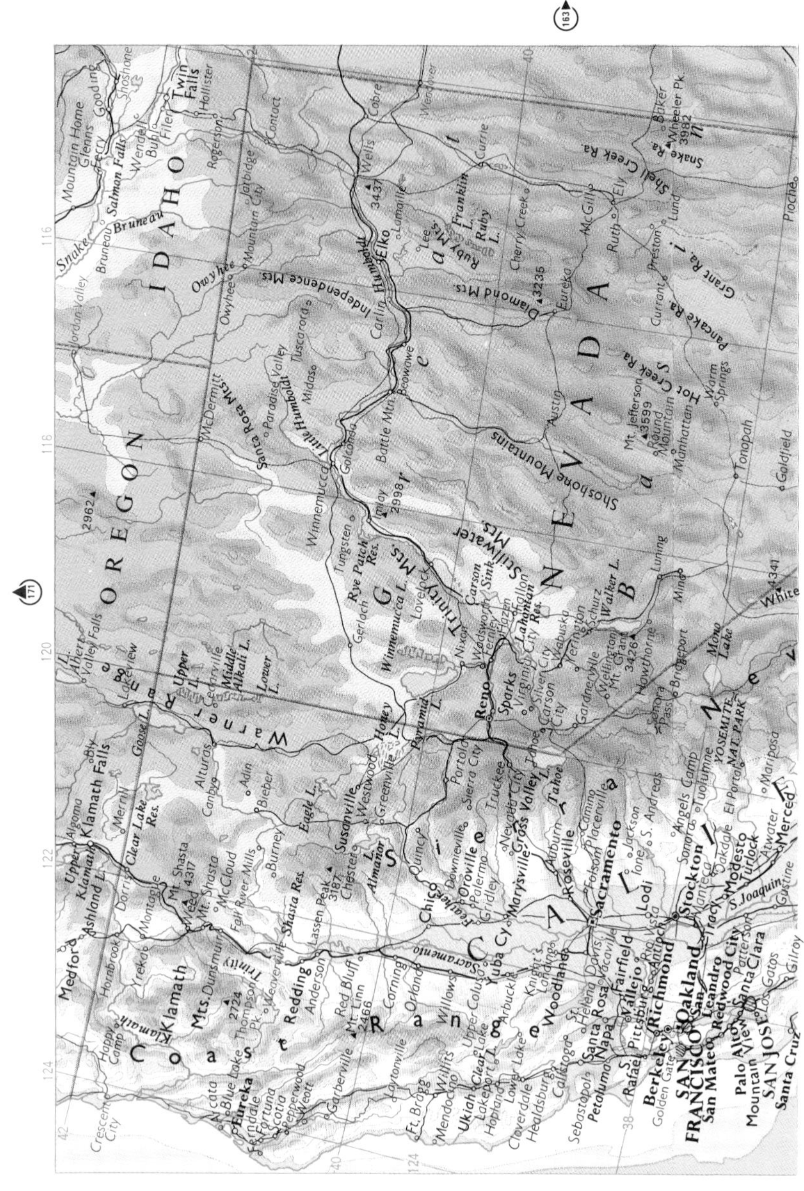
OREGON
IDAHO
NEVADA
CALIFORNIA
Sacramento
SAN FRANCISCO
Oakland
SAN JOSE
Reno
Sparks
Carson City
Stockton
Modesto
Merced
Eureka
Redding
Chico
Klamath Falls
Medford
Elko
Ely
Winnemucca
Tonopah
Goldfield
Twin Falls
Lake Tahoe
Mono Lake
Walker L.
Pyramid L.
Shasta Res.
Goose L.
Eagle L.
Clear Lake Res.
Mt. Shasta
4317
Lassen Peak
3187
Wheeler Pk.
3982
Santa Rosa
Berkeley
Richmond
Vallejo
Fairfield
Napa
Petaluma
Santa Cruz
Palo Alto
Mountain View
Santa Clara
Redwood City
San Mateo
Lodi
Marysville
Oroville
Yuba City
Woodland
Ukiah
Crescent City
Alturas
Susanville
Truckee
Lovelock
Fallon
Battle Mtn.
Carlin
Wells
Austin
Eureka
Independence Mts.
Shoshone Mountains
Diamond Mts.
Ruby Mts.
Trinity Mts.
Stillwater Mts.
Santa Rosa Mts.
Snake Ra.
Schell Creek Ra.
Grant Ra.
Pancake Ra.
Hot Creek Ra.
Warner
YOSEMITE NAT. PARK

1 : 6 000 000

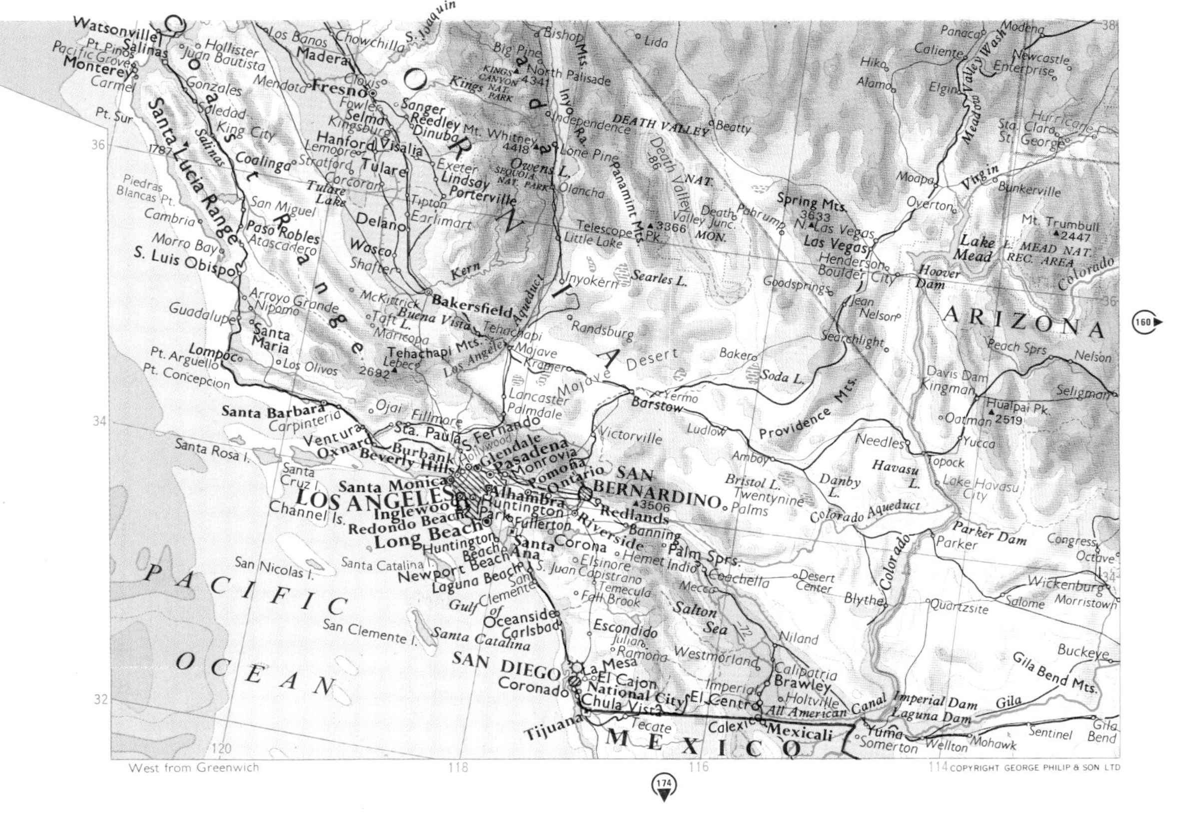
160
174
ARIZONA
MEXICO
PACIFIC OCEAN
Coast Range
Mojave Desert
Watsonville
Salinas
Monterey
Pacific Grove
Carmel
Pt. Pinos
Pt. Sur
Hollister
S. Juan Bautista
Gonzales
Soledad
King City
Salinas
Santa Lucia Range
1787
Piedras Blancas Pt.
Cambria
Morro Bay
S. Luis Obispo
Paso Robles
Atascadero
San Miguel
Coalinga
Arroyo Grande
Nipomo
Guadalupe
Santa Maria
Lompoc
Pt. Arguello
Pt. Concepcion
Los Olivos
Santa Barbara
Carpinteria
Ventura
Oxnard
Santa Rosa I.
Santa Cruz I.
Channel Is.
San Nicolas I.
San Clemente I.
Santa Catalina I.
Gulf of Santa Catalina
Los Banos
Madera
Chowchilla
S. Joaquin
Mendota
Fresno
Clovis
Sanger
Reedley
Dinuba
Fowler
Selma
Kingsburg
Hanford
Visalia
Lemoore
Stratford
Tulare
Tulare Lake
Corcoran
Exeter
Lindsay
Porterville
Tipton
Earlimart
Delano
Wasco
Shafter
McKittrick
Taft
Buena Vista
Maricopa
Bakersfield
Kern
Tehachapi Mts.
Tehachapi
Lebec
2682
Ojai
Fillmore
Sta. Paula
S. Fernando
Hollywood
Burbank
Beverly Hills
Santa Monica
LOS ANGELES
Inglewood
Redondo Beach
Long Beach
Huntington Beach
Huntington Park
Newport Beach
Laguna Beach
San Clemente
Oceanside
Carlsbad
Escondido
Ramona
Julian
La Mesa
El Cajon
National City
Chula Vista
SAN DIEGO
Coronado
Tijuana
Tecate
Glendale
Pasadena
Monrovia
Alhambra
Pomona
Ontario
Fullerton
Santa Ana
Corona
Riverside
SAN BERNARDINO
Redlands
3506
Banning
Palm Sprs.
Hemet
Elsinore
Temecula
S. Juan Capistrano
Fall Brook
Indio
Coachella
Mecca
Salton Sea
-72
Westmorland
Imperial
El Centro
Calexico
Mexicali
Holtville
Brawley
Calipatria
Niland
All American Canal
Desert Center
Blythe
Colorado
Colorado Aqueduct
Danby L.
Twentynine Palms
Bristol L.
Amboy
Ludlow
Barstow
Yermo
Victorville
Lancaster
Palmdale
Mojave
Kramer
Los Angeles Aqueduct
Randsburg
Inyokern
Searles L.
Little Lake
Olancha
Owens L.
Lone Pine
Independence
Inyo Ra.
Bishop
Big Pine
North Palisade 4341
Mt. Whitney 4418
KINGS CANYON NAT. PARK
SEQUOIA NAT. PARK
Kings
Telescope Pk. 3366
Panamint Mts.
Death Valley
-86
DEATH VALLEY NAT. MON.
Death Valley Junc.
Beatty
Lida
Pahrump
Spring Mts.
3633
N. Las Vegas
Las Vegas
Henderson
Boulder City
Goodsprings
Jean
Nelson
Searchlight
Providence Mts.
Soda L.
Baker
Needles
Havasu L.
Topock
Lake Havasu City
Parker Dam
Parker
Quartzsite
Yuma
Somerton
Imperial Dam
Laguna Dam
Wellton
Mohawk
Gila
Sentinel
Gila Bend Mts.
Gila Bend
Buckeye
Salome
Wickenburg
Morristown
Congress
Octave
Yucca
Oatman
Kingman
Hualpai Pk.
2519
Davis Dam
Peach Sprs
Seligman
Nelson
Hoover Dam
Lake Mead
L. MEAD NAT. REC. AREA
Mt. Trumbull 2447
Bunkerville
Overton
Moapa
Virgin
Meadow Valley Wash
Alamo
Hiko
Caliente
Elgin
Panaca
Modena
Newcastle
Enterprise
St. George
Sta. Clara
Hurricane
38
36
34
32
120
118
116
114
West from Greenwich

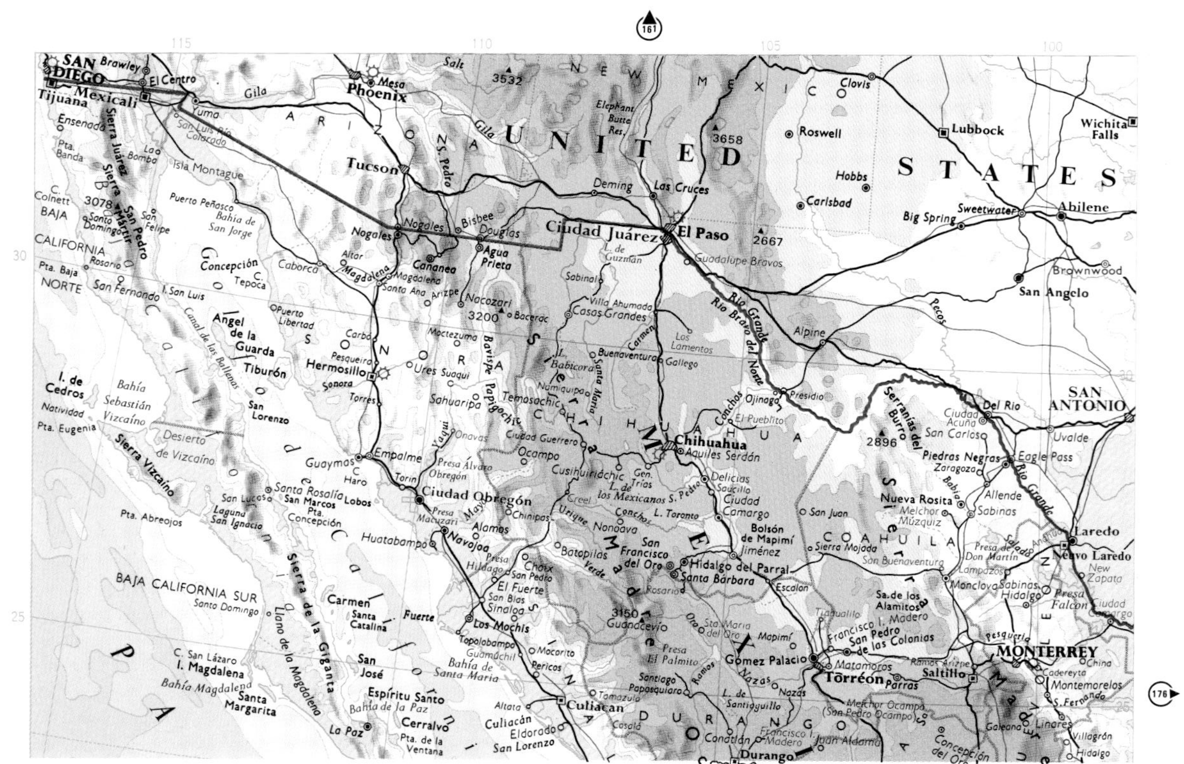

1 : 12 000 000

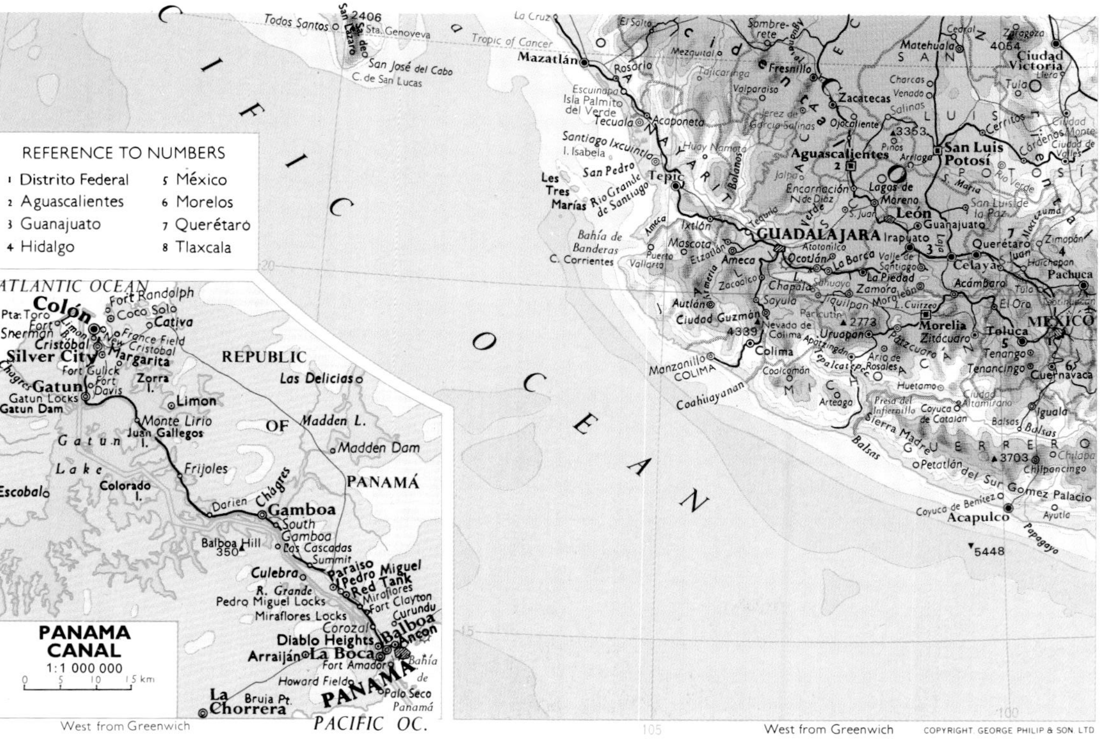

REFERENCE TO NUMBERS

1 Distrito Federal 5 México
2 Aguascalientes   6 Morelos
3 Guanajuato   7 Querétaro
4 Hidalgo   8 Tlaxcala

PANAMA CANAL
1:1 000 000
0   5   0   5 km

West from Greenwich

West from Greenwich

COPYRIGHT GEORGE PHILIP & SON LTD

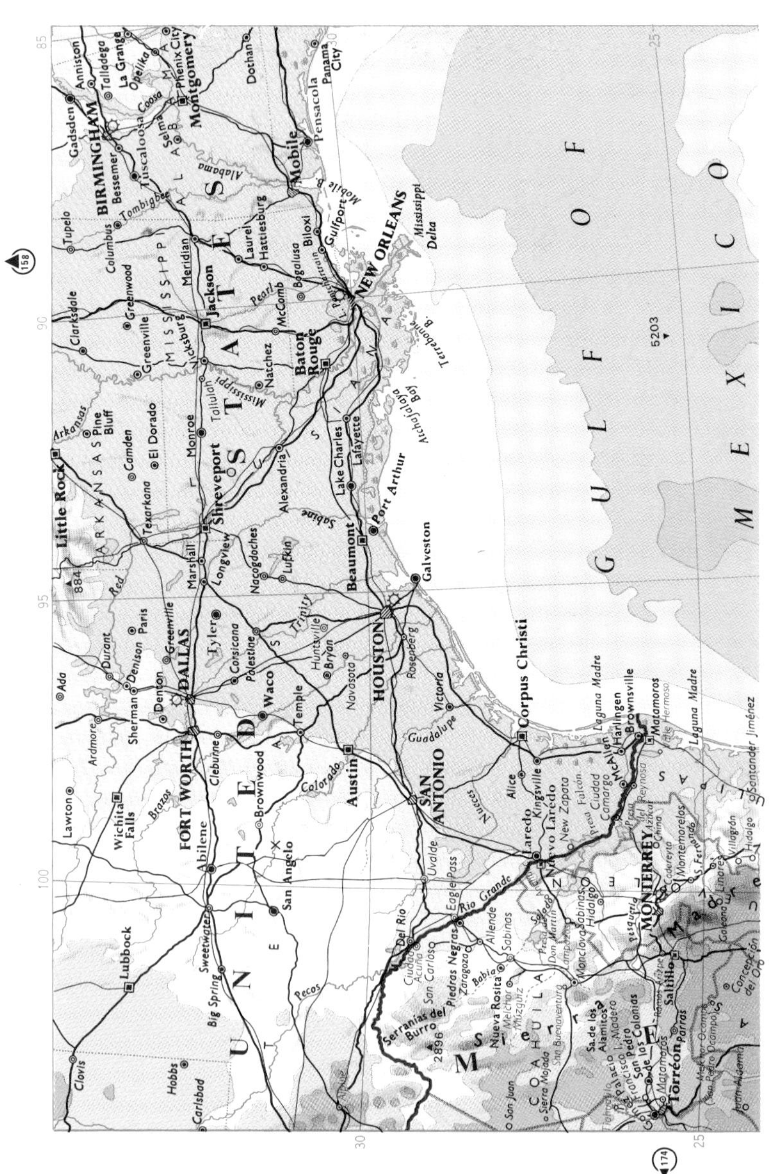

1 : 12 000 000

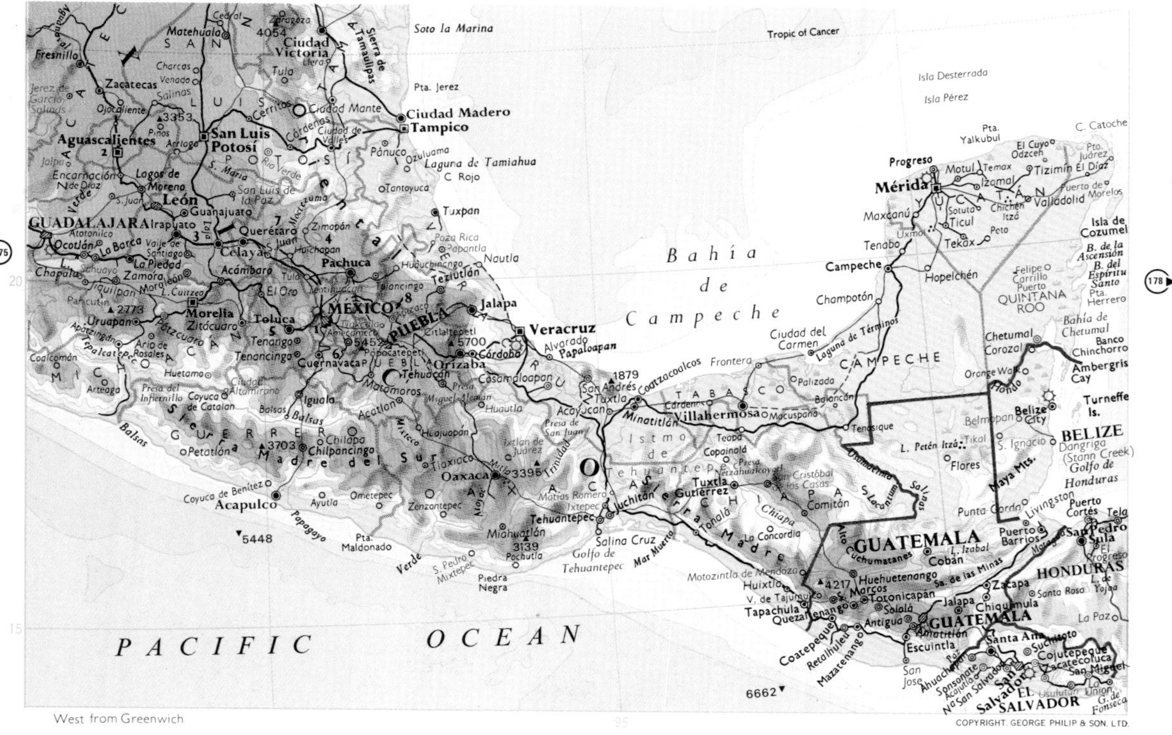

West from Greenwich

Tropic of Cancer

PACIFIC OCEAN

Bahia de Campeche

MEXICO

GUATEMALA

BELIZE
(Spanish Honduras)

HONDURAS

SAN SALVADOR

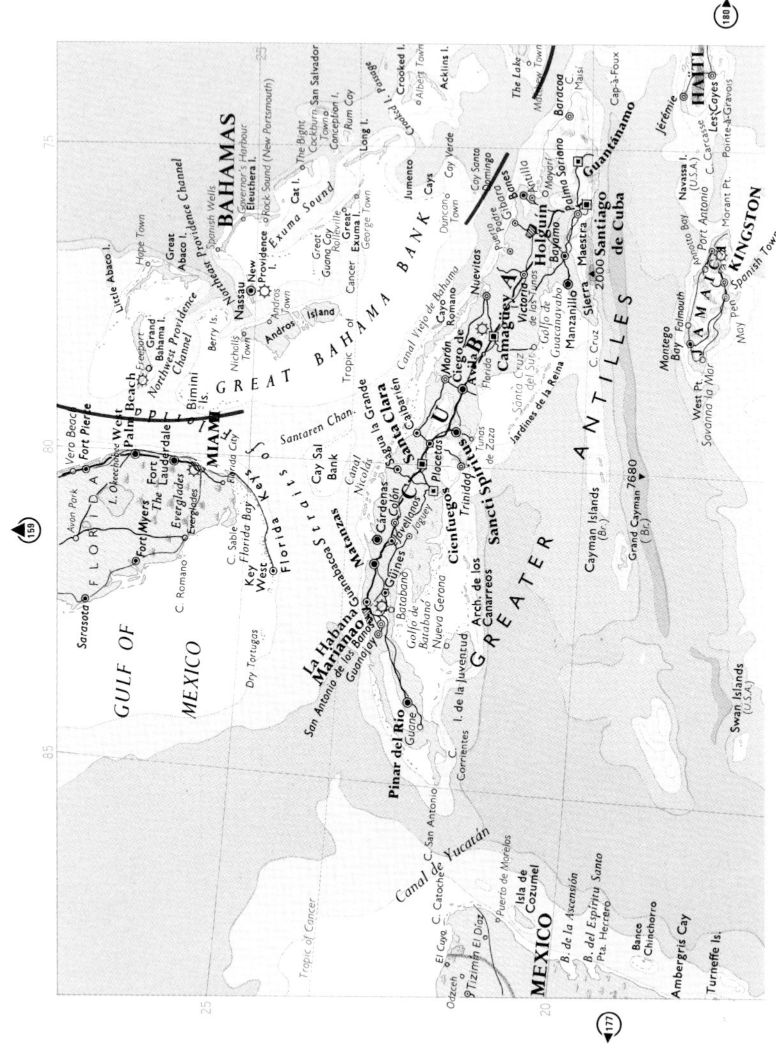
GULF OF MEXICO
BAHAMAS
GREAT BAHAMA BANK
GREATER ANTILLES
CUBA
JAMAICA
HAITI
MEXICO
FLORIDA
Florida Straits
Florida Keys
MIAMI
La Habana
Marianao
Pinar del Río
Matanzas
Cárdenas
Santa Clara
Cienfuegos
Sancti Spíritus
Ciego de Avila
Camagüey
Holguín
Santiago de Cuba
Guantánamo
Bayamo
Manzanillo
Nassau
Freeport
KINGSTON
Spanish Town
Montego Bay
Cayman Islands (Br.)
Grand Cayman (Br.)
Swan Islands (U.S.A.)
Canal de Yucatán
Isla de Cozumel
Ambergris Cay
Turneffe Is.
Tropic of Cancer
Exuma Sound
Northwest Providence Channel
Northeast Providence Channel
Santaren Chan.
Jardines de la Reina
Sierra Maestra
Navassa I. (U.S.A.)

1 : 12 000 000

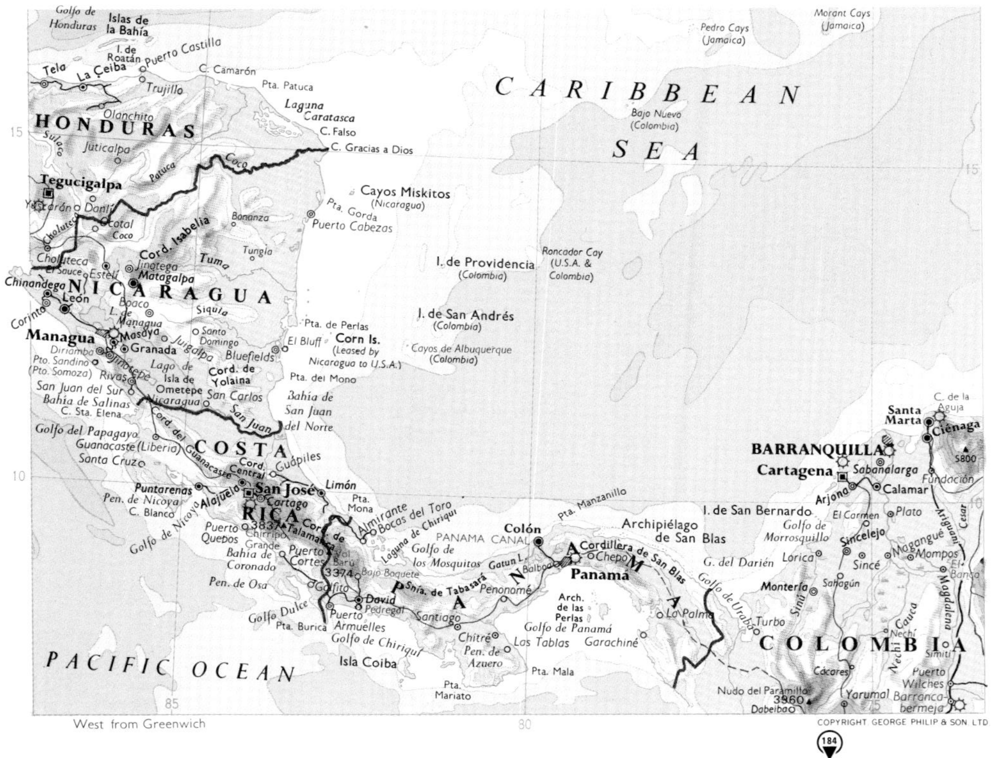

CARIBBEAN SEA

Morant Cays (Jamaica)

Pedro Cays (Jamaica)

Bajo Nuevo (Colombia)

Roncador Cay (U.S.A. & Colombia)

I. de Providencia (Colombia)

I. de San Andrés (Colombia)

Cayos de Albuquerque (Colombia)

Gulfo de Honduras

Islas de la Bahía

I. de Roatán puerto Castilla

La Ceiba

Tela

Trujillo

C. Camarón

Laguna Caratasca

C. Falso

Cayos Miskitos (Nicaragua)

Pta. Gorda

Puerto Cabezas

Pta. de Perlas

Corn Is. Leased by Nicaragua to U.S.A.

El Bluff Bluefields

Pta. del Mono

Bahía de San Juan del Norte

HONDURAS

Tegucigalpa

NICARAGUA

Managua

León

Chinandega

Masaya

Granada

Lago de Nicaragua

Isla de Ometepe

Rivas

San Juan del Sur

Bahía de Salinas

C. Sta. Elena

COSTA RICA

San José

Cartago

Puntarenas

Pen. de Nicoya

C. Blanco

Golfo de Papagayo

Guanacaste (Liberia)

Santa Cruz

Puerto Quepos

Bahía de Coronado

Pen. de Osa

Golfo Dulce

Pta. Burica

PACIFIC OCEAN

PANAMA

Colón

PANAMA CANAL

Golfo de los Mosquitos

Archipiélago de San Blas

Cordillera de San Blas

Arch. de las Perlas

Golfo de Panamá

Chitré

Los Tablos

Pen. de Azuero

Pta. Mala

Pta. Mariato

Isla Coiba

Golfo de Chiriquí

David

Puerto Armuelles

Bocas del Toro

Almirante

Golfo de los Mosquitos

COLOMBIA

BARRANQUILLA

Cartagena

Santa Marta

Ciénaga

Magdalena

Calamar

El Carmen

Plato

I. de San Bernardo

Golfo de Morrosquillo

Lorica

Montería

Sincé

Sahagún

Golfo de Urabá

Turbo

Nudo del Paramillo 3960

Dabeiba

La Palma

Gorgoné

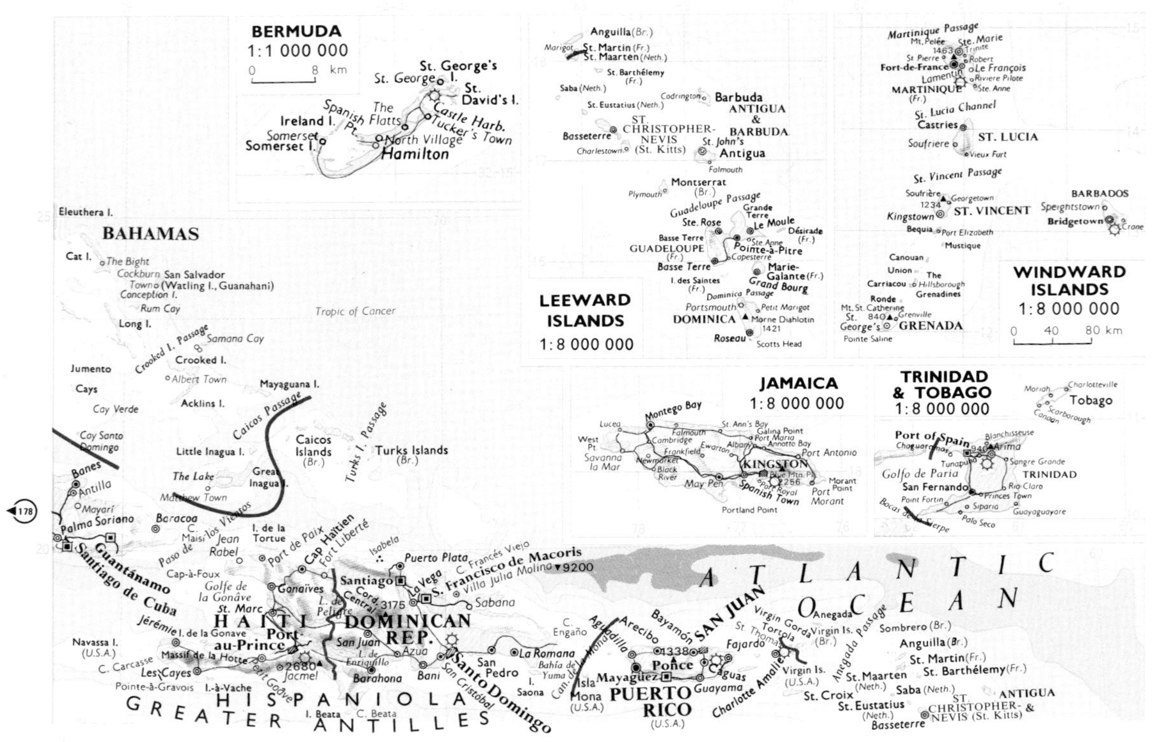

WINDWARD
ISLANDS
1:8 000 000
0   40   80 km

BARBADOS
Speightstown
Bridgetown© Crane

Martinique Passage
Ste Marie
Mt. Pelée St. François
St. Pierre le-Robert Le François
Fort-de-France Rivière-Pilote
Lamentin Ste. Anne
MARTINIQUE (Fr.)
Castries
St. Lucia Channel ST. LUCIA
Soufrière© Vieux Fort

St. Vincent Passage
Soufrière Georgetown
1234 ST. VINCENT
Kingstown© Bequia Port Elizabeth
Grenadines
Canouan
Union
Carriacou © Hillsborough
Mt. St. Catherine© Grenville
GRENADA
St. George's
Pointe Saline

TRINIDAD
& TOBAGO
1:8 000 000

Tobago
Charlotteville
Scarborough

Port of Spain Sangre Grande
Chaguanas TRINIDAD
Pos Couva
San Fernando
Golfo de Paria Siparia
Gulf of Paria Princes Town
Point Fortin
Icacos Point Guayaguayare

Anguilla (Br.)
Sombrero (Br.)
St. Martin (Fr.)
St. Barthélemy (Fr.)
St. Maarten (Neth.)
Saba (Neth.)
St. Croix St. Christopher
St. Eustatius ANTIGUA
(Neth.) NEVIS (St. Kitts) &
Basseterre

LEEWARD
ISLANDS
1:8 000 000

Anguilla (Br.)
Marigot St. Martin (Fr.)
St. Maarten (Neth.)
(Fr.)
Saba (Neth.)
St. Eustatius (Neth.)
Charlestown© NEVIS (St. Kitts)
Bosseterre
ST.
CHRISTOPHER
NEVIS
(St. Kitts)
Codrington© Barbuda
ANTIGUA
&
St. John's©
Antigua
Falmouth
Montserrat
Plymouth©
Guadeloupe (Fr.) Grande
Ste. Rose Terre
Basse Terre Le Moule
Pointe-à-Pitre
I. des Saintes Marie-
GUADELOUPE Grande Bourg
Basse Terre Galante (Fr.)
Portsmouth© Port Morgot Marie-
DOMINICA © Marine Dominica Galante
Roseau 1421
Scots Head

JAMAICA
1:8 000 000

St. Ann's Bay
Montego Bay Ocho Rios
Falmouth
Spanish Town KINGSTON
May Pen
Savanna- Portland Point
la-Mar Morant Point

ATLANTIC

OCEAN

SAN JUAN

Virgin Gorda
Virgin Is.
Virgin Virgin Is. (Br.)
Is. (U.S.A.)
Fajardo
Caguas
PUERTO
Mayagüez Ponce RICO
(U.S.A.)
Isla Mona
(U.S.A.)
Arecibo
Aguadilla
Bayamón 913389
Guayama

BERMUDA
1:1 000 000
0   8 km

St. George's St.
St. George I. David's I.
The Castle Harb.
Spanish Flatts© Tucker's Town
Ireland I. Pt. North Village's Town
Somerset I. Hamilton
Somerset I.

Tropic of Cancer

Turks Islands
Turks I. Passage
Caicos
Islands
(Br.)
Grand
Turk

BAHAMAS

Eleuthera I.
Cat I. ©The Bight
Cockburn San Salvador
Town© (Watling I. Guanahani)
Conception© I.
Rum Cay
Long I.
Crooked I.
Acklins I.
Little Inagua I.
Mayaguana I.
The Lake
Great
Inagua
Matthew
Town

Jumento
Cays
Cay Verde
Cay Santo
Domingo

Navassa I.
(U.S.A.)
C. Carcasse
Les Cayes
Pointe-à-Gravois

Santiago de Cuba
Guantánamo
Banes
©Moperí
Antilla
Holguín
Palma Soriano

Baracoa
Cap-à-Foux
Golfe de
la Gonâve
I. de la Gonâve
HAITI Port-
au-Prince
Massif de la Hotte
Jérémie©
Jérémie
Cayes Jacmel
Paso de los
Vientos
Môle St. Nicolas
Tortue
I. de la Tortue
Port-de-Paix
Gonaïves
St. Marc
Cap Haïtien
3175
San Juan
DOMINICAN
REP.

Puerto Plata
Francisco de Macoris
©San Francisco Julio Molina ▼9200
Santiago Vega
3087
Baní
San Cristóbal
Barahona
C. Beata I. Beata

San
Pedro
de Macoris
SANTO
DOMINGO
San
Pedro
La Romana
Bahía de
Yuma
Saona
I. Saona

HISPANIOLA

GREATER ANTILLES

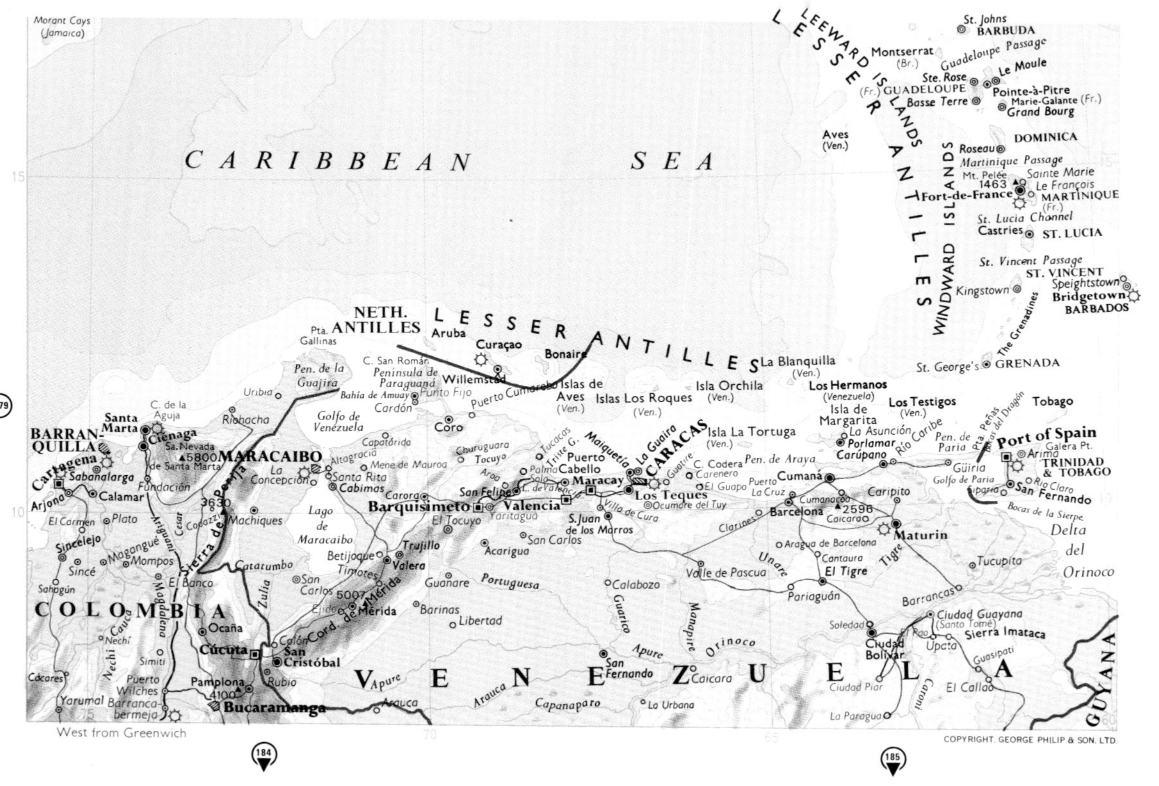

Morant Cays
(Jamaica)

CARIBBEAN SEA

LEEWARD ISLANDS
LESSER
St. Johns
BARBUDA
Montserrat
Guadeloupe Passage
Ste. Rose
Le Moule
(Fr.) GUADELOUPE
Pointe-à-Pitre
Basse Terre
Grand Bourg
Marie-Galante (Fr.)
DOMINICA
Roseau
Martinique Passage
Mt. Pelée
1463
Sainte Marie
Le François
(Fr.) MARTINIQUE
Fort-de-France
St. Lucia Channel
Castries
ST. LUCIA
St. Vincent Passage
Kingstown
ST. VINCENT
The Grenadines
St. George's
GRENADA
Speightstown
Bridgetown
BARBADOS
WINDWARD ISLANDS
ANTILLES

Aves
(Ven.)

Los Testigos
(Ven.)
Isla de
Margarita
Porlamar
La Asunción
Pampatar
Pta. de Piedras
Pen. de Araya

Los Hermanos
(Ven.)

Tobago
TRINIDAD
& TOBAGO
Port of Spain
Valera Pt.
San Fernando
Bocas de la Sierpe
del
Orinoco
Delta

GUIANA

NETH. ANTILLES
Aruba
Curaçao
Bonaire
Willemstad
C. San Roman
Peninsula de
Paraguaná
Punto Fijo
Cardón

La Blanquilla
(Ven.)
Isla Orchila
(Ven.)
Islas Los Roques
(Ven.)
Islas de
Aves
(Ven.)
La Orchila

Isla La Tortuga
(Ven.)

CARACAS
La Guaira
Maiquetía
Puerto
Cabello
Maracay
Valencia
Los Teques
San Felipe
Villa de Cura
El Guapo
Higuerote
C. Codera
El Tigre
Barcelona
Cumaná
Puerto La Cruz
Caripito
Maturín
Caripe
2590
Sierra Imataca

Barquisimeto
Acarigua
Guanare
San Carlos
Portuguesa
Barinas
Libertad
Apure
San
Fernando

Calabozo
Guárico
Valle de Pascua
Unare
Pariaguán
Soledad
Ciudad
Bolívar
Ciudad Pilar
Barrancas

V E N E Z U E L A

Maracaibo
Lago
de
Maracaibo
La
Concepción
Machiques
Cabimas
Santa Rita
Menegrande
Mene de Mauroa
El Tigre
Cordón
Bahía de Amuay
Coro
Capatárida
Dabajuro
Carora
Trujillo
Valera
Betijoque
Mérida
Barinas
San Cristóbal
Rubio
Táriba

Gulfo de
Venezuela
Pra. de la
Gallinas
Pen. de la
Guajira
Uribia

CARIBBEAN SEA

COLOMBIA
BARRAN-
QUILLA
Santa Marta
Ciénaga
Fundación
Sierra Nevada de Santa Marta
5800
Valledupar
Sabanalarga
Cartagena
Calamar
El Banco
Magdalena
Mompós
Plato
Ocaña
Cúcuta
Pamplona
Bucaramanga

West from Greenwich

179
184
185

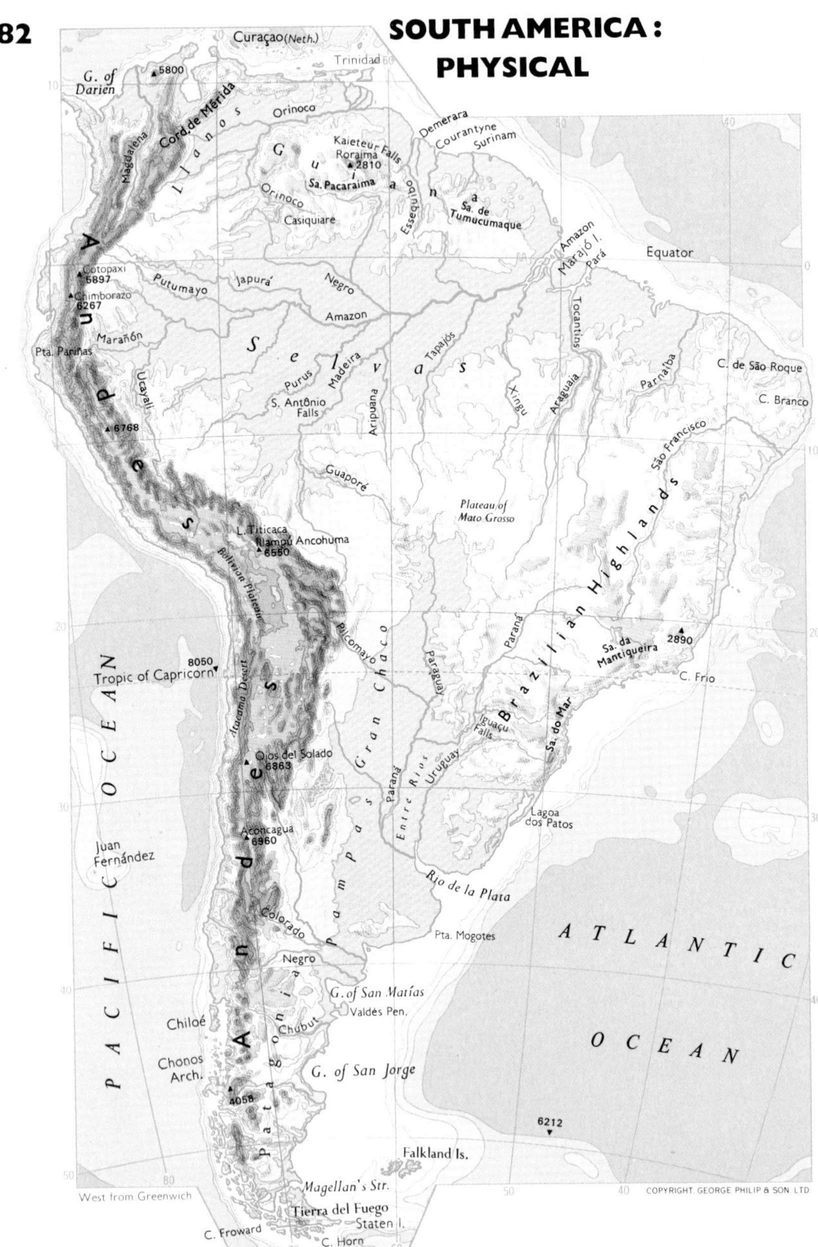

Curaçao (Neth.)

Trinidad

G. of
Darién ▲5800

Orinoco

L l a n o s

Kaieteur Falls
Roraima
▲2810

Courantyne
Surinam
Demerara

G
u
Orinoco
Sa. Pacaraima
a
r
a
n
a

Sa. de
Tumucumaque

Casiquiare

Esseguibo

Amazon
Marajó I.
Pará

Equator

Magdalena

Cord. de Mérida

A
n
d
e
s

Cotopaxi
▲5897
Chimborazo
▲6267

Putumayo

Japurá

Negro

Amazon

Tocantins

C. de São Roque
C. Branco

Pta. Pariñas

Marañón

Ucayali

S
e
l
v
a
s

Purus

Madeira

S. Antônio
Falls

Aripuanã

Tapajós

Xingu

Araguaia

Parnaíba

Parnaíba

▲6768

Guaporé

São Francisco

Plateau of
Mato Grosso

B
r
a
z
i
l
i
a
n

H
i
g
h
l
a
n
d
s

L. Titicaca
Illampú Ancohuma
▲6550

Balsean Plateau

Pilcomayo

G
r
a
n

C
h
a
c
o

Paraguay

Paraná

Sa. da
Mantiqueira
▲2890

C. Frio

8050

Tropic of Capricorn

Atacama Desert

Juan
Fernández

Ojos del Solado
▲6863

Paraná

Entre Ríos

Uruguay

Iguaçu
Falls

Sa. do Mar

P
A
C
I
F
I
C

O
C
E
A
N

Aconcagua
▲6960

P
a
m
p
a
s

Lagoa
dos Patos

Colorado

Rio de la Plata

A T L A N T I C

A
n
d
e
s

Negro

Pta. Mogotes

Chiloé

P
a
t
a
g
o
n
i
a

G. of San Matías
Valdés Pen.

O C E A N

Chubut

Chonos
Arch.

G. of San Jorge

▲4058

6212
▼

Falkland Is.

West from Greenwich

Magellan's Str.

Tierra del Fuego

COPYRIGHT GEORGE PHILIP & SON LTD

C. Froward

Staten I.

C. Horn

1 : 50 000 000

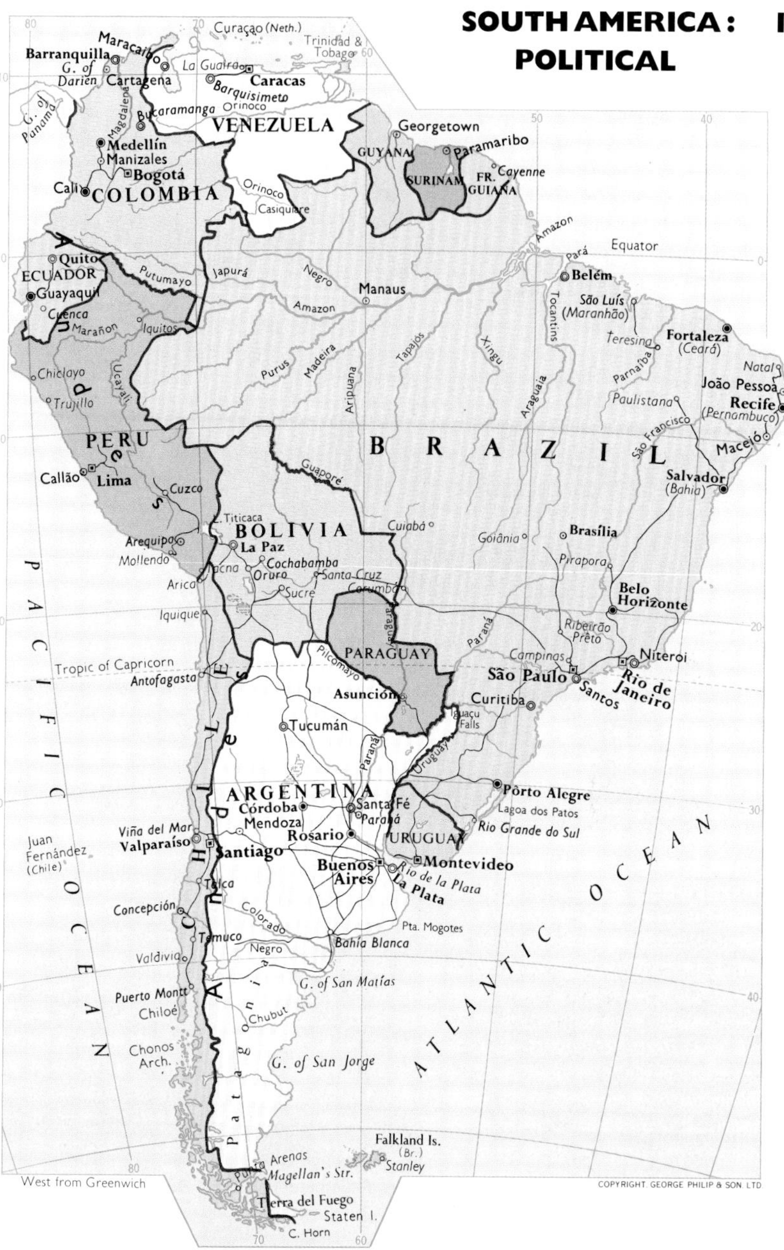

80
Curaçao (Neth.)
Trinidad &
Tobago 60
Maracaibo
Barranquilla
G. of
Darien Cartagena
La Guaira
Barquisimeto
Caracas
Georgetown
Bucaramanga Orinoco
G. of
Panama
Medellín
Manizales
Bogotá
VENEZUELA
GUYANA
SURINAM
FR.
GUIANA
Paramaribo
Cayenne
Cali COLOMBIA
Orinoco
Casiquiare
Amazon
Quito
ECUADOR
Guayaquil
Cuenca
Marañón Iquitos
Putumayo Japurá
Negro
Manaus
Pará
Equator
Belém
Chiclayo
Trujillo
Ucayali
Purus
Amazon
Madeira
Aripuana
Tapajos
Xingu
Araguaia
Tocantins
São Luís
(Maranhão)
Teresina
Parnaíba
Paulistana
Fortaleza
(Ceará)
Natal
João Pessoa
Recife
(Pernambuco)
Maceió
PERU
Callāo Lima
Cuzco
B R A Z I L
Arequipa
Mollendo
Titicaca
BOLIVIA
La Paz
cna Cochabamba
Arica Orūro Santa Cruz
Iquique Sucre Corumbá
Guaporé
Cuiabá
São Francisco
Goiânia
Brasília
Pirapora
Ribeirão
Prêto
Belo
Horizonte
P A C I F I C
Tropic of Capricorn
Antofagasta
PARAGUAY
Pilcomayo
Asunción
Campinas
São Paulo Santos
Curitiba
Iguaçú
Falls
Niteroi
Rio de
Janeiro
Paraná
Uruguay
Tucumán
Juan
Fernández
(Chile)
Viña del Mar
Valparaíso
ARGENTINA
Córdoba
Mendoza
Santiago
Rosario
Santa Fé
Paraná
URUGUAY
Buenos
Aires La Plata
Montevideo
Río de la Plata
Pôrto Alegre
Lagoa dos Patos
Rio Grande do Sul
O C E A N
30
Concepción
Talca
Temuco
Valdivia
Colorado
Negro
Bahía Blanca
Pta. Mogotes
A T L A N T I C
O C E A N
Puerto Montt
Chiloé
G. of San Matías
40
Chonos
Arch.
Chubut
G. of San Jorge
Patagonia
West from Greenwich
Falkland Is.
(Br.)
Arenas
Magellan's Str. Stanley
Tierra del Fuego
Staten I.
C. Horn
70 60

COPYRIGHT GEORGE PHILIP & SON LTD.

1 : 50 000 000

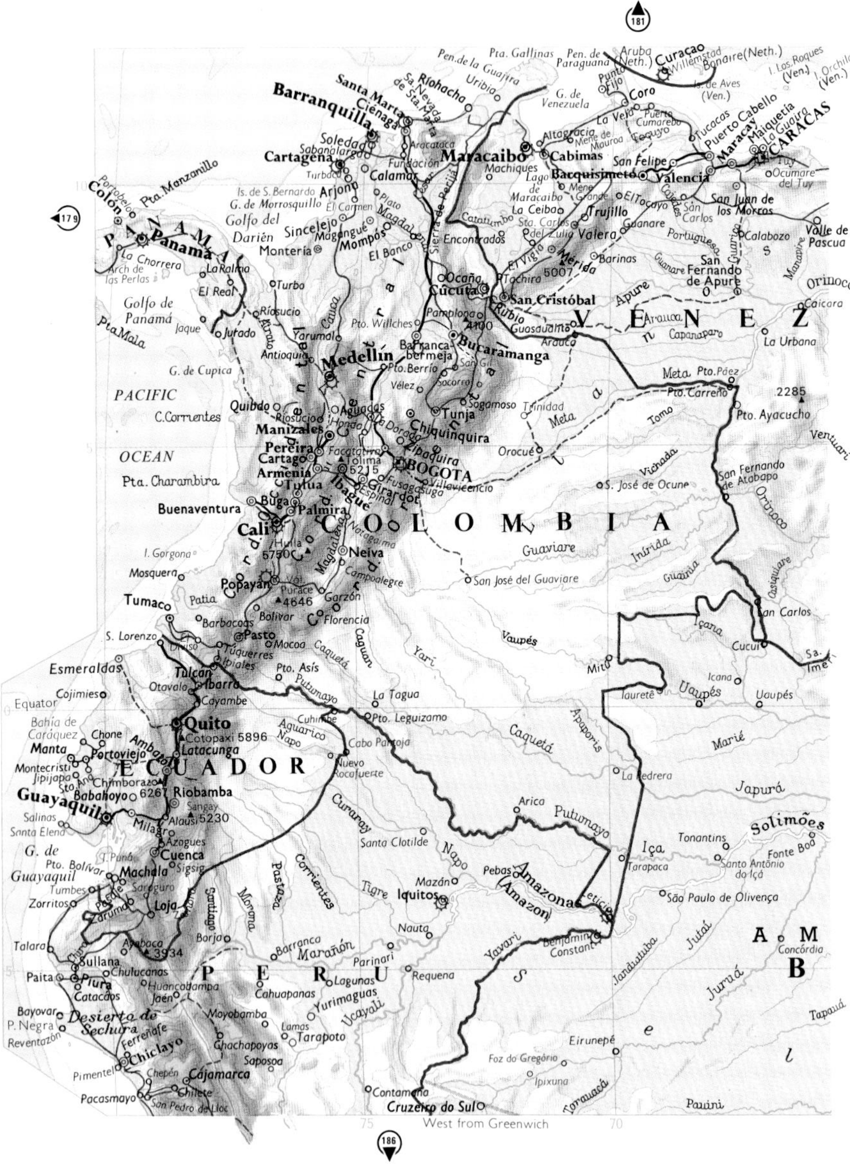
Barranquilla
Cartagena
Maracaibo
Medellín
BOGOTA
COLOMBIA
VENEZ
CARACAS
ECUADOR
Quito
Guayaquil
PERU
Iquitos
PANAMA
Panamá
PACIFIC
OCEAN
Cali
Bucaramanga
Cúcuta
Valencia
Barquisimeto
Amazonas (Amazon)
West from Greenwich

1 : 16 000 000

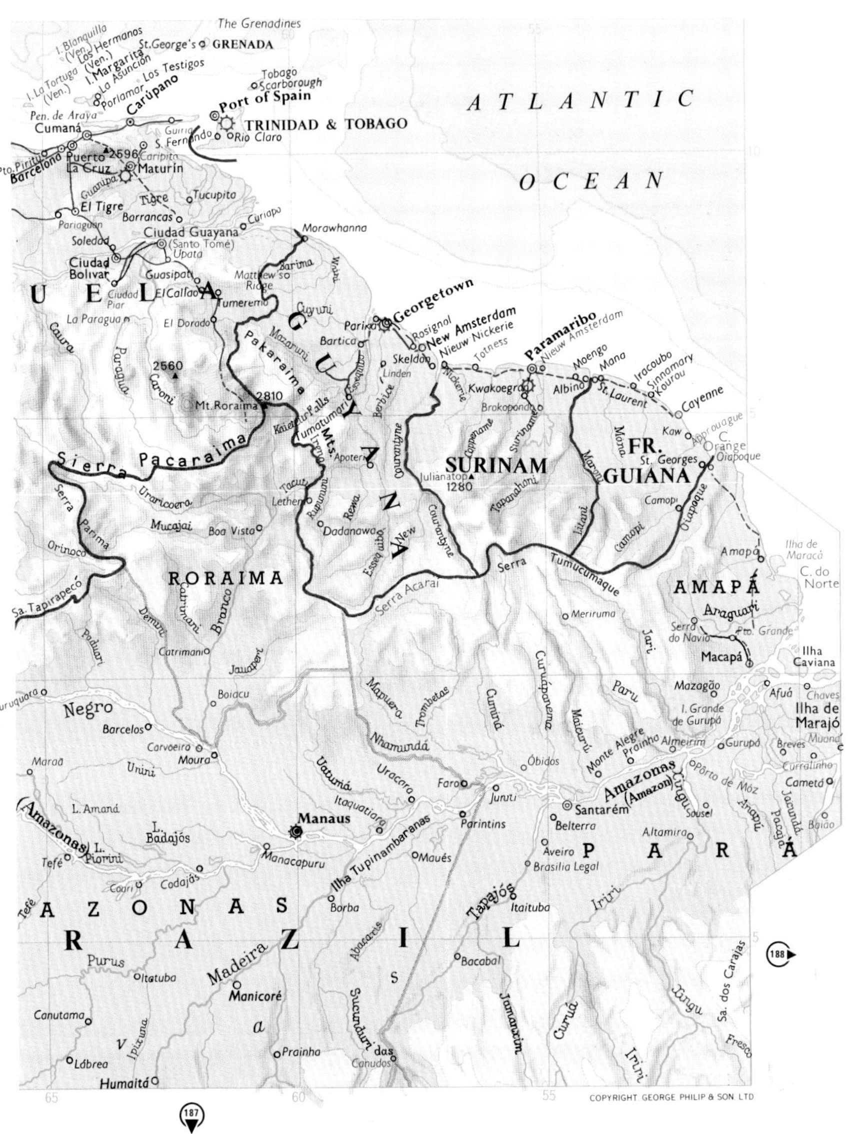
ATLANTIC
OCEAN
TRINIDAD & TOBAGO
Port of Spain
GRENADA
Georgetown
GUYANA
SURINAM
Paramaribo
FR. GUIANA
Cayenne
RORAIMA
AMAPÁ
Macapá
Manaus
Santarém
PARÁ
BRAZIL
Sierra Pacaraima
Serra Tumucumaque
Amazonas (Amazon)
COPYRIGHT GEORGE PHILIP & SON LTD.

188

187

184

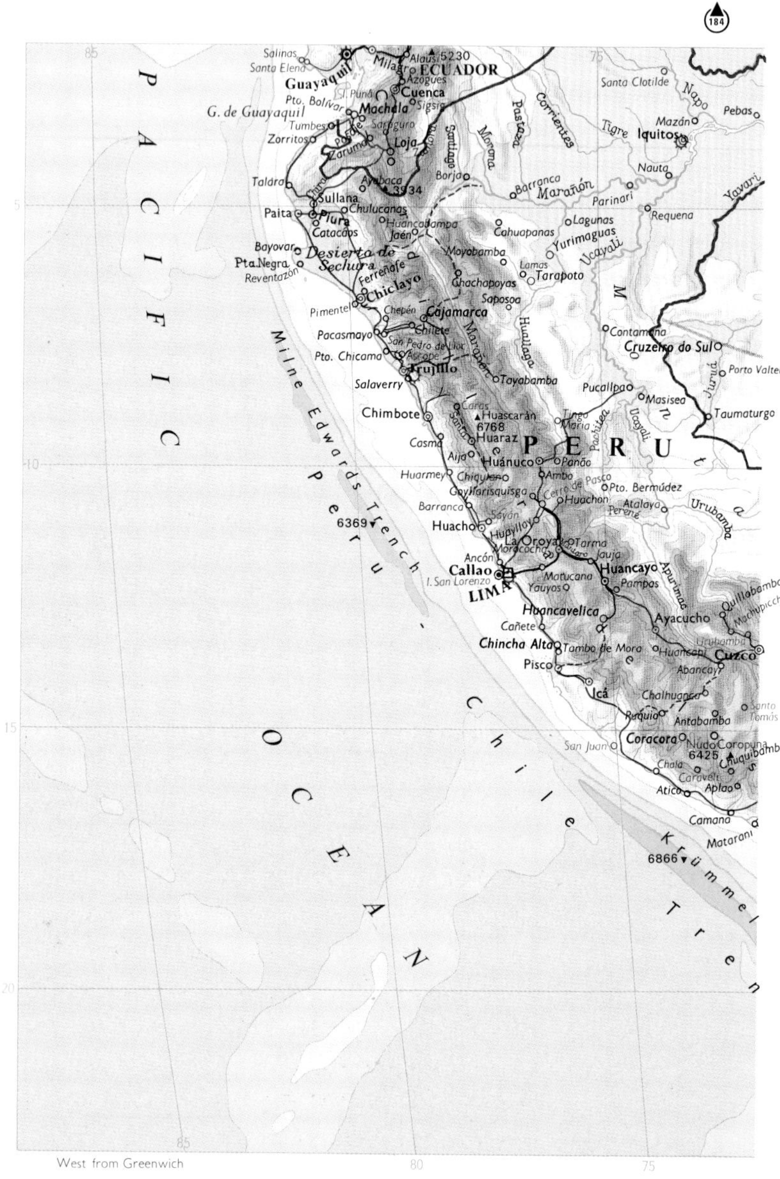
PACIFIC OCEAN
ECUADOR
PERU
Guayaquil
Cuenca
Machala
Loja
G. de Guayaquil
Salinas
Santa Elena
Milagro
Alausí
5230
Azogues
Pto. Bolívar
Tumbes
Zorritos
Zaruma
Saraguro
Sigsig
Talara
Sullana
Paita
Piura
Catacaos
Chulucanas
Huancabamba
Jaén
Bayovar
Pta.Negra
Reventazón
Desierto de Sechura
Ferreñafe
Chiclayo
Pimentel
Chepén
Cajamarca
Chilete
Pacasmayo
San Pedro de Lloc
Pto. Chicama
Ascope
Trujillo
Salaverry
Chimbote
Casma
Huarmey
Barranca
Huacho
Ancón
Callao
LIMA
I. San Lorenzo
Cañete
Chincha Alta
Pisco
Icá
Huancavelica
Huancayo
Ayacucho
Cuzco
Abancay
Coracora
Chala
Atico
Camana
Matarani
Aplao
Caravelí
Coropuna
6425
Chuquibamba
Antabamba
Santo Tomás
San Juan
Iquitos
Nauta
Requena
Pebas
Mazán
Santa Clotilde
Napo
Tigre
Pastaza
Corrientes
Morona
Santiago
Borja
Barranca
Marañón
Parinari
Lagunas
Yurimaguas
Cahuapanas
Moyobamba
Lamas
Tarapoto
Chachapoyas
Saposoa
Huallaga
Ucayali
Contamana
Cruzeiro do Sul
Porto Valter
Juruá
Taumaturgo
Yavari
Pucallpa
Masisea
Tayabamba
Huascarán
6768
Huaraz
Caras
Aija
Tingo María
Huánuco
Panão
Ambo
Chiquián
Cerro de Pasco
Pto. Bermúdez
Huachon
Atalaya
Perené
Urubamba
Huaylillas
La Oroya
Morococha
Tarma
Jauja
Matucana
Yauyos
Pampas
Apurímac
Quillabamba
Machupicchu
Tambo de Mora
Huancapi
Chalhuanca
Puquio
Milne Edwards Trench
6369
Peru-Chile Trench
Krümmel Trench
6866
3934
West from Greenwich
85
80
75
5
10
15
20

1 : 16 000 000

Page 187 — Map of western Brazil, Bolivia, and surrounding regions.

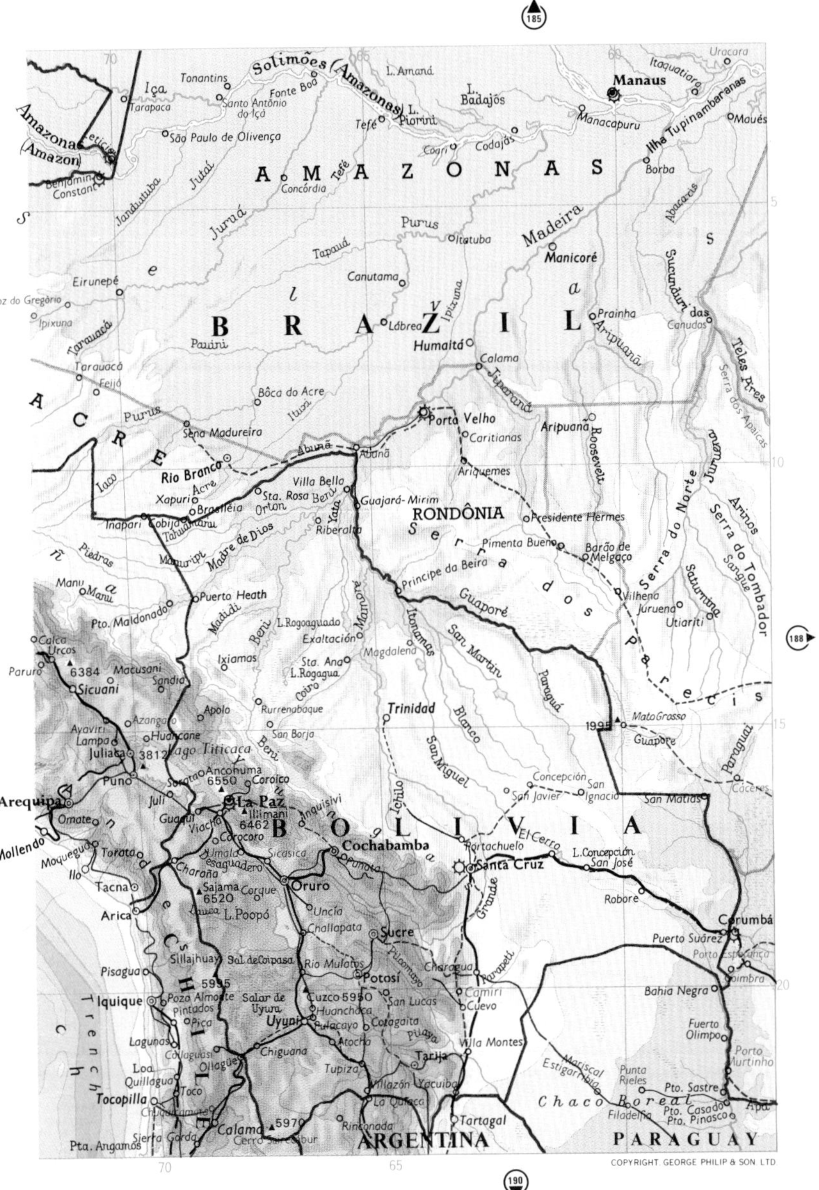

Manaus

Solimões (Amazonas)

Içá · Tonantins · Santo Antônio do Içá · Fonte Boa · L. Amanã · I. Badajós · Manacapuru · Maués · Itaquatiara · Uracara

Tarapacá · São Paulo de Olivença · Tefé · Florini · Coari · Codajás · Borba · Ilha Tupinambaranas

Amazonas (Amazon) · Benjamin Constant · A M A Z O N A S · Concórdia · Abacaxis

Juruá · Jutaí · Japurá · Purus · Itatuba · Madeira · Manicoré · Abunã · Sucundurí

Eirunepé · Canutama · Prainha · Aripuanã · das · Canudos · Teles Pires · Serra dos Apiacás

Foz do Gregório · Ipixuna · B R A Z I L · Lábrea · Humaitá · Calama · Aripuanã

Tarauacá · Feijó · Bôca do Acre · Iuzá · Porto Velho · Caritianas · Aripuanã · Roosevelt · Serra do Norte · Arinos · Serra do Tombador · Sangue

A C R E · Purus · Sena Madureira · Abunã · Abunã · Ariquemes · Presidente Hermes · Vilhena · Jurueno · Utiariti

Iaco · Rio Branco · Acre · Villa Bella · Guajará-Mirim · R O N D Ô N I A · Pimenta Bueno · Barão de Melgaço

Xapuri · Brasiléia · Sta. Rosa · Abunã · Serra · dos · Parecis

Inápari · Cobija · Tahuamanu · Orton · Riberalta · Príncipe da Beira · Guaporé

Piedras · Manuripe · Madre de Dios · Beni · L. Rogoaguado · Iténez · San Martín · Sararé

Manu · Pto. Maldonado · Puerto Heath · Madidi · Exaltación · Magdalena · MatoGrosso · Guaporé

Calca · Urcos · 6384 · Macusani · Sandia · Apolo · Rurrenabaque · Trinidad · Blanco · Paraguai

Sicuani · Ayaviri · Azángaro · San Borja · San Miguel · Concepción · San Ignacio · San Matias · Cáceres

Lampa · Juliaca · 3812 · Lago Titicaca · Ancohuma 6550 · Coroico · San Javier · San José

Arequipa · Puno · Juli · Guaqui · La Paz · Illimani 6462 · Aiquisivi · Concepción · Robore · Corumbá

Omate · Viacha · Coracaro · B O L I V I A · El Cerro · Santa Cruz · L. Concepción · Puerto Suárez

Mollendo · Moquegua · Torata · Charaña · Desaguadero · Sicasica · Cochabamba · Portachuelo · Coimbra

Ilo · Tacna · Salama 6520 · Corque · Oruro · Grande · Bahía Negra

Arica · Huari · L. Poópo · Uncía · Challapata · Sucre · Camiri · Fuerte Olimpo

Pisagua · Sillajhuay · Sal. de Coipasa · Rio Mulatos · Potosí · Camiri · Cuevo · Porto Murtinho

Iquique · 5995 · Poza Almonte · Salar de Uyuni · Cuzco 5950 · Huanchaca · San Lucas · Villa Montes · Pto. Sastre

Pintados · Pica · Ollacora · Cotagaita · Pugio · Mariscal Estigarribia · Punta Rieles · Pto. Casado · Pto. Pinasco

Lagunas · Colaguasa · Chiguana · Tupiza · Tarija · Filadelfia · Aba

Loa · Quilloguo · Toco · Oxlague · Villazón · Yacuiba · La Quiaca · Chaco Boreal

Tocopilla · Calama 5970 · Rinconada · Tartagal

Pta. Angamos · Sierra Gorda · Cerro · A R G E N T I N A · P A R A G U A Y

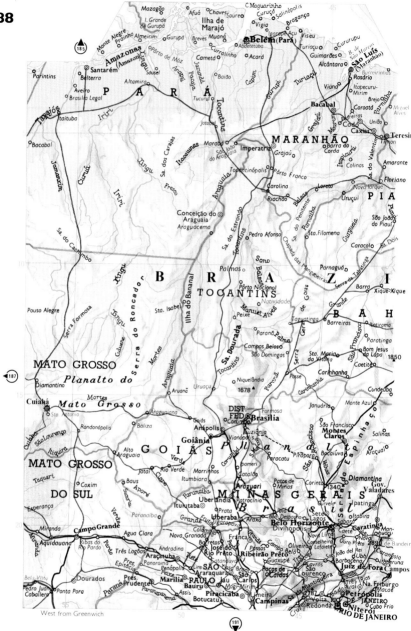

1 : 16 000 000

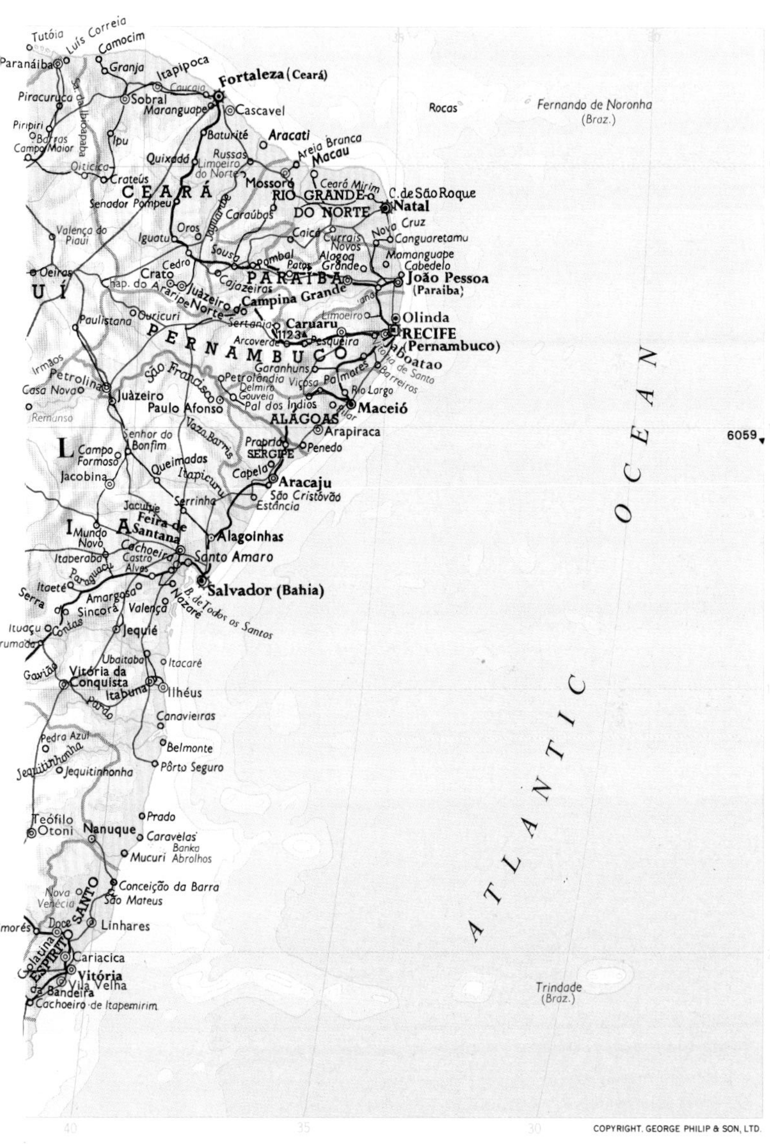

Tutóia
Luís Correia
Camocim
Paranaíba
Granja
Itapipoca
Caucaia
Fortaleza (Ceará)
Piracuruca
Sobral
Maranguape
Cascavel
Rocas
Fernando de Noronha (Braz.)
Piripiri
Ibu
Baturité
Aracati
Areia Branca
Barras
Campo Maior
Quixadá
Limoeiro do Norte
Macau
Crateús
Russas
Ceará Mirim
CEARÁ
Mossoró
RIO GRANDE
C. de São Roque
Senador Pompeu
Caraúbas
DO NORTE
Natal
Valença do Piauí
Oros
Iguatu
Caicó
Currais Novos
Nova Cruz
Conguaretamu
Cedro
Sousa
Pombal
Alagoa Grande
Mamanguape
Cabedelo
Oeiras
Crato
Juàzeiro do
Cajazeiras
Patos
João Pessoa
Chap. do Araripe
Norte
PARAÍBA
(Paraíba)
Paulistana
Ouricuri
Campina Grande
Efmoeiro
Olinda
PERNAMBUCO
Sertania
Caruaru
RECIFE
Irmãos
Petrolina
São Francisco
Arcoverde
Pesqueira
(Pernambuco)
Casa Nova
Juàzeiro
Garanhuns
Goatao
Remanso
Paulo Afonso
Petrolândia
Delmira
Viçosa
Palmares
Rio Largo
Senhor do
Pau dos Indios
Gouveia
Maceió
Campo
Bonfim
Vaza-Barris
ALAGOAS
Formoso
Queimadas
Proprió
Arapiraca
Jacobina
Itapicuru
Capela
Penedo
SERGIPE
Jacutinga
Feira de
Aracaju
Mundo Novo
Santana
São Cristóvão
Itaberaba
Cachoeira
Serrinha
Estância
Paraguaçu
Castro Alves
Alagoinhas
Itaetê
Amargosa
Santo Amaro
Serra
Sincará
Nazaré
Salvador (Bahia)
Ituaçu
Contas
Valença
B. de Todos os Santos
rumado
Jequié
Gavião
Ubaitaba
Itacaré
Vitória da
Conquista
Itabuna
Ilhéus
Pedra Azul
Prado
Canavieiras
Jequitinhonha
Jequitinhonha
Belmonte
Pôrto Seguro
Teófilo
Prado
Otoni
Nanuque
Caravelas
Mucuri
Banka
Abrolhos
Nova
Conceição da Barra
Venecia
Doce
São Mateus
imorés
ESPIRITO SANTO
Linhares
Cariacica
Vitória
Vila Velha
Bandeira
Cachoeiro de Itapemirim
Trindade (Braz.)

6059

ATLANTIC OCEAN

187

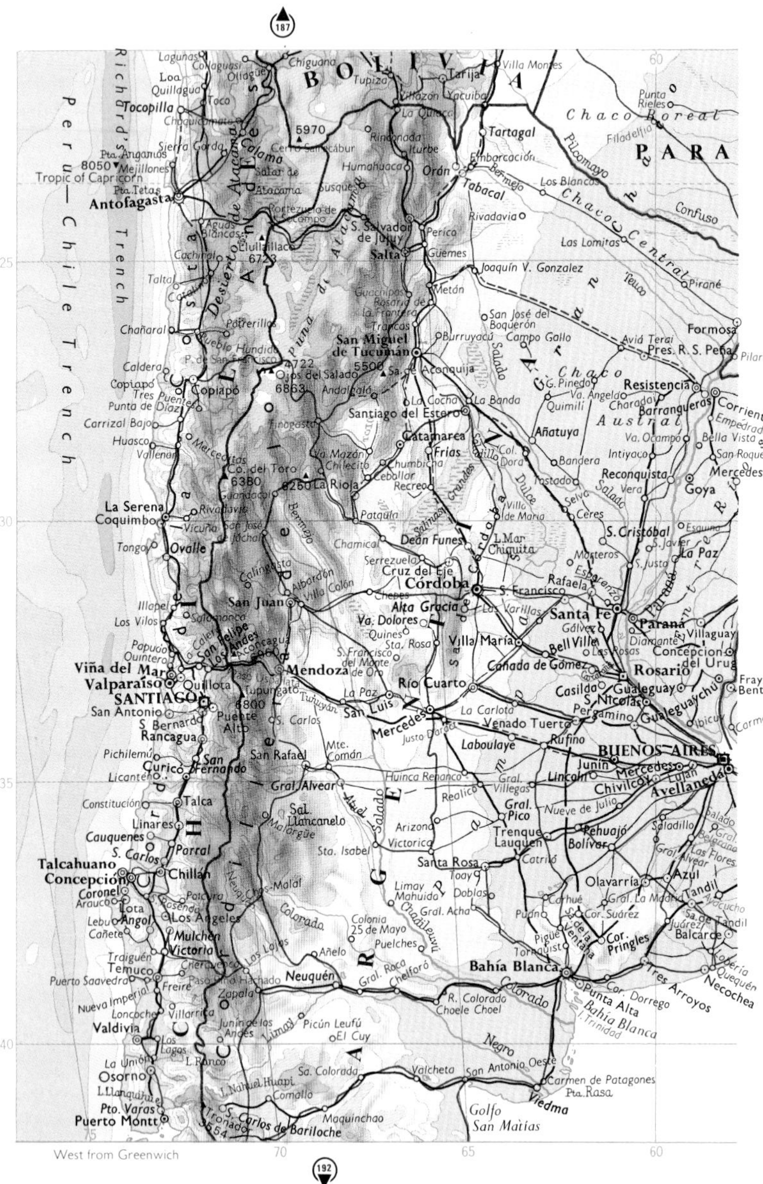
BOLIVIA
PARA
Chaco Boreal
Chaco Central
Chaco Austral
Peru — Chile Trench
Richards Trench
Tropic of Capricorn
Desierto de Atacama
Puna de Atacama
Tocopilla
Antofagasta
Mejillones
Taltal
Chañaral
Caldera
Copiapó
Vallenar
La Serena
Coquimbo
Ovalle
Illapel
Los Vilos
Viña del Mar
Valparaíso
SANTIAGO
San Antonio
Rancagua
Curicó
San Fernando
Talca
Linares
Cauquenes
Parral
Chillán
Talcahuano
Concepción
Coronel
Lota
Los Angeles
Angol
Mulchén
Victoria
Temuco
Valdivia
Osorno
Puerto Montt
Calama
Tarija
Villa Montes
Tupiza
Yacuiba
Tartagal
Orán
Tabacal
Embarcación
Pilcomayo
Bermejo
Salta
S. Salvador de Jujuy
Humahuaca
Rivadavia
Las Lomitas
Formosa
Pirané
Joaquín V. González
San Miguel de Tucumán
Santiago del Estero
La Banda
Catamarca
La Rioja
Chilecito
Añatuya
Resistencia
Corrientes
Barranqueras
Pres. R. S. Peña
Reconquista
Goya
Mercedes
Esquina
La Paz
S. Cristóbal
Dean Funes
Cruz del Eje
Córdoba
San Francisco
Rafaela
Santa Fe
Paraná
Alta Gracia
Villa María
Bell Ville
Rosario
Villaguay
Concepción del Uruguay
Cañada de Gómez
Río Cuarto
San Juan
Mendoza
San Luis
Mercedes
Aconcagua
Tupungato
San Rafael
Gral. Alvear
Venado Tuerto
Rufino
Laboulaye
Pergamino
San Nicolás
Gualeguay
Gualeguaychú
BUENOS AIRES
Junín
Chivilcoy
Lincoln
Avellaneda
Gral. Pico
Trenque Lauquen
Pehuajó
Bolívar
Nueve de Julio
Santa Rosa
Olavarría
Azul
Tandil
Gral. Acha
Cor. Pringles
Bahía Blanca
Tres Arroyos
Necochea
Balcarce
Punta Alta
Neuquén
Zapala
Colorado
Negro
Choele Choel
Viedma
Carmen de Patagones
San Antonio Oeste
Golfo San Matías
S. Carlos de Bariloche
El Cuy
Valcheta
Maquinchao
West from Greenwich
70
65
60
25
30
35
40

192

1 : 16 000 000

188

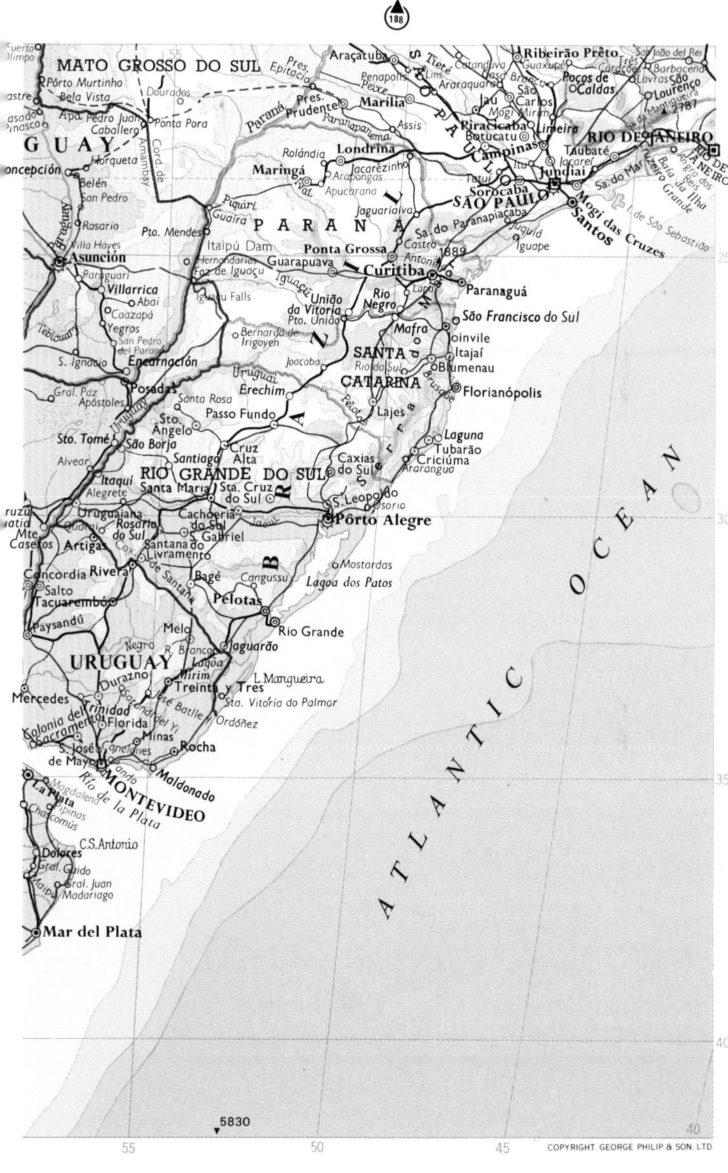
MATO GROSSO DO SUL
PARANÁ
SÃO PAULO
RIO DE JANEIRO
SANTA CATARINA
RIO GRANDE DO SUL
URUGUAY
BRAZIL
ATLANTIC OCEAN
Asunción
Curitiba
Pôrto Alegre
MONTEVIDEO
Mar del Plata
Florianópolis
Santos
Campinas
Londrina
Ponta Grossa
Pelotas
Rio Grande
Lagoa dos Patos
Posadas
Encarnación
Villarrica
Paranaguá
Joinvile
Blumenau
Caxias do Sul
Passo Fundo
Santa Maria
Rivera
Paysandú
Maldonado
La Plata
Dolores
5830
2787
1889

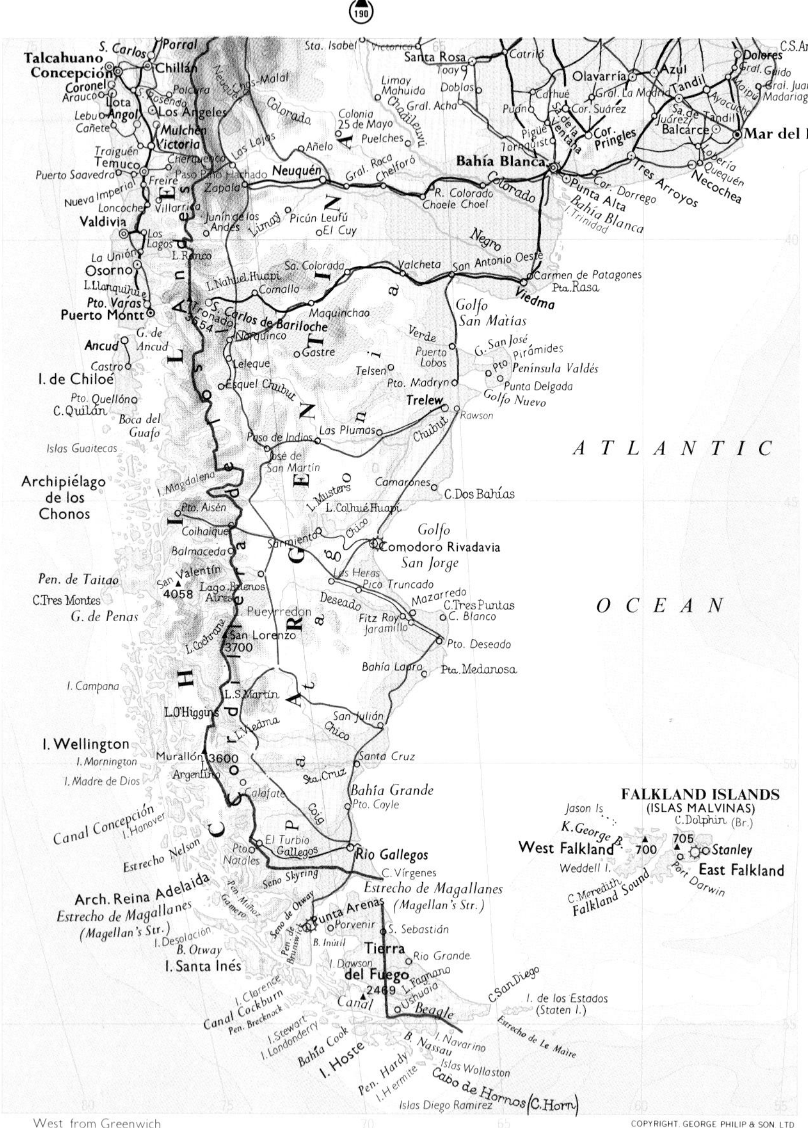

Talcahuano S. Carlos Porral Sta. Isabel Victorica Santa Rosa Catriló Dolores C.S.Ant
Concepción Chillán Malal Toay Olavarría Azul Gral. Guido
Coronel Polcura Limay Doblas Cafhué Gral. La Madrid Tandil Gral. Juan
Arauco Resendo Mahuida Gral. Acha Pudng Cor. Suárez Sa. de Madariago
Lebu Angol Los Ángeles Colonia Pirgue Juárez Tandil Mar del P.
Cañete Mulchén 25 de Mayo Tornquist Cor. Balcarce
Traiguén Victoria Añelo Puelches Pringles Necochea
Temuco Chelforó Bahía Blanca Punta Alta Tres Arroyos Quequén
Puerto Saavedra Freire Paso Rio Machado Neuquén Gral. Roca Cor. Dorrego
Nueva Imperial Zapala R. Colorado Bahía Blanca
Loncoche Villarrica Choele Choel Colorado I.Trinidad
Valdivia Junín de los Picún Leufú Negro
Los Andes Limay El Cuy San Antonio Oeste
Lagos Carmen de Patagones
La Unión I. Ranco Sa. Colorada Valcheta Pta. Rasa
Osorno Comallo Viedma
L.Llanquihue I.Nahuel Huapi Golfo G: San José Pirámides
Pto. Varas S. Carlos de Bariloche San Matías Pto Península Valdés
Puerto Montt Maquinchao Verde Lobos
G. de Ñorquinco Puerto Punta Delgada
Ancud Ancud Gastre Telsen Madryn Golfo Nuevo
Castro Leleque Trelew
I. de Chiloé Esquel Chubut Rawson
Pto. Quellóno Pto. Lobos
C.Quilán Boca del Las Plumas Chubut
Guafo Paso de Indios
Islas Guaitecas José de A T L A N T I C
San Martín
Archipiélago Magdalena Camarones
de los I. Musters C.Dos Bahías
Chonos Pta. Aisén L.Colhué Huapi
Coihaique Chico
Balmaceda Sarmiento Golfo
Comodoro Rivadavia
Pen. de Taitao Las Heras San Jorge
C.Tres Montes San Valentín Lago Buenos Pico Truncado O C E A N
G. de Penas 4058 Aires Mazarredo C.Tres Puntas
Deseado C. Blanco
San Lorenzo Fitz Roy Pto. Deseado
3700 Jaramillo
I. Campana Bahía Laura Pta. Medanosa
L.S.Martín
I. Wellington L.O'Higgins Piedra San Julián
I. Mornington Chico
I. Madre de Dios Murallón 3600 Santa Cruz
Argentino FALKLAND ISLANDS
Calafate Bahía Grande (ISLAS MALVINAS)
Canal Concepción Pto. Cayle Jason Is C.Dolphin (Br.)
I. Hanover El Turbio K.George B 705
Estrecho Nelson Pto. Gallegos West Falkland 700 Stanley
Natales Río Gallegos Weddell I. East Falkland
Arch. Reina Adelaida Seno Skyring C. Vírgenes C.Meredith Port Darwin
Estrecho de Magallanes Estrecho de Magallanes Falkland Sound
(Magellan's Str.) (Magellan's Str.)
Desolación Punta Arenas B. Otway Porvenir S. Sebastián
I. Santa Inés B. Inutil Tierra Río Grande
I. Dawson del Fuego I. de los Estados
C.Clarence 2469 Fagnano (Staten I.)
Canal Cockburn Pen. Brecknock Canal Ushuaia C.San Diego
I. Stewart Beagle Estrecho de Le Maire
I. Londonderry I.Navarino
I. Hoste Pen. Hardy B. Nassau Islas Wollaston
I.Hermite Cabo de Hornos (C. Horn)
Islas Diego Ramírez

1 : 16 000 000

INDEX

Abbreviations used

Ala. – *Alabama*
Arch. – *Archipelago*
Ark. – *Arkansas*
Austral. – *Australia*
B. – *Baie, Bahia, Bay, Boca, Bucht, Bugt*
B.C. – *British Columbia*
Bangla. – *Bangladesh*
Br. – *British*
C. – *Cabo, Cap, Cape, Coast, Costa*
C. Rica – *Costa Rica*
Calif. – *California*
Cap. Terr. – *Capital Territory*
Cat. – *Cataract*
Cent. – *Central*
Chan. – *Channel*
Colo. – *Colorado*
Conn. – *Connecticut*
Cord. – *Cordillera*
D.C. – *District of Columbia*
Del. – *Delaware*
Dét. – *Détroit*
Dom. Rep. – *Dominican Republic*
Domin. – *Dominica*
E. – *East, Eastern*
Est. – *Estrecho*
Falk. Is. – *Falkland Islands*
Fla. – *Florida*
Fr. Gui. – *French Guiana*
G. – *Golfe, Golfo, Gulf, Guba, Gebel*
Ga. – *Georgia*
Gt. – *Great*
Guat. – *Guatemala*
Hants. – *Hampshire*
Hd. – *Head*
Hond. – *Honduras*
Hts. – *Heights*
I. (s) – *Ile, Ilha, Insel, Isla, Island(s)*
I. of W. – *Isle of Wight*
Ill. – *Illinois*
Ind. – *Indiana*
Ind. Oc. – *Indian Ocean*
J. – *Jabal, Jazira*
K. – *Kap, Kapp*
Kans. – *Kansas*
Ky. – *Kentucky*

L. – *Lac, Lacul, Lago, Lagoa, Lake, Limni, Loch, Lough*
La. – *Louisiana*
Lag. – *Laguna*
Lancs. – *Lancashire*
Man. – *Manitoba*
Mass. – *Massachusetts*
Md. – *Maryland*
Mich. – *Michigan*
Minn. – *Minnesota*
Miss. – *Mississippi*
Mo. – *Missouri*
Mont. – *Montana*
Mt.(s) – *Mont, Monta, Monti, Muntii, Montaña, Mount, Mountain(s)*
N. – *North, Northern*
N.B. – *New Brunswick*
M.C. – *North Carolina*
N. Dak. – *North Dakota*
N.H. – *New Hampshire*
N.J. – *New Jersey*
N. Mex. – *New Mexico*
N.S.W. – *New South Wales*
N.W.T. – *North West Territories*
N.Y. – *New York*
N.Z. – *New Zealand*
Nebr. – *Nebraska*
Neth. – *Netherlands*
Nev. – *Nevada*
Nfld. – *Newfoundland*
Nic. – *Nicaragua*
Okla. – *Oklahoma*
Ont. – *Ontario*
Oreg. – *Oregon*
Os. – *Ostrov*
Oz. – *Ozero*
P. – *Pass, Passo, Pasul, Pulau*
P.E.I. – *Prince Edward Island*
Pa. – *Pennsylvania*
Pac. Oc. – *Pacific Ocean*
Papua N.G. – *Papua New Guinea*
Pen. – *Peninsula*
Pk. – *Peak*
Plat. – *Plateau*

P-ov. – *Poluostrov*
Pt. – *Point*
Pta. – *Ponta, Punta*
Queens. – *Queensland*
R. – *Rio, River, Rivière*
R.I. – *Rhode Island*
Ra.(s) – *Range(s)*
Raj. – *Rajasthan*
Rep. – *Republic*
Res. – *Reserve, Reservoir*
S. – *South, Southern, Sea, Sur*
S.C. – *South Carolina*
S. Africa – *South Africa*
S. Dak. – *South Dakota*
Sa. – *Serra, Sierra*
Salop. – *Shropshire*
Sard. – *Sardinia*
Sask. – *Saskatchewan*
Sd. – *Sound*
Sev. – *Severnaya*
Si. Arabia – *Saudi Arabia*
St. – *Saint*
Sta. – *Santa*
Ste. – *Sainte*
Str. – *Strait, Stretto*
Switz. – *Switzerland*
Tas. – *Tasmania*
Tenn. – *Tennessee*
Terr. – *Territory*
Tex. – *Texas*
Tipp. – *Tipperary*
Trin. & Tob. – *Trinidad and Tobago*
U.K. – *United Kingdom*
U.S.A. – *United States of America*
Ut. P. – *Uttar Pradesh*
Va. – *Virginia*
Vic. – *Victoria*
Vol. – *Volcano*
Vt. – *Vermont*
Wash. – *Washington*
W. – *West, Western, Wadi*
W. Va. – *West Virginia*
Wis. – *Wisconsin*
Worcs. – *Worcestershire*
Yorks. – *Yorkshire*

Introduction to Index

The number printed in bold type against each entry indicates the map page where the feature can be found. This is followed by its geographical coordinates. The first coordinate indicates latitude, i.e. distance north or south of the Equator. The second coordinate indicates longitude, i.e. distance east or west of the meridian of Greenwich in England (shown as 0° longitude). Both latitude and longitude are measured in degrees and minutes (with 60 minutes in a degree), and appear on the map as horizontal and vertical gridlines respectively. Thus the entry for Paris in France reads:

Paris, France . . . . **39** 48 50N 2 20 E

This entry indicates that Paris is on page **39**, at latitude 48 degrees 50 minutes north (approximately five-sixths of the distance between horizontal gridlines 48 and 49, marked on either side of the page) and at longitude 2 degrees 20 minutes east (approximately one-third of the distance between vertical gridlines 2 and 3, marked at top and bottom of the page). Paris can be found where lines extended from these two points cross on the page. The geographical coordinates are sometimes only approximate but are close enough for the place to be located. Rivers have been indexed to their mouth or confluence.

An open square □ signifies that the name refers to an administrative subdivision of a country while a solid square ■ follows the name of a country. An arrow → follows the name of a river.

The alphabetical order of names composed of two or more words is governed primarily by the first word and then by the second. This rule applies even if the second word is a description or its abbreviation, R., L., I., for example:

North Walsham
Northallerton
Northampton
Northern Circars
Northumberland Is.
Northumberland Str.

Names composed of a proper name (Gibraltar) and a description (Strait of) are positioned alphabetically by the proper name. This is the case where the definite article follows a proper name (Mans, Le). If the same word occurs in the name of a town and a geographical feature, the town name is listed first followed by the name or names of the geographical features.

Names beginning with M', Mc are all indexed as if they were spelt Mac. All names beginning St. are alphabetised under Saint, but Sankt, Sint, Santa and San are all spelt in full and are alphabetised accordingly.

If the same place name occurs twice or more times in the index and all are in the same country, each is followed by the name of the administrative subdivision in which it is located. The names are placed in the alphabetical order of the subdivisions. If the same place name occurs twice or more in the index and the places are in different countries they will be followed by their country names, the latter governing the alphabetical order. In a mixture of these situations the primary order is fixed by the alphabetical sequence of the countries and the secondary order by that of the country subdivisions.

A

Aachen 42 50 47N 6 4 E
Aalborg = Ålborg 61 57 2N 9 54 E
Aalsmeer 40 52 17N 4 43 E
Aalst 42 50 56N 4 2 E
Aalten 41 51 56N 6 35 E
Aarhus = Århus 61 56 8N 10 11 E
Aba 131 5 10N 7 19 E
Ābādān 84 30 22N 48 20 E
Ābādeh 85 31 8N 52 40 E
Abadla 126 31 2N 2 45W
Abai 191 25 58S 55 54W
Abakan 74 53 40N 91 10 E
Abancay 186 13 35S 72 55W
Abariringa I. 122 2 50S 171 40W
Abashiri 103 44 0N 144 15 E
Abashiri-Wan 103 44 0N 144 30 E
Abaya, L. 133 6 30N 37 50 E
Abbay = Nîl el Azraq → 129 15 38N 32 31 E
Abbeville, France 38 50 6N 1 49 E
Abbeville, U.S.A. 165 34 12N 82 21W
Abéché 129 13 50N 20 35 E
Abeokuta 131 7 3N 3 19 E
Aberaeron 26 52 15N 4 16W
Aberayron = Aberaeron 26 52 15N 4 16W
Aberdare 27 51 43N 3 27W
Aberdeen, U.K. 33 57 9N 2 6W
Aberdeen, S. Dak., U.S.A. 163 45 30N 98 30W
Aberdeen, Wash., U.S.A. 171 47 0N 123 50W
Aberdovey 26 52 33N 4 3W
Aberfeldy 33 56 37N 3 50W
Abergavenny 26 51 49N 3 1W
Aberystwyth 26 52 25N 4 6W
Abha 82 18 0N 42 34 E
Abidjan 130 5 26N 3 58W
Abilene 161 32 22N 99 40W
Abington 25 55 30N 3 42W
Abkhaz Rep. □ 70 43 0N 41 0 E
Abohar 89 30 10N 74 10 E
Abomey 131 7 10N 2 5 E
Abong-Mbang 131 4 0N 13 8 E
Abrud 56 46 19N 23 5 E
Abruzzi □ 47 42 15N 14 0 E
Absaroka Ra. 163 44 40N 110 0W
Abū al Khaşīb 84 30 25N 48 0 E
Abū 'Alī 84 27 20N 49 27 E
Abū 'Arīsh 82 16 58N 45 20 E
Abu Dhabi = Abū Z̧āby 85 24 28N 54 22 E
Abu Hamed 129 19 32N 33 13 E
Abū Z̧āby 85 24 28N 54 22 E
Abunã 187 9 40S 65 20W
Abunã → 187 9 41S 65 20W
Abut Hd. 123 43 7S 170 15 E
Acámbaro 177 20 2N 100 44W
Acaponeta 175 22 30N 105 22W
Acapulco 177 16 51N 99 56W
Acatlán 177 18 10N 98 3W
Acayucan 177 17 57N 94 55W
Accra 130 5 35N 0 6W
Accrington 28 53 46N 2 22W
Achill I. 34 53 58N 10 5W
Achinsk 74 56 20N 90 20 E
Aconcagua, Cerro 190 32 39S 70 0W
Aconquija, Mt. 190 27 0S 66 0W
Açores, Is. dos = Azores 126 38 44N 29 0W
Acre = 'Akko 80 32 55N 35 4 E
Acre □ 187 9 1S 71 0W
Ad Dawhah 85 25 15N 51 35 E
Ada 168 34 50N 96 45W
Adamaoua, Massif de l' 131 7 20N 12 20 E
Adamawa Highlands = Adamaoua, Massif de l' 131 7 20N 12 20 E
Adaminaby 117 36 0S 148 45 E
Adams, Mt. 171 46 10N 121 28W
Adam's Bridge 90 9 15N 79 40 E
Adana 80 37 0N 35 16 E
Adapazarı 80 40 48N 30 25 E
Adare, C. 15 71 0S 171 0 E
Addis Ababa = Addis Abeba 133 9 2N 38 42 E
Addis Abeba 133 9 2N 38 42 E
Adelaide 119 34 52S 138 30 E
Adelaide Pen. 145 68 15N 97 30W
Adélie, Terre 15 68 0S 140 0 E
Aden = Al 'Adan 83 12 45N 45 0 E
Aden, G. of 133 13 0N 50 0 E
Adige → 47 45 9N 12 20 E
Adirondack Mts. 151 44 0N 74 15W
Admiralty Is. 115 2 0S 147 0 E
Adoni 90 15 33N 77 18W
Adrian 167 41 55N 84 0W
Adriatic Sea 52 43 0N 16 0 E
Adwa 132 14 15N 38 52 E
Adzhar Rep. □ 70 42 0N 42 0 E
Ægean Sea 55 37 0N 25 0 E
Æolian Is. = Eólie, I. 49 38 30N 14 50 E
Aerht'ai Shan 100 46 40N 92 45 E
Afars & Issas, Terr. of = Djibouti ■ 133 12 0N 43 0 E
Afghanistan ■ 87 33 0N 65 0 E
Afuá 188 0 15S 50 20W
Afyonkarahisar 80 38 45N 30 33 E
Agadir 126 30 28N 9 35W
Agano → 103 37 57N 139 8 E
Agartala 93 23 50N 91 23 E
Agen 36 44 12N 0 38 E
Ageo 107 35 58N 139 36 E
Aghil Pass 89 36 15N 76 35 E
Agra 89 27 17N 77 58 E
Ağri Daği 81 39 50N 44 15 E
Água Clara 188 20 25S 52 45W
Agua Prieta 174 31 18N 109 34W
Aguadas 184 5 40N 75 38W
Aguadilla 180 18 27N 67 10W
Aguas Blancas 190 24 15S 69 55W
Aguascalientes 175 21 53N 102 18W
Aguascalientes □ 175 22 0N 102 30W
Agulhas, Kaap 136 34 52S 20 0 E
Ahaggar 127 23 0N 6 30 E
Ahaura → 123 42 21S 171 34 E
Ahmadabad 91 23 0N 72 40 E
Ahmadnagar 91 19 7N 74 46 E
Ahmedabad = Ahmadabad 91 23 0N 72 40 E
Ahmednagar = Ahmadnagar 91 19 7N 74 46 E
Ahvāz 84 31 20N 48 40 E
Ahvenanmaa = Åland 66 60 15N 20 0 E
Ahwar 83 13 30N 46 40 E
Aigle, L' 39 48 46N 0 38 E
Aigues-Mortes 37 43 35N 4 12 E
Aiken 170 33 34N 81 50W
Ailsa Craig 30 55 15N 5 7W
Aimorés 189 19 30S 41 4W
Aïn Ben Tili 126 25 59N 9 27W
Aioi 109 34 48N 134 28 E
Aïr 127 18 30N 8 0 E
Airdrie 31 55 53N 3 57W
Aire → 29 53 42N 0 55W
Airlie Beach 121 20 16S 148 43 E
Aisne → 37 49 26N 2 50 E
Aix-en-Provence 37 43 32N 5 27 E
Aix-la-Chapelle = Aachen 42 50 47N 6 4 E
Aix-les-Bains 37 45 41N 5 53 E
Aizuwakamatsu 105 37 30N 139 56 E
Ajaccio 36 41 55N 8 40 E
Ajanta Ra. 91 20 28N 75 50 E
Ajmer 91 26 28N 74 37 E
Akaishi-Dake 107 35 27N 138 9 E
Akaishi-Sammyaku 107 35 25N 138 10 E
Akashi 109 34 45N 135 0 E
Akershus fylke □ 60 60 0N 11 10 E
Akhelóös → 54 38 36N 21 14 E
Akhisar 80 38 56N 27 48 E
Aki 109 33 30N 133 54 E
Aki-Nada 109 34 5N 132 40 E
Akita 103 39 45N 140 7 E
'Akko 80 32 55N 35 4 E
Aklavik 144 68 12N 135 0W
Akō 109 34 45N 134 24 E
Akola 91 20 42N 77 2 E
Akranes 64 64 19N 21 58W
Akron 167 41 7N 81 31W

Aksaray	80	38 25N	34	2 E
Aksarka	69	66 31N	67	50 E
Akşehir	80	38 18N	31	30 E
Aksum	132	14 5N	38	40 E
Aktyubinsk	70	50 17N	57	10 E
Akune	108	32 1N	130	12 E
Akureyri	64	65 40N	18	6W
Al 'Adan	83	12 45N	45	0 E
Al Amādīyah	81	37 5N	43	30 E
Al Amārah	84	31 55N	47	15 E
Al 'Aqabah	80	29 31N	35	0 E
Al Baṣrah	84	30 30N	47	50 E
Al Ḥadīthah	81	31 28N	37	8 E
Al Hāmad	80	31 30N	39	30 E
Al Ḥasakah	81	36 35N	40	45 E
Al Ḥawrah	83	13 50N	47	35 E
Al Ḥayy	84	32 5N	46	5 E
Al Ḥillah, Iraq	84	32 30N	44	25 E
Al Ḥillah, Si. Arabia	83	23 35N	46	50 E
Al Hindīyah	84	32 30N	44	10 E
Al Ḥudaydah	82	14 50N	43	0 E
Al Hūfuf	84	25 25N	49	45 E
Al Jāfūrah	84	25 0N	50	15 E
Al Jawf, Libya	128	24 10N	23	24 E
Al Jawf, Si. Arabia	82	29 55N	39	40 E
Al Jazirah	81	33 30N	44	0 E
Al Khalīl	80	31 32N	35	6 E
Al Kūt	84	32 30N	46	0 E
Al Kuwayt	84	29 30N	47	30 E
Al Lādhiqīyah	80	35 30N	35	45 E
Al Lidām	82	20 33N	44	45 E
Al Luḥayyah	82	15 45N	42	40 E
Al Madīnah	82	24 35N	39	52 E
Al Manāmāh	85	26 10N	50	30 E
Al Marj	128	32 25N	20	30 E
Al Mawṣil	81	36 15N	43	5 E
Al Mubarraz	84	25 30N	49	40 E
Al Muḥarraq	85	26 15N	50	40 E
Al Mukallā	83	14 33N	49	2 E
Al Qaṭif	84	26 35N	50	0 E
Al Quds = Jerusalem	80	31 47N	35	10 E
Al Qunfudhah	82	19 3N	41	4 E
Al Qurnah	84	31 1N	47	25 E
Al 'Ubaylah	83	21 59N	50	57 E
Al 'Uthmānīyah	84	25 5N	49	22 E
Al Wajh	82	26 10N	36	30 E
Alabama □	169	33 0N	87	0W
Alabama ⟶	169	31 8N	87	57W
Alagoas □	189	9 0S	36	0W
Alagoinhas	189	12 7S	38	20W
Alajuela	179	10 2N	84	8W
Alamogordo	161	32 59N	106	0W
Álamos	174	27 1N	108	56W
Alamosa	163	37 30N	106	0W
Åland	66	60 15N	20	0 E
Alaska □	142	65 0N	150	0W
Alaska, G. of	142	58 0N	145	0W
Alaska Pen.	142	56 0N	160	0W
Alaska Range	142	62 50N	151	0W
Alba Iulia	56	46 8N	23	39 E
Albacete	51	39 0N	1	50W
Albania ■	52	41 0N	20	0 E
Albany, Australia	120	35 1S	117	58 E
Albany, Ga., U.S.A.	170	31 40N	84	10W
Albany, N.Y., U.S.A.	164	42 35N	73	47W
Albany, Oreg., U.S.A.	171	44 41N	123	0W
Albany ⟶	140	52 17N	81	31W
Albemarle	165	35 27N	80	15W
Albemarle Sd.	165	36 0N	76	30W
Albert	38	50 0N	2	38 E
Albert, L. = Mobutu Sese				
Seko, L.	132	1 30N	31	0 E
Albert Lea	166	43 32N	93	20W
Alberta □	155	54 40N	115	0W
Albertville = Kalemie	135	5 55S	29	9 E
Albi	37	43 56N	2	9 E
Albion	167	42 15N	84	45W
Ålborg	61	57 2N	9	54 E
Alborz, Reshteh-ye Kūhhā-ye	86	36 0N	52	0 E
Albuquerque	161	35 5N	106	47W
Alburquerque	50	39 15N	6	59W

Albury	117	36 3S	146	56 E
Alcântara	188	2 20S	44	30W
Alcázar de San Juan	50	39 24N	3	12W
Alcira	51	39 9N	0	30W
Aldan ⟶	75	63 28N	129	35 E
Aldeburgh	25	52 9N	1	35 E
Alderney	36	49 42N	2	12W
Aldershot	25	51 15N	0	43W
Alençon	39	48 27N	0	4 E
Aleppo = Ḥalab	80	36 10N	37	15 E
Alès	37	44 9N	4	5 E
Alessándria	46	44 54N	8	37 E
Ålesund	65	62 28N	6	12 E
Aleutian Is.	142	52 0N	175	0W
Alexander Arch.	143	57 0N	135	0W
Alexander City	169	32 58N	85	57W
Alexandra, Australia	117	37 8S	145	40 E
Alexandra, N.Z.	123	45 14S	169	25 E
Alexandretta = İskenderun	80	36 32N	36	10 E
Alexandria = El Iskandarîya	128	31 0N	30	0 E
Alexandria, La., U.S.A.	168	31 20N	92	30W
Alexandria, Va., U.S.A.	164	38 47N	77	1W
Alexandrina, L.	119	35 25S	139	10 E
Alexandroúpolis	55	40 50N	25	54 E
Alexis Creek	154	52 10N	123	20W
Alfreton	29	53 6N	1	22W
Algarve	50	36 58N	8	20W
Alger	127	36 42N	3	8 E
Algeria ■	127	35 10N	3	11 E
Algiers = Alger	127	36 42N	3	8 E
Algoa B.	136	33 50S	25	45 E
Alhambra	173	34 2N	118	10W
Alicante	51	38 23N	0	30W
Alice Springs	114	23 40S	133	50 E
Aligarh	89	27 55N	78	10 E
Alipur Duar	92	26 30N	89	35 E
Aliquippa	164	40 38N	80	18W
Alkmaar	40	52 37N	4	45 E
Allahabad	92	25 25N	81	58 E
Allegheny Mts.	165	38 0N	80	0W
Allen, Bog of	35	53 15N	7	0W
Allende	174	28 20N	100	51W
Allentown	164	40 36N	75	30W
Alleppey	90	9 30N	76	28 E
Aller ⟶	42	52 57N	9	10 E
Allier ⟶	37	46 57N	3	4 E
Alloa	31	56 7N	3	49W
Alma, Canada	148	48 35N	71	40W
Alma, U.S.A.	167	43 25N	84	40W
Alma Ata	71	43 15N	76	57 E
Almada	50	38 40N	9	9W
Almelo	41	52 22N	6	42 E
Almería	51	36 52N	2	27W
Almirante	179	9 10N	82	30W
Alor	113	8 15S	124	30 E
Alor Setar	96	6 7N	100	22 E
Alpena	150	45 6N	83	24W
Alphen	40	51 29N	4	58 E
Alpine	161	30 25N	103	35W
Alps	16	47 0N	8	0 E
Alsace	37	48 15N	7	25 E
Alsask	152	51 21N	109	59W
Alston	28	54 48N	2	26W
Alta Gracia	190	31 40S	64	30W
Altagracia	184	10 45N	71	30W
Altai = Aerht'ai Shan	100	46 40N	92	45 E
Altamaha ⟶	170	31 19N	81	17W
Altamira	188	3 12S	52	10W
Alto Adige = Trentino-Alto				
Adige □	47	46 30N	11	0 E
Alton	166	38 55N	90	5W
Altona	43	53 32N	9	56 E
Altoona	164	40 32N	78	24W
Altun Shan	100	38 30N	88	0 E
Alvarado	177	18 46N	95	46W
Älvsborgs län □	60	58 30N	12	30 E
Alwar	89	27 38N	76	34 E
Alxa Zuoqi	98	38 50N	105	40 E
Am-Timan	129	11 0N	20	10 E
Amadjuak	146	64 0N	72	39W
Amadjuak L.	146	65 0N	71	8W

Amagasaki **106** 34 42N 135 20 E
Amagi **108** 33 25N 130 39 E
Amakusa-Nada **108** 32 35N 130 5 E
Amalner **91** 21 5N 75 5 E
Amapá **185** 2 5N 50 50W
Amapá □ **185** 1 40N 52 0W
Amarillo **161** 35 14N 101 46W
Amasya **80** 40 40N 35 50 E
Amatitlán **177** 14 29N 90 38W
Amazon = Amazonas → **185** 0 5S 50 0W
Amazonas □ **185** 4 0S 62 0W
Amazonas → **185** 0 5S 50 0W
Ambala **89** 30 23N 76 56 E
Ambato **184** 1 5S 78 42W
Ambikapur **92** 23 15N 83 15 E
Ambleside **28** 54 26N 2 58W
Ambo **186** 10 5S 76 10W
Ambon **113** 3 35S 128 20 E
Amboyna I. **112** 7 50N 112 50 E
Amderma **69** 69 45N 61 30 E
Ameca **175** 20 33N 104 2W
Ameca, R. → **175** 20 41N 105 18W
Ameland **41** 53 27N 5 45 E
American Highland **14** 73 0S 75 0 E
American Samoa ■ **123** 14 20S 170 40W
Americus **170** 32 0N 84 10W
Amersfoort **40** 52 9N 5 23 E
Amery **143** 56 34N 94 3W
Ames **166** 42 0N 93 40W
Amga → **75** 62 38N 134 32 E
Amgu **75** 45 45N 137 15 E
Amgun → **75** 52 56N 139 38 E
Amherst **148** 45 48N 64 8W
Amherstburg **150** 42 6N 83 6W
Amiens **38** 49 54N 2 16 E
Amlwch **26** 53 24N 4 21W
'Ammān **80** 31 57N 35 52 E
Amorgós **55** 36 50N 25 57 E
Amos **151** 48 35N 78 5W
Amoy = Xiamen **99** 24 25N 118 4 E
Amravati **91** 20 55N 77 45 E
Amreli **91** 21 35N 71 17 E
Amritsar **89** 31 35N 74 57 E
Amsterdam, Neths. **40** 52 23N 4 54 E
Amsterdam, U.S.A. **164** 42 58N 74 10W
Amudarya → **70** 43 40N 59 0 E
Amundsen Gulf **145** 71 0N 124 0W
Amundsen Sea **15** 72 0S 115 0W
Amur → **75** 52 56N 141 10 E
An Nafūd **82** 28 15N 41 0 E
An Najaf **84** 32 3N 44 15 E
An Nāşirīyah **84** 31 0N 46 15 E
An Nhon **95** 13 55N 109 7 E
An Nu'ayrīyah **84** 27 30N 48 30 E
An Uaimh **34** 53 39N 6 40W
Anabar → **72** 73 8N 113 36 E
Anaconda **163** 46 7N 113 0W
Anacortes **171** 48 30N 122 40W
Anadolu **80** 38 0N 30 0 E
Anadyr → **73** 64 55N 176 5 E
Anadyrskiy Zaliv **73** 64 0N 180 0 E
Anaheim **173** 33 50N 118 0W
Anambas Is. **111** 3 20N 106 30 E
Anamur **80** 36 8N 32 58 E
Anan **109** 33 54N 134 40 E
Anápolis **188** 16 15S 48 50W
Anārak **85** 33 25N 53 40 E
Anatolia = Anadolu **80** 38 0N 30 0 E
Añatuya **190** 28 20S 62 50W
Anchorage **142** 61 10N 149 50W
Ancohuma, Nevada **187** 16 0S 68 50W
Ancona **47** 43 37N 13 30 E
Ancud **192** 42 0S 73 50W
Ancud, G. de **192** 42 0S 73 0W
Åndalsnes **65** 62 35N 7 43 E
Andalucía □ **50** 37 35N 5 0W
Andalusia **169** 31 19N 86 30W
Andalusia □ = Andalucía □ **50** 37 35N 5 0W
Andaman Is. **94** 12 30N 92 30 E
Andaman Sea **94** 13 0N 96 0 E
Andaman Str. **94** 12 15N 92 20 E
Andelys, Les **39** 49 15N 1 25 E
Anderson, Ind., U.S.A. **167** 40 5N 85 40W
Anderson, S.C., U.S.A. **165** 34 32N 82 40W
Andes, Cord. de los **182** 20 0S 68 0W
Andhra Pradesh □ **91** 16 0N 79 0 E
Andikíthira **55** 35 52N 23 15 E
Andizhan **71** 41 10N 72 0 E
Andorra ■ **36** 42 30N 1 30 E
Andover **24** 51 13N 1 29W
Andreanof Is. **142** 52 0N 178 0W
Andrewilla **118** 26 31S 139 17 E
Ándria **49** 41 13N 16 17 E
Andropov = Rybinsk **68** 58 5N 38 50 E
Ándros **55** 37 50N 24 57 E
Andros I. **178** 24 30N 78 0W
Angara → **74** 58 30N 97 0 E
Angarsk **74** 52 30N 104 0 E
Angaston **119** 34 30S 139 8 E
Ånge **66** 62 31N 15 35 E
Ängelholm **61** 56 15N 12 58 E
Angels Camp **172** 38 8N 120 30W
Ångerman → **66** 64 0N 17 20 E
Angers **36** 47 30N 0 35W
Angkor **95** 13 22N 103 50 E
Anglesey **26** 53 17N 4 20W
Angmagssalik **147** 65 40N 37 20W
Angol **190** 37 56S 72 45W
Angola ■ **134** 12 0S 18 0 E
Angoulême **36** 45 39N 0 10 E
Angoumois **36** 45 50N 0 25 E
Anguilla **180** 18 14N 63 5W
Angus, Braes of **33** 56 51N 3 10W
Anhui □ **99** 32 0N 117 0 E
Anhwei □ = Anhui □ **99** 32 0N 117 0 E
Anin **94** 15 36N 97 50 E
Anjō **106** 34 57N 137 5 E
Anjou **36** 47 20N 0 15W
Anju **98** 39 36N 125 40 E
Ankang **99** 32 40N 109 1 E
Ankara **80** 40 0N 32 54 E
Ann Arbor **167** 42 17N 83 45W
Annaba **127** 36 50N 7 46 E
Annam = Trung-Phan **95** 16 0N 108 0 E
Annamitique, Chaîne **95** 17 0N 106 0 E
Annan **31** 55 0N 3 17W
Annapolis **164** 39 0N 76 30W
Annecy **37** 45 55N 6 8 E
Anniston **169** 33 45N 85 50W
Annobón **131** 1 25S 5 36 E
Annonay **37** 45 15N 4 40 E
Annotto Bay **180** 18 17N 77 3W
Anqing **99** 30 30N 117 3 E
Anse, L' **150** 46 47N 88 28W
Anshan **98** 41 3N 122 58 E
Anshun **99** 26 18N 105 57 E
Anstruther **31** 56 14N 2 40W
Antabamba **186** 14 40S 73 0W
Antakya **80** 36 14N 36 10 E
Antalya **80** 36 52N 30 45 E
Antalya Körfezi **80** 36 15N 31 30 E
Antananarivo **137** 18 55S 47 31 E
Antarctic Pen. **14** 67 0S 60 0W
Antarctica **14** 90 0S 0 0 E
Anti Atlas **126** 30 0N 8 30W
Antibes **37** 43 34N 7 6 E
Anticosti, Î. d' **148** 49 30N 63 0W
Antigo **150** 45 8N 89 5W
Antigua, Guatemala **177** 14 34N 90 41W
Antigua, W. Indies **180** 17 0N 61 50W
Antigua and Barbuda ■ **180** 17 20N 61 48W
Antilla **178** 20 40N 75 50W
Antioch **172** 38 7N 121 45W
Antioquia **184** 6 40N 75 55W
Antipodes Is. **11** 49 45S 178 40 E
Antofagasta **190** 23 50S 70 30W
Antrim **34** 54 43N 6 13W
Antrim, Mts. of **34** 54 57N 6 8W
Antsiranana **137** 12 25S 49 20 E
Antwerp = Antwerpen **42** 51 13N 4 25 E
Antwerpen **42** 51 13N 4 25 E
Anvers = Antwerpen **42** 51 13N 4 25 E

Anvik 142 62 37N 160 20W
Anxious B. 119 33 24S 134 45 E
Anyang 98 36 5N 114 21 E
Anzhero-Sudzhensk 71 56 10N 86 0 E
Ánzio 46 41 28N 12 37 E
Aoga-Shima 105 32 28N 139 46 E
Aomori 103 40 45N 140 45 E
Apalachee B. 170 30 0N 84 0W
Apalachicola 170 29 40N 85 0W
Apalachicola → 170 29 40N 85 0W
Aparri 112 18 22N 121 38 E
Apatzingan 175 19 5N 102 21W
Apeldoorn 41 52 13N 5 57 E
Apennines 16 44 20N 10 20 E
Apizaco 177 19 25N 98 9W
Aplao 186 16 0S 72 40W
Apolo 187 14 30S 68 30W
Apostle Is. 150 47 0N 90 30W
Apostolos Andreas, C. 80 35 42N 34 35 E
Appalachian Mts. 138 38 0N 80 0W
Appingedam 41 53 19N 6 51 E
Appleby 28 54 35N 2 29W
Appleton 167 44 17N 88 25W
Apulia = Púglia □ 49 41 0N 16 30 E
Apure → 184 7 37N 66 25W
Aqabah = Al 'Aqabah 80 29 31N 35 0 E
Aquidauana 188 20 30S 55 50W
Áquila, L' 47 42 21N 13 24 E
Aquiles Serdán 174 28 36N 105 53W
Ar Riyāḍ 83 24 41N 46 42 E
Ar Ruṭbah 81 33 0N 40 15 E
Ara 92 25 35N 84 32 E
Arab, Bahr el → 129 9 50N 29 0 E
Arab, Shatt al 84 30 0N 48 31 E
Arabia 76 25 0N 45 0 E
Arabian Gulf = Gulf, The 85 27 0N 50 0 E
Arabian Sea 76 16 0N 65 0 E
Aracaju 189 10 55S 37 4W
Aracati 189 4 30S 37 44W
Araçatuba 188 21 10S 50 30W
Arad 56 46 10N 21 20 E
Arafura Sea 113 9 0S 135 0 E
Aragón □ 51 41 25N 1 0W
Araguacema 188 8 50S 49 20W
Araguaia → 188 5 21S 48 41W
Araguari 188 18 38S 48 11W
Arāk 84 34 0N 49 40 E
Arakan Coast 93 19 0N 94 0 E
Arakan Yoma 93 20 0N 94 40 E
Araks = Aras, Rūd-e → 81 39 10N 47 10 E
Aral Sea = Aralskoye More 70 44 30N 60 0 E
Aralsk 70 46 50N 61 20 E
Aralskoye More 70 44 30N 60 0 E
Aran I. 34 55 0N 8 30W
Aran Is. 35 53 5N 9 42W
Aranjuez 50 40 1N 3 40W
Aransas Pass 158 27 55N 97 9W
Arao 108 32 59N 130 25 E
Araraquara 188 21 50S 48 0W
Ararat 119 37 16S 143 0 E
Ararat, Mt. = Ağri Daği 81 39 50N 44 15 E
Aras, Rūd-e → 81 39 10N 47 10 E
Araya, Pen. de 185 10 40N 64 0W
Arbīl 81 36 15N 44 5 E
Arbroath 31 56 34N 2 35W
Arcachon 36 44 40N 1 10W
Arcadia 170 27 20N 81 50W
Archangel = Arkhangelsk 69 64 40N 41 0 E
Arcot 90 12 53N 79 20 E
Arctic Bay 146 73 1N 85 7W
Arctic Ocean 12 78 0N 160 0W
Arctic Red River 144 67 15N 134 0W
Ardabīl 81 38 15N 48 18 E
Ardennes 42 50 0N 5 10 E
Ardgour 32 56 45N 5 25W
Ardlethan 117 34 22S 146 53 E
Ardmore 168 34 10N 97 5W
Ardnacrusha 35 52 43N 8 38W
Ardnamurchan, Pt. of 32 56 44N 6 14W
Ards Pen. 34 54 30N 5 25W
Arecibo 180 18 29N 66 42W
Arequipa 187 16 20S 71 30W
Arezzo 46 43 28N 11 50 E
Argentan 39 48 45N 0 1W
Argentário, Mte. 46 42 23N 11 11 E
Argentina ■ 190 35 0S 66 0W
Argentino, L. 192 50 10S 73 0W
Árgos 54 37 40N 22 43 E
Argostólion 54 38 12N 20 33 E
Argun → 74 53 20N 121 28 E
Århus 61 56 8N 10 11 E
Arica, Chile 187 18 32S 70 20W
Arica, Colombia 184 2 0S 71 50W
Arida 106 34 5N 135 8 E
Arima 180 10 38N 61 17W
Ario de Rosales 175 19 12N 101 43W
Aripuanã 187 9 25S 60 30W
Aripuanã → 187 5 7S 60 25W
Ariquemes 187 9 55S 63 6W
Arisaig 32 56 55N 5 50W
Aristazabal I. 154 52 40N 129 10W
Arizona □ 160 34 20N 111 30W
Arjona 184 10 14N 75 22W
Arkadelphia 168 34 5N 93 0W
Arkansas □ 168 35 0N 92 30W
Arkansas → 168 33 48N 91 4W
Arkansas City 158 37 4N 97 3W
Arkhangelsk 69 64 40N 41 0 E
Arklow 35 52 48N 6 10W
Arkticheskiy, Mys 72 81 10N 95 0 E
Arles 37 43 41N 4 40 E
Arlington 164 38 52N 77 5W
Armagh 34 54 22N 6 40W
Armavir 70 45 2N 41 7 E
Armenia 184 4 35N 75 45W
Armenia ■ 70 40 0N 41 0 E
Armentières 38 50 40N 2 50 E
Armidale 116 30 30S 151 40 E
Armstrong 155 50 25N 119 10W
Arnaouti, C. 80 35 6N 32 17 E
Arnaud → 146 59 59N 69 46W
Arnhem 41 51 58N 5 55 E
Arnhem, C. 115 12 20S 137 30 E
Arnhem Land 114 13 10S 134 30 E
Arnprior 151 45 26N 76 21W
Arran 30 55 34N 5 12W
Arras 38 50 17N 2 46 E
Arriaga 177 16 14N 93 54W
Árta 54 39 8N 21 2 E
Artigas 191 30 20S 56 30W
Artois 38 50 20N 2 30 E
Aru, Kepulauan 113 6 0S 134 30 E
Arua 132 3 1N 30 58 E
Aruanã 188 14 54S 51 10W
Aruba 181 12 30N 70 0W
Arusha 135 3 20S 36 40 E
Arvida 148 48 25N 71 14W
Arys 71 42 26N 68 48 E
'As Saffānīyah 84 28 5N 48 50 E
As Samāwah 84 31 15N 45 15 E
As Sulaymānīyah 83 24 9N 47 18 E
As Sumaymānīyah 81 35 35N 45 29 E
As Suwaydā' 80 32 40N 36 30 E
As Ṣuwayrah 84 32 55N 45 0 E
Asahi 107 35 43N 140 39 E
Asahi-Gawa → 109 34 36N 133 58 E
Asahigawa 103 43 46N 142 22 E
Asama-Yama 107 36 24N 138 31 E
Asamankese 130 5 50N 0 40W
Asansol 92 23 40N 87 1 E
Asbestos 148 45 47N 71 58W
Ascension I. 125 8 0S 14 15W
Áscoli Piceno 47 42 51N 13 34 E
Aseb 133 13 0N 42 40 E
Ash Shām, Bādiyat 80 32 0N 40 0 E
Ash Shāmīyah 84 31 55N 44 35 E
Ash Shāriqah 85 25 23N 55 26 E
Ash Shaṭrah 84 31 30N 46 10 E
Ashburton 123 43 53S 171 48 E
Ashby-de-la-Zouch 28 52 45N 1 29W
Ashcroft 155 50 40N 121 20W
Asheboro 165 35 43N 79 46W

Asheville 165 35 39N 82 30W
Ashford, Australia 116 29 15S 151 3 E
Ashford, U.K. 25 51 8N 0 53 E
Ashikaga 107 36 28N 139 29 E
Ashizuri-Zaki 109 32 44N 133 0 E
Ashkhabad 70 38 0N 57 50 E
Ashland, Kans., U.S.A. 156 37 13N 99 43W
Ashland, Ky., U.S.A. 165 38 25N 82 40W
Ashland, Oreg., U.S.A. 171 42 10N 122 38W
Ashland, Wis., U.S.A. 150 46 40N 90 52W
Ashq'elon 80 31 42N 34 35 E
Ashtabula 164 41 52N 80 50W
Ashton-under-Lyne 28 53 30N 2 8W
Ashuanipi, L. 147 52 45N 66 15W
Asinara I. 48 41 5N 8 15 E
'Asīr □ 82 18 40N 42 30 E
Asir, Ras 133 11 55N 51 10 E
Asmara = Asmera 132 15 19N 38 55 E
Asmera 132 15 19N 38 55 E
Aso 108 33 0N 131 5 E
Aso-Zan 108 32 53N 131 6 E
Aspiring, Mt. 123 44 23S 168 46 E
Assam □ 93 26 0N 93 0 E
Assen 41 53 0N 6 35 E
Assiniboia 152 49 40N 105 59W
Assiniboine → 153 49 53N 97 8W
Assisi 46 43 4N 12 36 E
Asti 46 44 54N 8 11 E
Astipálaia 55 36 32N 26 22 E
Astoria 171 46 16N 123 50W
Astrakhan 70 46 25N 48 5 E
Asturias □ 50 43 15N 6 0W
Asunción 191 25 10S 57 30W
Aswân 128 24 4N 32 57 E
Asyût 128 27 11N 31 4 E
At Ţafīlah 80 30 45N 35 30 E
At Ta'if 82 21 5N 40 27 E
Atacama, Desierto de 190 24 0S 69 20W
Atacama, Salar de 190 23 30S 68 20W
Atalaya 186 10 45S 73 50W
Atami 107 35 5N 139 4 E
Atbara 129 17 42N 33 59 E
'Atbara → 129 17 40N 33 56 E
Atchafalaya B. 168 29 30N 91 20W
Atchison 166 39 40N 95 10W
Athabasca 155 54 45N 113 20W
Athabasca → 145 58 40N 110 50W
Athabasca, L. 145 59 15N 109 15W
Athenry 35 53 18N 8 45W
Athens = Athínai 55 37 58N 23 46 E
Athens, Ala., U.S.A. 169 34 49N 86 58W
Athens, Ga., U.S.A. 165 33 56N 83 24W
Athens, Ohio, U.S.A. 167 39 25N 82 6W
Athens, Tenn., U.S.A. 169 35 45N 84 38W
Athens, Tex., U.S.A. 168 32 11N 95 48W
Atherton 121 17 17S 145 30 E
Athínai 55 37 58N 23 46 E
Athlone 34 53 26N 7 57W
Atholl, Forest of 33 56 51N 3 50W
Áthos 55 40 9N 24 22 E
Athy 35 53 0N 7 0W
Atico 186 16 14S 73 40W
Atlanta 170 33 50N 84 24W
Atlantic 166 41 25N 95 0W
Atlantic City 164 39 25N 74 25W
Atlantic Ocean 9 0 0 20 0W
Atlas Mts. = Haut Atlas 126 32 30N 5 0W
Atmore 169 31 2N 87 30W
Atsugi 107 35 25N 139 21 E
Atsumi 106 34 35N 137 4 E
Atsumi-Wan 106 34 44N 137 13 E
Attawapiskat → 140 52 57N 82 18W
Attleboro 164 41 56N 71 18W
Aubagne 37 43 17N 5 37 E
Aube → 37 48 34N 3 43 E
Aubenas 37 44 37N 4 24 E
Auburn, Ala., U.S.A. 169 32 37N 85 30W
Auburn, N.Y., U.S.A. 164 42 57N 76 39W
Auckland 122 36 52S 174 46 E
Auckland Is. 15 50 40S 166 5 E
Aude → 37 43 13N 3 14 E
Augsburg 43 48 22N 10 54 E
Augusta, Ga., U.S.A. 170 33 29N 81 59W
Augusta, Maine, U.S.A. 148 44 20N 69 46W
Aunis 36 46 5N 0 50W
Aurangabad 91 19 50N 75 23 E
Aurillac 37 44 55N 2 26 E
Aurora 167 41 42N 88 12W
Aust-Agder fylke □ 60 58 55N 7 40 E
Austin, Minn., U.S.A. 166 43 37N 92 59W
Austin, Tex., U.S.A. 161 30 20N 97 45W
Austral Is. = Tubuai Is. 123 25 0S 150 0W
Australia ■ 114 23 0S 135 0 E
Australian Alps 117 36 30S 148 30 E
Australian Cap. Terr. □ 117 35 30S 149 0 E
Austria ■ 45 47 0N 14 0 E
Autlán 175 19 40N 104 30W
Auvergne 37 45 20N 3 15 E
Auxerre 39 47 48N 3 32 E
Avalon Pen. 149 47 30N 53 20W
Aveiro 185 3 10S 55 5W
Avellaneda 190 34 50S 58 10W
Aves, I. de 181 15 45N 63 55W
Avesnes-sur-Helpe 38 50 8N 3 55 E
Aveyron → 36 44 7N 1 5 E
Aviemore 33 57 11N 3 50W
Avignon 37 43 57N 4 50 E
Ávila 50 40 39N 4 43W
Avon □ 27 51 30N 2 40W
Avon →, Avon, U.K. 24 51 30N 2 43W
Avon →, Hants., U.K. 24 50 44N 1 45W
Avonmouth 27 51 30N 2 42W
Avranches 36 48 40N 1 20W
Awaji-Shima 109 34 30N 134 50 E
Aweil 129 8 42N 27 20 E
Axel Heiberg I. 12 80 0N 90 0W
Axminster 27 50 47N 3 1W
Ayabe 106 35 20N 135 20 E
Ayacucho 186 13 0S 74 0W
Ayios Evstrátios 55 39 34N 24 58 E
Ayon, Ostrov 73 69 50N 169 0 E
Ayr, Australia 121 19 35S 147 25 E
Ayr, U.K. 31 55 28N 4 37W
Ayre, Pt. of 28 54 27N 4 21W
Aytos 53 42 42N 27 16 E
Ayutla 177 16 58N 99 17W
Az Ẓahrān 84 26 10N 50 7 E
Az Zubayr 84 30 20N 47 50 E
Azamgarh 92 26 5N 83 13 E
Azbine = Aïr 127 18 30N 8 0 E
Azerbaijan ■ 70 40 20N 48 0 E
Azores 126 38 44N 29 0W
Azov Sea = Azovskoye More 68 46 0N 36 30 E
Azovskoye More 68 46 0N 36 30 E
Azúa de Compostela 180 18 25N 70 44W
Azuero, Pen. de 179 7 30N 80 30W
Azul 190 36 42S 59 43W

B

Ba Ngoi = Cam Lam 95 11 54N 109 10 E
Baarn 40 52 12N 5 17 E
Bāb el Māndeb 133 12 35N 43 25 E
Babahoyo 184 1 40S 79 30W
Babinda 121 17 20S 145 56 E
Babine L. 154 54 48N 126 0W
Bābol 86 36 40N 52 50 E
Babuyan Is. 112 19 10N 121 40 E
Babylon 84 32 40N 44 30 E
Bac Ninh 95 21 13N 106 4 E
Bac Phan 95 22 0N 105 0 E
Bac Quang 95 22 30N 104 48 E
Bacabal 188 4 15S 44 45W
Bacău 57 46 35N 26 55 E
Back → 145 65 10N 104 0W
Bacolod 112 10 40N 122 57 E
Bad Lands 163 43 40N 102 10W
Badajoz 50 38 50N 6 59W
Badakhshān □ 87 36 30N 71 0 E

Name	Page	Lat.	Long.
Badalona	**51**	41 26N	2 15 E
Badanah	**82**	30 58N	41 30 E
Baden-Baden	**42**	48 45N	8 15 E
Baden-Württemberg □	**42**	48 40N	9 0 E
Bādghīsāt □	**87**	35 0N	63 0 E
Badin	**88**	24 38N	68 54 E
Baffin □	**146**	70 0N	80 0W
Baffin B.	**13**	72 0N	64 0W
Baffin I.	**146**	68 0N	75 0W
Bafra	**80**	41 34N	35 54 E
Bāft	**85**	29 15N	56 38 E
Bagé	**191**	31 20S	54 15W
Baghdād	**84**	33 20N	44 30 E
Baghlān	**87**	36 12N	69 0 E
Baghlān □	**87**	36 0N	68 30 E
Bahamas ■	**178**	24 0N	75 0W
Baharampur	**92**	24 2N	88 27 E
Bahawalpur	**89**	29 24N	71 40 E
Bahía = Salvador	**189**	13 0S	38 30W
Bahía □	**189**	12 0S	42 0W
Bahía Blanca	**190**	38 35S	62 13W
Bahr el Jebel →	**129**	7 30N	30 30 E
Bahraich	**92**	27 38N	81 37 E
Bahrain ■	**85**	26 0N	50 35 E
Baia Mare	**56**	47 40N	23 35 E
Baie Comeau	**148**	49 12N	68 10W
Baie-St-Paul	**148**	47 28N	70 32W
Ba'ījī	**81**	35 0N	43 30 E
Baikal, L. = Baykal, Oz.	**74**	53 0N	108 0 E
Baile Atha Cliath = Dublin	**35**	53 20N	6 18W
Bailleul	**38**	50 44N	2 41 E
Bainbridge	**170**	30 53N	84 34W
Baird Mts.	**142**	67 10N	160 15W
Bairnsdale	**117**	37 48S	147 36 E
Baiyin	**98**	36 45N	104 14 E
Baja	**59**	46 12N	18 59 E
Baja California	**174**	31 10N	115 12W
Baja California Norte □	**174**	30 0N	115 0W
Baja California Sur □	**174**	25 50N	111 50W
Bajimba, Mt.	**116**	29 17S	152 6 E
Baker	**171**	44 50N	117 55W
Baker I.	**122**	0 10N	176 35W
Baker Lake	**145**	64 20N	96 3W
Bakersfield	**173**	35 25N	119 0W
Bākhtarān	**84**	34 23N	47 0 E
Bakony Forest = Bakony Hegység	**59**	47 10N	17 30 E
Bakony Hegység	**59**	47 10N	17 30 E
Baku	**70**	40 25N	49 45 E
Bala	**26**	52 54N	3 36W
Balabac, Str.	**112**	7 53N	117 5 E
Balabakk	**80**	34 0N	36 10 E
Balaghat	**91**	21 49N	80 12 E
Balaghat Ra.	**91**	18 50N	76 30 E
Balaklava	**119**	34 7S	138 22 E
Balakovo	**68**	52 4N	47 55 E
Balaton	**59**	46 50N	17 40 E
Balboa	**179**	9 0N	79 30W
Balbriggan	**34**	53 35N	6 10W
Balcarce	**190**	38 0S	58 10W
Balclutha	**123**	46 15S	169 45 E
Baldy Peak	**161**	33 50N	109 30W
Baleares, Islas	**51**	39 30N	3 0 E
Balearic Is. = Baleares, Islas	**51**	39 30N	3 0 E
Bali	**111**	8 20S	115 0 E
Balikesir	**80**	39 35N	27 58 E
Balikpapan	**111**	1 10S	116 55 E
Balkan Mts. = Stara Planina	**53**	43 15N	23 0 E
Balkan Pen.	**17**	42 0N	22 0 E
Balkh □	**87**	36 30N	67 0 E
Balkhash	**71**	46 50N	74 50 E
Balkhash, Ozero	**71**	46 0N	74 50 E
Ballachulish	**32**	56 40N	5 10W
Ballarat	**117**	37 33S	143 50 E
Ballard, L.	**120**	29 20S	120 10 E
Ballater	**33**	57 2N	3 2W
Ballina, Australia	**116**	28 50S	153 31 E
Ballina, Mayo, Ireland	**34**	54 7N	9 10W
Ballina, Tipp., Ireland	**35**	52 49N	8 27W
Ballinasloe	**35**	53 20N	8 12W
Ballinrobe	**34**	53 36N	9 13W
Ballycastle	**34**	55 12N	6 15W
Ballymena	**34**	54 53N	6 18W
Ballymoney	**34**	55 5N	6 30W
Ballyshannon	**34**	54 30N	8 10W
Balmaceda	**192**	46 0S	71 50W
Balmoral	**33**	57 3N	3 13W
Balrampur	**92**	27 30N	82 20 E
Balranald	**117**	34 38S	143 33 E
Balsas, R. →	**177**	17 55N	102 10W
Baltic Sea	**16**	56 0N	20 0 E
Baltimore	**164**	39 18N	76 37W
Baluchistan □	**88**	27 30N	65 0 E
Bamako	**130**	12 34N	7 55W
Bambari	**129**	5 40N	20 35 E
Bamberg	**43**	49 54N	10 53 E
Bāmīān □	**87**	35 0N	67 0 E
Ban Aranyaprathet	**95**	13 41N	102 30 E
Ban Don = Surat Thani	**96**	9 6N	99 20 E
Ban Houei Sai	**95**	20 22N	100 32 E
Ban Khe Bo	**95**	19 10N	104 39 E
Ban Khun Yuam	**94**	18 49N	97 57 E
Ban Nong Pling	**94**	15 40N	100 10 E
Ban Phai	**95**	16 4N	102 44 E
Banaras = Varanasi	**92**	25 22N	83 0 E
Banbridge	**34**	54 21N	6 17W
Banbury	**25**	52 4N	1 21W
Bancroft	**151**	45 3N	77 51W
Banda	**91**	25 30N	80 26 E
Banda, Kepulauan	**113**	4 37S	129 50 E
Banda Aceh	**111**	5 35N	95 20 E
Banda Banda, Mt.	**116**	31 10S	152 28 E
Banda Sea	**113**	6 0S	130 0 E
Bandar = Machilipatnam	**92**	16 12N	81 8 E
Bandār 'Abbās	**85**	27 15N	56 15 E
Bandar-e Anzalī	**81**	37 30N	49 30 E
Bandar-e Khomeyni	**84**	30 30N	49 5 E
Bandar-e Lengeh	**85**	26 35N	54 58 E
Bandar-e Nakhīlū	**85**	26 58N	53 30 E
Bandar-e Torkeman	**86**	37 0N	54 10 E
Bandar Seri Begawan	**112**	4 52N	115 0 E
Bandeira, Pico da	**188**	20 26S	41 47W
Bandırma	**80**	40 20N	28 0 E
Bandon	**35**	51 44N	8 45W
Bandung	**111**	6 54S	107 36 E
Banes	**178**	21 0N	75 42W
Banff, Canada	**155**	51 10N	115 34W
Banff, U.K.	**33**	57 40N	2 32W
Bangalore	**90**	12 59N	77 40 E
Bangassou	**129**	4 55N	23 7 E
Banggai	**113**	1 40S	123 30 E
Banghāzī	**128**	32 11N	20 3 E
Bangka, Selat	**111**	2 30S	105 30 E
Bangkok	**94**	13 45N	100 35 E
Bangladesh ■	**92**	24 0N	90 0 E
Bangor, N. Ireland, U.K.	**34**	54 40N	5 40W
Bangor, Wales, U.K.	**26**	53 13N	4 9W
Bangor, U.S.A.	**148**	44 48N	68 42W
Bangui	**131**	4 23N	18 35 E
Bangweulu, L.	**135**	11 0S	30 0 E
Bani	**180**	18 16N	70 22W
Banja Luka	**52**	44 49N	17 11 E
Banjarmasin	**111**	3 20S	114 35 E
Banjul	**130**	13 28N	16 40W
Bankipore	**92**	25 35N	85 10 E
Banks I., B.C., Canada	**154**	53 20N	130 0W
Banks I., N.W.T., Canada	**145**	73 15N	121 30W
Banks Pen.	**123**	43 45S	173 15 E
Banks Str.	**119**	40 40S	148 10 E
Bann →	**34**	54 30N	6 31W
Banning	**173**	33 58N	116 52W
Bannockburn	**31**	56 5N	3 55W
Bannu	**89**	33 0N	70 18 E
Bantry	**35**	51 40N	9 28W
Baoding	**98**	38 50N	115 28 E
Baoji	**99**	34 20N	107 5 E
Baotou	**98**	40 32N	110 2 E
Ba'qūbah	**81**	33 45N	44 50 E
Bar	**52**	42 8N	19 8 E
Bar Harbor	**148**	44 15N	68 20W
Baraboo	**166**	43 28N	89 46W
Baracoa	**178**	20 20N	74 30W

Name	Page	Lat °	′	N/S	Long °	′	E/W
Barahona	180	18	13	N	71	7	W
Barail Range	93	25	15	N	93	20	E
Baramula	89	34	15	N	74	20	E
Baran	91	25	9	N	76	40	E
Baranof I.	143	57	0	N	135	10	W
Baranovichi	68	53	10	N	26	0	E
Barbacoas	184	1	45	N	78	0	W
Barbados ■	180	13	0	N	59	30	W
Barbuda I.	180	17	30	N	61	40	W
Barca, La	175	20	17	N	102	34	W
Barcaldine	121	23	43	S	145	6	E
Barcelona, Spain	51	41	21	N	2	10	E
Barcelona, Venezuela	185	10	10	N	64	40	W
Barcelos	185	1	0	S	63	0	W
Barddhaman	92	23	14	N	87	39	E
Bardera	133	2	20	N	42	27	E
Bardsey I.	26	52	46	N	4	47	W
Bareilly	89	28	22	N	79	27	E
Barentin	38	49	33	N	0	58	E
Barents Sea	13	73	0	N	39	0	E
Bargara	121	24	50	S	152	25	E
Bari	49	41	6	N	16	52	E
Bari Doab	89	30	20	N	73	0	E
Barīm	82	12	39	N	43	25	E
Barinas	184	8	36	N	70	15	W
Barisal	92	22	45	N	90	20	E
Barito →	111	4	0	S	114	50	E
Barlee, L.	120	29	15	S	119	30	E
Barletta	49	41	20	N	16	17	E
Barmer	91	25	45	N	71	20	E
Barmera	119	34	15	S	140	28	E
Barmouth	26	52	44	N	4	3	W
Barnard Castle	28	54	33	N	1	55	W
Barnaul	71	53	20	N	83	40	E
Barneveld	41	52	7	N	5	36	E
Barnsley	28	53	33	N	1	29	W
Barnstaple	27	51	5	N	4	3	W
Baro	131	8	35	N	6	18	E
Baroda = Vadodara	91	22	20	N	73	10	E
Barpeta	93	26	20	N	91	10	E
Barquisimeto	184	10	4	N	69	19	W
Barra	32	57	0	N	7	30	W
Barra Hd.	32	56	47	N	7	40	W
Barraba	116	30	21	S	150	35	E
Barranca	186	10	45	S	77	50	W
Barrancabermeja	184	7	0	N	73	50	W
Barrancas	185	8	55	N	62	5	W
Barranqueras	190	27	30	S	59	0	W
Barranquilla	184	11	0	N	74	50	W
Barre	151	44	15	N	72	30	W
Barreiros	188	8	49	S	35	12	W
Barrhead	155	54	10	N	114	24	W
Barrie	151	44	24	N	79	40	W
Barrier Ra.	118	31	0	S	141	30	E
Barrington Tops	116	32	6	S	151	28	E
Barrow →	35	52	10	N	6	57	W
Barrow, Pt.	138	71	22	N	156	30	W
Barrow-in-Furness	28	54	8	N	3	15	W
Barry	27	51	23	N	3	19	W
Barry's Bay	151	45	29	N	77	41	W
Barsi	91	18	10	N	75	50	E
Barstow	173	34	58	N	117	2	W
Bartica	185	6	25	N	58	40	W
Bartow	170	27	53	N	81	49	W
Basel	44	47	35	N	7	35	E
Bashi Channel	99	21	15	N	122	0	E
Bashkir Rep. □	69	54	0	N	57	0	E
Basilan	112	6	35	N	122	0	E
Basildon	25	51	34	N	0	29	E
Basilicata □	49	40	30	N	16	0	E
Basim = Washim	91	20	3	N	77	0	E
Basle = Basel	44	47	35	N	7	35	E
Basoka	134	1	16	N	23	40	E
Basque Provinces = Vascongadas	50	42	50	N	2	45	W
Basra = Al Başrah	84	30	30	N	47	50	E
Bass Rock	31	56	5	N	2	40	W
Bass Str.	117	39	15	S	146	30	E
Bassano	155	50	48	N	112	20	W
Basse-Terre	180	16	0	N	61	40	W
Bassein	93	16	45	N	94	30	E
Basseterre	180	17	17	N	62	43	W
Basti	92	26	52	N	82	55	E
Bastia	36	42	40	N	9	30	E
Batabanó	178	22	40	N	82	20	W
Batamay	74	63	30	N	129	15	E
Batan Is.	112	20	25	N	121	59	E
Batang	101	30	1	N	99	0	E
Batavia	164	43	0	N	78	10	W
Batemans Bay	117	35	44	S	150	11	E
Batesville	168	35	48	N	91	40	W
Bath, U.K.	27	51	22	N	2	22	W
Bath, Maine, U.S.A.	148	43	50	N	69	49	W
Bath, N.Y., U.S.A.	164	42	20	N	77	17	W
Bathurst = Banjul	130	13	28	N	16	40	W
Bathurst, Australia	117	33	25	S	149	31	E
Bathurst, Canada	148	47	37	N	65	43	W
Bathurst, C.	145	70	34	N	128	0	W
Bathurst Inlet	145	66	50	N	108	1	W
Batlow	117	35	31	S	148	9	E
Batman	81	37	55	N	41	5	E
Batna	127	35	34	N	6	15	E
Baton Rouge	168	30	30	N	91	5	W
Batopilas	174	27	1	N	107	44	W
Battambang	95	13	7	N	103	12	E
Batticaloa	90	7	43	N	81	45	E
Battle	25	50	55	N	0	30	E
Battle Creek	167	42	20	N	85	6	W
Battle Harbour	147	52	16	N	55	35	W
Battleford	152	52	45	N	108	15	W
Batu Gajah	96	4	28	N	101	3	E
Batu Is.	111	0	30	S	98	25	E
Batumi	70	41	30	N	41	30	E
Bauchi	131	10	22	N	9	48	E
Bauru	188	22	10	S	49	0	W
Bavaria = Bayern □	43	49	7	N	11	30	E
Bawdwin	93	23	5	N	97	20	E
Bawean	111	5	46	S	112	35	E
Bawku	130	11	3	N	0	19	W
Bay City	167	43	35	N	83	51	W
Bay Shore	164	40	44	N	73	15	W
Bayamo	178	20	20	N	76	40	W
Bayamón	180	18	24	N	66	10	W
Bayan Har Shan	101	34	0	N	98	0	E
Bayan Hot = Alxa Zuoqi	98	38	50	N	105	40	E
Bayern □	43	49	7	N	11	30	E
Bayeux	36	49	17	N	0	42	W
Bayfield	150	43	34	N	81	42	W
Baykal, Oz.	74	53	0	N	108	0	E
Baykonur	71	47	48	N	65	50	E
Bayonne	36	43	30	N	1	28	W
Bayreuth	43	49	56	N	11	35	E
Bayrūt	80	33	53	N	35	31	E
Baytown	168	29	42	N	94	57	W
Beachy Head	25	50	44	N	0	16	E
Beagle, Canal	192	55	0	S	68	30	W
Béarn	36	43	8	N	0	36	W
Beauce, Plaine de la	37	48	10	N	1	45	E
Beaudesert	116	27	59	S	153	0	E
Beaufort	170	32	25	N	80	40	W
Beaufort Sea	12	72	0	N	140	0	W
Beaugency	39	47	47	N	1	38	E
Beauharnois	151	45	20	N	73	52	W
Beauly	33	57	29	N	4	27	W
Beaumaris	26	53	16	N	4	7	W
Beaumont	168	30	5	N	94	8	W
Beaumont-sur-Oise	39	49	9	N	2	17	E
Beauséjour	153	50	5	N	96	35	W
Beauvais	38	49	25	N	2	8	E
Beauval	152	55	9	N	107	37	W
Beaver	142	66	20	N	147	30	W
Beaver →	152	55	26	N	107	45	W
Beaver Falls	164	40	44	N	80	20	W
Beaverlodge	155	55	11	N	119	29	W
Beawar	91	26	3	N	74	18	E
Bečej	52	45	36	N	20	3	E
Béchar	127	31	38	N	2	18	W
Beckley	165	37	50	N	81	8	W
Bedford, U.K.	25	52	8	N	0	29	W
Bedford, U.S.A.	167	38	50	N	86	30	W
Bedford □	25	52	4	N	0	28	W
Beenleigh	116	27	43	S	153	10	E

Be'er Sheva' — 80 31 15N 34 48 E
Beersheba = Be'er Sheva' — 80 31 15N 34 48 E
Beeston — 29 52 55N 1 11W
Bega — 117 36 41S 149 51 E
Behbehān — 84 30 30N 50 15 E
Beibei — 99 29 47N 106 22 E
Beihai — 99 21 28N 109 6 E
Beijing — 98 39 55N 116 20 E
Beira — 137 19 50S 34 52 E
Beira-Alta — 50 40 35N 7 35W
Beira-Baixa — 50 40 2N 7 30W
Beira-Litoral — 50 40 5N 8 30W
Beirut = Bayrūt — 80 33 53N 35 31 E
Bejaia — 127 36 42N 5 2 E
Békéscsaba — 59 46 40N 21 5 E
Bela — 92 25 50N 82 0 E
Bela Crkva — 52 44 55N 21 27 E
Belaya Tserkov — 68 49 45N 30 10 E
Belcher Is. — 140 56 15N 78 45W
Belém — 188 1 20S 48 30W
Belfast, U.K. — 34 54 35N 5 56W
Belfast, U.S.A. — 148 44 30N 69 0W
Belfort — 37 47 38N 6 50 E
Belgaum — 91 15 55N 74 35 E
Belgium ■ — 42 50 30N 5 0 E
Belgorod — 68 50 35N 36 35 E
Belgrade = Beograd — 52 44 50N 20 37 E
Belitung — 111 3 10S 107 50 E
Belize ■ — 177 17 0N 88 30W
Belize City — 177 17 25N 88 0W
Bell Peninsula — 146 63 50N 82 0W
Bell Ville — 190 32 40S 62 40W
Bella Coola — 154 52 25N 126 40W
Bellaire — 164 40 1N 80 46W
Bellary — 90 15 10N 76 56 E
Belle Fourche → — 163 44 25N 102 19W
Belle Glade — 170 26 43N 80 38W
Belle Isle — 147 51 57N 55 25W
Belle Isle, Str. of — 141 51 30N 56 30W
Bellefontaine — 167 40 20N 83 45W
Belleville, Canada — 151 44 10N 77 23W
Belleville, U.S.A. — 166 38 30N 90 0W
Bellevue — 155 49 35N 114 22W
Bellin — 146 60 0N 70 0W
Bellingham — 171 48 45N 122 27W
Bellingshausen Sea — 14 66 0S 80 0W
Belmont — 117 33 4S 151 42 E
Belmopan — 177 17 18N 88 30W
Belo Horizonte — 188 19 55S 43 56W
Belogorsk — 75 51 0N 128 20 E
Beloit — 166 42 35N 89 0W
Belomorsk — 68 64 35N 34 30 E
Belorussia ■ — 68 53 30N 27 0 E
Belovo — 71 54 30N 86 0 E
Beloye More — 69 66 30N 38 0 E
Beloye Ozero — 68 45 15N 46 50 E
Belper — 28 53 2N 1 29W
Belukha — 71 49 50N 86 50 E
Belyy, Ostrov — 69 73 30N 71 0 E
Bemidji — 156 47 30N 94 50W
Ben Lomond, N.S.W., Australia — 116 30 1S 151 40 E
Ben Lomond, Tas., Australia — 119 41 38S 147 42 E
Ben Macdhui — 33 57 4N 3 40W
Ben More, Central, U.K. — 32 56 23N 4 31W
Ben More, Strath., U.K. — 30 56 26N 6 2W
Ben More Assynt — 32 58 7N 4 51W
Ben Nevis — 32 56 48N 5 0W
Benalla — 117 36 30S 146 0 E
Benares = Varanasi — 92 25 22N 83 0 E
Benbecula — 32 57 26N 7 21W
Benbonyathe, Mt. — 118 30 25S 139 11 E
Bencubbin — 120 30 48S 117 52 E
Bend — 171 44 2N 121 15W
Bendemeer — 116 30 53S 151 8 E
Bender Beila — 133 9 30N 50 48 E
Bendigo — 117 36 40S 144 15 E
Benevento — 49 41 7N 14 45 E
Bengal, Bay of — 92 15 0N 90 0 E
Bengbu — 99 32 58N 117 20 E
Benghazi = Banghāzī — 128 32 11N 20 3 E

Benguela — 134 12 37S 13 25 E
Beni → — 187 10 23S 65 24W
Beni Suef — 128 29 5N 31 6 E
Benidorm — 51 38 33N 0 9W
Benin ■ — 131 10 0N 2 0 E
Benin, Bight of — 131 5 0N 3 0 E
Benin City — 131 6 20N 5 31 E
Benjamin Constant — 187 4 40S 70 15W
Bennett — 144 59 56N 134 53W
Bennettsville — 165 34 38N 79 39W
Benton — 168 34 30N 92 35W
Benue → — 131 7 48N 6 46 E
Benxi — 98 41 20N 123 48 E
Beograd — 52 44 50N 20 37 E
Beppu — 108 33 15N 131 30 E
Berau, Teluk — 113 2 30S 132 30 E
Berber — 129 18 0N 34 0 E
Berbera — 133 10 30N 45 2 E
Berck-sur-Mer — 38 50 25N 1 36 E
Berezniki — 69 59 24N 56 46 E
Bérgamo — 46 45 42N 9 40 E
Bergen, Neths. — 40 52 40N 4 43 E
Bergen, Norway — 60 60 23N 5 20 E
Bergen-op-Zoom — 40 51 30N 4 18 E
Bergerac — 36 44 51N 0 30 E
Berhala, Selat — 111 1 0S 104 15 E
Berhampore = Baharampur — 92 24 2N 88 27 E
Berhampur — 92 19 15N 84 54 E
Bering Sea — 142 58 0N 167 0 E
Bering Str. — 142 66 0N 170 0W
Berkeley — 172 37 52N 122 20W
Berkshire □ — 25 51 30N 1 20W
Berkshire Downs — 24 51 30N 1 30W
Berlin, Germany — 43 52 32N 13 24 E
Berlin, U.S.A. — 148 44 29N 71 10W
Bermuda ■ — 180 32 45N 65 0W
Bern — 44 46 57N 7 28 E
Bernay — 39 49 5N 0 35 E
Berne = Bern — 44 46 57N 7 28 E
Berri — 119 34 14S 140 35 E
Berry — 37 47 0N 2 0 E
Bertoua — 131 4 30N 13 45 E
Berwick-upon-Tweed — 31 55 47N 2 0W
Berwyn Mts. — 26 52 54N 3 26W
Besançon — 37 47 15N 6 0 E
Bessemer, Ala., U.S.A. — 169 33 25N 86 57W
Bessemer, Mich., U.S.A. — 156 46 27N 90 0W
Bethel — 142 60 50N 161 50W
Bethlehem — 164 40 39N 75 24W
Béthune — 38 50 30N 2 38 E
Betsiboka → — 137 16 3S 46 36 E
Beverley — 29 53 52N 0 26W
Beverly Hills — 173 34 4N 118 29W
Beverwijk — 40 52 28N 4 38 E
Bexhill — 24 50 51N 0 29 E
Beyneu — 70 45 10N 55 3 E
Beyşehir Gölü — 80 37 40N 31 45 E
Béziers — 37 43 20N 3 12 E
Bezwada = Vijayawada — 92 16 31N 80 39 E
Bhadravati — 90 13 49N 75 40 E
Bhagalpur — 92 25 10N 87 0 E
Bhakra Dam — 89 31 30N 76 45 E
Bhandara — 91 21 5N 79 42 E
Bhanrer Ra. — 91 23 40N 79 45 E
Bharat = India ■ — 78 20 0N 78 0 E
Bharatpur — 89 27 15N 77 30 E
Bharuch — 91 21 47N 73 0 E
Bhatpara — 92 22 50N 88 25 E
Bhaunagar = Bhavnagar — 91 21 45N 72 10 E
Bhavnagar — 91 21 45N 72 10 E
Bhilwara — 91 25 25N 74 38 E
Bhima → — 91 16 25N 77 17 E
Bhiwandi — 91 19 20N 73 0 E
Bhiwani — 89 28 50N 76 9 E
Bhopal — 91 23 20N 77 30 E
Bhubaneshwar — 92 20 15N 85 50 E
Bhusaval — 91 21 3N 75 46 E
Bhutan ■ — 92 27 25N 90 30 E
Biafra, B. of = Bonny, Bight of — 131 3 30N 9 20 E
Biała Podlaska — 58 52 4N 23 6 E

Białystok	**58** 53 10N	23 10 E
Biarritz	**36** 43 29N	1 33W
Bibai	**103** 43 19N	141 52 E
Bicester	**25** 51 53N	1 9W
Biche, L. la	**155** 54 50N	112 3W
Bidar	**91** 17 55N	77 35 E
Biddeford	**148** 43 30N	70 28W
Bideford	**27** 51 1N	4 13W
Bié, Planalto de	**136** 12 0S	16 0 E
Bieber	**172** 41 4N	121 6W
Biel	**44** 47 8N	7 14 E
Bielé Karpaty	**59** 49 5N	18 0 E
Bielefeld	**42** 52 2N	8 31 E
Bielsko-Biała	**59** 49 50N	19 2 E
Bien Hoa	**95** 10 57N	106 49 E
Bienne = Biel	**44** 47 8N	7 14 E
Bienville, L.	**146** 55 5N	72 40W
Big Belt Mts.	**163** 46 50N	111 30W
Big Cypress Swamp	**170** 26 12N	81 10W
Big Horn Mts. = Bighorn Mts.	**163** 44 30N	107 30W
Big Rapids	**167** 43 42N	85 27W
Big Sioux →	**156** 42 30N	96 25W
Big Spring	**161** 32 10N	101 25W
Big Stone Gap	**165** 36 52N	82 45W
Big Trout L.	**153** 53 40N	90 0W
Biggar, Canada	**152** 52 4N	108 0W
Biggar, U.K.	**31** 55 38N	3 31W
Bighorn →	**163** 46 9N	107 28W
Bighorn Mts.	**163** 44 30N	107 30W
Bihar	**92** 25 5N	85 40 E
Bihar □	**92** 25 0N	86 0 E
Bijagós, Arquipélago dos	**130** 11 15N	16 10W
Bijapur	**91** 16 50N	75 55 E
Bijeljina	**52** 44 46N	19 17 E
Bikaner	**89** 28 2N	73 18 E
Bikin	**75** 46 50N	134 20 E
Bilaspur	**92** 22 2N	82 15 E
Bilauk Taungdan	**94** 13 0N	99 0 E
Bilbao	**50** 43 16N	2 56W
Billingham	**29** 54 36N	1 18W
Billings	**163** 45 43N	108 29W
Billiton Is. = Belitung	**111** 3 10S	107 50 E
Bilma	**127** 18 50N	13 30 E
Biloela	**121** 24 24S	150 31 E
Biloxi	**169** 30 24N	88 53W
Bina-Etawah	**91** 24 13N	78 14 E
Bīnālūd, Kūh-e	**86** 36 30N	58 30 E
Bindi Bindi	**120** 30 37S	116 22 E
Bingara	**116** 29 52S	150 36 E
Bingerville	**130** 5 18N	3 49W
Bingham	**148** 45 5N	69 50W
Binghamton	**164** 42 9N	75 54W
Binh Dinh = An Nhon	**95** 13 55N	109 7 E
Binnaway	**116** 31 28S	149 24 E
Binzert = Bizerte	**127** 37 15N	9 50 E
Bioko	**131** 3 30N	8 40 E
Bir Mogrein	**126** 25 10N	11 25W
Birchip	**119** 35 56S	142 55 E
Bird I. = Aves, I. de	**181** 15 45N	63 55W
Birdum	**114** 15 39S	133 13 E
Birkenhead	**28** 53 24N	3 1W
Birmingham, U.K.	**24** 52 30N	1 55W
Birmingham, U.S.A.	**169** 33 31N	86 50W
Birobidzhan	**75** 48 50N	132 50 E
Birr	**35** 53 7N	7 55W
Bisai	**106** 35 16N	136 44 E
Biscay, B. of	**36** 45 0N	2 0W
Biscostasing	**150** 47 18N	82 9W
Bishkek	**71** 42 54N	74 46 E
Bishop Auckland	**28** 54 40N	1 40W
Bishop's Stortford	**25** 51 52N	0 11 E
Bismarck	**163** 46 49N	100 49W
Bismarck Arch.	**115** 2 30S	150 0 E
Bissagos = Bijagós,		
Arquipélago dos	**130** 11 15N	16 10W
Bissau	**130** 11 45N	15 45W
Bitola	**52** 41 5N	21 10 E
Bitolj = Bitola	**52** 41 5N	21 10 E
Bitterroot Range	**162** 46 0N	114 20W
Biu	**131** 10 40N	12 3 E
Biwa-Ko	**106** 35 15N	136 10 E
Biysk	**71** 52 40N	85 0 E
Bizen	**109** 34 43N	134 8 E
Bizerte	**127** 37 15N	9 50 E
Bjørnøya	**13** 74 30N	19 0 E
Black → = Da →	**95** 21 15N	105 20 E
Black Diamond	**155** 50 45N	114 14W
Black Forest = Schwarzwald	**42** 48 0N	8 0 E
Black Hills	**163** 44 0N	103 50W
Black Mts.	**26** 51 52N	3 5W
Black Sea	**17** 43 30N	35 0 E
Blackall	**121** 24 25S	145 45 E
Blackburn	**28** 53 44N	2 30W
Blackpool	**28** 53 48N	3 3W
Blackwater	**121** 23 35S	148 53 E
Blackwater →, Meath,		
Ireland	**34** 53 46N	7 0W
Blackwater →, Munster,		
Ireland	**35** 51 55N	7 50W
Blackwater →, U.K.	**34** 54 31N	6 35W
Blackwell	**168** 36 55N	97 20W
Blaenau Ffestiniog	**26** 53 0N	3 57W
Blagoveshchensk	**75** 50 20N	127 30 E
Blair Atholl	**33** 56 46N	3 50W
Blairmore	**155** 49 40N	114 25W
Blanc, Mont	**37** 45 48N	6 50 E
Blanca Peak	**163** 37 35N	105 29W
Blanche L.	**118** 29 15S	139 40 E
Blanco, C.	**171** 42 50N	124 40W
Blandford Forum	**24** 50 52N	2 10W
Blantyre	**137** 15 45S	35 0 E
Blarney	**35** 51 57N	8 35W
Blaydon	**28** 54 56N	1 47W
Blayney	**117** 33 32S	149 14 E
Blekinge län □	**61** 56 20N	15 20 E
Blenheim	**123** 41 38S	173 57 E
Bletchley	**25** 51 59N	0 44W
Blida	**127** 36 30N	2 49 E
Blind River	**150** 46 10N	82 58W
Blitar	**111** 8 5S	112 11 E
Bloemfontein	**137** 29 6S	26 14 E
Blois	**36** 47 35N	1 20 E
Bloody Foreland	**34** 55 10N	8 18W
Bloomington, Ill., U.S.A.	**166** 40 27N	89 0W
Bloomington, Ind., U.S.A.	**167** 39 10N	86 30W
Bloomsburg	**164** 41 0N	76 30W
Blue Mts., Oreg., U.S.A.	**171** 45 15N	119 0W
Blue Mts., Pa., U.S.A.	**164** 40 30N	76 30W
Blue Nile = Nîl el Azraq →	**129** 15 38N	32 31 E
Blue Ridge Mts.	**165** 36 30N	80 15W
Bluefield	**165** 37 18N	81 14W
Bluefields	**179** 12 20N	83 50W
Bluestack, mt.	**34** 54 46N	8 5W
Bluff	**123** 46 37S	168 20 E
Blumenau	**191** 27 0S	49 0W
Blyth	**28** 55 8N	1 32W
Bo	**130** 7 55N	11 50W
Bo Hai	**98** 39 0N	120 0 E
Boa Vista	**185** 2 48N	60 30W
Boaco	**179** 12 29N	85 35W
Bobadah	**116** 32 19S	146 41 E
Bobcaygeon	**151** 44 33N	78 33W
Bobo-Dioulasso	**130** 11 8N	4 13W
Bobraomby, Tanjon' i	**137** 12 40S	49 10 E
Bobruysk	**68** 53 10N	29 15 E
Bôca do Acre	**187** 8 50S	67 27W
Boca Raton	**170** 26 21N	80 5W
Bocas del Toro	**179** 9 15N	82 20W
Bocholt	**42** 51 50N	6 35 E
Bochum	**42** 51 28N	7 12 E
Boden	**67** 65 50N	21 42 E
Bodensee	**44** 47 35N	9 25 E
Bodhan	**91** 18 40N	77 44 E
Bodmin	**27** 50 28N	4 44W
Bodmin Moor	**27** 50 33N	4 36W
Bodø	**64** 67 17N	14 24 E
Bogalusa	**169** 30 50N	89 55W
Boggabilla	**116** 28 36S	150 24 E
Boggabri	**116** 30 45S	150 0 E
Boggeragh Mts.	**35** 52 2N	8 55W
Bognor Regis	**25** 50 47N	0 40W
Bogong, Mt.	**117** 36 47S	147 17 E

Bogor 111 6 36S 106 48 E
Bogota 184 4 34N 74 0W
Boguchany 74 58 40N 97 30 E
Bohain 38 49 59N 3 28 E
Bohemian Forest = Böhmerwald 43 49 30N 12 40 E
Böhmerwald 43 49 30N 12 40 E
Bohol 112 9 50N 124 10 E
Bohol Sea 112 9 0N 124 0 E
Bohotleh 133 8 20N 46 25 E
Boise 162 43 43N 116 9W
Boissevain 153 49 15N 100 5W
Boké 130 10 56N 14 17W
Bolan Pass 88 29 50N 67 20 E
Bolaños, R. → 175 21 12N 104 5W
Bolbec 38 49 30N 0 30 E
Bolgatanga 130 10 44N 0 53W
Bolívar 190 36 15S 60 53W
Bolivia ■ 187 17 6S 64 0W
Bollnäs 60 61 21N 16 24 E
Bollon 116 28 2S 147 29 E
Bologna 47 44 30N 11 20 E
Boloven, Cao Nguyen 95 15 10N 106 30 E
Bolsena, L. di 46 42 35N 11 55 E
Bolshevik, Ostrov 72 78 30N 102 0 E
Bolshoi Kavkas 70 42 50N 44 0 E
Bolshoy Begichev, Ostrov 72 74 20N 112 30 E
Bolsward 41 53 3N 5 32 E
Bolton 28 53 35N 2 26W
Bolzano 47 46 30N 11 20 E
Boma 134 5 50S 13 4 E
Bombala 117 36 56S 149 15 E
Bombay 91 18 55N 72 50 E
Bomu → 129 4 40N 23 30 E
Bon, C. 127 37 1N 11 2 E
Bonaire 181 12 10N 68 15W
Bonavista 149 48 40N 53 5W
Bonifacio, Bouches de 48 41 12N 9 15 E
Bonn 42 50 43N 7 6 E
Bonneval 39 48 11N 1 24 E
Bonnie Rock 120 30 29S 118 22 E
Bonny, Bight of 131 3 30N 9 20 E
Bonnyville 152 54 20N 110 45W
Bonthe 130 7 30N 12 33W
Boonah 116 27 58S 152 41 E
Boone 166 42 5N 93 53W
Boonville 167 38 3N 87 13W
Boorowa 117 34 28S 148 44 E
Boothia, Gulf of 146 71 0N 90 0W
Boothia Pen. 145 71 0N 94 0W
Bootle 28 53 28N 3 1W
Bôr 129 6 10N 31 40 E
Borås 60 57 43N 12 56 E
Borāzjān 85 29 22N 51 10 E
Bordeaux 36 44 50N 0 36W
Borders □ 31 55 35N 2 50W
Bordertown 119 36 19S 140 45 E
Bordj Omar Driss 127 28 10N 6 40 E
Borger 161 35 40N 101 20W
Borja 186 4 20S 77 40W
Borlänge 60 60 29N 15 26 E
Borneo 111 1 0N 115 0 E
Bornholm 61 55 10N 15 0 E
Borujerd 84 33 55N 48 50 E
Borzya 74 50 24N 116 31 E
Boscastle 27 50 42N 4 42W
Boshan 98 36 28N 117 49 E
Bosna → 52 45 4N 18 29 E
Bosnia-Herzegovina ■ 52 44 0N 18 0 E
Bōsō-Hantō 107 35 20N 140 20 E
Bosporus = Karadeniz Boğazı 80 41 10N 29 10 E
Bossangoa 131 6 35N 17 30 E
Bossembélé 131 5 25N 17 40 E
Bossier City 168 32 28N 93 48W
Bosten Hu 100 41 55N 87 40 E
Boston, U.K. 29 52 59N 0 2W
Boston, U.S.A. 164 42 20N 71 0W
Bothnia, G. of 67 63 0N 20 0 E
Botletle → 136 20 10S 23 15 E
Botoşani 57 47 42N 26 41 E
Botswana ■ 136 22 0S 24 0 E
Botucatu 188 22 55S 48 30W
Bou Djébéha 126 18 25N 2 45W
Bouaké 130 7 40N 5 2W
Bougie = Bejaia 127 36 42N 5 2 E
Boulogne-sur-Mer 38 50 42N 1 36 E
Bourbonnais 37 46 28N 3 0 E
Bourem 130 17 0N 0 24W
Bourg-en-Bresse 37 46 13N 5 12 E
Bourges 37 47 9N 2 25 E
Bourgogne 37 47 0N 4 30 E
Bourke 116 30 8S 145 55 E
Bournemouth 24 50 43N 1 53W
Bousso 131 10 34N 16 52 E
Bouvet I. = Bouvetøya 14 54 26S 3 24 E
Bouvetøya 14 54 26S 3 24 E
Bowen 121 20 0S 148 16 E
Bowland, Forest of 28 54 0N 2 30W
Bowling Green, Ky., U.S.A. 169 37 0N 86 25W
Bowling Green, Ohio, U.S.A. 167 41 22N 83 40W
Bowling Green, C. 121 19 19S 147 25 E
Bowmanville 151 43 55N 78 41W
Bowral 117 34 26S 150 27 E
Boyle 34 53 58N 8 19W
Boyne → 34 53 43N 6 15W
Boyne City 150 45 13N 85 1W
Boyup Brook 120 33 50S 116 23 E
Bozeman 163 45 40N 111 0W
Bozen = Bolzano 47 46 30N 11 20 E
Brač 52 43 20N 16 40 E
Bracciano, L. di 46 42 8N 12 11 E
Bracebridge 151 45 2N 79 19W
Bräcke 66 62 45N 15 26 E
Brad 56 46 10N 22 50 E
Bradenton 170 27 25N 82 35W
Bradford, U.K. 28 53 47N 1 45W
Bradford, U.S.A. 164 41 58N 78 41W
Braemar 33 57 2N 3 20W
Braga 50 41 35N 8 25W
Bragança, Brazil 188 1 0S 47 2W
Bragança, Portugal 50 41 48N 6 50W
Brahmanbaria 93 23 58N 91 15 E
Brahmani → 92 20 39N 86 46 E
Brahmaputra → 93 24 2N 90 59 E
Braidwood 117 35 27S 149 49 E
Brăila 57 45 19N 27 59 E
Brainerd 156 46 20N 94 10W
Braintree 25 51 53N 0 34 E
Brampton 151 43 45N 79 45W
Branco → 185 1 20S 61 50W
Branco, Cabo 182 7 9S 34 47W
Brandenburg 43 52 24N 12 33 E
Brandon 153 49 50N 99 57W
Brantford 151 43 10N 80 15W
Brasil, Planalto 188 18 0S 46 30W
Brasília 188 15 47S 47 55 E
Braşov 57 45 38N 25 35 E
Brassey, Banjaran 111 5 0N 117 15 E
Brasstown Bald, Mt. 165 34 54N 83 45W
Bratislava 59 48 10N 17 7 E
Bratsk 74 56 10N 101 30 E
Brattleboro 164 42 53N 72 37W
Braunschweig 43 52 17N 10 28 E
Brava 133 1 20N 44 8 E
Bravo del Norte → 174 25 57N 97 9W
Brawley 173 32 58N 115 30W
Bray 35 53 12N 6 6W
Brazil 167 39 32N 87 8W
Brazil ■ 188 10 0S 50 0W
Brazilian Highlands = Brasil, Planalto 188 18 0S 46 30W
Brazos → 168 28 53N 95 23W
Brazzaville 134 4 9S 15 12 E
Brčko 52 44 54N 18 46 E
Breadalbane 31 56 30N 4 15W
Bream Bay 122 35 56S 174 28 E
Brecon 26 51 57N 3 23W
Brecon Beacons 26 51 53N 3 27W
Breda 40 51 35N 4 45 E
Breiðafjörður 64 65 15N 23 15W
Bremen 42 53 4N 8 47 E

Bremerhaven	42	53	34N	8	35 E
Bremerton	171	47	30N	122	38W
Brenham	168	30	5N	96	27W
Brentwood	25	51	37N	0	19 E
Bréscia	46	45	33N	10	13 E
Breslau = Wrocław	58	51	5N	17	5 E
Brest, France	36	48	24N	4	31W
Brest, U.S.S.R.	68	52	10N	23	40 E
Bretagne	36	48	0N	3	0W
Bretçu	57	46	7N	26	18 E
Breton Sd.	169	29	40N	89	12W
Brett, C.	122	35	10S	174	20 E
Brewer	148	44	43N	68	50W
Brewster	171	48	10N	119	51W
Brewton	169	31	9N	87	2W
Brezhnev = Naberezhnyye Chelny	68	55	42N	52	19 E
Briançon	37	44	54N	6	39 E
Bridgend	27	51	30N	3	35W
Bridgeport	164	41	12N	73	12W
Bridgeton	164	39	29N	75	10W
Bridgetown, Australia	120	33	58S	116	7 E
Bridgetown, Barbados	180	13	0N	59	30W
Bridgnorth	24	52	33N	2	25W
Bridgwater	27	51	7N	3	0W
Bridlington	29	54	6N	0	11W
Bridport	27	50	43N	2	45W
Brigham City	163	41	30N	112	1W
Bright	117	36	42S	146	56 E
Brighton, Australia	119	42	42S	147	16 E
Brighton, U.K.	25	50	50N	0	9W
Brindisi	49	40	39N	17	55 E
Brisbane	116	27	25S	153	2 E
Bristol, U.K.	27	51	26N	2	35W
Bristol, Conn., U.S.A.	164	41	44N	72	57W
Bristol, Tenn., U.S.A.	165	36	36N	82	11W
Bristol B.	142	58	0N	160	0W
Bristol Channel	27	51	18N	4	30W
Bristow	168	35	55N	96	28W
British Columbia □	154	55	0N	125	15W
British Guiana = Guyana ■	185	5	0N	59	0W
British Honduras = Belize ■	177	17	0N	88	30W
British Isles	18	55	0N	4	0W
Brittany = Bretagne	36	48	0N	3	0W
Brive-la-Gaillarde	36	45	10N	1	32 E
Brlik	71	44	0N	74	5 E
Brno	59	49	10N	16	35 E
Broach = Bharuch	91	21	47N	73	0 E
Broad Law	31	55	30N	3	22W
Broad Sd.	121	22	0S	149	45 E
Broads, The	29	52	45N	1	30 E
Brochet	145	57	53N	101	40W
Brockton	164	42	8N	71	2W
Brockville	151	44	35N	75	41W
Brod	52	41	35N	21	17 E
Brodeur Pen.	146	72	30N	88	10W
Broken Hill = Kabwe	135	14	30S	28	29 E
Broken Hill	118	31	58S	141	29 E
Bromley	25	51	20N	0	5 E
Brookhaven	169	31	40N	90	25W
Brooks	155	50	35N	111	55W
Brooks Ra.	142	68	40N	147	0W
Brosna →	35	53	8N	8	0W
Brough	28	54	32N	2	19W
Broughty Ferry	31	56	29N	2	50W
Brouwershaven	40	51	45N	3	55 E
Brownsville	158	25	56N	97	25W
Brownwood	161	31	45N	99	0W
Bruay-en-Artois	38	50	29N	2	33 E
Bruce, Mt.	114	22	37S	118	8 E
Bruce Rock	120	31	52S	118	8 E
Bruck an der Leitha	45	48	1N	16	47 E
Bruges = Brugge	42	51	13N	3	13 E
Brugge	42	51	13N	3	13 E
Brunei = Bandar Seri Begawan	112	4	52N	115	0 E
Brunei ■	111	4	50N	115	0 E
Bruno	152	52	20N	105	30W
Brunswick = Braunschweig	43	52	17N	10	28 E
Brunswick, Ga., U.S.A.	170	31	10N	81	30W
Brunswick, Maine, U.S.A.	148	43	53N	69	50W
Bruny I.	119	43	20S	147	15 E
Brussel	42	50	51N	4	21 E
Bruthen	117	37	42S	147	50 E
Bruton	27	51	6N	2	28W
Bryan, Ohio, U.S.A.	167	41	30N	84	30W
Bryan, Tex., U.S.A.	168	30	40N	96	27W
Bryan, Mt.	119	33	30S	139	0 E
Bryansk	68	53	13N	34	25 E
Brzeg	58	50	52N	17	30 E
Bucaramanga	184	7	0N	73	0W
Buchan	33	57	32N	2	8W
Buchan Ness	33	57	29N	1	48W
Buchanan	130	5	57N	10	2W
Buchans	149	48	50N	56	52W
Bucharest = Bucureşti	57	44	27N	26	10 E
Buckhannon	165	39	2N	80	10W
Buckhaven	31	56	10N	3	2W
Buckingham, Canada	151	45	37N	75	24W
Buckingham, U.K.	25	52	0N	0	59W
Buckingham □	25	51	50N	0	55W
Buckleboo	118	32	54S	136	12 E
Bucureşti	57	44	27N	26	10 E
Bucyrus	167	40	48N	83	0W
Budalin	93	22	20N	95	10 E
Budapest	59	47	29N	19	5 E
Budaun	89	28	5N	79	10 E
Bude	27	50	49N	4	33W
Budgewoi Lake	117	33	13S	151	34 E
Buenaventura, Colombia	184	3	53N	77	4W
Buenaventura, Mexico	174	29	51N	107	29W
Buenos Aires	190	34	30S	58	20W
Buffalo	164	42	55N	78	50W
Bug →	58	52	31N	21	5 E
Buga	184	4	0N	76	15W
Bugun Shara	100	49	0N	104	0 E
Builth Wells	26	52	10N	3	26W
Buir Nur	98	47	50N	117	42 E
Bujumbura	135	3	16S	29	18 E
Bukachacha	74	52	55N	116	50 E
Bukavu	23	2	20S	28	52 E
Bukhara	70	39	48N	64	25 E
Bukit Mertajam	96	5	22N	100	28 E
Bukittinggi	111	0	20S	100	20 E
Bukoba	135	1	20S	31	49 E
Bukuru	131	9	42N	8	48 E
Bulahdelah	117	32	23S	152	13 E
Bulandshahr	89	28	28N	77	51 E
Bulawayo	137	20	7S	28	32 E
Bulgaria ■	53	42	35N	25	30 E
Bull Shoals L.	168	36	40N	93	5W
Bully-les-Mines	38	50	27N	2	44 E
Bulsar = Valsad	91	20	40N	72	58 E
Bulun	72	70	37N	127	30 E
Bunbury	120	33	20S	115	35 E
Buncrana	34	55	8N	7	28W
Bundaberg	116	24	54S	152	22 E
Bundi	91	25	30N	75	35 E
Bundoran	34	54	24N	8	17W
Bungo-Suidō	109	33	0N	132	15 E
Buorkhaya, Mys	72	71	50N	132	40 E
Bûr Sa'îd	128	31	16N	32	18 E
Bûr Sûdân	129	19	32N	37	9 E
Buraymī, Al Wāhāt al	83	24	10N	55	43 E
Burbank	173	34	9N	118	23W
Burdur	80	37	45N	30	22 E
Burdwan = Barddhaman	92	23	14N	87	39 E
Burgas	53	42	33N	27	29 E
Burgenland □	45	47	20N	16	20 E
Burgos	50	42	21N	3	41W
Burgundy = Bourgogne	37	47	0N	4	30 E
Burin	149	47	1N	55	14W
Burkina Faso ■	130	12	0N	1	0W
Burlington, Canada	151	43	18N	79	45W
Burlington, Iowa, U.S.A.	166	40	50N	91	5W
Burlington, N.C., U.S.A.	165	36	7N	79	27W
Burlington, N.J., U.S.A.	164	40	5N	74	50W
Burlington, Vt., U.S.A.	151	44	27N	73	14W
Burma ■	93	21	0N	96	30 E
Burnie	119	41	4S	145	56 E
Burnley	28	53	47N	2	15W
Burns	171	43	40N	119	4W

Burns Lake **154** 54 20N 125 45W
Burra . . . . **119** 33 40S 138 55 E
Bursa . . . . **80** 40 15N 29 5 E
Burton-upon-Trent **28** 52 48N 1 39W
Buru . . . . **113** 3 30S 126 30 E
Burundi ■ . . . . **135** 3 15S 30 0 E
Bury **28** 53 36N 2 19W
Bury St. Edmunds . . . . **25** 52 15N 0 42 E
Buryat Rep. □ . . . . **74** 53 0N 110 0 E
Buskerud fylke □ . . . . **60** 60 13N 9 0 E
Busselton . . . . **120** 33 42S 115 15 E
Bussum . . . . **40** 52 16N 5 10 E
Bute **30** 55 48N 5 2W
Butiaba . . . . **132** 1 50N 31 20 E
Butler **164** 40 52N 79 52W
Butte **163** 46 0N 112 31W
Butterworth . . . . **96** 5 24N 100 23 E
Butuan . . . . **112** 8 57N 125 33 E
Butung . . . . **113** 5 0S 122 45 E
Buxton **28** 53 16N 1 54W
Buyaga . . . . **74** 59 50N 127 0 E
Buzău . . . . **57** 45 10N 26 50 E
Buzen . . . . **108** 33 35N 131 5 E
Buzzards Bay **164** 41 45N 70 38W
Bydgoszcz . . . . **58** 53 10N 18 0 E
Byelorussia = Belorussia ■ . **68** 53 30N 27 0 E
Bylot I. **146** 73 13N 78 34W
Byrd Land **15** 79 30S 125 0W
Byron Bay . . . . **116** 28 43S 153 37 E
Byrranga, Gory . . . . **72** 75 0N 100 0 E
Bytom . . . . **58** 50 25N 18 54 E

C

Cabimas **184** 10 23N 71 25W
Cabinda . . . . **134** 5 33S 12 11 E
Cabinda □ . . . . **134** 5 0S 12 30 E
Cabo Pantoja **184** 1 0S 75 10W
Cabonga, Réservoir **151** 47 20N 76 40W
Caboolture . . . . **116** 27 5S 152 58 E
Cabora Bassa Dam . . . . **137** 15 20S 32 50 E
Caborca **174** 30 40N 112 10W
Cabot Strait **149** 47 15N 59 40W
Cabrera, I. . . . . **51** 39 8N 2 57 E
Cabri **152** 50 35N 108 25W
Čačak . . . . **52** 43 54N 20 20 E
Cáceres **50** 39 26N 6 23W
Cache Bay **151** 46 22N 80 0W
Cachoeira **189** 12 30S 39 0W
Cachoeira de Itapemirim **189** 20 51S 41 7W
Cachoeira do Sul **191** 30 3S 52 53W
Cader Idris **26** 52 43N 3 56W
Cadibarrawirracanna, L. . . . . **118** 28 52S 135 27 E
Cadillac, Canada **151** 48 14N 78 23W
Cadillac, U.S.A. **167** 44 16N 85 25W
Cádiz **50** 36 30N 6 20W
Cádiz, G. de **50** 36 40N 7 0W
Caen **36** 49 10N 0 22W
Caernarfon **26** 53 8N 4 17W
Caernarfon B. **26** 53 4N 4 40W
Caernarvon = Caernarfon . . **26** 53 8N 4 17W
Caerphilly **27** 51 34N 3 13W
Cagayan de Oro . . . . **112** 8 30N 124 40 E
Cágliari . . . . **48** 39 15N 9 6 E
Caguas **180** 18 14N 66 4W
Caha Mts. **35** 51 45N 9 40W
Caher **35** 52 23N 7 56W
Cahors . . . . **36** 44 27N 1 27 E
Cahuapanas **186** 5 15S 77 0W
Caibarién **178** 22 30N 79 30W
Caicos Is. **180** 21 40N 71 40W
Cairngorm Mts. **33** 57 6N 3 42W
Cairns . . . . **121** 16 57S 145 45 E
Cairo = El Qâhira . . . . **128** 30 1N 31 14 E
Cairo **169** 37 0N 89 10W
Cajamarca **186** 7 5S 78 28W
Calabar . . . . **131** 4 57N 8 20 E
Calabozo **184** 9 0N 67 28W

Calábria □ . . . . **49** 39 24N 16 30 E
Calais, France . . . . **38** 50 57N 1 56 E
Calais, U.S.A. **148** 45 11N 67 20W
Calama, Brazil **187** 8 0S 62 50W
Calama, Chile **190** 22 30S 68 55W
Calamar **184** 10 15N 74 55W
Calamian Group . . . . **112** 11 50N 119 55 E
Calca **187** 13 22S 72 0W
Calcutta . . . . **92** 22 36N 88 24 E
Caldwell **171** 43 45N 116 42W
Calgary **155** 51 0N 114 10W
Cali **184** 3 25N 76 35W
Calicut . . . . **90** 11 15N 75 43 E
California □ **172** 37 25N 120 0W
California, Golfo de **174** 28 0N 112 0W
Callander **31** 56 15N 4 14W
Callao **186** 12 0S 77 0W
Caloundra . . . . **116** 26 45S 153 10 E
Caltanissetta . . . . **49** 37 30N 14 3 E
Cam Lam . . . . **95** 11 54N 109 10 E
Cam Ranh . . . . **95** 11 54N 109 12 E
Camagüey **178** 21 20N 78 0W
Camaná **186** 16 30S 72 50W
Camargue . . . . **37** 43 34N 4 34 E
Camarones **192** 44 50S 65 40W
Cambay = Khambhat . . . . **91** 22 23N 72 33 E
Cambodia ■ . . . . **95** 12 15N 105 0 E
Camborne **27** 50 13N 5 18W
Cambrai . . . . **38** 50 11N 3 14 E
Cambrian Mts. **26** 52 25N 3 52W
Cambridge, Canada **151** 43 23N 80 15W
Cambridge, N.Z. . . . . **122** 37 54S 175 29 E
Cambridge, U.K. . . . . **25** 52 13N 0 8 E
Cambridge, Mass., U.S.A. . . . **164** 42 20N 71 8W
Cambridge, Md., U.S.A. **164** 38 33N 76 2W
Cambridge, Ohio, U.S.A. **167** 40 1N 81 35W
Cambridge Bay **145** 69 10N 105 0W
Cambridge Gulf . . . . **114** 14 55S 128 15 E
Cambridgeshire □ . . . . **25** 52 12N 0 7 E
Camden, Ark., U.S.A. **168** 33 40N 92 50W
Camden, N.J., U.S.A. **164** 39 57N 75 7W
Camden, S.C., U.S.A. **165** 34 17N 80 34W
Cameroon ■ . . . . **131** 6 0N 12 30 E
Cameroun, Mt. . . . . **131** 4 13N 9 10 E
Cametá **188** 2 12S 49 30W
Camiri **187** 20 3S 63 31W
Camocim **189** 2 55S 40 50W
Campagna . . . . **46** 40 40N 15 5 E
Campania □ . . . . **49** 40 50N 14 45 E
Campbell I. . . . . **15** 52 30S 169 0 E
Campbell River **154** 50 5S 125 20W
Campbellton **148** 47 57N 66 43W
Campbelltown, Australia . . . . **117** 34 4S 150 49 E
Campbeltown, U.K. **30** 57 34N 4 2W
Campeche **177** 19 51N 90 32W
Campeche □ **177** 19 0N 90 30W
Campeche, B. de **177** 20 0N 94 0W
Camperdown . . . . **119** 38 14S 143 9 E
Camperville **153** 51 59N 100 9W
Campina Grande **189** 7 20S 35 47W
Campinas **188** 22 50S 47 0W
Campo Grande **188** 20 25S 54 40W
Campos **188** 21 50S 41 20W
Camrose **155** 53 0N 112 50W
Can Tho . . . . **95** 10 2N 105 46 E
Canada ■ **139** 60 0N 100 0W
Cañada de Gómez **190** 32 40S 61 30W
Canadian → **158** 35 27N 95 3W
Çanakkale Boğazi . . . . **80** 40 0N 26 0 E
Cananea **174** 30 57N 110 18W
Canarias, Is. **126** 28 30N 16 0W
Canary Is. = Canarias, Islas **126** 28 30N 16 0W
Canaveral, C. **170** 28 28N 80 31W
Canberra . . . . **117** 35 15S 149 8 E
Candala . . . . **133** 11 30N 49 58 E
Candia = Iráklion . . . . **55** 35 20N 25 12 E
Canea = Khaniá . . . . **55** 35 30N 24 4 E
Çankırı . . . . **80** 40 40N 33 37 E
Canmore **155** 51 7N 115 18W
Canna **32** 57 3N 6 33W
Cannanore . . . . **90** 11 53N 75 27 E

Name	Page	Lat.	Long.
Cannes	**37**	43 32N	7 0 E
Cannock	**28**	52 42N	2 2W
Canora	**152**	51 40N	102 30W
Canowindra	**117**	33 35S	148 38 E
Canso	**149**	45 20N	61 0W
Cantabrian Mts. = Cantábrica, Cordillera	**50**	43 0N	5 10W
Cantábrica, Cordillera	**50**	43 0N	5 10W
Canterbury	**25**	51 17N	1 5 E
Canterbury □	**123**	43 45S	171 19 E
Canterbury Bight	**123**	44 16S	171 55 E
Canterbury Plains	**123**	43 55S	171 22 E
Canton = Guangzhou	**99**	23 5N	113 10 E
Canton, Ill., U.S.A.	**166**	40 32N	90 0W
Canton, Miss., U.S.A.	**169**	32 40N	90 1W
Canton, Ohio, U.S.A.	**167**	40 47N	81 22W
Canutama	**185**	6 30S	64 20W
Cap-Chat	**148**	49 6N	66 40W
Cap-de-la-Madeleine	**151**	46 22N	72 31W
Cap-Haïtien	**180**	19 40N	72 20W
Cape Barren I.	**119**	40 25S	148 15 E
Cape Breton I.	**149**	46 0N	60 30W
Cape Coast	**130**	5 5N	1 15W
Cape Dorset	**146**	64 14N	76 32W
Cape Fear →	**165**	34 30N	78 25W
Cape Girardeau	**169**	37 20N	89 30W
Cape May	**164**	39 1N	74 53W
Cape Montague	**149**	46 5N	62 25W
Cape Province □	**136**	32 0S	23 0 E
Cape Town	**136**	33 55S	18 22 E
Cape Verde Is. ■	**9**	17 10N	25 20W
Cape York Peninsula	**115**	12 0S	142 30 E
Caquetá →	**184**	1 15S	69 15W
Caracal	**57**	44 8N	24 22 E
Caracas	**184**	10 30N	66 55W
Caratinga	**188**	19 50S	42 10W
Carberry	**153**	49 50N	99 25W
Carbonara, C.	**48**	39 8N	9 30 E
Carbondale	**166**	37 45N	89 10W
Carbonear	**149**	47 42N	53 13W
Carcassonne	**37**	43 13N	2 20 E
Carcross	**144**	60 13N	134 45W
Cárdenas, Cuba	**178**	23 0N	81 30W
Cárdenas, Mexico	**177**	21 0N	99 40W
Cardiff	**27**	51 28N	3 11W
Cardigan	**26**	52 6N	4 41W
Cardigan B.	**26**	52 30N	4 30W
Cardston	**155**	49 15N	113 20W
Cardwell	**121**	18 14S	146 2 E
Caribbean Sea	**181**	15 0N	75 0W
Cariboo Mts.	**155**	53 0N	121 0W
Caribou	**148**	46 55N	68 0W
Caribou Mts.	**145**	59 12N	115 40W
Carinhanha	**188**	14 15S	44 46W
Carinthia = Kärnten □	**45**	46 52N	13 30 E
Carlisle, U.K.	**28**	54 54N	2 55W
Carlisle, U.S.A.	**164**	40 12N	77 10W
Carlow	**35**	52 50N	6 58W
Carlow □	**35**	52 43N	6 50W
Carlsbad, Calif., U.S.A.	**173**	33 11N	117 25W
Carlsbad, N. Mex., U.S.A.	**161**	32 20N	104 14W
Carlyle	**152**	49 40N	102 20W
Carmacks	**144**	62 5N	136 16W
Carman	**153**	49 30N	98 0W
Carmarthen	**26**	51 52N	4 20W
Carmarthen B.	**27**	51 40N	4 30W
Carnarvon	**120**	24 51S	113 42 E
Carnegie, L.	**114**	26 5S	122 30 E
Carniche, Alpi	**47**	46 36N	13 0 E
Carnsore Pt.	**35**	52 10N	6 20W
Caroline Is.	**122**	8 0N	150 0 E
Caroona	**116**	31 24S	150 26 E
Carpathians, Mts.	**17**	49 50N	21 0 E
Carpaţii Meridionali	**57**	45 30N	25 0 E
Carpentaria, G. of	**115**	14 0S	139 0 E
Carrara	**46**	44 5N	10 7 E
Carrick-on-Shannon	**34**	53 57N	8 7W
Carrick-on-Suir	**35**	52 22N	7 30W
Carrickfergus	**34**	54 43N	5 50W
Carrickmacross	**34**	54 0N	6 43W
Carroll	**166**	42 2N	94 55W
Carrollton	**170**	33 36N	85 5W
Carse of Gowrie	**31**	56 30N	3 10W
Carson City	**172**	39 12N	119 46W
Carstairs	**31**	55 42N	3 41W
Cartagena, Colombia	**184**	10 25N	75 33W
Cartagena, Spain	**51**	37 38N	0 59W
Cartago, Colombia	**184**	4 45N	75 55W
Cartago, Costa Rica	**179**	9 50N	85 52W
Cartersville	**169**	34 11N	84 48W
Carthage	**168**	37 10N	94 20W
Cartwright	**147**	53 41N	56 58W
Caruaru	**189**	8 15S	35 55W
Carúpano	**185**	10 39N	63 15W
Caruthersville	**169**	36 10N	89 40W
Carvin	**38**	50 30N	2 57 E
Casablanca	**126**	33 36N	7 36W
Casas Grandes	**174**	30 22N	107 57W
Cascade Ra.	**171**	47 0N	121 30W
Casilda	**190**	33 10S	61 10W
Casino	**116**	28 52S	153 3 E
Casiquiare →	**184**	2 1N	67 7W
Casma	**186**	9 30S	78 20W
Casper	**163**	42 52N	106 20W
Caspian Sea	**70**	43 0N	50 0 E
Cassiar Mts.	**144**	59 30N	130 30W
Castellón de la Plana	**51**	39 58N	0 3W
Castelsarrasin	**36**	44 2N	1 7 E
Casterton	**119**	37 30S	141 30 E
Castilla La Nueva	**50**	39 45N	3 20W
Castilla La Vieja	**50**	41 55N	4 0W
Castle Douglas	**31**	54 57N	3 57W
Castlebar	**34**	53 52N	9 17W
Castleblaney	**34**	54 7N	6 44W
Castlegar	**155**	49 20N	117 40W
Castlemaine	**117**	37 2S	144 12 E
Castlereagh	**34**	53 47N	8 30W
Castletown	**28**	58 35N	3 22W
Castletown Bearhaven	**35**	51 40N	9 54W
Castor	**155**	52 15N	111 50W
Castres	**37**	43 37N	2 13 E
Castricum	**40**	52 33N	4 40 E
Castries	**180**	14 0N	60 50W
Castro	**192**	42 30S	73 50W
Cat I.	**178**	24 30N	75 30W
Catacáos	**186**	5 20S	80 45W
Catalonia = Cataluña □	**51**	41 40N	1 15 E
Cataluña □	**51**	41 40N	1 15 E
Catamarca	**190**	28 30S	65 50W
Catanduanes	**112**	13 50N	124 20 E
Catánia	**49**	37 31N	15 4 E
Catanzaro	**49**	38 54N	16 38 E
Catoche, C.	**177**	21 35N	87 5W
Catskill Mts.	**164**	42 15N	74 15W
Cauca →	**184**	8 54N	74 28W
Caucasus Mts. = Bolshoi Kavkas	**70**	42 50N	44 0 E
Caudry	**38**	50 7N	3 22 E
Cauquenes	**190**	36 0S	72 22W
Cavaillon	**37**	43 50N	5 2 E
Cavan	**34**	54 0N	7 22W
Cawnpore = Kanpur	**91**	26 28N	80 20 E
Caxias	**188**	4 55S	43 20W
Caxias do Sul	**191**	29 10S	51 10W
Cayenne	**185**	5 0N	52 18W
Cayes, Les	**180**	18 15N	73 46W
Cayman Is.	**178**	19 40N	80 30W
Ceanannus Mor	**34**	53 42N	6 53W
Ceará = Fortaleza	**189**	3 45S	38 35W
Ceará □	**189**	5 0S	40 0W
Cebu	**112**	10 18N	123 54 E
Cedar →	**166**	41 17N	91 21W
Cedar City	**162**	37 41N	113 3W
Cedar Falls	**166**	42 39N	92 29W
Cedar L.	**152**	53 10N	100 0W
Cedar Rapids	**166**	42 0N	91 38W
Cedartown	**169**	34 1N	85 15W
Ceduna	**118**	32 7S	133 46 E
Cegléd	**59**	47 11N	19 47 E
Ceiba, La	**179**	15 40N	86 50W
Celaya	**177**	20 31N	100 37W
Celebes = Sulawesi □	**113**	2 0S	120 0 E

Celebes Sea	113	3	0N	123 0 E
Center	168	31	50N	94 10W
Centerville	166	40	45N	92 57W
Central □	31	56	10N	4 30W
Central, Cordillera	184	5	0N	75 0W
Central African Republic ■	129	7	0N	20 0 E
Central Makran Range	88	26	30N	64 15 E
Central Russian Uplands	17	54	0N	36 0 E
Central Siberian Plateau	77	65	0N	105 0 E
Centralia	166	38	32N	89 5W
Cephalonia = Kefallinia	54	38	20N	20 30 E
Ceram = Seram	113	3	10S	129 0 E
Ceram Sea = Seram Sea	113	2	30S	128 30 E
Cerignola	49	41	17N	15 53 E
Cerigo = Kithira	55	36	9N	23 0 E
Cerritos	177	22	26N	100 17W
Cesena	47	44	9N	12 14 E
Ceskomoravská Vrchovina	59	49	30N	15 40 E
Český Těšin	59	49	45N	18 39 E
Cessnock	117	32	50S	151 21 E
Cetinje	52	42	23N	18 59 E
Ceuta	126	35	52N	5 18W
Cévennes	37	44	10N	3 50 E
Ceylon = Sri Lanka ■	90	7	30N	80 50 E
Chachapoyas	186	6	15S	77 50W
Chachoengsao	95	13	42N	101 5 E
Chad ■	131	15	0N	17 15 E
Chad, L. = Tchad, L.	131	13	30N	14 30 E
Chadron	163	42	50N	103 0W
Chagos Arch.	76	6	0S	72 0 E
Chāh Bahār	85	25	20N	60 40 E
Chakradharpur	92	22	45N	85 40 E
Chala	186	15	48S	74 20W
Chalcis = Khalkis	55	38	27N	23 42 E
Chalhuanca	186	14	15S	73 15W
Chalisgaon	91	20	30N	75 10 E
Challapata	187	18	53S	66 50W
Chalon-sur-Saône	37	46	48N	4 50 E
Châlons-sur-Marne	37	48	58N	4 20 E
Chambal →►	91	26	29N	79 15 E
Chambersburg	164	39	53N	77 41W
Chambéry	37	45	34N	5 55 E
Chamonix	37	45	55N	6 51 E
Champagne	37	49	0N	4 40 E
Champaign	167	40	8N	88 14W
Champlain, L.	151	44	30N	73 20W
Chañaral	190	26	23S	70 40W
Chandigarh	89	30	43N	76 47 E
Chandler	118	27	0S	133 19 E
Chang Jiang →►	99	31	48N	121 10 E
Changchiak'ou = Zhangjiakou	98	40	48N	114 55 E
Ch'angchou = Changzhou	99	31	47N	119 58 E
Changchun	98	43	57N	125 17 E
Changde	99	29	4N	111 35 E
Changhai = Shanghai	99	31	15N	121 26 E
Changsha	99	28	12N	113 0 E
Changzhi	98	36	10N	113 6 E
Changzhou	99	31	47N	119 58 E
Channel Is.	36	49	30N	2 40W
Channel-Port aux Basques	149	47	30N	59 9W
Chanthaburi	95	12	38N	102 12 E
Chantilly	39	49	12N	2 29 E
Chanute	166	37	45N	95 25W
Chao Phraya →►	94	13	32N	100 36 E
Ch'aoan	99	23	41N	116 33 E
Chapala, L. de	175	20	15N	103 0W
Chapayevsk	68	53	0N	49 40 E
Chapel Hill	165	35	53N	79 3W
Chapleau	150	47	50N	83 24W
Charagua	187	19	45S	63 10W
Charaña	187	17	30S	69 25W
Chard	27	50	52N	2 59W
Chardzhou	70	39	6N	63 34 E
Chari →►	131	12	58N	14 31 E
Chārīkār	87	35	0N	69 10 E
Charleroi	42	50	24N	4 27 E
Charles, C.	165	37	10N	75 59W
Charles City	166	43	2N	92 41W
Charleston, S.C., U.S.A.	170	32	47N	79 56W
Charleston, W. Va., U.S.A.	165	38	24N	81 36W
Charleville = Rath Luirc	35	52	21N	8 40W
Charleville	116	26	24S	146 15 E
Charleville-Mézières	37	49	44N	4 40 E
Charlotte, Mich., U.S.A.	167	42	36N	84 48W
Charlotte, N.C., U.S.A.	165	35	16N	80 46W
Charlotte Amalie	180	18	22N	64 56W
Charlotte Harbor	170	26	58N	82 4W
Charlottenburg	43	52	31N	13 15 E
Charlottesville	165	38	1N	78 30W
Charlottetown	149	46	14N	63 8W
Charlton, Australia	117	36	16S	143 24 E
Charlton, U.S.A.	166	40	59N	93 20W
Charters Towers	121	20	5S	146 13 E
Chartres	39	48	29N	1 30 E
Chascomús	191	35	30S	58 0W
Château-du-Loir	39	47	40N	0 25 E
Château-Thierry	39	49	3N	3 20 E
Châteaubriant	36	47	43N	1 23W
Châteaudun	39	48	3N	1 20 E
Châteauroux	37	46	50N	1 40 E
Châtellerault	36	46	50N	0 30 E
Chatham, N.B., Canada	148	47	2N	65 28W
Chatham, Ont., Canada	141	42	24N	82 11W
Chatham, U.K.	25	51	22N	0 32 E
Chatta-Hantō	106	34	45N	136 55 E
Chattahoochee →►	170	30	43N	84 51W
Chattanooga	169	35	2N	85 17W
Chaumont	37	48	7N	5 8 E
Chauny	38	49	37N	3 12 E
Cheboksary	68	56	8N	47 12 E
Cheboygan	150	45	38N	84 29W
Checheno-Ingush Rep. □	70	43	30N	45 29 E
Chegdomyn	75	51	7N	133 1 E
Chegga	126	25	27N	5 40W
Chehalis	171	46	44N	122 59W
Cheju Do	99	33	29N	126 34 E
Chekiang = Zhejiang □	99	29	0N	120 0 E
Chelforó	190	39	0S	66 33W
Chelkar Tengiz, Solonchak	70	48	0N	62 30 E
Chełm	58	51	8N	23 30 E
Chełmża	58	53	10N	18 39 E
Cheltenham	24	51	55N	2 5W
Chelyabinsk	71	55	10N	61 24 E
Chemainus	154	48	55N	123 42W
Chemnitz	43	50	50N	12 55 E
Chemult	171	43	14N	121 47W
Chen, Gora	73	65	16N	141 50 E
Chencha	132	6	15N	37 32 E
Chenchiang = Zhenjiang	99	32	11N	119 26 E
Chengchou = Zhengzhou	99	34	45N	113 34 E
Chengde	98	40	59N	117 58 E
Chengdu	99	30	38N	104 2 F
Ch'engtu = Chengdu	99	30	38N	104 2 E
Cheo Reo	95	13	25N	108 28 E
Chepstow	27	51	38N	2 40W
Cher →►	36	47	21N	0 29 E
Cherbourg	36	49	39N	1 40W
Cheremkhovo	74	53	8N	103 1 E
Cherepovets	68	59	5N	37 55 E
Cherkassy	68	49	27N	32 4 E
Chernigov	68	51	28N	31 20 E
Chernovtsy	68	48	15N	25 52 E
Chernoye	72	70	30N	89 10 E
Cherokee	166	42	40N	95 30W
Cherrapunji	93	25	17N	91 47 E
Cherskiy	73	68	45N	161 18 E
Cherskogo Khrebet	73	65	0N	143 0 E
Cherwell →►	25	51	46N	1 18W
Chesapeake	165	36	43N	76 15W
Chesapeake Bay	165	38	0N	76 12W
Cheshire □	28	53	14N	2 30W
Cheshskaya Guba	69	67	20N	47 0 E
Chester, U.K.	28	53	12N	2 53W
Chester, Pa., U.S.A.	164	39	54N	75 20W
Chester, S.C., U.S.A.	165	34	44N	81 13W
Chesterfield	28	53	14N	1 26W
Chesterfield Inlet	145	63	30N	90 45W
Chetumal	177	18	30N	88 18W
Cheviot, The	31	55	29N	2 8W
Cheviot Hills	31	55	20N	2 30W
Chew Bahir	132	4	40N	36 50 E

Name	Page	Lat.	Long.
Cheyenne	**163**	41 9N	104 49W
Cheyenne →	**163**	44 40N	101 15W
Chhapra	**92**	25 48N	84 44 E
Chiamussu = Jiamusi	**98**	46 40N	130 26 E
Chiang Mai	**94**	18 47N	98 59 E
Chiapa →	**177**	16 42N	93 0W
Chiapas □	**177**	16 30N	92 30W
Chiba	**107**	35 30N	140 7 E
Chibougamau	**151**	49 56N	74 24W
Chicago	**167**	41 53N	87 40W
Chicago Heights	**167**	41 29N	87 37W
Chichagof I.	**143**	58 0N	136 0W
Chichester	**25**	50 50N	0 47W
Chichibu	**107**	36 5N	139 10 E
Ch'ich'ihaerh = Qiqihar	**98**	47 26N	124 0 E
Chiclayo	**186**	6 42S	79 50W
Chico	**172**	39 45N	121 54W
Chicopee	**164**	42 6N	72 37W
Chicoutimi	**148**	48 28N	71 5W
Chidambaram	**90**	11 20N	79 45 E
Chidley C.	**146**	60 23N	64 26W
Chigasaki	**107**	35 19N	139 24 E
Chihli, G. of = Bo Hai	**98**	39 0N	120 0 E
Chihuahua	**174**	28 38N	106 5W
Chihuahua □	**174**	28 30N	106 0W
Chikugo	**108**	33 14N	130 28 E
Chilapa	**177**	17 40N	99 11W
Childress	**161**	34 30N	100 15W
Chile ■	**190**	35 0S	72 0W
Chilin = Jilin	**98**	43 44N	126 30 E
Chilka L.	**92**	19 40N	85 25 E
Chillán	**190**	36 40S	72 10W
Chillicothe, Mo., U.S.A.	**166**	39 45N	93 30W
Chillicothe, Ohio, U.S.A.	**167**	39 20N	82 58W
Chilliwack	**154**	49 10N	121 54W
Chiloé, I. de	**192**	42 30S	73 50W
Chilpancingo	**177**	17 30N	99 30W
Chiltern Hills	**25**	51 44N	0 42W
Chimborazo	**184**	1 29S	78 55W
Chimbote	**186**	9 0S	78 35W
Chimkent	**71**	42 18N	69 36 E
Chin □	**93**	22 0N	93 0 E
China ■	**79**	30 0N	110 0 E
Chinan = Jinan	**98**	36 38N	117 1 E
Chinandega	**179**	12 35N	87 12W
Chincha Alta	**186**	13 25S	76 7W
Chinchilla	**116**	26 45S	150 38 E
Chinchou = Jinzhou	**98**	41 5N	121 3 E
Chindwin →	**93**	21 26N	95 15 E
Ch'ingtao = Qingdao	**98**	36 5N	120 20 E
Chinju	**98**	35 12N	128 2 E
Chinnampo	**98**	38 52N	125 10 E
Chino	**107**	35 59N	138 9 E
Chinon	**36**	47 10N	0 15 E
Chippenham	**24**	51 27N	2 7W
Chippewa Falls	**166**	44 55N	91 22W
Chiquián	**186**	10 10S	77 0W
Chiquimula	**177**	14 51N	89 37W
Chiquinquira	**184**	5 37N	73 50W
Chirala	**90**	15 50N	80 26 E
Chirchik	**71**	41 29N	69 35 E
Chita	**74**	52 0N	113 35 E
Chitral	**89**	35 50N	71 56 E
Chitré	**179**	7 59N	80 27W
Chittagong	**93**	22 19N	91 48 E
Chittagong □	**93**	24 5N	91 0 E
Chivilcoy	**190**	34 55S	60 0W
Chkalov = Orenburg	**70**	51 45N	55 6 E
Chōfu	**107**	35 39N	139 33 E
Choix	**174**	26 43N	108 17W
Chojnice	**58**	53 42N	17 32 E
Cholet	**36**	47 4N	0 52W
Choluteca	**179**	13 20N	87 14W
Chon Buri	**95**	13 21N	101 1 E
Chongjin	**98**	41 47N	129 50 E
Chŏngju	**98**	36 39N	127 27 E
Chongqing	**99**	29 35N	106 25 E
Chŏnju	**98**	35 50N	127 4 E
Chonos, Arch. de los	**192**	45 0S	75 0W
Chorley	**28**	53 39N	2 39W
Chorzów	**58**	50 18N	18 57 E
Chōshi	**107**	35 45N	140 51 E
Christchurch, N.Z.	**123**	43 33S	172 47 E
Christchurch, U.K.	**24**	50 44N	1 33W
Christianshåb	**147**	68 50N	51 18W
Christmas I. = Kiritimati	**123**	1 58N	157 27W
Christmas I.	**111**	10 30S	105 40 E
Ch'uanchou = Quanzhou	**99**	24 55N	118 34 E
Chūbu □	**106**	36 45N	137 30 E
Chubut →	**192**	43 20S	65 5W
Chūgoku □	**109**	35 0N	133 0 E
Chūgoku-Sanchi	**109**	35 0N	133 0 E
Chukotskiy Khrebet	**73**	68 0N	175 0 E
Chukotskoye More	**73**	68 0N	175 0W
Chula Vista	**173**	32 39N	117 8W
Chulman	**74**	56 52N	124 52 E
Chulucanas	**186**	5 8S	80 10W
Chumikan	**75**	54 40N	135 10 E
Chumphon	**94**	10 35N	99 14 E
Chunchŏn	**98**	37 58N	127 44 E
Chungking = Chongqing	**99**	29 35N	106 25 E
Chuquibamba	**186**	15 47S	72 44W
Chur	**44**	46 52N	9 32 E
Churchill →, Man., Canada	**143**	58 47N	94 12W
Churchill →, Nfld., Canada	**147**	53 19N	60 10W
Churchill, C.	**143**	58 46N	93 12W
Churchill Falls	**147**	53 36N	64 19W
Churchill Pk.	**144**	58 10N	125 10W
Churu	**89**	28 20N	74 50 E
Chuvash Rep.□	**68**	55 30N	47 0 E
Chuxiong	**101**	25 2N	101 28 E
Cicero	**167**	41 48N	87 48W
Ciego de Avila	**178**	21 50N	78 50W
Ciénaga	**184**	11 1N	74 15W
Cienfuegos	**178**	22 10N	80 30W
Cimarron →	**161**	36 10N	96 17W
Cincinnati	**167**	39 10N	84 26W
Cinto, Mt.	**36**	42 24N	8 54 E
Ciotat, La	**37**	43 12N	5 36 E
Circle	**142**	65 50N	144 10W
Circleville	**167**	39 35N	82 57W
Cirebon	**111**	6 45S	108 32 E
Cirencester	**24**	51 43N	1 59W
Citlaltépetl, Volcán	**177**	19 1N	97 16W
Ciudad Acuña	**174**	29 20N	100 58W
Ciudad Bolívar	**185**	8 5N	63 36W
Ciudad Camargo, Chihuahua, Mexico	**174**	27 40N	105 10W
Ciudad Camargo, Tamaulipas, Mexico	**176**	26 19N	98 50W
Ciudad de Valles	**177**	21 59N	99 1W
Ciudad del Carmen	**177**	18 38N	91 50W
Ciudad Guayana	**185**	8 0N	62 30W
Ciudad Guzmán	**175**	19 41N	103 29W
Ciudad Juárez	**174**	31 44N	106 29W
Ciudad Madero	**177**	22 16N	97 50W
Ciudad Mante	**177**	22 44N	98 57W
Ciudad Obregón	**174**	27 29N	109 56W
Ciudad Real	**50**	38 59N	3 55W
Ciudad Rodrigo	**50**	40 35N	6 32W
Ciudad Trujillo = Santo Domingo	**180**	18 30N	64 54W
Ciudad Victoria	**177**	23 44N	99 8W
Çivril	**80**	38 20N	29 43 E
Cizre	**81**	37 19N	42 10 E
Clare	**119**	33 50S	138 37 E
Clare □	**35**	52 20N	9 0W
Clare →	**35**	53 22N	9 5W
Clare I.	**34**	53 48N	10 0W
Claremont	**164**	43 23N	72 20W
Claremore	**168**	36 40N	95 37W
Claremorris	**34**	53 45N	9 0W
Claresholm	**155**	50 0N	113 33W
Clark Fork →	**162**	48 9N	116 15W
Clarksburg	**164**	39 18N	80 21W
Clarksdale	**169**	34 12N	90 33W
Clarkston	**171**	46 28N	117 2W
Clarksville	**169**	36 32N	87 20W
Clear, C.	**20**	51 26N	9 30W
Clearwater, Canada	**155**	51 38N	120 2W
Clearwater, U.S.A.	**170**	27 58N	82 45W
Cleburne	**168**	32 18N	97 25W

Clee Hills **24** 52 26N 2 35W
Cleethorpes **29** 53 33N 0 2W
Cleeve Hill **24** 51 54N 2 0W
Clermont, Australia .... **121** 22 49S 147 39 E
Clermont, France .... **39** 49 23N 2 24 E
Clermont-Ferrand .... **37** 45 46N 3 4 E
Clevedon **27** 51 26N 2 52W
Cleveland, Miss., U.S.A. . **169** 33 43N 90 43W
Cleveland, Ohio, U.S.A. .. **167** 41 28N 81 43W
Cleveland, Tenn., U.S.A. . **169** 35 9N 84 52W
Cleveland, Tex., U.S.A. .. **169** 30 18N 95 0W
Cleveland □ .... **29** 54 35N 1 8 E
Cleveleys **28** 53 52N 3 3W
Clew B. **34** 53 54N 9 50W
Clifton Beach .... **121** 16 46S 145 39 E
Clifton Forge **165** 37 49N 79 51W
Clinton, Canada **150** 43 37N 81 32W
Clinton, Iowa, U.S.A. ... **166** 41 50N 90 12W
Clinton, Mass., U.S.A. .. **164** 42 26N 71 40W
Clinton, Mo., U.S.A. **166** 38 20N 93 46W
Clinton, Okla., U.S.A. ... **161** 35 30N 99 0W
Clinton, S.C., U.S.A. ... **165** 34 30N 81 54W
Clinton Colden L. **145** 63 58N 107 27W
Clonakilty **35** 51 37N 8 53W
Cloncurry .... **115** 20 40S 140 28 E
Clones **34** 54 10N 7 13W
Clonmel **35** 52 22N 7 42W
Clovis **161** 34 20N 103 10W
Cluj-Napoca .... **56** 46 47N 23 38 E
Clunes .... **117** 37 20S 143 45 E
Clwyd □ **26** 53 5N 3 20W
Clyde ⟶ **31** 55 56N 4 29W
Clyde, Firth of **30** 55 20N 5 0W
Clydebank **31** 55 54N 4 25W
Coahuila □ **174** 27 20N 102 0W
Coaldale **155** 49 45N 112 35W
Coalinga **173** 36 10N 120 21W
Coalville **29** 52 43N 1 21W
Coast Mts. **144** 55 0N 129 0W
Coast Ranges **173** 41 0N 123 0W
Coatbridge **31** 55 52N 4 2W
Coatepeque **177** 14 46N 91 55W
Coats I. **146** 62 30N 83 0W
Coats Land **14** 77 0S 25 0W
Coatzacoalcos **177** 18 9N 94 25W
Cobalt **151** 47 25N 79 42W
Cobán **177** 15 30N 90 21W
Cobar .... **116** 31 27S 145 48 E
Cóbh **35** 51 50N 8 18W
Cobham .... **118** 30 18S 142 7 E
Cobourg **151** 43 58N 78 10W
Cobram .... **117** 35 54S 145 40 E
Cocanada = Kakinada .... **92** 16 57N 82 11 E
Cochabamba **187** 17 26S 66 10W
Cochin China = Nam-Phan . **95** 10 30N 106 0 E
Cochran **170** 32 25N 83 23W
Cochrane **151** 49 0N 81 0W
Cockburn, Canal **192** 54 30S 72 0W
Coco ⟶ **179** 15 0N 83 8W
Coco Chan. .... **94** 13 50N 93 25 E
Cocos Is. .... **111** 12 10S 96 55 E
Cod, C. **164** 42 8N 70 10W
Codajás **185** 3 55S 62 0W
Codó **185** 4 30S 43 55W
Cœur d'Alene **171** 47 45N 116 51W
Coffs Harbour .... **116** 30 16S 153 5 E
Cohoes **164** 42 47N 73 42W
Cohuna .... **117** 35 45S 144 15 E
Coiba, I. **179** 7 30N 81 40W
Coihaique **192** 45 30S 71 45W
Coimbatore .... **90** 11 2N 76 59 E
Coimbra **50** 40 15N 8 27W
Cojimies **184** 0 20N 80 0W
Cojutepequé **177** 13 41N 88 54W
Colac .... **117** 38 21S 143 35 E
Colchester .... **25** 51 54N 0 55 E
Coldstream **31** 55 39N 2 14W
Coleman **155** 49 40N 114 30W
Coleraine, Australia .... **119** 37 36S 141 40 E
Coleraine, U.K. **34** 55 8N 6 40W
Colima **175** 19 14N 103 43W

Colima □ **175** 19 10N 104 0W
Coll **30** 56 40N 6 35W
College Park **170** 33 42N 84 27W
Collie .... **120** 33 22S 116 8 E
Collingwood **151** 44 29N 80 13W
Collinsville .... **121** 20 30S 147 56 E
Collooney **34** 54 11N 8 28W
Colmar .... **37** 48 5N 7 20 E
Colne **28** 53 51N 2 11W
Cologne = Köln .... **42** 50 56N 6 58 E
Colomb-Béchar = Béchar .. **127** 31 38N 2 18W
Colômbia **188** 20 10S 48 40W
Colombia ■ **184** 3 45N 73 0W
Colombo .... **90** 6 56N 79 58 E
Colón, Cuba **178** 22 42N 80 54W
Colón, Panama **179** 9 20N 79 54W
Colonia **191** 34 25S 57 50W
Colonsay **30** 56 4N 6 12W
Colorado □ **163** 37 40N 106 0W
Colorado ⟶, Argentina .. **190** 39 50S 62 8W
Colorado ⟶, Calif., U.S.A. **173** 34 45N 114 40W
Colorado ⟶, Tex., U.S.A. . **161** 28 36N 95 58W
Colorado Desert **160** 34 20N 116 0W
Colorado Plateau **161** 36 40N 110 30W
Colorado Springs **163** 38 55N 104 50W
Columbia, Miss., U.S.A. ... **169** 31 16N 89 50W
Columbia, Mo., U.S.A. **166** 38 58N 92 20W
Columbia, S.C., U.S.A. ... **165** 34 0N 81 0W
Columbia, Tenn., U.S.A. .. **169** 35 40N 87 0W
Columbia ⟶ **171** 46 15N 124 5W
Columbia, District of □ ... **164** 38 55N 77 0W
Columbia Basin **171** 47 30N 118 30W
Columbretes, Is. .... **51** 39 50N 0 50 E
Columbus, Ga., U.S.A. ... **170** 32 30N 84 58W
Columbus, Ind., U.S.A. ... **167** 39 14N 85 55W
Columbus, Miss., U.S.A. .. **169** 33 30N 88 26W
Columbus, Ohio, U.S.A. ... **167** 39 57N 83 1W
Colwyn Bay **26** 53 17N 3 44W
Comeragh Mts. **35** 52 17N 7 35W
Comilla .... **93** 23 28N 91 10 E
Comitán **177** 16 18N 92 9W
Committee B. **146** 68 30N 86 30W
Communism Pk. =
  Kommunizma, Pik ...... **71** 39 0N 72 2 E
Como .... **46** 45 48N 9 5 E
Como, L. di .... **46** 46 5N 9 17 E
Comodoro Rivadavia ... **192** 45 50S 67 40W
Comorin, C. .... **90** 8 3N 77 40 E
Comoro Is. ■ .... **125** 12 10S 44 15 E
Comox **154** 49 42N 124 55W
Compiègne .... **38** 49 24N 2 50 E
Côn Dao .... **95** 8 45N 106 45 E
Conakry **130** 9 29N 13 49W
Conceição da Barra **189** 18 35S 39 45W
Concepción, Argentina .. **191** 27 20S 65 35W
Concepción, Chile **190** 36 50S 73 0W
Concepción, Est. de ... **192** 50 30S 74 55W
Concepción del Oro **174** 24 38N 101 25W
Concepción del Uruguay .. **190** 32 35S 58 20W
Conchos, R. ⟶ **174** 29 35N 104 25W
Concord, Calif., U.S.A. .. **172** 37 59N 122 2W
Concord, N.C., U.S.A. ... **165** 35 28N 80 35W
Concord, N.H., U.S.A. ... **164** 43 12N 71 30W
Concordia, Argentina ... **190** 31 20S 58 2W
Concordia, U.S.A. **161** 39 35N 97 40W
Condamine .... **155** 26 56S 150 9 E
Condé .... **38** 50 26N 3 34 E
Condobolin .... **117** 33 4S 147 6 E
Congleton **28** 53 10N 2 12W
Congo = Zaïre ⟶ ...... **134** 6 4S 12 24 E
Congo (Kinshasa) = Zaïre ■ **134** 3 0S 23 0 E
Congo ■ .... **134** 1 0S 16 0 E
Congo Basin .... **124** 0 10S 24 30 E
Conjeeveram = Kanchipuram **90** 12 52N 79 45 E
Connacht **34** 53 23N 8 40W
Conneaut **164** 41 55N 80 32W
Connecticut □ **164** 41 40N 72 40W
Connecticut ⟶ **157** 41 17N 72 21W
Connemara **34** 53 29N 9 45W
Connors Ra. .... **121** 21 40S 149 10 E
Consett **28** 54 52N 1 50W

212 Constance

Constance = Konstanz .... **44** 47 39N 9 10 E
Constance, L. = Bodensee . **44** 47 35N 9 25 E
Constanţa .... **57** 44 14N 28 38 E
Constantine .... **127** 36 25N 6 42 E
Contamana **186** 7 19S 74 55W
Conway = Conwy **26** 53 17N 3 50W
Conway = Conwy → **26** 53 18N 3 50W
Conway, N.H., U.S.A. **148** 43 58N 71 8W
Conway, S.C., U.S.A. **165** 33 49N 79 2W
Conwy **26** 53 17N 3 50W
Conwy → **26** 53 18N 3 50W
Cook, Mt. .... **123** 43 36S 170 9 E
Cook Inlet **142** 59 0N 151 0W
Cook Is. **123** 17 0S 160 0W
Cook Strait .... **123** 41 15S 174 29 E
Cookeville **169** 36 12N 85 30W
Cookstown **34** 54 40N 6 43W
Coolah .... **116** 31 48S 149 41 E
Coolamon .... **117** 34 46S 147 8 E
Coolangatta .... **116** 28 11S 153 29 E
Coolgardie .... **120** 30 55S 121 8 E
Cooma .... **117** 36 12S 149 8 E
Coonabarabran .... **116** 31 14S 149 18 E
Coonamble .... **116** 30 56S 148 27 E
Cooper Cr. → .... **118** 12 7S 132 41 E
Coorong, The .... **119** 35 50S 139 20 E
Coorow .... **120** 29 53S 116 2 E
Coos Bay **171** 43 26N 124 7W
Cootamundra .... **117** 34 36S 148 1 E
Copenhagen = København . **61** 55 41N 12 34 E
Copiapó **190** 27 30S 70 20W
Copper Center **142** 62 10N 145 25W
Coppermine **145** 67 50N 115 5W
Coppermine → **145** 67 49N 116 4W
Coquilhatville = Mbandaka . **134** 0 1N 18 18 E
Coquimbo **190** 30 0S 71 20W
Coracora **186** 15 5S 73 45W
Coral Gables **170** 25 45N 80 16W
Coral Harbour **146** 64 8N 83 10W
Coral Sea .... **121** 15 0S 150 0 E
Corbeil-Essonnes ...... **39** 48 36N 2 26 E
Corbin **165** 37 0N 84 3W
Corby **25** 52 29N 0 41W
Cordele **170** 31 55N 83 49W
Córdoba, Argentina **190** 31 20S 64 10W
Córdoba, Mexico **177** 18 53N 96 56W
Córdoba, Spain **50** 37 50N 4 50W
Córdoba, Sierra de **190** 31 10S 64 25W
Cordova **142** 60 36N 145 45W
Corfu = Kérkira .... **54** 39 38N 19 50 E
Corinth = Kórinthos ... **54** 37 56N 22 55 E
Corinth **169** 34 54N 88 30W
Corinth, G. of = Korinthiakós
Kólpos .... **54** 38 16N 22 30 E
Corinto, Brazil **188** 18 20S 44 30W
Corinto, Nic. **179** 12 30N 87 10W
Cork **35** 51 54N 8 30W
Cork □ **35** 51 50N 8 50W
Çorlu .... **80** 41 11N 27 49 E
Corn Is. = Maíz, Islas del . **179** 12 15N 83 4W
Corner Brook **140** 48 57N 57 58W
Cornwall **151** 45 2N 74 44W
Cornwall □ **27** 50 26N 4 40W
Coro **184** 11 25N 69 41W
Coroatá **188** 4 8S 44 0W
Corocoro **187** 17 15S 68 28W
Coroico **187** 16 0S 67 50W
Coromandel Coast ..... **90** 12 30N 81 0 E
Corona **173** 33 49N 117 36W
Coronado **173** 32 45N 117 9W
Coronation Gulf **145** 68 25N 110 0W
Coronel **190** 37 0S 73 10W
Coronel Pringles **190** 38 0S 61 30W
Corowa .... **117** 35 58S 146 21 E
Corozal **177** 9 19N 75 18W
Corpus Christi **161** 27 50N 97 28W
Corrib, L. **34** 53 5N 9 10W
Corrientes **190** 27 30S 58 45W
Corrientes, C., Colombia . **184** 5 30N 77 34W
Corrientes, C., Cuba ... **178** 21 43N 84 30W
Corrientes, C., Mexico .. **175** 20 25N 105 42W

Corrigin .... **120** 32 20S 117 53 E
Corse .... **36** 42 0N 9 0 E
Corsica = Corse ...... **36** 42 0N 9 0 E
Corsicana **168** 32 5N 96 30W
Cortez **163** 37 24N 108 35W
Cortland **164** 42 35N 76 11W
Çorum .... **80** 40 30N 34 57 E
Corumbá **187** 19 0S 57 30W
Coruña, La **50** 43 20N 8 25W
Corunna = Coruña, La . **50** 43 20N 8 25W
Corvallis **171** 44 36N 123 15W
Cosamaloapan **177** 18 23N 95 50W
Cosenza .... **49** 39 17N 16 14 E
Coshocton **167** 40 17N 81 51W
Costa Blanca **51** 38 25N 0 10W
Costa Brava .... **51** 41 30N 3 0 E
Costa del Sol **50** 36 30N 4 30W
Costa Dorada .... **51** 40 45N 1 15 E
Costa Rica ■ **179** 10 0N 84 0W
Cotagaita **187** 20 45S 65 40W
Côte d'Or .... **37** 47 10N 4 50 E
Coteau des Prairies ... **156** 44 30N 97 0W
Cotonou .... **131** 6 20N 2 25 E
Cotopaxi, Vol. **184** 0 40S 78 30W
Cotswold Hills **24** 51 42N 2 10W
Cottbus .... **43** 51 44N 14 20 E
Coulommiers .... **39** 48 50N 3 3 E
Council **142** 64 55N 163 45W
Council Bluffs **166** 41 20N 95 50W
Courantyne → **185** 5 55N 57 5W
Courtrai = Kortrijk .... **42** 50 50N 3 17 E
Coventry **24** 52 25N 1 31W
Covington, Ga., U.S.A. . **170** 33 36N 83 50W
Covington, Ky., U.S.A. . **167** 39 5N 84 30W
Cowdenbeath **31** 56 7N 3 20W
Cowes **25** 50 45N 1 18W
Cowra .... **117** 33 49S 148 42 E
Coxim **188** 18 30S 54 55W
Cracow = Kraków ..... **58** 50 4N 19 57 E
Craigavon = Lurgan ... **34** 54 28N 6 20W
Craiova .... **57** 44 21N 23 48 E
Cranbrook, Australia ... **120** 34 18S 117 33 E
Cranbrook, Canada **155** 49 30N 115 46W
Crateús **189** 5 10S 40 39W
Crato **189** 7 10S 39 25W
Crawfordsville **167** 40 2N 86 51W
Crawley **24** 51 7N 0 10W
Creil .... **39** 49 15N 2 34 E
Cremona .... **46** 45 8N 10 2 E
Crépy-en-Valois ...... **39** 49 14N 2 54 E
Cres .... **52** 44 58N 14 25 E
Crescent City **172** 41 45N 124 12W
Creston, Canada **155** 49 10N 116 31W
Creston, U.S.A. **166** 41 0N 94 20W
Crestview **169** 30 45N 86 35W
Crete = Kriti .... **55** 35 15N 25 0 E
Creuse → .... **36** 47 0N 0 34 E
Creusot, Le .... **37** 46 50N 4 24 E
Crewe **28** 53 6N 2 28W
Criciúma **191** 28 40S 49 23W
Crieff **31** 56 22N 3 50W
Crimea = Krymskiy P-ov. . **68** 45 0N 34 0 E
Crişul Alb → .... **56** 46 42N 21 17 E
Crişul Negru → .... **56** 46 38N 22 26 E
Crna Gora = Montenegro □ . **52** 42 40N 19 20 E
Crna Gora .... **52** 42 10N 21 30 E
Croatia ■ .... **52** 45 20N 18 0 E
Crockett **168** 31 20N 95 30W
Cromarty **33** 57 40N 4 2W
Cromer .... **29** 52 56N 1 18 E
Crooked I. **180** 22 50N 74 10W
Crookwell .... **117** 34 28S 149 24 E
Cross Fell **28** 54 44N 2 29W
Cross L. **153** 54 45N 97 30W
Crosse, La **166** 43 48N 91 13W
Crowley **168** 30 15N 92 20W
Crowsnest Pass **155** 49 40N 114 40W
Cruz, C. **178** 19 50N 77 50W
Cruz Alta **191** 28 45S 53 40W
Cruz del Eje **190** 30 45S 64 50W
Cruzeiro do Sul **186** 7 35S 72 35W

Crystal Brook **119** 33 21S 138 12 E
Cu Lao Hon **95** 10 54N 108 18 E
Cuando → **134** 14 0S 19 30 E
Cuanza → **134** 9 2S 13 30 E
Cuba ■ **178** 22 0N 79 0W
Cubango → **134** 18 50S 22 25 E
Cucuí **184** 1 12N 66 50W
Cúcuta **184** 7 54N 72 31W
Cuddalore **90** 11 46N 79 45 E
Cuddapah **90** 14 30N 78 47 E
Cue **120** 27 25S 117 54 E
Cuenca, Ecuador **184** 2 50S 79 9W
Cuenca, Spain **51** 40 5N 2 10W
Cuenca, Serranía de **51** 39 55N 1 50W
Cuernavaca **177** 18 55N 99 15W
Cuevo **187** 20 15S 63 30W
Cuiabá **188** 15 30S 56 0W
Cuillin Hills **32** 57 14N 6 15W
Cuitzeo, L. de **175** 19 55N 101 5W
Culcairn **117** 35 41S 147 3 E
Culiacán **174** 24 48N 107 24W
Cullarin Range **117** 34 30S 149 30 E
Culloden Moor **33** 57 29N 4 7W
Culverden **123** 42 47S 172 49 E
Cumaná **185** 10 30N 64 5W
Cumberland **164** 39 40N 78 43W
Cumberland → **169** 36 15N 87 0W
Cumberland Is. **121** 20 35S 149 10 E
Cumberland Pen. **146** 67 0N 64 0W
Cumberland Plat. **169** 36 0N 84 30W
Cumberland Sd. **146** 65 30N 66 0W
Cumbria □ **28** 54 35N 2 55W
Cumbrian Mts. **28** 54 30N 3 0W
Cumbum **90** 15 40N 79 10 E
Cummins **119** 34 16S 135 43 E
Cumnock **31** 55 27N 4 18W
Cunene → **134** 17 20S 11 50 E
Cunnamulla **116** 28 2S 145 38 E
Curaçao **181** 12 10N 69 0W
Curaray → **184** 2 20S 74 5W
Curiapo **185** 8 33N 61 5W
Curicó **190** 34 55S 71 20W
Curitiba **191** 25 20S 49 10W
Curtis Group **117** 39 30S 146 37 E
Curuá → **188** 5 23S 54 22W
Curuçá **188** 0 43S 47 50W
Curuzú Cuatiá **191** 29 50S 58 5W
Cushing **168** 35 59N 96 46W
Cusihuiriáchic **174** 28 14N 106 50W
Cuthbert **170** 31 47N 84 47W
Cuttack **92** 20 25N 85 57 E
Cuxhaven **42** 53 51N 8 41 E
Cuyahoga Falls **167** 41 8N 81 30W
Cuzco, Bolivia **187** 20 0S 66 50W
Cuzco, Peru **186** 13 32S 72 0W
Cwmbran **27** 51 39N 3 0W
Cypress Hills **152** 49 40N 109 30W
Cyprus ■ **80** 35 0N 33 0 E
Cyrenaica **124** 27 0N 23 0 E
Czech Republic ■ **59** 49 0N 15 0 E
Czeremcha **58** 52 31N 23 21 E
Częstochowa **58** 50 49N 19 7 E

D

Da → **95** 21 15N 105 20 E
Da Hinggan Ling **98** 48 0N 121 0 E
Da Nang **95** 16 4N 108 13 E
Da Yunhe → **99** 34 25N 120 5 E
Daba Shan **99** 32 0N 109 0 E
Dacca = Dhaka **92** 23 43N 90 26 E
Dacca □ = Dhaka □ **93** 24 25N 90 25 E
Dadanawa **185** 2 50N 59 30W
Dadra and Nagar Haveli □ **91** 20 5N 73 0 E
Daghestan Rep. □ **70** 42 30N 47 0 E
Dahomey = Benin ■ **131** 10 0N 2 0 E
Dai-Sen **109** 35 22N 133 32 E
Daiō-Misaki **106** 34 15N 136 45 E
Daisetsu-Zan **103** 43 30N 142 57 E
Daito **109** 35 19N 132 58 E
Dajarra **115** 21 42S 139 30 E
Dakar **130** 14 34N 17 29W
Dakhla **126** 23 50N 15 53W
Dakhla, El Wâhât el- **128** 25 30N 28 50 E
Đakovica **52** 42 22N 20 26 E
Dalandzadgad **98** 43 27N 104 30 E
Dalbeattie **31** 54 55N 3 50W
Dalby **116** 27 10S 151 17 E
Dalhousie **148** 48 5N 66 26W
Dali **99** 25 40N 100 10 E
Dalian **98** 38 50N 121 40 E
Daliang Shan **99** 28 0N 102 45 E
Dallas, Oreg., U.S.A. **171** 45 0N 123 15W
Dallas, Tex., U.S.A. **168** 32 50N 96 50W
Dalmacija **52** 43 20N 17 0 E
Dalmatia = Dalmacija **52** 43 20N 17 0 E
Daloa **130** 7 0N 6 30W
Dalton **169** 34 47N 84 58W
Daly Waters **114** 16 15S 133 24 E
Daman **91** 20 25N 72 57 E
Damaraland **136** 21 0S 17 0 E
Damascus = Dimashq **80** 33 30N 36 18 E
Damāvand **86** 35 47N 52 0 E
Damāvand, Qolleh-ye **86** 35 56N 52 10 E
Dampier **114** 20 41S 116 42 E
Dampier Arch. **114** 20 38S 116 32 E
Danbury **164** 41 23N 73 29W
Dandenong **117** 38 0S 145 15 E
Dandong **98** 40 10N 124 20 E
Dangriga **177** 17 0N 88 13W
Dannevirke **122** 40 12S 176 8 E
Dansville **164** 42 32N 77 41W
Danville, Ill., U.S.A. **167** 40 10N 87 40W
Danville, Ky., U.S.A. **167** 37 40N 84 45W
Danville, Va., U.S.A. **165** 36 40N 79 20W
Danzig = Gdańsk **58** 54 22N 18 40 E
Dar es Salaam **135** 6 50S 39 12 E
Darbhanga **92** 26 15N 85 55 E
Dardanelles = Çanakkale Boğazi **80** 40 0N 26 0 E
Dârfûr **129** 13 40N 24 0 E
Dargan Ata **70** 40 29N 62 10 E
Dargaville **122** 35 57S 173 52 E
Darién, G. del **184** 9 0N 77 0W
Darjeeling = Darjiling **92** 27 3N 88 18 E
Darjiling **92** 27 3N 88 18 E
Darling → **119** 34 4S 141 54 E
Darling Downs **116** 27 30S 150 30 E
Darling Ra. **120** 32 30S 116 0 E
Darlington **28** 54 33N 1 33W
Darmstadt **42** 49 51N 8 40 E
Darnley, C. **14** 68 0S 69 0 E
Dart → **27** 50 24N 3 36W
Dartmoor **27** 50 36N 4 0W
Dartmouth, Canada **149** 44 40N 63 30W
Dartmouth, U.K. **27** 50 21N 3 35W
Darwin **114** 12 25S 130 51 E
Dasht-e Kavīr **86** 34 30N 55 0 E
Dasht-e Lūt **85** 31 30N 58 0 E
Dasht-e Mārgow **87** 30 40N 62 30 E
Datia **91** 25 39N 78 27 E
Datong **98** 40 6N 113 18 E
Daugavpils **68** 55 53N 26 32 E
Dauphin **153** 51 9N 100 5W
Dauphiné **37** 45 15N 5 25 E
Davangere **90** 14 25N 75 55 E
Davao **112** 7 0N 125 40 E
Davenport **166** 41 30N 90 40W
Daventry **24** 52 16N 1 10W
David **179** 8 30N 82 30W
Davis Sea **15** 66 0S 92 0 E
Davis Str. **146** 65 0N 58 0W
Davos **44** 46 48N 9 49 E
Dawson **144** 64 10N 139 30W
Dawson Creek **155** 55 45N 120 15W
Dawson Range **121** 24 30S 149 48 E
Daylesford **117** 37 21S 144 9 E
Dayr az Zawr **81** 35 20N 40 5 E
Dayton, Ohio, U.S.A. **167** 39 45N 84 10W

Dayton, Wash., U.S.A. 171 46 20N 118 10W
Daytona Beach 170 29 14N 81 0W
De Aar .... 136 30 39S 24 0 E
De Land 170 29 1N 81 19W
De Ridder 168 30 48N 93 15W
De Soto 166 38 7N 90 33W
Deakin .... 114 30 46S 128 0 E
Deal .... 25 51 13N 1 25 E
Dean, Forest of 24 51 50N 2 35W
Deán Funes 190 30 20S 64 20W
Dease ~► 144 59 56N 128 32W
Dease Lake 144 58 25N 130 6W
Death Valley 173 36 19N 116 52W
Deauville .... 38 49 23N 0 2 E
Debar .... 52 41 31N 20 30 E
Debre Markos .... 132 10 20N 37 40 E
Debre Tabor .... 132 11 50N 38 26 E
Debrecen .... 59 47 33N 21 42 E
Decatur, Ala., U.S.A. 169 34 35N 87 0W
Decatur, Ga., U.S.A. 170 33 47N 84 17W
Decatur, Ill., U.S.A. 166 39 50N 89 0W
Deccan .... 76 18 0N 79 0 E
Dedéagach =
    Alexandroúpolis ...... 55 40 50N 25 54 E
Dee ~►, Scotland, U.K. .. 33 57 4N 2 7W
Dee ~►, Wales, U.K. 26 53 15N 3 7W
Deepwater .... 116 29 25S 151 51 E
Deer Lake 149 49 11N 57 27W
Defiance 167 41 20N 84 20W
Deh Bid .... 85 30 39N 53 11 E
Dehra Dun .... 89 30 20N 78 4 E
Dej .... 56 47 10N 23 52 E
Del Rio 161 29 23N 100 50W
Delano 173 35 48N 119 13W
Delaware □ 164 39 0N 75 40W
Delaware ~► 164 39 20N 75 25W
Delaware B. 157 38 50N 75 0W
Delft .... 40 52 1N 4 22 E
Delfzijl .... 41 53 20N 6 55 E
Delgado, C. .... 137 10 45S 40 40 E
Delgo .... 129 20 6N 30 40 E
Delhi .... 89 28 38N 77 17 E
Delice ~► .... 80 39 45N 34 15 E
Delicias 174 28 13N 105 28W
Delong, Ostrova .... 72 76 40N 149 20 E
Deloraine .... 119 41 30S 146 40 E
Delray Beach 170 26 27N 80 4W
Demanda, Sierra de la ... 50 42 15N 3 0W
Dembidolo .... 132 8 34N 34 50 E
Deming 161 32 10N 107 50W
Demopolis 169 32 30N 87 48W
Den Burg .... 40 53 3N 4 47 E
Den Haag = 's-Gravenhage 40 52 7N 4 17 E
Den Helder .... 40 52 57N 4 45 E
Den Oever .... 40 52 56N 5 2 E
Denain .... 38 50 20N 3 22 E
Denbigh 26 53 12N 3 26W
Denham .... 120 25 56S 113 31 E
Deniliquin .... 117 35 30S 144 58 E
Denison 168 33 50N 96 40W
Denizli .... 80 37 42N 29 2 E
Denmark .... 120 34 59S 117 25 E
Denmark ■ .... 61 55 30N 9 0 E
Denmark Str. 13 66 0N 30 0W
Denton 168 33 12N 97 10W
D'Entrecasteaux Is. ..... 115 9 0S 151 0 E
Denver 163 39 45N 105 0W
Deolali .... 91 19 58N 73 50 E
Deoria .... 92 26 31N 83 48 E
Deosai Mts. .... 89 35 40N 75 0 E
Dera Ghazi Khan .... 89 30 5N 70 43 E
Dera Ismail Khan .... 89 31 50N 70 50 E
Derby 28 52 55N 1 28W
Derby □ 28 52 55N 1 28W
Derg, L. 35 53 0N 8 20W
Derry = Londonderry 34 55 0N 7 20W
Derryveagh Mts. 34 55 0N 8 40W
Derwent ~►, Cumb., U.K. . 28 54 42N 3 22W
Derwent ~►, Derby, U.K. . 29 52 53N 1 17W
Derwent ~►, N. Yorks., U.K. 29 53 45N 0 57W
Derwent Water, L. 28 54 35N 3 9W

Des Moines 166 41 35N 93 37W
Des Moines ~► 166 40 23N 91 25W
Deschutes ~► 171 45 30N 121 0W
Dese .... 133 11 5N 39 40 E
Despeñaperros, Paso 50 38 24N 3 30W
Dessau .... 43 51 49N 12 15 E
Dessye = Dese .... 133 11 5N 39 40 E
Desvrès .... 38 50 40N 1 48 E
Detroit 167 42 23N 83 5W
Deurne .... 41 51 27N 5 49 E
Deutsche Bucht .... 42 54 10N 7 51 E
Devakottai .... 90 9 55N 78 45 E
Deventer .... 41 52 15N 6 10 E
Devizes 24 51 21N 2 0W
Devon I. 13 75 10N 85 0W
Devonport, Australia .... 119 41 10S 146 22 E
Devonport, N.Z. .... 122 36 49S 174 49 E
Devonport, U.K. 27 50 23N 4 11W
Devonshire □ 27 50 50N 3 40W
Dewsbury 28 53 42N 1 38W
Dezful .... 84 32 20N 48 30 E
Dezhneva, Mys 73 66 5N 169 40W
Dhahran = Az Zahrān .... 84 26 10N 50 7 E
Dhaka .... 92 23 43N 90 26 E
Dhaka □ .... 93 24 25N 90 25 E
Dhamar .... 83 14 30N 44 20 E
Dhar .... 91 22 35N 75 26 E
Dharmapuri .... 90 12 10N 78 10 E
Dharwad .... 90 15 22N 75 15 E
Dhidhimótikhon .... 55 41 22N 26 29 E
Dhikti .... 55 35 8N 25 22 E
Dhodhekánisos .... 55 36 35N 27 0 E
Dhuburi .... 92 26 2N 89 59 E
Dhule .... 91 20 58N 74 50 E
Di Linh, Cao Nguyen .... 95 11 30N 108 0 E
Diamantina 188 18 17S 43 40W
Diamantina ~► .... 115 26 45S 139 10 E
Diamantino 188 14 30S 56 30W
Dibrugarh .... 93 27 29N 94 55 E
Dickinson 163 46 50N 102 48W
Didsbury 155 51 35N 114 10W
Diefenbaker L. 152 51 0N 106 55W
Dieppe .... 38 49 54N 1 4 E
Dieren .... 41 52 3N 6 6 E
Digby 148 44 38N 65 50W
Digne .... 37 44 5N 6 12 E
Dijlah, Nahr ~► .... 81 31 0N 47 25 E
Dijon .... 37 47 20N 5 0 E
Dila .... 133 6 21N 38 22 E
Dillon 165 34 26N 79 20W
Dimashq .... 80 33 30N 36 18 E
Dimboola .... 119 36 28S 142 7 E
Dîmbovița ~► .... 57 44 14N 26 13 E
Dimitrovgrad .... 53 42 5N 25 35 E
Dimitrovo = Pernik ..... 53 42 35N 23 2 E
Dinan 36 48 28N 2 2W
Dinara Planina .... 52 44 0N 16 30 E
Dinaric Alps = Dinara Planina 52 44 0N 16 30 E
Dindigul .... 90 10 25N 78 0 E
Dingle 35 52 9N 10 17W
Dingle B. 35 52 3N 10 20W
Dingwall 33 57 36N 4 26W
Dinuba 173 36 31N 119 22W
Dire Dawa .... 133 9 35N 41 45 E
Diriamba 179 11 51N 86 19W
Dirranbandi .... 116 28 33S 148 17 E
Disappointment L. ...... 114 23 20S 122 40 E
Discovery B. .... 119 38 10S 140 40 E
Disko 146 69 45N 53 30W
Diss .... 25 52 23N 1 6 E
Diu .... 91 20 45N 70 58 E
Dives-sur-Mer 39 49 18N 0 8W
Dixon 166 41 50N 89 30W
Dixon Entrance 154 54 30N 132 0W
Diyarbakir .... 81 37 55N 40 18 E
Djakarta = Jakarta ..... 111 6 9S 106 49 E
Djelfa .... 130 34 40N 3 15 E
Djerid, Chott .... 127 33 42N 8 30 E
Djibouti .... 133 11 30N 43 5 E
Djibouti ■ .... 133 12 0N 43 0 E
Djoum .... 131 2 41N 12 35 E

Dmitriya Lapteva, Proliv **72** 73 0N 140 0 E
Dnepr → **68** 46 30N 32 18 E
Dnepropetrovsk **68** 48 30N 35 0 E
Dnestr → **68** 46 18N 30 17 E
Dnestrovski = Belgorod **68** 50 35N 36 35 E
Dnieper = Dnepr → **68** 46 30N 32 18 E
Dniester = Dnestr → **68** 46 18N 30 17 E
Dobrich **53** 43 37N 27 49 E
Dobruja **57** 44 30N 28 15 E
Dodecanese = Dhodhekánisos **55** 36 35N 27 0 E
Dodge City **161** 37 42N 100 0W
Dodoma **135** 6 8S 35 45 E
Doesburg **41** 52 1N 6 9 E
Doetinchem **41** 51 59N 6 18 E
Dogger Bank **124** 54 50N 2 0 E
Doi Luang **95** 18 30N 101 0 E
Dojran **54** 41 10N 22 45 E
Dokkum **41** 53 20N 5 59 E
Dolbeau **148** 48 53N 72 18W
Dole **37** 47 7N 5 31 E
Dolgellau **26** 52 44N 3 53W
Dolgelley = Dolgellau **26** 52 44N 3 53W
Dolomites = Dolomiti **47** 46 30N 11 40 E
Dolomiti **47** 46 30N 11 40 E
Dolores **191** 36 20S 57 40W
Dolphin and Union Str. **145** 69 5N 114 45W
Domel I. = Letsôk-aw Kyun **94** 11 30N 98 25 E
Dominica ■ **180** 15 20N 61 20W
Dominican Rep. ■ **180** 19 0N 70 30W
Don →, Russia **68** 47 4N 39 18 E
Don →, U.K. **33** 57 14N 2 5W
Donaghadee **34** 54 38N 5 32W
Donau → **42** 48 10N 17 0 E
Doncaster **29** 53 31N 1 9W
Dondra Head **90** 5 55N 80 40 E
Donegal **34** 54 39N 8 8W
Donegal □ **34** 54 53N 8 0W
Donegal B. **34** 54 30N 8 35W
Donetsk **68** 48 0N 37 45 E
Dongara **120** 29 14S 114 57 E
Dongen **40** 51 38N 4 56 E
Dongting Hu **99** 29 18N 112 45 E
Donnelly's Crossing **122** 35 42S 173 38 E
Donnybrook **120** 33 34S 115 48 E
Doon → **31** 55 26N 4 41W
Dorada, La **184** 5 30N 74 40W
Dorchester **27** 50 42N 2 28W
Dorchester, C. **146** 65 27N 77 27W
Dordogne □ **36** 45 5N 0 40 E
Dordrecht **40** 51 48N 4 39 E
Dornoch **33** 57 52N 4 0W
Dorrigo **116** 30 20S 152 44 E
Dorris **172** 41 59N 121 58W
Dorset □ **27** 50 48N 2 25W
Dortmund **42** 51 32N 7 28 E
Dothan **169** 31 10N 85 25W
Douai **38** 50 21N 3 4 E
Douala **131** 4 0N 9 45 E
Douarnenez **36** 48 6N 4 21W
Douglas, U.K. **28** 54 9N 4 29W
Douglas, U.S.A. **170** 31 32N 82 52W
Doullens **38** 50 10N 2 20 E
Dounreay **33** 58 34N 3 44W
Dourados **188** 22 9S 54 50W
Douro → **50** 41 8N 8 40W
Douro Litoral □ **50** 41 10N 8 20W
Dove → **28** 52 51N 1 36W
Dover, U.K. **25** 51 7N 1 19 E
Dover, Del., U.S.A. **164** 39 10N 75 31W
Dover, N.H., U.S.A. **164** 43 12N 70 51W
Dover, Str. of **38** 51 0N 1 30 E
Dovey → **26** 52 32N 4 0W
Downham Market **25** 52 36N 0 22 E
Downpatrick **34** 54 20N 5 43W
Drachten **41** 53 7N 6 5 E
Dragoman, Prokhod **53** 43 0N 22 53 E
Draguignan **37** 43 30N 6 27 E
Drakensberg **137** 31 0S 28 0 E
Dráma **55** 41 9N 24 10 E
Drammen **60** 59 42N 10 12 E
Drau = Drava → **59** 45 33N 18 55 E
Drava → **59** 45 33N 18 55 E
Drayton Valley **155** 53 12N 114 58W
Drenthe □ **41** 52 52N 6 40 E
Dresden **43** 51 2N 13 45 E
Dreux **39** 48 44N 1 23 E
Driffield **29** 54 0N 0 25W
Drin i zi → **52** 41 37N 20 28 E
Drina → **52** 44 53N 19 21 E
Drogheda **34** 53 45N 6 20W
Droitwich **24** 52 16N 2 10W
Dronne → **36** 45 2N 0 9W
Dronning Maud Land **14** 72 30S 12 0 E
Drumheller **155** 51 25N 112 40W
Drummond Ra. **121** 23 45S 147 10 E
Drummondville **151** 45 55N 72 25W
Dryden **153** 49 47N 92 50W
Du Bois **164** 41 8N 78 46W
Du Quoin **166** 38 0N 89 10W
Dubai = Dubayy **85** 25 18N 55 20 E
Dubawnt → **145** 64 33N 100 6W
Dubawnt, L. **143** 63 4N 101 42W
Dubayy **85** 25 18N 55 20 E
Dubbo **116** 32 11S 148 35 E
Dublin, Ireland **35** 53 20N 6 18W
Dublin, U.S.A. **170** 32 30N 82 34W
Dublin □ **34** 53 24N 6 20W
Dubrovnik **52** 42 39N 18 6 E
Dubuque **166** 42 30N 90 41W
Dudley **24** 52 30N 2 5W
Dugi Otok **52** 44 0N 15 0 E
Duisburg **42** 51 27N 6 42 E
Duluth **150** 46 48N 92 10W
Dumbarton **31** 55 58N 4 35W
Dumfries **31** 55 4N 3 37W
Dumfries & Galloway □ **31** 55 0N 4 0W
Dun Laoghaire **35** 53 17N 6 9W
Dunărea → **57** 45 30N 8 15 E
Dunaújváros **59** 47 0N 18 57 E
Dunbar **31** 56 0N 2 32W
Dunblane **31** 56 10N 3 58W
Duncan, Canada **154** 48 45N 123 40W
Duncan, U.S.A. **161** 34 25N 98 0W
Duncan Pass. **94** 11 0N 92 30 E
Dundalk **34** 54 1N 6 25W
Dundas, Canada **151** 43 17N 79 59W
Dundas, Greenland **13** 77 0N 69 0W
Dundee **31** 56 29N 3 0W
Dundrum **34** 54 17N 5 50W
Dunedin **123** 45 50S 170 33 E
Dunedoo **116** 32 0S 149 25 E
Dunfermline **31** 56 5N 3 28W
Dungannon **34** 54 30N 6 47W
Dungarvan **35** 52 6N 7 40W
Dungeness **25** 50 54N 0 59 E
Dungog **117** 32 22S 151 46 E
Dunhuang **100** 40 8N 94 36 E
Dunkeld **33** 56 34N 3 36W
Dunkerque **38** 51 2N 2 20 E
Dunkery Beacon **27** 51 15N 3 37W
Dunkirk = Dunkerque **38** 51 2N 2 20 E
Dunkirk **164** 42 30N 79 18W
Dúnleary = Dun Laoghaire **35** 53 17N 6 9W
Dunmore **164** 41 27N 75 38W
Dunn **165** 35 18N 78 36W
Dunnet Hd. **33** 58 38N 3 22W
Duns **31** 55 47N 2 20W
Dunsmuir **172** 41 10N 122 18W
Dunstan Mts. **123** 44 53S 169 35 E
Durance → **37** 43 55N 4 45 E
Durango, Mexico **174** 24 3N 104 39W
Durango, U.S.A. **163** 37 16N 107 50W
Durango □ **174** 24 50N 104 50W
Durant **168** 34 0N 96 25W
Durazno **191** 33 25S 56 31W
Durban **137** 29 49S 31 1 E
Durg **92** 21 15N 81 22 E
Durham, U.K. **28** 54 47N 1 34W
Durham, U.S.A. **165** 36 0N 78 55W
Durham □ **28** 54 42N 1 45W
Durmitor **52** 43 10N 19 0 E

Place	Map	Lat°	Lat′	N/S	Long°	Long′	E/W
Durness	32	58	34	N	4	45	W
D'Urville I.	122	40	50	S	173	55	E
Dushanbe	71	38	33	N	68	48	E
Düsseldorf	42	51	15	N	6	46	E
Duwādimi	82	24	35	N	44	15	E
Duyun	99	26	18	N	107	29	E
Duzce	80	40	50	N	31	10	E
Duzdab = Zāhedān	86	29	30	N	60	50	E
Dvina, Sev. →	69	64	32	N	40	30	E
Dvinsk = Daugavpils	68	55	53	N	26	32	E
Dyer, C.	146	66	40	N	61	0	W
Dyersburg	169	36	2	N	89	20	W
Dyfed □	26	52	0	N	4	30	W
Dysart	121	22	32	S	148	23	E
Dzamin Üüd	98	43	50	N	111	58	E
Dzerzhinsk	68	53	40	N	27	1	E
Dzhalal-Abad	71	40	56	N	73	0	E
Dzhalinda	75	53	26	N	124	0	E
Dzhambul	71	42	54	N	71	22	E
Dzhardzhan	72	68	10	N	124	10	E
Dzhetygara	71	52	11	N	61	12	E
Dzhezkazgan	71	47	44	N	67	40	E
Dzhugdzur, Khrebet	75	57	30	N	138	0	E
Dzuumod	98	47	45	N	106	58	E

E

Place	Map	Lat°	Lat′	N/S	Long°	Long′	E/W
Eagle	142	64	44	N	141	7	W
Eagle Pass	161	28	45	N	100	35	W
Eagle River	150	45	55	N	89	17	W
Ealing	25	51	30	N	0	19	W
Earn →	31	56	20	N	3	19	W
Easley	165	34	52	N	82	35	W
East Angus	148	45	30	N	71	40	W
East Bengal	92	24	0	N	90	0	E
East Beskids = Vychodné Beskydy	59	49	30	N	22	0	E
East C.	122	37	42	S	178	35	E
East Chicago	167	41	40	N	87	30	W
East China Sea	99	30	5	N	126	0	E
East Falkland	192	51	30	S	58	30	W
East Indies	77	0	0		120	0	E
East Kilbride	31	55	46	N	4	10	W
East Liverpool	164	40	39	N	80	35	W
East London	137	33	0	S	27	55	E
East Main = Eastmain	140	52	10	N	78	30	W
East Pakistan = Bangladesh ■	92	24	0	N	90	0	E
East Point	170	33	40	N	84	28	W
East St. Louis	166	38	37	N	90	4	W
East Schelde → = Oosterschelde	40	51	33	N	4	0	E
East Siberian Sea	73	73	0	N	160	0	E
East Sussex □	25	51	0	N	0	20	E
Eastbourne, N.Z.	123	41	19	S	174	55	E
Eastbourne, U.K.	25	50	46	N	0	18	E
Eastern Ghats	90	14	0	N	78	50	E
Eastleigh	25	50	58	N	1	21	W
Eastmain	140	52	10	N	78	30	W
Eastmain →	140	52	27	N	78	26	W
Easton	164	40	41	N	75	15	W
Eau Claire	166	44	46	N	91	30	W
Eau Claire, L. à l'	146	56	10	N	74	25	W
Ebbw Vale	26	51	47	N	3	12	W
Eboli	49	40	39	N	15	2	E
Ebro →	51	40	43	N	0	54	E
Echizen-Misaki	106	35	59	N	135	57	E
Echo Bay	145	46	29	N	84	4	W
Echuca	117	36	10	S	144	20	E
Ecuador ■	184	2	0	S	78	0	W
Ed Dâmer	129	17	27	N	34	0	E
Edam	40	52	31	N	5	3	E
Eddystone	27	50	11	N	4	16	W
Ede	41	52	4	N	5	40	E
Eden	117	37	3	S	149	55	E
Eden →	28	54	57	N	3	2	W
Edenhope	119	37	4	S	141	19	E
Edge Hill	24	52	7	N	1	28	W
Edhessa	54	40	48	N	22	5	E
Edinburgh	31	55	57	N	3	12	W
Edirne	80	41	40	N	26	34	E
Edmonton, Australia	121	17	2	S	145	46	E
Edmonton, Canada	155	53	30	N	113	30	W
Edmundston	148	47	23	N	68	20	W
Edson	155	53	35	N	116	28	W
Edward, L.	132	0	25	S	29	40	E
Edward VII Land	15	80	0	S	150	0	W
Edwards Plat.	161	30	30	N	101	5	W
Effingham	167	39	8	N	88	30	W
Égadi, Ísole	48	37	55	N	12	16	E
Eger	59	47	53	N	20	27	E
Egmont, Mt.	122	39	17	S	174	5	E
Eğridir Gölü	80	37	53	N	30	50	E
Egypt ■	128	28	0	N	31	0	E
Eifel	42	50	10	N	6	45	E
Eigg	32	56	54	N	6	10	W
Eil	133	8	0	N	49	50	E
Eindhoven	41	51	26	N	5	30	E
Eirunepé	187	6	35	S	69	53	W
El Aaiún	126	27	9	N	13	12	W
El Cajon	173	32	49	N	117	0	W
El Callao	185	7	18	N	61	50	W
El Centro	173	32	50	N	115	40	W
El Cerro	187	17	30	S	61	40	W
El Dere	133	3	50	N	47	8	E
El Djouf	126	20	0	N	11	30	E
El Dorado	168	33	10	N	92	40	W
El Escorial	50	40	35	N	4	7	W
El Faiyûm	128	29	19	N	30	50	E
El Fâsher	129	13	33	N	25	26	E
El Ferrol	50	43	29	N	8	15	W
El Fuerte	174	26	25	N	108	39	W
El Geteina	129	14	50	N	32	27	E
El Iskandarîya	128	31	0	N	30	0	E
El Jadida	126	33	11	N	8	17	W
El Khârga	128	25	30	N	30	33	E
El Khartûm	129	15	31	N	32	35	E
El Mahalla el Kubra	128	31	0	N	31	0	E
El Minyâ	128	28	7	N	30	33	E
El Obeid	129	13	8	N	30	10	E
El Oro	177	27	15	N	103	30	W
El Paso	161	31	50	N	106	30	W
El Progreso	177	15	26	N	87	51	W
El Qâhira	128	30	1	N	31	14	E
El Qasr	128	25	44	N	28	42	E
El Salvador ■	177	13	50	N	89	0	W
El Suweis	128	29	58	N	32	31	E
El Tigre	185	8	44	N	64	15	W
El Turbio	192	51	45	S	72	5	W
Elat	80	29	30	N	34	56	E
Elâzığ	81	38	37	N	39	14	E
Elba	46	42	48	N	10	15	E
Elbasani	52	41	9	N	20	9	E
Elbe →	42	53	50	N	9	0	E
Elbert, Mt.	163	39	5	N	106	27	W
Elberton	165	34	7	N	82	51	W
Elbeuf	39	49	17	N	1	2	E
Elbing = Elbląg	58	54	10	N	19	25	E
Elbląg	58	54	10	N	19	25	E
Elbrus	70	43	21	N	42	30	E
Elburg	41	52	26	N	5	50	E
Elburz Mts. = Alborz, Reshteh-ye Kühhä-ye	86	36	0	N	52	0	E
Elche	51	38	15	N	0	42	W
Eldorado	174	24	20	N	107	22	W
Eldorado Springs	166	37	54	N	93	59	W
Eldoret	132	0	30	N	35	17	E
Eleanora, Peak	120	32	57	S	121	9	E
Electra	161	34	0	N	99	0	W
Elephant Butte Res.	161	33	45	N	107	30	W
Eleuthera	178	25	0	N	76	20	W
Elgin, U.K.	33	57	39	N	3	20	W
Elgin, Ill., U.S.A.	167	42	0	N	88	20	W
Elgin, Oreg., U.S.A.	171	45	37	N	118	0	W
Elgon, Mt.	132	1	10	N	34	30	E
Elisabethville = Lubumbashi	135	11	40	S	27	28	E
Elizabeth, Australia	119	34	42	S	138	41	E
Elizabeth, U.S.A.	164	40	37	N	74	12	W
Elizabeth City	165	36	18	N	76	16	W

Elizabethton **165** 36 20N 82 13W
Elizabethtown **167** 37 40N 85 54W
Elk Point **152** 53 54N 110 55W
Elkhart **167** 41 42N 85 55W
Elkins **165** 38 53N 79 53W
Elko **172** 40 50N 115 50W
Ellensburg **171** 47 0N 120 30W
Ellery, Mt. **117** 37 28S 148 47 E
Ellesmere I. **13** 79 30N 80 0W
Ellesmere Port **28** 53 17N 2 55W
Ellice Is. = Tuvalu ■ **122** 8 0S 178 0 E
Elliot Lake **150** 46 25N 82 35W
Ellore = Eluru **92** 16 48N 81 8 E
Ellsworth Land **14** 76 0S 89 0W
Ellsworth Mts. **14** 78 30S 85 0W
Elmhurst **167** 41 52N 87 58W
Elmira **164** 42 8N 76 49W
Elrose **152** 51 12N 108 0W
Eluru **92** 16 48N 81 8 E
Elvas **50** 38 50N 7 10W
Elwood **167** 40 20N 85 50W
Ely **172** 39 10N 114 50W
Elyria **167** 41 22N 82 8W
Emāmrūd **86** 36 30N 55 0 E
Emba → **70** 46 38N 53 14 E
Emden **42** 53 22N 7 12 E
Emerald **121** 23 32S 148 10 E
Emilia-Romagna □ **46** 44 33N 10 40 E
Emmeloord **41** 52 44N 5 46 E
Emmen **41** 52 48N 6 57 E
Empalme **174** 27 58N 110 51W
Emporia, Kans., U.S.A. **158** 38 25N 96 10W
Emporia, Va., U.S.A. **165** 36 41N 77 32W
Ems → **42** 52 37N 9 26 E
En Nahud **129** 12 45N 28 25 E
Ena **106** 35 25N 137 25 E
Ena-San **106** 35 26N 137 36 E
Encarnación **191** 27 15S 55 50W
Encarnación de Díaz **175** 21 31N 102 14W
Encontrados **184** 9 3N 72 14W
Enderby **155** 50 35N 119 10W
Enderby Land **14** 66 0S 53 0 E
Endicott **164** 42 6N 76 2W
Engaño, C. **180** 18 30N 68 20W
Engels = Pokrovsk **68** 51 28N 46 6 E
Enggano **111** 5 20S 102 40 E
England □ **21** 53 0N 2 0W
English Bazar = Ingraj Bazar **92** 24 58N 88 10 E
English Channel **16** 50 0N 2 0W
Enid **161** 36 26N 97 52W
Enkhuizen **40** 52 42N 5 17 E
Ennedi **129** 17 15N 22 0 E
Ennis **35** 52 51N 8 59W
Enniscorthy **35** 52 30N 6 35W
Enniskillen **34** 54 20N 7 40W
Enriquillo, L. **180** 18 20N 72 5W
Enschede **41** 52 13N 6 53 E
Ensenada **174** 31 52N 116 37W
Enshū-Nada **106** 34 27N 137 38 E
Entebbe **132** 0 4N 32 28 E
Enterprise **171** 45 30N 117 18W
Entre Ríos □ **190** 30 30S 58 30W
Enugu **131** 6 20N 7 30 E
Enzan **107** 35 42N 138 44 E
Eólie, I. **49** 38 30N 14 50 E
Epe **41** 52 21N 5 59 E
Épernay **39** 49 3N 3 56 E
Ephesus **80** 37 50N 27 33 E
Épinal **37** 48 10N 6 27 E
Epping **25** 51 42N 0 8 E
Equatorial Guinea ■ **134** 2 0S 8 0 E
Er Rif **126** 35 1N 4 1W
Erāwadī Myit → = Irrawaddy → **93** 15 50N 95 6 E
Ercha **73** 69 45N 147 20 E
Ercıyaş Dağı **80** 38 30N 35 30 E
Erebus, Mt. **15** 77 35S 167 0 E
Erechim **191** 27 35S 52 15W
Ereğli **80** 41 15N 31 30 E
Erfurt **43** 50 58N 11 2 E
Erg Chech **126** 50 59N 11 0 E
Erie **164** 42 10N 80 7W
Erie, L. **151** 42 15N 81 0W
Erímanthos **54** 37 57N 21 50 E
Erimo-misaki **103** 41 50N 143 15 E
Eritrea ■ **132** 14 0N 41 0 E
Ermoúpolis = Síros **55** 37 28N 24 57 E
Erne, Lough **34** 54 26N 7 46W
Erode **90** 11 24N 77 45 E
Erramala Hills **90** 15 30N 78 15 E
Erris Hd. **34** 54 19N 10 0W
Erzgebirge **43** 50 25N 13 0 E
Erzincan **81** 39 46N 39 30 E
Erzurum **81** 39 57N 41 15 E
Es Sînâ' **128** 29 0N 34 0 E
Esan-Misaki **103** 41 40N 141 10 E
Esashi **103** 41 52N 140 7 E
Esbjerg **61** 55 29N 8 29 E
Escanaba **150** 45 44N 87 5W
Escondido **173** 33 9N 117 4W
Escuintla **177** 14 20N 90 48W
Eşfahān **85** 33 0N 53 0 E
Esh Sham = Dimashq **80** 33 30N 36 18 E
Esk → **29** 54 27N 0 36W
Eskilstuna **60** 59 22N 16 32 E
Eskimo Pt. **145** 61 10N 94 15W
Eskişehir **80** 39 50N 30 35 E
Eslāmābād-e Gharb **84** 34 10N 46 30 E
Esmeraldas **184** 1 0N 79 40W
Espanola **151** 46 15N 81 46W
Esperance **114** 33 45S 121 55 E
Espinazo, Sierra del = Espinhaço, Serra do **188** 17 30S 43 30W
Espinhaço, Serra do **188** 17 30S 43 30W
Espírito Santo □ **189** 20 0S 40 45W
Essaouira **126** 31 32N 9 42W
Essen **42** 51 28N 6 59 E
Essequibo → **185** 6 50N 58 30W
Essex □ **25** 51 48N 0 30 E
Estados, I. de los **192** 54 40S 64 30W
Estelí **179** 13 9N 86 22W
Estevan **152** 49 10N 102 59W
Estherville **166** 43 25N 94 50W
Estonia ■ **68** 58 30N 25 30 E
Estoril **50** 38 42N 9 23W
Estrêla, Serra da **50** 40 10N 7 45W
Estremadura **50** 39 0N 9 0W
Étampes **39** 48 26N 2 10 E
Étaples **38** 50 30N 1 39 E
Etawah **91** 26 48N 79 6 E
Ethiopia ■ **133** 8 0N 40 0 E
Ethiopian Highlands **132** 10 0N 37 0 E
Etna **49** 37 45N 15 0 E
Etosha Pan **136** 18 40S 16 30 E
Etzatlán **175** 20 46N 104 5W
Euboea = Évvoia **55** 38 30N 24 0 E
Euclid **167** 41 32N 81 31W
Eucumbene, L. **117** 36 2S 148 40 E
Eufaula **169** 35 20N 95 33W
Eugene **171** 44 0N 123 8W
Eupen **42** 50 37N 6 3 E
Euphrates = Furāt, Nahr al → **84** 31 0N 47 25 E
Eureka, Calif., U.S.A. **172** 40 50N 124 0W
Eureka, Nev., U.S.A. **172** 39 32N 116 2W
Euroa **117** 36 44S 145 35 E
Europa, Pta. de **50** 36 3N 5 21W
Europa Pt. = Europa, Pta. de **50** 36 3N 5 21W
Europoort **40** 51 57N 4 10 E
Euston **119** 34 30S 142 46 E
Eutsuk L. **154** 53 20N 126 45W
Evans Head **116** 29 7S 153 27 E
Evanston **167** 42 0N 87 40W
Evansville **167** 38 0N 87 35W
Everard, L. **118** 31 30S 135 0 E
Everest, Mt. **92** 28 5N 86 58 E
Everett **171** 48 0N 122 10W
Everglades **170** 26 0N 80 30W
Evesham **24** 52 6N 1 57W
Évora **50** 38 33N 7 57W
Évreux **39** 49 0N 1 8 E
Évvoia **55** 38 30N 24 0 E

Place	Page	°	′	Lat	°	′	Long
Excelsior Springs	166	39	20N		94	10W	
Exe ➤	27	50	38N		3	27W	
Exeter	27	50	43N		3	31W	
Exmoor	27	51	10N		3	59W	
Exmouth	27	50	37N		3	26W	
Extremadura □	50	39	30N		6	5W	
Eyasi, L.	135	3	30S		35	0 E	
Eye Pen.	32	58	13N		6	10W	
Eyre, L.	118	29	30S		137	26 E	
Eyre Mts.	123	45	25S		168	25 E	
Eyre Pen.	119	33	30S		137	17 E	

F

Place	Page	°	′	Lat	°	′	Long
Facatativá	184	4	49N		74	22W	
Faddeyevskiy, Ostrov	72	76	0N		150	0 E	
Fair Hd.	34	55	14N		6	10W	
Fairbanks	142	64	50N		147	50W	
Fairfield, N.Z.	123	45	54S		170	24 E	
Fairfield, Ala., U.S.A.	169	33	30N		87	0W	
Fairfield, Calif., U.S.A.	172	38	14N		122	1W	
Fairfield, Tex., U.S.A.	168	31	40N		96	0W	
Fairmont, Minn., U.S.A.	166	43	37N		94	30W	
Fairmont, W. Va., U.S.A.	164	39	29N		80	10W	
Fairview	155	56	5N		118	25W	
Fairweather, Mt.	143	58	55N		137	45W	
Faisalabad	89	31	30N		73	5 E	
Faizabad	92	26	45N		82	10 E	
Fajardo	180	18	20N		65	39W	
Fakenham	29	52	50N		0	51 E	
Falam	93	23	0N		93	45 E	
Falkirk	31	56	0N		3	47W	
Falkland Is.	192	51	30S		59	0W	
Falköping	60	58	12N		13	33 E	
Fall River	164	41	45N		71	5W	
Falls City	166	40	0N		95	40W	
Falmouth, Jamaica	180	18	30N		77	40W	
Falmouth, U.K.	27	50	9N		5	5W	
Famagusta	80	35	8N		33	55 E	
Farāh	87	32	20N		62	7 E	
Farāh □	87	32	25N		62	10 E	
Fareham	25	50	52N		1	11W	
Farewell, C.	122	40	29S		172	43 E	
Farewell C. = Farvel, Kap	147	59	48N		43	55W	
Fargo	156	46	52N		96	40W	
Farmington, N.H., U.S.A.	157	43	25N		71	3W	
Farmington, N. Mex., U.S.A.	161	36	45N		108	28W	
Farnborough	25	51	17N		0	46W	
Faro	50	37	2N		7	55W	
Faroe Is.	16	62	0N		7	0W	
Fars □	85	29	30N		55	0 E	
Fársala	54	39	17N		22	23 E	
Farvel, Kap	147	59	48N		43	55W	
Fāryāb □	87	36	0N		65	0 E	
Fatehgarh	89	27	25N		79	35 E	
Fatehpur, Raj., India	92	28	0N		74	40 E	
Fatehpur, Ut. P., India	89	25	56N		81	13 E	
Faxaflói	64	64	29N		23	0W	
Fayetteville, Ark., U.S.A.	168	36	0N		94	5W	
Fayetteville, N.C., U.S.A.	165	35	0N		78	58W	
Fazilka	89	30	27N		74	2 E	
Fdérik	126	22	40N		12	45W	
Fear, C.	165	33	51N		78	0W	
Fécamp	38	49	45N		0	22 E	
Feilding	122	40	13S		175	35 E	
Feira de Santana	189	12	15S		38	57W	
Felixstowe	25	51	58N		1	22 E	
Fengjie	99	31	5N		109	36 E	
Fens, The	29	52	45N		0	2 E	
Fenyang	98	37	19N		111	46 E	
Ferfer	133	5	4N		45	9 E	
Fergana	71	40	23N		71	19 E	
Fergus Falls	156	46	18N		96	7W	
Fermoy	35	52	4N		8	18W	
Fernando de Noronha	189	4	0S		33	10W	
Fernando Póo = Bioko	131	3	30N		8	40 E	
Fernie	155	49	30N		115	5W	
Ferrara	47	44	50N		11	36 E	
Ferté-Bernard, La	39	48	10N		0	40 E	
Fès	126	34	0N		5	0W	
Feuilles ➤	146	58	47N		70	4W	
Feyzābād	87	37	7N		70	33 E	
Fezzan	124	27	0N		15	0 E	
Fianarantsoa	137	21	26S		47	5 E	
Fichtelgebirge	43	50	10N		12	0 E	
Fife □	31	56	13N		3	2W	
Fife Ness	31	56	17N		2	35W	
Fiji ■	122	17	20S		179	0 E	
Filey	29	54	13N		0	18W	
Findlay	167	41	0N		83	41W	
Finisterre, C.	50	42	50N		9	19W	
Finland ■	67	63	0N		27	0 E	
Finland, G. of	67	60	0N		26	0 E	
Finlay ➤	144	57	0N		125	10W	
Finley	117	35	38S		145	35 E	
Firenze	47	43	47N		11	15 E	
Firozabad	89	27	10N		78	25 E	
Fishguard	26	51	59N		4	59W	
Fiskenæsset	147	63	5N		50	45W	
Fitchburg	164	42	35N		71	47W	
Fitzgerald	170	31	45N		83	16W	
Fitzroy ➤	121	23	32S		150	52 E	
Fiume = Rijeka	52	45	20N		14	21 E	
Flagstaff	160	35	10N		111	40W	
Flamborough Hd.	29	54	8N		0	4W	
Flannan Is.	32	58	9N		7	52W	
Flattery, C.	171	48	21N		124	43W	
Flèche, La	39	47	42N		0	4W	
Fleetwood	28	53	55N		3	1W	
Flekkefjord	60	58	18N		6	39 E	
Flensburg	43	54	46N		9	28 E	
Flers	36	48	47N		0	33W	
Flin Flon	152	54	46N		101	53W	
Flinders I.	117	40	0S		148	0 E	
Flinders Ranges	118	31	30S		138	30 E	
Flinders Reefs	121	17	37S		148	31 E	
Flint, U.K.	26	53	15N		3	7W	
Flint, U.S.A.	167	43	5N		83	40W	
Flint ➤	170	30	52N		84	38W	
Flodden	31	55	37N		2	8W	
Flora	167	38	40N		88	30W	
Florence = Firenze	47	43	47N		11	15 E	
Florence, Ala., U.S.A.	169	34	50N		87	40W	
Florence, S.C., U.S.A.	165	34	12N		79	44W	
Flores, Guatemala	177	16	59N		89	50W	
Flores, Indonesia	113	8	35S		121	0 E	
Flores Sea	113	6	30S		124	0 E	
Floriano	188	6	50S		43	0W	
Florianópolis	191	27	30S		48	30W	
Florida	191	34	7S		56	10W	
Florida □	170	28	30N		82	0W	
Florida, Straits of	159	25	0N		80	0W	
Florida B.	159	25	0N		81	20W	
Florida Keys	159	25	0N		80	40W	
Flórina	54	40	48N		21	26 E	
Flushing = Vlissingen	40	51	26N		3	34 E	
Fly ➤	115	8	25S		143	0 E	
Foam Lake	152	51	40N		103	32W	
Fóggia	49	41	28N		15	31 E	
Foix	36	42	58N		1	38 E	
Folda	64	64	41N		10	50 E	
Folkestone	25	51	5N		1	11 E	
Follette, La	169	36	23N		84	9W	
Fond-du-Lac, Canada	145	59	19N		107	12W	
Fond du Lac, U.S.A.	167	43	46N		88	26W	
Fontainebleau	39	48	24N		2	40 E	
Fonte Boa	184	2	33S		66	0W	
Foochow = Fuzhou	99	26	5N		119	16 E	
Forbes	117	33	22S		148	0 E	
Forestburg	155	52	35N		112	1W	
Forestville	148	48	48N		69	2W	
Forfar	33	56	40N		2	53W	
Forli	47	44	14N		12	2 E	
Formby Pt.	28	53	33N		3	7W	
Formentera	51	38	43N		1	27 E	
Formosa = Taiwan ■	99	23	30N		121	0 E	
Formosa	191	26	15S		58	10W	
Forrest City	169	35	0N		90	50W	
Fort Albany	140	52	15N		81	35W	

Fort Augustus **32** 57 9N 4 40W
Fort Chipewyan **145** 58 42N 111 8W
Fort Collins **163** 40 30N 105 4W
Fort-Coulonge **151** 45 50N 76 45W
Fort-de-France **180** 14 36N 61 2W
Fort Dodge **166** 42 29N 94 10W
Fort Frances **153** 48 36N 93 24W
Fort Franklin **145** 65 10N 123 30W
Fort George **140** 53 50N 79 0W
Fort Good-Hope **144** 66 14N 128 40W
Fort Hertz = Putao . . . . **93** 27 28N 97 30 E
Fort Kent **148** 47 12N 68 30W
Fort-Lamy = Ndjamena . . . . **131** 12 10N 14 59 E
Fort Lauderdale **170** 26 10N 80 5W
Fort Liard **144** 60 14N 123 30W
Fort Mackay **143** 57 12N 111 41W
Fort Macleod **155** 49 45N 113 30W
Fort McMurray **155** 56 44N 111 7W
Fort McPherson **144** 67 30N 134 55W
Fort Madison **166** 40 39N 91 20W
Fort Morgan **163** 40 10N 103 50W
Fort Myers **170** 26 39N 81 51W
Fort Nelson **144** 58 50N 122 44W
Fort Nelson → **144** 59 32N 124 0W
Fort Payne **169** 34 25N 85 44W
Fort Peck L. **163** 47 40N 107 0W
Fort Pierce **170** 27 29N 80 19W
Fort Providence **145** 61 3N 117 40W
Fort Qu'Appelle **152** 50 45N 103 50W
Fort Resolution **145** 61 10N 113 40W
Fort Rupert **140** 51 30N 78 40W
Fort St. James **154** 54 30N 124 10W
Fort St. John **155** 56 15N 120 50W
Fort Sandeman . . . . **88** 31 20N 69 31 E
Fort Saskatchewan **155** 53 40N 113 15W
Fort Scott **166** 37 50N 94 40W
Fort Severn **140** 56 0N 87 40W
Fort Shevchenko . . . . **70** 43 40N 51 20 E
Fort Simpson **144** 61 45N 121 15W
Fort Smith, Canada **145** 60 0N 111 51W
Fort Smith, U.S.A. **168** 35 25N 94 25W
Fort Smith Region □ **145** 63 0N 120 0W
Fort Trinquet = Bir Mogrein **126** 25 10N 11 25W
Fort Valley **170** 32 33N 83 52W
Fort Vermilion **145** 58 24N 116 0W
Fort Wayne **167** 41 5N 85 10W
Fort William **32** 56 48N 5 8W
Fort Worth **168** 32 45N 97 25W
Fort Yukon **142** 66 35N 145 20W
Fortaleza **189** 3 45S 38 35W
Forth → **31** 56 9N 4 18W
Forth, Firth of **31** 56 5N 2 55W
Fortuna **172** 40 38N 124 8W
Foshan . . . . **99** 23 4N 113 5 E
Foster . . . . **117** 38 40S 146 15 E
Fougères **36** 48 21N 1 14W
Foula, I. **30** 60 10N 2 5W
Foulness I. . . . . **24** 51 36N 0 55 E
Fourmies . . . . **38** 50 1N 4 2 E
Foúrnoi . . . . **55** 37 36N 26 32 E
Fouta Djalon **130** 11 20N 12 10W
Foveaux Str. . . . . **123** 46 42S 168 10 E
Fowey **27** 50 20N 4 39W
Foxe Basin **146** 66 0N 77 0W
Foxe Chan. **146** 65 0N 80 0W
Foxe Pen. **146** 65 0N 76 0W
Foxton . . . . **122** 40 29S 175 18 E
Foyle, Lough **34** 55 6N 7 8W
Foynes **35** 52 37N 9 5W
Franca **188** 20 33S 47 30W
France ■ . . . . **37** 47 0N 3 0 E
Franche-Comté . . . . **37** 46 30N 5 50 E
François **180** 14 38N 60 57W
Franeker . . . . **41** 53 12N 5 33 E
Frankfort, Ind., U.S.A. **167** 40 20N 86 33W
Frankfort, Ky., U.S.A. **165** 38 12N 84 52W
Frankfurt am Main . . . . **42** 50 7N 8 40 E
Frankfurt an der Oder . . . . . **43** 52 50N 14 31 E
Fränkische Alb . . . . **43** 49 20N 11 30 E
Franklin, La., U.S.A. **168** 29 45N 91 30W
Franklin, N.H., U.S.A. **164** 43 28N 71 39W
Franklin, W. Va., U.S.A. **165** 38 38N 79 21W
Franklin D. Roosevelt L. **162** 48 30N 118 16W
Franklin Mts. **145** 65 0N 125 0W
Franklin Str. **145** 72 0N 96 0W
Frankston . . . . **117** 38 8S 145 8 E
Franz **150** 48 25N 84 30W
Fraser → **154** 49 7N 123 11W
Fraser, Mt. . . . . **120** 25 35S 118 20 E
Fraser I. . . . . **116** 25 15S 153 10 E
Fraserburgh **33** 57 41N 2 0W
Fray Bentos **190** 33 10S 58 15W
Frederick **164** 39 25N 77 23W
Fredericksburg **165** 38 16N 77 29W
Fredericton **148** 45 57N 66 40W
Frederikshavn . . . . **61** 57 28N 10 31 E
Fredrikstad . . . . **60** 59 13N 10 57 E
Freeport, Bahamas **178** 26 30N 78 47W
Freeport, Ill., U.S.A. **166** 42 18N 89 40W
Freeport, N.Y., U.S.A. **164** 40 39N 73 35W
Freeport, Tex., U.S.A. **158** 28 55N 95 22W
Freetown **130** 8 30N 13 17W
Freiberg . . . . **42** 50 55N 13 20 E
Freibourg = Fribourg . . . . . . **44** 46 49N 7 9 E
Fréjus . . . . **37** 43 25N 6 44 E
Fremantle . . . . **120** 32 7S 115 47 E
Fremont, Calif., U.S.A. **172** 37 32N 122 1W
Fremont, Nebr., U.S.A. **166** 41 30N 96 30W
French Guiana ■ **185** 4 0N 53 0W
French Pass . . . . **123** 40 55S 173 55 E
French Terr. of Afars & Issas
= Djibouti ■ . . . . **133** 12 0N 43 0 E
Fresnillo **175** 23 10N 102 53W
Fresno **173** 36 47N 119 50W
Fria, C. . . . . **136** 18 0S 12 0 E
Frías **190** 28 40S 65 5W
Fribourg . . . . **44** 46 49N 7 9 E
Friendly, Is. = Tonga ■ **123** 19 50S 174 30W
Friesland □ . . . . **41** 53 5N 5 50 E
Frio, C. **182** 22 50S 41 50W
Friuli-Venezia Giulia □ . . . . . **47** 46 0N 13 0 E
Frobisher B. **146** 62 30N 66 0W
Frobisher Bay **146** 63 44N 68 31W
Frobisher L. **152** 56 20N 108 15W
Frome **27** 51 16N 2 17W
Frome, L. . . . . **118** 30 45S 139 45 E
Frome Downs . . . . **118** 31 13S 139 45 E
Front Range **163** 40 0N 105 40W
Front Royal **164** 38 55N 78 10W
Frontera **177** 18 32N 92 38W
Frostburg **164** 39 43N 78 57W
Frunze = Bishkek . . . . **71** 42 54N 74 46 E
Frutal **188** 20 0S 49 0W
Fuchou = Fuzhou . . . . **99** 26 5N 119 16 E
Fuchū, Hiroshima, Japan . . . **109** 34 34N 133 14 E
Fūchū, Tōkyō, Japan . . . . . . **107** 35 40N 139 29 E
Fuerte, R. → **174** 25 54N 109 22W
Fuji . . . . **107** 35 9N 138 39 E
Fuji-no-miya . . . . **107** 35 10N 138 40 E
Fuji-San . . . . **107** 35 22N 138 44 E
Fuji-yoshida . . . . **107** 35 30N 138 46 E
Fujian □ . . . . **99** 26 0N 118 0 E
Fujieda . . . . **107** 34 52N 138 16 E
Fujisawa . . . . **107** 35 22N 139 29 E
Fukaya . . . . **107** 36 12N 139 12 E
Fukien = Fujian □ . . . . **99** 26 0N 118 0 E
Fukuchiyama . . . . **106** 35 19N 135 9 E
Fukue-Shima . . . . **104** 32 40N 128 45 E
Fukui . . . . **106** 36 0N 136 10 E
Fukuoka . . . . **108** 33 39N 130 21 E
Fukushima . . . . **103** 37 44N 140 28 E
Fukuyama . . . . **109** 34 35N 133 20 E
Fulton, Mo., U.S.A. **166** 38 50N 91 55W
Fulton, N.Y., U.S.A. **164** 43 20N 76 22W
Funabashi . . . . **107** 35 45N 140 0 E
Funchal **126** 32 38N 16 54W
Fundación **184** 10 31N 74 11W
Fundy, B. of **148** 45 0N 66 0W
Furāt, Nahr al → . . . . **84** 31 0N 47 25 E
Furneaux Group . . . . **119** 40 10S 147 50 E
Furness **28** 54 14N 3 8W
Fürth . . . . **43** 49 29N 11 0 E

Fury and Hecla Str. **146** 69 56N 84 0W
Fushun .... **98** 41 50N 123 55 E
Fuxin .... **98** 42 5N 121 48 E
Fuzhou .... **99** 26 5N 119 16 E
Fylde **28** 53 50N   2 58W
Fyn .... **61** 55 20N 10 30 E
Fyne, L. **30** 56 0N   5 20W

G

Gabès, Golfe de .... **127** 34 0N 10 30 E
Gabon ■ .... **134** 0 10S 10 0 E
Gaborone .... **137** 24 45S 25 57 E
Gachsārān .... **85** 30 15N 50 45 E
Gadag .... **90** 15 30N 75 45 E
Gadsden **169** 34 1N 86 0W
Gaeta .... **49** 41 12N 13 35 E
Gaffney **165** 35 3N 81 40W
Gagnon **141** 51 50N 68 5W
Gainesville, Fla., U.S.A. **170** 29 38N 82 20W
Gainesville, Ga., U.S.A. **165** 34 17N 83 47W
Gainesville, Tex., U.S.A. **168** 33 40N 97 10W
Gainsborough **29** 53 23N   0 46W
Gairdner L. .... **118** 31 30S 136 0 E
Galápagos **10** 0 0 89 0W
Galas ⤳ .... **96** 4 55N 101 57 E
Galashiels **31** 55 37N   2 50W
Galaţi .... **57** 45 27N 28 2 E
Galatina .... **49** 40 10N 18 10 E
Galdhøpiggen .... **60** 61 38N   8 18 E
Galesburg **166** 40 57N 90 23W
Galicia □ **50** 42 43N   7 45W
Galilee, L. .... **121** 22 20S 145 50 E
Gallatin **169** 36 24N 86 27W
Galle .... **90** 6 5N 80 10 E
Gallinas, Pta. **184** 12 28N 71 40W
Gallipoli = Gelibolu .... **80** 40 28N 26 43 E
Gallipoli .... **49** 40 8N 18 0 E
Gällivare .... **66** 67 9N 20 40 E
Galloway **31** 55 0N   4 25W
Galloway, Mull of **30** 54 38N   4 50W
Gallup **161** 35 30N 108 45W
Galty Mts. **35** 52 22N   8 10W
Galveston **168** 29 15N 94 48W
Galveston B. **168** 29 30N 94 50W
Galway **35** 53 16N   9 4W
Galway □ **34** 53 16N   9 3W
Gamagori .... **106** 34 50N 137 14 E
Gambia ■ **130** 13 25N 16 0W
Gambia ⤳ **130** 13 28N 16 34W
Gand = Gent .... **42** 51 2N   3 42 E
Gander **149** 48 58N 54 35W
Gandhi Sagar .... **91** 24 40N 75 40 E
Gandi .... **131** 12 55N   5 49 E
Ganga ⤳ .... **92** 23 20N 90 30 E
Ganges = Ganga ⤳ ..... **92** 23 20N 90 30 E
Gangtok .... **92** 27 20N 88 37 E
Gannett Pk. **163** 43 15N 109 38W
Gansu □ .... **98** 36 0N 104 0 E
Ganzhou .... **99** 25 51N 114 56 E
Gao **130** 16 15N   0 5W
Gaoxiong .... **99** 22 38N 120 18 E
Garachiné **179** 8 0N 78 12W
Garanhuns **189** 8 50S 36 30W
Garberville **172** 40 11N 123 50W
Garda, L. di .... **46** 45 40N 10 40 E
Garden City **161** 38 0N 100 45W
Garden Grove **173** 33 47N 117 55W
Gardēz .... **87** 33 37N 69 9 E
Garmsār .... **86** 35 20N 52 25 E
Garonne ⤳ **36** 45 2N   0 36W
Garoua .... **131** 9 19N 13 21 E
Garrison Res. = Sakakawea,
  L. **163** 47 30N 102 0W
Garry L. **145** 65 58N 100 18W
Garvie Mts. .... **123** 45 30S 168 50 E
Garwa = Garoua .... **131** 9 19N 13 21 E
Gary **167** 41 35N 87 20W

Garzón **184** 2 10N 75 40W
Gascogne .... **36** 43 45N   0 20 E
Gascony = Gascogne .... **36** 43 45N   0 20 E
Gaspé **148** 48 52N 64 30W
Gaspé, C. de **148** 48 48N 64 7W
Gaspé, Pén. de **148** 48 45N 65 40W
Gastonia **165** 35 17N 81 10W
Gastre **192** 42 20S 69 15W
Gata, C. de **51** 36 41N   2 13W
Gateshead **28** 54 57N   1 37W
Gauhati .... **93** 26 10N 91 45 E
Gävle .... **60** 60 40N 17 9 E
Gävleborgs län □ .... **60** 61 30N 16 15 E
Gawilgarh Hills .... **91** 21 15N 76 45 E
Gawler .... **119** 34 30S 138 42 E
Gawler Ranges .... **114** 32 30S 135 45 E
Gaxun Nur .... **100** 42 22N 100 30 E
Gaya .... **92** 24 47N 85 4 E
Gaylord **150** 45 1N 84 41W
Gayndah .... **116** 25 35S 151 32 E
Gaza .... **80** 31 30N 34 28 E
Gaziantep .... **80** 37 6N 37 23 E
Gdańsk .... **58** 54 22N 18 40 E
Gdańska, Zatoka .... **58** 54 30N 19 20 E
Gdynia .... **58** 54 35N 18 33 E
Gedaref .... **129** 14 2N 35 28 E
Geelong .... **117** 38 10S 144 22 E
Gejiu .... **99** 23 20N 103 10 E
Gelderland □ .... **41** 52 5N   6 10 E
Geldermalsen .... **40** 51 53N   5 17 E
Geldrop .... **41** 51 25N   5 32 E
Geleen .... **41** 50 57N   5 49 E
Gelibolu .... **80** 40 28N 26 43 E
Gelsenkirchen .... **42** 51 30N   7 5 E
Gemert .... **41** 51 33N   5 41 E
General Alvear **190** 35 0S 67 40W
General Pico **190** 35 45S 63 50W
Geneva = Genève .... **44** 46 12N   6 9 E
Geneva **164** 42 53N 77 0W
Geneva, L. = Léman, Lac .. **44** 46 26N   6 30 E
Genève .... **44** 46 12N   6 9 E
Genk .... **41** 50 58N   5 32 E
Genkai-Nada .... **108** 34 0N 130 0 E
Gennargentu, Mti. del .... **48** 40 0N   9 10 E
Genoa = Génova .... **46** 44 24N   8 56 E
Génova .... **46** 44 24N   8 56 E
Génova, Golfo di .... **46** 44 0N   9 0 E
Gent .... **42** 51 2N   3 42 E
George, L. .... **132** 0 5N 30 10 E
George River = Port
  Nouveau-Québec **146** 58 30N 65 59W
George Town .... **96** 5 25N 100 15 E
Georgetown, Australia .... **119** 18 17S 143 33 E
Georgetown, Canada **151** 43 40N 79 56W
Georgetown, Guyana **185** 6 50N 58 12W
Georgetown, U.S.A. **170** 33 22N 79 15W
Georgia □ **170** 32 0N 82 0W
Georgia ■ .... **70** 42 0N 43 0 E
Georgian B. **151** 45 15N 81 0W
Gera .... **43** 50 53N 12 11 E
Geraldton, Australia ...... **120** 28 48S 114 32 E
Geraldton, Canada **150** 49 44N 86 59W
Gereshk .... **87** 31 47N 64 35 E
Germany ■ .... **18** 52 0N 12 0 E
Germiston .... **137** 26 15S 28 10 E
Gerona .... **51** 41 58N   2 46 E
Ghana ■ **130** 6 0N   1 0W
Ghat .... **127** 24 59N 10 11 E
Ghawdex = Gozo .... **49** 36 0N 14 13 E
Ghaziabad .... **89** 28 42N 77 26 E
Ghazipur .... **92** 25 38N 83 35 E
Ghaznī .... **87** 33 30N 68 28 E
Ghaznī □ .... **87** 32 10N 68 20 E
Ghent = Gent .... **42** 51 2N   3 42 E
Ghowr □ .... **87** 34 0N 64 20 E
Ghulam Mohammad Barrage **88** 25 30N 68 20 E
Giant's Causeway **34** 55 15N   6 30W
Gibara **178** 21 9N 76 11W
Gibraltar **50** 36 7N   5 22W
Gibraltar, Str. of **50** 35 55N   5 40W
Gien .... **39** 47 40N   2 36 E

Place	Page	Lat.	Long.
Gifu	**106**	35 30N	136 45 E
Gigha	**30**	55 42N	5 45W
Gijón	**50**	43 32N	5 42W
Gila →	**173**	32 43N	114 33W
Gīlān □	**81**	37 0N	50 0 E
Gilbert Is. = Kiribati ■	**122**	1 0N	176 0 E
Gilford I.	**154**	50 40N	126 30W
Gilgandra	**116**	31 43S	148 39 E
Gilgit	**89**	35 50N	74 15 E
Gillingham	**25**	51 23N	0 34 E
Gingin	**120**	31 22S	115 54 E
Gippsland	**117**	37 45S	147 15 E
Girardot	**184**	4 18N	74 48W
Giresun	**81**	40 55N	38 30 E
Gironde →	**36**	45 32N	1 7W
Girvan	**30**	55 15N	4 50W
Gisborne	**122**	38 39S	178 5 E
Gisors	**39**	49 15N	1 47 E
Gizhiga	**73**	62 3N	160 30 E
Gizhiginskaya, Guba	**73**	61 0N	158 0 E
Giźycko	**58**	54 2N	21 48 E
Gjoa Haven	**145**	68 20N	96 8W
Glace Bay	**149**	46 11N	59 58W
Gladstone, Queens., Australia	**121**	23 52S	151 16 E
Gladstone, S. Austral., Australia	**118**	33 15S	138 22 E
Gláma	**64**	65 48N	23 0W
Glasgow, U.K.	**31**	55 52N	4 14W
Glasgow, U.S.A.	**169**	37 2N	85 55W
Glastonbury	**27**	51 9N	2 42W
Gleiwitz = Gliwice	**58**	50 22N	18 41 E
Glen Coe	**32**	56 40N	5 0W
Glen Innes	**116**	29 44S	151 44 E
Glen Mor	**33**	57 12N	4 37 E
Glenburgh	**120**	25 26S	116 6 E
Glendale	**173**	34 7N	118 18W
Glendive	**163**	47 7N	104 40W
Glenelg	**119**	34 58S	138 31 E
Glenns Ferry	**172**	43 0N	115 15W
Glenorchy	**119**	42 49S	147 18 E
Glenrothes	**31**	56 12N	3 11W
Glens Falls	**164**	43 20N	73 40W
Gliwice	**58**	50 22N	18 41 E
Głogów	**58**	51 37N	16 5 E
Glossop	**28**	53 27N	1 56W
Gloucester	**24**	51 52N	2 15W
Gloucestershire □	**24**	51 44N	2 10W
Gloversville	**164**	43 5N	74 18W
Gniezno	**58**	52 30N	17 35 E
Go Cong	**95**	10 22N	106 40 E
Goa	**91**	15 33N	73 59 E
Goa □	**90**	15 33N	73 59 E
Goat Fell	**30**	55 37N	5 11W
Goba	**133**	7 1N	39 59 E
Gobi	**98**	44 0N	111 0 E
Gobō	**106**	33 53N	135 10 E
Godavari →	**91**	16 25N	82 18 E
Godbout	**148**	49 20N	67 38W
Goderich	**150**	43 45N	81 41W
Godhra	**91**	22 49N	73 40 E
Gods L.	**153**	54 40N	94 15W
Godthåb	**147**	64 10N	51 35W
Goeie Hoop, Kaap die	**136**	34 24S	18 30 E
Goeree	**40**	51 50N	4 0 E
Goes	**40**	51 30N	3 55 E
Gogama	**151**	47 35N	81 43W
Goiânia	**188**	16 43S	49 20W
Goiás □	**188**	12 10S	48 0W
Goirle	**40**	51 31N	5 4 E
Gojō	**106**	34 21N	135 42 E
Gökçeada	**55**	40 10N	25 50 E
Gold Coast, Australia	**116**	28 0S	153 25 E
Gold Coast, W. Afr.	**124**	4 0N	1 40W
Golden Bay	**122**	40 40S	172 50 E
Golden Gate	**172**	37 54N	122 30W
Golden Hinde	**154**	49 40N	125 44W
Golden Vale	**35**	52 33N	8 17W
Goldfield	**172**	37 45N	117 13W
Goldsboro	**165**	35 24N	77 59W
Goldsworthy	**114**	20 21S	119 30 E
Golfo Aranci	**48**	41 0N	9 35 E
Gomel	**68**	52 28N	31 0 E
Gómez Palacio	**174**	25 34N	103 30W
Gonābād	**86**	34 15N	58 45 E
Gonaïves	**180**	19 20N	72 42W
Gonda	**92**	27 9N	81 58 E
Gonder	**132**	12 39N	37 30 E
Good Hope, C. of = Goeie Hoop, Kaap die	**136**	34 24S	18 30 E
Goole	**29**	53 42N	0 52W
Goondiwindi	**116**	28 30S	150 21 E
Goose Bay	**147**	53 15N	60 20W
Gorakhpur	**92**	26 47N	83 23 E
Gordonvale	**121**	17 5S	145 50 E
Gore, Ethiopia	**132**	8 12N	35 32 E
Gore, N.Z.	**123**	46 5S	168 58 E
Gorey	**35**	52 41N	6 18W
Gorinchem	**40**	51 50N	4 59 E
Gorkiy = Nizhniy Novgorod	**68**	56 20N	44 0 E
Görlitz	**43**	51 10N	14 59 E
Gorna Oryakhovitsa	**53**	43 7N	25 40 E
Gort	**35**	53 4N	8 50W
Gorzów Wielkopolski	**58**	52 43N	15 15 E
Gosford	**117**	33 23S	151 18 E
Gospič	**52**	44 35N	15 23 E
Gosport	**25**	50 48N	1 8W
Göteborg	**60**	57 43N	11 59 E
Göteborgs och Bohus län □	**60**	58 30N	11 30 E
Gotemba	**107**	35 18N	138 56 E
Gotha	**43**	50 56N	10 42 E
Gotland	**60**	57 30N	18 33 E
Gōtsu	**109**	35 0N	132 14 E
Gottwaldov = Zlin	**59**	49 14N	17 40 E
Gouda	**40**	52 1N	4 42 E
Gouin, Rés.	**151**	48 35N	74 40W
Goulburn	**117**	34 44S	149 44 E
Goundam	**130**	16 25N	3 45W
Gournay-en-Bray	**38**	49 29N	1 44 E
Governador Valadares	**188**	18 15S	41 57W
Governor's Harbour	**178**	25 10N	76 14W
Gower, The	**27**	51 35N	4 10W
Goya	**190**	29 10S	59 10W
Gozo	**49**	36 0N	14 13 E
Graaff-Reinet	**136**	32 13S	24 32 E
Gracias a Dios, C.	**179**	15 0N	83 10W
Grafton	**116**	29 38S	152 58 E
Graham	**165**	36 5N	79 22W
Graham I.	**154**	53 40N	132 30W
Graham Land	**14**	65 0S	64 0W
Grahamstown	**137**	33 19S	26 31 E
Grain Coast	**124**	4 20N	10 0W
Grampian □	**33**	57 0N	3 0W
Grampian Mts.	**33**	56 50N	4 0W
Grampians, The	**119**	37 0S	142 20 E
Gran Chaco	**190**	25 0S	61 0W
Gran Sasso d'Italia	**47**	42 25N	13 30 E
Granada, Nic.	**179**	11 58N	86 0W
Granada, Spain	**50**	37 10N	3 35W
Granby	**151**	45 25N	72 45W
Grand Bank	**149**	47 6N	55 48W
Grand Bassam	**130**	5 10N	3 49W
Grand Canyon	**160**	36 3N	112 9W
Grand Cayman	**178**	19 20N	81 20W
Grand Cess	**130**	4 40N	8 12W
Grand Falls	**149**	48 56N	55 40W
Grand Forks, Canada	**155**	49 0N	118 30W
Grand Forks, U.S.A.	**156**	48 0N	97 3W
Grand Island	**163**	40 59N	98 25W
Grand Junction	**163**	39 0N	108 30W
Grand Mère	**151**	46 36N	72 40W
Grand Portage	**150**	47 58N	89 41W
Grand Rapids, Canada	**153**	53 12N	99 19W
Grand Rapids, U.S.A.	**167**	42 57N	86 40W
Grand St.-Bernard, Col. du	**44**	45 53N	7 11 E
Grand Teton	**163**	43 54N	111 50W
Grand View	**153**	51 10N	100 42W
Grande →, Bolivia	**187**	15 51S	64 39W
Grande →, Brazil	**188**	20 6S	51 4W
Grande, B.	**192**	50 30S	68 20W
Grande, La	**171**	45 15N	118 0W
Grande, La →	**140**	53 50N	79 0W
Grande Baleine, R. de la →	**140**	55 16N	77 47W

Grande de Santiago, R. →►	**175**	21 36N	105 26W
Grande Prairie	**155**	55 10N	118 50W
Grande-Rivière	**148**	48 26N	64 30W
Grange, La	**170**	33 4N	85 0W
Grangemouth	**31**	56 1N	3 43W
Grangeville	**162**	45 57N	116 4W
Granite City	**166**	38 45N	90 3W
Grant, Mt.	**172**	38 34N	118 48W
Grantham	**29**	52 55N	0 39W
Grantown-on-Spey	**33**	57 19N	3 36W
Grants Pass	**171**	42 30N	123 22W
Grass Valley	**172**	39 18N	121 0W
Grasse	**37**	43 38N	6 56 E
Gravelbourg	**152**	49 50N	106 35W
Gravelines	**38**	51 0N	2 10 E
's-Gravenhage	**40**	52 7N	4 17 E
Gravesend	**25**	51 25N	0 22 E
Grayling	**167**	44 40N	84 42W
Graz	**45**	47 4N	15 27 E
Great Abaco I.	**178**	26 25N	77 10W
Great Australian Bight	**114**	33 30S	130 0 E
Great Bahama Bank	**178**	23 15N	78 0W
Great Barrier I.	**122**	36 11S	175 25 E
Great Barrier Reef	**121**	18 0S	146 50 E
Great Basin	**172**	40 0N	116 30W
Great Bear L.	**145**	65 30N	120 0W
Great Britain	**16**	54 0N	2 15W
Great Divide, The	**117**	35 0S	149 17 E
Great Dividing Ra.	**121**	23 0S	146 0 E
Great Exuma I.	**178**	23 30N	75 50W
Great Falls	**163**	47 27N	111 12W
Great Inagua I.	**180**	21 0N	73 20W
Great Indian Desert = Thar Desert	**89**	28 0N	72 0 E
Great Orme's Head	**26**	53 20N	3 52W
Great Ouse →►	**29**	52 47N	0 22 E
Great Plains	**138**	47 0N	105 0W
Great Salt Lake	**162**	41 0N	112 30W
Great Salt Lake Desert	**162**	40 20N	113 50W
Great Slave L.	**145**	61 23N	115 38W
Great Wall	**98**	38 30N	109 30 E
Great Whernside	**28**	54 9N	1 59W
Great Yarmouth	**29**	52 40N	1 45 E
Greater Antilles	**181**	17 40N	74 0W
Greater Manchester □	**28**	53 30N	2 15W
Greater Sunda Is.	**111**	2 30S	110 0 E
Gredos, Sierra de	**50**	40 20N	5 0W
Greece ■	**54**	40 0N	23 0 E
Greeley	**163**	40 30N	104 40W
Green →►, Ky., U.S.A.	**167**	37 54N	87 30W
Green →►, Utah, U.S.A.	**163**	38 11N	109 53W
Green Bay	**167**	44 30N	88 0W
Greenfield	**164**	42 38N	72 38W
Greenland □	**147**	66 0N	45 0W
Greenland Sea	**13**	73 0N	10 0W
Greenock	**30**	55 57N	4 46W
Greensboro	**165**	36 7N	79 46W
Greenville, Ala., U.S.A.	**169**	31 50N	86 37W
Greenville, Mich., U.S.A.	**167**	43 12N	85 14W
Greenville, Miss., U.S.A.	**168**	33 25N	91 0W
Greenville, N.C., U.S.A.	**165**	35 37N	77 26W
Greenville, S.C., U.S.A.	**165**	34 54N	82 24W
Greenville, Tenn., U.S.A.	**165**	36 13N	82 51W
Greenwood, Miss., U.S.A.	**169**	33 30N	90 4W
Greenwood, S.C., U.S.A.	**165**	34 13N	82 13W
Grenada	**169**	33 45N	89 50W
Grenada ■	**180**	12 10N	61 40W
Grenoble	**37**	45 12N	5 42 E
Grenville	**117**	37 46S	143 52 E
Gretna Green	**31**	55 0N	3 3W
Grey Range	**116**	27 0S	143 30 E
Grey Res.	**149**	48 20N	56 30W
Greymouth	**123**	42 29S	171 13 E
Griffin	**170**	33 17N	84 14W
Griffith	**117**	34 18S	146 2 E
Grimsby	**29**	53 35N	0 5W
Grimshaw	**155**	56 10N	117 40W
Grinnell	**166**	41 45N	92 43W
Grodno	**68**	53 42N	23 52 E
Groningen	**41**	53 15N	6 35 E
Groningen □	**41**	53 16N	6 40 E
Grootfontein	**136**	19 31S	18 6 E
Groznyy	**70**	43 20N	45 45 E
Grudziądz	**58**	53 30N	18 47 E
Grytviken	**14**	53 50S	37 10W
Gt. Stour = Stour →►	**25**	51 15N	1 20 E
Guadalajara, Mexico	**175**	20 40N	103 20W
Guadalajara, Spain	**50**	40 37N	3 12W
Guadalquivir →►	**50**	36 47N	6 22W
Guadalupe = Guadeloupe ■	**180**	16 20N	61 40W
Guadalupe Bravos	**174**	31 23N	106 7W
Guadarrama, Sierra de	**50**	41 0N	4 0W
Guadeloupe ■	**180**	16 20N	61 40W
Guadiana →►	**50**	37 14N	7 22W
Guadix	**50**	37 18N	3 11W
Guaira	**191**	24 5S	54 10W
Guajará-Mirim	**187**	10 50S	65 20W
Gualeguay	**190**	33 10S	59 14W
Gualeguaychú	**190**	33 3S	59 31W
Guam	**10**	13 27N	144 45 E
Guanabacoa	**178**	23 8N	82 18W
Guanacaste, Cordillera del	**179**	10 40N	85 4W
Guanahani = San Salvador	**178**	24 0N	74 40W
Guanajay	**178**	22 56N	82 42W
Guanajuato	**177**	21 1N	101 15W
Guanajuato □	**177**	21 0N	101 0W
Guanare	**184**	8 42N	69 12W
Guangdong □	**99**	23 0N	113 0 E
Guangxi Zhuangzu Zizhiqu □	**99**	24 0N	109 0 E
Guangzhou	**99**	23 5N	113 10 E
Guantánamo	**178**	20 10N	75 14W
Guaporé →►	**187**	11 55S	65 4W
Guaqui	**187**	16 41S	68 54W
Guarapuava	**191**	25 20S	51 30W
Guarda	**50**	40 32N	7 20W
Guardafui, C. = Asir, Ras	**133**	11 55N	51 10 E
Guatemala	**177**	14 40N	90 22W
Guatemala ■	**177**	15 40N	90 30W
Guaviare →►	**184**	4 3N	67 44W
Guayama	**180**	17 59N	66 7W
Guayaquil	**184**	2 15S	79 52W
Guayaquil, G. de	**186**	3 10S	81 0W
Guaymas	**174**	27 56N	110 54W
Guddu Barrage	**89**	28 30N	69 50 E
Gudur	**90**	14 12N	79 55 E
Guelph	**151**	43 35N	80 20W
Guernica	**50**	43 19N	2 40W
Guernsey	**36**	49 30N	2 35W
Guerrero □	**177**	17 40N	100 0W
Guilin	**99**	25 18N	110 15 E
Guimarães	**188**	2 9S	44 42W
Guinea ■	**130**	10 20N	10 0W
Guinea, Gulf of	**130**	3 0N	2 30 E
Guinea-Bissau ■	**130**	12 0N	15 0W
Güines	**178**	22 50N	82 0W
Guiyang	**99**	26 32N	106 40 E
Guizhou □	**99**	27 0N	107 0 E
Gujarat □	**91**	23 20N	71 0 E
Gujranwala	**89**	32 10N	74 12 E
Gujrat	**89**	32 40N	74 2 E
Gulbarga	**91**	17 20N	76 50 E
Gulf, The	**85**	27 0N	50 0 E
Gulfport	**169**	30 21N	89 3W
Gulgong	**116**	32 20S	149 49 E
Gull Lake	**152**	50 10N	108 29W
Gümüsane	**81**	40 30N	39 30 E
Guna	**91**	24 40N	77 19 E
Gundagai	**117**	35 3S	148 6 E
Gunnedah	**116**	30 59S	150 15 E
Gunningbar Cr. →►	**116**	31 14S	147 6 E
Guntakal	**90**	15 11N	77 27 E
Guntersville	**169**	34 18N	86 16W
Guntur	**92**	16 23N	80 30 E
Gurdaspur	**89**	32 5N	75 31 E
Gurgaon	**89**	28 27N	77 1 E
Gurkha	**92**	28 5N	84 40 E
Gurupi →►	**188**	1 13S	46 6W
Guryev	**70**	47 5N	52 0 E
Gusau	**131**	12 12N	6 40 E
Guthrie	**168**	35 55N	97 30W
Guyana ■	**185**	5 0N	59 0W
Guyenne	**36**	44 30N	0 40 E

Guyra	116	30 15S	151	40 E
Gwalior	91	26 12N	78	10 E
Gwent □	27	51 45N	2	55W
Gweru	137	19 28S	29	45 E
Gwynedd □	26	53 0N	4	0W
Gyandzha	70	40 45N	46	20 E
Gyaring Hu	101	34 50N	97	40 E
Gydanskiy P-ov.	69	70 0N	78	0 E
Gympie	116	26 11S	152	38 E
Gyoda	107	36 10N	139	30 E
Gyöngyös	59	47 48N	20	0 E
Györ	59	47 41N	17	40 E
Gypsumville	153	51 45N	98	40W

H

Ha 'Arava	80	30 50N	35	20 E
Ha Giang	95	22 50N	104	59 E
Haarlem	40	52 23N	4	39 E
Habana, La	178	23 8N	82	22W
Hachijō-Jima	105	33 5N	139	45 E
Hachinohe	103	40 30N	141	29 E
Hachiōji	107	35 40N	139	20 E
Hadera	80	32 27N	34	55 E
Hadhramaut = Hadramawt	83	15 30N	49	30 E
Hadiya	82	25 30N	36	56 E
Hadramawt	83	15 30N	49	30 E
Hadrians Wall	28	55 0N	2	30W
Haeju	98	38 3N	125	45 E
Haerhpin = Harbin	98	45 48N	126	40 E
Hafar al Bāṭin	82	28 25N	46	0 E
Hafnarfjörður	64	64 4N	21	57W
Haft-Gel	84	31 30N	49	32 E
Hagen	42	51 21N	7	29 E
Hagerstown	164	39 39N	77	46W
Hagi	108	34 30N	131	22 E
Hags Hd.	35	52 57N	9	30W
Hague, The = 's-Gravenhage	40	52 7N	4	17 E
Hai'an	99	32 37N	120	27 E
Haifa = Ḥefa	80	32 46N	35	0 E
Haikou	99	20 1N	110	16 E
Ḥā'il	82	27 28N	41	45 E
Hailar	98	49 10N	119	38 E
Hailey	162	43 30N	114	15W
Haileybury	151	47 30N	79	38W
Hainan	99	19 0N	110	0 E
Hainan Dao	99	19 0N	109	30 E
Haiphong	95	20 47N	106	41 E
Haiti ■	180	19 0N	72	30W
Hakken-Zan	106	34 10N	135	54 E
Hakodate	103	41 45N	140	44 E
Ḥalab	80	36 10N	37	15 E
Halaib	129	22 12N	36	30 E
Halberstadt	43	51 53N	11	2 E
Halfmoon Bay	123	46 50S	168	5 E
Halifax, Canada	148	44 38N	63	35W
Halifax, U.K.	28	53 43N	1	51W
Halifax B.	121	18 50S	147	0 E
Hallands län □	61	56 50N	12	50 E
Halle	43	51 29N	12	0 E
Halls Creek	114	18 16S	127	38 E
Halmahera	113	0 40N	128	0 E
Halmstad	61	56 41N	12	52 E
Hälsingborg = Helsingborg	61	56 3N	12	42 E
Hamada	109	34 56N	132	4 E
Hamadān	81	34 52N	48	32 E
Hamadān □	81	35 0N	49	0 E
Hamāh	80	35 5N	36	40 E
Hamakita	107	34 45N	137	47 E
Hamamatsu	106	34 45N	137	45 E
Hamar	60	60 48N	11	7 E
Hamburg	43	53 32N	9	59 E
Hämeenlinna	67	61 0N	24	28 E
Hamelin Pool	120	26 22S	114	20 E
Hameln	42	52 7N	9	24 E
Hamhung	98	39 54N	127	30 E
Hamilton, Australia	119	37 45S	142	2 E
Hamilton, Bermuda	180	32 15N	64	45W

Hamilton, Canada	151	43 15N	79	50W
Hamilton, N.Z.	122	37 47S	175	19 E
Hamilton, U.K.	31	55 47N	4	2W
Hamilton, U.S.A.	167	39 20N	84	35W
Hamm	42	51 40N	7	49 E
Hammerfest	67	70 39N	23	41 E
Hammond, Ind., U.S.A.	167	41 40N	87	30W
Hammond, La., U.S.A.	169	30 32N	90	30W
Hampshire □	25	51 3N	1	20W
Hampshire Downs	25	51 10N	1	10W
Hampton	165	37 4N	76	18W
Hanamaki	103	39 23N	141	7 E
Hancock	150	47 10N	88	40W
Handa	106	34 53N	137	0 E
Handan	98	36 35N	114	28 E
Haney	154	49 12N	122	40W
Hanford	173	36 23N	119	39W
Hangayn Nuruu	100	47 30N	100	0 E
Hangchou = Hangzhou	99	30 18N	120	11 E
Hangö	67	59 50N	22	57 E
Hangu	98	39 18N	117	53 E
Hangzhou	99	30 18N	120	11 E
Hanna	155	51 40N	111	54W
Hannibal	166	39 42N	91	22W
Hannover	42	52 23N	9	43 E
Hanoi	95	21 5N	105	55 E
Hanover = Hannover	42	52 23N	9	43 E
Hanover, N.H., U.S.A.	148	43 43N	72	17W
Hanover, Pa., U.S.A.	164	39 46N	76	59W
Hansi	89	29 10N	75	57 E
Hanyū	107	36 10N	139	32 E
Hanzhong	99	33 10N	107	1 E
Haora	92	22 37N	88	20 E
Haparanda	67	65 52N	24	8 E
Ḥaraḍ, Si. Arabia	83	24 22N	49	0 E
Ḥaraḍ, Yemen	83	16 26N	43	5 E
Harare	137	17 43S	31	2 E
Harbin	98	45 48N	126	40 E
Harbour Breton	149	47 29N	55	50W
Harbour Grace	149	47 40N	53	22W
Hardap Dam	136	24 32S	17	50 E
Hardenberg	41	52 34N	6	37 E
Harderwijk	41	52 21N	5	38 E
Hardinxveld	40	51 49N	4	53 E
Hardwar = Haridwar	89	29 58N	78	9 E
Harer	133	9 20N	42	8 E
Harfleur	38	49 30N	0	10 E
Hargeisa	133	9 30N	44	2 E
Hari →	111	1 16S	104	5 E
Haridwar	89	29 58N	78	9 E
Harima-Nada	109	34 30N	134	35 E
Harīrūd →	86	34 20N	62	30 E
Harlech	26	52 52N	4	7W
Harlingen, Neths.	41	53 11N	5	25 E
Harlingen, U.S.A.	161	26 20N	97	50W
Harlow	25	51 47N	0	9 E
Harney Basin	171	43 30N	119	0W
Härnösand	66	62 38N	18	0 E
Harriman	169	36 0N	84	35W
Harris	32	57 50N	6	55W
Harris L.	118	31 10S	135	10 E
Harrisburg, Ill., U.S.A.	167	37 42N	88	30W
Harrisburg, Pa., U.S.A.	164	40 18N	76	52W
Harrison	168	36 10N	93	4W
Harrison, C.	147	54 55N	57	55W
Harrison B.	142	70 25N	151	30W
Harrisonburg	165	38 28N	78	52W
Harrogate	28	53 59N	1	32W
Harrow	25	51 35N	0	15W
Hartford	164	41 47N	72	41W
Hartland Pt.	27	51 2N	4	32W
Hartlepool	29	54 42N	1	11W
Hartsville	165	34 23N	80	2W
Harvey, Australia	120	33 5S	115	54 E
Harvey, U.S.A.	167	41 40N	87	40W
Harwich	25	51 56N	1	18 E
Haryana □	89	29 0N	76	10 E
Hashima	106	35 20N	136	40 E
Hashimoto	106	34 19N	135	37 E
Hastings, N.Z.	122	39 39S	176	52 E
Hastings, U.K.	25	50 51N	0	36 E

Hastings, U.S.A.	**163**	40 34N	98	22W
Hastings Ra.	**116**	31 15S	152	14 E
Hatano	**107**	35 22N	139	14 E
Hathras	**89**	27 36N	78	6 E
Hatteras, C.	**165**	35 10N	75	30W
Hattiesburg	**169**	31 20N	89	20W
Hatvan	**59**	47 40N	19	45 E
Hau Bon = Cheo Reo	**95**	13 25N	108	28 E
Hauraki Gulf	**122**	36 35S	175	5 E
Haut Atlas	**126**	32 30N	5	0W
Havana = Habana, La	**178**	23 8N	82	22W
Havant	**25**	50 51N	0	59W
Havelock	**151**	44 26N	77	53W
Haverfordwest	**26**	51 48N	4	59W
Haverhill	**164**	42 50N	71	2W
Havre	**163**	48 34N	109	40W
Havre, Le	**38**	49 30N	0	5 E
Hawaii □	**160**	20 30N	157	0W
Hawaiian Is.	**160**	20 30N	156	0W
Hawea Lake	**123**	44 28S	169	19 E
Hawera	**122**	39 35S	174	19 E
Hawick	**31**	55 25N	2	48W
Hawke B.	**122**	39 25S	177	20 E
Hawkesbury	**151**	45 37N	74	37W
Hawthorne	**172**	38 31N	118	37W
Hay, Australia	**117**	34 30S	144	51 E
Hay, U.K.	**26**	52 4N	3	9W
Hay River	**145**	60 51N	115	44W
Hayward's Heath	**25**	51 0N	0	5W
Hazard	**165**	37 18N	83	10W
Hazaribag	**92**	23 58N	85	26 E
Hazebrouck	**38**	50 42N	2	31 E
Hazelton	**154**	55 20N	127	42W
Hazleton	**164**	40 58N	76	0W
Healdsburg	**172**	38 33N	122	51W
Healesville	**117**	37 35S	145	30 E
Heanor	**29**	53 1N	1	20W
Hearst	**150**	49 40N	83	41W
Hebei □	**98**	39 0N	116	0 E
Hebel	**116**	28 58S	147	47 E
Hebrides	**16**	57 30N	7	0W
Hebron = Al Khalīl	**80**	31 32N	35	6 E
Hebron	**147**	58 5N	62	30W
Hecate Str.	**154**	53 10N	130	30W
Hechuan	**99**	30 2N	106	12 E
Hedmark fylke □	**60**	61 17N	11	40 E
Heemstede	**40**	52 22N	4	37 E
Heerenveen	**41**	52 57N	5	55 E
Heerlen	**41**	50 55N	6	0 E
Hefa	**80**	32 46N	35	0 E
Hefei	**99**	31 52N	117	18 E
Hegang	**98**	47 20N	130	19 E
Heidelberg	**42**	49 23N	8	41 E
Heilbronn	**42**	49 8N	9	13 E
Heilongjiang □	**98**	48 0N	126	0 E
Heilunkiang = Heilongjiang □	**98**	48 0N	126	0 E
Heinze Is.	**94**	14 25N	97	45 E
Hekimhan	**81**	38 50N	38	0 E
Hekinan	**106**	34 52N	137	0 E
Hekla	**16**	63 56N	19	35W
Helena, Ark., U.S.A.	**169**	34 30N	90	35W
Helena, Mont., U.S.A.	**163**	46 40N	112	0W
Helensburgh	**30**	56 0N	4	44W
Helmand →	**87**	31 12N	61	34 E
Helmond	**41**	51 29N	5	41 E
Helmsdale	**33**	58 7N	3	40W
Helsingborg	**61**	56 3N	12	42 E
Helsinki	**67**	60 15N	25	3 E
Helston	**27**	50 7N	5	17W
Helvellyn	**28**	54 31N	3	1W
Hemel Hempstead	**25**	51 45N	0	28W
Hempstead	**164**	30 5N	96	5W
Henan □	**99**	34 0N	114	0 E
Henderson	**165**	36 20N	78	25W
Hendersonville	**165**	35 21N	82	28W
Hengelo	**41**	52 16N	6	48 E
Hengyang	**99**	26 51N	112	30 E
Hénin-Beaumont	**38**	50 25N	2	58 E
Hennebont	**36**	47 49N	3	19W
Henrietta Maria C.	**140**	55 9N	82	20W
Henty	**117**	35 30S	147	0 E
Henzada	**93**	17 38N	95	26 E
Herät	**87**	34 20N	62	7 E
Herät □	**87**	35 0N	62	0 E
Herbert →	**121**	18 31S	146	17 E
Herbiers, Les	**36**	46 52N	1	0W
Hercegnovi	**52**	42 30N	18	33 E
Hercegovina = Bosnia & Herzegovina □	**52**	44 0N	18	0 E
Hereford	**24**	52 4N	2	42W
Hereford and Worcester □	**24**	52 10N	2	30W
Herford	**42**	52 7N	8	40 E
Hermosillo	**174**	29 4N	110	58W
Heroica = Caborca	**174**	30 40N	112	10W
Heroica Nogales = Nogales	**174**	31 20N	110	56W
Heron Bay	**150**	48 40N	86	25W
Herrin	**166**	37 50N	89	0W
Hertford □	**25**	51 51N	0	5W
's-Hertogenbosch	**40**	51 42N	5	17 E
Hesse = Hessen □	**42**	50 40N	9	20 E
Hessen □	**42**	50 40N	9	20 E
Hewett, C.	**146**	70 16N	67	45W
Hexham	**28**	54 58N	2	7W
Heysham	**28**	54 5N	2	53W
Heywood	**119**	38 8S	141	37 E
Hi-no-Misaki	**109**	35 26N	132	38 E
Hialeach	**170**	25 49N	80	17W
Hibiki-Nada	**108**	34 0N	130	0 E
Hickory	**165**	35 46N	81	17W
Hida-Gawa →	**106**	35 26N	137	3 E
Hida-Sammyaku	**106**	36 30N	137	40 E
Hida-Sanchi	**106**	36 10N	137	0 E
Hidaka	**109**	35 30N	134	44 E
Hidalgo □	**177**	20 30N	99	0W
Hidalgo del Parral	**174**	26 56N	105	40W
Higashi-matsuyama	**107**	36 2N	139	25 E
Higashiōsaka	**106**	34 40N	135	37 E
Higasi-Suidō	**108**	34 0N	129	30 E
High Atlas = Haut Atlas	**126**	32 30N	5	0W
High Point	**165**	35 57N	79	58W
High Prairie	**155**	55 30N	116	30W
Highland □	**32**	57 30N	5	0W
Highland Park	**167**	42 10N	87	50W
Ḥijārah, Ṣaḥrā' al	**84**	30 25N	44	30 E
Hikari	**108**	33 58N	131	58 E
Hikone	**106**	35 15N	136	10 E
Hildesheim	**43**	52 9N	9	55 E
Hillegom	**40**	52 18N	4	35 E
Hillsboro	**171**	45 31N	123	0W
Hillston	**117**	33 30S	145	31 E
Hilo	**160**	19 44N	155	5W
Hilversum	**40**	52 14N	5	10 E
Himachal Pradesh □	**89**	31 30N	77	0 E
Himalaya, Mts.	**101**	29 0N	84	0 E
Hime-Jima	**108**	33 43N	131	40 E
Himeji	**109**	34 50N	134	40 E
Himi	**106**	36 50N	137	0 E
Ḥimṣ	**80**	34 40N	36	45 E
Hinchinbrook I.	**121**	18 20S	146	15 E
Hinckley	**25**	52 33N	1	21W
Hindmarsh	**119**	34 54S	138	34 E
Hindu Kush	**89**	36 0N	71	0 E
Hindupur	**90**	13 49N	77	32 E
Hines Creek	**155**	56 20N	118	40W
Hingoli	**91**	19 41N	77	15 E
Hinton	**165**	37 40N	80	51W
Hirado	**108**	33 22N	129	33 E
Hirakarta	**106**	34 48N	135	40 E
Hirakud Dam	**92**	21 32N	83	45 E
Hirata	**109**	35 24N	132	49 E
Hiratsuka	**107**	35 19N	139	21 E
Hirosaki	**103**	40 34N	140	28 E
Hiroshima	**109**	34 24N	132	30 E
Hirson	**38**	49 55N	4	4 E
Hispaniola	**180**	19 0N	71	0W
Hita	**108**	33 20N	130	58 E
Hitachi	**107**	36 36N	140	39 E
Hitachiota	**107**	36 30N	140	30 E
Hitchin	**25**	51 57N	0	16W
Hitoyoshi	**108**	32 13N	130	45 E
Hitra	**65**	63 30N	8	45 E
Hiuchi-Nada	**109**	34 5N	133	20 E

Ho Chi Minh City = Thanh
Pho Ho Chi Minh .... **95** 10 58N 106 40 E
Hoa Binh .... **95** 20 50N 105 20 E
Hobart .... **119** 42 50S 147 21 E
Hobbs **161** 32 40N 103 3W
Hodaka-Dake .... **106** 36 17N 137 39 E
Hódmezövásárhely .... **59** 46 28N 20 22 E
Hoek van Holland .... **40** 52 0N   4 7 E
Hofsjökull **64** 64 49N 18 48W
Hōfu .... **108** 34 3N 131 34 E
Hogan Group .... **117** 39 13S 147 1 E
Hoh Xil Shan .... **101** 35 0N 89 0 E
Hohhot .... **98** 40 52N 111 40 E
Hōjō .... **109** 33 58N 132 46 E
Hokitika .... **123** 42 42S 171 0 E
Hokkaidō □ .... **103** 43 30N 143 0 E
Holbrook .... **117** 35 42S 147 18 E
Holderness **29** 53 45N   0 5W
Holdrege **163** 40 26N 99 22W
Holguin **178** 20 50N 76 20W
Holland **167** 42 47N 86 7W
Holly Springs **169** 34 45N 89 25W
Hollywood, Calif., U.S.A. .. **173** 34 7N 118 25W
Hollywood, Fla., U.S.A. **170** 26 0N 80 9W
Holsteinsborg **147** 66 40N 53 30W
Holsworthy **27** 50 48N   4 21W
Holt **64** 63 33N 19 48W
Holy I., Scotland, U.K. **31** 55 31N   5 4W
Holy I., Wales, U.K. **26** 53 17N   4 37W
Holyhead **26** 53 18N   4 38W
Holyoke **164** 42 14N 72 37W
Hombori **130** 15 20N   1 38W
Home Hill .... **121** 19 43S 147 25 E
Homer **142** 59 40N 151 35W
Homs = Ḥimṣ .... **80** 34 40N 36 45 E
Honan = Henan □ .... **99** 34 0N 114 0 E
Hondo .... **108** 32 27N 130 12 E
Honduras ■ **179** 14 40N 86 30W
Honduras, Golfo de **177** 16 50N 87 0W
Hong Kong ■ .... **99** 22 11N 114 14 E
Hongha ─► .... **95** 22 0N 104 0 E
Hongshui He ─► .... **99** 23 48N 109 30 E
Honiton **27** 50 48N   3 11W
Honolulu **160** 21 19N 157 52W
Honshū .... **106** 36 0N 138 0 E
Hoogeveen .... **41** 52 44N   6 30 E
Hook Hd. **35** 52 8N   6 57W
Hook of Holland = Hoek van
Holland .... **40** 52 0N   4 7 E
Hoorn .... **40** 52 38N   5 4 E
Hope, Canada .... **154** 49 25N 121 25 E
Hope, U.S.A. **168** 33 40N 93 36W
Hope Town **178** 26 35N 76 57W
Hopedale **147** 55 28N 60 13W
Hopei = Hebei □ .... **98** 39 0N 116 0 E
Hopelchén **177** 19 46N 89 51W
Hopetoun, Vic., Australia ... **119** 35 42S 142 22 E
Hopetoun, W. Austral.,
Australia .... **120** 33 57S 120 7 E
Hopkinsville **169** 36 52N 87 26W
Hoquiam **171** 46 50N 123 55W
Hordaland fylke □ .... **60** 60 25N   6 15 E
Hormoz .... **85** 27 35N 55 0 E
Hormuz Str. .... **85** 26 30N 56 30 E
Horn, Cape = Hornos, Cabo
de **192** 55 50S 67 30W
Hornavan .... **66** 66 15N 17 30 E
Hornell **164** 42 23N 77 41W
Hornos, Cabo de **192** 55 50S 67 30W
Hornsby .... **117** 33 42S 151 2 E
Hornsea **29** 53 55N   0 10W
Horqin Youyi Qianqi .... **98** 46 5N 122 3 E
Horsens .... **61** 55 52N   9 51 E
Horsham .... **119** 36 44S 142 13 E
Horton ─► **145** 69 56N 126 52W
Hoshiarpur .... **89** 31 30N 75 58 E
Hospet .... **90** 15 15N 76 20 E
Hospitalet de Llobregat .... **51** 41 21N   2 6 E
Hoste, I. **192** 55 0S 69 0W
Hot Springs **168** 34 30N 93 0W
Houghton **150** 47 9N 88 39W

Houghton-le-Spring **28** 54 51N   1 28W
Houhora .... **122** 34 49S 173 9 E
Houlton **148** 46 5N 67 50W
Houma **169** 29 35N 90 44W
Houston, Canada **154** 54 25N 126 39W
Houston, U.S.A. **168** 29 50N 95 20W
Houtman Abrolhos .... **120** 28 43S 113 48 E
Hovd .... **100** 48 2N 91 37 E
Hove **25** 50 50N   0 10W
Howe, C. .... **117** 37 30S 150 0 E
Howrah = Haora .... **92** 22 37N 88 20 E
Hoy I. **33** 58 50N   3 15W
Hradec Králové .... **58** 50 15N 15 50 E
Hrvatska = Croatia ■ .... **52** 45 20N 18 0 E
Hsiamen = Xiamen ...... **99** 24 25N 118 4 E
Hsian = Xi'an .... **99** 34 15N 109 0 E
Hsinhailien = Lianyungang . **99** 34 40N 119 11 E
Hsüchou = Xuzhou ...... **99** 34 18N 117 10 E
Hua Hin .... **94** 12 34N 99 58 E
Huacho **186** 11 10S 77 35W
Huainan .... **99** 32 38N 116 58 E
Huallaga ─► **186** 5 0S 75 30W
Huambo .... **134** 12 42S 15 54 E
Huancane **187** 15 10S 69 44W
Huancavelica **186** 12 50S 75 5W
Huancayo **186** 12 5S 75 12W
Huanchaca **187** 20 15S 66 40W
Huang Hai = Yellow Sea ... **99** 35 0N 123 0 E
Huang Ho ─► .... **98** 37 30N 118 50 E
Huangshi .... **99** 30 10N 115 3 E
Huánuco **186** 9 55S 76 15W
Huaraz **186** 9 30S 77 32W
Huascarán **186** 9 8S 77 36W
Huasco **190** 28 30S 71 15W
Huatabampo **174** 26 50N 109 38W
Huautla **177** 17 51N 100 5W
Hubei □ .... **99** 31 0N 112 0 E
Hubli-Dharwad = Dharwad . **90** 15 22N 75 15 E
Huddersfield **28** 53 38N   1 49W
Hudiksvall .... **66** 61 43N 17 10 E
Hudson **164** 42 15N 73 46W
Hudson ─► **164** 40 42N 74 2W
Hudson Bay **146** 52 51N 102 23W
Hudson Str. **146** 62 0N 70 0W
Hudson's Hope **155** 56 0N 121 54W
Hue .... **95** 16 30N 107 35 E
Huehuetenango **177** 15 20N 91 28W
Huelva **50** 37 18N   6 57W
Huesca **51** 42 8N   0 25W
Hughenden .... **121** 20 52S 144 10 E
Huila, Nevado del **184** 3 0N 76 0W
Huinca Renancó **190** 34 51S 64 22W
Huixtla **177** 15 9N 92 28W
Huizen .... **40** 52 18N   5 14 E
Hukawng Valley .... **93** 26 30N 96 30 E
Hull, Canada **151** 45 25N 75 44W
Hull, U.K. **29** 53 45N   0 20W
Hulst .... **40** 51 17N   4 2 E
Hulun Nur .... **98** 49 0N 117 30 E
Humaitá **187** 27 2S 58 31W
Humber ─► **29** 53 40N   0 10W
Humberside □ **29** 53 50N   0 30W
Humboldt, Canada **152** 52 15N 105 9W
Humboldt, U.S.A. **169** 35 50N 88 55W
Humboldt ─► **172** 40 2N 118 31W
Hume, L. .... **117** 36 0S 147 0 E
Húnaflói **64** 65 50N 20 50W
Hunan □ .... **99** 27 30N 111 30 E
Hunedoara .... **56** 45 40N 22 50 E
Hungary ■ .... **59** 47 20N 19 20 E
Hungary, Plain of .... **17** 47 0N 20 0 E
Hüngnam .... **98** 39 49N 127 45 E
Hunsrück .... **42** 49 30N   7 0 E
Hunstanton .... **29** 52 57N   0 30 E
Hunter Ra. .... **117** 32 45S 150 15 E
Huntingdon **25** 52 20N   0 11W
Huntington, Ind., U.S.A. ... **167** 40 52N 85 30W
Huntington, W. Va., U.S.A. . **165** 38 20N 82 30W
Huntington Beach **173** 33 40N 118 0W
Huntly .... **122** 37 34S 175 11 E
Huntsville, Canada **151** 45 20N 79 14W

Place	Page	Lat.	Long.
Huntsville, Ala., U.S.A.	**169**	34 45N	86 35W
Huntsville, Tex., U.S.A.	**168**	30 45N	95 35W
Huonville	**119**	43 0S	147 5 E
Hupeh = Hubei □	**99**	31 0N	112 0 E
Huron, L.	**150**	45 0N	83 0W
Hurricane	**173**	37 10N	113 12W
Húsavík	**64**	66 3N	17 21W
Hutchinson	**161**	38 3N	97 59W
Hvar	**52**	43 11N	16 28 E
Hwang Ho = Huang Ho →	**98**	37 30N	118 50 E
Hwange	**137**	18 18S	26 30 E
Hyden	**120**	32 24S	118 53 E
Hyderabad, India	**91**	17 22N	78 29 E
Hyderabad, Pakistan	**88**	25 23N	68 24 E
Hyères	**37**	43 8N	6 9 E
Hyndman Pk.	**162**	43 50N	114 10W
Hythe	**24**	51 4N	1 5 E
Hyūga	**108**	32 25N	131 35 E

I

Place	Page	Lat.	Long.
Iaşi	**57**	47 10N	27 40 E
Ibadan	**131**	7 22N	3 58 E
Ibagué	**184**	4 20N	75 20W
Ibara	**109**	34 36N	133 28 E
Ibaraki	**106**	34 49N	135 34 E
Ibarra	**184**	0 21N	78 7W
Iberian Peninsula	**16**	40 0N	5 0W
Ibiza	**51**	38 54N	1 26 E
Ibuki-Sanchi	**106**	35 25N	136 18 E
Ibusuki	**108**	31 12N	130 40 E
Icá	**186**	14 0S	75 48W
Iça →	**184**	2 55S	67 58W
Iceland ■	**64**	65 0N	19 0W
Icha	**73**	55 30N	156 0 E
Ich'ang = Yichang	**99**	30 40N	111 20 E
Ichchapuram	**92**	19 10N	84 40 E
Ichihara	**107**	35 28N	140 5 E
Ichikawa	**107**	35 44N	139 55 E
Ichinomiya	**106**	35 18N	136 48 E
Ichinoseki	**103**	38 55N	141 8 E
Idaho □	**162**	44 10N	114 0W
Idaho Falls	**163**	43 30N	112 1W
Ídhi Óros	**55**	35 15N	24 45 E
Ídhra	**55**	37 20N	23 28 E
Ierápetra	**55**	35 0N	25 44 E
Ife	**131**	7 30N	4 31 E
Igloolik	**146**	69 20N	81 49W
Iguaçu →	**191**	25 36S	54 36W
Iguaçu, Cat. del	**191**	25 41S	54 26W
Iguaçu Falls = Iguaçu, Cat. del	**191**	25 41S	54 26W
Iguala de la Independencia	**177**	18 21N	99 32W
Iguassu = Iguaçu →	**191**	25 36S	54 36W
Iida	**107**	35 35N	137 50 E
Iisalmi	**67**	63 32N	27 10 E
Iizuka	**108**	33 38N	130 42 E
IJmuiden	**40**	52 28N	4 35 E
IJsselmeer	**40**	52 45N	5 20 E
IJsselstein	**40**	52 1N	5 2 E
Ikaría	**55**	37 35N	26 10 E
Ikeda	**109**	34 1N	133 48 E
Iki	**108**	33 45N	129 42 E
Iki-Kaikyō	**108**	33 40N	129 45 E
Île-de-France	**37**	49 0N	2 20 E
Ilebo	**134**	4 17S	20 55 E
Ilfracombe	**27**	51 13N	4 8W
Ilhéus	**189**	14 49S	39 2W
Ili →	**71**	45 53N	77 10 E
Iliamna L.	**142**	59 35N	155 30W
Iliodhrómia	**55**	39 12N	23 50 E
Ilkeston	**29**	52 59N	1 19W
Illampu = Ancohuma, Nevada	**187**	16 0S	68 50W
Illinois □	**166**	40 15N	89 30W
Illinois →	**166**	38 55N	90 28W
Ilo	**187**	17 40S	71 20W
Iloilo	**112**	10 45N	122 33 E
Ilorin	**131**	8 30N	4 35 E
Imabari	**109**	34 4N	133 0 E
Imari	**108**	33 15N	129 52 E
Imatra	**67**	61 12N	28 48 E
Immingham	**29**	53 37N	0 12W
Imperial	**152**	51 21N	105 28W
Imphal	**92**	24 48N	93 56 E
İmroz = Gökçeada	**55**	40 10N	25 50 E
Ina	**107**	35 50N	138 0 E
Iñapari	**187**	11 0S	69 40W
Inari	**67**	68 54N	27 5 E
Inarijärvi	**67**	69 0N	28 0 E
Inazawa	**106**	35 15N	136 47 E
Inchon	**98**	37 27N	126 40 E
Indalsälven →	**66**	62 36N	17 30 E
Independence, Kans., U.S.A.	**166**	37 10N	95 43W
Independence, Mo., U.S.A.	**166**	39 3N	94 25W
India ■	**78**	20 0N	78 0 E
Indian Head	**152**	50 30N	103 41W
Indiana	**164**	40 38N	79 9W
Indiana □	**167**	40 0N	86 0W
Indianapolis	**167**	39 42N	86 10W
Indigirka →	**73**	70 48N	148 54 E
Indonesia ■	**111**	5 0S	115 0 E
Indore	**91**	22 42N	75 53 E
Indre →	**36**	47 16N	0 19 E
Indus →	**88**	24 20N	67 47 E
Indus, Mouth of the	**88**	24 0N	68 0 E
İnebolu	**80**	41 55N	33 40 E
İnegöl	**80**	40 5N	29 31 E
Ingersoll	**151**	43 4N	80 55W
Ingham	**121**	18 43S	146 10 E
Ingleborough	**28**	54 11N	2 23W
Inglewood, N.Z.	**122**	39 9S	174 14 E
Inglewood, U.S.A.	**173**	33 58N	118 21W
Ingolstadt	**43**	48 45N	11 26 E
Ingraj Bazar	**92**	24 58N	88 10 E
Inhambane	**137**	23 54S	35 30 E
Ining = Yining	**100**	43 58N	81 10 E
Inishmore	**35**	53 8N	9 45W
Inishowen	**34**	55 14N	7 15W
Inn →	**43**	48 35N	13 28 E
Innamincka	**118**	27 44S	140 46 E
Inner Hebrides	**32**	57 0N	6 30W
Inner Mongolia = Nei Monggol Zizhiqu □	**98**	42 0N	112 0 E
Innisfail, Australia	**121**	17 33S	146 5 E
Innisfail, Canada	**155**	52 0N	113 57W
In'no-shima	**109**	34 19N	133 10 E
Innsbruck	**45**	47 16N	11 23 E
Inoucdjouac	**146**	58 25N	78 15W
Inowrocław	**58**	52 50N	18 12 E
Inquisivi	**187**	16 50S	67 10W
Insein	**93**	16 50N	96 5 E
Interlaken	**44**	46 41N	7 50 E
Inuvik	**144**	68 16N	133 40W
Inuvik □	**144**	70 0N	130 0W
Inuyama	**106**	35 23N	136 56 E
Inveraray	**30**	56 13N	5 5W
Invercargill	**123**	46 24S	168 24 E
Inverell	**116**	29 45S	151 8 E
Invergordon	**33**	57 41N	4 10W
Inverness	**33**	57 29N	4 12W
Investigator Group	**119**	34 45S	134 20 E
Investigator Str.	**119**	35 30S	137 0 E
Ioánnina	**54**	39 42N	20 47 E
Iola	**166**	38 0N	95 20W
Iona	**30**	56 20N	6 25W
Ionian Is. = Iónioi Nísoi	**54**	38 40N	20 0 E
Ionian Sea	**54**	37 30N	17 30 E
Iónioi Nísoi	**54**	38 40N	20 0 E
Íos	**55**	36 41N	25 20 E
Iowa □	**166**	42 18N	93 30W
Iowa City	**166**	41 40N	91 35W
Iowa Falls	**166**	42 30N	93 15W
Ipiales	**184**	0 50N	77 37W
Ipin = Yibin	**99**	28 45N	104 32 E
Ípiros □	**54**	39 30N	20 30 E
Ipoh	**96**	4 35N	101 5 E
Ipswich, Australia	**116**	27 35S	152 40 E
Ipswich, U.K.	**25**	52 4N	1 9 E
Iquique	**187**	20 19S	70 5W

Name	Page	Lat.	Long.
Iquitos	**186**	3 45S	73 10W
Iracoubo	**185**	5 30N	53 10W
Iráklion	**55**	35 20N	25 12 E
Iran ■	**86**	33 0N	53 0 E
Iran Ra.	**111**	2 20N	114 50 E
Irapuato	**177**	20 41N	101 28W
Iraq ■	**81**	33 0N	44 0 E
Irbid	**80**	32 35N	35 48 E
Ireland ■	**34**	53 0N	8 0W
Irian Jaya □	**113**	4 0S	137 0 E
Iriri →	**188**	3 52S	52 37W
Irish Republic ■	**20**	53 0N	8 0W
Irish Sea	**20**	54 0N	5 0W
Irkutsk	**74**	52 18N	104 20 E
Irō-Zaki	**107**	34 36N	138 51 E
Iron Gate = Portile de Fier	**56**	44 42N	22 30 E
Iron Knob	**118**	32 46S	137 8 E
Iron Mountain	**150**	45 49N	88 4W
Ironbridge	**24**	52 38N	2 29W
Ironton	**167**	38 35N	82 40W
Ironwood	**150**	46 30N	90 10W
Iroquois Falls	**151**	48 46N	80 41W
Irrawaddy →	**93**	15 50N	95 6 E
Irtysh →	**69**	61 4N	68 52 E
Irumu	**135**	1 32N	29 53 E
Irún	**51**	43 20N	1 52W
Irvine	**31**	55 37N	4 40W
Irvinestown	**34**	54 28N	7 38W
Ísafjörður	**64**	66 5N	23 9W
Isahaya	**108**	32 52N	130 2 E
Íschia	**49**	40 45N	13 51 E
Ise	**106**	34 25N	136 45 E
Ise-Wan	**106**	34 43N	136 43 E
Isère →	**37**	44 59N	4 51 E
Isesaki	**107**	36 19N	139 12 E
Ishikari-Wan	**103**	43 25N	141 1 E
Ishinomaki	**103**	38 32N	141 20 E
Ishioka	**107**	36 11N	140 16 E
Ishkuman	**89**	36 30N	73 50 E
Ishpeming	**150**	46 30N	87 40W
İskenderun	**80**	36 32N	36 10 E
Islamabad	**89**	33 40N	73 10 E
Island L.	**153**	53 47N	94 25W
Island Pond	**148**	48 25N	56 23W
Islay	**30**	55 46N	6 10W
Isle-Adam, L'	**39**	49 6N	2 14 E
Isle Royale	**150**	48 0N	88 50W
İsparta	**80**	37 47N	30 30 E
Israel ■	**80**	32 0N	34 50 E
Issoire	**37**	45 32N	3 15 E
Issyk-Kul, Ozero	**71**	42 25N	77 15 E
İstanbul	**80**	41 0N	29 0 E
Istra	**52**	45 10N	14 0 E
Istria = Istra	**52**	45 10N	14 0 E
Itabuna	**189**	14 48S	39 16W
Itaituba	**185**	4 10S	55 50W
Itajaí	**191**	27 50S	48 39W
Italy ■	**19**	42 0N	13 0 E
Itaquatiara	**185**	2 58S	58 30W
Itaquí	**191**	29 8S	56 30W
Itchen →	**24**	50 57N	1 20W
Ithaca = Itháki	**54**	38 25N	20 40 E
Ithaca	**164**	42 25N	76 30W
Itháki	**54**	38 25N	20 40 E
Ito	**107**	34 58N	139 5 E
Ituaçu	**189**	13 50S	41 18W
Ituiutaba	**188**	19 0S	49 25W
Iturup, Ostrov	**75**	45 0N	148 0 E
Ivano-Frankovsk	**68**	48 40N	24 40 E
Ivanovo, Belorussia	**68**	52 7N	25 29 E
Ivanovo, Russia	**68**	57 5N	41 0 E
Ivigtut	**147**	61 14N	48 12W
Iviza = Ibiza	**51**	38 54N	1 26 E
Ivory Coast ■	**130**	7 30N	5 0W
Iwai-Jima	**108**	33 47N	131 58 E
Iwaki	**105**	37 3N	140 55 E
Iwakuni	**109**	34 15N	132 8 E
Iwami	**109**	35 32N	134 15 E
Iwamizawa	**103**	43 12N	141 46 E
Iwanuma	**103**	38 7N	140 51 E
Iwata	**107**	34 42N	137 51 E
Iwo	**131**	7 39N	4 9 E
Ixiamas	**187**	13 50S	68 5W
Ixtepec	**177**	16 34N	95 6W
Ixtlán	**175**	20 11N	102 24W
Ixtlán de Juárez	**177**	17 23N	96 28W
Iyo	**109**	33 45N	132 45 E
Iyo-mishima	**109**	33 58N	133 30 E
Iyo-Nada	**109**	33 40N	132 20 E
Izamal	**177**	20 56N	89 1W
Izhevsk	**69**	56 51N	53 14 E
İzmir	**80**	38 25N	27 8 E
İzmit	**80**	40 45N	29 50 E
Izu-Hantō	**107**	34 45N	139 0 E
Izumi	**108**	32 5N	130 22 E
Izumi-sano	**106**	34 23N	135 18 E
Izumiotsu	**106**	34 30N	135 24 E
Izumo	**109**	35 20N	132 46 E

J

Name	Page	Lat.	Long.
Jabalpur	**91**	23 9N	79 58 E
Jacarèzinho	**191**	23 5S	50 0W
Jackson, Mich., U.S.A.	**167**	42 18N	84 25W
Jackson, Miss., U.S.A.	**169**	32 20N	90 10W
Jackson, Tenn., U.S.A.	**169**	35 40N	88 50W
Jacksonville, Fla., U.S.A.	**170**	30 15N	81 38W
Jacksonville, Ill., U.S.A.	**166**	39 42N	90 15W
Jacksonville, N.C., U.S.A.	**165**	34 50N	77 29W
Jacksonville, Tex., U.S.A.	**168**	31 58N	95 19W
Jacmel	**180**	18 14N	72 32W
Jacobabad	**88**	28 20N	68 29 E
Jacques Cartier, Dét. de	**149**	50 0N	63 30W
Jadotville = Likasi	**135**	10 55S	26 48 E
Jaén, Peru	**186**	5 25S	78 40W
Jaén, Spain	**50**	37 44N	3 43W
Jaffa = Tel Aviv-Yafo	**80**	32 4N	34 48 E
Jaffna	**90**	9 45N	80 2 E
Jagdalpur	**92**	19 3N	82 0 E
Jaguariaíva	**191**	24 10S	49 50W
Jagüey Grande	**178**	22 35N	81 7W
Jahrom	**85**	28 30N	53 31 E
Jaipur	**91**	27 0N	75 50 E
Jakarta	**111**	6 9S	106 49 E
Jalalabad	**87**	34 30N	70 29 E
Jalapa, Guatemala	**177**	14 39N	89 59W
Jalapa, Mexico	**177**	17 43N	92 49W
Jalgaon	**91**	21 0N	75 42 E
Jalisco □	**175**	20 20N	103 40W
Jalna	**91**	19 48N	75 38 E
Jalón →	**51**	41 47N	1 4W
Jalpaiguri	**92**	26 32N	88 46 E
Jamaica ■	**180**	18 10N	77 30W
Jamalpur, Bangla.	**92**	24 52N	89 56 E
Jamalpur, India	**92**	25 18N	86 28 E
Jambi	**111**	1 38S	103 30 E
James →	**163**	42 52N	97 18W
James B.	**140**	51 30N	80 0W
Jamestown, Australia	**118**	33 10S	138 32 E
Jamestown, N. Dak., U.S.A.	**163**	46 54N	98 42W
Jamestown, N.Y., U.S.A.	**164**	42 5N	79 18W
Jamkhandi	**91**	16 30N	75 15 E
Jammu	**89**	32 43N	74 54 E
Jammu & Kashmir □	**89**	34 25N	77 0 E
Jamnagar	**90**	22 30N	70 6 E
Jamshedpur	**92**	22 44N	86 12 E
Jan Mayen Is.	**13**	71 0N	9 0W
Janesville	**166**	42 39N	89 1W
Januária	**188**	15 25S	44 25W
Jaora	**91**	23 40N	75 10 E
Japan ■	**79**	36 0N	136 0 E
Japan, Sea of	**102**	40 0N	135 0 E
Japurá →	**185**	3 8S	64 46W
Jargalant = Hovd	**100**	48 2N	91 37 E
Jargeau	**39**	47 50N	2 1 E
Jarosław	**58**	50 2N	22 42 E
Jāsk	**85**	25 38N	57 45 E
Jasło	**59**	49 45N	21 30 E
Jasper, Canada	**155**	52 55N	118 5W

Jasper, U.S.A. **169** 33 48N 87 16W
Jassy = Iaşi . . . . **57** 47 10N 27 40 E
Jataí **188** 17 58S 51 48W
Jaú **188** 22 10S 48 30W
Jaunpur . . . . **92** 25 46N 82 44 E
Java, I. . . . . **111** 7 0S 110 0 E
Java Sea . . . . **111** 4 35S 107 15 E
Javhlant = Ulyasutay . . . . . . **100** 47 56N 97 28 E
Jean Marie River **144** 61 32N 120 38W
Jean Rabel **180** 19 50N 73 5W
Jedburgh **31** 55 28N 2 33W
Jędrzejów . . . . **58** 50 35N 20 15 E
Jefferson, Mt. **171** 44 45N 121 50W
Jefferson City **166** 38 34N 92 10W
Jeffersonville **167** 38 20N 85 42W
Jelenia Góra . . . . **58** 50 50N 15 45 E
Jena . . . . **43** 50 56N 11 33 E
Jenkins **165** 37 13N 82 41W
Jennings **168** 30 10N 92 45W
Jeparit . . . . **119** 36 8S 142 1 E
Jequié **189** 13 51S 40 5W
Jequitinhonha **189** 16 30S 41 0W
Jérémie **180** 18 40N 74 10W
Jerez de Garcia Salinas . . . **175** 22 39N 103 0W
Jerez de la Frontera **50** 36 41N 6 7W
Jerez de los Caballeros **50** 38 20N 6 45W
Jericho . . . . **121** 23 38S 146 6 E
Jerilderie . . . . **117** 35 20S 145 41 E
Jerome **148** 47 37N 82 14W
Jersey, I. **36** 49 13N 2 7W
Jersey City **164** 40 41N 74 8W
Jerseyville **166** 39 5N 90 20W
Jerusalem . . . . **80** 31 47N 35 10 E
Jesselton = Kota Kinabalu . **112** 6 0N 116 4 E
Jhang Maghiana . . . . **89** 31 15N 72 22 E
Jhansi . . . . **91** 25 30N 78 36 E
Jharsuguda . . . . **92** 21 56N 84 5 E
Jhelum ⟶ . . . . **89** 31 20N 72 10 E
Jhunjhunu . . . . **89** 28 10N 75 30 E
Jiamusi . . . . **98** 46 40N 130 26 E
Ji'an . . . . **99** 27 6N 114 59 E
Jiangmen . . . . **99** 22 32N 113 0 E
Jiangsu □ . . . . **99** 33 0N 120 0 E
Jiangxi □ . . . . **99** 27 30N 116 0 E
Jian'ou . . . . **99** 27 3N 118 17 E
Jiao Xian . . . . **98** 36 18N 120 1 E
Jiaozuo . . . . **99** 35 16N 113 12 E
Jiaxing . . . . **99** 30 49N 120 45 E
Jiayi . . . . **99** 23 30N 120 24 E
Jibuti = Djibouti ■ . . . . **133** 12 0N 43 0 E
Jiddah . . . . **82** 21 29N 39 10 E
Jido . . . . **93** 29 2N 94 58 E
Jihlava . . . . **59** 49 28N 15 35 E
Jilin . . . . **98** 43 44N 126 30 E
Jilong . . . . **99** 25 8N 121 42 E
Jima . . . . **132** 7 40N 36 47 E
Jiménez **174** 27 8N 104 54W
Jinan . . . . **98** 36 38N 117 1 E
Jingdezhen . . . . **99** 29 20N 117 11 E
Jining, Nei Mongol Zizhiqu,
China . . . . **98** 41 5N 113 0 E
Jining, Shandong, China . . . **99** 35 22N 116 34 E
Jinja . . . . **132** 0 25N 33 12 E
Jinnah Barrage . . . . **89** 32 58N 71 33 E
Jinotega **179** 13 6N 85 59W
Jinotepe **179** 11 50N 86 10W
Jinshi . . . . **99** 29 40N 111 50 E
Jinzhou . . . . **98** 41 5N 121 3 E
Jipijapa **184** 1 0S 80 40W
Jiquilpan de Juárez **175** 19 59N 102 43W
Jisr ash Shughūr . . . . **80** 35 49N 36 18 E
Jiujiang . . . . **99** 29 42N 115 58 E
Jixi . . . . **98** 45 20N 130 50 E
João Pessoa **189** 7 10S 34 52W
Jodhpur . . . . **91** 26 23N 73 8 E
Joensuu . . . . **67** 62 37N 29 49 E
Jogjakarta = Yogyakarta . . . **111** 7 49S 110 22 E
Jōhana . . . . **106** 36 30N 136 57 E
Johannesburg . . . . **137** 26 10S 28 2 E
John o' Groats **33** 58 39N 3 3W
Johnson City, N.Y., U.S.A. . . **164** 42 7N 75 57W

Johnson City, Tenn., U.S.A. . **165** 36 18N 82 21W
Johnston **31** 51 45N 5 5W
Johnstown, N.Y., U.S.A. **164** 43 1N 74 20W
Johnstown, Pa., U.S.A. **164** 40 19N 78 53W
Johor □ . . . . **96** 2 5N 103 20 E
Johor Baharu . . . . **96** 1 28N 103 46 E
Joigny . . . . **39** 48 0N 3 20 E
Joinvile . . . . **191** 26 15S 48 55 E
Joliet **167** 41 30N 88 0W
Joliette **151** 46 3N 73 24W
Jolo . . . . **112** 6 0N 121 0 E
Jonesboro **169** 35 50N 90 45W
Jönköping . . . . **60** 57 45N 14 10 E
Jönköpings län □ . . . . **61** 57 30N 14 30 E
Jonquière **148** 48 27N 71 14W
Joplin **168** 37 0N 94 31W
Jordan ■ . . . . **80** 31 0N 36 0 E
Jordan ⟶ . . . . **80** 31 48N 35 32 E
Jorhat . . . . **93** 26 45N 94 12 E
José de San Martín **192** 44 4S 70 26W
Jowzjān □ . . . . **87** 36 10N 66 0 E
Juan de Fuca Str. **142** 48 15N 124 0W
Juan Fernández, Arch. de . . **183** 33 50S 80 0W
Juàzeiro **189** 9 30S 40 30W
Juàzeiro do Norte **189** 7 10S 39 18W
Jubbulpore = Jabalpur . . . . **91** 23 9N 79 58 E
Júcar ⟶ **51** 39 5N 0 10W
Juchitán de Zaragoza **177** 16 26N 95 1W
Jugoslavia = Yugoslavia ■ . **52** 44 0N 21 0 E
Juiz de Fora **188** 21 43S 43 19W
Juli **187** 16 10S 69 25W
Juliaca **187** 15 25S 70 10W
Julianehåb **147** 60 43N 46 0W
Jullundur . . . . **89** 31 20N 75 40 E
Jumla . . . . **92** 29 15N 82 13 E
Jumna = Yamuna ⟶ . . . . . . **92** 25 30N 81 53 E
Junagadh . . . . **91** 21 30N 70 30 E
Jundiaí **191** 24 30S 47 0W
Juneau **143** 58 20N 134 20W
Junee . . . . **117** 34 53S 147 35 E
Junggar Pendi . . . . **100** 44 30N 86 0 E
Junín **190** 34 33S 60 57W
Jura, Europe . . . . **37** 46 35N 6 5 E
Jura, U.K. **30** 56 0N 5 50W
Jurado **184** 7 7N 77 46W
Juruá ⟶ **184** 2 37S 65 44W
Juruena **187** 13 0S 58 10W
Juruena ⟶ **187** 7 20S 58 3W
Juticalpa **179** 14 40N 86 12W
Jutland = Jylland . . . . **61** 56 25N 9 30 E
Juventud, I. de la **178** 21 40N 82 40W
Jylland . . . . **61** 56 25N 9 30 E
Jyväskylä . . . . **67** 62 14N 25 50 E

K

Kaapstad = Cape Town . . . . **136** 33 55S 18 22 E
Kabala **130** 9 38N 11 37W
Kabardino-Balkar Rep. □ . . . **70** 43 30N 43 30 E
Kabarega Falls . . . . **132** 2 15N 31 30 E
Kabīr Kūh . . . . **84** 33 0N 47 30 E
Kābul . . . . **87** 34 28N 69 11 E
Kābul □ . . . . **87** 34 30N 69 0 E
Kabwe . . . . **135** 14 30S 28 29 E
Kachin □ . . . . **93** 26 0N 97 30 E
Kadan Kyun . . . . **94** 12 30N 98 20 E
Kadina . . . . **119** 34 0S 137 43 E
Kaduna . . . . **131** 10 30N 7 21 E
Kaédi **126** 16 9N 13 28W
Kāf . . . . **80** 31 25N 37 29 E
Kafirévs, Ákra . . . . **55** 38 9N 24 38 E
Kafue ⟶ . . . . **135** 15 30S 26 0 E
Kaga . . . . **106** 36 16N 136 15 E
Kagoshima . . . . **108** 31 35N 130 33 E
Kagoshima-Wan . . . . **108** 31 25N 130 40 E
Kai, Kepulauan **113** 5 55S 132 45W
Kaieteur Falls **185** 5 1N 59 10W
Kaifeng . . . . **99** 34 49N 114 30 E

Name	Page	Lat.	Long.
Kaikoura Ra.	**123**	41 59S	173 41 E
Kailua	**160**	19 39N	156 0W
Kaimanawa Mts.	**122**	39 15S	175 56 E
Kainan	**106**	34 9N	135 12 E
Kainji Res.	**131**	10 1N	4 40 E
Kaipara Harbour	**122**	36 25S	174 14 E
Kaiserslautern	**42**	49 30N	7 43 E
Kaitaia	**122**	35 8S	173 17 E
Kajaani	**67**	64 17N	27 46 E
Kajana = Kajaani	**67**	64 17N	27 46 E
Kakabeka Falls	**150**	48 24N	89 37W
Kakamigahara	**106**	35 28N	136 48 E
Kakanui Mts.	**123**	45 10S	170 30 E
Kakegawa	**107**	34 45N	138 1 E
Kakinada	**92**	16 57N	82 11 E
Kakogawa	**109**	34 46N	134 51 E
Kalabáka	**54**	39 42N	21 39 E
Kalahari	**136**	24 0S	21 30 E
Kalamata	**54**	37 3N	22 10 E
Kalamazoo	**167**	42 20N	85 35W
Kalamazoo →	**167**	42 40N	86 12W
Kalat	**88**	29 8N	66 31 E
Kalaupapa	**160**	21 12N	156 59W
Kalemie	**135**	5 55S	29 9 E
Kalgan = Zhangjiakou	**98**	40 48N	114 55 E
Kalgoorlie-Boulder	**120**	30 40S	121 22 E
Kálimnos	**55**	37 0N	27 0 E
Kalinin = Tver	**68**	56 55N	35 55 E
Kaliningrad	**68**	54 42N	20 32 E
Kalispell	**162**	48 10N	114 22W
Kalisz	**58**	51 45N	18 8 E
Kalmar	**61**	56 40N	16 20 E
Kalmar län □	**61**	57 25N	16 0 E
Kalmyk Rep. □	**70**	46 5N	46 1 E
Kalocsa	**59**	46 32N	19 0 E
Kaluga	**68**	54 35N	36 10 E
Kama →	**68**	55 45N	52 0 E
Kamaishi	**103**	39 16N	141 53 E
Kamakura	**107**	35 19N	139 33 E
Kamaran	**82**	15 21N	42 35 E
Kamchatka, P-ov.	**73**	57 0N	160 0 E
Kamenka	**69**	53 10N	44 5 E
Kamensk Uralskiy	**69**	56 25N	62 2 E
Kamenskoye	**73**	62 45N	165 30 E
Kameoka	**106**	35 0N	135 35 E
Kameyama	**106**	34 51N	136 27 E
Kami-koshiki-Jima	**108**	31 50N	129 52 E
Kamioka	**106**	36 25N	137 15 E
Kamloops	**155**	50 40N	120 20W
Kampala	**132**	0 20N	32 30 E
Kampar	**96**	4 18N	101 9 E
Kampen	**41**	52 33N	5 53 E
Kampot	**95**	10 36N	104 10 E
Kampuchea = Cambodia ■	**95**	12 15N	105 0 E
Kamsack	**152**	51 34N	101 54W
Kamui-Misaki	**103**	43 20N	140 21 E
Kamyshin	**68**	50 10N	45 24 E
Kananga	**134**	5 55S	22 18 E
Kanawha →	**165**	38 50N	82 8W
Kanazawa	**106**	36 30N	136 38 E
Kanchenjunga	**92**	27 50N	88 10 E
Kanchipuram	**90**	12 52N	79 45 E
Kandahar = Qandahār	**87**	31 32N	65 30 E
Kandalaksha	**69**	67 9N	32 30 E
Kandi	**131**	11 7N	2 55 E
Kandos	**117**	32 45S	149 58 E
Kandy	**90**	7 18N	80 43 E
Kangar	**97**	6 27N	100 12 E
Kangaroo I.	**119**	35 45S	137 0 E
Kangean Is.	**113**	6 55S	115 23 E
Kangnŭng	**98**	37 45N	128 54 E
Kangto	**93**	27 50N	92 35 E
Kaniapiskau →	**146**	56 40N	69 30W
Kanin, P-ov.	**69**	68 0N	45 0 E
Kaniva	**119**	36 22S	141 18 E
Kankakee	**167**	41 6N	87 50W
Kankakee →	**167**	41 23N	88 16W
Kankan	**130**	10 23N	9 15W
Kanmuri-Yama	**109**	34 30N	132 4 E
Kannapolis	**165**	35 32N	80 37W
Kano	**131**	12 2N	8 30 E
Kan'onji	**109**	34 7N	133 39 E
Kanoya	**108**	31 25N	130 50 E
Kanpur	**91**	26 28N	80 20 E
Kansas □	**161**	38 40N	98 0W
Kansas →	**158**	39 7N	94 36W
Kansas City, Kans., U.S.A.	**166**	39 0N	94 40W
Kansas City, Mo., U.S.A.	**166**	39 3N	94 30W
Kansk	**74**	56 20N	95 37 E
Kansu = Gansu □	**98**	36 0N	104 0 E
Kantō □	**107**	36 15N	139 30 E
Kantō-Sanchi	**107**	35 59N	138 50 E
Kanuma	**107**	36 34N	139 42 E
Kaohsiung = Gaoxiong	**99**	22 38N	120 18 E
Kaolack	**130**	14 5N	16 8W
Kāpīsā □	**87**	35 0N	69 20 E
Kapoeta	**129**	4 50N	33 35 E
Kapuas →	**111**	0 25S	109 20 E
Kapunda	**119**	34 20S	138 56 E
Kapuskasing	**150**	49 25N	82 30W
Kaputar, Mt.	**116**	30 15S	150 10 E
Kara Bogaz Gol, Zaliv	**70**	41 0N	53 30 E
Kara Kalpak Rep. □	**70**	43 0N	60 0 E
Kara Kum = Karakum, Peski	**70**	39 30N	60 0 E
Kara Sea	**69**	75 0N	70 0 E
Karabük	**80**	41 12N	32 37 E
Karachi	**88**	24 53N	67 0 E
Karad	**91**	17 15N	74 10 E
Karadeniz Boğazı	**80**	41 10N	29 10 E
Karaganda	**71**	49 50N	73 10 E
Karaj	**86**	35 48N	51 0 E
Karakoram Pass	**89**	35 33N	77 50 E
Karakoram Ra.	**89**	35 30N	77 0 E
Karakum, Peski	**70**	39 30N	60 0 E
Karaman	**80**	37 14N	33 13 E
Karamea Bight	**123**	41 22S	171 40 E
Karasuk	**71**	53 44N	78 2 E
Karatau, Khrebet	**71**	43 30N	69 30 E
Karbalā	**84**	32 36N	44 3 E
Karelian Rep. □	**68**	65 30N	32 30 E
Karen	**94**	12 49N	92 53 E
Kariba Lake	**137**	16 40S	28 25 E
Karimata I.	**111**	1 40S	109 0 E
Karimnagar	**91**	18 26N	79 10 E
Karimunjawa, Kepulauan	**111**	5 50S	110 30 E
Kariya	**106**	34 58N	137 1 E
Karl-Marx-Stadt = Chemnitz	**43**	50 50N	12 55 E
Karlskrona	**61**	56 10N	15 35 E
Karlsruhe	**42**	49 3N	8 23 E
Karlstad	**60**	59 23N	13 30 E
Karnal	**89**	29 42N	77 2 E
Karnaphuli Res.	**93**	22 40N	92 20 E
Karnataka □	**90**	13 15N	77 0 E
Kärnten □	**45**	46 52N	13 30 E
Kárpathos	**55**	35 37N	27 10 E
Kars	**81**	40 40N	43 5 E
Karshi	**70**	38 53N	65 48 E
Kasai →	**134**	3 30S	16 10 E
Kasaoka	**109**	34 30N	133 30 E
Kaseda	**108**	31 25N	130 19 E
Kāshān	**86**	34 5N	51 30 E
Kashi	**100**	39 30N	76 2 E
Kashihara	**106**	34 27N	135 46 E
Kashima	**108**	33 7N	130 6 E
Kashima-Nada	**107**	36 0N	140 45 E
Kashiwa	**107**	35 52N	139 59 E
Kāshmar	**86**	35 16N	58 26 E
Kashmir	**78**	34 0N	76 0 E
Kashun Noerh = Gaxun Nur	**100**	42 22N	100 30 E
Kásos	**55**	35 20N	26 55 E
Kassala	**129**	16 0N	36 0 E
Kassel	**42**	51 19N	9 32 E
Kastoría	**54**	40 30N	21 19 E
Kasugai	**106**	35 12N	136 59 E
Kasukabe	**107**	35 58N	139 49 E
Kasumiga-Ura	**107**	36 0N	140 25 E
Kasur	**89**	31 5N	74 25 E
Katanning	**120**	33 40S	117 33 E
Katha	**93**	24 10N	96 30 E
Katherîna, Gebel	**128**	28 30N	33 57 E
Katherine	**114**	14 27S	132 20 E
Kathiawar	**91**	22 20N	71 0 E

Place	Page	Lat.	Long.
Katihar	**92**	25 34N	87 36 E
Katmandu	**92**	27 45N	85 20 E
Katoomba	**117**	33 41S	150 19 E
Katowice	**58**	50 17N	19 5 E
Katsuta	**107**	36 25N	140 31 E
Katsuura	**107**	35 10N	140 20 E
Katsuyama	**106**	36 3N	136 30 E
Kattegatt	**61**	57 0N	11 20 E
Katwijk-aan-Zee	**40**	52 12N	4 24 E
Kauai	**160**	22 0N	159 30W
Kaukauna	**167**	44 20N	88 13W
Kaunas	**68**	54 54N	23 54 E
Kawachi-Nagano	**106**	34 28N	135 31 E
Kawagoe	**107**	35 55N	139 29 E
Kawaguchi	**107**	35 52N	139 45 E
Kawanoe	**109**	34 1N	133 34 E
Kawarau	**122**	45 3S	168 45 E
Kawasaki	**107**	35 35N	139 42 E
Kayah □	**93**	19 15N	97 15 E
Kayes	**130**	14 25N	11 30W
Kayseri	**80**	38 45N	35 30 E
Kazachinskoye	**74**	56 16N	107 36 E
Kazachye	**72**	70 52N	135 58 E
Kazakhstan ■	**71**	50 0N	70 0 E
Kazan	**68**	55 48N	49 3 E
Kazanlúk	**53**	42 38N	25 20 E
Kāzerūn	**85**	29 38N	51 40 E
Kazo	**107**	36 7N	139 36 E
Kéa	**55**	37 35N	24 22 E
Keaau	**160**	19 37N	155 3W
Kebnekaise	**66**	67 53N	18 33 E
Kecskemét	**59**	46 57N	19 42 E
Kedah □	**96**	5 50N	100 40 E
Kediri	**111**	7 51S	112 1 E
Keeling Is. = Cocos Is.	**111**	12 10S	96 55 E
Keene	**164**	42 57N	72 17W
Keetmanshoop	**136**	26 35S	18 8 E
Keewatin	**153**	49 46N	94 34W
Keewatin □	**145**	63 20N	95 0W
Kefallinía	**54**	38 20N	20 30 E
Keflavík	**64**	64 2N	22 35W
Keighley	**28**	53 52N	1 54W
Keith, Australia	**119**	36 6S	140 20 E
Keith, U.K.	**33**	57 33N	2 58W
Kelang	**96**	3 2N	101 26 E
Kelantan □	**96**	5 10N	102 0 E
Kelantan →	**96**	6 13N	102 14 E
Kellerberrin	**120**	31 36S	117 38 E
Kellogg	**162**	47 30N	116 5W
Kells = Ceanannus Mor	**34**	53 42N	6 53W
Kelowna	**155**	49 50N	119 25W
Kelso, U.K.	**31**	55 36N	2 27W
Kelso, U.S.A.	**171**	46 10N	122 57W
Keluang	**96**	2 3N	103 18 E
Kelvington	**152**	52 10N	103 30W
Kemerovo	**71**	55 20N	86 5 E
Kemi	**67**	65 44N	24 34 E
Kemi →	**67**	67 30N	28 30 E
Kempsey	**116**	31 1S	152 50 E
Kendal	**28**	54 19N	2 44W
Keng Tung	**93**	21 0N	99 30 E
Kenitra	**126**	34 15N	6 40W
Kenmare	**35**	51 52N	9 35W
Kennewick	**171**	46 11N	119 2W
Keno Hill	**144**	63 57N	135 18W
Kenora	**153**	49 47N	94 29W
Kenosha	**167**	42 33N	87 48W
Kent	**164**	41 8N	81 20W
Kent □	**25**	51 12N	0 40 E
Kent Group	**117**	39 30S	147 20 E
Kent Pen.	**145**	68 30N	107 0W
Kentucky □	**167**	37 20N	85 0W
Kentucky →	**167**	38 41N	85 11W
Kenya ■	**133**	1 0N	38 0 E
Kenya, Mt.	**132**	0 10S	37 18 E
Keokuk	**166**	40 25N	91 24W
Kepsut	**80**	39 40N	28 9 E
Kerala □	**90**	11 0N	76 15 E
Kerang	**117**	35 40S	143 55 E
Kerch	**68**	45 20N	36 20 E
Kerki	**70**	37 50N	65 12 E
Kérkira	**54**	39 38N	19 50 E
Kerkrade	**41**	50 53N	6 4 E
Kermadec Is.	**122**	30 0S	178 15W
Kermān	**85**	30 15N	57 1 E
Kermān □	**85**	30 0N	57 0 E
Kermānshāh = Bākhtarān	**84**	34 23N	47 0 E
Kerrobert	**152**	52 0N	109 11W
Kerry □	**35**	52 7N	9 35W
Kerulen →	**98**	48 48N	117 0 E
Kestenga	**68**	66 0N	31 50 E
Keswick	**28**	54 35N	3 9W
Ketchikan	**143**	55 25N	131 40W
Kettering	**156**	39 41N	84 10W
Kewanee	**166**	41 18N	89 55W
Keweenaw B.	**150**	46 56N	88 23W
Key West	**159**	24 33N	82 0W
Keyser	**164**	39 26N	79 0W
Khabarovsk	**75**	48 30N	135 5 E
Khalkhāl	**81**	37 37N	48 32 E
Khalkís	**55**	38 27N	23 42 E
Khalmer Yu	**69**	67 58N	65 1 E
Khambhat	**91**	22 23N	72 33 E
Khambhat, G. of	**91**	20 45N	72 30 E
Khamir	**82**	16 0N	44 0 E
Khānābād	**87**	36 45N	69 5 E
Khānaqīn	**81**	34 23N	45 25 E
Khandwa	**91**	21 49N	76 22 E
Khanewal	**89**	30 20N	71 55 E
Khaniá	**55**	35 30N	24 4 E
Khanka, Ozero	**75**	45 0N	132 24 E
Kharagpur	**92**	22 20N	87 25 E
Kharkov	**68**	49 58N	36 20 E
Khartoum = El Khartûm	**129**	15 31N	32 35 E
Khashm el Girba	**129**	14 59N	35 58 E
Khaskovo	**53**	41 56N	25 30 E
Khatanga	**72**	72 0N	102 20 E
Khatanga →	**72**	72 55N	106 0 E
Khenchela	**127**	35 28N	7 11 E
Kherson	**68**	46 35N	32 35 E
Kheta →	**72**	71 54N	102 6 E
Khíos, I.	**55**	38 20N	26 0 E
Khmer Rep. = Cambodia ■	**95**	12 15N	105 0 E
Khodzhent	**71**	40 17N	69 37 E
Khojak P.	**88**	30 55N	66 30 E
Kholm	**87**	36 45N	67 40 E
Khon Kaen	**95**	16 30N	102 47 E
Khoper →	**68**	49 30N	42 20 E
Khorāsān □	**86**	34 0N	58 0 E
Khorat = Nakhon Ratchasima	**95**	14 59N	102 12 E
Khorat, Cao Nguyen	**95**	15 30N	102 50 E
Khorog	**71**	37 30N	71 36 E
Khorramābād	**84**	33 30N	48 25 E
Khorrāmshahr	**84**	30 29N	48 15 E
Khulna	**92**	22 45N	89 34 E
Khulna □	**92**	22 25N	89 35 E
Khushab	**89**	32 20N	72 20 E
Khūzestān □	**84**	31 0N	49 0 E
Khvor	**86**	33 45N	55 0 E
Khvoy	**81**	38 35N	45 0 E
Khyber Pass	**89**	34 10N	71 8 E
Kiama	**117**	34 40S	150 50 E
Kiangsi = Jiangxi □	**99**	27 30N	116 0 E
Kiangsu = Jiangsu □	**99**	33 0N	120 0 E
Kichiga	**73**	59 50N	163 5 E
Kicking Horse Pass	**155**	51 28N	116 16W
Kidderminster	**24**	52 24N	2 13W
Kidnappers, C.	**122**	39 38S	177 5 E
Kiel	**43**	54 16N	10 8 E
Kielce	**58**	50 52N	20 42 E
Kieler Bucht	**42**	54 30N	10 30 E
Kiev = Kiyev	**68**	50 30N	30 28 E
Kigali	**135**	1 59S	30 4 E
Kii-Hantō	**106**	34 0N	135 45 E
Kii-Sanchi	**106**	34 20N	136 0 E
Kii-Suidō	**109**	33 40N	135 0 E
Kikládhes □	**55**	37 0N	25 0 E
Kikuchi	**108**	32 59N	130 47 E
Kilcoy	**116**	26 59S	152 30 E
Kildare □	**35**	53 10N	6 50W
Kilimanjaro	**132**	3 7S	37 20 E
Kilis	**80**	36 50N	37 10 E

Kilkenny 35 52 40N 7 17W
Kilkenny □ 35 52 35N 7 15W
Killala B. 34 54 20N 9 12W
Killarney, Canada 153 49 10N 99 40W
Killarney, Ireland 35 52 2N 9 30W
Killary Harbour 34 53 38N 9 52W
Killiecrankie, Pass of 33 56 44N 3 46W
Kilmarnock 31 55 36N 4 30W
Kilmore .... 117 37 25S 144 53 E
Kilrush 35 52 39N 9 30W
Kimba .... 118 33 8S 136 23 E
Kimberley, Australia .... 114 16 20S 127 0 E
Kimberley, Canada 155 49 40N 115 59W
Kimberley, S. Africa .... 136 28 43S 24 46 E
Kinabalu .... 112 6 3N 116 14 E
Kincardine 150 44 10N 81 40W
Kindersley 152 51 30N 109 10W
Kindia 130 10 0N 12 52W
King Frederick VI Land =
  Kong Frederik VI.s Kyst .. 147 63 0N 43 0W
King George Is. 140 57 20N 80 30W
King I. = Kadan Kyun ..... 94 12 30N 98 20 E
King I., Australia .... 119 39 50S 144 0 E
King I., Canada 154 52 10N 127 40W
King Sd. .... 114 16 50S 123 20 E
King William I. 145 69 10N 97 25W
Kingaroy .... 116 26 32S 151 51 E
Kingman 173 35 12N 114 2W
King's Lynn .... 29 52 45N 0 25 E
Kingscote .... 119 35 40S 137 38 E
Kingsport 165 36 33N 82 36W
Kingston, Canada 151 44 14N 76 30W
Kingston, Jamaica 180 18 0N 76 50W
Kingston, N.Z. .... 123 45 20S 168 43 E
Kingston, U.S.A. 164 41 55N 74 0W
Kingston South East ..... 119 36 51S 139 55 E
Kingstown 180 13 10N 61 10W
Kingsville 150 42 2N 82 45W
Kingussie 33 57 5N 4 2W
Kinistino 152 52 57N 105 2W
Kinki □ .... 106 33 30N 136 0 E
Kinnairds Hd. 33 57 40N 2 0W
Kinsale, Old Hd. of 35 51 37N 8 32W
Kinshasa .... 134 4 20S 15 15 E
Kinston 165 35 18N 77 35W
Kintyre 30 55 30N 5 35W
Kintyre, Mull of 30 55 17N 5 55W
Kinu-Gawa → .... 107 35 36N 139 57 E
Kiparissia .... 54 37 15N 21 40 E
Kirensk .... 74 57 50N 107 55 E
Kirghizia ■ .... 71 42 0N 75 0 E
Kiribati ■ .... 122 1 0N 176 0 E
Kırıkkale .... 80 39 51N 33 32 E
Kirin = Jilin .... 98 43 44N 126 30 E
Kiritimati 123 1 58N 157 27W
Kirkcaldy 31 56 7N 3 10W
Kirkcudbright 31 54 50N 4 3W
Kirkee .... 91 18 34N 73 56 E
Kirkintilloch 31 55 57N 4 10W
Kirkland Lake 151 48 9N 80 2W
Kirksville 166 40 8N 92 35W
Kirkūk .... 81 35 30N 44 21 E
Kirkwall 33 58 59N 2 59W
Kirov = Vyatka .... 69 58 35N 49 40 E
Kirovabad = Gyandzha .... 70 40 45N 46 20 E
Kirovograd = Yelizavetgrad . 68 48 35N 32 20 E
Kirthar Range .... 88 27 0N 67 0 E
Kiruna .... 66 67 52N 20 15 E
Kiryū .... 107 36 24N 139 20 E
Kisangani .... 135 0 35N 25 15 E
Kisarazu .... 107 35 23N 139 55 E
Kiselevsk .... 71 54 5N 86 39 E
Kishangarh .... 89 27 50N 70 30 E
Kishinev .... 68 47 0N 28 50 E
Kishiwada .... 106 34 28N 135 22 E
Kiskunfélegyháza .... 59 46 42N 19 53 E
Kiso-Gawa → .... 106 35 20N 136 45 E
Kisumu .... 132 0 3S 34 45 E
Kita 130 13 5N 9 25W
Kita-Ura .... 107 36 0N 140 34 E
Kitakami-Gawa → .... 103 38 25N 141 19 E

Kitakyūshū .... 108 33 50N 130 50 E
Kitale .... 132 1 0N 35 0 E
Kitami .... 103 43 48N 143 54 E
Kitchener 151 43 27N 80 29W
Kithira .... 55 36 9N 23 0 E
Kithnos .... 55 37 26N 24 27 E
Kitikmeot □ 145 70 0N 110 0W
Kitimat 154 54 3N 128 38W
Kitsuki .... 108 33 25N 131 37 E
Kittakittaooloo, L. .... 118 28 3S 138 14 E
Kitwe .... 135 12 54S 28 13 E
Kiyev .... 68 50 30N 30 28 E
Klagenfurt .... 45 46 38N 14 20 E
Klaipeda .... 68 55 43N 21 10 E
Klamath → 172 41 40N 124 4W
Klamath Falls 171 42 20N 121 50W
Klamath Mts. 172 41 20N 123 0W
Kleena Kleene 154 52 0N 124 59W
Klondike 144 64 0N 139 26W
Kluane L. 144 61 15N 138 40W
Klyuchevsk .... 73 55 50N 160 30 E
Knaresborough 28 54 1N 1 29W
Knockmealdown Mts. 35 52 16N 8 0W
Knossos .... 55 35 16N 25 10 E
Knoxville, Iowa, U.S.A. 166 41 20N 93 5W
Knoxville, Tenn., U.S.A. ... 165 35 58N 83 57W
Ko Chang .... 95 12 0N 102 20 E
Ko Kut .... 95 11 40N 102 32 E
Koartac 146 60 55N 69 40W
Kobarid .... 52 46 15N 13 30 E
Kobayashi .... 108 31 56N 130 59 E
Kobdo = Hovd .... 100 48 2N 91 37 E
Kōbe .... 106 34 45N 135 10 E
København .... 61 55 41N 12 34 E
Koblenz .... 42 50 21N 7 36 E
Kobroor, Kepulauan ...... 113 6 10S 134 30 E
Kočani .... 53 41 55N 22 25 E
Kōchi .... 109 33 30N 133 35 E
Kochiu = Gejiu .... 99 23 20N 103 10 E
Kodaira .... 107 35 44N 139 29 E
Kodiak I. 142 57 30N 152 45W
Kōfu .... 107 35 40N 138 30 E
Koga .... 107 36 11N 139 43 E
Kogota .... 103 38 33N 141 3 E
Koh-i-Bābā .... 87 34 30N 67 0 E
Kohat .... 89 33 40N 71 29 E
Kokand .... 71 40 30N 70 57 E
Kokchetav .... 71 53 20N 69 25 E
Koko Kyunzu .... 94 14 10N 93 25 E
Kokomo 167 40 30N 86 6W
Kokopo .... 115 4 22S 152 19 E
Koksoak → 146 58 30N 68 10W
Kokubu .... 108 31 44N 130 46 E
Kola Pen. = Kolskiy
  Poluostrov .... 69 67 30N 38 0 E
Kolar .... 90 13 12N 78 15 E
Kolar Gold Fields .... 90 12 58N 78 16 E
Kolarovgrad .... 53 43 18N 26 55 E
Kolding .... 61 55 30N 9 29 E
Kolguyev, Ostrov .... 69 69 20N 48 30 E
Kolhapur .... 91 16 43N 74 15 E
Köln .... 42 50 56N 6 58 E
Koło .... 58 52 14N 18 40 E
Kolomna .... 68 55 8N 38 45 E
Kolskiy Poluostrov ...... 69 67 30N 38 0 E
Kolyma → .... 73 69 30N 161 0 E
Komagene .... 107 35 44N 137 58 E
Komaki .... 106 35 17N 136 55 E
Komandorskiye, Is. ...... 73 55 0N 167 0 E
Komárno .... 59 47 49N 18 5 E
Komatsu .... 106 36 25N 136 30 E
Komatsujima .... 109 34 0N 134 35 E
Komi Rep. □ .... 69 64 0N 55 0 E
Kommunizma, Pik .... 71 39 0N 72 2 E
Komoro .... 107 36 19N 138 26 E
Kompong Cham .... 95 12 0N 105 30 E
Kompong Chhnang ...... 95 12 20N 104 35 E
Kompong Som .... 95 10 38N 103 30 E
Komsomolets, Ostrov .... 72 80 30N 95 0 E
Komsomolsk .... 75 50 30N 137 0 E
Konarhá □ .... 87 35 30N 71 3 E

Place	Page	Lat	Long
Kong	**130**	8 54N	4 36W
Kong, Koh	**95**	11 20N	103 0 E
Kong Christian X.s Land	**13**	74 0N	29 0W
Kong Frederik VI.s Kyst	**147**	63 0N	43 0W
Kong Frederik VIII.s Land	**13**	78 30N	26 0W
Kongor	**129**	7 1N	31 27 E
Königsberg = Kaliningrad	**68**	54 42N	20 32 E
Konin	**58**	52 12N	18 15 E
Konjic	**52**	43 42N	17 58 E
Konosha	**68**	61 0N	40 5 E
Konstanz	**44**	47 39N	9 10 E
Kontagora	**131**	10 23N	5 27 E
Konya	**80**	37 52N	32 35 E
Konya Ovasi	**80**	38 30N	33 0 E
Koolyanobbing	**120**	30 48S	119 36 E
Kopaonik Planina	**52**	43 10N	21 50 E
Kopeysk	**71**	55 7N	61 37 E
Kopparberg	**60**	59 52N	15 0 E
Koppeh Dāgh	**86**	38 0N	58 0 E
Korab	**52**	41 44N	20 40 E
Korça	**52**	40 37N	20 50 E
Korčula	**52**	42 57N	17 8 E
Kordestān □	**81**	36 0N	47 0 E
Korea Bay	**98**	39 0N	124 0 E
Korea Strait	**104**	34 0N	129 30 E
Korhogo	**130**	9 29N	5 28W
Korinthiakós Kólpos	**54**	38 16N	22 30 E
Kórinthos	**54**	37 56N	22 55 E
Kōriyama	**105**	37 24N	140 23 E
Koroit	**119**	38 18S	142 24 E
Kortrijk	**42**	50 50N	3 17 E
Koryakskiy Khrebet	**73**	61 0N	171 0 E
Kos	**55**	36 50N	27 15 E
Kosciusko	**169**	33 3N	89 34W
Kosciusko, Mt.	**117**	36 27S	148 16 E
Koshigaya	**107**	35 54N	139 48 E
K'oshih = Kashi	**100**	39 30N	76 2 E
Koshiki-Rettō	**108**	31 45N	129 49 E
Kōshoku	**107**	36 38N	138 6 E
Košice	**59**	48 42N	21 15 E
Kosovska-Mitrovica	**52**	42 54N	20 52 E
Kôstî	**129**	13 8N	32 43 E
Kostroma	**68**	57 50N	40 58 E
Koszalin	**58**	53 50N	16 8 E
Kota	**91**	25 14N	75 49 E
Kota Baharu	**96**	6 7N	102 14 E
Kota Kinabalu	**112**	6 0N	116 4 E
Kotelnich	**68**	58 20N	48 10 E
Kotka	**67**	60 28N	26 58 E
Kotlas	**69**	61 15N	47 0 E
Kotor	**52**	42 25N	18 47 E
Kotuy →	**77**	71 54N	102 6 E
Kotzebue	**142**	66 50N	162 40W
Kowloon	**99**	22 20N	114 15 E
Kōyama	**108**	31 20N	130 56 E
Koyukuk →	**142**	64 56N	157 30W
Kozáni	**55**	40 19N	21 47 E
Kozhikode = Calicut	**90**	11 15N	75 43 E
Kōzu-Shima	**107**	34 13N	139 10 E
Kra, Isthmus of = Kra, Kho Khot	**94**	10 15N	99 30 E
Kra, Kho Khot	**94**	10 15N	99 30 E
Kragujevac	**52**	44 2N	20 56 E
Kraków	**58**	50 4N	19 57 E
Kraljevo	**52**	43 44N	20 41 E
Krasnodar	**68**	45 5N	39 0 E
Krasnovodsk	**70**	40 0N	52 52 E
Krasnoyarsk	**74**	56 8N	93 0 E
Krasnyy Kut	**68**	50 50N	47 0 E
Kratie	**95**	12 32N	106 10 E
Kravanh, Chuor Phnum	**95**	12 0N	103 32 E
Krefeld	**42**	51 20N	6 32 E
Kremenchug	**68**	49 5N	33 25 E
Krishna →	**91**	15 57N	80 59 E
Krishnanagar	**92**	23 24N	88 33 E
Kristiansand	**60**	58 9N	8 1 E
Kristianstad	**61**	56 2N	14 9 E
Kristianstads län □	**61**	56 15N	14 0 E
Kristiansund	**65**	63 7N	7 45 E
Kríti	**55**	35 15N	25 0 E
Krivoy Rog	**68**	47 51N	33 20 E
Krk	**52**	45 8N	14 40 E
Kronobergs län □	**61**	56 45N	14 30 E
Kronshtadt	**68**	60 5N	29 45 E
Krotoszyn	**58**	51 42N	17 23 E
Krugersdorp	**137**	26 5S	27 46 E
Krung Thep = Bangkok	**94**	13 45N	100 35 E
Kruševac	**52**	43 35N	21 28 E
Krymskiy P-ov.	**68**	45 0N	34 0 E
Kuala Dungun	**96**	4 45N	103 25 E
Kuala Kangsar	**96**	4 46N	100 56 E
Kuala Lipis	**96**	4 10N	102 3 E
Kuala Lumpur	**96**	3 9N	101 41 E
Kuala Pilah	**96**	2 45N	102 15 E
Kuala Trengganu	**96**	5 20N	103 8 E
Kuangchou = Guangzhou	**99**	23 5N	113 10 E
Kuantan	**96**	3 49N	103 20 E
Kubak	**88**	27 10N	63 10 E
Kuban →	**68**	45 20N	37 30 E
Kubokawa	**109**	33 12N	133 8 E
Kuchinoerabu-Jima	**104**	30 28N	130 11 E
Kucing	**111**	1 33N	110 25 E
Kudamatsu	**108**	34 0N	131 52 E
Kueiyang = Guiyang	**99**	26 32N	106 40 E
Kūh-e-Jebāl Bārez	**85**	29 0N	58 0 E
Kūh-e Sorkh	**86**	35 30N	58 45 E
Kūhhā-ye-Bashākerd	**85**	26 45N	59 0 E
Kūhhā-ye Sabalān	**81**	38 15N	47 45 E
Kuji	**103**	40 11N	141 46 E
Kuldja = Yining	**100**	43 58N	81 10 E
Kulunda	**71**	52 35N	78 57 E
Kumagaya	**107**	36 9N	139 22 E
Kumamoto	**108**	32 45N	130 45 E
Kumano	**106**	33 54N	136 5 E
Kumano-Nada	**106**	33 47N	136 20 E
Kumasi	**130**	6 41N	1 38W
Kumayri	**70**	40 47N	43 50 E
Kumon Bum	**93**	26 30N	97 15 E
Kunashir, Ostrov	**75**	44 0N	146 0 E
Kunimi-Dake	**109**	32 33N	131 1 E
Kunlun Shan	**100**	36 0N	86 30 E
Kunming	**101**	25 1N	102 41 E
Kunsan	**98**	35 59N	126 45 E
Kuopio	**67**	62 53N	27 35 E
Kupang	**113**	10 19S	123 39 E
Kurashiki	**109**	34 40N	133 50 E
Kurayoshi	**109**	35 26N	133 50 E
Kure	**109**	34 14N	132 32 E
Kurgan	**71**	55 26N	65 18 E
Kuril Is. = Kurilskiye Ostrova	**75**	45 0N	150 0 E
Kurilskiye Ostrova	**75**	45 0N	150 0 E
Kurnool	**90**	15 45N	78 0 E
Kurobe-Gawe →	**106**	36 55N	137 25 E
Kurri Kurri	**117**	32 50S	151 28 E
Kursk	**68**	51 42N	36 11 E
Kuršumlija	**52**	43 9N	21 19 E
Kurume	**108**	33 15N	130 30 E
Kurunegala	**90**	7 30N	80 23 E
Kusatsu	**106**	34 58N	135 57 E
Kushikino	**108**	31 44N	130 16 E
Kushima	**108**	31 29N	131 14 E
Kushimoto	**106**	33 28N	135 47 E
Kushiro	**103**	43 0N	144 25 E
Kushka	**70**	35 20N	62 18 E
Kushtia	**92**	23 55N	89 5 E
Kuskokwim Bay	**142**	59 50N	162 56W
Kustanay	**71**	53 10N	63 35 E
Kusu	**108**	33 16N	131 9 E
Kütahya	**80**	39 30N	30 2 E
Kutaisi	**70**	42 19N	42 40 E
Kutaraja = Banda Aceh	**111**	5 35N	95 20 E
Kutno	**58**	52 15N	19 23 E
Kuujjuaq	**146**	58 6N	68 15W
Kuwait = Al Kuwayt	**84**	29 30N	47 30 E
Kuwait ■	**84**	29 30N	47 30 E
Kuwana	**106**	35 0N	136 43 E
Kuybyshev = Samara	**68**	53 8N	50 6 E
Kwakoegron	**185**	5 12N	55 25W
Kwangju	**98**	35 9N	126 54 E
Kwangsi-Chuang = Guangxi Zhuangzu Zizhiqu □	**99**	24 0N	109 0 E
Kwangtung = Guangdong □	**99**	23 0N	113 0 E

Kweichow = Guizhou □ ... **99** 27 0N 107 0 E
Kwinana New Town .... **120** 32 15S 115 47 E
Kyabram .... **117** 36 19S 145 4 E
Kyaukpadaung .... **93** 20 52N 95 8 E
Kyle of Lochalsh **32** 57 17N 5 43W
Kyneton .... **117** 37 10S 144 29 E
Kyō-ga-Saki .... **106** 35 45N 135 15 E
Kyoga, L. .... **132** 1 35N 33 0 E
Kyogle .... **116** 28 40S 153 0 E
Kyōto .... **106** 35 0N 135 45 E
Kyrenia .... **80** 35 20N 33 20 E
Kyūshū .... **108** 33 0N 131 0 E
Kyūshū □ .... **108** 33 0N 131 0 E
Kyūshū-Sanchi .... **108** 32 35N 131 17 E
Kyustendil .... **53** 42 16N 22 41 E
Kyzyl .... **74** 51 50N 94 30 E
Kyzylkum, Peski .... **70** 42 30N 65 0 E
Kzyl-Orda .... **71** 44 48N 65 28 E

L

Labe = Elbe → .... **42** 53 50N 9 0 E
Laboulaye **190** 34 10S 63 30W
Labrador, Coast of □ **147** 53 20N 61 0W
Lábrea **187** 7 15S 64 51W
Lac la Martre **145** 63 8N 117 16W
Laccadive Is. =
　Lakshadweep Is. .... **78** 10 0N 72 30 E
Lachine **151** 45 30N 73 40W
Lachute **151** 45 39N 74 21W
Lackawanna **164** 42 49N 78 50W
Lacombe **155** 52 30N 113 44W
Laconia **148** 43 32N 71 30W
Ladakh Ra. .... **89** 34 0N 78 0 E
Ladoga, L. = Ladozhskoye
　Ozero .... **68** 61 15N 30 30 E
Ladozhskoye Ozero .... **68** 61 15N 30 30 E
Ladysmith **154** 49 0N 123 49W
Lae .... **115** 6 40S 147 2 E
Lafayette, Ind., U.S.A. **167** 40 25N 86 54W
Lafayette, La., U.S.A. **168** 30 18N 92 0W
Laghmān □ .... **87** 34 20N 70 0 E
Laghouat .... **127** 33 50N 2 59 E
Lagny .... **39** 48 52N 2 40 E
Lagos, Nigeria .... **131** 6 25N 3 27 E
Lagos, Portugal **50** 37 5N 8 41W
Lagos de Moreno **175** 21 21N 101 55W
Laguna **191** 28 30S 48 50W
Laguna Beach **173** 33 31N 117 52W
Laguna Madre **158** 27 0N 97 20W
Lagunas, Chile **187** 21 0S 69 45W
Lagunas, Peru **186** 5 10S 75 35W
Lahore .... **89** 31 32N 74 22 E
Lahti .... **67** 60 58N 25 40 E
Lahtis = Lahti .... **67** 60 58N 25 40 E
Laï .... **131** 9 25N 16 18 E
Laidley .... **116** 27 39S 152 20 E
Lairg **33** 58 1N 4 24W
Laja, R. de la → **177** 20 55N 100 46W
Lajes **191** 27 48S 50 20W
Lake Cargelligo .... **117** 33 15S 146 22 E
Lake Charles **168** 30 15N 93 10W
Lake City, Fla., U.S.A. **170** 30 10N 82 40W
Lake City, S.C., U.S.A. **165** 33 51N 79 44W
Lake Grace .... **120** 33 7S 118 28 E
Lake Harbour **146** 62 50N 69 50W
Lake Worth **170** 26 36N 80 3W
Lakeland **170** 28 0N 82 0W
Lakes Entrance .... **117** 37 50S 148 0 E
Lakewood **167** 41 28N 81 50W
Lakshadweep Is. .... **78** 10 0N 72 30 E
Lala Ghat .... **93** 24 30N 92 40 E
Lalitpur .... **91** 24 42N 78 28 E
Lamar **163** 38 9N 102 35W
Lambi Kyun .... **96** 10 50N 98 20 E
Lameroo .... **119** 35 19S 140 33 E
Lamia .... **54** 38 55N 22 26 E
Lammermuir Hills **31** 55 50N 2 40W

Lamon Bay .... **112** 14 30N 122 20 E
Lampa **187** 15 22S 70 22W
Lampang .... **94** 18 16N 99 32 E
Lampeter **26** 52 6N 4 6W
Lamu .... **133** 2 16S 40 55 E
Lanark **31** 55 40N 3 48W
Lancang Jiang → ...... **101** 21 40N 101 10 E
Lancashire □ **28** 53 40N 2 30W
Lancaster, U.K. **28** 54 3N 2 48W
Lancaster, U.S.A. **164** 40 4N 76 19W
Lancaster Sd. **146** 74 13N 84 0W
Lanchow = Lanzhou ..... **99** 36 1N 103 52 E
Landes, Les **36** 44 20N 1 0W
Land's End **27** 50 4N 5 43W
Landskrona .... **61** 55 53N 12 50 E
Lanett **169** 33 0N 85 15W
Langjökull **64** 64 39N 20 12W
Langlade **149** 46 50N 56 20W
Langøya .... **64** 68 45N 14 50 E
Langres, Plateau de ...... **37** 47 45N 5 3 E
Languedoc .... **37** 43 58N 4 0 E
Lannion **36** 48 46N 3 29W
Lansing **167** 42 47N 84 40W
Lanzhou .... **99** 36 1N 103 52 E
Laois □ **35** 53 0N 7 20W
Laon .... **38** 49 33N 3 35 E
Laona **150** 45 32N 88 41W
Laos ■ .... **95** 17 45N 105 0 E
Lapeer **167** 43 3N 83 20W
Lapland = Lappland ..... **67** 68 7N 24 0 E
Lappland .... **67** 68 7N 24 0 E
Laptev Sea .... **72** 76 0N 125 0 E
Laramie **163** 41 20N 105 38W
Laramie Mts. **163** 42 0N 105 30W
Laredo **161** 27 34N 99 29W
Laren .... **40** 52 16N 5 14 E
Largs **30** 55 48N 4 51W
Lárisa .... **54** 39 49N 22 28 E
Larkana .... **88** 27 32N 68 18 E
Larnaca .... **80** 35 0N 33 35 E
Larne **34** 54 52N 5 50W
Laryak .... **69** 61 15N 80 0 E
Las Cruces **161** 32 18N 106 50W
Las Lajas **190** 38 30S 70 25W
Las Palmas **126** 28 7N 15 26W
Las Vegas, N. Mex., U.S.A. . **161** 35 35N 105 10W
Las Vegas, Nev., U.S.A. ... **173** 36 10N 115 5W
Lashio .... **93** 22 56N 97 45 E
Latacunga **184** 0 50S 78 35W
Latakia = Al Lādhiqīyah .... **80** 35 30N 35 45 E
Latium = Lazio □ .... **46** 42 10N 12 30 E
Latrobe .... **119** 41 14S 146 30 E
Latur .... **91** 18 25N 76 40 E
Latvia ■ .... **68** 56 50N 24 0 E
Lauchhammer .... **43** 51 35N 13 48 E
Launceston, Australia ..... **119** 41 24S 147 8 E
Launceston, U.K. **27** 50 38N 4 21W
Launglon Bok .... **94** 13 50N 97 54 E
Laurel **169** 31 41N 89 9W
Laurens **165** 34 32N 82 2W
Laurentian Plat. **138** 52 0N 70 0W
Laurinburg **165** 34 50N 79 25W
Lausanne .... **44** 46 32N 6 38 E
Laut, Pulau .... **111** 3 40S 116 10 E
Laut Ketil, Kepulauan ..... **113** 4 45S 115 40 E
Lauzon **148** 46 48N 71 10W
Laval **36** 48 4N 0 48W
Lávrion .... **55** 37 40N 24 4 E
Lawrence, Kans., U.S.A. ... **166** 39 0N 95 10W
Lawrence, Mass., U.S.A. ... **164** 42 40N 71 9W
Lawrenceburg **169** 35 12N 87 19W
Lawton **161** 34 33N 98 25W
Lazio □ .... **46** 42 10N 12 30 E
Lea → **25** 51 30N 0 10W
Leader **152** 50 50N 109 30W
Leadhills **31** 55 25N 3 47W
Leadville **163** 39 17N 106 23W
Leamington, Canada **150** 42 3N 82 36W
Leamington, U.K. **24** 52 18N 1 32W
Leavenworth **166** 39 25N 95 0W
Lebanon, Mo., U.S.A. **166** 37 40N 92 40W

Lebanon, Oreg., U.S.A. 171 44 31N 122 57W
Lebanon, Pa., U.S.A. 164 40 20N 76 28W
Lebanon, Tenn., U.S.A. 169 36 15N 86 20W
Lebanon ■ . . . . 80 34 0N 36 0 E
Lecce . . . . 49 40 20N 18 10 E
Ledbury 24 52 3N 2 25W
Leduc 155 53 15N 113 30W
Leeds 28 53 48N 1 34W
Leek 28 53 7N 2 2W
Leerdam . . . . 40 51 54N 5 6 E
Leesburg 170 28 47N 81 52W
Leeton . . . . 117 34 33S 146 23 E
Leeuwarden . . . . 41 53 15N 5 48 E
Leeuwin, C. . . . . 120 34 20S 115 9 E
Leeward Is. 181 16 30N 63 30W
Leghorn = Livorno . . . . 46 43 32N 10 18 E
Legnica . . . . 58 51 12N 16 10 E
Leicester 25 52 39N 1 9W
Leicester □ 25 52 40N 1 10W
Leichhardt . . . . 121 33 53S 151 9 E
Leiden . . . . 40 52 9N 4 30 E
Leigh Creek South . . . . 118 30 38S 138 26 E
Leinster . . . . 120 27 51S 120 36 E
Leinster □ 35 53 0N 7 10W
Leinster, Mt. 35 52 38N 6 47W
Leipzig . . . . 43 51 20N 12 23 E
Leith 31 55 59N 3 10W
Leith Hill 24 51 10N 0 23W
Leitrim 34 54 0N 8 5W
Lek → . . . . 40 51 54N 4 35 E
Leleque 192 42 28S 71 0W
Léman, Lac . . . . 44 46 26N 6 30 E
Lemmer . . . . 41 52 51N 5 43 E
Lena → . . . . 72 72 52N 126 40 E
Leninabad = Khodzhent . . . 71 40 17N 69 37 E
Leninakan = Kumayri . . . . . . 70 40 47N 43 50 E
Leningrad = Sankt-Peterburg 68 59 55N 30 20 E
Leninsk-Kuznetskiy . . . . 71 54 44N 86 10 E
Leninskoye . . . . 75 47 56N 132 38 E
Lenoir City 165 35 40N 84 20W
Lens, Belgium . . . . 38 50 33N 3 54 E
Lens, France . . . . 37 50 26N 2 50 E
Lensk . . . . 74 60 48N 114 55 E
Leominster, U.K. 24 52 15N 2 43W
Leominster, U.S.A. 164 42 32N 71 45W
León, Mexico 177 21 7N 101 40W
León, Nic. 179 12 20N 86 51W
León, Spain 50 42 38N 5 34W
León □ 50 42 40N 5 55W
Leongatha . . . . 117 38 30S 145 58 E
Léopold II, Lac = Mai-Ndombe, L. . . . . 134 2 0S 18 20 E
Léopoldville = Kinshasa . . . 134 4 20S 15 15 E
Lérida . . . . 51 41 37N 0 39 E
Lerwick 30 60 10N 1 10W
Lesbos, I. = Lésvos . . . . 55 39 10N 26 20 E
Lesotho ■ . . . . 137 29 40S 28 0 E
Lesozavodsk . . . . 75 45 30N 133 29 E
Lesser Antilles 181 15 0N 61 0W
Lesser Slave L. 155 55 30N 115 25W
Lésvos . . . . 55 39 10N 26 20 E
Letchworth 25 51 58N 0 13W
Lethbridge 155 49 45N 112 45W
Leti, Kepulauan . . . . 113 8 10S 128 0 E
Leticia 184 4 9S 70 0W
Letsôk-aw Kyun . . . . 94 11 30N 98 25 E
Letterkenny 34 54 57N 7 42W
Leuven . . . . 42 50 52N 4 42 E
Levanger . . . . 65 63 45N 11 19 E
Levin . . . . 122 40 37S 175 18 E
Lévis 148 46 48N 71 9W
Levkás . . . . 54 38 40N 20 43 E
Levkôsia = Nicosia . . . . 80 35 10N 33 25 E
Lewes . . . . 25 50 53N 0 2 E
Lewis 32 58 10N 6 40W
Lewis, Butt of 32 58 30N 6 12W
Lewis Ra. 162 48 0N 113 15W
Lewisporte 149 49 15N 55 3W
Lewiston . . . . 148 44 3N 70 10 E
Lexington, Ky., U.S.A. 165 38 6N 84 30W
Lexington, Mo., U.S.A. 166 39 7N 93 55W
Lexington, N.C., U.S.A. 165 35 50N 80 13W
Lexington, Oreg., U.S.A. . . . 171 45 29N 119 46W
Lexington Park 165 38 16N 76 27W
Leyte . . . . 112 11 0N 125 0 E
Lhasa . . . . 101 29 50N 91 3 E
Lhazê . . . . 101 29 5N 87 38 E
Lianyungang . . . . 99 34 40N 119 11 E
Liaoning □ . . . . 98 41 40N 122 30 E
Liaoyuan . . . . 98 42 58N 125 2 E
Liard → 144 61 51N 121 18W
Libau = Liepaja . . . . 68 56 30N 21 0 E
Liberec . . . . 58 50 47N 15 7 E
Liberia ■ 130 6 30N 9 30W
Lîbîya, Sahrâ' . . . . 128 27 35N 25 0 E
Libreville . . . . 134 0 25N 9 26 E
Libya ■ . . . . 127 27 0N 17 0 E
Lichfield 28 52 40N 1 50W
Liechtenstein ■ . . . . 44 47 8N 9 35 E
Liège . . . . 42 50 38N 5 35 E
Liegnitz = Legnica . . . . 58 51 12N 16 10 E
Lienyünchiangshih = Lianyungang . . . . 99 34 40N 119 11 E
Liepaja . . . . 68 56 30N 21 0 E
Liévin . . . . 38 50 24N 2 47 E
Liffey → 35 53 21N 6 20W
Lifford 34 54 50N 7 30W
Liguria □ . . . . 46 44 30N 9 0 E
Ligurian Sea . . . . 46 43 20N 9 0 E
Lihou Reefs and Cays . . . . . 121 17 25S 151 40 E
Lihue 160 21 59N 159 24W
Likasi . . . . 135 10 55S 26 48 E
Lille, Belgium . . . . 38 51 15N 4 50 E
Lille, France . . . . 37 50 38N 3 3 E
Lille Bælt . . . . 61 55 20N 9 45 E
Lillehammer . . . . 60 61 8N 10 30 E
Lillers . . . . 38 50 35N 2 28 E
Lillooet 154 50 44N 121 57W
Lilongwe . . . . 137 14 0S 33 48 E
Lima, Peru 186 12 0S 77 0W
Lima, U.S.A. 167 40 42N 84 5W
Limassol . . . . 80 34 42N 33 1 E
Limavady 34 55 3N 6 58W
Limbe . . . . 137 15 55S 35 2 E
Limburg □ . . . . 41 51 20N 5 55 E
Limeira 188 22 35S 47 28W
Limerick 35 52 40N 8 38W
Limerick □ 35 52 30N 8 50W
Limfjorden . . . . 61 56 55N 9 0 E
Límnos . . . . 55 39 50N 25 5 E
Limoges . . . . 36 45 50N 1 15 E
Limón 179 10 0N 83 2W
Limousin . . . . 36 46 0N 1 0 E
Limpopo → . . . . 137 25 15S 33 30 E
Linares, Chile 190 35 50S 71 40W
Linares, Mexico 176 24 50N 99 40W
Linares, Spain 50 38 10N 3 40W
Lincoln, Argentina 190 34 55S 61 30W
Lincoln, U.K. 29 53 14N 0 32W
Lincoln, Ill., U.S.A. 166 40 10N 89 20W
Lincoln, Maine, U.S.A. 148 45 27N 68 29W
Lincoln, Nebr., U.S.A. 156 40 50N 96 42W
Lincoln □ 29 53 14N 0 32W
Lincoln Sea 12 84 0N 55 0W
Lincoln Wolds 29 53 20N 0 5W
Lindsay, Canada 151 44 22N 78 43W
Lindsay, U.S.A. 173 36 14N 119 6W
Línea de la Concepción, La . 50 36 15N 5 23W
Lingga, Kepulauan . . . . 111 0 10S 104 30 E
Linguéré 130 15 25N 15 5W
Linköping . . . . 60 58 28N 15 36 E
Linlithgow 31 55 58N 3 38W
Linxia . . . . 99 35 36N 103 10 E
Linz . . . . 45 48 18N 14 18 E
Lion, G. du . . . . 37 43 0N 4 0 E
Lípari, Is. . . . . 49 38 30N 14 50 E
Lipetsk . . . . 68 52 37N 39 35 E
Lippe → . . . . 42 51 39N 6 38 E
Lisboa 50 38 42N 9 10W
Lisbon = Lisboa 50 38 42N 9 10W
Lisburn 34 54 30N 6 9W
Lisburne, C. 142 68 50N 166 0W

Lisieux	39 49 10N	0 12 E
Lismore	116 28 44S	153 21 E
Lister, Mt.	15 78 0S	162 0 E
Listowel	35 52 27N	9 30W
Litchfield	166 39 10N	89 40W
Lithgow	117 33 25S	150 8 E
Lithuania ■	68 55 30N	24 0 E
Little Andaman I.	94 10 40N	92 15 E
Little Barrier I.	122 36 12S	175 8 E
Little Current	150 45 55N	82 0W
Little Falls	164 43 3N	74 50W
Little Minch	32 57 35N	6 45W
Little Rann	91 23 25N	71 25 E
Little Rock	168 34 41N	92 10W
Littlehampton	25 50 48N	0 32W
Liuzhou	99 24 22N	109 22 E
Liverpool, Australia	117 33 54S	150 58 E
Liverpool, Canada	148 44 5N	64 41W
Liverpool, U.K.	28 53 25N	3 0W
Liverpool Plains	116 31 15S	150 15 E
Livingston, Guatemala	177 15 50N	88 50W
Livingston, U.K.	31 55 52N	3 33W
Livingston, Mont., U.S.A.	163 45 40N	110 40W
Livingston, Tex., U.S.A.	168 30 44N	94 54W
Livingstone	135 17 46S	25 52 E
Livonia	167 42 25N	83 23W
Livorno	46 43 32N	10 18 E
Lizard Pt.	27 49 57N	5 11W
Ljubljana	52 46 4N	14 33 E
Ljusnan →	66 61 12N	17 8 E
Llandeilo	26 51 53N	4 0W
Llandovery	26 51 59N	3 49W
Llandrindod Wells	26 52 15N	3 23W
Llandudno	26 53 19N	3 51W
Llanelli	27 51 41N	4 11W
Llanes	50 43 25N	4 50W
Llangollen	26 52 58N	3 10W
Llanidloes	26 52 28N	3 31W
Llano Estacado	161 34 0N	103 0W
Llanos	184 5 0N	71 35W
Lloydminster	152 53 17N	110 0W
Loc Ninh	95 11 50N	106 34 E
Lochaber	32 56 55N	5 0W
Lochboisdale	32 57 10N	7 20W
Lochem	41 52 9N	6 26 E
Lochgilphead	30 56 2N	5 37W
Lochinver	32 58 9N	5 15W
Lochmaddy	32 57 36N	7 10W
Lochy, L.	32 56 58N	4 55W
Lock Haven	164 41 7N	77 31W
Lockhart	117 35 14S	146 40 E
Lockport	164 43 12N	78 42W
Lodi	172 38 12N	121 16W
Łódź	58 51 45N	19 27 E
Lofoten	64 68 30N	15 0 E
Logan, Utah, U.S.A.	163 41 45N	111 50W
Logan, W. Va., U.S.A.	165 37 51N	81 59W
Logan, Mt.	144 60 31N	140 22W
Logansport	167 40 45N	86 21W
Logroño	51 42 28N	2 27W
Loire →	36 47 16N	2 10W
Loja	184 3 59S	79 16W
Lokka	67 67 55N	27 35 E
Lolland	61 54 45N	11 30 E
Lom	53 43 48N	23 12 E
Lomami →	134 0 46N	24 16 E
Lombardia □	46 45 35N	9 45 E
Lombardy = Lombardia □	46 45 35N	9 45 E
Lombok	113 8 45S	116 30 E
Lomé	130 6 9N	1 20 E
Lomond, L.	31 56 8N	4 38W
Lompoc	173 34 41N	120 32W
Łomza	58 53 10N	22 2 E
London, Canada	150 42 59N	81 15W
London, U.K.	25 51 30N	0 5W
Londonderry	34 55 0N	7 20W
Londrina	191 23 18S	51 10W
Long Beach	173 33 46N	118 12W
Long I., Bahamas	178 23 20N	75 10W
Long I., U.S.A.	164 40 50N	73 20W
Long Range Mts.	149 49 30N	57 30W
Long Xuyen	95 10 19N	105 28 E
Longford, Australia	119 41 32S	147 3 E
Longford, Ireland	34 53 43N	7 50W
Longford □	34 53 42N	7 45W
Longlac	150 49 45N	86 25W
Longmont	163 40 10N	105 4W
Longreach	121 23 28S	144 14 E
Longview, Tex., U.S.A.	168 32 30N	94 45W
Longview, Wash., U.S.A.	171 46 9N	122 58W
Looe	27 50 24N	4 25W
Loop Hd.	35 52 34N	9 55W
Lop Nor	100 40 20N	90 10 E
Lopez, C.	134 0 47S	8 40 E
Lorain	167 41 28N	82 55W
Lorca	51 37 41N	1 42W
Lord Howe I.	122 31 33S	159 6 E
Lordsburg	161 32 22N	108 45W
Lorient	36 47 45N	3 23W
Lorn	30 56 26N	5 10W
Lorn, Firth of	30 56 20N	5 40W
Lorraine	37 49 0N	6 0 E
Los Alamos	161 35 57N	106 17W
Los Andes	190 32 50S	70 40W
Los Angeles, Chile	190 37 28S	72 23W
Los Angeles, U.S.A.	173 34 0N	118 10W
Los Angeles Aqueduct	173 35 25N	118 0W
Los Hermanos	181 11 45N	84 25W
Los Mochis	174 25 45N	108 57W
Los Testigos	181 11 23N	63 6W
Lošinj	52 44 30N	14 30 E
Lossiemouth	33 57 43N	3 17W
Lot →	36 44 18N	0 20 E
Lota	190 37 5S	73 10W
Lothian □	31 55 50N	3 0W
Loughborough	29 52 46N	1 11W
Loughrea	35 53 11N	8 33W
Louisbourg	149 45 55N	60 0W
Louise I.	154 52 55N	131 50W
Louisiana □	168 30 50N	92 0W
Louisville, Ky., U.S.A.	167 38 15N	85 45W
Louisville, Miss., U.S.A.	169 33 7N	89 3W
Lourdes	36 43 6N	0 3W
Lourenço-Marques = Maputo	137 25 58S	32 32 E
Louth	29 53 23N	0 0 E
Louth □	34 53 55N	6 30W
Louvain = Leuven	42 50 52N	4 42 E
Louviers	39 49 12N	1 10 E
Lowell	164 42 38N	71 19W
Lower Austria = Niederösterreich □	45 48 25N	15 40 E
Lower California = Baja California	174 31 10N	115 12W
Lower Hutt	123 41 10S	174 55 E
Lower Saxony = Niedersachsen □	42 52 45N	9 0 E
Lowestoft	25 52 29N	1 44 E
Łowicz	58 52 6N	19 55 E
Loxton	119 34 28S	140 31 E
Loyalty Is. = Loyauté, Is.	122 21 0S	167 30 E
Loyang = Luoyang	99 34 40N	112 26 E
Loyauté, Is.	122 21 0S	167 30 E
Lualaba →	135 0 26N	25 20 E
Luan Chau	95 21 38N	103 24 E
Luanda	134 8 50S	13 15 E
Luang Prabang	95 19 52N	102 10 E
Luarca	50 43 32N	6 32W
Lubbock	161 33 40N	101 53W
Lübeck	43 53 52N	10 41 E
Lublin	58 51 12N	22 38 E
Lubnān, J.	80 33 50N	35 45 E
Lubumbashi	135 11 40S	27 28 E
Lucca	46 43 50N	10 30 E
Luce Bay	30 54 45N	4 48W
Lučenec	59 48 18N	19 42 E
Lucerne = Luzern	44 47 3N	8 18 E
Lucknow	92 26 50N	81 0 E
Lüda = Dalian	98 38 50N	121 40 E
Lüderitz	136 26 41S	15 8 E
Ludhiana	89 30 57N	75 56 E
Ludington	167 43 58N	86 27W
Ludlow	24 52 23N	2 42W

Ludwigshafen	**42**	49 27N	8 27 E
Lufkin	**168**	31 25N	94 40W
Lugano	**44**	46 0N	8 57 E
Lugansk	**68**	48 38N	39 15 E
Lugo	**50**	43 2N	7 35W
Lugovoye	**71**	42 55N	72 43 E
Luján	**190**	34 45S	59 5W
Łuków	**58**	51 55N	22 23 E
Lule älv →	**67**	65 35N	22 10 E
Luleå	**67**	65 35N	22 10 E
Lüleburgaz	**80**	41 23N	27 22 E
Lulua →	**134**	6 30S	22 50 E
Luluabourg = Kananga	**134**	5 55S	22 18 E
Lumberton	**165**	34 37N	78 59W
Lundy	**27**	51 10N	4 41W
Lune →	**28**	54 0N	2 51W
Lüneburg	**43**	53 15N	10 23 E
Lüneburg Heath = Lüneburger Heide	**43**	53 0N	10 0 E
Lüneburger Heide	**43**	53 0N	10 0 E
Lūni →	**91**	24 41N	71 14 E
Luoyang	**99**	34 40N	112 26 E
Lurgan	**34**	54 28N	6 20W
Lusaka	**135**	15 28S	28 16 E
Luta = Dalian	**98**	38 50N	121 40 E
Luton	**25**	51 53N	0 24W
Lutsk	**68**	50 50N	25 15 E
Luvua →	**135**	6 50S	27 30 E
Luxembourg	**42**	49 37N	6 9 E
Luxembourg ■	**42**	50 0N	6 0 E
Luzern	**44**	47 3N	8 18 E
Luzhou	**99**	28 52N	105 20 E
Luziânia	**188**	16 20S	48 0W
Luzon	**112**	16 0N	121 0 E
Lvov	**68**	49 50N	24 0 E
Lyakhovskiye, Ostrova	**72**	73 40N	141 0 E
Lyallpur = Faisalabad	**89**	31 30N	73 5 E
Lyell I.	**154**	52 40N	131 35W
Lyell Range	**123**	41 38S	172 20 E
Lyme Regis	**27**	50 44N	2 57W
Lymington	**24**	50 46N	1 32W
Lynchburg	**165**	37 23N	79 10W
Lynn	**164**	42 28N	70 57W
Lynn Lake	**152**	56 51N	101 3W
Lynton	**27**	51 14N	3 50W
Lyon	**37**	45 46N	4 50 E
Lyons = Lyon	**37**	45 46N	4 50 E
Lytham St. Anne's	**28**	53 45N	2 58W
Lyttelton	**122**	43 35S	172 44 E

M

Ma'ān	**80**	30 12N	35 44 E
Ma'anshan	**99**	31 44N	118 29 E
Ma'arrat an Nu'mān	**80**	35 43N	36 43 E
Maas →	**40**	51 45N	4 32 E
Maaseik	**41**	51 6N	5 45 E
Maastricht	**41**	50 50N	5 40 E
Mablethorpe	**29**	53 21N	0 14 E
McAlester	**168**	34 57N	95 46W
Macao = Macau ■	**99**	22 16N	113 35 E
Macapá	**185**	0 5N	51 4W
Macau	**189**	5 0S	36 40W
Macau ■	**99**	22 16N	113 35 E
McBride	**155**	53 20N	120 19W
Macclesfield	**28**	53 16N	2 9W
McClure Str.	**12**	75 0N	119 0W
McComb	**169**	31 13N	90 30W
McCook	**163**	40 15N	100 35W
McDermitt	**172**	42 0N	117 45W
Macdonald L.	**114**	23 30S	129 0 E
Macdonnell Ranges	**114**	23 40S	133 0 E
McDouall Peak	**118**	29 51S	134 55 E
Macduff	**33**	57 40N	2 30W
Macedonia ■	**55**	41 39N	22 0 E
Maceió	**189**	9 40S	35 41W
Macfarlane, L.	**118**	32 0S	136 40 E
Macgillycuddy's Reeks	**35**	52 2N	9 45W
Machala	**184**	3 20S	79 57W
Machida	**107**	35 28N	139 23 E
Machilipatnam	**92**	16 12N	81 8 E
Machiques	**184**	10 4N	72 34W
Machynlleth	**26**	52 36N	3 51W
Mackay	**121**	21 8S	149 11 E
Mackay, L.	**114**	22 30S	129 0 E
McKeesport	**164**	40 21N	79 50W
Mackenzie →	**144**	69 10N	134 20W
Mackenzie Bay	**12**	69 0N	137 30W
Mackenzie Mts.	**144**	64 0N	130 0W
McKinley, Mt.	**142**	63 2N	151 0W
McKinley Sea	**13**	84 0N	10 0W
McKinney	**168**	33 10N	96 40W
Macksville	**116**	30 40S	152 56 E
Maclean	**116**	29 26S	153 16 E
McLennan	**155**	55 42N	116 50W
MacLeod Lake	**154**	54 58N	123 0W
M'Clintock Chan.	**145**	72 0N	102 0W
McMinnville, Oreg., U.S.A.	**171**	45 16N	123 11W
McMinnville, Tenn., U.S.A.	**169**	35 43N	85 45W
McMurdo Sd.	**15**	77 0S	170 0 E
McMurray = Fort McMurray	**155**	56 44N	111 7W
McNaughton L.	**155**	52 0N	118 10W
Macomb	**166**	40 25N	90 40W
Mâcon, France	**37**	46 19N	4 50 E
Macon, U.S.A.	**170**	32 50N	83 37W
McPherson	**161**	38 25N	97 40W
Macpherson Ra.	**116**	28 15S	153 15 E
Macquarie →	**116**	30 5S	147 30 E
Macquarie Is.	**15**	54 36S	158 55 E
MacRobertson Land	**14**	71 0S	64 0 E
Macroom	**35**	51 54N	8 57W
Madagascar ■	**137**	20 0S	47 0 E
Madang	**115**	5 12S	145 49 E
Madaripur	**93**	23 19N	90 15 E
Made	**40**	51 41N	4 49 E
Madeira	**126**	32 50N	17 0W
Madeira →	**185**	3 22S	58 45W
Madeleine, Îs. de la	**149**	47 30N	61 40W
Madera	**173**	37 0N	120 1W
Madhya Pradesh □	**91**	21 50N	81 0 E
Madison, Fla., U.S.A.	**170**	30 29N	83 39W
Madison, Ind., U.S.A.	**167**	38 42N	85 20W
Madison, Wis., U.S.A.	**166**	43 5N	89 25W
Madisonville	**167**	37 20N	87 30W
Madiun	**111**	7 38S	111 32 E
Madras = Tamil Nadu □	**90**	11 0N	77 0 E
Madras, India	**90**	13 8N	80 19 E
Madras, U.S.A.	**171**	44 40N	121 10W
Madre, Laguna	**176**	25 0N	97 30W
Madre de Dios →	**187**	10 59S	66 8W
Madre del Sur, Sa.	**177**	17 0N	100 0W
Madre Occidental, Sa.	**174**	25 0N	105 0W
Madre Oriental, Sa.	**177**	22 0N	99 30W
Madrid	**50**	40 25N	3 45W
Madura, Selat	**111**	7 30S	113 20 E
Madurai	**90**	9 55N	78 10 E
Madurantakam	**90**	12 30N	79 50 E
Mae Rim	**94**	18 54N	98 57 E
Maebashi	**107**	36 24N	139 4 E
Maesteg	**27**	51 36N	3 40W
Maestra, Sierra	**178**	20 15N	77 0W
Mafeking	**152**	52 40N	101 10W
Maffra	**117**	37 53S	146 58 E
Mafia	**135**	7 45S	39 50 E
Mafikeng	**136**	25 50S	25 38 E
Mafra	**191**	26 10S	50 0W
Magadan	**73**	59 38N	150 50 E
Magallanes, Estrecho de	**192**	52 30S	75 0W
Magangué	**184**	9 14N	74 45W
Magdalena, Bolivia	**187**	13 13S	63 57W
Magdalena, Mexico	**174**	30 38N	110 57W
Magdalena →	**184**	11 6N	74 51W
Magdeburg	**43**	52 8N	11 36 E
Magelang	**111**	7 29S	110 13 E
Magellan's Str. = Magallanes, Estrecho de	**192**	52 30S	75 0W
Magherafelt	**34**	54 44N	6 37W
Magnitogorsk	**71**	53 27N	59 4 E
Magog	**148**	45 18N	72 9W

Place	Page	Lat.	Long.
Magosa = Famagusta	**80**	35 8N	33 55 E
Magrath	**155**	49 25N	112 50W
Mahābād	**81**	36 50N	45 45 E
Mahajanga □	**137**	17 0S	47 0 E
Mahakam →	**111**	0 35S	117 17 E
Maḩallāt	**86**	33 55N	50 30 E
Mahanadi →	**92**	20 20N	86 25 E
Maharashtra □	**91**	20 30N	75 30 E
Mahbubnagar	**91**	16 45N	77 59 E
Mahia Pen.	**122**	39 9S	177 55 E
Mahón	**51**	39 53N	4 16 E
Mahone Bay	**148**	44 30N	64 20W
Mahukona	**160**	20 11N	155 52W
Mai-Ndombe, L.	**134**	2 0S	18 20 E
Maidenhead	**25**	51 31N	0 42W
Maiduguri	**131**	12 0N	13 20 E
Maikala Ra.	**92**	22 0N	81 0 E
Main →	**42**	50 0N	8 18 E
Maine	**36**	48 0N	0 0 E
Maine □	**148**	45 20N	69 0W
Mainland, Orkney, U.K.	**33**	59 0N	3 10W
Mainland, Shet., U.K.	**30**	60 15N	1 22W
Mainpuri	**89**	27 18N	79 4 E
Mainz	**42**	50 0N	8 17 E
Maiquetía	**184**	10 36N	66 57W
Maisi, Pta. de	**178**	20 10N	74 10W
Maitland, N.S.W., Australia	**117**	32 33S	151 36 E
Maitland, S. Austral., Australia	**119**	34 23S	137 40 E
Maiz, Islas del	**179**	12 15N	83 4W
Maizuru	**106**	35 25N	135 22 E
Majorca, I. = Mallorca	**51**	39 30N	3 0 E
Makarikari = Makgadikgadi Salt Pans	**136**	20 40S	25 45 E
Makasar = Ujung Pandang	**113**	5 10S	119 20 E
Makasar, Selat	**113**	1 0S	118 20 E
Makedhonía = Macedonia □	**55**	41 39N	22 0 E
Makena	**160**	20 39N	156 27W
Makeyevka	**68**	48 0N	38 0 E
Makgadikgadi Salt Pans	**136**	20 40S	25 45 E
Makhachkala	**70**	43 0N	47 30 E
Makkah	**82**	21 30N	39 54 E
Makó	**59**	46 14N	20 33 E
Makran Coast Range	**88**	25 40N	64 0 E
Makurazaki	**108**	31 15N	130 20 E
Makurdi	**131**	7 43N	8 35 E
Malabar Coast	**90**	11 0N	75 0 E
Malacca, Str. of	**111**	3 0N	101 0 E
Malad City	**162**	42 10N	112 20 E
Málaga	**50**	36 43N	4 23W
Malakal	**129**	9 33N	31 50 E
Malang	**111**	7 59S	112 45 E
Mälaren	**60**	59 30N	17 10 E
Malatya	**81**	38 25N	38 20 E
Malawi ■	**137**	13 0S	34 0 E
Malawi, L.	**137**	12 30S	34 30 E
Malay Pen.	**97**	7 25N	100 0 E
Malāyer	**84**	34 19N	48 51 E
Malaysia ■	**111**	5 0N	110 0 E
Malbaie, La	**148**	47 40N	70 10W
Malbork	**58**	54 3N	19 1 E
Malcolm	**120**	28 51S	121 25 E
Maldives ■	**78**	7 0N	73 0 E
Maldonado	**191**	35 0S	55 0W
Malebo, Pool	**134**	4 17S	15 20 E
Malegaon	**91**	20 30N	74 38 E
Mali ■	**130**	15 0N	2 0W
Mali Kyun	**94**	13 0N	98 20 E
Malin Hd.	**34**	55 18N	7 24W
Malindi	**133**	3 12S	40 5 E
Malines = Mechelen	**42**	51 2N	4 29 E
Mallaig	**32**	57 0N	5 50W
Mallorca	**51**	39 30N	3 0 E
Mallow	**35**	52 8N	8 40W
Malmédy	**42**	50 25N	6 2 E
Malmö	**61**	55 36N	12 59 E
Malmöhus län □	**61**	55 45N	13 30 E
Malone	**151**	44 50N	74 19W
Malta ■	**49**	35 50N	14 30 E
Malton	**29**	54 9N	0 48W
Maluku	**113**	1 0S	127 0 E
Malvern, U.K.	**24**	52 7N	2 19W
Malvern, U.S.A.	**168**	34 22N	92 50W
Malvern Hills	**24**	52 0N	2 19W
Malvinas, Is. = Falkland Is.	**192**	51 30S	59 0W
Mamers	**39**	48 21N	0 22 E
Mamoré →	**187**	10 23S	65 53W
Mamou	**130**	10 15N	12 0W
Man	**130**	7 30N	7 40W
Man, I. of	**28**	54 15N	4 30W
Mana, Fr. Guiana	**185**	5 45N	53 55W
Mana, U.S.A.	**160**	22 3N	159 45W
Manaar, Gulf of = Mannar, G. of	**90**	8 30N	79 0 E
Manacapuru	**185**	3 16S	60 37W
Manado	**113**	1 29N	124 51 E
Managua	**179**	12 6N	86 20W
Manaos = Manaus	**185**	3 0S	60 0W
Manapouri	**123**	45 34S	167 39 E
Manaung	**93**	18 45N	93 40 E
Manaus	**185**	3 0S	60 0W
Mancha, La	**50**	39 10N	2 54W
Manchester, U.K.	**28**	53 30N	2 15W
Manchester, U.S.A.	**164**	42 58N	71 29W
Mandalay	**93**	22 0N	96 4 E
Mandale = Mandalay	**93**	22 0N	96 4 E
Mandurah	**120**	32 36S	115 48 E
Manfredónia, G. di	**49**	41 30N	16 10 E
Mangalore	**90**	12 55N	74 47 E
Mangla Dam	**89**	33 9N	73 44 E
Mangole	**113**	1 50S	125 55 E
Mangonui	**122**	35 1S	173 32 E
Mangyshlak P-ov.	**70**	44 30N	52 30 E
Manhattan	**158**	39 10N	96 40W
Manicoré	**185**	5 48S	61 16W
Manicouagan →	**148**	49 30N	68 30W
Manila	**112**	14 40N	121 3 E
Manilla	**116**	30 45S	150 43 E
Manipur □	**93**	25 0N	94 0 E
Manisa	**80**	38 38N	27 30 E
Manistee	**167**	44 15N	86 20W
Manistique	**150**	45 59N	86 18W
Manitoba □	**153**	55 30N	97 0W
Manitoba, L.	**153**	51 0N	98 45W
Manitoulin I.	**150**	45 40N	82 30W
Manitowoc	**167**	44 8N	87 40W
Manizales	**184**	5 5N	75 32W
Manjil	**81**	36 46N	49 30 E
Manjimup	**120**	34 15S	116 6 E
Mankato	**166**	44 8N	93 59W
Manly	**117**	33 48S	151 17 E
Mannar, G. of	**90**	8 30N	79 0 E
Mannar I.	**90**	9 5N	79 45 E
Mannheim	**42**	49 28N	8 29 E
Mannum	**119**	34 50S	139 20 E
Manosque	**37**	43 49N	5 47 E
Manouane, L.	**148**	50 45N	70 45W
Mans, Le	**39**	48 0N	0 10 E
Mansel I.	**146**	62 0N	80 0W
Mansfield, Australia	**117**	37 4S	146 6 E
Mansfield, U.K.	**29**	53 8N	1 12W
Mansfield, U.S.A.	**167**	40 45N	82 30W
Manta	**184**	1 0S	80 40W
Mantes-la-Jolie	**39**	49 0N	1 41 E
Mantiqueira, Serra da	**188**	22 0S	44 0W
Mántova	**46**	45 20N	10 42 E
Mantua = Mántova	**46**	45 20N	10 42 E
Manu	**187**	12 10S	70 51W
Manukau	**122**	35 14S	173 13 E
Manyara, L.	**135**	3 40S	35 50 E
Manzanillo, Cuba	**178**	20 20N	77 31W
Manzanillo, Mexico	**175**	19 3N	104 20W
Manzhouli	**98**	49 35N	117 25 E
Mapimí	**174**	25 49N	103 51W
Maple	**152**	43 51N	79 31W
Maputo	**137**	25 58S	32 32 E
Maquinchao	**192**	41 15S	68 50W
Mar, Serra do	**191**	25 30S	49 0W
Mar Chiquita, L.	**190**	30 40S	62 50W
Mar del Plata	**191**	38 0S	57 30W
Mar Menor, L.	**51**	37 40N	0 45W
Marabá	**188**	5 20S	49 5W
Maracaibo	**184**	10 40N	71 37W

Place	Page	Lat.	Long.
Maracaibo, Lago de	**184**	9 40N	71 30W
Maracay	**184**	10 15N	67 28W
Marajó, Ilha de	**188**	1 0S	49 30W
Maranhão = São Luís	**188**	2 39S	44 15W
Maranhão □	**188**	5 0S	46 0W
Marañón →	**186**	4 30S	73 35W
Maraş	**80**	37 37N	36 53 E
Marathón	**55**	38 11N	23 58 E
Marbella	**50**	36 30N	4 57W
Marble Bar	**114**	21 9S	119 44 E
March	**25**	52 33N	0 5 E
Marché	**36**	46 0N	1 20 E
Marche □	**47**	43 22N	13 10 E
Marchena	**50**	37 18N	5 23W
Marches = Marche □	**47**	43 22N	13 10 E
Mardan	**89**	34 20N	72 0 E
Mardin	**81**	37 20N	40 43 E
Mareeba	**121**	16 59S	145 28 E
Margarita	**175**	9 20N	79 55W
Margarita I.	**185**	11 0N	64 0W
Margate	**25**	51 23N	1 24 E
Mari Rep. □	**68**	56 30N	48 0 E
Maria van Diemen, C.	**122**	34 29S	172 40 E
Marianao	**178**	23 8N	82 24W
Marianna	**169**	30 45N	85 15W
Maribor	**52**	46 36N	15 40 E
Maricourt	**146**	61 30N	72 0W
Marie-Galante	**180**	15 56N	61 16W
Marienberg	**41**	52 30N	6 35 E
Marietta, Ga., U.S.A.	**169**	34 0N	84 30W
Marietta, Ohio, U.S.A.	**164**	39 27N	81 27W
Marília	**188**	22 13S	50 0W
Marín	**50**	42 23N	8 42W
Marinette	**167**	45 4N	87 40W
Maringá	**191**	23 26S	52 2W
Marion, Ill., U.S.A.	**166**	37 45N	88 55W
Marion, Ind., U.S.A.	**167**	40 35N	85 40W
Marion, Ohio, U.S.A.	**167**	40 38N	83 8W
Mariupol	**68**	47 5N	37 31 E
Marken	**40**	52 26N	5 12 E
Market Drayton	**28**	52 55N	2 30W
Market Harborough	**25**	52 29N	0 55W
Market Rasen	**29**	53 24N	0 20W
Markham, Mt.	**15**	83 0S	164 0 E
Marlborough	**24**	51 26N	1 44W
Marlborough □	**123**	41 45S	173 33 E
Marlborough Downs	**24**	51 25N	1 55W
Marlin	**168**	31 25N	96 50W
Marmagao	**91**	15 25N	73 56 E
Marmara, Sea of = Marmara Denizi	**80**	40 45N	28 15 E
Marmara Denizi	**80**	40 45N	28 15 E
Marmaris	**80**	36 50N	28 14 E
Marne →	**39**	8 23N	18 36 E
Maroochydore	**116**	26 29S	153 5 E
Marquesas Is.	**123**	9 30S	140 0W
Marquette	**150**	46 30N	87 21W
Marrakech	**126**	31 9N	8 0W
Marree	**118**	29 39S	138 1 E
Marsabit	**133**	2 18N	38 0 E
Marseille	**37**	43 18N	5 23 E
Marseilles = Marseille	**37**	43 18N	5 23 E
Marshall, Minn., U.S.A.	**166**	44 25N	95 45W
Marshall, Mo., U.S.A.	**166**	39 8N	93 15W
Marshall, Tex., U.S.A.	**168**	32 29N	94 20W
Marshalltown	**166**	42 5N	92 56W
Marshfield	**166**	44 42N	90 10W
Martaban, G. of	**93**	16 5N	96 30 E
Martha's Vineyard	**164**	41 25N	70 35W
Martigues	**37**	43 24N	5 4 E
Martinique	**180**	14 40N	61 0W
Martinsburg	**164**	39 30N	77 57W
Martinsville, Ind., U.S.A.	**167**	39 29N	86 23W
Martinsville, Va., U.S.A.	**165**	36 41N	79 52W
Marton	**122**	40 4S	175 23 E
Marugame	**109**	34 15N	133 40 E
Maruoka	**106**	36 9N	136 16 E
Marwar	**91**	25 43N	73 45 E
Mary	**70**	37 40N	61 50 E
Maryborough = Port Laoise	**35**	53 2N	7 20W
Maryborough, Queens., Australia	**116**	25 31S	152 37 E
Maryborough, Vic., Australia	**117**	37 0S	143 44 E
Maryland □	**164**	39 10N	76 40W
Maryport	**28**	54 43N	3 30W
Marysville	**172**	39 14N	121 40W
Maryville	**165**	35 50N	84 0W
Marzūq	**127**	25 53N	13 57 E
Masan	**98**	35 11N	128 32 E
Masaya	**179**	12 0N	86 7W
Masbate, I.	**112**	12 21N	123 36 E
Mascota	**175**	20 32N	104 49W
Maseru	**137**	29 18S	27 30 E
Mashhad	**86**	36 20N	59 35 E
Masisea	**186**	8 35S	74 22W
Masjed Soleyman	**84**	31 55N	49 18 E
Mask, L.	**34**	53 36N	9 24W
Mason City	**166**	43 9N	93 12W
Masqat	**83**	23 37N	58 36 E
Massachusetts □	**164**	42 25N	72 0W
Massawa = Mitsiwa	**132**	15 35N	39 25 E
Massena	**151**	44 52N	74 55W
Massif Central	**37**	45 30N	2 21 E
Massillon	**167**	40 47N	81 30W
Mastanli = Momchilgrad	**53**	41 33N	25 23 E
Masterton	**123**	40 56S	175 39 E
Mastūrah	**82**	23 7N	38 52 E
Masuda	**108**	34 40N	131 51 E
Matachewan	**151**	47 56N	80 39W
Matadi	**134**	5 52S	13 31 E
Matagalpa	**179**	13 0N	85 58W
Matamoros, Coahuila, Mexico	**174**	25 32N	103 15W
Matamoros, Puebla, Mexico	**177**	18 2N	98 17W
Matane	**148**	48 50N	67 33W
Matanzas	**178**	23 0N	81 40W
Matapan, C. = Taínaron, Ákra	**54**	36 22N	22 27 E
Matarani	**186**	77 0S	72 10W
Matehuala	**177**	23 39N	100 39W
Mathura	**89**	27 30N	77 40 E
Matlock	**28**	53 8N	1 32W
Mato Grosso □	**188**	14 0S	55 0W
Mato Grosso, Planalto do	**188**	15 0S	59 57W
Matopo Hills	**137**	20 36S	28 20 E
Matrah	**83**	23 37N	58 30 E
Matsubara	**106**	34 33N	135 34 E
Matsudo	**107**	35 47N	139 54 E
Matsue	**109**	35 25N	133 10 E
Matsumoto	**107**	36 15N	138 0 E
Matsusaka	**106**	34 34N	136 32 E
Matsutō	**106**	36 31N	136 34 E
Matsuura	**108**	33 20N	129 49 E
Matsuyama	**109**	33 45N	132 45 E
Mattancheri	**90**	9 50N	76 15 E
Mattawa	**151**	46 20N	78 45W
Matterhorn	**44**	45 58N	7 39 E
Matucana	**186**	11 55S	76 25W
Maturín	**185**	9 45N	63 11W
Mau Ranipur	**91**	25 16N	79 8 E
Maubeuge	**38**	50 17N	3 57 E
Maudin Sun	**93**	16 0N	94 30 E
Maui	**160**	20 45N	156 20 E
Maulamyaing	**93**	16 30N	97 40 E
Mauna Kea	**160**	19 50N	155 28W
Mauna Loa	**160**	21 8N	157 10W
Maungmagan Kyunzu	**94**	14 0N	97 48 E
Mauritania ■	**126**	20 50N	10 0W
Mauritius ■	**9**	20 0S	57 0 E
Mawlaik	**93**	23 40N	94 26 E
May Pen	**180**	17 58N	77 15W
Maya →	**75**	54 31N	134 41 E
Mayagüez	**180**	18 12N	67 9W
Mayerthorpe	**155**	53 57N	115 8W
Mayfield	**169**	36 45N	88 40W
Maykop	**70**	44 35N	40 25 E
Maynooth	**34**	53 22N	6 38W
Mayo	**144**	63 38N	135 57W
Mayo □	**34**	53 47N	9 7W
Mayor I.	**122**	37 16S	176 17 E
Maysville	**167**	38 39N	83 46W
Mazagán = El Jadida	**126**	33 11N	8 17W
Mazán	**186**	3 30S	73 0W
Mazar-e Sharīf	**87**	36 41N	67 0 E
Mazarredo	**192**	47 10S	66 50W

Mazatenango 177 14 35N 91 30W
Mazatlán 175 23 13N 106 25W
Mbandaka 134 0 1N 18 18 E
Mdina 49 35 51N 14 25 E
Mead, L. 173 36 1N 114 44W
Meadville 164 41 39N 80 9W
Meander River 145 59 2N 117 42W
Meath □ 34 53 32N 6 40W
Meaux 39 48 58N 2 50 E
Mecca = Makkah 82 21 30N 39 54 E
Mechelen 42 51 2N 4 29 E
Mecklenburger Bucht 42 54 20N 11 40 E
Medan 111 3 40N 98 38 E
Medellín 184 6 15N 75 35W
Medford 171 42 20N 122 52W
Mediaş 57 46 9N 24 22 E
Medicine Hat 152 50 0N 110 45W
Medina = Al Madīnah 82 24 35N 39 52 E
Medina 167 41 9N 81 50W
Medina del Campo 50 41 18N 4 55W
Mediterranean Sea 124 35 0N 15 0 E
Medley 152 54 25N 110 16W
Médoc 36 45 10N 0 56W
Medvezhi, Ostrava 73 71 0N 161 0 E
Medway → 25 51 28N 0 45 E
Meekatharra 120 26 32S 118 29 E
Meerut 89 29 1N 77 42 E
Mega 133 3 57N 38 19 E
Mégantic, L. 148 45 32N 70 53W
Mégara 55 37 58N 23 22 E
Meghalaya □ 93 25 50N 91 0 E
Mei Xian 99 24 16N 116 6 E
Meknès 126 33 57N 5 33W
Mekong → 95 9 30N 106 15 E
Melaka 96 2 15N 102 15 E
Melaka □ 96 2 15N 102 15 E
Melanesia 122 4 0S 155 0 E
Melbourne 117 37 50S 145 0 E
Melchor Muzquiz 174 27 53N 101 31W
Melfort 152 52 50N 104 37W
Melilla 126 35 21N 2 57W
Melitopol 68 46 50N 35 22 E
Melo 191 32 20S 54 10W
Melrose 31 53 35N 2 44W
Melton Mowbray 29 52 46N 0 52W
Melun 39 48 32N 2 39 E
Melville 152 50 55N 102 50W
Melville, L. 147 53 30N 60 0W
Melville I., Australia 114 11 30S 131 0 E
Melville I., Canada 12 75 30N 112 0W
Melville Pen. 146 68 0N 84 0W
Memel = Klaipeda 68 55 43N 21 10 E
Memphis 169 35 7N 90 0W
Menai Strait 26 53 14N 4 10W
Ménaka 131 15 59N 2 18 E
Menan = Chao Phraya → 94 13 32N 100 36 E
Menasha 167 44 13N 88 27W
Mende 37 44 31N 3 30 E
Mendip Hills 27 51 17N 2 40W
Mendocino 172 39 26N 123 50W
Mendoza 190 32 50S 68 52W
Menindee 118 32 20S 142 25 E
Menindee, L. 118 32 20S 142 25 E
Menominee 150 45 9N 87 39W
Menorca 51 40 0N 4 0 E
Mentawai, Kepulauan 111 2 0S 99 0 E
Menzies 120 29 40S 120 58 E
Meppel 41 52 42N 6 12 E
Merbein 119 34 10S 142 2 E
Merca 133 1 48N 44 50 E
Merced 172 37 18N 120 30W
Mercedes, Buenos Aires, Argentina 190 34 40S 59 30W
Mercedes, Corrientes, Argentina 191 29 10S 58 5W
Mercedes, San Luis, Argentina 190 33 40S 65 21W
Mercedes, Uruguay 191 33 12S 58 0W
Mere 24 51 5N 2 16W
Mergui Arch. = Myeik Kyunzu 94 11 30N 97 30 E
Mérida, Mexico 177 20 58N 89 37W
Mérida, Spain 50 38 55N 6 25W
Mérida, Venezuela 184 8 24N 71 8W
Mérida, Cord. de 182 9 0N 71 0W
Meriden 164 41 33N 72 47W
Meridian 169 32 20N 88 42W
Merowe 129 18 29N 31 46 E
Merredin 120 31 28S 118 18 E
Merrill 156 45 11N 89 41W
Merritt 155 50 10N 120 45W
Merriwa 116 32 6S 150 22 E
Mersey → 28 53 20N 2 56W
Merseyside □ 28 53 25N 2 55W
Mersin 80 36 51N 34 36 E
Merthyr Tydfil 27 51 45N 3 23W
Méru 39 49 13N 2 8 E
Merville 38 50 38N 2 38 E
Mesa 160 33 20N 111 56W
Mesa, La 173 32 48N 117 5W
Meshed = Mashhad 86 36 20N 59 35 E
Mesolóngion 54 38 21N 21 28 E
Mesopotamia = Al Jazirah 81 33 30N 44 0 E
Mesquite 173 36 47N 114 6W
Messina, Italy 49 38 10N 15 32 E
Messina, S. Africa 137 22 20S 30 0 E
Messina, Str. di 49 38 5N 15 35 E
Messíni 54 37 4N 22 1 E
Meta → 184 6 12N 67 28W
Metairie 169 29 59N 90 9W
Metán 190 25 30S 65 0W
Metropolis 169 37 10N 88 47W
Metz 37 49 8N 6 10 E
Meuse → 42 50 45N 5 41 E
Mexia 168 31 38N 96 32W
Mexicali 174 32 40N 115 29W
México, Mexico 177 19 20N 99 10W
Mexico, U.S.A. 166 39 10N 91 55W
México □ 177 19 20N 99 30W
Mexico ■ 174 20 0N 100 0W
Mexico, G. of 138 25 0N 90 0W
Mezen → 69 66 11N 43 59 E
Mhow 91 22 33N 75 50 E
Miahuatlán 177 16 21N 96 36W
Miami 170 25 45N 80 15W
Miami Beach 170 25 49N 80 6W
Mīāneh 81 37 30N 47 40 E
Mianwali 89 32 38N 71 28 E
Miaoli 99 24 37N 120 49 E
Miass 69 54 59N 60 6 E
Michigan □ 167 44 40N 85 40W
Michigan, L. 150 44 0N 87 0W
Michigan City 167 41 42N 86 56W
Michikamau L. 147 54 20N 63 10W
Michipicoten 150 47 55N 84 55W
Michoacán □ 175 19 10N 101 50W
Michurinsk 68 52 58N 40 27 E
Micronesia 122 11 0N 160 0 E
Mid Glamorgan □ 27 51 40N 3 25W
Middelburg 40 51 30N 3 36 E
Middle Andaman I. 94 12 30N 92 30 E
Middlesboro 165 36 36N 83 43W
Middlesbrough 29 54 35N 1 14W
Middleton 148 44 57N 65 4W
Middletown, Conn., U.S.A. 164 41 37N 72 40W
Middletown, N.Y., U.S.A. 164 41 28N 74 28W
Middletown, Ohio, U.S.A. 167 39 29N 84 25W
Midland, Canada 151 44 45N 79 50W
Midland, Mich., U.S.A. 167 43 37N 84 17W
Midland, Tex., U.S.A. 161 32 0N 102 3W
Międzyrzec Podlaski 58 51 58N 22 45 E
Miercurea Ciuc 57 46 21N 25 48 E
Mieres 50 43 18N 5 48W
Migennes 39 47 58N 3 31 E
Mihara 109 34 24N 133 5 E
Miki 109 34 48N 134 59 E
Míkonos 55 37 30N 25 25 E
Mikuni-Tōge 107 36 50N 138 50 E
Mikura-Jima 107 33 52N 139 36 E
Milagro 184 2 11S 79 36W
Milan = Milano 46 45 28N 9 10 E
Milano 46 45 28N 9 10 E
Milâs 80 37 20N 27 50 E

Mildura . . . . **119** 34 13S 142 9 E
Miles . . . . **116** 26 40S 150 9 E
Miles City **163** 46 24N 105 50W
Milford **164** 38 52N 75 27W
Milford Haven **27** 51 43N 5 2W
Milk —▶ **163** 48 5N 106 15W
Millau . . . . **37** 44 8N 3 4 E
Millicent . . . . **119** 37 34S 140 21 E
Millinocket **148** 45 45N 68 45W
Millmerran . . . . **116** 27 53S 151 16 E
Millom **28** 54 13N 3 16W
Millville **164** 39 22N 75 0W
Milne Inlet **146** 72 30N 80 0W
Milos . . . . **55** 36 44N 24 25 E
Milton Keynes **25** 52 3N 0 42W
Milwaukee **167** 43 9N 87 58W
Milwaukie **171** 45 27N 122 39W
Minamata . . . . **108** 32 10N 130 30 E
Minas **191** 34 20S 55 10W
Minas Gerais □ **188** 18 50S 46 0W
Minatitlán **177** 17 59N 94 31W
Mindanao . . . . **112** 8 0N 125 0 E
Mindanao Sea = Bohol Sea **112** 9 0N 124 0 E
Minden **168** 32 40N 93 20W
Mindoro . . . . **112** 13 0N 121 0 E
Mindoro Strait . . . . **112** 12 30N 120 30 E
Mine . . . . **108** 34 12N 131 7 E
Minehead **27** 51 12N 3 29W
Mineral Wells **161** 32 50N 98 5W
Mingan **148** 50 20N 64 0W
Mingenew . . . . **120** 29 12S 115 21 E
Minho □ **50** 41 25N 8 20W
Minneapolis **166** 44 58N 93 20W
Minnedosa **153** 50 14N 99 50W
Minnesota □ **156** 46 40N 94 0W
Mino . . . . **106** 35 32N 136 55 E
Mino-Kamo . . . . **106** 35 23N 137 2 E
Mino-Mikawa-Kōgen . . . . . . **106** 35 10N 137 23 E
Minorca = Menorca . . . . **51** 40 0N 4 0 E
Minot **163** 48 10N 101 15W
Minsk . . . . **68** 53 52N 27 30 E
Mintaka Pass . . . . **89** 37 0N 74 58 E
Miquelon, I. **149** 47 2N 56 20W
Miraj . . . . **91** 16 50N 74 45 E
Miranda do Douro **50** 41 30N 6 16W
Mirpur Khas . . . . **88** 25 30N 69 0 E
Mirzapur . . . . **92** 25 10N 82 34 E
Mirzapur-cum-Vindhyachal =
    Mirzapur . . . . **92** 25 10N 82 34 E
Miscou I. **148** 47 57N 64 31W
Mishawaka **167** 41 40N 86 8W
Mishima . . . . **107** 35 10N 138 52 E
Miskitos, Cayos **179** 14 26N 82 50W
Miskolc . . . . **59** 48 7N 20 50 E
Misool . . . . **113** 1 52S 130 10 E
Misrātah . . . . **127** 32 24N 15 3 E
Mission City **154** 49 10N 122 15W
Mississippi □ **169** 33 0N 90 0W
Mississippi —▶ **169** 29 0N 89 15W
Mississippi, Delta of the **169** 29 15N 90 30W
Missoula **162** 46 52N 114 0W
Missouri □ **166** 38 25N 92 30W
Missouri —▶ **166** 38 50N 90 8W
Mistassini L. **151** 51 0N 73 30W
Mitaka . . . . **107** 35 40N 139 33 E
Mitchell, Australia . . . . **116** 26 29S 147 58 E
Mitchell, U.S.A. **163** 43 40N 98 0W
Mitchell —▶ . . . . **115** 15 12S 141 35 E
Mitilini . . . . **55** 39 6N 26 35 E
Mito . . . . **107** 36 20N 140 30 E
Mitsiwa . . . . **132** 15 35N 39 25 E
Mitsukaidō . . . . **107** 36 1N 139 59 E
Mittagong . . . . **117** 34 28S 150 29 E
Mitú **184** 1 8N 70 3W
Miura . . . . **107** 35 12N 139 40 E
Miyake-Jima . . . . **107** 34 0N 139 30 E
Miyako . . . . **103** 39 40N 141 59 E
Miyakonojō . . . . **108** 31 40N 131 5 E
Miyanojō . . . . **108** 31 54N 130 27 E
Miyazaki . . . . **108** 31 56N 131 30 E
Miyazu . . . . **106** 35 35N 135 10 E

Miyoshi . . . . **109** 34 48N 132 51 E
Mizamis = Ozamis . . . . **112** 8 15N 123 50 E
Mizen Hd. **35** 51 27N 9 50W
Mizoram □ . . . . **93** 23 30N 92 40 E
Mizunami . . . . **106** 35 22N 137 15 E
Mława . . . . **58** 53 9N 20 25 E
Mobara . . . . **107** 35 25N 140 18 E
Moberley **166** 39 25N 92 25W
Mobile **169** 30 41N 88 3W
Mobutu Sese Seko, L. . . . . . **132** 1 30N 31 0 E
Moçâmedes = Namibe . . . . . **134** 15 7S 12 11 E
Moctezuma, R. —▶ **177** 21 59N 98 34W
Módena . . . . **46** 44 39N 10 55 E
Modesto **172** 37 43N 121 0W
Moe . . . . **117** 38 12S 146 19 E
Moei —▶ . . . . **94** 17 25N 98 10 E
Moengo **185** 5 45N 54 20W
Moffat **31** 55 20N 3 27W
Mogadishu = Muqdisho . . . **133** 2 2N 45 25 E
Mogador = Essaouira **126** 31 32N 9 42W
Mogami —▶ . . . . **103** 38 45N 140 0 E
Mogi das Cruzes **191** 23 31S 46 11W
Mogilev . . . . **68** 53 55N 30 18 E
Mointy . . . . **71** 47 10N 73 18 E
Moisie **148** 50 12N 66 1W
Mojave Desert **173** 35 0N 116 30W
Mold **26** 53 10N 3 10W
Moldavia ■ . . . . **68** 47 0N 28 0 E
Molde . . . . **65** 62 45N 7 9 E
Molfetta . . . . **49** 41 12N 16 35 E
Moline **166** 41 30N 90 30W
Molise □ . . . . **49** 41 45N 14 30 E
Mollendo **187** 17 0S 72 0W
Mölndal . . . . **60** 57 40N 12 3 E
Molong . . . . **117** 33 5S 148 54 E
Molopo —▶ . . . . **136** 28 30S 20 13 E
Molotov = Perm . . . . **69** 58 0N 57 10 E
Molucca Sea . . . . **113** 4 0S 124 0 E
Moluccas = Maluku . . . . **113** 1 0S 127 0 E
Mombasa . . . . **135** 4 2S 39 43 E
Mombetsu . . . . **103** 42 27N 142 4 E
Momchilgrad . . . . **53** 41 33N 25 23 E
Mompós **184** 9 14N 74 26W
Møn . . . . **61** 54 57N 12 15 E
Mona, Canal de la **180** 18 30N 67 45W
Monach Is. **32** 57 32N 7 40W
Monaco ■ . . . . **37** 43 46N 7 23 E
Monaghan **34** 54 15N 6 58W
Monaghan □ **34** 54 10N 7 0W
Monastir = Bitola . . . . **52** 41 5N 21 10 E
Mönchengladbach . . . . **42** 51 12N 6 23 E
Monchique **50** 37 19N 8 38W
Monclova **174** 26 50N 101 30W
Moncton **148** 46 7N 64 51W
Monessen **164** 40 9N 79 50W
Monforte **50** 39 6N 7 25W
Mongalla . . . . **129** 5 8N 31 42 E
Monghyr = Munger . . . . **92** 25 23N 86 30 E
Mongolia ■ . . . . **98** 47 0N 103 0 E
Monmouth, U.K. **26** 51 48N 2 43W
Monmouth, U.S.A. **166** 40 50N 90 40W
Monroe, La., U.S.A. **168** 32 32N 92 4W
Monroe, Mich., U.S.A. **167** 41 55N 83 26W
Monroe, N.C., U.S.A. **165** 35 2N 80 37W
Monrovia, Liberia **130** 6 18N 10 47W
Monrovia, U.S.A. **173** 34 7N 118 1W
Mons . . . . **42** 50 27N 3 58 E
Mont-de-Marsan **36** 43 54N 0 31W
Mont Laurier **151** 46 35N 75 30W
Montague **172** 41 47N 122 30W
Montana □ **163** 47 0N 110 0W
Montargis . . . . **39** 48 0N 2 43 E
Montauban . . . . **36** 44 0N 1 21 E
Montbéliard . . . . **37** 47 31N 6 48 E
Montceau-les-Mines . . . . . . **37** 46 40N 4 23 E
Montdidier . . . . **38** 49 38N 2 35 E
Monte-Carlo . . . . **37** 43 46N 7 23 E
Monte Caseros **191** 30 10S 57 50W
Montego Bay **180** 18 30N 78 0W
Montélimar . . . . **37** 44 33N 4 45 E
Montemorelos **176** 25 11N 99 42W

Montenegro □	52	42	40N	19	20 E
Monterey	173	36	35N	121	57W
Monteria	184	8	46N	75	53W
Monterrey	176	25	40N	100	30W
Montes Claros	188	16	30S	43	50W
Montevideo, Uruguay	191	34	50S	56	11W
Montevideo, U.S.A.	166	44	55N	95	40W
Montgomery = Sahiwal	89	30	45N	73	8 E
Montgomery, U.K.	26	52	34N	3	9W
Montgomery, U.S.A.	169	32	20N	86	20W
Montluçon	37	46	22N	2	36 E
Montmagny	148	46	58N	70	34W
Montmorency	148	46	53N	71	11W
Montpelier, Idaho, U.S.A.	163	42	15N	111	20W
Montpelier, Vt., U.S.A.	151	44	15N	72	38W
Montpellier	37	43	37N	3	52 E
Montréal	151	45	31N	73	34W
Montrose, U.K.	33	56	43N	2	28W
Montrose, U.S.A.	163	38	30N	107	52W
Montserrat	180	16	40N	62	10W
Monywa	93	22	7N	95	11 E
Monze, C.	88	24	47N	66	37 E
Mo'oka	107	36	26N	140	1 E
Moonta	119	34	6S	137	32 E
Moora	120	30	37S	115	58 E
Moorfoot Hills	31	55	44N	3	8W
Moorhead	156	46	51N	96	44W
Mooroopna	117	36	25S	145	22 E
Moose Jaw	152	50	24N	105	30W
Moosehead L.	148	45	34N	69	40W
Moosomin	152	50	9N	101	40W
Moosonee	140	51	17N	80	39W
Mopti	130	14	30N	4	0W
Moradabad	89	28	50N	78	50 E
Moranbah	121	22	1S	148	6 E
Moratuwa	90	6	45N	79	55 E
Morava →►	59	48	10N	16	59 E
Moravian Hts. = Ceskomoravská Vrchovina	59	49	30N	15	40 E
Morawa	120	29	13S	116	0 E
Morawhanna	185	8	30N	59	40W
Moray Firth	33	57	50N	3	30W
Morden	153	49	15N	98	10W
Mordovian Rep.□	68	54	20N	44	30 E
Møre og Romsdal fylke □	65	62	30N	8	0 E
Morecambe	28	54	5N	2	52W
Morecambe B.	28	54	7N	3	0W
Moree	116	29	28S	149	54 E
Morehead City	165	34	46N	76	44W
Morelia	175	19	42N	101	7W
Morelos □	177	18	45N	99	0W
Morena, Sierra	50	38	20N	4	0W
Moresby I.	154	52	30N	131	40W
Morgan City	168	29	40N	91	15W
Morganton	165	35	46N	81	48W
Morgantown	164	39	39N	79	58W
Moriguchi	106	34	44N	135	34 E
Morlaix	36	48	36N	3	52W
Mornington	117	38	15S	145	5 E
Moro G.	112	6	30N	123	0 E
Morocco ■	126	32	0N	5	50W
Moroleón	177	20	8N	101	12W
Morón	178	22	8N	78	39W
Morotai	113	2	10N	128	30 E
Morrilton	168	35	10N	92	45W
Morrinhos	188	17	45S	49	10W
Morris	153	49	25N	97	22W
Morristown	165	36	18N	83	20W
Mortes, R. das →►	188	11	45S	50	44W
Mortlake	119	38	5S	142	50 E
Moruya	117	35	58S	150	3 E
Morvern	30	56	38N	5	44W
Morwell	117	38	10S	146	22 E
Moscos Is.	94	14	0N	97	30 E
Moscow = Moskva	68	55	45N	37	35 E
Moscow	171	46	45N	116	59W
Mosel →►	42	50	22N	7	36 E
Moselle = Mosel →►	42	50	22N	7	36 E
Mosgiel	123	45	53S	170	21 E
Mosjøen	65	65	51N	13	12 E
Moskva	68	55	45N	37	35 E
Mosquera	184	2	35N	78	24W
Mosquitos, Golfo de los	179	9	15N	81	10W
Moss Vale	117	34	32S	150	25 E
Mosselbaai	136	34	11S	22	8 E
Mossman	121	16	21S	145	15 E
Mossoró	189	5	10S	37	15W
Mostaganem	127	35	54N	0	5 E
Mostar	52	43	22N	17	50 E
Mosul = Al Mawşil	81	36	15N	43	5 E
Motala	60	58	32N	15	1 E
Motherwell	31	55	48N	4	0W
Motihari	92	26	30N	84	55 E
Motueka	123	41	7S	173	1 E
Motul	177	21	6N	89	17W
Moúdhros	55	39	50N	25	18 E
Moule	180	16	20N	61	22W
Moulins	37	46	35N	3	19 E
Moultrie	170	31	11N	83	47W
Moundsville	164	39	53N	80	43W
Mount Airy	165	36	31N	80	37W
Mount Barker, S. Austral., Australia	119	35	5S	138	52 E
Mount Barker, W. Austral., Australia	120	34	38S	117	40 E
Mount Carmel	167	38	20N	87	48W
Mount Forest	151	43	59N	80	43W
Mount Gambier	119	37	50S	140	46 E
Mount Isa	115	20	42S	139	26 E
Mount Lofty Ra.	119	34	35S	139	5 E
Mount Magnet	120	28	2S	117	47 E
Mount Maunganui	122	37	40S	176	14 E
Mount Morgan	121	23	40S	150	25 E
Mount Pearl	149	47	31N	52	47W
Mount Pleasant, Mich., U.S.A.	167	43	35N	84	47W
Mount Pleasant, Tex., U.S.A.	168	33	5N	95	0W
Mount Sterling	165	38	0N	84	0W
Mount Vernon, Ill., U.S.A.	166	38	17N	88	57W
Mount Vernon, N.Y., U.S.A.	164	40	57N	73	49W
Mount Vernon, Wash., U.S.A.	171	48	25N	122	20W
Mount Whaleback	114	23	18S	119	44 E
Mountain City	172	41	54N	116	0W
Mountain View	172	37	26N	122	5W
Moura, Australia	121	24	35S	149	58 E
Moura, Brazil	185	1	32S	61	38W
Mourne →►	34	54	45N	7	39W
Mourne Mts.	34	54	10N	6	0W
Moyale	133	3	30N	39	0 E
Mozambique ■	137	19	0S	35	0 E
Mozambique Chan.	137	20	0S	39	0 E
Mu Us Shamo	98	39	0N	109	0 E
Muaná	188	1	25S	49	15W
Muang Chiang Rai	94	19	52N	99	50 E
Muck	32	56	50N	6	15W
Mucuri	189	18	0S	39	36W
Mudanjiang	98	44	38N	129	30 E
Mudgee	117	32	32S	149	31 E
Muğla	80	37	15N	28	22 E
Mukden = Shenyang	98	41	50N	123	25 E
Mukhtuya = Lensk	74	60	48N	114	55 E
Mukinbudin	120	30	55S	118	5 E
Muktsar	89	30	30N	74	30 E
Mulchén	190	37	45S	72	20W
Mulgrave	149	45	38N	61	31W
Mulhacén	50	37	4N	3	20W
Mülheim	42	51	26N	6	53 E
Mulhouse	37	47	40N	7	20 E
Mull	30	56	27N	6	0W
Muller, Pegunungan	111	0	30N	113	30 E
Mullet Pen.	34	54	10N	10	2W
Mullewa	120	28	29S	115	30 E
Mullingar	34	53	31N	7	20W
Mullumbimby	116	28	30S	153	30 E
Multan	89	30	15N	71	36 E
Muna	113	5	0S	122	30 E
München	43	48	8N	11	33 E
Munchen-Gladbach = Mönchengladbach	42	51	12N	6	23 E
Muncie	167	40	10N	85	20W
Mundo Novo	189	11	50S	40	29W
Mungana	121	17	8S	144	27 E
Munger	92	25	23N	86	30 E

Place	Map	Latitude	Longitude
Munich = München	43	48 8N	11 33 E
Munising	150	46 25N	86 39W
Munku-Sardyk	74	51 45N	100 20 E
Münster	42	51 58N	7 37 E
Munster □	35	52 20N	8 40W
Muqdisho	133	2 2N	45 25 E
Murallón, Cuerro	192	49 48S	73 30W
Murchison →►	120	27 45S	114 0 E
Murchison Falls = Kabarega Falls	132	2 15N	31 30 E
Murcia	51	38 20N	1 10W
Murcia □	51	37 50N	1 30W
Mureş →►	56	46 15N	20 13 E
Mureşul = Mureş →►	56	46 15N	20 13 E
Murfreesboro	169	35 50N	86 21W
Murgon	116	26 15S	151 54 E
Müritz See	43	53 25N	12 40 E
Murmansk	69	68 57N	33 10 E
Muroran	103	42 25N	141 0 E
Muroto	109	33 18N	134 9 E
Muroto-Misaki	109	33 15N	134 10 E
Murphysboro	166	37 50N	89 20W
Murray	169	36 40N	88 20W
Murray →►	119	35 20S	139 22 E
Murray Bridge	119	35 6S	139 14 E
Murrumbidgee →►	117	34 43S	143 12 E
Murrurundi	116	31 42S	150 51 E
Murtoa	119	36 35S	142 28 E
Murupara	122	38 28S	176 42 E
Murwillumbah	116	28 18S	153 27 E
Muş	81	38 45N	41 30 E
Musashino	107	35 42N	139 34 E
Muscat = Masqat	83	23 37N	58 36 E
Muscat & Oman = Oman ■	83	23 0N	58 0 E
Muscatine	166	41 25N	91 5W
Musgrave Ras.	114	26 0S	132 0 E
Musi →►	111	2 20S	104 56 E
Muskegon	167	43 15N	86 17W
Muskegon →►	167	43 25N	86 0W
Muskegon Hts.	167	43 12N	86 17W
Muskogee	168	35 50N	95 25W
Musselburgh	31	55 57N	3 3W
Muswellbrook	116	32 16S	150 56 E
Mutare	137	18 58S	32 38 E
Mutsu	103	41 5N	140 55 E
Mutsu-Wan	103	41 5N	140 55 E
Muzaffargarh	89	30 5N	71 14 E
Muzaffarnagar	89	29 26N	77 40 E
Muzaffarpur	92	26 7N	85 23 E
Mwanza	135	2 30S	32 58 E
Mweru, L.	135	9 0S	28 40 E
My Tho	95	10 29N	106 23 E
Myanaung	93	18 18N	95 22 E
Myeik Kyunzu	94	11 30N	97 30 E
Myingyan	93	21 30N	95 20 E
Myitkyina	93	25 24N	97 26 E
Myrdalsjökull	64	63 40N	19 6W
Myrtle Point	171	43 0N	124 4W
Mysore = Karnataka □	90	13 15N	77 0 E
Mysore	90	12 17N	76 41 E

N

Place	Map	Latitude	Longitude
Naaldwijk	40	51 59N	4 13 E
Nabari	106	34 37N	136 5 E
Naberezhnyye Chelny	68	55 42N	52 19 E
Nablus = Nābulus	80	32 14N	35 15 E
Nābulus	80	32 14N	35 15 E
Nacogdoches	168	31 33N	94 39W
Nacozari	174	30 24N	109 39W
Nadiad	91	22 41N	72 56 E
Nadym	69	65 35N	72 42 E
Nagahama	106	35 23N	136 16 E
Nagaland □	93	26 0N	94 30 E
Nagano	107	36 40N	138 10 E
Nagaoka	105	37 27N	138 51 E
Nagappattinam	90	10 46N	79 51 E
Nagasaki	108	32 47N	129 50 E
Nagato	108	34 19N	131 5 E
Nagercoil	90	8 12N	77 26 E
Nagornyy	75	55 58N	124 57 E
Nagoya	106	35 10N	136 50 E
Nagpur	91	21 8N	79 10 E
Nahanni Butte	144	61 2N	123 31W
Nahāvand	84	34 10N	48 22 E
Naicam	152	52 30N	104 30W
Nain	147	56 34N	61 40W
Nainpur	91	22 30N	80 10 E
Nairn	33	57 35N	3 54W
Nairobi	132	1 17S	36 48 E
Naivasha	132	0 40S	36 30 E
Najafābād	85	32 40N	51 15 E
Najibabad	89	29 40N	78 20 E
Naka →►	107	36 20N	140 36 E
Naka-no-Shima	104	29 51N	129 46 E
Nakama	108	33 56N	130 43 E
Nakamura	109	33 0N	133 0 E
Nakano	107	36 45N	138 22 E
Nakanojō	107	36 35N	138 51 E
Nakatsu	108	33 34N	131 15 E
Nakatsugawa	106	35 29N	137 30 E
Nakhichevan Rep. □	70	39 14N	45 30 E
Nakhodka	75	42 53N	132 54 E
Nakhon Phanom	95	17 23N	104 43 E
Nakhon Ratchasima	95	14 59N	102 12 E
Nakhon Sawan	94	15 35N	100 10 E
Nakhon Si Thammarat	96	8 29N	100 0 E
Nakina	140	50 10N	86 40W
Nakskov	61	54 50N	11 8 E
Nakuru	132	0 15S	36 4 E
Nalchik	70	43 30N	43 33 E
Nalgonda	91	17 6N	79 15 E
Nam Co	101	30 30N	90 45 E
Nam Dinh	95	20 25N	106 5 E
Nam-Phan	95	10 30N	106 0 E
Nam Tha	95	20 58N	101 30 E
Nam Tok	94	14 21N	99 4 E
Namaland	136	24 30S	17 0 E
Namangan	71	41 0N	71 40 E
Nambour	116	26 32S	152 58 E
Nambucca Heads	116	30 37S	153 0 E
Namerikawa	106	36 46N	137 20 E
Namib Desert = Namib-Woestyn	124	22 30S	15 0 E
Namib-Woestyn	124	22 30S	15 0 E
Namibe	134	15 7S	12 11 E
Namibia ■	136	22 0S	18 9 E
Nampa	171	43 34N	116 34W
Namsos	65	64 29N	11 30 E
Namur	42	50 27N	4 52 E
Nanaimo	154	49 10N	124 0W
Nanango	116	26 40S	152 0 E
Nanao	105	37 0N	137 0 E
Nanchang	99	28 42N	115 55 E
Nanching = Nanjing	99	32 3N	118 47 E
Nanching	99	32 3N	118 47 E
Nancy	37	48 42N	6 12 E
Nanda Devi	101	30 23N	79 59 E
Nandan	109	34 10N	134 42 E
Nanded	91	19 10N	77 20 E
Nandurbar	91	21 20N	74 15 E
Nanga Parbat	89	35 10N	74 35 E
Nangarhár □	87	34 20N	70 0 E
Nanjing	99	32 3N	118 47 E
Nanking = Nanching	99	32 3N	118 47 E
Nanking = Nanjing	99	32 3N	118 47 E
Nankoku	109	33 39N	133 44 E
Nanning	99	22 48N	108 20 E
Nanping	99	26 38N	118 10 E
Nantes	36	47 12N	1 33W
Nanticoke	164	41 12N	76 1W
Nanton	155	50 21N	113 46W
Nanuque	189	17 50S	40 21W
Napa	172	38 18N	122 17W
Napier	122	39 30S	176 56 E
Naples = Nápoli	49	40 50N	14 17 E
Napo →►	186	3 20S	72 40W
Nápoli	49	40 50N	14 17 E
Nara, Japan	106	34 40N	135 49 E

Name	Page	Lat	Long
Nara, Mali	130	15 10N	7 20W
Naracoorte	119	36 58S	140 45 E
Narasapur	92	16 26N	81 40 E
Narayanganj	92	23 40N	90 33 E
Narayanpet	91	16 45N	77 30 E
Narbonne	37	43 11N	3 0 E
Narita	107	35 47N	140 19 E
Narmada ~►	91	21 38N	72 36 E
Narooma	117	36 14S	150 4 E
Narrabri	116	30 19S	149 46 E
Narrandera	117	34 42S	146 31 E
Narrogin	120	32 58S	117 14 E
Narromine	116	32 12S	148 12 E
Naruto	109	34 11N	134 37 E
Narvik	64	68 28N	17 26 E
Narym	71	59 0N	81 30 E
Naser, Buheirat en	128	23 0N	32 30 E
Nashua	164	42 50N	71 25W
Nashville	169	36 12N	86 46W
Nasik	91	19 58N	73 50 E
Nasirabad	91	26 15N	74 45 E
Nassau	178	25 0N	77 20W
Nasser, L. = Naser, Buheirat			
en	128	23 0N	32 30 E
Nässjö	60	57 39N	14 42 E
Natal	189	5 47S	35 13W
Natal □	137	28 30S	30 30 E
Natashquan	149	50 14N	61 46W
Natchez	168	31 35N	91 25W
Natchitoches	168	31 47N	93 4W
Nathalia	117	36 1S	145 13 E
National City	173	32 39N	117 7W
Natuna Besar, Kepulauan	111	4 0N	108 15 E
Natuna Selatan, Kepulauan	111	2 45N	109 0 E
Nauru ■	122	1 0S	166 0 E
Nauta	186	4 31S	73 35W
Nautanwa	92	27 20N	83 25 E
Nautla	177	20 20N	96 50W
Navarra □	51	42 40N	1 40W
Navojoa	174	27 0N	109 30W
Navsari	91	20 57N	72 59 E
Nawabshah	88	26 15N	68 25 E
Nawalgarh	89	27 50N	75 15 E
Náxos	55	37 8N	25 25 E
Nãy Band	87	27 20N	52 40 E
Nayakhan	73	61 56N	159 0 E
Nayarit □	175	22 0N	105 0W
Ndélé	129	8 25N	20 36 E
Ndjamena	131	12 10N	14 59 E
Ndola	135	13 0S	28 34 E
Neagh, Lough	34	54 35N	6 25W
Near Is.	142	53 0N	172 0 E
Neath	27	51 39N	3 49W
Nebraska □	163	41 30N	100 0W
Nebraska City	166	40 40N	95 52W
Nebrodi Mts.	49	37 55N	14 45 E
Neches ~►	168	29 55N	93 52W
Neckar ~►	42	49 31N	8 26 E
Necochea	190	38 30S	58 50W
Needles, The	24	50 39N	1 35W
Neenah	167	44 10N	88 30W
Neepawa	153	50 15N	99 30W
Negapatam = Nagappattinam	90	10 46N	79 51 E
Negeri Sembilan □	96	2 45N	102 10 E
Negotin	53	44 16N	22 37 E
Negra, Pta.	186	6 6S	81 10W
Negro ~►, Argentina	190	41 2S	62 47W
Negro ~►, Brazil	185	3 0S	60 0W
Negros	112	9 30N	122 40 E
Nehbandãn	85	31 35N	60 5 E
Nei Monggol Zizhiqu □	98	42 0N	112 0 E
Neijiang	99	29 35N	104 55 E
Neiva	184	2 56N	75 18W
Nellore	90	14 27N	79 59 E
Nelson, Canada	155	49 30N	117 20W
Nelson, N.Z.	123	41 18S	173 16 E
Nelson, U.K.	28	53 50N	2 14W
Nelson ~►	153	54 33N	98 2W
Néma	126	16 40N	7 15W
Neman ~►	68	55 25N	21 10 E
Nemours	39	48 16N	2 40 E
Nemunas = Neman ~►	68	55 25N	21 10 E
Nemuro	103	43 20N	145 35 E
Nemuro-Kaikyõ	103	43 30N	145 30 E
Nenagh	35	52 52N	8 11W
Nenana	142	64 30N	149 20W
Nene ~►	29	52 38N	0 13 E
Neosho	168	36 56N	94 28W
Neosho ~►	168	35 59N	95 10W
Nepal ■	92	28 0N	84 30 E
Nephi	162	39 43N	111 52W
Ness, Loch	33	57 15N	4 30W
Netanya	80	32 20N	34 51 E
Netherlands ■	41	52 0N	5 30 E
Netherlands Antilles ■	181	12 15N	69 0W
Netherlands Guiana =			
Surinam ■	185	4 0N	56 0W
Nettilling L.	146	66 30N	71 0W
Netzahualcoyotl, Presa	177	17 10N	93 30W
Neuchâtel	44	47 0N	6 55 E
Neuchâtel, Lac de	44	46 53N	6 50 E
Neuquén	190	38 55S	68 0 E
Neuse ~►	165	35 5N	76 30W
Neusiedler See	45	47 50N	16 47 E
Nevada	166	37 51N	94 22W
Nevada □	172	39 20N	117 0W
Nevada, Sierra, Spain	50	37 3N	3 15W
Nevada, Sierra, U.S.A.	172	39 0N	120 30W
Nevada City	172	39 20N	121 0W
Nevada de Sta. Marta, Sa.	184	10 55N	73 50W
Nevers	37	47 0N	3 9 E
New Albany	167	38 20N	85 50W
New Amsterdam	185	6 15N	57 36W
New Bedford	164	41 40N	70 52W
New Bern	165	35 8N	77 3W
New Braunfels	161	29 43N	98 9W
New Brighton	123	43 29S	172 43 E
New Britain, Papua N. G.	115	5 50S	150 20 E
New Britain, U.S.A.	164	41 41N	72 47W
New Brunswick	164	40 30N	74 28W
New Brunswick □	148	46 50N	66 30W
New Caledonia = Nouvelle			
Calédonie	122	21 0S	165 0 E
New Castile = Castilla La			
Nueva	50	39 45N	3 20W
New Castle, Ind., U.S.A.	164	39 55N	85 23W
New Castle, Pa., U.S.A.	164	41 0N	80 20W
New England Ra.	116	30 20S	151 45 E
New Forest	24	50 53N	1 40W
New Glasgow	149	45 35N	62 36W
New Hampshire □	164	43 40N	71 40W
New Haven	164	41 20N	72 54W
New Hebrides = Vanuatu ■	122	15 0S	168 0 E
New Iberia	168	30 2N	91 54W
New Ireland	115	3 20S	151 50 E
New Jersey □	164	40 30N	74 10W
New Kensington	164	40 36N	79 43W
New London	164	41 23N	72 8W
New Mexico □	161	34 30N	106 0W
New Norfolk	119	42 46S	147 2 E
New Orleans	169	30 0N	90 5W
New Philadelphia	164	40 29N	81 25W
New Plymouth	122	39 4S	174 5 E
New Providence	178	25 25N	78 35W
New Radnor	26	52 15N	3 10W
New Siberian Is. =			
Novosibirskiye Ostrova	72	75 0N	142 0 E
New South Wales □	116	33 0S	146 0 E
New Ulm	166	44 15N	94 30W
New Waterford	149	46 13N	60 4W
New Westminster	154	49 13N	122 55W
New York □	164	42 40N	76 0W
New York City	164	40 45N	74 0W
New Zealand ■	122	40 0S	176 0 E
Newark, N.J., U.S.A.	164	40 41N	74 12W
Newark, N.Y., U.S.A.	164	43 2N	77 10W
Newark, Ohio, U.S.A.	167	40 5N	82 24W
Newark-on-Trent	29	53 6N	0 48W
Newberry, Mich., U.S.A.	150	46 20N	85 30W
Newberry, S.C., U.S.A.	165	34 17N	81 37W
Newburgh	164	41 30N	74 1W
Newburyport	164	42 48N	70 50W

Newcastle, Australia .... **117** 33 0S 151 46 E
Newcastle, Canada **148** 47 1N 65 38W
Newcastle, U.K. **34** 54 13N 5 54W
Newcastle Emlyn **26** 52 2N 4 29W
Newcastle-under-Lyme **28** 53 2N 2 15W
Newcastle-upon-Tyne **28** 54 59N 1 37W
Newfoundland □ **149** 53 0N 58 0W
Newhaven .... **25** 50 47N 0 4 E
Newmarket .... **25** 52 15N 0 23 E
Newnan **170** 33 22N 84 48W
Newport, Gwent, U.K. **27** 51 35N 3 0W
Newport, I. of W., U.K. **25** 50 42N 1 18W
Newport, Ark., U.S.A. **168** 35 38N 91 15W
Newport, Ky., U.S.A. **167** 39 5N 84 23W
Newport, Oreg., U.S.A. **171** 44 41N 124 2W
Newport, R.I., U.S.A. **164** 41 13N 71 19W
Newport, Vt., U.S.A. **148** 44 57N 72 17W
Newport Beach **173** 33 40N 117 58W
Newport News **165** 37 2N 76 30W
Newquay **27** 50 24N 5 6W
Newry **34** 54 10N 6 20W
Newton, Iowa, U.S.A. **166** 41 40N 93 3W
Newton, Mass., U.S.A. **164** 42 21N 71 10W
Newton Abbot **27** 50 32N 3 37W
Newton Stewart **31** 54 57N 4 30W
Newtonmore **33** 57 4N 4 7W
Newtown **26** 52 31N 3 19W
Newtownards **34** 54 37N 5 40W
Ngaoundéré .... **131** 7 15N 13 35 E
Ngoring Hu .... **101** 34 55N 97 5 E
Nguru .... **131** 12 56N 10 29 E
Nha Trang .... **95** 12 16N 109 10 E
Nhill .... **119** 36 18S 141 40 E
Niagara Falls, Canada **151** 43 7N 79 5W
Niagara Falls, U.S.A. **164** 43 5N 79 0W
Niamey .... **131** 13 27N 2 6 E
Nias .... **111** 1 0N 97 30 E
Nicaragua ■ **179** 11 40N 85 30W
Nicaragua, Lago de **179** 12 0N 85 30W
Nice .... **37** 43 42N 7 14 E
Nichinan .... **108** 31 38N 131 23 E
Nicobar Is. .... **8** 9 0N 93 0 E
Nicosia .... **80** 35 10N 33 25 E
Nicoya, Pen. de **179** 9 45N 85 40W
Nidd ⟶ **28** 54 1N 1 32W
Niederösterreich □ ...... **45** 48 25N 15 40 E
Niedersachsen □ .... **42** 52 45N 9 0 E
Nieuw Nickerie **185** 6 0N 56 59W
Niger ■ .... **131** 13 30N 10 0 E
Niger ⟶ .... **131** 5 33N 6 33 E
Nigeria ■ .... **131** 8 30N 8 0 E
Nii-Jima .... **107** 34 20N 139 15 E
Niigata .... **103** 37 58N 139 0 E
Niihama .... **109** 33 55N 133 16 E
Niimi .... **109** 34 59N 133 28 E
Nijkerk .... **41** 52 13N 5 30 E
Nijmegen .... **41** 51 50N 5 52 E
Nikki .... **131** 9 58N 3 12 E
Nikkō .... **107** 36 45N 139 35 E
Nikolayev .... **68** 46 58N 32 0 E
Nikolayevsk-na-Amur ..... **75** 53 8N 140 44 E
Nikolskoye .... **73** 55 12N 166 0 E
Nikšić .... **52** 42 50N 18 57 E
Nîl, Nahr en ⟶ .... **128** 30 10N 31 6 E
Nîl el Abyad ⟶ .... **129** 15 38N 32 31 E
Nîl el Azraq ⟶ .... **129** 15 38N 32 31 E
Nile = Nîl, Nahr en ⟶ ... **128** 30 10N 31 6 E
Niles **164** 41 8N 80 40W
Nîmes .... **37** 43 50N 4 23 E
Nimule .... **129** 3 32N 32 3 E
Nīnawá .... **81** 36 25N 43 10 E
Nineveh = Nīnawá .... **81** 36 25N 43 10 E
Ningbo .... **99** 29 51N 121 28 E
Ningde .... **99** 26 38N 119 23 E
Ningpo = Ningbo .... **99** 29 51N 121 28 E
Ningsia Hui A.R. = Ningxia
 Huizu Zizhiqu □ .... **98** 38 0N 106 0 E
Ningxia Huizu Zizhiqu □ ... **98** 38 0N 106 0 E
Niobrara ⟶ **163** 42 45N 98 0W
Nioro du Sahel **130** 15 15N 9 30W
Niort **36** 46 19N 0 29W

Nipawin **152** 53 20N 104 0W
Nipigon **150** 49 0N 88 17W
Nipigon, L. **150** 49 50N 88 30W
Niš .... **53** 43 19N 21 58 E
Nişāb .... **83** 14 25N 46 29 E
Nishinomiya .... **106** 34 45N 135 20 E
Nishio .... **106** 34 52N 137 3 E
Nishiwaki .... **109** 34 59N 134 58 E
Niterói **188** 22 52S 43 0W
Nith ⟶ **31** 55 20N 3 5W
Nitra .... **59** 48 19N 18 4 E
Nivernais .... **37** 47 0N 3 40 E
Nizamabad .... **91** 18 45N 78 7 E
Nizhne Kolymsk .... **73** 68 34N 160 55 E
Nizhneudinsk .... **74** 54 54N 99 3 E
Nizhnevartovsk .... **69** 60 56N 76 38 E
Nizhniy Novgorod .... **68** 56 20N 44 0 E
Nizhniy Tagil .... **69** 57 55N 59 57 E
Nizhnyaya Tunguska ⟶ ... **74** 64 20N 93 0 E
Nizké Tatry .... **59** 48 55N 20 0 E
Nkongsamba .... **131** 4 55N 9 55 E
Noatak **142** 67 32N 162 59W
Nobeoka .... **108** 32 36N 131 41 E
Noda .... **107** 35 56N 139 52 E
Nogales **174** 31 20N 110 56W
Nōgata .... **108** 33 48N 130 44 E
Nogent-le-Rotrou .... **39** 48 20N 0 50 E
Noi ⟶ .... **94** 14 50N 100 15 E
Noirmoutier, Î. de **36** 46 58N 2 10W
Nojima-Zaki .... **107** 34 54N 139 53 E
Nok Kundi .... **88** 28 50N 62 45 E
Nome **142** 64 30N 165 24W
Nong Khae .... **95** 14 29N 100 53 E
Nong Khai .... **95** 17 50N 102 46 E
Nonoava **174** 27 28N 106 44W
Noord Brabant □ .... **40** 51 40N 5 0 E
Noord Holland □ .... **40** 52 30N 4 45 E
Noordbeveland .... **40** 51 35N 3 50 E
Noordoostpolder .... **41** 52 45N 5 45 E
Noordwijk aan Zee ...... **40** 52 14N 4 26 E
Nootka I. **154** 49 32N 126 42W
Nord-Trøndelag fylke □ ... **65** 64 20N 12 0 E
Nordaustlandet .... **13** 79 14N 23 0 E
Nordegg **155** 52 29N 116 5W
Nordkapp .... **67** 71 10N 25 44 E
Nordkinn .... **67** 71 8N 27 40 E
Nordland fylke □ .... **65** 65 40N 13 0 E
Nordrhein-Westfalen □ ... **42** 51 45N 7 30 E
Nordvik .... **72** 74 2N 111 32 E
Nore ⟶ **35** 52 40N 7 20W
Norfolk **165** 36 40N 76 15W
Norfolk □ .... **29** 52 39N 1 0 E
Norfolk I. .... **122** 28 58S 168 3 E
Norilsk .... **72** 69 20N 88 6 E
Norman **168** 35 12N 97 30W
Norman Wells **144** 65 17N 126 51W
Normandie .... **39** 48 45N 0 10 E
Normandin **151** 48 49N 72 31W
Normandy = Normandie ... **39** 48 45N 0 10 E
Normanton .... **115** 17 40S 141 10 E
Norquinco **192** 41 51S 70 55W
Norristown **164** 40 9N 75 21W
Norrköping .... **60** 58 37N 16 11 E
Norrland □ .... **66** 66 50N 18 0 E
Norseman .... **114** 32 8S 121 43 E
Norsk .... **75** 52 30N 130 0 E
North Andaman I. .... **94** 13 15N 92 40 E
North Battleford **152** 52 50N 108 17W
North Bay **151** 46 20N 79 30W
North Bend **171** 43 28N 124 14W
North Berwick **31** 56 4N 2 44W
North C. .... **122** 34 23S 173 4 E
North Carolina □ **165** 35 30N 80 0W
North Channel, Br. Is. **30** 55 0N 5 30W
North Channel, Canada ... **150** 46 0N 83 0W
North Dakota □ **163** 47 30N 100 0W
North Downs .... **25** 51 17N 0 30 E
North European Plain ..... **17** 55 0N 20 0 E
North I. .... **122** 38 0S 175 0 E
North Korea ■ .... **98** 40 0N 127 0 E
North Minch **32** 58 5N 5 55W

North Ossetian Rep. □	....	**70**	43	30N	44	30 E
North Platte	....	**163**	41	10N	100	50W
North Platte ⟶	....	**163**	41	15N	100	45W
North Pole	....	**12**	90	0N	0	0 E
North Ronaldsay	....	**33**	59	20N	2	30W
North Saskatchewan ⟶	..	**143**	53	15N	105	5W
North Sea	....	**16**	56	0N	4	0 E
North Sentinel I.	....	**94**	11	35N	92	15 E
North Sporades = Voríai						
Sporádhes	....	**55**	39	15N	23	30 E
North Sydney	....	**149**	46	12N	60	15W
North Tonawanda	....	**164**	43	5N	78	50W
North Uist	....	**32**	57	40N	7	15W
North Vancouver	....	**154**	49	25N	123	3W
North Walsham	....	**29**	52	49N	1	22 E
North West Frontier □	....	**89**	34	0N	71	0 E
North West Highlands	....	**32**	57	35N	5	2W
North West River	....	**147**	53	30N	60	10W
North West Territories □	...	**145**	67	0N	110	0W
North York Moors	....	**29**	54	25N	0	50W
North Yorkshire □	....	**28**	54	15N	1	25W
Northallerton	....	**28**	54	20N	1	26W
Northam	....	**120**	31	35S	116	42 E
Northampton, Australia	....	**120**	28	27S	114	33 E
Northampton, U.K.	....	**25**	52	14N	0	54W
Northampton, U.S.A.	......	**164**	42	22N	72	31W
Northampton □	....	**25**	52	16N	0	55W
Northcliffe	....	**120**	34	39S	116	7 E
Northern Circars	....	**92**	17	30N	82	30 E
Northern Ireland □	....	**34**	54	45N	7	0W
Northern Territory □	......	**114**	16	0S	133	0 E
Northfield	....	**166**	44	30N	93	10W
Northumberland □	....	**28**	55	12N	2	0W
Northumberland Is.	....	**121**	21	30S	149	50 E
Northumberland Str.	......	**148**	46	20N	64	0W
Northwich	....	**28**	53	16N	2	30W
Norton Sd.	....	**142**	64	0N	164	0W
Norwalk	....	**164**	41	9N	73	25W
Norway ■	....	**18**	63	0N	11	0 E
Norwegian Sea	....	**16**	66	0N	1	0 E
Norwich	....	**29**	52	38N	1	17 E
Nos Kaliakra	....	**53**	43	21N	28	30 E
Noshiro	....	**103**	40	12N	140	0 E
Noss Hd.	....	**33**	58	29N	3	4W
Nossob ⟶	....	**136**	26	55S	20	37 E
Noteć ⟶	....	**58**	52	44N	15	26 E
Notre Dame de Koartac =						
Koartac	....	**146**	60	55N	69	40W
Nottaway ⟶	....	**140**	51	22N	78	55W
Nottingham	....	**29**	52	57N	1	10W
Nottingham □	....	**29**	53	10N	1	0W
Nouâdhibou	....	**126**	20	54N	17	0W
Nouâdhibou, Ras	....	**126**	20	50N	17	0W
Nouakchott	....	**126**	18	9N	15	58W
Noumea	....	**122**	22	17S	166	30 E
Nouveau Comptoir	......	**140**	53	0N	78	49W
Nouvelle Calédonie	......	**122**	21	0S	165	0 E
Nova Friburgo	....	**188**	22	16S	42	30W
Nova Granada	....	**188**	20	30S	49	20W
Nova Lisboa = Huambo	..	**134**	12	42S	15	54 E
Nova Scotia □	....	**149**	45	10N	63	0W
Novara	....	**46**	45	27N	8	36 E
Novaya Sibir, Ostrov	.....	**72**	75	10N	150	0 E
Novaya Zemlya	....	**69**	75	0N	56	0 E
Novgorod	....	**68**	58	30N	31	25 E
Novi Pazar	....	**52**	43	12N	20	28 E
Novi Sad	....	**52**	45	18N	19	52 E
Novocherkassk	....	**68**	47	27N	40	5 E
Novokuznetsk	....	**71**	53	45N	87	10 E
Novomoskovsk	....	**68**	54	5N	38	15 E
Novorossiysk	....	**68**	44	43N	37	46 E
Novosibirsk	....	**71**	55	0N	83	5 E
Novosibirskiye Ostrova	...	**72**	75	0N	142	0 E
Nowgong	....	**93**	26	20N	92	50 E
Nowra	....	**117**	34	53S	150	35 E
Nowy Sącz	....	**59**	49	40N	20	41 E
Noyon	....	**38**	49	34N	3	0 E
Nûbîya, Es Sahrâ En	.....	**129**	21	30N	33	30 E
Nueces ⟶	....	**161**	27	50N	97	30W
Nueltin L.	....	**145**	60	30N	99	30W
Nueva Gerona	....	**178**	21	53N	82	49W

Nueva Rosita	....	**174**	27	57N	101	13W
Nuevitas	....	**178**	21	30N	77	20W
Nuevo Laredo	....	**176**	27	30N	99	30W
Nuevo Leon □	....	**176**	25	40N	100	0W
Nuhaka	....	**122**	39	3S	177	45 E
Nukey Bluff, Mt.	....	**118**	32	26S	135	29 E
Nukus	....	**70**	42	20N	59	7 E
Nulato	....	**142**	64	40N	158	10W
Nullarbor Plain	....	**114**	30	45S	129	0 E
Numan	....	**131**	9	29N	12	3 E
Numazu	....	**107**	35	7N	138	51 E
Numurkah	....	**117**	36	5S	145	26 E
Nuneaton	....	**25**	52	32N	1	29W
Nunivak	....	**142**	60	0N	166	0W
Nunspeet	....	**41**	52	21N	5	45 E
Nuoro	....	**48**	40	20N	9	20 E
Nuremburg = Nürnberg	..	**43**	49	26N	11	5 E
Nuriootpa	....	**119**	34	27S	139	0 E
Nürnberg	....	**43**	49	26N	11	5 E
Nurran, L. = Terewah, L.	...	**116**	29	52S	147	35 E
Nutak	....	**147**	57	28N	61	59W
Nuweveldberge	....	**136**	32	10S	21	45 E
Nuyts Arch.	....	**118**	32	35S	133	20 E
Nyaake	....	**130**	4	52N	7	37W
Nyainqentanglha Shan	...	**101**	30	0N	90	0 E
Nyasa, L. = Malawi, L.	...	**137**	12	30S	34	30 E
Nyíregyháza	....	**59**	47	58N	21	47 E
Nyngan	....	**116**	31	30S	147	8 E
Nysa	....	**58**	50	30N	17	22 E

O

Oahe L.	....	**163**	45	30N	100	25W
Oahu	....	**160**	21	30N	158	0W
Oak Hill	....	**165**	38	0N	81	7W
Oak Park	....	**167**	41	55N	87	45W
Oak Ridge	....	**169**	36	1N	84	12W
Oakengates	....	**28**	52	42N	2	29W
Oakey	....	**116**	27	25S	151	43 E
Oakham	....	**29**	52	40N	0	43W
Oakland	....	**172**	37	50N	122	18W
Oakridge	....	**171**	43	47N	122	31W
Oamaru	....	**123**	45	5S	170	59 E
Oaxaca	....	**177**	17	2N	96	40W
Oaxaca □	....	**177**	17	0N	96	30W
Ob ⟶	....	**69**	66	45N	69	30 E
Oba	....	**150**	49	4N	84	7W
Obama	....	**106**	35	30N	135	45 E
Oban	....	**30**	56	25N	5	30W
Obbia	....	**133**	5	25N	48	30 E
Oberhausen	....	**42**	51	28N	6	50 E
Oberon	....	**117**	33	45S	149	52 E
Oberösterreich □	....	**45**	48	10N	14	0 E
Obi, Is.	....	**113**	1	30S	127	30 E
Obihiro	....	**103**	42	56N	143	12 E
Obskaya Guba	....	**69**	69	0N	73	0 E
Ocala	....	**170**	29	11N	82	5W
Ocampo	....	**174**	28	11N	108	23W
Ocaña	....	**184**	8	15N	73	20W
Occidental, Cordillera	....	**184**	5	0N	76	0W
Ocean City	....	**164**	39	18N	74	34W
Oceanside	....	**173**	33	13N	117	26W
Ochil Hills	....	**31**	56	14N	3	40W
Oconee ⟶	....	**170**	31	58N	82	32W
Oconto	....	**167**	44	52N	87	53W
Ocotlán	....	**175**	20	21N	102	46W
Ōda	....	**109**	35	11N	132	30 E
Ódáðahraun	....	**64**	65	5N	17	0W
Odate	....	**103**	40	16N	140	34 E
Odawara	....	**107**	35	20N	139	6 E
Ödemiş	....	**80**	38	15N	28	0 E
Odense	....	**61**	55	22N	10	23 E
Oder ⟶	....	**58**	53	33N	14	38 E
Odessa, Ukraine	....	**68**	46	30N	30	45 E
Odessa, U.S.A.	....	**161**	31	51N	102	23W
Odra ⟶	....	**58**	53	33N	14	38 E
Odžak	....	**52**	45	3N	18	18 E
Offaly □	....	**35**	53	15N	7	30W

Offenbach ... **42** 50 6N 8 46 E
Oga-Hantō ... **103** 39 58N 139 47 E
Ogaden ... **133** 7 30N 45 30 E
Ōgaki ... **106** 35 21N 136 37 E
Ogbomosho ... **131** 8 1N 4 11 E
Ogden ... **163** 41 13N 112 1W
Ogdensburg ... **151** 44 40N 75 27W
Ohio □ ... **167** 40 20N 14 10 E
Ohio → ... **167** 38 0N 86 0W
Ohrid ... **52** 41 8N 20 52 E
Ohridsko, Jezero ... **52** 41 8N 20 52 E
Oil City ... **164** 41 26N 79 40W
Oise → ... **38** 49 0N 2 4 E
Oisterwijk ... **40** 51 35N 5 12 E
Ōita ... **108** 33 14N 131 36 E
Ojos del Salado, Cerro ... **190** 27 0S 68 40W
Oka → ... **68** 56 20N 43 59 E
Okawa ... **108** 33 9N 130 21 E
Okaya ... **107** 36 0N 138 10 E
Okayama ... **109** 34 40N 133 54 E
Okazaki ... **106** 34 57N 137 10 E
Okeechobee, L. ... **170** 27 0N 80 50W
Okehampton ... **27** 50 44N 4 1W
Okha ... **75** 53 40N 143 0 E
Okhotsk ... **75** 59 20N 143 10 E
Okhotsk, Sea of ... **77** 55 0N 145 0 E
Okhotsko Kolymskoye ... **73** 63 0N 157 0 E
Oki-no-Shima ... **109** 32 44N 132 33 E
Oki-Shotō ... **109** 36 5N 133 15 E
Okinawa-Jima ... **99** 26 32N 128 0 E
Oklahoma □ ... **161** 35 20N 97 30W
Oklahoma City ... **161** 35 25N 97 30W
Okmulgee ... **168** 35 38N 96 0W
Oktabrsk ... **70** 49 28N 57 25 E
Oktyabrskoy Revolyutsii, Os. **72** 79 30N 97 0 E
Oktyabrskoye ... **69** 62 28N 66 3 E
Ōkuchi ... **108** 32 4N 130 37 E
Okuru ... **123** 43 55S 168 55 E
Okushiri-Tō ... **103** 42 15N 139 30 E
Olanchito ... **179** 15 30N 86 30W
Öland ... **61** 56 45N 16 38 E
Olary ... **118** 32 18S 140 19 E
Olavarría ... **190** 36 55S 60 20W
Old Castile = Castilla La Vieja **50** 41 55N 4 0W
Old Town ... **148** 45 0N 68 41W
Oldenburg ... **42** 53 10N 8 10 E
Oldenzaal ... **41** 52 19N 6 53 E
Oldham ... **28** 53 33N 2 8W
Olds ... **155** 51 50N 114 10W
Olekma → ... **74** 60 22N 120 42 E
Olekminsk ... **74** 60 25N 120 30 E
Olenek ... **72** 68 28N 112 18 E
Olenek → ... **72** 73 0N 120 10 E
Oléron, Île d' ... **36** 45 55N 1 15W
Oleśnica ... **58** 51 13N 17 22 E
Olifants → ... **137** 24 5S 31 20 E
Ólimbos, Óros ... **54** 40 6N 22 23 E
Oliveira ... **188** 20 39S 44 50W
Oliver ... **155** 49 13N 119 37W
Ollagüe ... **187** 21 15S 68 10W
Olney ... **167** 38 40N 88 0W
Olomouc ... **59** 49 38N 17 12 E
Olsztyn ... **58** 53 48N 20 29 E
Olt → ... **57** 43 50N 24 40 E
Olympia, Greece ... **54** 37 39N 21 39 E
Olympia, U.S.A. ... **171** 47 0N 122 58W
Olympic Mts. ... **171** 47 50N 123 45W
Olympus, Mt. = Ólimbos, Óros ... **54** 40 6N 22 23 E
Olympus, Mt. ... **171** 47 52N 123 40W
Ōmachi ... **107** 36 30N 137 50 E
Omae-Zaki ... **107** 34 36N 138 14 E
Omagh ... **34** 54 36N 7 20W
Omaha ... **166** 41 15N 96 0W
Omak ... **171** 48 24N 119 31W
Oman ■ ... **83** 23 0N 58 0 E
Oman, G. of ... **83** 24 30N 58 30 E
Omdurmân ... **129** 15 40N 32 28 E
Ōme ... **107** 35 47N 139 15 E
Omeo ... **117** 37 6S 147 36 E
Omihachiman ... **106** 35 7N 136 3 E
Ōmiya ... **107** 35 54N 139 38 E
Omo → ... **132** 6 25N 36 10 E
Omolon → ... **73** 68 42N 158 36 E
Omono-Gawa → ... **103** 39 46N 140 3 E
Omsk ... **71** 55 0N 73 12 E
Ōmura ... **108** 32 56N 130 0 E
Ōmuta ... **108** 33 0N 130 26 E
Onega ... **68** 64 0N 38 10 E
Onega, L. = Onezhskoye Ozero ... **68** 62 0N 35 30 E
Onehunga ... **122** 36 55S 174 48 E
Oneida ... **164** 43 5N 75 40W
Onekotan, Ostrov ... **75** 49 25N 154 45 E
Onezhskoye Ozero ... **68** 62 0N 35 30 E
Ongerup ... **120** 33 58S 118 28 E
Ongole ... **90** 15 33N 80 2 E
Onguren ... **74** 53 38N 107 36 E
Onitsha ... **131** 6 6N 6 42 E
Ono, Fukui, Japan ... **106** 35 59N 136 29 E
Ono, Hyōgo, Japan ... **109** 34 51N 134 56 E
Onoda ... **108** 34 2N 131 25 E
Onomichi ... **109** 34 25N 133 12 E
Onslow ... **114** 21 40S 115 12 E
Onslow B. ... **165** 34 20N 77 20W
Ontake-San ... **106** 35 53N 137 29 E
Ontario ... **173** 34 2N 117 40W
Ontario □ ... **140** 52 0N 88 10W
Ontario, L. ... **151** 43 40N 78 0W
Oodnadatta ... **118** 27 33S 135 30 E
Ooldea ... **114** 30 27S 131 50 E
Oostende ... **42** 51 15N 2 50 E
Oosterhout ... **40** 51 39N 4 47 E
Oosterschelde ... **40** 51 33N 4 0 E
Opala ... **73** 51 58N 156 30 E
Opava ... **58** 49 57N 17 58 E
Opelousas ... **168** 30 35N 92 7W
Ophir ... **142** 63 10N 156 40W
Opole ... **58** 50 42N 17 58 E
Oporto = Porto ... **50** 41 8N 8 40W
Opp ... **169** 31 19N 86 13W
Oppland fylke □ ... **60** 61 15N 9 40 E
Opua ... **122** 35 19S 174 9 E
Oradea ... **56** 47 2N 21 58 E
Öræfajökull ... **64** 64 2N 16 39W
Orai ... **91** 25 58N 79 30 E
Oran, Algeria ... **127** 35 45N 0 39W
Oran, Argentina ... **190** 23 10S 64 20W
Orange, Australia ... **117** 33 15S 149 7 E
Orange, France ... **37** 44 8N 4 47 E
Orange, U.S.A. ... **168** 30 10N 93 50W
Orange → = Oranje → .. **136** 28 41S 16 28 E
Orange, C. ... **185** 4 20N 51 30W
Orangeburg ... **170** 33 35N 80 53W
Oranje → ... **136** 28 41S 16 28 E
Oraşul Stalin = Braşov ... **57** 45 38N 25 35 E
Orbost ... **117** 37 40S 148 29 E
Orchies ... **38** 50 28N 3 14 E
Ordos = Mu Us Shamo ... **98** 39 0N 109 0 E
Ordu ... **81** 40 55N 37 53 E
Ordzhonikidze = Vladikavkaz **70** 43 0N 44 35 E
Ore Mts. = Erzgebirge ... **43** 50 25N 13 0 E
Örebro ... **60** 59 20N 15 18 E
Oregon □ ... **171** 44 0N 121 0W
Oregon City ... **171** 45 21N 122 35W
Orel ... **68** 52 57N 36 3 E
Orenburg ... **70** 51 45N 55 6 E
Orense ... **50** 42 19N 7 55W
Orepuki ... **123** 46 19S 167 46 E
Orford Ness ... **24** 52 6N 1 31 E
Oriental, Cordillera ... **184** 6 0N 73 0W
Orillia ... **151** 44 40N 79 24W
Orinoco → ... **185** 9 15N 61 30W
Orissa □ ... **92** 20 0N 84 0 E
Oristano ... **48** 39 54N 8 35 E
Oristano, Golfo di ... **48** 39 50N 8 22 E
Orizaba ... **177** 18 51N 97 6W
Orkney Is. ... **33** 59 0N 3 0W
Orland ... **172** 39 46N 122 12W
Orlando ... **170** 28 30N 81 25W
Orléanais ... **39** 48 0N 2 0 E
Orléans ... **39** 47 54N 1 52 E

Ormara 88 25 16N 64 33 E
Ormskirk 28 53 35N 2 53W
Örnsköldsvik 66 63 17N 18 40 E
Orocué 184 4 48N 71 20W
Oroville 172 39 31N 121 30W
Orsha 68 54 30N 30 25 E
Orsk 70 51 12N 58 34 E
Ortegal, C. 50 43 43N 7 52W
Orūmīyeh 81 37 40N 45 0 E
Orūmīyeh, Daryācheh-ye 81 37 50N 45 30 E
Oruro 187 18 0S 67 9W
Oruzgān □ 87 33 30N 66 0 E
Oryakhovo 53 43 40N 23 57 E
Osage → 166 38 35N 91 57W
Ōsaka 106 34 40N 135 30 E
Osceola 169 35 40N 90 0W
Ösel = Saaremaa 68 58 30N 22 30 E
Osh 71 40 37N 72 49 E
Oshawa 151 43 50N 78 50W
Oshima 107 33 55N 132 14 E
Oshkosh 167 44 3N 88 35W
Oshogbo 131 7 48N 4 37 E
Osijek 52 45 34N 18 41 E
Oskaloosa 166 41 18N 92 40W
Oslo 60 59 55N 10 45 E
Osmaniye 80 37 5N 36 10 E
Osnabrück 42 52 16N 8 2 E
Osorno 190 40 25S 73 0W
Oss 41 51 46N 5 32 E
Ossa, Mt. 119 41 52S 146 3 E
Ostend = Oostende 42 51 15N 2 50 E
Östergötlands län □ 60 58 35N 15 45 E
Östersund 66 63 10N 14 38 E
Østfold fylke □ 60 59 25N 11 25 E
Ostfriesische Inseln 42 53 45N 7 15 E
Ostia 46 41 40N 12 20 E
Ostrava 59 49 51N 18 18 E
Ostróda 58 53 42N 19 58 E
Ostrołeka 58 53 4N 21 32 E
Ostrów Mazowiecka 58 52 50N 21 51 E
Ostrów Wielkopolski 58 51 36N 17 44 E
Ōsumi-Kaikyō 104 30 55N 131 0 E
Ōsumi-Shotō 104 30 30N 130 0 E
Oswego 164 43 29N 76 30W
Oswestry 28 52 52N 3 3W
Ōta 107 36 18N 139 22 E
Otago □ 123 44 44S 169 10 E
Ōtake 109 34 12N 132 13 E
Otaki 122 40 45S 175 10 E
Otaru 103 43 10N 141 0 E
Otaru-Wan = Ishikari-Wan 103 43 25N 141 1 E
Otira Gorge 123 42 53S 171 33 E
Otoineppu 103 44 44N 142 16 E
Otranto 49 40 9N 18 28 E
Otranto, C. d' 49 40 7N 18 30 E
Otranto, Str. of 52 40 15N 18 40 E
Ōtsu 106 35 0N 135 50 E
Ottawa, Canada 151 45 27N 75 42W
Ottawa, U.S.A. 166 38 40N 95 6W
Ottawa → = Outaouais → 140 45 27N 74 8W
Ottawa Is. 146 59 35N 80 10W
Otter Rapids, Ont., Canada 151 50 11N 81 39W
Otter Rapids, Sask., Canada 152 55 38N 104 44W
Ottumwa 166 41 0N 92 25W
Otwock 58 52 5N 21 20 E
Ouachita → 168 31 38N 91 49W
Ouachita Mts. 168 34 50N 94 30W
Ouagadougou 130 12 25N 1 30W
Ouahran = Oran 127 35 45N 0 39W
Ouargla 127 31 59N 5 16 E
Oubangi → 131 1 0N 17 50 E
Oudenbosch 40 51 35N 4 32 E
Oudtshoorn 136 33 35S 22 14 E
Ouessant, Île d' 36 48 28N 5 6W
Oujda 127 34 41N 1 55W
Oulu 67 65 1N 25 29 E
Oulujärvi 67 64 25N 27 15 E
Oulujoki → 67 65 1N 25 30 E
Ouse → 29 54 3N 0 7 E
Outaouais → 140 45 27N 74 8W
Outer Hebrides 32 57 30N 7 40W
Outlook 152 51 30N 107 0W
Outreau 38 50 40N 1 36 E
Ouyen 119 35 1S 142 22 E
Ovalle 190 30 33S 71 18W
Overflakkee 40 51 44N 4 10 E
Overijssel □ 41 52 25N 6 35 E
Oviedo 50 43 25N 5 50W
Owaka 123 46 27S 169 40 E
Owase 106 34 7N 136 12 E
Owatonna 166 44 3N 93 10W
Owen Sound 151 44 35N 80 55W
Owen Stanley Range 115 8 30S 147 0 E
Owensboro 167 37 40N 87 5W
Owosso 167 43 0N 84 10W
Owyhee → 171 43 46N 117 2W
Oxford, U.K. 25 51 45N 1 15W
Oxford, U.S.A. 165 36 19N 78 36W
Oxford □ 25 51 45N 1 15W
Oxford L. 153 54 51N 95 37W
Oxnard 173 34 10N 119 14W
Oyabe 106 36 47N 136 56 E
Oyama 107 36 18N 139 48 E
Oyana 108 32 32N 130 30 E
Oyo 131 7 46N 3 56 E
Oyonnax 37 46 16N 5 40 E
Ozamis 112 8 15N 123 50 E
Ozark 169 31 29N 85 39W
Ozark Plateau 168 37 20N 91 40W
Ozarks, L. of 166 38 10N 92 40W
Ozu, Ehime, Japan 109 33 30N 132 33 E
Ozu, Kumamoto, Japan 108 32 52N 130 52 E

P

Paarl 136 33 45S 18 56 E
Pabna 92 24 1N 89 18 E
Pacaraima, Sierra 185 4 0N 62 30W
Pacasmayo 186 7 20S 79 35W
Pachuca 177 20 10N 98 40W
Padang 111 1 0S 100 20 E
Pádova 47 45 24N 11 52 E
Padstow 27 50 33N 4 57W
Padua = Pádova 47 45 24N 11 52 E
Paducah 169 37 0N 88 40W
Pag 52 44 30N 14 50 E
Pagalu = Annobón 131 1 25S 5 36 E
Pagastikós Kólpos 54 39 15N 23 0 E
Page 160 36 57N 111 27W
Pahala 160 19 12N 155 25W
Pahang □ 96 3 30N 102 45 E
Pahiatua 122 40 27S 175 50 E
Paignton 27 50 26N 3 33W
Painesville 167 41 42N 81 18W
Paint Hills = Nouveau Comptoir 140 53 0N 78 49W
Painted Desert 160 36 0N 111 30W
Paisley 31 55 51N 4 27W
Paita 186 5 11S 81 9W
Pak Sane 95 18 22N 103 39 E
Pakistan ■ 78 30 0N 70 0 E
Pakistan, East = Bangladesh ■ 92 24 0N 90 0 E
Pakokku 93 21 20N 95 0 E
Pakse 95 15 5N 105 52 E
Paktīā □ 87 33 0N 69 15 E
Palanpur 91 24 10N 72 25 E
Palatka 170 29 40N 81 40W
Palawan 112 9 30N 118 30 E
Palembang 111 3 0S 104 50 E
Palencia 50 42 1N 4 34W
Palermo 48 38 8N 13 20 E
Palestine 168 31 42N 95 35W
Palghat 90 10 46N 76 42 E
Pali 91 25 50N 73 20 E
Palizada 177 18 15N 92 5W
Palk Bay 90 9 30N 79 15 E
Palk Strait 90 10 0N 79 45 E
Palm Is. 121 18 40S 146 35 E
Palm Springs 173 33 51N 116 35W

Place	Page	Lat.	Long.
Palma, La	**179**	8 15N	78 0W
Palma de Mallorca	**51**	39 35N	2 39 E
Palma Soriano	**178**	20 15N	76 0W
Palmas, C.	**130**	4 27N	7 46W
Palmer Land	**14**	73 0S	60 0W
Palmerston North	**122**	40 21S	175 39 E
Palmi	**49**	38 21N	15 51 E
Palmira	**184**	3 32N	76 16W
Palmyra = Tudmur	**80**	34 36N	38 15 E
Palo Alto	**172**	37 25N	122 8W
Pamirs	**71**	37 40N	73 0 E
Pamlico Sd.	**165**	35 20N	76 0W
Pampa	**161**	35 35N	100 58W
Pampas	**190**	35 0S	63 0W
Pamplona	**51**	42 48N	1 38W
Panaca	**173**	37 51N	114 23W
Panaji	**91**	15 25N	73 50 E
Panamá	**179**	9 0N	79 25W
Panama ■	**179**	8 48N	79 55W
Panamá, Golfo de	**179**	8 4N	79 20W
Panama Canal	**175**	9 10N	79 37W
Panama City	**169**	30 10N	85 41W
Panay	**112**	11 10N	122 30 E
Pančevo	**52**	44 52N	20 41 E
Pandharpur	**91**	17 41N	75 20 E
Pangfou = Bengbu	**99**	32 58N	117 20 E
Pangkalpinang	**111**	2 0S	106 0 E
Pangnirtung	**146**	66 8N	65 54W
Panjim = Panaji	**91**	15 25N	73 50 E
Panjinad Barrage	**89**	29 22N	71 15 E
Pantelleria	**48**	36 52N	12 0 E
Pánuco	**177**	22 3N	98 10W
Paoting = Baoding	**98**	38 50N	115 28 E
Paot'ou = Baotou	**98**	40 32N	110 2 E
Papien Chiang = Da →	**95**	21 15N	105 20 E
Papua, Gulf of	**115**	9 0S	144 50 E
Papua New Guinea ■	**115**	8 0S	145 0 E
Pará = Belém	**188**	1 20S	48 30W
Pará □	**188**	3 20S	52 0W
Paracatu	**188**	17 10S	46 50W
Paragua, La	**185**	6 50N	63 20W
Paraguay ■	**191**	23 0S	57 0W
Paraguay →	**191**	27 18S	58 38W
Paraíba = João Pessoa	**189**	7 10S	34 52W
Paraíba □	**189**	7 0S	36 0W
Parakou	**131**	9 25N	2 40 E
Paramaribo	**185**	5 50N	55 10W
Paraná	**190**	31 45S	60 30W
Paraná □	**191**	24 30S	51 0W
Paraná →	**190**	33 43S	59 15W
Paranaguá	**191**	25 30S	48 30W
Paranaíba →	**188**	20 6S	51 4W
Parbhani	**91**	19 8N	76 52 E
Parecis, Serra dos	**187**	13 0S	60 0W
Parent	**151**	47 55N	74 35W
Paria, Golfo de	**180**	10 20N	62 0W
Parika	**185**	6 50N	58 20W
Parintins	**185**	2 40S	56 50W
Paripart Kyun	**94**	14 55S	93 45 E
Paris, France	**39**	48 50N	2 20 E
Paris, Tenn., U.S.A.	**169**	36 20N	88 20W
Paris, Tex., U.S.A.	**168**	33 40N	95 30W
Park Range	**163**	40 0N	106 30W
Parker	**173**	34 8N	114 16W
Parkersburg	**164**	39 18N	81 31W
Parkes	**117**	33 9S	148 11 E
Parma	**46**	44 50N	10 20 E
Parnaguá	**188**	10 10S	44 38W
Parnaíba	**189**	2 54S	41 47W
Parnaíba →	**188**	3 0S	41 50W
Parnassós	**54**	38 35N	22 30 E
Pärnu	**68**	58 28N	24 33 E
Páros	**55**	37 5N	25 12 E
Parral	**190**	36 10S	71 52W
Parramatta	**117**	33 48S	151 1 E
Parras	**174**	25 30N	102 20W
Parrett →	**27**	51 7N	2 58W
Parry Is.	**12**	77 0N	110 0W
Parry Sound	**151**	45 20N	80 0W
Parsons	**166**	37 20N	95 17W
Paruro	**187**	13 45S	71 50W
Parvān □	**87**	35 0N	69 0 E
Pasadena, Calif., U.S.A.	**173**	34 5N	118 9W
Pasadena, Tex., U.S.A.	**168**	29 45N	95 14W
Pasaje	**184**	3 23S	79 50W
Pascagoula	**169**	30 21N	88 30W
Pasco	**171**	46 10N	119 0W
Pasco, Cerro de	**186**	10 45S	76 10W
Paso Robles	**173**	35 40N	120 45W
Passero, C.	**49**	36 42N	15 8 E
Passo Fundo	**191**	28 10S	52 20W
Pasto	**184**	1 13N	77 17W
Patagonia	**192**	45 0S	69 0W
Patan	**91**	23 54N	72 14 E
Patchogue	**164**	40 46N	73 1W
Paterson	**164**	40 55N	74 10W
Pathankot	**89**	32 18N	75 45 E
Patiala	**89**	30 23N	76 26 E
Patkai Bum	**93**	27 0N	95 30 E
Pátmos	**55**	37 21N	26 36 E
Patna	**92**	25 35N	85 12 E
Patos, Lag. dos	**191**	31 20S	51 0 E
Patos de Minas	**188**	18 35S	46 32W
Pátrai	**54**	38 14N	21 47 E
Patuca →	**179**	15 50N	84 18W
Pátzcuaro	**175**	19 32N	101 36W
Pau	**36**	43 19N	0 25W
Paulistana	**189**	8 9S	41 9W
Paulo Afonso	**189**	9 21S	38 15W
Pavia	**46**	45 10N	9 10 E
Pavlodar	**71**	52 33N	77 0 E
Pavlovo	**74**	63 5N	115 25 E
Pawtucket	**164**	41 51N	71 22W
Payette	**171**	44 0N	117 0W
Payne Bay = Bellin	**146**	60 0N	70 0W
Payne L.	**146**	59 30N	74 30W
Paynes Find	**120**	29 15S	117 42 E
Paysandú	**191**	32 19S	58 8W
Paz, La, Argentina	**190**	30 50S	59 45W
Paz, La, Bolivia	**187**	16 20S	68 10W
Paz, La, Mexico	**174**	24 10N	110 18W
Pazardzhik	**53**	42 12N	24 20 E
Peace →	**145**	59 0N	111 25W
Peace River	**155**	56 15N	117 18W
Peak, The	**28**	53 24N	1 53W
Peak Hill	**116**	32 47S	148 11 E
Pearl City	**160**	21 24N	158 0W
Pearl Harbor	**160**	21 20N	158 0W
Peary Land	**13**	82 40N	33 0W
Pebas	**186**	3 10S	71 46W
Pechenga	**69**	69 30N	31 25 E
Pechora →	**69**	68 13N	54 15 E
Pechorskaya Guba	**69**	68 40N	54 0 E
Pecos	**161**	31 25N	103 35W
Pecos →	**161**	29 42N	102 30W
Pécs	**59**	46 5N	18 15 E
Pedro Afonso	**188**	9 0S	48 10W
Pedro Juan Caballero	**191**	22 30S	55 40W
Peebles	**31**	55 40N	3 12W
Peekskill	**164**	41 18N	73 57W
Peel	**28**	54 14N	4 40W
Peel →	**144**	67 0N	135 0W
Pegasus Bay	**123**	43 20S	173 10 E
Pegu	**93**	17 20N	96 29 E
Pegu Yoma	**93**	19 0N	96 0 E
Pehuajó	**190**	35 45S	62 0W
Peip'ing = Beijing	**98**	39 55N	116 20 E
Pekalongan	**111**	6 53S	109 40 E
Pekan	**96**	3 30N	103 25 E
Pekanbaru	**111**	0 30N	101 15 E
Pekin	**166**	40 35N	89 40W
Peking = Beijing	**98**	39 55N	116 20 E
Peleng	**113**	1 20S	123 30 E
Pelly →	**144**	62 47N	137 19W
Pelly Bay	**146**	68 38N	89 50W
Peloponnes = Pelopónnisos □	**54**	37 10N	22 0 E
Pelopónnisos □	**54**	37 10N	22 0 E
Peloro, C.	**49**	38 15N	15 40 E
Pelorus Sound	**123**	40 59S	173 59 E
Pelotas	**191**	31 42S	52 23W
Pelvoux, Massif de	**37**	44 52N	6 20 E
Pematangsiantar	**111**	2 57N	99 5 E
Pemba	**135**	5 0S	39 45 E

Name	Page	Lat °	Lat ′	N/S	Long °	Long ′	E/W
Pembroke, Canada	151	45	50N		77	7W	
Pembroke, U.K.	27	51	41N		4	57W	
Pen-y-Ghent	28	54	10N		2	15W	
Penas, G. de	192	47	0S		75	0W	
Pench'i = Benxi	98	41	20N		123	48 E	
Pendembu	130	9	7N		12	14W	
Pendleton	171	45	35N		118	50W	
Penetanguishene	151	44	50N		79	55W	
Penguin	119	41	8S		146	6 E	
Penicuik	31	55	50N		3	14W	
Peninsular Malaysia □	96	4	0N		102	0 E	
Pennines	28	54	50N		2	20W	
Pennsylvania □	164	40	50N		78	0W	
Penola	119	37	25S		140	21 E	
Penonomé	179	8	31N		80	21W	
Penrith, Australia	117	33	43S		150	38 E	
Penrith, U.K.	28	54	40N		2	45W	
Pensacola	169	30	30N		87	10W	
Pensacola Mts.	14	84	0S		40	0W	
Penshurst	119	37	49S		142	20 E	
Penticton	155	49	30N		119	38W	
Pentland Firth	33	58	43N		3	10W	
Pentland Hills	31	55	48N		3	25W	
Penza	68	53	15N		45	5 E	
Penzance	27	50	7N		5	32W	
Penzhinskaya Guba	73	61	30N		163	0 E	
Peoria	166	40	40N		89	40W	
Perak □	96	5	0N		101	0 E	
Perche	36	48	31N		1	1 E	
Pereira	184	4	49N		75	43W	
Perenjori	120	29	26S		116	16 E	
Pergamino	190	33	52S		60	30W	
Périgueux	36	45	10N		0	42 E	
Perlis □	96	6	30N		100	15 E	
Perm	69	58	0N		57	10 E	
Pernambuco = Recife	189	8	0S		35	0W	
Pernambuco □	189	8	0S		37	0W	
Pernatty Lagoon	118	31	30S		137	12 E	
Pernik	53	42	35N		23	2 E	
Peron Pen.	120	26	0S		113	10 E	
Péronne	38	49	55N		2	57 E	
Perouse Str., La	77	45	40N		142	0 E	
Perpignan	37	42	42N		2	53 E	
Perry, Iowa, U.S.A.	166	41	48N		94	5W	
Perry, Okla., U.S.A.	168	36	20N		97	20W	
Persepolis	85	29	55N		52	50 E	
Persia = Iran ■	86	33	0N		53	0 E	
Persian Gulf = Gulf, The	85	27	0N		50	0 E	
Perth, Australia	120	31	57S		115	52 E	
Perth, Canada	151	44	55N		76	15W	
Perth, U.K.	31	56	24N		3	27W	
Perth Amboy	164	40	31N		74	16W	
Peru	167	40	42N		86	0W	
Peru ■	186	8	0S		75	0W	
Perúgia	46	43	6N		12	24 E	
Pervouralsk	69	56	55N		60	0 E	
Pésaro	47	43	55N		12	53 E	
Pescara	47	42	28N		14	13 E	
Peshawar	89	34	2N		71	37 E	
Pesqueria →	176	25	54N		99	11W	
Petah Tiqwa	80	32	6N		34	53 E	
Petaling Jaya	96	3	4N		101	42 E	
Petaluma	172	38	13N		122	39W	
Petatlán	177	17	31N		101	16W	
Peterborough, Australia	118	32	58S		138	51 E	
Peterborough, Canada	151	44	20N		78	20W	
Peterborough, U.K.	25	52	35N		0	14W	
Peterhead	33	57	30N		1	49W	
Peterlee	29	54	45N		1	18W	
Petersburg, Alaska, U.S.A.	143	56	50N		133	0W	
Petersburg, Va., U.S.A.	164	37	17N		77	26W	
Petit Goâve	180	18	27N		72	51W	
Petitsikapau, L.	147	54	37N		66	25W	
Petlad	91	22	30N		72	45 E	
Petone	123	41	13S		174	53 E	
Petoskey	150	45	22N		84	57W	
Petrich	53	41	24N		23	13 E	
Petrolia	150	42	54N		82	9W	
Petrolina	189	9	24S		40	30W	
Petropavlovsk	71	54	53N		69	13 E	
Petropavlovsk-Kamchatskiy	73	53	3N		158	43 E	
Petrópolis	188	22	33S		43	9W	
Petrovaradin	52	45	16N		19	55 E	
Petrozavodsk	68	61	41N		34	20 E	
Pevek	73	69	41N		171	19 E	
Pforzheim	42	48	53N		8	43 E	
Phan Rang	95	11	34N		109	0 E	
Phangan, Ko	96	9	45N		100	0 E	
Phenix City	169	32	30N		85	0W	
Philadelphia	164	40	0N		75	10W	
Philippi	55	41	1N		24	16 E	
Philippines ■	112	12	0N		123	0 E	
Philippopolis = Plovdiv	53	42	8N		24	44 E	
Phitsanulok	94	16	50N		100	12 E	
Phnom Penh	95	11	33N		104	55 E	
Phoenix	160	33	30N		112	10W	
Phoenix Is.	123	3	30S		172	0W	
Phra Chedi Sam Ong	94	15	16N		98	23 E	
Phuket	96	7	52N		98	22 E	
Piacenza	46	45	2N		9	42 E	
Piauí □	188	7	0S		43	0W	
Picardie	38	50	0N		2	15 E	
Picardie, Plaine de	37	50	0N		2	0 E	
Picardy = Picardie	38	50	0N		2	15 E	
Picayune	169	30	31N		89	40W	
Pickering	29	54	15N		0	46W	
Picton, Australia	117	34	12S		150	34 E	
Picton, N.Z.	123	41	18S		174	3 E	
Pictou	149	45	41N		62	42W	
Pidurutalagala	90	7	10N		80	50 E	
Piedad, La	175	20	20N		102	1W	
Piedmont = Piemonte □	46	45	0N		7	30 E	
Piedmont Plat.	165	34	0N		81	30W	
Piedras Negras	174	28	42N		100	31W	
Piemonte □	46	45	0N		7	30 E	
Pierre	163	44	23N		100	20W	
Pietermaritzburg	137	29	35S		30	25 E	
Pietrosul	57	47	35N		24	43 E	
Pikeville	165	37	30N		82	30W	
Pilcomayo →	190	25	21S		57	42W	
Pilsen = Plzen	43	49	45N		13	22 E	
Pimenta Bueno	187	11	35S		61	10W	
Pinang □	96	5	20N		100	20 E	
Pinar del Río	178	22	26N		83	40W	
Pinaroo	119	35	17S		140	53 E	
Pinawa	153	50	9N		95	50W	
Pincher Creek	155	49	30N		113	57W	
Pinczów	58	50	30N		20	35 E	
Pindos Óros	54	40	0N		21	0 E	
Pindus Mts. = Pindos Óros	54	40	0N		21	0 E	
Pine Bluff	168	34	10N		92	0W	
Pine Pass	155	55	25N		122	42W	
Pineville	168	31	22N		92	30W	
Ping →	94	15	42N		100	9 E	
Pingdong	99	22	39N		120	30 E	
Pingliang	99	35	35N		106	31 E	
Pingxiang	99	22	6N		106	46 E	
Piniós →	54	37	48N		21	20 E	
Pinjarra	120	32	37S		115	52 E	
Piombino	46	42	54N		10	30 E	
Piotrków Trybunalski	58	51	23N		19	43 E	
Piqua	167	40	10N		84	10W	
Piracicaba	188	22	45S		47	40W	
Piræus = Piraiévs	55	37	57N		23	42 E	
Piraiévs	55	37	57N		23	42 E	
Pirapora	188	17	20S		44	56W	
Pirgos	54	37	40N		21	27 E	
Pirin Planina	53	41	40N		23	30 E	
Pirineos	51	42	40N		1	0 E	
Pisa	46	43	43N		10	23 E	
Pisagua	187	19	40S		70	15W	
Pisco	186	13	50S		76	12W	
Pistóia	46	43	57N		10	53 E	
Pitcairn I.	10	25	5S		130	5W	
Piteå	67	65	20N		21	25 E	
Piteşti	57	44	52N		24	54 E	
Pithiviers	39	48	10N		2	13 E	
Pitlochry	33	56	43N		3	43W	
Pitt I.	154	53	30N		129	50W	
Pittsburg, Kans., U.S.A.	166	37	21N		94	43W	
Pittsburg, Tex., U.S.A.	168	32	59N		94	59W	
Pittsburgh	164	40	25N		79	55W	
Pittsfield	164	42	28N		73	17W	
Pittsworth	116	27	41S		151	37 E	

Place	Page	Lat D	Lat M	N/S	Lon D	Lon M	E/W
Piura	186	5	15S		80	38W	
Placentia	149	47	20N		54	0W	
Placerville	172	38	47N		120	51W	
Placetas	178	22	15N		79	44W	
Plainfield	164	40	37N		74	28W	
Plainview	161	34	10N		101	40W	
Plaster Rock	148	46	53N		67	22W	
Plata, La	191	35	0S		57	55W	
Plata, Río de la	191	34	45S		57	30W	
Platte →	163	39	16N		94	50W	
Plattsburg	151	44	41N		73	30W	
Plauen	43	50	29N		12	9 E	
Pleasantville	164	39	25N		74	30W	
Plenty, Bay of	122	37	45S		177	0 E	
Plessisville	148	46	14N		71	47W	
Pleven	53	43	26N		24	37 E	
Płock	58	52	32N		19	40 E	
Ploiești	57	44	57N		26	5 E	
Plovdiv	53	42	8N		24	44 E	
Plymouth	27	50	23N		4	9W	
Plzen	43	49	45N		13	22 E	
Po →	47	44	57N		12	4 E	
Po Hai = Bo Hai	98	39	0N		120	0 E	
Pobeda	73	65	12N		146	12 E	
Pobedy Pik	71	40	45N		79	58 E	
Pocatello	163	42	50N		112	25W	
Pochutla	177	15	50N		96	31W	
Poços de Caldas	188	21	50S		46	33W	
Podgorica	52	42	30N		19	19 E	
Podkamennaya Tunguska →	74	61	50N		90	13 E	
Point Edward	150	43	0N		82	30W	
Pointe-à-Pitre	180	16	10N		61	30W	
Pointe Noire	134	4	48S		11	53 E	
Poissy	39	48	55N		2	0 E	
Poitiers	36	46	35N		0	20 E	
Poitou, Plaines et Seuil du ..	36	46	30N		0	1W	
Pokaran	91	27	0N		71	50 E	
Pokrovsk	68	51	28N		46	6 E	
Pola = Pula	52	44	54N		13	57 E	
Poland ■	58	52	0N		20	0 E	
Polden Hills	27	51	7N		2	50W	
Polesye	17	52	0N		28	10 E	
Polillo Is.	112	14	56N		122	0 E	
Políyiros	55	40	23N		23	25 E	
Pollachi	90	10	35N		77	0 E	
Polotsk	68	55	30N		28	50 E	
Poltava	68	49	35N		34	35 E	
Polynesia	123	10	0S		162	0W	
Pomona	173	34	2N		117	49W	
Pompano Beach	170	26	12N		80	6W	
Ponca City	168	36	40N		97	5W	
Ponce	180	18	1N		66	37W	
Pond Inlet	146	72	40N		77	0W	
Pondicherry	90	11	59N		79	50 E	
Ponnyadaung	93	22	0N		94	10 E	
Ponoka	155	52	42N		113	40W	
Pont-Audemer	39	49	21N		0	30 E	
Ponta Grossa	191	25	7S		50	10W	
Ponta Pora	188	22	20S		55	35W	
Pontchartrain, L.	169	30	12N		90	0W	
Pontefract	29	53	42N		1	19W	
Pontevedra	50	42	26N		8	40W	
Pontiac	167	42	40N		83	20W	
Pontianak	111	0	3S		109	15 E	
Pontine Is. = Ponziane, Isole	48	40	55N		13	0 E	
Pontoise	39	49	3N		2	5 E	
Pontypool	27	51	42N		3	1W	
Pontypridd	27	51	36N		3	21W	
Ponziane, Isole	48	40	55N		13	0 E	
Poochera	118	32	43S		134	51 E	
Poole	24	50	42N		1	58W	
Pooley I.	154	52	45N		128	15W	
Poona = Pune	91	18	29N		73	57 E	
Poopó, Lago de	187	18	30S		67	35W	
Popayán	184	2	27N		76	36W	
Poplar Bluff	169	36	45N		90	22W	
Popocatépetl, Volcán	177	19	2N		98	38W	
Porcher I.	154	53	50N		130	30W	
Porcupine →	142	66	35N		145	15W	
Pori	67	61	29N		21	48 E	
Porkkala	67	59	59N		24	26 E	
Port Adelaide	119	34	46S		138	30 E	
Port Alberni	154	49	40N		124	50W	
Port Albert	115	38	42S		146	42 E	
Port Alfred	148	48	18N		70	53W	
Port Angeles	171	48	7N		123	30W	
Port Antonio	180	18	10N		76	30W	
Port Arthur	168	30	0N		94	0W	
Port-au-Prince	180	18	40N		72	20W	
Port Augusta	118	32	30S		137	50 E	
Port Blair	94	11	40N		92	30 E	
Port-Cartier	148	50	2N		66	50W	
Port Chalmers	123	45	49S		170	30 E	
Port Colborne	151	42	50N		79	10W	
Port Coquitlam	154	49	15N		122	45W	
Port Darwin	192	51	50S		59	0W	
Port-de-Paix	180	19	50N		72	50W	
Port Elgin	150	44	25N		81	25W	
Port Elizabeth	136	33	58S		25	40 E	
Port Erin	28	54	5N		4	45W	
Port Etienne = Nouâdhibou .	126	20	54N		17	0W	
Port Fairy	119	38	22S		142	12 E	
Port Glasgow	30	55	57N		4	40W	
Port Harcourt	131	4	40N		7	10 E	
Port Harrison = Inoucdjouac	146	58	25N		78	15W	
Port Hawkesbury	149	45	36N		61	22W	
Port Hope	151	43	56N		78	20W	
Port Huron	167	43	0N		82	28W	
Port Kembla	117	34	52S		150	49 E	
Port Laoise	35	53	2N		7	20W	
Port Lavaca	158	28	38N		96	38W	
Port Lincoln	119	34	42S		135	52 E	
Port Lyautey = Kenitra	126	34	15N		6	40W	
Port Macquarie	116	31	25S		152	25 E	
Port Morant	180	17	54N		76	19W	
Port Moresby	115	9	24S		147	8 E	
Port Nelson	143	57	3N		92	36W	
Port Nolloth	136	29	17S		16	52 E	
Port Nouveau-Québec	146	58	30N		65	59W	
Port of Spain	180	10	40N		61	31W	
Port Phillip B.	117	38	10S		144	50 E	
Port Pirie	118	33	10S		138	1 E	
Port Said = Bûr Sa'îd	128	31	16N		32	18 E	
Port Simpson	154	54	30N		130	20W	
Port Stanley	150	42	40N		81	10W	
Port Sudan = Bûr Sûdân	129	19	32N		37	9 E	
Port Talbot	27	51	35N		3	48W	
Port Townsend	171	48	7N		122	50W	
Portadown	34	54	27N		6	26W	
Portage La Prairie	153	49	58N		98	18W	
Portarlington	35	53	10N		7	10W	
Porte, La	167	41	36N		86	43W	
Porterville	173	36	5N		119	0W	
Porthcawl	27	51	28N		3	42W	
Porthmadog	26	52	55N		4	13W	
Portile de Fier	56	44	42N		22	30 E	
Portland, Australia	119	38	20S		141	35 E	
Portland, Maine, U.S.A.	148	43	40N		70	15W	
Portland, Oreg., U.S.A.	171	45	35N		122	40W	
Portland, Bill of	24	50	31N		2	27W	
Portland Prom.	146	58	40N		78	33W	
Porto	50	41	8N		8	40W	
Pôrto Alegre	191	30	5S		51	10W	
Porto Empédocle	48	37	18N		13	30 E	
Porto Mendes	191	24	30S		54	15W	
Porto Novo	131	6	23N		2	42 E	
Pôrto Seguro	189	16	26S		39	5W	
Pôrto Velho	187	8	46S		63	54W	
Portoferráio	46	42	50N		10	20 E	
Portoscuso	48	39	12N		8	22 E	
Portovíejo	184	1	7S		80	28W	
Portpatrick	30	54	50N		5	7W	
Portree	32	57	25N		6	11W	
Portrush	34	55	13N		6	40W	
Portsmouth, Domin.	180	15	34N		61	27W	
Portsmouth, U.K.	25	50	48N		1	6W	
Portsmouth, N.H., U.S.A.	164	43	5N		70	45W	
Portsmouth, Ohio, U.S.A.	167	38	45N		83	0W	
Portsmouth, Va., U.S.A.	165	36	50N		76	20W	
Porttipahta	67	68	5N		26	40 E	
Portugal ■	50	40	0N		7	0W	
Portuguese-Guinea = Guinea-Bissau ■	130	12	0N		15	0W	

Name	Page	Lat	Long
Portuguese Timor ■ = Timor	113	9 0S	125 0 E
Portumna	35	53 5N	8 12W
Porvenir	192	53 10S	70 16W
Posadas	191	27 30S	55 50W
Poshan = Boshan	98	36 28N	117 49 E
Poste-de-la-Baleine	140	55 17N	77 45W
Potchefstroom	137	26 41S	27 7 E
Potenza	49	40 40N	15 50 E
Potomac →	165	38 0N	76 23W
Potosí	187	19 38S	65 50W
Potsdam, Germany	43	52 23N	13 4 E
Potsdam, U.S.A.	151	44 40N	74 59W
Pottsville	164	40 39N	76 12W
Pouce Coupé	155	55 40N	120 10W
Poughkeepsie	164	41 40N	73 57W
Poulaphouca Res.	35	53 8N	6 30W
Póvoa de Varzim	50	41 25N	8 46W
Powell, L.	163	37 25N	110 45W
Powell River	154	49 50N	124 35W
Powys □	26	52 20N	3 20W
Poyang Hu	99	29 10N	116 10 E
Poyarkovo	75	49 36N	128 41 E
Poznań	58	52 25N	16 55 E
Prachuap Khiri Khan	94	11 49N	99 48 E
Prague = Praha	58	50 5N	14 22 E
Praha	58	50 5N	14 22 E
Prainha, Amazonas, Brazil	187	7 10S	60 30W
Prainha, Pará, Brazil	185	1 45S	53 30W
Prairie du Chien	166	43 1N	91 9W
Prato	46	43 53N	11 5 E
Pratt	161	37 40N	98 45W
Prepansko Jezero	52	40 55N	21 0 E
Preparis North Channel	94	15 12N	93 40 E
Preparis South Channel	94	14 36N	93 40 E
Prescott	160	34 35N	112 30W
Preservation Inlet	123	46 8S	166 35 E
Presidencia Roque Saenz Peña	190	26 45S	60 30W
Presidente Prudente	188	22 5S	51 25W
Presidio	161	29 30N	104 20W
Prespa, L. = Prepansko Jezero	52	40 55N	21 0 E
Presque Isle	148	46 40N	68 0W
Preston, Borders, U.K.	28	55 48N	2 18W
Preston, Lancs., U.K.	21	53 46N	2 42W
Prestonpans	31	55 58N	3 0W
Prestwick	31	55 30N	4 38W
Pretoria	137	25 44S	28 12 E
Préveza	55	38 57N	20 47 E
Prichard	169	30 47N	88 5W
Prilep	52	41 21N	21 37 E
Prince Albert	152	53 15N	105 50W
Prince Albert Pen.	145	72 30N	116 0W
Prince Albert Sd.	145	70 25N	115 0W
Prince Charles I.	146	67 47N	76 12W
Prince Edward I. □	148	46 20N	63 20W
Prince George	154	53 55N	122 50W
Prince of Wales I., Canada	145	73 0N	99 0W
Prince of Wales I., U.S.A.	143	55 30N	133 0W
Prince Patrick I.	12	77 0N	120 0W
Prince Rupert	154	54 20N	130 20W
Princess Royal I.	154	53 0N	128 40W
Princeton	155	49 27N	120 30W
Principe, I. de	131	1 37N	7 27 E
Principe da Beira	187	12 20S	64 30W
Pripet = Pripyat →	68	51 20N	30 9 E
Pripet Marshes = Polesye	17	52 0N	28 10 E
Pripyat →	68	51 20N	30 9 E
Pripyat Marshes = Polesye	17	52 0N	28 10 E
Priština	52	42 40N	21 13 E
Privolzhskaya Vozvyshennost	17	51 0N	46 0 E
Prizren	52	42 13N	20 45 E
Proddatur	90	14 45N	78 30 E
Progreso	177	21 17N	89 40W
Prokopyevsk	71	54 0N	86 45 E
Proserpine	121	20 21S	148 36 E
Provence	37	43 40N	5 46 E
Providence	164	41 50N	71 28W
Provo	163	40 16N	111 37W
Prudhoe Bay	142	70 20N	148 20W
Pruszków	58	52 9N	20 49 E
Prut →	57	46 3N	28 10 E
Przemyśl	58	49 50N	22 45 E
Przeworsk	58	50 6N	22 32 E
Pskov	68	57 50N	28 25 E
Pucallpa	186	8 25S	74 30W
Puebla	177	19 3N	98 12W
Puebla □	177	18 50N	98 0W
Pueblo	163	38 20N	104 40W
Puelches	190	38 5S	65 51W
Puente Alto	190	33 32S	70 35W
Puerto Armuelles	179	8 20N	82 51W
Puerto Ayacucho	184	5 40N	67 35W
Puerto Barrios	177	15 40N	88 32W
Puerto Cabello	184	10 28N	68 1W
Puerto Cabezas	179	14 0N	83 30W
Puerto Castilla	179	16 0N	86 0W
Puerto Cortes, Costa Rica	179	8 55N	84 0W
Puerto Cortés, Honduras	177	15 51N	88 0W
Puerto Heath	187	12 34S	68 39W
Puerto La Cruz	185	10 13N	64 38W
Puerto Libertad	174	29 55N	112 41W
Puerto Lobos	192	42 0S	65 3W
Puerto Maldonado	187	12 30S	69 10W
Puerto Montt	190	41 28S	73 0W
Puerto Padre	178	21 13N	76 35W
Puerto Pinasco	191	22 36S	57 50W
Puerto Plata	180	19 48N	70 45W
Puerto Quepos	179	9 29N	84 6W
Puerto Rico ■	180	18 15N	66 45W
Puerto Vallarta	175	20 37N	105 15W
Puertollano	50	38 43N	4 7W
Puget Sd.	171	47 15N	122 30W
Púglia □	49	41 0N	16 30 E
Pula	52	44 54N	13 57 E
Pulaski, Tenn., U.S.A.	169	35 10N	87 0W
Pulaski, Va., U.S.A.	165	37 4N	80 49W
Pulicat, L.	90	13 40N	80 15 E
Pullman	171	46 49N	117 10W
Punakha	92	27 42N	89 52 E
Punata	187	17 32S	65 50W
Pune	91	18 29N	73 57 E
Punjab □, India	89	31 0N	76 0 E
Punjab □, Pakistan	89	30 0N	72 0 E
Puno	187	15 55S	70 3W
Punta Alta	190	38 53S	62 4W
Punta Arenas	192	53 10S	71 0W
Punta Gorda	177	16 10N	88 45W
Puntabie	118	32 12S	134 13 E
Puntarenas	179	10 0N	84 50W
Punto Fijo	184	11 50N	70 13W
Puquio	186	14 45S	74 10W
Pur →	69	67 31N	77 55 E
Purbeck, Isle of	24	50 40N	2 5W
Purmerend	40	52 30N	4 58 E
Purnia	92	25 45N	87 31 E
Pursat	95	12 34N	103 50 E
Purus →	185	3 42S	61 28W
Pusan	98	35 5N	129 0 E
Putao	93	27 28N	97 30 E
Putorana, Gory	72	69 0N	95 0 E
Putumayo →	184	3 7S	67 58W
Puy, Le	37	45 2N	3 53 E
Puy-de-Dôme	37	45 46N	2 57 E
Puyallup	171	47 10N	122 22W
Pwllheli	26	52 54N	4 26W
Pyasina →	72	73 30N	87 0 E
Pyatigorsk	70	44 2N	43 6 E
Pyinmana	93	19 45N	96 12 E
Pyôngyang	98	39 0N	125 30 E
Pyramid L.	172	40 0N	119 30W
Pyrénées	124	42 45N	0 18 E

Q

Name	Page	Lat	Long
Qā'emshahr	86	36 30N	52 55 E
Qahremānshahr = Bākhtarān	84	34 23N	47 0 E
Qaidam Pendi	100	37 0N	95 0 E
Qal'at al Akhḍar	82	28 0N	37 10 E
Qamar, Ghubbat al	83	16 20N	52 30 E
Qamdo	101	31 15N	97 6 E

Qandahār	87	31 32N	65	30 E
Qasr-e Qand	85	26 15N	60	45 E
Qatar ■	85	25 30N	51	15 E
Qāyen	86	33 40N	59	10 E
Qazvin	81	36 15N	50	0 E
Qena	128	26 10N	32	43 E
Qeshm	85	26 55N	56	10 E
Qilian Shan	100	38 30N	96	0 E
Qingdao	98	36 5N	120	20 E
Qinghai □	101	36 0N	98	0 E
Qinghai Hu	100	36 40N	100	10 E
Qinhuangdao	98	39 56N	119	30 E
Qiqihar	98	47 26N	124	0 E
Qom	86	34 40N	51	0 E
Qomsheh	85	32 0N	51	55 E
Qondūz □	87	36 50N	68	50 E
Qu Xian	99	30 48N	106	58 E
Quang Ngai	95	15 13N	108	58 E
Quantock Hills	27	51 8N	3	10W
Quanzhou	99	24 55N	118	34 E
Quatsino	154	50 30N	127	40W
Queanbeyan	117	35 17S	149	14 E
Québec	148	46 52N	71	13W
Québec □	140	50 0N	70	0W
Queen Alexandra Ra.	15	85 0S	170	0 E
Queen Charlotte	154	53 15N	132	2W
Queen Charlotte Is.	154	53 20N	132	10W
Queen Charlotte Str.	154	51 0N	128	0W
Queen Elizabeth Is.	138	76 0N	95	0W
Queen Mary Land	15	70 0S	95	0 E
Queen Maud G.	145	68 15N	102	30W
Queen Maud Mts.	15	86 0S	160	0W
Queenscliff	117	38 16S	144	39 E
Queensland □	115	22 0S	142	0 E
Queenstown, Australia	119	42 4S	145	35 E
Queenstown, N.Z.	123	45 1S	168	40 E
Quelimane	137	17 53S	36	58 E
Quelpart = Cheju Do	99	33 29N	126	34 E
Querétaro	177	20 36N	100	23W
Querétaro □	177	21 0N	99	55W
Quesnel	154	53 0N	122	30W
Quetta	88	30 15N	66	55 E
Quezaltenango	177	14 50N	91	30W
Quezon City	112	14 38N	121	0 E
Qui Nhon	95	13 40N	109	13 E
Quibdo	184	5 42N	76	40W
Quillabamba	186	12 50S	72	50W
Quilon	90	8 50N	76	38 E
Quilpie	116	26 35S	144	11 E
Quimper	36	48 0N	4	9W
Quincy, Calif., U.S.A.	172	39 56N	121	0W
Quincy, Fla., U.S.A.	170	30 34N	84	34W
Quincy, Ill., U.S.A.	166	39 55N	91	20W
Quincy, Mass., U.S.A.	164	42 14N	71	0W
Quintana Roo □	177	19 40N	88	30W
Quirindi	116	31 28S	150	40 E
Quitman	170	30 49N	83	35W
Quito	184	0 15S	78	35W
Quixadá	189	4 55S	39	0W
Quorn	118	32 25S	138	0 E
Quseir	128	26 7N	34	16 E

R

Raahe	67	64 40N	24	28 E
Raasay	32	57 25N	6	4W
Rabat	126	34 2N	6	48W
Rabaul	115	4 24S	152	18 E
Rābigh	82	22 50N	39	5 E
Race, C.	149	46 40N	53	5W
Rach Gia	95	10 5N	105	5 E
Racibórz	58	50 7N	18	18 E
Racine	167	42 41N	87	51W
Radium Hot Springs	155	50 35N	116	2W
Radnor Forest	26	52 17N	3	10W
Radom	58	51 23N	21	12 E
Radomir	53	42 37N	23	4 E
Radstock	27	51 17N	2	25W
Radville	152	49 30N	104	15W

Rae	145	62 50N	116	3W
Rae Bareli	92	26 18N	81	20 E
Raetihi	122	39 25S	175	17 E
Rafaela	190	31 10S	61	30W
Rafḥā	82	29 35N	43	35 E
Rafsanjān	85	30 30N	56	5 E
Ragama	90	7 0N	79	50 E
Raglan	122	37 55S	174	55 E
Ragusa	49	36 56N	14	42 E
Rahaeng = Tak	94	16 52N	99	8 E
Raichur	91	16 10N	77	20 E
Rainier, Mt.	171	46 50N	121	50W
Rainy L.	153	48 42N	93	10W
Rainy River	153	48 43N	94	29W
Raipur	92	21 17N	81	45 E
Rajahmundry	92	17 1N	81	48 E
Rajapalaiyam	90	9 25N	77	35 E
Rajasthan □	91	26 45N	73	30 E
Rajasthan Canal	89	28 0N	72	0 E
Rajkot	91	22 15N	70	56 E
Rajshahi □	92	25 0N	89	0 E
Raleigh	165	35 47N	78	39W
Raleigh B.	165	34 50N	76	15W
Rambouillet	39	48 40N	1	48 E
Rampur	89	28 50N	79	5 E
Ramsey	28	54 20N	4	21W
Rancagua	190	34 10S	70	50W
Ranchi	92	23 19N	85	27 E
Rangiora	123	43 19S	172	36 E
Rangoon	93	16 45N	96	20 E
Rangpur	92	25 42N	89	22 E
Raniwara	91	24 50N	72	10 E
Rankin Inlet	145	62 30N	93	0W
Rankins Springs	117	33 49S	146	14 E
Rannoch, L.	33	56 41N	4	20W
Rannoch Moor	30	56 38N	4	48W
Rapid City	163	44 0N	103	0W
Ras Dashen	132	13 8N	38	26 E
Rasa, Punta	192	40 50S	62	15W
Rasht	81	37 20N	49	40 E
Rat Is.	142	51 50N	178	15 E
Ratangarh	89	28 5N	74	35 E
Rath Luirc	35	52 21N	8	40W
Rathlin I.	34	55 18N	6	14W
Ratibor = Racibórz	58	50 7N	18	18 E
Ratlam	91	23 20N	75	0 E
Ratnagiri	91	16 57N	73	18 E
Rattray Hd.	33	57 38N	1	50W
Raub	96	3 47N	101	52 E
Raukumara Ra.	122	38 5S	177	55 E
Ravenna	47	44 28N	12	15 E
Ravenshoe	121	17 37S	145	29 E
Ravensthorpe	120	33 35S	120	2 E
Rawalpindi	89	33 38N	73	8 E
Rawlins	163	41 50N	107	20W
Ray, C.	149	47 33N	59	15W
Raymond	155	49 30N	112	35W
Razgrad	53	43 33N	26	34 E
Ré, Île de	36	46 12N	1	30W
Reading, U.K.	25	51 27N	0	57W
Reading, U.S.A.	164	40 20N	75	53W
Reay Forest	32	58 20N	4	55W
Rebun-Tō	103	45 23N	141	2 E
Recife	189	8 0S	35	0W
Reconquista	190	29 10S	59	45W
Recreo	190	29 25S	65	10W
Red →►	168	31 0N	91	40W
Red Bluff	172	40 11N	122	11W
Red Cliffs	119	34 19S	142	11 E
Red Deer	155	52 20N	113	50W
Red Lake	153	51 3N	93	49W
Red Oak	166	41 0N	95	10W
Red Sea	128	25 0N	36	0 E
Red Tower Pass = Turnu				
Rosu Pasul	57	45 33N	24	17 E
Red Wing	166	44 32N	92	35W
Redcar	29	54 37N	1	4W
Redcliff	152	50 10N	110	50W
Redcliffe	116	27 12S	153	0 E
Redding	172	40 30N	122	25W
Redditch	24	52 18N	1	57W
Redlands	173	34 0N	117	11W

Redruth 27 50 14N 5 14W
Redwater 155 53 55N 113 6W
Redwood City 172 37 30N 122 15W
Ree, L. 34 53 35N 8 0W
Reedley 173 36 36N 119 27W
Regensburg 43 49 1N 12 7 E
Réggio di Calábria 49 38 7N 15 38 E
Réggio nell' Emilia 46 44 42N 10 38 E
Regina 152 50 27N 104 35W
Rehovot 80 31 54N 34 48 E
Reichenbach 43 50 36N 12 19 E
Reidsville 165 36 21N 79 40W
Reims 39 49 15N 4 0 E
Reina Adelaida, Arch. 192 52 20S 74 0W
Reindeer L. 143 57 15N 102 15W
Reliance 145 63 0N 109 20W
Remanso 189 9 41S 42 4W
Remarkable, Mt. 118 32 48S 138 10 E
Remscheid 42 51 11N 7 12 E
Rendsburg 42 54 18N 9 41 E
Renfrew, Canada 151 45 30N 76 40W
Renfrew, U.K. 31 55 52N 4 24W
Renkum 41 51 58N 5 43 E
Renmark 119 34 11S 140 43 E
Rennes 36 48 7N 1 41W
Reno 172 39 30N 119 50W
Republic 150 46 25N 87 59W
Republican → 163 39 3N 96 48W
Repulse Bay 146 66 30N 86 30W
Requena 186 5 5S 73 52W
Resht = Rasht 81 37 20N 49 40 E
Resistencia 190 27 30S 59 0W
Resolution I., Canada 146 61 30N 65 0W
Resolution I., N.Z. 123 45 40S 166 40 E
Retalhuleu 177 14 33N 91 46W
Réthímnon 55 35 18N 24 30 E
Réunion 9 22 0S 56 0 E
Reval = Tallinn 68 59 22N 24 48 E
Revelstoke 155 51 0N 118 10W
Revilla Gigedo, Is. 139 18 40N 112 0W
Rewa 92 24 33N 81 25 E
Rewari 89 28 15N 76 40 E
Rexburg 163 43 55N 111 50W
Rey Malabo 131 3 45N 8 50 E
Reykjavík 64 64 10N 21 57 E
Reynosa 176 26 5N 98 18W
Rhayader 26 52 19N 3 30W
Rhein → 42 51 52N 6 20 E
Rheinland-Pfalz □ 42 50 0N 7 0 E
Rhin = Rhein → 42 51 52N 6 20 E
Rhine = Rhein → 42 51 52N 6 20 E
Rhineland-Palatinate = Rheinland-Pfalz □ 42 50 0N 7 0 E
Rhinelander 150 45 38N 89 29W
Rhode Island □ 164 41 38N 71 37W
Rhodes = Ródhos 55 36 15N 28 10 E
Rhodesia = Zimbabwe ■ 137 20 0S 30 0 E
Rhodope Mts. = Rhodopi Planina 53 41 40N 24 20 E
Rhodopi Planina 53 41 40N 24 20 E
Rhön 42 50 24N 9 58 E
Rhondda 27 51 39N 3 30W
Rhône → 37 43 28N 4 42 E
Rhum 32 57 0N 6 20W
Rhyl 26 53 19N 3 29W
Rhymney 27 51 45N 3 17W
Riachão 188 7 20S 46 37W
Riau, Kepulauan 111 0 30N 104 20 E
Ribatejo □ 50 39 15N 8 30W
Ribble → 28 54 13N 2 20W
Ribeirão Prêto 188 21 10S 47 50W
Riberalta 187 11 0S 66 0W
Riccarton 123 43 32S 172 37 E
Richland 171 46 15N 119 15W
Richmond, Australia 116 20 43S 143 8 E
Richmond, N.Z. 123 41 20S 173 12 E
Richmond, N. Yorks., U.K. 28 54 24N 1 43W
Richmond, Surrey, U.K. 25 51 28N 0 18W
Richmond, Calif., U.S.A. 172 37 58N 122 21W
Richmond, Ind., U.S.A. 167 39 50N 84 50W
Richmond, Ky., U.S.A. 165 37 40N 84 20W
Richmond, Va., U.S.A. 165 37 33N 77 27W
Richwood 165 38 17N 80 32W
Ridgeway 164 42 56S 147 16 E
Riga 68 56 53N 24 8 E
Rīgestān □ 87 30 15N 65 0 E
Rigolet 147 54 10N 58 23W
Rijeka 52 45 20N 14 21 E
Rijssen 41 52 19N 6 30 E
Rijswijk 40 52 4N 4 22 E
Rímini 47 44 3N 12 33 E
Rîmnicu Vîlcea 57 45 9N 24 21 E
Rimouski 148 48 27N 68 30W
Rinía 55 37 23N 25 13 E
Rio Branco 187 9 58S 67 49W
Rio Claro 180 10 20N 61 25W
Río Cuarto 190 33 10S 64 25W
Rio de Janeiro 188 23 0S 43 12W
Rio de Janeiro □ 188 22 50S 43 0W
Río Gallegos 192 51 35S 69 15W
Rio Grande 191 32 0S 52 20W
Rio Grande → 161 25 57N 97 9W
Rio Grande do Norte □ 189 5 40S 36 0W
Rio Grande do Sul □ 191 30 0S 53 0W
Río Mulatos 187 19 40S 66 50W
Rio Negro 191 26 0S 50 0W
Rio Verde 188 17 50S 51 0W
Ríobamba 184 1 50S 78 45W
Ríohacha 184 11 33N 72 55W
Rioja, La 190 29 20S 67 0W
Rioja, La □ 50 42 20N 2 20W
Ríosucio 184 7 27N 77 7W
Ripon 28 54 8N 1 31W
Rishiri-Tō 103 45 11N 141 15 E
Ritchies Archipelago 94 12 5N 94 0 E
Rivas 179 11 30N 85 50W
Riverhead 164 40 53N 72 40W
Riverside 173 34 0N 117 22W
Riverton 153 51 1N 97 0W
Riviera di Levante 46 44 23N 9 15 E
Riviera di Ponente 46 43 50N 7 58 E
Rivière-du-Loup 148 47 50N 69 30W
Riyadh = Ar Riyāḑ 83 24 41N 46 42 E
Roanne 37 46 3N 4 4 E
Roanoke, Ala., U.S.A. 169 33 9N 85 23W
Roanoke, Va., U.S.A. 165 37 19N 79 55W
Roanoke → 165 35 56N 76 43W
Roanoke Rapids 165 36 28N 77 42W
Robinvale 119 34 40S 142 45 E
Roblin 152 51 14N 101 21W
Roboré 187 18 10S 59 45W
Robson, Mt. 155 53 10N 119 10W
Roca, C. da 50 38 40N 9 31W
Rocha 191 34 30S 54 25W
Rochdale 28 53 36N 2 10W
Roche-sur-Yon, La 36 46 40N 1 25W
Rochefort 36 45 56N 0 57W
Rochelle, La 36 46 10N 1 9W
Rochester, Minn., U.S.A. 166 44 1N 92 28W
Rochester, N.H., U.S.A. 164 43 19N 70 57W
Rochester, N.Y., U.S.A. 164 43 10N 77 40W
Rock Hill 165 34 55N 81 2W
Rock Island 166 41 30N 90 35W
Rock Sprs. 163 41 40N 109 10W
Rockall 16 57 37N 13 42W
Rockford 166 42 20N 89 0W
Rockglen 152 49 11N 105 57W
Rockhampton 119 23 22S 150 32 E
Rockingham 120 32 15S 115 38 E
Rockland 148 44 6N 69 6W
Rocky Mount 165 35 55N 77 48W
Rocky Mountain House 155 52 22N 114 55W
Rocky Mts. 138 55 0N 121 0W
Ródhos 55 36 15N 28 10 E
Roebourne 114 20 44S 117 9 E
Roermond 41 51 12N 6 0 E
Roes Welcome Sd. 146 65 0N 87 0W
Rogaland fylke □ 60 59 12N 6 20 E
Rogers 168 36 20N 94 5W
Rohri 88 27 45N 68 51 E
Rohtak 89 28 55N 76 43 E
Rojo, C. 177 21 33N 97 20W
Rolla 166 37 56N 91 42W
Roma, Australia 116 26 32S 148 49 E

Place	Page	Lat.	Long.
Roma, Italy	**46**	41 54N	12 30 E
Romaine →	**141**	50 18N	63 47W
Roman	**57**	46 57N	26 55 E
Romana, La	**180**	18 27N	68 57W
Romania ■	**57**	46 0N	25 0 E
Romans	**37**	45 3N	5 3 E
Romanzof, C.	**142**	62 0N	165 50W
Rome = Roma	**46**	41 54N	12 30 E
Rome, Ga., U.S.A.	**169**	34 20N	85 0W
Rome, N.Y., U.S.A.	**164**	43 14N	75 29W
Romilly	**39**	48 31N	3 44 E
Romney Marsh	**25**	51 0N	1 0 E
Rona	**32**	57 33N	6 0W
Rondônia □	**187**	11 0S	63 0W
Rong, Koh	**95**	10 45N	103 15 E
Ronge, L. la	**152**	55 6N	105 17W
Roosendaal	**40**	51 32N	4 29 E
Roraima □	**185**	2 0N	61 30W
Roraima, Mt.	**185**	5 10N	60 40W
Rosario, Argentina	**190**	33 0S	60 40W
Rosário, Brazil	**188**	3 0S	44 15W
Rosario, Mexico	**175**	22 58N	105 53W
Rosario, Paraguay	**191**	24 30S	57 35W
Rosário do Sul	**191**	30 15S	54 55W
Roscommon	**34**	53 38N	8 11W
Roscommon □	**34**	53 40N	8 15W
Roscrea	**35**	52 58N	7 50W
Roseau	**180**	15 20N	61 24W
Roseburg	**171**	43 10N	123 20W
Rosenberg	**168**	29 30N	95 48W
Rosendaël	**38**	51 3N	2 24 E
Rosetown	**152**	51 35N	107 59W
Roseville	**172**	38 46N	121 17W
Rosewood	**116**	27 38S	152 36 E
Roskilde	**61**	55 38N	12 3 E
Ross on Wye	**24**	51 55N	2 34W
Ross Sea	**15**	74 0S	178 0 E
Rossan Pt.	**34**	54 42N	8 47W
Rossland	**155**	49 6N	117 50W
Rosslare	**35**	52 17N	6 23W
Røssvatnet	**65**	65 45N	14 5 E
Rosthern	**152**	52 40N	106 20W
Rostock	**43**	54 4N	12 9 E
Rostov	**68**	47 15N	39 45 E
Roswell	**161**	33 26N	104 32W
Rosyth	**31**	56 2N	3 26W
Rother →	**25**	50 59N	0 40 E
Rotherham	**29**	53 26N	1 21W
Rothesay	**30**	55 50N	5 3W
Roto	**117**	33 0S	145 30 E
Rotorua	**122**	38 9S	176 16 E
Rotorua, L.	**122**	38 5S	176 18 E
Rotterdam	**40**	51 55N	4 30 E
Rotuma	**122**	12 25S	177 5 E
Roubaix	**37**	50 40N	3 10 E
Rouen	**38**	49 27N	1 4 E
Round Mt.	**116**	30 26S	152 16 E
Roussillon	**37**	42 30N	2 35 E
Rouyn	**151**	48 20N	79 0W
Rovaniemi	**67**	66 29N	25 41 E
Rovno	**68**	50 40N	26 10 E
Ruahine Ra.	**122**	39 55S	176 2 E
Ruapehu	**122**	39 17S	175 35 E
Rub' al Khali	**83**	18 0N	48 0 E
Rubh a' Mhail	**30**	55 55N	6 10W
Rubio	**184**	7 43N	72 22W
Rubtsovsk	**71**	51 30N	81 10 E
Rudnyy	**71**	52 57N	63 7 E
Rudolf, Ostrov	**69**	81 45N	58 30 E
Rufiji →	**135**	7 50S	39 15 E
Rufino	**190**	34 20S	62 50W
Rugby	**25**	52 23N	1 16W
Rügen	**43**	54 22N	13 25 E
Ruhr →	**42**	51 25N	6 44 E
Rukwa L.	**135**	8 0S	32 20 E
Rumania = Romania ■	**57**	46 0N	25 0 E
Rumford	**148**	44 30N	70 30W
Rumoi	**103**	43 56N	141 39W
Runcorn	**28**	53 20N	2 44W
Rupat	**111**	1 45N	101 40 E
Rupert →	**140**	51 29N	78 45W
Rupert House = Fort Rupert	**140**	51 30N	78 40W
Ruschuk = Ruse	**53**	43 48N	25 59 E
Ruse	**53**	43 48N	25 59 E
Russell	**152**	50 50N	101 20W
Russellville, Ala., U.S.A.	**169**	34 30N	87 44W
Russellville, Ark., U.S.A.	**168**	35 15N	93 8W
Russia ■	**78**	60 0N	100 0 E
Ruston	**168**	32 30N	92 58W
Rutherglen	**31**	55 50N	4 11W
Rutland I.	**94**	11 25N	92 40 E
Ruwenzori	**132**	0 30N	29 55 E
Rwanda ■	**135**	2 0S	30 0 E
Ryan, L.	**30**	55 0N	5 2W
Ryazan	**68**	54 40N	39 40 E
Rybache	**71**	46 40N	81 20 E
Rybinsk	**68**	58 5N	38 50 E
Ryde	**25**	50 44N	1 9W
Rye	**25**	50 57N	0 46 E
Rylstone	**117**	32 46S	149 58 E
Ryōhaku-Sanchi	**106**	36 9N	136 49 E
Ryūgasaki	**107**	35 54N	140 11 E
Rzeszów	**58**	50 5N	21 58 E

S

Place	Page	Lat.	Long.
Sa Dec	**95**	10 20N	105 46 E
Saar →	**42**	49 41N	6 32 E
Saarbrücken	**42**	49 15N	6 58 E
Saaremaa	**68**	58 30N	22 30 E
Saarland □	**42**	49 15N	7 0 E
Sabadell	**51**	41 28N	2 7 E
Sabae	**106**	35 57N	136 11 E
Sabah □	**112**	6 0N	117 0 E
Sábana de la Mar	**180**	19 7N	69 24W
Sabhah	**127**	27 9N	14 29 E
Sabi →	**137**	18 50S	31 40 E
Sabinas	**174**	27 51N	101 7W
Sabinas Hidalgo, R. →	**176**	26 50N	99 35W
Sabine →	**158**	30 0N	93 35W
Sable, C., Canada	**148**	43 29N	65 38W
Sable, C., U.S.A.	**159**	25 13N	81 0W
Sable I.	**149**	44 0N	60 0W
Sabrina Coast	**15**	68 0S	120 0 E
Sabzevār	**86**	36 15N	57 40 E
Saco	**148**	43 30N	70 27W
Sacramento	**172**	38 33N	121 30 E
Sacramento →	**172**	38 3N	121 56W
Sacramento Mts.	**161**	32 30N	105 30W
Sado, Shima	**103**	38 15N	138 30 E
Safed Koh	**87**	34 0N	70 0 E
Saffron Walden	**25**	52 2N	0 15 E
Safi	**126**	32 18N	9 20W
Saga	**108**	33 15N	130 16 E
Sagami-Nada	**107**	34 58N	139 30 E
Sagami-Wan	**107**	35 15N	139 25 E
Sagamihara	**107**	35 33N	139 25 E
Sagar	**91**	14 14N	75 6 E
Sagara	**107**	34 41N	138 12 E
Saginaw	**167**	43 26N	83 55W
Saginaw B.	**167**	43 50N	83 40W
Saglouc	**146**	62 14N	75 38W
Sagres	**50**	37 0N	8 58W
Sagua la Grande	**178**	22 50N	80 10W
Saguenay →	**148**	48 22N	71 0W
Sahara	**126**	23 0N	5 0 E
Saharanpur	**89**	29 58N	77 33 E
Saharien, Atlas	**127**	33 30N	1 0 E
Sahiwal	**89**	30 45N	73 8 E
Sahuaripa	**174**	29 3N	109 14W
Saigō	**109**	36 12N	133 20 E
Saigon = Thanh Pho Ho Chi Minh	**95**	10 58N	106 40 E
Saijō, Ehime, Japan	**109**	33 55N	133 11 E
Saijō, Hiroshima, Japan	**109**	34 25N	132 45 E
Saikhoa Ghat	**93**	27 50N	95 40 E
Saiki	**108**	32 58N	131 51 E
Saimaa	**67**	61 15N	28 15 E
Şa'in Dezh	**81**	36 40N	46 25 E
St. Abb's Head	**31**	55 55N	2 10W
St. Albans, U.K.	**25**	51 44N	0 19W

St. Albans, U.S.A. 151 44 49N 73 7W
St. Alban's Head 24 50 34N 2 3W
St. Albert 155 53 37N 113 32W
St. Andrews 31 56 20N 2 48W
St. Arnaud .... 119 36 40S 143 16 E
St. Asaph 26 53 15N 3 27W
St-Augustin-Saguenay 141 51 13N 58 38W
St. Augustine 170 29 52N 81 20W
St. Austell 27 50 20N 4 48W
St. Bee's Hd. .... 28 54 30N 3 38 E
St. Boniface 153 49 53N 97 5W
St. Bride's B. 26 51 48N 5 15W
St-Brieuc 36 48 30N 2 46W
St. Catharines 151 43 10N 79 15W
St. Charles 166 38 46N 90 30W
St. Christopher-Nevis ■ ... 180 17 20N 62 40W
St. Cloud 156 45 30N 94 11W
St. Croix 180 17 45N 64 45W
St. David's 26 51 54N 5 16W
St. David's Head 26 51 55N 5 16W
St-Denis .... 39 48 56N 2 22 E
St-Dizier .... 37 48 40N 5 0 E
St. Elias, Mt. 144 60 14N 140 50W
St. Elias Mts. 144 60 33N 139 28W
St-Étienne .... 37 45 27N 4 22 E
St-Félicien 151 48 40N 72 25W
St. Gallen .... 44 47 25N 9 20 E
St. George, Australia ..... 116 28 1S 148 30 E
St. George, Bermuda 180 32 24N 64 42W
St. Georges, Fr. Guiana .. 185 4 0N 52 0W
St. George's, Grenada ... 180 12 5N 61 43W
St. George's Channel 20 52 0N 6 0W
St. Gotthard P. = San
  Gottardo, Paso del .... 44 46 33N 8 33 E
St. Helena 125 15 55S 5 44W
St. Helena B. .... 136 32 40S 18 10 E
St. Helens, Australia ..... 119 41 20S 148 15 E
St. Helens, U.K. 28 53 28N 2 44W
St. Helens, U.S.A. 171 45 55N 122 50W
St. Helier 36 49 11N 2 6W
St-Hyacinthe 151 45 40N 72 58W
St. Ives, Cambs., U.K. 25 52 20N 0 5W
St. Ives, Corn., U.K. 27 50 13N 5 29W
St-Jean 151 45 20N 73 20W
St-Jérôme 151 45 47N 74 0W
St. John 148 45 20N 66 8W
St. John's 149 47 35N 52 40W
St. John's → 170 30 20N 81 30W
St. Johnsbury 148 44 25N 72 1W
St. Joseph, Mich., U.S.A. ... 167 42 5N 86 30W
St. Joseph, Mo., U.S.A. ... 166 39 46N 94 50W
St. Kilda, N.Z. .... 123 45 53S 170 31 E
St. Kilda, U.K. 22 57 9N 8 34W
St. Lawrence 149 46 54N 55 23W
St. Lawrence → 148 49 30N 66 0W
St. Lawrence, Gulf of 149 48 25N 62 0W
St. Lawrence I. 142 63 0N 170 0W
St. Leonard 148 47 12N 67 58W
St-Louis 130 16 8N 16 27W
St. Louis 166 38 40N 90 12W
St. Lucia ■ 180 14 0N 60 50W
St. Maarten 180 18 0N 63 5W
St-Malo 36 48 39N 2 1W
St-Marc 180 19 10N 72 41W
St-Martin, I. 180 18 0N 63 0W
St. Mary Pk. .... 118 31 32S 138 34 E
St. Marys 164 41 27N 78 33W
St. Matthews, I. = Zadetkyi
  Kyun .... 94 10 0N 98 25 E
St. Michael's Mt. 27 50 7N 5 30W
St. Moritz .... 44 46 30N 9 51 E
St-Nazaire 36 47 17N 2 12W
St. Neots 25 52 14N 0 16W
St-Omer .... 38 50 45N 2 15 E
St. Pascal 148 47 32N 69 48W
St. Paul 166 44 54N 93 5W
St. Paul, I. 149 47 12N 60 9W
St-Petersburg = Sankt-
  Peterburg .... 68 59 55N 30 20 E
St. Petersburg 170 27 45N 82 40W
St-Pierre et Miquelon □ ... 149 46 55N 56 10W
St-Quentin .... 38 49 50N 3 16 E

St-Raphaël .... 37 43 25N 6 46 E
St-Servan-sur-Mer 36 48 38N 2 0W
St. Thomas, Canada 151 42 45N 81 10W
St. Thomas, W. Indies ... 180 18 21N 64 55W
St-Tropez .... 37 43 17N 6 38 E
St. Vincent and the
  Grenadines ■ 180 13 0N 61 10W
Ste-Adresse .... 38 49 31N 0 5 E
Ste. Anne de Beaupré 148 47 2N 70 58W
Ste. Marie 180 14 48N 61 1W
Ste-Rose 180 16 20N 61 45W
Ste. Rose du lac 153 51 4N 99 30W
Saintes 36 45 45N 0 37W
Saintonge 36 45 40N 0 50W
Saito .... 108 32 3N 131 24 E
Sajama 187 18 7S 69 0W
Sakai .... 106 34 30N 135 30 E
Sakaide .... 109 34 15N 133 50 E
Sakaiminato .... 109 35 38N 133 11 E
Sakakawea, L. 163 47 30N 102 0W
Sakata .... 103 38 55N 139 50 E
Sakhalin .... 79 51 0N 143 0 E
Sakhalinskiy Zaliv .... 75 54 0N 141 0 E
Saku .... 107 36 17N 138 31 E
Sakura .... 107 35 43N 140 14 E
Sakurai .... 106 34 30N 135 51 E
Salaberry-de-Valleyfield ... 151 45 15N 74 8W
Salado → 190 31 40S 60 41W
Salado, R. → 176 26 52N 99 19W
Salamanca, Spain 50 40 58N 5 39W
Salamanca, U.S.A. 164 42 10N 78 42W
Salamis .... 55 37 56N 23 30 E
Salcombe 27 50 14N 3 47W
Sale .... 117 38 6S 147 6 E
Salem, India .... 90 11 40N 78 11 E
Salem, Mass., U.S.A. 164 42 29N 70 53W
Salem, Oreg., U.S.A. 171 45 0N 123 0W
Salem, Va., U.S.A. 165 37 19N 80 8W
Salerno .... 49 40 40N 14 44 E
Salford 28 53 30N 2 17W
Salida 163 38 35N 106 0W
Salina, Italy .... 49 38 35N 14 50 E
Salina, U.S.A. 161 38 50N 97 40W
Salina Cruz 177 16 10N 95 12W
Salinas, Ecuador 184 2 10S 80 58W
Salinas, U.S.A. 173 36 40N 121 41W
Salinas → 173 36 45N 121 48W
Salinas Grandes 190 30 0S 65 0W
Salisbury = Harare ..... 137 17 43S 31 2 E
Salisbury, U.K. 24 51 4N 1 48W
Salisbury, Md., U.S.A. ... 165 38 20N 75 38W
Salisbury, N.C., U.S.A. ... 165 35 20N 80 29W
Salisbury Plain 24 51 13N 1 50W
Salle, La 166 41 20N 89 6W
Salmon 162 45 12N 113 56W
Salmon → 171 45 51N 116 46W
Salmon Arm 155 50 40N 119 15W
Salmon River Mts. 162 45 0N 114 30W
Salon-de-Provence ..... 37 43 39N 5 6 E
Salonica = Thessaloniki .. 54 40 38N 22 58 E
Salop = Shropshire □ ... 24 52 36N 2 45W
Salt Fork → 161 36 37N 97 7W
Salt Lake City 163 40 45N 111 58W
Salta 190 24 57S 65 25W
Saltcoats 30 55 38N 4 47W
Saltillo 174 25 25N 101 0W
Salto 191 31 27S 57 50W
Salton Sea 173 33 20N 115 50W
Salûm .... 128 31 31N 25 7 E
Salvador 189 13 0S 38 30W
Salween → .... 93 16 31N 97 37 E
Salzburg .... 45 47 48N 13 2 E
Salzburg □ .... 45 47 15N 13 0 E
Salzgitter .... 43 52 13N 10 22 E
Sam Neua .... 95 20 29N 104 0 E
Sama .... 69 60 12N 60 22 E
Samangán □ .... 87 36 15N 68 3 E
Samar .... 112 12 0N 125 0 E
Samara .... 68 53 8N 50 6 E
Samarkand .... 70 39 40N 66 55 E
Sãmarrã .... 81 34 12N 43 52 E
Sambalpur ■ .... 92 21 28N 84 4 E

Sambhal **89** 28 35N 78 37 E
Sámos **55** 37 45N 26 50 E
Samothráki **55** 40 28N 25 28 E
Samsun **80** 41 15N 36 22 E
Samut Prakan **95** 13 32N 100 40 E
Samut Sakhon **94** 13 31N 100 13 E
Samut Songkhram → **94** 13 24N 100 1 E
San Andreas **172** 38 0N 120 39W
San Andres Mts. **161** 33 0N 106 45W
San Andrés Tuxtla **177** 18 27N 95 13W
San Angelo **161** 31 30N 100 30W
San Antonio, Chile **190** 33 40S 71 40W
San Antonio, U.S.A. **161** 29 30N 98 30W
San Antonio, C., Argentina **191** 36 15S 56 40W
San Antonio, C., Cuba **178** 21 50N 84 57W
San Antonio de los Baños **178** 22 54N 82 31W
San Antônio Falls **182** 9 30S 65 0W
San Antonio Oeste **192** 40 40S 65 0W
San Bernardino **173** 34 7N 117 18W
San Bernardino Str. **112** 13 0N 125 0 E
San Bernardo **190** 33 40S 70 50W
San Blas, C. **169** 29 40N 85 12W
San Carlos, Chile **190** 36 10S 72 0W
San Carlos, Mexico **174** 29 1N 100 51W
San Carlos, Nic. **179** 11 12N 84 50W
San Carlos de Bariloche **192** 41 10S 71 25W
San Clemente I. **173** 32 53N 118 30W
San Cristóbal, Argentina **190** 30 20S 61 10W
San Cristóbal, Dom. Rep. **180** 18 25N 70 6W
San Cristóbal, Venezuela **184** 16 50N 92 40W
San Cristóbal de las Casas **177** 16 45N 92 38W
San Diego **173** 32 43N 117 10W
San Felipe, Chile **190** 32 43S 70 42W
San Felipe, Colombia **184** 1 55N 67 6W
San Fernando, Chile **190** 34 30S 71 0W
San Fernando, Mexico **174** 30 0N 115 10W
San Fernando, Trin. & Tob. **180** 10 20N 61 30W
San Fernando, U.S.A. **173** 34 15N 118 29W
San Fernando de Apure **184** 7 54N 67 15W
San Francisco **172** 37 47N 122 30W
San Francisco de Macorîs **180** 19 19N 70 15W
San Francisco del Oro **174** 26 52N 105 51W
San Gabriel **191** 0 36N 77 49W
San Gottardo, Paso del **44** 46 33N 8 33 E
San Ignacio **187** 16 20S 60 55W
San Joaquin → **172** 37 4N 121 51W
San Jorge, Golfo **192** 46 0S 66 0W
San Jorge, G. de **51** 40 50N 0 55W
San José, Bolivia **187** 17 53S 60 50W
San José, Costa Rica **179** 10 0N 84 2W
San Jose, U.S.A. **172** 37 20N 121 53W
San José de Mayo **191** 34 27S 56 40W
San José del Cabo **175** 23 3N 109 41W
San José del Guaviare **184** 2 35N 72 38W
San Juan, Argentina **190** 31 30S 68 30W
San Juan, Dom. Rep. **180** 18 49N 71 12W
San Juan, Puerto Rico **180** 18 28N 66 8W
San Juan → **179** 10 56N 83 42W
San Juan de los Morros **184** 9 55N 67 21W
San Juan Mts. **163** 38 30N 108 30W
San Julián **192** 49 15S 67 45W
San Leandro **172** 37 40N 122 6W
San Lorenzo **184** 1 15N 78 50W
San Lucas, C. de **175** 22 50N 110 0W
San Luis **190** 33 20S 66 20W
San Luis de la Paz **177** 21 18N 100 31W
San Luis Obispo **173** 35 21N 120 38W
San Luis Potosí **177** 22 9N 100 59W
San Luis Potosí □ **177** 22 30N 100 30W
San Marcos **177** 14 59N 91 52W
San Marino ■ **47** 43 56N 12 25 E
San Mateo **172** 37 32N 122 19W
San Matías **187** 16 25S 58 20W
San Matías, Golfo **192** 41 30S 64 0W
San Miguel **177** 13 30N 88 12W
San Miguel de Tucumán **190** 26 50S 65 20W
San Pedro → **175** 21 45N 105 30W
San Pedro de las Colonias **174** 25 45N 102 59W
San Pedro de Macorís **180** 18 30N 69 18W
San Pedro Sula **177** 15 30N 88 0W
San Rafael, Argentina **190** 34 40S 68 21W
San Rafael, U.S.A. **172** 37 59N 122 32W
San Roque **190** 28 25S 58 45W
San Salvador, Bahamas **178** 24 0N 74 40W
San Salvador, El Salv. **177** 13 40N 89 10W
San Salvador de Jujuy **190** 24 10S 64 48W
San Sebastián **51** 43 17N 1 58W
San Valentin, Mte. **192** 46 30S 73 30W
Sana' **82** 15 27N 44 12 E
Sanandaj **81** 35 18N 47 1 E
Sancti-Spíritus **178** 21 52N 79 33W
Sanda **106** 34 53N 135 14 E
Sandgate **116** 27 18S 153 3 E
Sandomierz **58** 50 40N 21 43 E
Sandpoint **171** 48 20N 116 34W
Sandringham **29** 52 50N 0 30 E
Sandstone **120** 27 59S 119 16 E
Sandusky **167** 41 25N 82 40W
Sandwip Chan. **93** 22 35N 91 35 E
Sandy C. **119** 41 25S 144 45 E
Sandy Lake **153** 53 0N 93 15W
Sanford, Fla., U.S.A. **170** 28 45N 81 20W
Sanford, Maine, U.S.A. **148** 43 28N 70 47W
Sanford, N.C., U.S.A. **165** 35 30N 79 10W
Sangay **184** 2 0S 78 20W
Sangihe, P. **113** 3 45N 125 30 E
Sangli **91** 16 55N 74 33 E
Sangre de Cristo Mts. **161** 37 0N 105 0W
Sankt-Peterburg **68** 59 55N 30 20 E
Sankuru → **134** 4 17S 20 25 E
Sanliurfa **81** 37 12N 38 50 E
Sano **107** 36 19N 139 35 E
Sanok **59** 49 35N 22 10 E
Sanquhar **31** 55 21N 3 56W
Sanshui **99** 23 10N 112 56 E
Santa Ana, Bolivia **187** 13 50S 65 40W
Santa Ana, Mexico **174** 30 33N 111 7W
Santa Ana, U.S.A. **173** 33 48N 117 55W
Santa Bárbara, Mexico **174** 26 48N 105 49W
Santa Barbara, U.S.A. **173** 34 25N 119 40W
Santa Barbara I. **160** 33 29N 119 2W
Santa Catarina □ **191** 27 25S 48 30W
Santa Clara, Cuba **178** 22 20N 80 0W
Santa Clara, U.S.A. **162** 37 21N 122 0W
Santa Clotilde **186** 2 33S 73 45W
Santa Cruz, Bolivia **187** 17 43S 63 10W
Santa Cruz, U.S.A. **172** 36 55N 122 1W
Santa Cruz, Is. **122** 10 30S 166 0 E
Santa Cruz de Tenerife **126** 28 28N 16 15W
Santa Cruz del Sur **178** 20 44N 78 0W
Santa Cruz do Sul **191** 29 42S 52 25W
Santa Fe, Argentina **190** 31 35S 60 41W
Santa Fe, U.S.A. **161** 35 40N 106 0W
Santa Inés, I. **192** 54 0S 73 0W
Santa Isabel = Rey Malabo **131** 3 45N 8 50 E
Santa Lucia Range **173** 36 0N 121 20W
Santa Maria, Brazil **191** 29 40S 53 48W
Santa Maria, U.S.A. **173** 34 58N 120 29W
Santa Maria da Vitória **188** 13 24S 44 12W
Santa Maria di Leuca, C. **49** 39 48N 18 20 E
Santa Marta **184** 11 15N 74 13W
Santa Maura = Levkás **54** 38 40N 20 43 E
Santa Monica **173** 34 0N 118 30W
Santa Rosa, Argentina **190** 36 40S 64 17W
Santa Rosa, U.S.A. **172** 38 26N 122 43W
Santa Rosa I., Calif., U.S.A. **173** 34 0N 120 6W
Santa Rosa I., Fla., U.S.A. **169** 30 23N 87 0W
Santa Rosalía **174** 27 19N 112 17W
Santana do Livramento **191** 30 55S 55 30W
Santander **50** 43 27N 3 51W
Santander Jiménez **176** 24 13N 98 28W
Santarém, Brazil **185** 2 25S 54 42W
Santarém, Portugal **50** 39 12N 8 42W
Santiago, Brazil **191** 29 11S 54 52W
Santiago, Chile **190** 33 24S 70 40W
Santiago, Panama **179** 8 0N 81 0W
Santiago de Compostela **50** 42 52N 8 37W
Santiago de Cuba **178** 20 0N 75 49W
Santiago de los Cabelleros **180** 19 30N 70 40W
Santiago del Estero **190** 27 50S 64 15W
Santiago Ixcuintla **175** 21 50N 105 11W
Santo Amaro **189** 12 30S 38 43W
Santo Ângelo **191** 28 15S 54 15W
Santo Domingo **180** 18 30N 64 54W

Santo Tomé 191 28 40S 56 5W
Santoña 50 43 29N 3 27W
Santos 191 24 0S 46 20W
São Borja 191 28 39S 56 0W
São Carlos 188 22 0S 47 50W
São Francisco → 189 10 30S 36 24W
São Francisco do Sul 191 26 15S 48 36W
São João del Rei 188 21 8S 44 15W
São José do Rio Prêto 188 20 50S 49 20W
São Leopoldo 191 29 50S 51 10W
São Lourenço 188 22 7S 45 3W
São Luís 188 2 39S 44 15W
São Paulo 191 23 32S 46 37W
São Paulo □ 188 22 0S 49 0W
São Paulo de Olivença 184 3 27S 68 48W
São Roque, C. de 189 5 30S 35 16W
São Tomé . . . . 131 0 10N 6 39 E
São Tomé & Principe ■ . . . . 131 0 12N 6 39 E
São Vicente, Cabo de 50 37 0N 9 0W
Saône → . . . . 37 45 44N 4 50 E
Sapporo . . . . 103 43 0N 141 21 E
Sapulpa 168 36 0N 96 0W
Saqqez . . . . 81 36 15N 46 20 E
Sar Planina . . . . 52 42 10N 21 0 E
Saragossa = Zaragoza 51 41 39N 0 53W
Sarajevo . . . . 52 43 52N 18 26 E
Saranac Lake 151 44 20N 74 10W
Sarangani B. . . . . 112 6 0N 125 13 E
Saransk . . . . 68 54 10N 45 10 E
Sarapul . . . . 69 56 28N 53 48 E
Sarasota 165 27 20N 82 30W
Saratoga Springs 164 43 5N 73 47W
Saratov . . . . 68 51 30N 46 2 E
Sarawak □ . . . . 111 2 0N 113 0 E
Sardegna . . . . 48 39 57N 9 0 E
Sardinia = Sardegna . . . . . . 48 39 57N 9 0 E
Sargodha . . . . 89 32 10N 72 40 E
Sarh . . . . 131 9 5N 18 23 E
Sārī . . . . 86 36 30N 53 4 E
Sarina . . . . 121 21 22S 149 13 E
Sarmiento 192 45 35S 69 5W
Sarnia 150 42 58N 82 23W
Saronikós Kólpos . . . . 55 37 45N 23 45 E
Sarre = Saar → . . . . 42 49 41N 6 32 E
Sarre, La 151 48 45N 79 15W
Sarthe → 36 47 33N 0 31W
Sasaram . . . . 92 24 57N 84 5 E
Sasebo . . . . 108 33 10N 129 43 E
Saskatchewan □ 152 54 40N 106 0W
Saskatchewan → 152 53 37N 100 40W
Saskatoon 152 52 10N 106 38W
Sassandra 130 5 0N 6 8W
Sássari . . . . 48 40 44N 8 33 E
Sata-Misaki . . . . 108 30 59N 130 40 E
Satara . . . . 91 17 44N 73 58 E
Satmala Hills . . . . 91 20 15N 74 40 E
Satna . . . . 92 24 35N 80 50 E
Satpura Ra. . . . . 91 21 25N 76 10 E
Sattahip . . . . 95 12 41N 100 54 E
Satu Mare . . . . 56 47 46N 22 55 E
Sauðarkrókur 64 65 45N 19 40W
Saudi Arabia ■ . . . . 82 26 0N 44 0 E
Sault Ste. Marie, Canada . . . 150 46 30N 84 20W
Sault Ste. Marie, U.S.A. 150 46 27N 84 22W
Saumur 36 47 15N 0 5W
Sava → . . . . 52 44 50N 20 26 E
Savanna la Mar 180 18 10N 78 10W
Savannah 170 32 4N 81 4W
Savannah → 170 32 2N 80 53W
Savannakhet . . . . 95 16 30N 104 49 E
Savoie □ . . . . 37 45 26N 6 35 E
Savona . . . . 46 44 19N 8 29 E
Sawankhalok . . . . 94 17 19N 99 50 E
Sawara . . . . 107 35 55N 140 30 E
Sawatch Mts. 163 38 30N 106 30W
Sawu, I. . . . . 113 10 35S 121 50 E
Sawu Sea . . . . 113 9 30S 121 50 E
Saxony, Lower =
  Niedersachsen □ . . . . 42 52 45N 9 0 E
Sayan, Zapadnyy . . . . 77 52 30N 94 0 E
Saydā . . . . 80 33 35N 35 25 E
Sayḩut . . . . 83 15 12N 51 10 E
Sayula 175 19 52N 103 36W
Sazan . . . . 52 40 30N 19 20 E
Scafell Pikes 28 54 26N 3 14W
Scalloway 30 60 9N 1 16W
Scandinavia . . . . 16 64 0N 12 0 E
Scapa Flow 33 58 52N 3 6W
Scarborough 29 54 17N 0 24W
Schaffhausen . . . . 44 47 42N 8 39 E
Schefferville 146 54 48N 66 50W
Schelde → . . . . 42 51 15N 4 16 E
Schenectady 164 42 50N 73 58W
Scheveningen . . . . 40 52 6N 4 16 E
Schiedam . . . . 40 51 55N 4 25 E
Schiermonnikoog . . . . 41 53 30N 6 15 E
Schleswig-Holstein □ . . . . . 42 54 10N 9 40 E
Schouten I. . . . . 119 42 20S 148 20 E
Schouten Is. . . . . 113 1 0S 136 0 E
Schouwen . . . . 40 51 43N 3 45 E
Schreiber 150 48 45N 87 20W
Schwäbische Alb . . . . 42 48 30N 9 30 E
Schwarzwald . . . . 42 48 0N 8 0 E
Schwerin . . . . 43 53 37N 11 22 E
Schwyz . . . . 44 47 2N 8 39 E
Scilly, Isles of 20 49 55N 6 15W
Scone, Australia . . . . 116 32 5S 150 52 E
Scone, U.K. 31 56 25N 3 26W
Scoresbysund 13 70 20N 23 0W
Scotia Sea 14 56 5S 56 0W
Scotland □ 23 57 0N 4 0W
Scottsbluff 163 41 55N 103 35W
Scottsdale . . . . 119 41 9S 147 31 E
Scranton 164 41 22N 75 41W
Scunthorpe 29 53 35N 0 38W
Scutari = Üsküdar . . . . 80 41 0N 29 5 E
Seaforth 150 43 35N 81 25W
Searcy 168 35 15N 91 45W
Seascale 28 54 24N 3 29W
Seattle 171 47 41N 122 15W
Sebastián Vizcaíno, B. 174 28 0N 114 30W
Sebastopol = Sevastopol . . 68 44 35N 33 30 E
Sebring 170 27 30N 81 26W
Sebta = Ceuta 126 35 52N 5 18W
Sebuku, Teluk . . . . 111 4 0N 118 10 E
Sechura, Desierto de 186 6 0S 80 30W
Seclin . . . . 38 50 33N 3 2 E
Sedalia 166 38 40N 93 18W
Segamat . . . . 96 2 30N 102 50 E
Ségou 130 13 30N 6 16W
Segovia = Coco → 179 15 0N 83 8W
Segovia 50 40 57N 4 10W
Séguéla 130 7 55N 6 40W
Segura → 51 38 6N 0 54W
Seine → . . . . 38 49 26N 0 26 E
Seistan . . . . 85 30 50N 61 0 E
Seki . . . . 106 35 29N 136 55 E
Sekondi-Takoradi 130 4 58N 1 45W
Selangor □ . . . . 96 3 10N 101 30 E
Selby 29 53 47N 1 5W
Sélibabi 130 15 10N 12 15W
Selkirk, Canada 153 50 10N 96 55W
Selkirk, U.K. 31 55 33N 2 50W
Selkirk Mts. 155 51 15N 117 40W
Selma, Ala., U.S.A. 169 32 30N 87 0W
Selma, Calif., U.S.A. 173 36 39N 119 39W
Selsey Bill 24 50 44N 0 47W
Selvas 187 6 30S 67 0W
Semarang . . . . 111 7 0S 110 26 E
Seminole 168 35 15N 96 45W
Semipalatinsk . . . . 71 50 30N 80 10 E
Semnān . . . . 86 35 55N 53 25 E
Semnān □ . . . . 86 36 0N 54 0 E
Sendai, Kagoshima, Japan . 108 31 50N 130 20 E
Sendai, Miyagi, Japan . . . . . 103 38 15N 140 53 E
Senegal ■ 130 14 30N 14 30W
Senegal → 126 15 48N 16 32W
Senge Khambab = Indus → 88 24 20N 67 47 E
Senhor-do-Bonfim 189 10 30S 40 10W
Senja I. . . . . 64 69 15N 17 30 E
Senlis . . . . 39 49 13N 2 35 E
Sennâr . . . . 129 13 30N 33 35 E
Senneterre 151 48 25N 77 15W

Place	Page	Lat.	Long.
Sens	**39**	48 11N	3 15 E
Senta	**52**	45 55N	20 3 E
Seoul = Sŏul	**98**	37 31N	126 58 E
Sept-Îles	**148**	50 13N	66 22W
Seram	**113**	3 10S	129 0 E
Seram Sea	**113**	2 30S	128 30 E
Seremban	**96**	2 43N	101 53 E
Serena, La	**190**	29 55S	71 10W
Sereth = Siret →	**57**	47 58N	26 5 E
Sergipe □	**189**	10 30S	37 30W
Sérifos	**55**	37 9N	24 30 E
Serny Zavod	**70**	39 59N	58 50 E
Serov	**69**	59 29N	60 35 E
Serowe	**137**	22 25S	26 43 E
Serpukhov	**68**	54 55N	37 28 E
Serra do Navio	**185**	0 59N	52 3W
Sérrai	**55**	41 5N	23 31 E
Sesheke	**134**	17 29S	24 13 E
Setana	**103**	42 26N	139 51 E
Sète	**37**	43 25N	3 42 E
Sétif	**127**	36 9N	5 26 E
Seto	**106**	35 14N	137 6 E
Setonaikai	**109**	34 20N	133 30 E
Settle	**28**	54 5N	2 18W
Setúbal	**50**	38 30N	8 58W
Sevastopol	**68**	44 35N	33 30 E
Seven Sisters	**154**	54 56N	128 10W
Severn →, Canada	**140**	56 2N	87 36W
Severn →, U.K.	**24**	51 35N	2 38W
Severnaya Zemlya	**72**	79 0N	100 0 E
Severodinsk	**69**	64 27N	39 58 E
Sevilla	**50**	37 23N	6 0W
Seville = Sevilla	**50**	37 23N	6 0W
Seward	**142**	60 6N	149 26W
Seward Pen.	**142**	65 0N	164 0W
Seychelles ■	**78**	5 0S	56 0 E
Seyðisfjörður	**64**	65 16N	14 0W
Seymour	**117**	37 0S	145 10 E
Seyne-sur-Mer, La	**37**	43 7N	5 52 E
Sézanne	**39**	48 40N	3 40 E
Sfax	**127**	34 49N	10 48 E
Sfîntu Gheorghe	**57**	45 52N	25 48 E
Shaanxi □	**99**	35 0N	109 0 E
Shaba □	**135**	8 0S	25 0 E
Shache	**100**	38 20N	77 10 E
Shaftesbury	**24**	51 0N	2 12W
Shahdād	**85**	30 30N	57 40 E
Shakhty	**68**	47 40N	40 16 E
Shamo = Gobi	**98**	44 0N	111 0 E
Shamokin	**164**	40 47N	76 33W
Shan □	**93**	21 30N	98 30 E
Shandong □	**99**	36 0N	118 0 E
Shanghai	**99**	31 15N	121 26 E
Shangqiu	**99**	34 26N	115 36 E
Shangrao	**99**	28 25N	117 59 E
Shangshui	**99**	33 42N	114 35 E
Shannon →	**35**	52 35N	9 30W
Shansi = Shanxi □	**98**	37 0N	112 0 E
Shantou	**99**	23 18N	116 40 E
Shantung = Shandong □	**99**	36 0N	118 0 E
Shanxi □	**98**	37 0N	112 0 E
Shaoguan	**99**	24 48N	113 35 E
Shaoxing	**99**	30 0N	120 35 E
Shaoyang	**99**	27 14N	111 25 E
Shap	**28**	54 32N	2 40W
Sharjah = Ash Shāriqah	**85**	25 23N	55 26 E
Shark B.	**120**	25 55S	113 32 E
Sharon	**164**	41 18N	80 30W
Shashi	**99**	30 25N	112 14 E
Shasta, Mt.	**172**	41 30N	122 12W
Shasta L.	**172**	40 50N	122 15W
Shaunavon	**152**	49 35N	108 25W
Shawano	**167**	44 45N	88 38W
Shawinigan	**151**	46 35N	72 50W
Shawnee	**168**	35 15N	97 0W
Shcherbakov = Andropov	**68**	58 5N	38 50 E
Shebele, Wabi →	**133**	2 0N	44 0 E
Sheboygan	**167**	43 46N	87 45W
Sheerness	**24**	51 26N	0 47 E
Sheffield	**28**	53 23N	1 28W
Shekhupura	**89**	31 42N	73 58 E

Place	Page	Lat.	Long.
Shelburne	**148**	43 47N	65 20W
Shelby, Mont., U.S.A.	**163**	48 30N	111 52W
Shelby, N.C., U.S.A.	**165**	35 18N	81 34W
Shelbyville, Ind., U.S.A.	**167**	39 30N	85 42W
Shelbyville, Tenn., U.S.A.	**169**	35 30N	86 25W
Shelikhova, Zaliv	**73**	59 30N	157 0 E
Shellharbour	**117**	34 31S	150 51 E
Shelton	**171**	47 15N	123 6W
Shenandoah	**166**	40 50N	95 25W
Shensi = Shaanxi □	**99**	35 0N	109 0 E
Shenyang	**98**	41 50N	123 25 E
Shepparton	**117**	36 23S	145 26 E
Sheppey, I. of	**24**	51 23N	0 50 E
Sherborne	**27**	50 56N	2 31W
Sherbrooke	**148**	45 28N	71 57W
Sheridan	**163**	44 50N	107 0W
Sherman	**168**	33 40N	96 35W
Sherridon	**152**	55 8N	101 5W
Sherwood Forest	**29**	53 5N	1 5W
Shetland Is.	**30**	60 30N	1 30W
Shibām	**83**	16 0N	48 36 E
Shibata	**103**	37 57N	139 20 E
Shibetsu	**103**	44 10N	142 23 E
Shibukawa	**107**	36 29N	139 0 E
Shibushi-Wan	**108**	31 24N	131 8 E
Shiel, L.	**32**	56 48N	5 32W
Shihchiachuangi = Shijiazhuang	**98**	38 2N	114 28 E
Shijiazhuang	**98**	38 2N	114 28 E
Shikarpur	**88**	27 57N	68 39 E
Shikine-Jima	**107**	34 19N	139 13 E
Shikoku	**109**	33 30N	133 30 E
Shikoku □	**109**	33 30N	133 30 E
Shikoku-Sanchi	**109**	33 30N	133 30 E
Shillong	**93**	25 35N	91 53 E
Shimabara	**108**	32 48N	130 20 E
Shimada	**107**	34 49N	138 10 E
Shimizu	**107**	35 0N	138 30 E
Shimo-Jima	**108**	32 15N	130 7 E
Shimo-Koshiki-Jima	**108**	31 40N	129 43 E
Shimoda	**107**	34 40N	138 57 E
Shimodate	**107**	36 20N	139 55 E
Shimoga	**90**	13 57N	75 32 E
Shimonoseki	**108**	33 58N	131 0 E
Shin, L.	**33**	58 7N	4 30W
Shin-Tone →	**107**	35 44N	140 51 E
Shinano →	**105**	36 50N	138 30 E
Shingū	**106**	33 40N	135 55 E
Shinji Ko	**109**	35 26N	132 57 E
Shinjō	**103**	38 46N	140 18 E
Shinminato	**106**	36 47N	137 4 E
Shinshiro	**106**	34 54N	137 30 E
Shio-no-Misaki	**106**	33 25N	135 45 E
Shiogama	**103**	38 19N	141 1 E
Shiojiri	**107**	36 6N	137 58 E
Shipka	**53**	42 46N	25 33 E
Shirane-San, Gumma, Japan	**107**	36 48N	139 22 E
Shirane-San, Yamanashi, Japan	**107**	35 42N	138 9 E
Shīrāz	**85**	29 42N	52 30 E
Shire →	**137**	17 42S	35 19 E
Shiriya-Zaki	**103**	41 25N	141 30 E
Shivpuri	**91**	25 26N	77 42 E
Shizuoka	**107**	35 0N	138 24 E
Shkoder = Shkodra	**52**	42 6N	19 20 E
Shkodra	**52**	42 6N	19 20 E
Shkumbini →	**52**	41 5N	19 50 E
Shō-Gawa →	**106**	36 47N	137 4 E
Shōbara	**109**	34 51N	133 1 E
Shoeburyness	**24**	51 31N	0 49 E
Sholapur = Solapur	**91**	17 43N	75 56 E
Shoshone	**172**	43 0N	114 27W
Shreveport	**168**	32 30N	93 50W
Shrewsbury	**28**	52 42N	2 45W
Shrirampur	**92**	22 44N	88 21 E
Shropshire □	**24**	52 36N	2 45W
Shuangyashan	**98**	46 37N	131 22 E
Siahan Range	**88**	27 30N	64 40 E
Sialkot	**89**	32 32N	74 30 E
Siam = Thailand ■	**95**	16 0N	102 0 E
Sian = Xi'an	**99**	34 15N	109 0 E

Siberia . . . . . 77 60 0N 100 0 E
Siberut . . . . . 111 1 30S 99 0 E
Sibi . . . . . 88 29 30N 67 54 E
Sibiu . . . . . 57 45 45N 24 9 E
Sichuan □ . . . . . 99 31 0N 104 0 E
Sicilia . . . . . 49 37 30N 14 30 E
Sicily = Sicilia . . . . . 49 37 30N 14 30 E
Sicuani 187 14 21S 71 10W
Sidi-bel-Abbès 127 35 13N 0 39W
Sidlaw Hills 31 56 32N 3 10W
Sidley, Mt. 15 77 2S 126 2W
Sidmouth 27 50 40N 3 13W
Sidney 154 48 39N 123 24W
Sidon = Saydā . . . . . 80 33 35N 35 25 E
Sidra, G. of = Surt, Khalīj . . 127 31 40N 18 30 E
Siedlce . . . . . 58 52 10N 22 20 E
Siena . . . . . 46 43 20N 11 20 E
Sierra Blanca Pk. 161 33 20N 105 54W
Sierra Leone ■ 130 9 0N 12 0W
Sífnos . . . . . 55 37 0N 24 45 E
Siglufjörður 64 66 12N 18 55W
Sihanoukville = Kompong Som . . . . . 95 10 38N 103 30 E
Siirt . . . . . 81 37 57N 41 55 E
Sikar . . . . . 89 27 33N 75 10 E
Sikeston 169 36 52N 89 35W
Sikhote Alin, Khrebet . . . . . 75 46 0N 136 0 E
Síkinos . . . . . 55 36 40N 25 8 E
Sikkim □ . . . . . 92 27 50N 88 30 E
Silchar . . . . . 93 24 49N 92 48 E
Silesia = Slask . . . . . 58 51 0N 16 30 E
Siling Co . . . . . 101 31 50N 89 20 E
Silloth 28 54 53N 3 25W
Simbirsk . . . . . 68 54 20N 48 25 E
Simcoe 151 42 50N 80 20W
Simenga . . . . . 74 62 42N 108 25 E
Simeulue . . . . . 111 2 45N 95 45 E
Simferopol . . . . . 68 44 55N 34 3 E
Simi Valley 173 34 16N 118 47W
Simla . . . . . 89 31 2N 77 9 E
Simplon Pass . . . . . 44 46 15N 8 0 E
Simushir, Ostrov . . . . . 75 46 50N 152 30 E
Sinai = Es Sînâ' . . . . . 128 29 0N 34 0 E
Sinaloa 174 25 50N 108 20W
Sinaloa □ 174 25 0N 107 30W
Sincelejo 184 9 18N 75 24W
Sinclair Mills 155 54 5N 121 40W
Sind □ . . . . . 88 26 0N 69 0 E
Sind Sagar Doab . . . . . 89 32 0N 71 30 E
Singa . . . . . 129 13 10N 33 57 E
Singapore ■ . . . . . 96 1 17N 103 51 E
Singapore, Straits of . . . . . 96 1 15N 104 0 E
Singkaling Hkamti . . . . . 92 26 0N 95 39 E
Singleton . . . . . 117 32 33S 151 0 E
Singora = Songkhla . . . . . 97 7 13N 100 37 E
Sinkiang Uighur = Xinjiang Uygur Zizhiqu □ . . . . . 100 42 0N 86 0 E
Sioux City 166 42 32N 96 25W
Sioux Falls 166 43 35N 96 40W
Sioux Lookout 153 50 10N 91 50W
Siping . . . . . 98 43 8N 124 21 E
Sipora . . . . . 111 2 18S 99 40 E
Siracusa . . . . . 49 37 4N 15 17 E
Sirajganj . . . . . 92 24 25N 89 47 E
Siret → . . . . . 57 47 58N 26 5 E
Síros . . . . . 55 37 28N 24 57 E
Sitapur . . . . . 92 27 38N 80 45 E
Sitka 143 57 9N 135 20W
Sittard . . . . . 41 51 0N 5 52 E
Sivas . . . . . 80 39 43N 36 58 E
Siverek . . . . . 81 37 50N 39 19 E
Sivrihisar . . . . . 80 39 30N 31 35 E
Sîwa . . . . . 128 29 11N 25 31 E
Siwalik Range . . . . . 92 28 0N 83 0 E
Sizewell . . . . . 24 52 13N 1 38 E
Sjumen = Kolarovgrad . . . . 53 43 18N 26 55 E
Skadarsko Jezero . . . . . 52 42 10N 19 20 E
Skagerrak . . . . . 60 57 30N 9 0 E
Skagway 143 59 23N 135 20W
Skaraborgs län □ . . . . . 60 58 20N 13 30 E
Skeena → 154 54 9N 130 5W
Skegness . . . . . 29 53 9N 0 20 E
Skellefte → . . . . . 66 65 30N 18 30 E
Skellefteå . . . . . 67 64 45N 20 58 E
Skerries, The 26 53 27N 4 40W
Skiddaw 28 54 39N 3 9W
Skien . . . . . 60 59 12N 9 35 E
Skierniewice . . . . . 58 51 58N 20 10 E
Skikda . . . . . 127 36 50N 6 58 E
Skipton 28 53 57N 2 1W
Skíros . . . . . 55 38 55N 24 34 E
Skopje . . . . . 52 42 1N 21 32 E
Skowhegan 148 44 49N 69 40W
Skull 35 51 32N 9 40W
Skye 32 57 15N 6 10W
Skyros = Skíros . . . . . 55 38 55N 24 34 E
Slaney → 35 52 52N 6 45W
Slask . . . . . 58 51 0N 16 30 E
Slave → 145 61 18N 113 39W
Slave Coast . . . . . 124 6 0N 2 30 E
Sleaford 29 53 0N 0 22W
Sliedrecht . . . . . 40 51 50N 4 45 E
Slieve Aughty 35 53 4N 8 30W
Slieve Bloom 35 53 4N 7 40W
Slieve Donard 34 54 10N 5 57W
Slieve Mish 35 52 12N 9 50W
Slievenamon 35 52 25N 7 37W
Sligo 34 54 17N 8 28W
Sligo □ 34 54 10N 8 35W
Slovak Republic ■ . . . . . 59 48 30N 20 0 E
Slovakian Ore Mts. = Slovenské Rudohorie . . . . 59 48 45N 20 0 E
Slovenia ■ . . . . . 52 45 58N 14 30 E
Slovenské Rudohorie . . . . . 59 48 45N 20 0 E
Słupsk . . . . . 58 54 30N 17 3 E
Slyne Hd. 34 53 25N 10 10W
Smara 126 32 9N 8 16W
Smithers 154 54 45N 127 10W
Smithfield 165 35 31N 78 16W
Smiths Falls 151 44 55N 76 0W
Smithton . . . . . 119 40 53S 145 6 E
Smolensk . . . . . 68 54 45N 32 0 E
Smolikas, Óros . . . . . 54 40 9N 20 58 E
Smyrna = İzmir . . . . . 80 38 25N 27 8 E
Snaefell, Iceland 64 64 48N 15 34W
Snaefell, U.K. 28 54 18N 4 26W
Snæfellsjökull 64 64 49N 23 46W
Snake → 171 46 12N 119 2W
Sneek . . . . . 41 53 2N 5 40 E
Snowdon 26 53 4N 4 8W
Snowdrift 145 62 24N 110 44W
Snowy Mts. . . . . . 117 36 30S 148 20 E
Sobat → . . . . . 129 8 32N 32 40 E
Sobral 177 3 50S 40 20W
Soch'e = Shache . . . . . 100 38 20N 77 10 E
Sochi . . . . . 70 43 35N 39 40 E
Société, Is. de la 123 17 0S 151 0W
Society Is. = Société, Is. de la 123 17 0S 151 0W
Socorro 161 34 4N 106 54W
Socotra . . . . . 78 12 30N 54 0 E
Söderhamn . . . . . 60 61 18N 17 10 E
Södermanlands län □ . . . . . 60 59 10N 16 30 E
Södertälje . . . . . 60 59 12N 17 39 E
Sodo . . . . . 132 7 0N 37 41 E
Sofala . . . . . 137 33 4S 149 43 E
Sofia = Sofiya . . . . . 53 42 45N 23 20 E
Sofiya . . . . . 53 42 45N 23 20 E
Sogn og Fjordane fylke □ . . 60 61 40N 6 0 E
Soissons . . . . . 39 49 25N 3 19 E
Sōja . . . . . 109 34 40N 133 45 E
Söke . . . . . 80 37 48N 27 28 E
Sol Iletsk . . . . . 70 51 10N 55 0 E
Solapur . . . . . 91 17 43N 75 56 E
Soledad, Colombia 184 10 55N 74 46W
Soledad, Venezuela 185 8 10N 63 34W
Solent, The 24 50 45N 1 25W
Solesmes . . . . . 38 50 10N 3 30 E
Solikamsk . . . . . 69 59 38N 56 50 E
Solimões = Amazonas → . 185 0 5S 50 0W
Sóller . . . . . 51 39 46N 2 43 E
Sololá . . . . . 177 14 49N 91 10 E

Solomon Is. ■ .... 122 6 0S 155 0 E
Solţānābād .... 86 36 29N 58 5 E
Solway Firth 31 54 45N 3 38W
Somali Rep. ■ .... 133 7 0N 47 0 E
Sombor .... 52 45 46N 19 9 E
Sombrerete 175 23 38N 103 39W
Somerset, Bermuda 180 32 16N 64 55W
Somerset, U.S.A. 169 37 5N 84 40W
Somerset □ 27 51 9N 3 0W
Somerset I. 145 73 30N 93 0W
Somme □ .... 36 50 0N 2 20 E
Somport, Puerto de 51 42 48N 0 31W
Søndre Strømfjord 147 66 59N 50 40W
Songkhla .... 97 7 13N 100 37 E
Sonora □ 174 29 20N 110 40W
Soochow = Suzhou ...... 99 31 19N 120 38 E
Sop's Arm 149 49 46N 56 56W
Sør-Rondane .... 14 72 0S 25 0 E
Sør-Trøndelag fylke □ ... 65 63 0N 10 0 E
Sorata 187 15 50S 68 40W
Sorel 151 46 0N 73 10W
Soria 51 41 43N 2 32W
Sorocaba 191 23 31S 47 27W
Sørøya .... 67 70 40N 22 30 E
Sorsogon .... 112 13 0N 124 0 E
Sosnowiec .... 58 50 20N 19 10 E
Sotteville-lès-Rouen ...... 38 49 24N 1 5 E
Sŏul .... 98 37 31N 126 58 E
Souris, Man., Canada 153 49 40N 100 20W
Souris, P.E.I., Canada 149 46 21N 62 15W
South Africa, Rep. of ■ ... 136 32 0S 17 0 E
South Australia □ .... 118 32 0S 139 0 E
South Bend 167 41 38N 86 20W
South Carolina □ 165 33 45N 81 0W
South Charleston 165 38 20N 81 40W
South China Sea .... 77 10 0N 113 0 E
South Dakota □ 163 45 0N 100 0W
South Downs 25 50 53N 0 10W
South Georgia 183 54 30S 37 0W
South Glamorgan □ 27 51 30N 3 20W
South Haven 167 42 22N 86 20W
South Island .... 123 44 0S 170 0 E
South Korea ■ .... 98 36 0N 128 0 E
South Orkney Is. 14 63 0S 45 0W
South Platte → 163 41 7N 100 42W
South Pole .... 14 90 0S 0 0 E
South Porcupine 151 48 30N 81 12W
South Ronaldsay 33 58 46N 2 58W
South Sandwich Is. 14 57 0S 27 0W
South Sentinel I. .... 94 11 1N 92 16 E
South Shetland Is. 14 62 0S 59 0W
South Shields 28 54 59N 1 26W
South Taranaki Bight ..... 122 39 40S 174 5 E
South Uist 32 57 20N 7 15W
South West Africa =
Namibia ■ .... 136 22 0S 18 9 E
South West Cape .... 123 47 16S 167 31 E
South Yorkshire □ 29 53 30N 1 20W
Southampton 25 50 54N 1 23W
Southampton I. 146 64 30N 84 0W
Southend-on-Sea .... 25 51 32N 0 42 E
Southern Alps .... 123 43 41S 170 11 E
Southern Cross .... 120 31 12S 119 15 E
Southern Indian L. 143 57 10N 98 30W
Southern Uplands 31 55 30N 3 3W
Southland □ .... 123 45 51S 168 13 E
Southport, Australia ...... 116 27 58S 153 25 E
Southport, U.K. 28 53 38N 3 1W
Southwold .... 25 52 19N 1 41 E
Sovetskaya Gavan ...... 75 48 50N 140 0 E
Sōya-Kaikyō = Perouse Str.,
La .... 77 45 40N 142 0 E
Spain ■ 50 40 0N 5 0W
Spalding 29 52 47N 0 9W
Spandau .... 43 52 35N 13 7 E
Spanish Fork 163 40 10N 111 37W
Spanish Town 180 18 0N 76 57W
Sparks 172 39 30N 119 45W
Sparta = Spárti .... 54 37 5N 22 25 E
Sparta 166 43 55N 90 47W
Spartanburg 165 35 0N 82 0W

Spárti .... 54 37 5N 22 25 E
Spartivento, C., Calabria, Italy 49 37 56N 16 4 E
Spartivento, C., Sard., Italy . 48 38 52N 8 50 E
Spassk-Dalniy .... 75 44 40N 132 48 E
Speightstown 180 13 15N 59 39W
Spence Bay 145 69 32N 93 32W
Spencer 166 43 5N 95 19W
Spencer G. .... 119 34 0S 137 20 E
Spenser Mts. .... 123 42 15S 172 45 E
Sperrin Mts. 34 54 50N 7 0W
Spessart .... 42 50 10N 9 20 E
Spey → 33 57 26N 3 25W
Spézia, La .... 46 44 8N 9 50 E
Spinazzola .... 49 40 58N 16 5 E
Spithead 25 50 43N 1 5W
Spitzbergen = Svalbard .... 13 78 0N 17 0 E
Split .... 52 43 31N 16 26 E
Splügenpass .... 44 46 30N 9 20 E
Spokane 171 47 45N 117 25W
Sporyy Navolok, Mys ..... 69 75 50N 68 40 E
Spratly, I. .... 112 8 20N 112 0 E
Spring Mts. 173 36 20N 115 43W
Springfield, Ill., U.S.A. 166 39 48N 89 40W
Springfield, Mass., U.S.A. .. 164 42 8N 72 37W
Springfield, Mo., U.S.A. ... 168 37 15N 93 20W
Springfield, Ohio, U.S.A. ... 167 39 58N 83 48W
Springfield, Oreg., U.S.A. .. 171 44 2N 123 0W
Springfield, Tenn., U.S.A. .. 169 36 35N 86 55W
Springfield, Vt., U.S.A. 164 43 20N 72 30W
Springhill 148 45 40N 64 4W
Springs .... 137 26 13S 28 25 E
Springwood .... 117 33 41S 150 33 E
Spurn Hd. .... 29 53 34N 0 8 E
Squamish 154 49 45N 123 10W
Sredinnyy Khrebet ...... 73 57 0N 160 0 E
Srednekolymsk .... 73 67 27N 153 40 E
Sremska Mitrovica ...... 52 44 59N 19 33 E
Srepok → .... 95 13 33N 106 16 E
Sretensk .... 74 52 10N 117 40 E
Sri Lanka ■ .... 90 7 30N 80 50 E
Srinagar .... 89 34 5N 74 50 E
Stadskanaal .... 41 53 4N 6 55 E
Staffa 30 56 26N 6 21W
Stafford 28 52 49N 2 9W
Stafford □ 28 52 53N 2 10W
Staines 25 51 26N 0 30W
Stalingrad = Volgograd ... 68 48 40N 44 25 E
Stalino = Donetsk .... 68 48 0N 37 45 E
Stalinogorsk =
Novomoskovsk .... 68 54 5N 38 15 E
Stalybridge 28 53 29N 2 4W
Stamford, U.K. 25 52 39N 0 29W
Stamford, U.S.A. 164 41 5N 73 30W
Stanislav = Ivano-Frankovsk 68 48 40N 24 40 E
Stanley, Canada 152 55 24N 104 22W
Stanley, Falk. Is. 192 51 40S 59 51W
Stanovoy Khrebet .... 75 55 0N 130 0 E
Stanthorpe .... 116 28 36S 151 59 E
Stara Planina .... 53 43 15N 23 0 E
Stara Zagora .... 53 42 26N 25 39 E
Starkville 169 33 26N 88 48W
Start Pt. 27 50 13N 3 38W
State College 164 40 47N 77 49W
Staten, I. = Estados, I. de los 192 54 40S 64 30W
Statesboro 170 32 26N 81 46W
Statesville 165 35 48N 80 51W
Staunton 165 38 7N 79 4W
Stavanger .... 60 58 57N 5 40 E
Staveren .... 40 52 53N 5 22 E
Stavropol .... 70 45 5N 42 0 E
Stawell .... 119 37 5S 142 47 E
Steenwijk .... 41 52 47N 6 7 E
Stefanie L. = Chew Bahir . 132 4 40N 36 50 E
Steiermark □ .... 45 47 26N 15 0 E
Steinbach 153 49 32N 96 40W
Steinkjer .... 65 63 59N 11 31 E
Stellarton 149 45 32N 62 30W
Stephenville 149 48 31N 58 35W
Stereá Ellas □ .... 54 38 50N 22 0 E
Sterling, Colo., U.S.A. ... 163 40 40N 103 15W
Sterling, Ill., U.S.A. 166 41 45N 89 45W

Place	Page	Lat.	Long.
Sterlitamak	**71**	53 40N	56 0 E
Stettin = Szczecin	**58**	53 27N	14 27 E
Stettler	**155**	52 19N	112 40W
Steubenville	**164**	40 21N	80 39W
Stevens Port	**166**	44 32N	89 34W
Stewart	**144**	63 19N	139 26W
Stewart I.	**123**	46 58S	167 54 E
Stikine →	**144**	56 40N	132 30W
Stillwater, Minn., U.S.A.	**166**	45 3N	92 47W
Stillwater, Okla., U.S.A.	**168**	36 5N	97 3W
Stillwater Ra.	**172**	39 45N	118 6W
Štip	**53**	41 42N	22 10 E
Stirling	**31**	56 7N	3 57W
Stirling Ra.	**120**	34 23S	118 0 E
Stockholm	**60**	59 20N	18 3 E
Stockholms län □	**60**	59 30N	18 20 E
Stockport	**28**	53 25N	2 11W
Stockton	**172**	38 0N	121 20W
Stockton-on-Tees	**29**	54 34N	1 20W
Stoke-on-Trent	**28**	53 1N	2 11W
Stonehaven	**33**	56 58N	2 11W
Stonehenge	**24**	51 9N	1 45W
Stonewall	**153**	50 10N	97 19W
Stora Lulevatten	**66**	67 10N	19 30 E
Storavan	**66**	65 45N	18 10 E
Store Bælt	**61**	55 20N	11 0 E
Storm B.	**119**	43 10S	147 30 E
Storm Lake	**166**	42 35N	95 11W
Stornoway	**32**	58 12N	6 23W
Storsjön	**66**	63 12N	14 18 E
Storuman	**66**	65 5N	17 10 E
Stour →, Here. & Worcs., U.K.	**24**	52 25N	2 13W
Stour →, Kent, U.K.	**25**	51 15N	1 20 E
Stour →, Suffolk, U.K.	**25**	51 55N	1 5 E
Stourbridge	**24**	52 28N	2 8W
Stowmarket	**25**	52 11N	1 0 E
Strabane	**34**	54 50N	7 28W
Stralsund	**43**	54 17N	13 5 E
Strangford, L.	**34**	54 30N	5 37W
Stranraer	**30**	54 54N	5 0W
Strasbourg	**37**	48 35N	7 42 E
Stratford, Canada	**151**	43 23N	81 0W
Stratford, N.Z.	**122**	39 20S	174 19 E
Stratford-on-Avon	**24**	52 12N	1 42W
Strath Spey	**33**	57 15N	3 40W
Strathalbyn	**119**	35 13S	138 53 E
Strathclyde □	**30**	56 0N	4 50W
Strathmore	**33**	56 40N	3 4W
Strathy Pt.	**33**	58 35N	4 0W
Streaky B.	**118**	32 51S	134 18 E
Streator	**167**	41 9N	88 52W
Strómboli	**49**	38 48N	15 12 E
Stromeferry	**32**	57 20N	5 33W
Stromness	**33**	58 58N	3 18W
Stronsay	**33**	59 8N	2 38W
Stroud	**24**	51 44N	2 12W
Strumica	**53**	41 28N	22 41 E
Stuart L.	**154**	54 30N	124 30W
Stung Treng	**95**	13 31N	105 58 E
Sturgeon Bay	**167**	44 52N	87 20W
Sturgeon Falls	**151**	46 25N	79 57W
Stuttgart, Germany	**42**	48 46N	9 10 E
Stuttgart, U.S.A.	**168**	34 30N	91 33W
Styria = Steiermark □	**45**	47 26N	15 0 E
Suakin	**129**	19 8N	37 20 E
Subotica	**52**	46 6N	19 49 E
Suchitoto	**177**	13 56N	89 0W
Suchou = Suzhou	**99**	31 19N	120 38 E
Süchow = Xuzhou	**99**	34 18N	117 10 E
Sucre	**187**	19 0S	65 15W
Sudan ■	**129**	15 0N	30 0 E
Sudbury, Canada	**151**	46 30N	81 0W
Sudbury, U.K.	**25**	52 2N	0 44 E
Sudetan Mts. = Sudety	**58**	50 20N	16 45 E
Sudety	**58**	50 20N	16 45 E
Suez = El Suweis	**128**	29 58N	32 31 E
Suez Canal = Suweis, Qanâl es	**128**	31 0N	32 20 E
Suffolk	**165**	36 47N	76 33W
Suffolk □	**25**	52 16N	1 0 E
Sugluk = Saglouc	**146**	62 14N	75 38W
Suhbaatar	**98**	50 17N	106 10 E
Suir →	**35**	52 15N	7 10W
Suita	**106**	34 45N	135 32 E
Sukhona →	**68**	60 30N	45 0 E
Sukhumi	**70**	43 0N	41 0 E
Sukkertoppen	**147**	65 26N	52 55W
Sukkur	**88**	27 42N	68 54 E
Sukkur Barrage	**88**	27 40N	68 50 E
Sukumo	**109**	32 56N	132 44 E
Sulaiman Range	**89**	30 30N	69 50 E
Sulawesi □	**113**	2 0S	120 0 E
Sulina	**57**	45 10N	29 40 E
Sulitjelma	**66**	67 9N	16 3 E
Sullana	**186**	4 52S	80 39W
Sullivan	**167**	39 5N	87 26W
Sullivan I. = Lambi Kyun	**96**	10 50N	98 20 E
Sulphur Springs	**168**	33 5N	95 36W
Sulu Arch.	**112**	6 0N	121 0 E
Sulu Sea	**112**	8 0N	120 0 E
Suluq	**128**	31 44N	20 14 E
Sumatera □	**111**	0 40N	100 20 E
Sumatra = Sumatera □	**111**	0 40N	100 20 E
Sumba	**113**	9 45S	119 35 E
Sumbawa	**113**	8 26S	117 30 E
Sumburgh Hd.	**30**	59 52N	1 17W
Summerland	**155**	49 32N	119 41W
Summerside	**148**	46 24N	63 47W
Sumoto	**109**	34 21N	134 54 E
Sumter	**165**	33 55N	80 22W
Sumy	**68**	50 57N	34 50 E
Sunbury, Australia	**117**	37 35S	144 44 E
Sunbury, U.S.A.	**164**	40 50N	76 46W
Sunda, Selat	**111**	6 20S	105 30 E
Sundarbans, The	**92**	22 0N	89 0 E
Sunderland	**28**	54 54N	1 22W
Sundsvall	**66**	62 23N	17 17 E
Sungei Patani	**96**	5 38N	100 29 E
Sungei Siput	**96**	4 51N	101 6 E
Sungurlu	**80**	40 12N	34 21 E
Sunnyside	**171**	46 24N	120 2W
Sunnyvale	**172**	37 23N	122 2W
Suntar	**74**	62 15N	117 30 E
Suō-Nada	**108**	33 50N	131 30 E
Superior	**150**	46 45N	92 5W
Superior, L.	**150**	47 40N	87 0W
Suphan Dağı	**81**	38 54N	42 48 E
Sūr	**80**	22 34N	59 32 E
Surabaja = Surabaya	**111**	7 17S	112 45 E
Surabaya	**111**	7 17S	112 45 E
Surakarta	**111**	7 35S	110 48 E
Surat	**91**	21 12N	72 55 E
Surat Thani	**96**	9 6N	99 20 E
Suratgarh	**89**	29 18N	73 55 E
Surgut	**69**	61 14N	73 20 E
Surin	**95**	14 50N	103 34 E
Surinam ■	**185**	4 0N	56 0W
Surrey □	**25**	51 16N	0 30W
Surt	**127**	31 11N	16 39 E
Surt, Khalīj	**127**	31 40N	18 30 E
Suruga-Wan	**107**	34 45N	138 30 E
Susaki	**109**	33 22N	133 17 E
Susanville	**172**	40 28N	120 40W
Susquehanna →	**164**	39 33N	76 5W
Sutherland Falls	**123**	44 48S	167 46 E
Sutlej →	**89**	29 23N	71 3 E
Sutton-in-Ashfield	**29**	53 7N	1 20W
Suva	**122**	18 6S	178 30 E
Suwa	**107**	36 2N	138 8 E
Suwa-Ko	**107**	36 3N	138 5 E
Suwannee →	**170**	29 18N	83 9W
Suwanose-Jima	**104**	29 38N	129 43 E
Suweis, Qanâl es	**128**	31 0N	32 20 E
Suzaka	**107**	36 39N	138 19 E
Suzhou	**99**	31 19N	120 38 E
Suzu-Misaki	**105**	37 31N	137 21 E
Svalbard	**13**	78 0N	17 0 E
Svartenhuk Halvø	**146**	71 50N	54 30W
Svendborg	**61**	55 4N	10 35 E
Sverdlovsk = Yekaterinburg	**69**	56 50N	60 30 E
Sverdrup Is.	**12**	79 0N	97 0W

Name	Page	Lat.	Long.
Svishtov	**53**	43 36N	25 23 E
Svobodnyy	**75**	51 20N	128 0 E
Swabian Alps = Schwäbische Alb	**42**	48 30N	9 30 E
Swakopmund	**136**	22 37S	14 30 E
Swale →	**28**	54 5N	1 20W
Swan Hill	**117**	35 20S	143 33 E
Swan Hills	**155**	54 42N	115 24W
Swan Islands	**178**	17 22N	83 57W
Swan River	**152**	52 10N	101 16W
Swanage	**24**	50 36N	1 59W
Swansea	**27**	51 37N	3 57W
Swartberge	**136**	33 20S	22 0 E
Swatow = Shantou	**99**	23 18N	116 40 E
Swaziland ■	**137**	26 30S	31 30 E
Sweden ■	**66**	57 0N	15 0 E
Sweetwater	**161**	32 30N	100 28W
Swift Current	**152**	50 20N	107 45W
Swindon	**24**	51 33N	1 47W
Switzerland ■	**44**	46 30N	8 0 E
Swords	**34**	53 27N	6 15W
Sydney, Australia	**117**	33 53S	151 10 E
Sydney, Canada	**149**	46 7N	60 7W
Sydney Mines	**149**	46 18N	60 15W
Sydprøven	**147**	60 30N	45 35W
Sydra G. of = Surt, Khalīj	**127**	31 40N	18 30 E
Syktyvkar	**69**	61 45N	50 40 E
Sylacauga	**169**	33 10N	86 15W
Sylhet	**92**	24 54N	91 52 E
Sylvan Lake	**155**	52 20N	114 3W
Syracuse	**164**	43 4N	76 11W
Syrdarya →	**71**	46 3N	61 0 E
Syria ■	**80**	35 0N	38 0 E
Syrian Desert	**76**	31 0N	40 0 E
Syzran	**68**	53 12N	48 30 E
Szczecin	**58**	53 27N	14 27 E
Szechwan = Sichuan □	**99**	31 0N	104 0 E
Szeged	**59**	46 16N	20 10 E
Székesfehérvár	**59**	47 15N	18 25 E
Szolnok	**59**	47 10N	20 15 E
Szombathely	**59**	47 14N	16 38 E

T

Name	Page	Lat.	Long.
Tabacal	**190**	23 15S	64 15W
Ţābah	**82**	26 55N	42 38 E
Tabasco □	**177**	18 0N	92 40W
Taber	**155**	49 47N	112 8W
Tablas	**112**	12 25N	122 2 E
Table Mt.	**136**	34 0S	18 22 E
Table Top, Mt.	**121**	23 24S	147 11 E
Tabora	**135**	5 2S	32 50 E
Tabrīz	**81**	38 7N	46 20 E
Tabūk	**82**	28 23N	36 36 E
Tachibana-Wan	**108**	32 45N	130 7 E
Tachikawa	**107**	35 42N	139 25 E
Tacna	**187**	18 0S	70 20W
Tacoma	**171**	47 15N	122 30W
Tacuarembó	**191**	31 45S	56 0W
Tademaït, Plateau du	**127**	28 30N	2 30 E
Tadoussac	**148**	48 11N	69 42W
Taegu	**98**	35 50N	128 37 E
Taejŏn	**98**	36 20N	127 28 E
Taganrog	**68**	47 12N	38 50 E
Tagish	**144**	60 19N	134 16W
Tagua, La	**184**	0 3N	74 40W
Tagus = Tajo →	**50**	38 40N	9 24W
Tahiti	**123**	17 37S	149 27W
Tahoua	**131**	14 57N	5 16 E
Taibei	**99**	25 4N	121 29 E
T'aichung = Taizhong	**99**	24 12N	120 35 E
Taidong	**99**	22 43N	121 9 E
Taihape	**122**	39 41S	175 48 E
Tailem Bend	**119**	35 12S	139 29 E
Taimyr = Taymyr, Poluostrov	**72**	75 0N	100 0 E
Tain	**33**	57 49N	4 4W
Tainan	**99**	23 17N	120 18 E
Taínaron, Ákra	**54**	36 22N	22 27 E
T'aipei = Taibei	**99**	25 4N	121 29 E
Taiping	**96**	4 51N	100 44 E
Taisha	**109**	35 24N	132 40 E
Taitao, Pen. de	**192**	46 30S	75 0W
Taiwan ■	**99**	23 30N	121 0 E
Taiyuan	**98**	37 52N	112 33 E
Taizhong	**99**	24 12N	120 35 E
Ta'izz	**83**	13 35N	44 2 E
Tajikistan ■	**71**	35 30N	70 0 E
Tajimi	**106**	35 19N	137 8 E
Tajo →	**50**	38 40N	9 24W
Tak	**94**	16 52N	99 8 E
Takachiho	**108**	32 42N	131 18 E
Takada	**105**	37 7N	138 15 E
Takahashi	**109**	34 51N	133 39 E
Takamatsu	**109**	34 20N	134 5 E
Takaoka	**106**	36 47N	137 0 E
Takapuna	**122**	36 47S	174 47 E
Takasago	**109**	34 45N	134 48 E
Takasaki	**107**	36 20N	139 0 E
Takatsuki	**106**	34 51N	135 37 E
Takawa	**108**	33 38N	130 51 E
Takayama	**106**	36 18N	137 11 E
Takayama-Bonchi	**106**	36 0N	137 18 E
Takefu	**106**	35 50N	136 10 E
Takehara	**109**	34 21N	132 55 E
Taketa	**108**	32 58N	131 24 E
Takhār □	**87**	36 40N	70 0 E
Takla Landing	**154**	55 30N	125 50W
Takla Makan	**76**	39 0N	83 0 E
Taku	**108**	33 18N	130 3 E
Talara	**186**	4 38S	81 18 E
Talaud, Kepulauan	**113**	4 30N	127 10 E
Talca	**190**	35 28S	71 40W
Talcahuano	**190**	36 40S	73 10W
Ţalesh, Kūhhā-ye	**81**	39 0N	48 30 E
Talguppa	**90**	14 10N	74 45 E
Taliabu	**113**	1 45S	125 0 E
Talkeetna	**142**	62 20N	150 9W
Tall 'Afar	**81**	36 22N	42 27 E
Talladega	**169**	33 28N	86 2W
Tallahassee	**170**	30 25N	84 15W
Tallangatta	**117**	36 15S	147 19 E
Tallinn	**68**	59 22N	24 48 E
Tallulah	**168**	32 25N	91 12W
Tamale	**130**	9 22N	0 50W
Tamana	**108**	32 58N	130 32 E
Tamano	**109**	34 29N	133 59 E
Tamanrasset	**127**	22 50N	5 30 E
Tamar →	**27**	50 33N	4 15W
Tamaulipas □	**176**	24 0N	98 45W
Tambellup	**120**	34 4S	117 37 E
Tambov	**68**	52 45N	41 28 E
Tamgak, Mts.	**127**	19 12N	8 35 E
Tamil Nadu □	**90**	11 0N	77 0 E
Tammerfors = Tampere	**67**	61 30N	23 50 E
Tamo Abu, Pegunungan	**111**	3 10N	115 0 E
Tampa	**170**	27 57N	82 38W
Tampa B.	**170**	27 40N	82 40W
Tampere	**67**	61 30N	23 50 E
Tampico	**177**	22 20N	97 50W
Tamrah	**83**	20 24N	45 25 E
Tamsagbulag	**98**	47 14N	117 21 E
Tamworth, Australia	**116**	31 7S	150 58 E
Tamworth, U.K.	**24**	52 38N	1 41W
Tana →, Kenya	**133**	2 32S	40 31 E
Tana →, Norway	**67**	70 30N	28 23 E
Tana, L.	**132**	13 5N	37 30 E
Tanabe	**106**	33 44N	135 22 E
Tanana	**142**	65 10N	152 15W
Tananarive = Antananarivo	**137**	18 55S	47 31 E
Tanba-Sanchi	**106**	35 7N	135 48 E
Tandil	**190**	37 15S	59 6W
Tando Adam	**88**	25 45N	68 40 E
Tane-ga-Shima	**104**	30 30N	131 0 E
Tanen Tong Dan	**93**	16 30N	98 30 E
Tanezrouft	**127**	23 9N	0 11 E
Tanga	**135**	5 5S	39 2 E
Tanganyika, L.	**135**	6 40S	30 0 E
Tanger	**126**	35 50N	5 49W
Tanggula Shan	**101**	32 40N	92 10 E

Place	Page	Latitude	Longitude
Tangier = Tanger	**126**	35 50N	5 49W
Tangshan	**98**	39 38N	118 10 E
Tanimbar, Kepulauan	**113**	7 30S	131 30 E
Taniyama	**108**	31 31N	130 31 E
Tanjore = Thanjavur	**90**	10 48N	79 12 E
Tannu Ola	**74**	51 0N	94 0 E
Tanout	**131**	14 50N	8 55 E
Tanta	**128**	30 45N	30 57 E
Tantung = Dandong	**98**	40 10N	124 20 E
Tanunda	**119**	34 30S	139 0 E
Tanzania ■	**135**	6 40S	34 0 E
Tapa Shan = Daba Shan	**99**	32 0N	109 0 E
Tapachula	**177**	14 54N	92 17W
Tapajós →	**185**	2 24S	54 41W
Tapanui	**123**	45 56S	169 18 E
Tapi →	**91**	21 8N	72 41 E
Tara →	**71**	56 42N	74 36 E
Tarabagatay, Khrebet	**71**	48 0N	83 0 E
Tarābulus, Lebanon	**80**	34 31N	35 50 E
Tarābulus, Libya	**127**	32 49N	13 7 E
Taranaki □	**122**	39 5S	174 51 E
Táranto	**49**	40 30N	17 11 E
Táranto, G. di	**49**	40 0N	17 15 E
Tarapoto	**186**	6 30S	76 20W
Tarare	**37**	45 54N	4 26 E
Tararua Range	**123**	40 45S	175 25 E
Tarauacá	**187**	8 6S	70 48W
Tarbela Dam	**89**	34 8N	72 52 E
Tarbert	**32**	57 54N	6 49W
Tarbes	**36**	43 15N	0 3 E
Tarcoola	**118**	30 44S	134 36 E
Taree	**116**	31 50S	152 30 E
Tarfaya	**126**	27 55N	12 55W
Tarifa	**50**	36 1N	5 36W
Tarija	**187**	21 30S	64 40W
Tarim →	**100**	41 5N	86 40 E
Tarim Pendi	**100**	40 0N	84 0 E
Tarko Sale	**69**	64 55N	77 50 E
Tarn →	**36**	44 5N	1 6 E
Tarnobrzeg	**58**	50 35N	21 41 E
Tarnów	**58**	50 3N	21 0 E
Tarragona	**51**	41 5N	1 17 E
Tarrasa	**51**	41 34N	2 1 E
Tarsus	**80**	36 58N	34 55 E
Tartagal	**190**	22 30S	63 50W
Tarṭūs	**80**	34 55N	35 55 E
Tarumizu	**108**	31 29N	130 42 E
Tarutao, Ko	**96**	6 33N	99 40 E
Taschereau	**151**	48 40N	78 40W
Tashi Chho Dzong = Thimphu	**92**	27 31N	89 45 E
Tashkent	**71**	41 20N	69 10 E
Tasman B.	**123**	40 59S	173 25 E
Tasman Mts.	**123**	41 3S	172 25 E
Tasman Sea	**122**	36 0S	160 0 E
Tasmania □	**119**	42 0S	146 30 E
Tatabánya	**59**	47 32N	18 25 E
Tatarsk	**71**	55 14N	76 0 E
Tateshina-Yama	**107**	36 8N	138 11 E
Tateyama	**107**	35 0N	139 50 E
Tatra = Tatry	**59**	49 20N	20 0 E
Tatry	**59**	49 20N	20 0 E
Tatsuno	**109**	34 52N	134 33 E
Tat'ung = Datong	**98**	40 6N	113 18 E
Taubaté	**191**	23 0S	45 36W
Tauern	**45**	47 15N	12 40 E
Taumarunui	**122**	38 53S	175 15 E
Taunggyi	**93**	20 50N	97 0 E
Taungup Taunggya	**93**	18 20N	93 40 E
Taunton, U.K.	**27**	51 1N	3 7W
Taunton, U.S.A.	**164**	41 54N	71 6W
Taunus	**42**	50 15N	8 20 E
Taupo	**122**	38 41S	176 7 E
Taupo, L.	**122**	38 46S	175 55 E
Tauranga	**122**	37 42S	176 11 E
Taurus Mts. = Toros Daglari	**80**	37 0N	35 0 E
Taverny	**39**	49 2N	2 13 E
Tavistock	**27**	50 33N	4 9W
Tavoy	**94**	14 2N	98 12 E
Tawas City	**167**	44 16N	83 31W
Tay →	**33**	56 37N	3 38W
Tayabamba	**186**	8 15S	77 16W
Taylor Mt.	**161**	35 16N	107 36W
Taymā	**82**	27 35N	38 45 E
Taymyr, Poluostrov	**72**	75 0N	100 0 E
Tayshet	**74**	55 58N	98 1 E
Tayside □	**31**	56 25N	3 30W
Taz →	**69**	67 32N	78 40 E
Tbilisi	**70**	41 43N	44 50 E
Tchad = Chad ■	**131**	15 0N	17 15 E
Tchad, L.	**131**	13 30N	14 30 E
Tch'eng-tou = Chengdu	**99**	30 38N	104 2 E
Tch'ong-k'ing = Chongqing	**99**	29 35N	106 25 E
Te Anau, L.	**123**	45 15S	167 45 E
Te Kuiti	**122**	38 20S	175 11 E
Tecuala	**175**	22 23N	105 27W
Tefé	**185**	3 25S	64 50W
Tegal	**111**	6 52S	109 8 E
Tegucigalpa	**179**	14 5N	87 14W
Tehachapi Mts.	**173**	35 0N	118 40W
Tehrān	**86**	35 44N	51 30 E
Tehuacán	**177**	18 27N	97 23W
Tehuantepec	**177**	16 21N	95 13W
Tehuantepec, G. de	**177**	16 0N	94 50W
Tehuantepec, Istmo de	**177**	17 0N	94 30W
Teifi →	**26**	52 4N	4 14W
Teignmouth	**27**	50 33N	3 30W
Tejo →	**50**	38 40N	9 24W
Tekax	**177**	20 12N	89 17W
Tekeli	**71**	44 50N	79 0 E
Tekirdağ	**80**	40 58N	27 30 E
Tel Aviv-Yafo	**80**	32 4N	34 48 E
Tela	**179**	15 40N	87 28W
Telanaipura = Jambi	**111**	1 38S	103 30 E
Telegraph Cr. →	**144**	58 0N	131 10W
Telemark fylke □	**60**	59 25N	8 30 E
Teles Pires →	**187**	7 21S	58 3W
Telford	**28**	52 42N	2 31W
Tell City	**167**	38 0N	86 44W
Teme →	**24**	52 23N	2 15W
Temerloh	**96**	3 27N	102 25 E
Temirtau	**71**	50 5N	72 56 E
Temora	**117**	34 30S	147 30 E
Temosachic	**174**	28 57N	107 51W
Temple	**158**	31 5N	97 22W
Temuco	**190**	38 45S	72 40W
Temuka	**123**	44 14S	171 17 E
Tenali	**91**	16 15N	80 35 E
Tenancingo	**177**	19 0N	99 33W
Tenango	**177**	19 7N	99 33W
Tenby	**27**	51 40N	4 42W
Tenerife	**126**	28 15N	16 35W
Teng Xian	**99**	35 5N	117 10 E
Tennessee □	**169**	36 0N	86 30W
Tennessee →	**169**	37 4N	88 34W
Tenri	**106**	34 39N	135 49 E
Tenryū	**107**	34 52N	137 49 E
Tenryū-Gawa →	**107**	35 39N	137 48 E
Tenterfield	**116**	29 0S	152 0 E
Teófilo Otoni	**189**	17 50S	41 30W
Tepic	**175**	21 30N	104 54W
Terang	**119**	38 15S	142 55 E
Terek →	**70**	44 0N	47 30 E
Terengganu □	**96**	4 55N	103 0 E
Teresina	**188**	5 9S	42 45W
Terewah, L.	**116**	29 52S	147 35 E
Termez	**70**	37 15N	67 15 E
Términos, L. de	**177**	18 37N	91 33W
Terneuzen	**40**	51 20N	3 50 E
Terni	**46**	42 34N	12 38 E
Terrace	**154**	54 30N	128 35W
Terre Haute	**167**	39 28N	87 24W
Terrell	**168**	32 44N	96 19W
Terschelling	**40**	53 25N	5 20 E
Teruel	**51**	40 22N	1 8W
Teshio	**103**	44 53N	141 44 E
Teslin	**144**	60 10N	132 43W
Test →	**24**	51 7N	1 30W
Tete	**137**	16 13S	33 33 E
Teteven	**53**	42 58N	24 17 E
Tétouan	**126**	35 35N	5 21W
Tetuán = Tétouan	**126**	35 35N	5 21W

Name	Page	Lat	Long
Teuco →	190	25 35S	60 11W
Teutoburger Wald	42	52 5N	8 20 E
Tevere →	46	41 44N	12 14 E
Tewkesbury	24	51 59N	2 8W
Texarkana, Ark., U.S.A.	168	33 25N	94 0W
Texarkana, Tex., U.S.A.	168	33 25N	94 3W
Texas □	161	31 40N	98 30W
Texel	40	53 5N	4 50 E
Teziutlán	177	19 49N	97 21W
Tezpur	93	26 40N	92 45 E
Thabana Ntlenyana	137	29 30S	29 16 E
Thailand ■	95	16 0N	102 0 E
Thailand, G. of	95	11 30N	101 0 E
Thal Desert	89	31 10N	71 30 E
Thame →	24	51 35N	1 8W
Thames	122	37 7S	175 34 E
Thames →	25	51 30N	0 35 E
Thane	91	19 12N	72 59 E
Thanh Hoa	95	19 48N	105 46 E
Thanh Pho Ho Chi Minh	95	10 58N	106 40 E
Thanjavur	90	10 48N	79 12 E
Thar Desert	89	28 0N	72 0 E
Thásos	55	40 40N	24 40 E
Thaungdut	93	24 30N	94 40 E
Thazi	93	21 0N	96 5 E
The Dalles	171	45 40N	121 11W
The Grenadines, Is.	180	12 40N	61 20W
The Hague = 's-Gravenhage	40	52 7N	4 17 E
The Macumba →	118	27 52S	137 12 E
The Neales →	118	28 8S	136 47 E
The Pas	152	53 45N	101 15W
The Rock	117	35 15S	147 2 E
The Warburton →	118	28 4S	137 28 E
Thebes = Thívai	55	38 19N	23 19 E
Thermaïkos Kólpos	54	40 15N	22 45 E
Thermopolis	163	43 35N	108 10W
Thessalía □	54	39 30N	22 0 E
Thessalon	150	46 20N	83 30W
Thessaloníki	54	40 38N	22 58 E
Thessaly = Thessalía □	54	39 30N	22 0 E
Thetford Mines	148	46 8N	71 18W
Thicket Portage	153	55 19N	97 42W
Thies	130	14 50N	16 51W
Thimphu	92	27 31N	89 45 E
Thionville	37	49 20N	6 10 E
Thíra	55	36 23N	25 27 E
Thirsk	29	54 15N	1 20W
Thisted	61	56 58N	8 40 E
Thívai	55	38 19N	23 19 E
Thomaston	170	32 54N	84 20W
Thomasville, Ga., U.S.A.	170	30 50N	84 0W
Thomasville, N.C., U.S.A.	165	35 55N	80 4W
Thon Buri	94	13 43N	100 29 E
Thornaby on Tees	29	54 36N	1 19W
Thrace = Thráki □	55	41 9N	25 30 E
Thráki □	55	41 9N	25 30 E
Three Hills	155	51 43N	113 15W
Three Hummock I.	119	40 25S	144 55 E
Thule	13	77 40N	69 0W
Thundelarra	120	28 53S	117 7 E
Thunder B.	150	45 0N	83 20W
Thunder Bay	150	48 20N	89 15W
Thüringer Wald	43	50 35N	11 0 E
Thurles	35	52 40N	7 53W
Thursday I.	115	10 30S	142 3 E
Thurso	33	58 34N	3 31W
Tian Shan	100	43 0N	84 0 E
Tianjin	98	39 8N	117 10 E
Tianshui	99	34 32N	105 40 E
Tiber = Tevere →	46	41 44N	12 14 E
Tibesti	127	21 0N	17 30 E
Tibet = Xizang □	101	32 0N	88 0 E
Tibooburra	118	29 26S	142 1 E
Ticul	177	20 24N	89 32W
Tiel	40	51 53N	5 26 E
Tien Shan	76	42 0N	80 0 E
Tien-tsin = Tianjin	98	39 8N	117 10 E
T'ienching = Tianjin	98	39 8N	117 10 E
Tientsin = Tianjin	98	39 8N	117 10 E
Tierra de Campos	50	42 10N	4 50W
Tierra del Fuego □	192	54 0S	67 45W
Tiffin	167	41 8N	83 10W
Tiflis = Tbilisi	70	41 43N	44 50 E
Tifton	170	31 28N	83 32W
Tignish	148	46 58N	64 2W
Tigris = Dijlah, Nahr →	81	31 0N	47 25 E
Tijuana	174	32 32N	117 1W
Tiksi	72	71 40N	128 45 E
Tilburg	40	51 31N	5 6 E
Tilbury	25	51 27N	0 24 E
Tillsonburg	151	42 53N	80 44W
Tílos	55	36 27N	27 27 E
Timaru	123	44 23S	171 14 E
Timbuktu = Tombouctou	130	16 50N	3 0W
Timişoara	56	45 43N	21 15 E
Timmins	151	48 28N	81 25W
Timor	113	9 0S	125 0 E
Timor Sea	113	10 0S	127 0 E
Tinaca Pt.	112	5 30N	125 25 E
Tindouf	126	27 42N	8 10W
Tinnevelly = Tirunelveli	90	8 45N	77 45 E
Tinogasta	190	28 5S	67 32W
Tínos	55	37 33N	25 8 E
Tioman, Pulau	96	2 50N	104 10 E
Tipperary	35	52 28N	8 10W
Tipperary □	35	52 37N	7 55W
Tipton	24	52 32N	2 4W
Tirana	52	41 18N	19 49 E
Tiraspol	68	46 55N	29 35 E
Tire	80	38 5N	27 50 E
Tirebolu	81	40 58N	38 45 E
Tiree	30	56 31N	6 55W
Tîrgu Mureş	57	46 31N	24 38 E
Tirol □	45	47 3N	10 43 E
Tiruchchirappalli	90	10 45N	78 45 E
Tirunelveli	90	8 45N	77 45 E
Tisa →	59	45 15N	20 17 E
Tisdale	152	52 50N	104 0W
Titicaca, L.	187	15 30S	69 30W
Titograd = Podgorica	52	42 30N	19 19 E
Titov Veles	53	41 46N	21 47 E
Titovo Užice	52	43 55N	19 50 E
Tiverton	27	50 54N	3 30W
Tívoli	46	41 58N	12 45 E
Tizimín	177	21 9N	88 9W
Tjirebon = Cirebon	111	6 45S	108 32 E
Tlaxcala □	177	19 25N	98 10W
Tlaxiaco	177	17 18N	97 40W
Tlemcen	127	34 52N	1 21W
To-Shima	107	34 31N	139 17 E
Toamasina	137	18 10S	49 25 E
Toba Kakar	88	31 30N	69 0 E
Tobago	180	11 10N	60 30W
Tobermory	30	56 37N	6 4W
Tobolsk	69	58 15N	68 10 E
Tobruk = Tubruq	128	32 7N	23 55 E
Tocantins →	188	1 45S	49 10W
Toccoa	165	34 32N	83 17W
Tochigi	107	36 25N	139 45 E
Tocopilla	190	22 5S	70 10W
Todos Santos	175	23 27N	110 13W
Tōgane	107	35 33N	140 22 E
Togliatti	68	53 32N	49 24 E
Togo ■	130	6 15N	1 35 E
Tōhoku □	103	39 50N	141 45 E
Tōjō	109	34 53N	133 16 E
Tokai	106	35 2N	136 55 E
Tokaj	58	48 8N	21 27 E
Tokara Kaikyō	104	30 0N	130 0 E
Tokat	80	40 22N	36 35 E
Tokelau Is.	123	9 0S	171 45W
Toki	106	35 18N	137 8 E
Tokoname	106	34 53N	136 51 E
Tokorozawa	107	35 47N	139 28 E
Tokushima	109	34 4N	134 34 E
Tokuyama	108	34 3N	131 50 E
Tōkyō	107	35 45N	139 45 E
Tōkyō-Wan	107	35 25N	139 47 E
Tolbukhin = Dobrich	53	43 37N	27 49 E
Toledo, Spain	50	39 50N	4 2W
Toledo, U.S.A.	167	41 37N	83 33W
Tolga	127	34 40N	5 22 E

Tolima, Vol.	184	4	40N	75	19W
Toluca	177	19	20N	99	40W
Tomakomai	103	42	38N	141	36 E
Tombigbee →	169	31	4N	87	58W
Tombouctou	130	16	50N	3	0W
Tomini, Teluk	113	0	10S	122	0 E
Tomsk	71	56	30N	85	5 E
Tonalá	177	16	4N	93	45W
Tonantins	184	2	45S	67	45W
Tonbridge	25	51	12N	0	18 E
Tong Xian	98	39	55N	116	35 E
Tonga ■	123	19	50S	174	30W
Tongchuan	99	35	6N	109	3 E
Tonghua	98	41	42N	125	58 E
Tongking, G. of	95	20	0N	108	0 E
Tongue	33	58	29N	4	25W
Tonk	91	26	6N	75	54 E
Tonkin = Bac Phan	95	22	0N	105	0 E
Tonlé Sap	95	13	0N	104	0 E
Tonopah	172	38	4N	117	12W
Tonoshō	109	34	29N	134	11 E
Tooele	162	40	30N	112	20W
Toowoomba	116	27	32S	151	56 E
Topeka	166	39	3N	95	40W
Toppenish	171	46	27N	120	16W
Torbay	27	50	26N	3	31W
Torino	46	45	4N	7	40 E
Tormes →	50	41	18N	6	29W
Torne älv →	67	65	50N	24	12 E
Torneå = Tornio	67	65	50N	24	12 E
Torneträsk	66	68	24N	19	15 E
Tornio	67	65	50N	24	12 E
Toro, Cerro del	190	29	10S	69	50W
Toronto, Australia	117	33	0S	151	30 E
Toronto, Canada	151	43	39N	79	20W
Toros Daglari	80	37	0N	35	0 E
Torquay	27	50	27N	3	31W
Torre Annunziata	49	40	45N	14	26 E
Tôrre de Moncorvo	50	41	12N	7	8W
Torremolinos	50	36	38N	4	30W
Torrens, L.	119	31	0S	137	50 E
Torreón	174	25	33N	103	26W
Torres Vedras	50	39	5N	9	15W
Torridge →	27	50	51N	4	10W
Torrington	164	41	50N	73	9W
Tortosa	51	40	49N	0	31 E
Tortosa, C.	51	40	41N	0	52 E
Toruń	58	53	0N	18	39 E
Tory I.	34	55	17N	8	12W
Tosa-Shimizu	109	32	52N	132	58 E
Tosa-Wan	109	33	15N	133	30 E
Toscana	46	43	30N	11	5 E
Tostado	190	29	15S	61	50W
Tosu	109	33	22N	130	31 E
Totnes	27	50	26N	3	41W
Totonicapán	177	14	58N	91	12W
Tottori	109	35	30N	134	15 E
Toubkal, Djebel	126	31	0N	8	0W
Touggourt	127	33	6N	6	4 E
Toulon	37	43	10N	5	55 E
Toulouse	36	43	37N	1	27 E
Toungoo	93	19	0N	96	30 E
Touraine	36	47	20N	0	30 E
Tourane = Da Nang	95	16	4N	108	13 E
Tourcoing	38	50	42N	3	10 E
Tournai	42	50	35N	3	25 E
Tours	36	47	22N	0	40 E
Townsville	121	19	15S	146	45 E
Towson	164	39	26N	76	34W
Toyama	106	36	40N	137	15 E
Toyama-Wan	105	37	0N	137	30 E
Toyohashi	106	34	45N	137	25 E
Toyokawa	106	34	48N	137	27 E
Toyonaka	106	34	50N	135	28 E
Toyooka	109	35	35N	134	48 E
Toyota	106	35	3N	137	7 E
Tozeur	127	33	56N	8	8 E
Trabzon	81	41	0N	39	45 E
Tracy	172	37	46N	121	27W
Trafalgar, C.	50	36	10N	6	2W
Trail	155	49	5N	117	40W
Tralee	35	52	16N	9	42W
Tralee B.	35	52	17N	9	55W
Tran Ninh, Cao Nguyen	95	19	30N	103	10 E
Trangan	113	6	40S	134	20 E
Trangie	116	32	4S	148	0 E
Transantarctic Mts.	15	85	0S	170	0W
Transcona	153	49	55N	97	0W
Transilvania	57	46	19N	25	0 E
Transkei	137	32	15S	28	15 E
Transvaal □	137	25	0S	29	0 E
Transylvania = Transilvania .	57	46	19N	25	0 E
Transylvanian Alps	17	45	30N	25	0 E
Trápani	48	38	1N	12	30 E
Traralgon	117	38	12S	146	34 E
Trasimeno, L.	46	43	10N	12	5 E
Travers, Mt.	123	42	1S	172	45 E
Traverse City	167	44	45N	85	39W
Travnik	52	44	17N	17	39 E
Tredegar	27	51	47N	3	16W
Tregaron	26	52	14N	3	56W
Treinta y Tres	191	33	16S	54	17W
Trelew	192	43	10S	65	20W
Trenque Lauquen	190	36	5S	62	45W
Trent →	29	53	33N	0	44W
Trentino-Alto Adige □	47	46	30N	11	0 E
Trento	47	46	5N	11	8 E
Trenton, Canada	151	44	10N	77	34W
Trenton, Mo., U.S.A.	166	40	5N	93	37W
Trenton, N.J., U.S.A.	164	40	15N	74	41W
Tréport, Le	38	50	3N	1	20 E
Tres Arroyos	190	38	26S	60	20W
Três Lagoas	188	20	50S	51	43W
Tres Montes, C.	192	46	50S	75	30W
Tres Puntas, C.	192	47	0S	66	0W
Treviso	47	45	40N	12	15 E
Trichinopoly = Tiruchchirappalli	90	10	45N	78	45 E
Trichur	90	10	30N	76	18 E
Trier	42	49	45N	6	37 E
Trieste	47	45	39N	13	45 E
Trikkala	54	39	34N	21	47 E
Trincomalee	90	8	38N	81	15 E
Trinidad, Bolivia	187	14	46S	64	50W
Trinidad, Colombia	184	5	25N	71	40W
Trinidad, Cuba	178	21	48N	80	0W
Trinidad, Uruguay	191	33	30S	56	50W
Trinidad, U.S.A.	163	37	15N	104	30W
Trinidad & Tobago ■	180	10	30N	61	20W
Trinity →	168	30	30N	95	0W
Trinity Mts.	172	40	20N	118	50W
Tripoli = Tarābulus, Lebanon	80	34	31N	35	50 E
Tripoli = Tarābulus, Libya	127	32	49N	13	7 E
Tripolis	54	37	31N	22	25 E
Tripura □	93	24	0N	92	0 E
Trivandrum	90	8	41N	77	0 E
Trois-Riviéres	151	46	25N	72	34W
Troitsk	71	54	10N	61	35 E
Trollhättan	60	58	17N	12	20 E
Tromsø	66	69	40N	18	56 E
Trondheim	65	63	36N	10	25 E
Trossachs, The	31	56	14N	4	24W
Trotternish	32	57	32N	6	15W
Trouville	38	49	21N	0	5 E
Trowbridge	24	51	18N	2	12W
Troy, Ala., U.S.A.	169	31	50N	85	58W
Troy, N.Y., U.S.A.	164	42	45N	73	39W
Troyes	39	48	19N	4	3 E
Trucial States = United Arab Emirates ■	85	23	50N	54	0 E
Trujillo, Honduras	179	16	0N	86	0W
Trujillo, Peru	186	8	6S	79	0W
Trujillo, Venezuela	184	9	22N	70	38W
Trundle	117	32	53S	147	35 E
Trung-Phan	95	16	0N	108	0 E
Truro, Canada	149	45	21N	63	14W
Truro, U.K.	27	50	17N	5	2W
Tselinograd	71	51	10N	71	30 E
Tsinan = Jinan	98	36	38N	117	1 E
Tsinghai = Qinghai □	101	36	0N	98	0 E
Tsingtao = Qingdao	98	36	5N	120	20 E
Tsu	106	34	45N	136	25 E

Tsuchiura	107	36 5N	140	15 E
Tsugaru-Kaikyō	103	41 35N	141	0 E
Tsukumi	108	33 4N	131	52 E
Tsukushi-Sanchi	108	33 25N	130	30 E
Tsuruga	106	35 45N	136	2 E
Tsurugi-San	109	33 51N	134	6 E
Tsuruoka	103	38 44N	139	50 E
Tsushima, Gifu, Japan	104	35 10N	136	43 E
Tsushima, Nagasaki, Japan	104	34 20N	129	20 E
Tuamotu Arch.	123	17 0S	144	0W
Tubarão	191	28 30S	49	0W
Tubruq	128	32 7N	23	55 E
Tubuai Is.	123	25 0S	150	0W
Tucacas	184	10 48N	68	19W
Tucson	160	32 14N	110	59W
Tucumcari	161	35 12N	103	45W
Tucupita	185	9 2N	62	3W
Tucuruí	188	3 42S	49	44W
Tudmur	80	34 36N	38	15 E
Tuktoyaktuk	144	69 27N	133	2W
Tula, Mexico	177	23 0N	99	43W
Tula, Russia	68	54 13N	37	38 E
Tulare	173	36 15N	119	26W
Tulcán	184	0 48N	77	43W
Tullahoma	169	35 23N	86	12W
Tullamore	35	53 17N	7	30W
Tully	121	17 56S	145	55 E
Tulsa	168	36 10N	96	0W
Tulua	184	4 6N	76	11W
Tuma →	179	13 6N	84	35W
Tumaco	184	1 50N	78	45W
Tumatumari	185	5 20N	58	55W
Tumbarumba	117	35 44S	148	0 E
Túmbes	186	3 37S	80	27W
Tumkur	90	13 18N	77	6 E
Tummel, L.	33	56 43N	3	55W
Tummo	127	22 45N	14	8 E
Tump	88	26 7N	62	16 E
Tumucumaque, Serra	188	2 0N	55	0W
Tumut	117	35 16S	148	13 E
Tunbridge Wells	25	51 7N	0	16 E
Tundzha →	53	41 40N	26	35 E
Tunis	127	36 50N	10	11 E
Tunisia ■	127	33 30N	9	10 E
Tunja	184	5 33N	73	25W
Tunxi	99	29 42N	118	25 E
Tupelo	169	34 15N	88	42W
Tupiza	187	21 30S	65	40W
Tupper L.	151	44 18N	74	30W
Tuque, La	151	47 30N	72	50W
Túquerres	184	1 5N	77	37W
Tura	92	25 30N	90	16 E
Turayf	82	31 41N	38	39 E
Turfan = Turpan	100	43 58N	89	10 E
Turfan Depression = Turpan Hami	100	42 40N	89	25 E
Türgovishte	53	43 17N	26	38 E
Turgutlu	80	38 30N	27	48 E
Turin = Torino	46	45 4N	7	40 E
Turkana, L.	132	3 30N	36	5 E
Turkestan	71	43 17N	68	16 E
Turkey ■	80	39 0N	36	0 E
Turkmenistan ■	70	39 0N	59	0 E
Turks Is.	180	21 20N	71	20W
Turku	67	60 30N	22	19 E
Turlock	172	37 30N	120	55W
Turnagain, C.	122	40 28S	176	38 E
Turnhout	42	51 19N	4	57 E
Túrnovo	53	43 5N	25	41 E
Turnu Rosu Pasul	57	45 33N	24	17 E
Turnu-Severin	56	44 39N	22	41 E
Turpan	100	43 58N	89	10 E
Turpan Hami	100	42 40N	89	25 E
Turukhansk	74	65 21N	88	5 E
Tuscaloosa	169	33 13N	87	31W
Tuscany = Toscana	46	43 30N	11	5 E
Tuskegee	169	32 24N	85	39W
Tutrakan	53	44 2N	26	40 E
Tuvalu ■	122	8 0S	178	0 E
Tuxpan	177	20 57N	97	24W
Tuxtla Gutiérrez	177	16 45N	93	7W
Tuy Hoa	95	13 5N	109	10 E
Tuyen Hoa	95	17 50N	106	10 E
Tuz Gölü	80	38 45N	33	30 E
Ţūz Khurmātū	81	34 56N	44	38 E
Tuzla	52	44 34N	18	41 E
Tver	68	56 55N	35	55 E
Tweed →	31	55 42N	2	10W
Tweed Heads	116	28 10S	153	31 E
Twin Falls	172	42 30N	114	30W
Two Harbors	156	47 1N	91	40W
Tyler	168	32 18N	95	18W
Tyne →	28	54 58N	1	28W
Tyne & Wear □	28	54 55N	1	35W
Tynemouth	28	55 1N	1	27W
Tyrol = Tirol □	45	47 3N	10	43 E
Tyrrhenian Sea	48	40 0N	12	30 E
Tyumen	69	57 11N	65	29 E
Tzukong = Zigong	99	29 15N	104	48 E

U

Uaupés	184	0 8S	67	5W
Ubangi = Oubangi →	131	1 0N	17	50 E
Ube	108	33 56N	131	15 E
Uberaba	188	19 50S	47	55W
Uberlândia	188	19 0S	48	20W
Ubon Ratchathani	95	15 15N	104	50 E
Ucayali →	186	4 30S	73	30W
Uchi Lake	153	51 5N	92	35W
Uchiura-Wan	103	42 25N	140	40 E
Uchur →	75	58 48N	130	35 E
Udaipur	91	24 36N	73	44 E
Uddevalla	60	58 21N	11	55 E
Udine	47	46 5N	13	10 E
Udmurt Rep. □	69	57 30N	52	30 E
Udon Thani	95	17 29N	102	46 E
Ueda	107	36 24N	138	16 E
Uelen	73	66 10N	170	0W
Uelzen	43	53 0N	10	33 E
Ueno	106	34 45N	136	8 E
Ufa	69	54 45N	55	55 E
Uganda ■	132	2 0N	32	0 E
Uinta Mts.	163	40 45N	110	30W
Uithuizen	41	53 24N	6	41 E
Uji	106	34 53N	135	48 E
Ujjain	91	23 9N	75	43 E
Ujpest	59	47 32N	19	6 E
Ujung Pandang	113	5 10S	119	20 E
Ukiah	172	39 10N	123	9W
Ukraine ■	68	49 0N	32	0 E
Ulaanbaatar	98	47 55N	106	53 E
Ulan Bator = Ulaanbaatar	98	47 55N	106	53 E
Ulan Ude	74	51 45N	107	40 E
Ulcinj	52	41 58N	19	10 E
Ulhasnagar	91	19 15N	73	10 E
Ulladulla	117	35 21S	150	29 E
Ullapool	32	57 54N	5	10W
Ullswater	28	54 35N	2	52W
Ulm	42	48 23N	10	0 E
Ulster □	34	54 35N	6	30W
Ulverston	28	54 13N	3	7W
Ulverstone	119	41 11S	146	11 E
Ulyanovsk = Simbirsk	68	54 20N	48	25 E
Ulyasutay	100	47 56N	97	28 E
Umbrella Mts.	123	45 35S	169	5 E
Umbria □	46	42 53N	12	30 E
Ume älv →	66	63 45N	20	20 E
Umeå	66	63 45N	20	20 E
Umm al Qaywayn	85	25 30N	55	35 E
Umm Lajj	85	25 0N	37	23 E
Umnak	142	53 20N	168	20W
Umpang	94	16 3N	98	54 E
Umtata	137	31 36S	28	49 E
Unalaska	142	53 40N	166	40W
Ungava B.	146	59 30N	67	30W
Ungava Pen.	146	60 0N	74	0W
União da Vitória	191	26 13S	51	5W
Unimak	142	55 0N	164	0W

Place	Page	Lat.	Long.
Union City	**169**	36 25N	89 0W
Uniontown	**164**	39 54N	79 45W
United Arab Emirates ■	**85**	23 50N	54 0 E
United Kingdom ■	**18**	55 0N	3 0W
United States of America ■	**139**	37 0N	96 0W
Unity	**152**	52 30N	109 5W
Unnao	**92**	26 35N	80 30 E
Unst	**30**	60 50N	0 55W
Uozu	**106**	36 48N	137 24 E
Upata	**185**	8 1N	62 24W
Upper Austria = Oberösterreich □	**45**	48 10N	14 0 E
Upper Hutt	**123**	41 8S	175 5 E
Upper Taimyr →	**72**	74 15N	99 48 E
Upper Volta = Burkina Faso ■	**130**	12 0N	1 0W
Uppsala	**60**	59 53N	17 38 E
Uppsala län □	**60**	60 0N	17 30 E
Ur	**84**	30 55N	46 25 E
Uracara	**185**	2 20S	57 50W
Urakawa	**103**	42 9N	142 47 E
Ural →	**70**	47 0N	51 48 E
Ural Mts. = Uralskie Gory	**69**	60 0N	59 0 E
Uralsk	**70**	51 20N	51 20 E
Uralskie Gory	**69**	60 0N	59 0 E
Uranium City	**145**	59 34N	108 37W
Urawa	**107**	35 50N	139 40 E
Urbana, Ill., U.S.A.	**167**	40 7N	88 12W
Urbana, Ohio, U.S.A.	**167**	40 9N	83 44W
Urbana, La	**184**	7 8N	66 56W
Urcos	**187**	13 40S	71 38W
Ures	**174**	29 26N	110 24W
Urfa = Sanliurfa	**81**	37 12N	38 50 E
Urgench	**70**	41 40N	60 41 E
Uribia	**184**	11 43N	72 16W
Urk	**41**	52 39N	5 36 E
Urmia = Orūmīyeh	**81**	37 40N	45 0 E
Urmia, L. = Orūmīyeh, Daryācheh-ye	**81**	37 50N	45 30 E
Uruapan	**175**	19 30N	102 0W
Uruçuí	**188**	7 20S	44 28W
Uruguaiana	**191**	29 50S	57 0W
Uruguay ■	**191**	32 30S	56 30W
Uruguay →	**191**	34 12S	58 18W
Urumchi = Ürümqi	**100**	43 45N	87 45 E
Ürümqi	**100**	43 45N	87 45 E
Urup, Os.	**75**	46 0N	151 0 E
Usa	**108**	33 31N	131 21 E
Uşak	**80**	38 43N	29 28 E
Usfan	**82**	21 58N	39 27 E
Ushant = Ouessant, Île d'	**36**	48 28N	5 6W
Ushibuka	**108**	32 11N	130 1 E
Ushuaia	**192**	54 50S	68 23W
Usk →	**26**	51 37N	2 56W
Üsküdar	**80**	41 0N	29 5 E
Usolye Sibirskoye	**74**	52 48N	103 40 E
Uspenskiy	**71**	48 41N	72 43 E
Ussuriysk	**75**	43 48N	131 59 E
Ust-Aldan = Batamay	**74**	63 30N	129 15 E
Ust-Ilimsk	**74**	58 3N	102 39 E
Ust-Kamchatsk	**73**	56 10N	162 28 E
Ust-Kamenogorsk	**71**	50 0N	82 36 E
Ust Maya	**75**	60 30N	134 28 E
Ust Olenek	**72**	73 0N	119 48 E
Ust Port	**69**	69 40N	84 26 E
Ust Urt = Ustyurt, Plato	**70**	44 0N	55 0 E
Ust Vorkuta	**69**	67 24N	64 0 E
Ústí nad Labem	**58**	50 41N	14 3 E
Ustica	**48**	38 42N	13 10 E
Ustinov	**69**	56 51N	53 14 E
Ustyurt, Plato	**70**	44 0N	55 0 E
Usu	**100**	44 27N	84 40 E
Usuki	**108**	33 8N	131 49 E
Usumbura = Bujumbura	**135**	3 16S	29 18 E
Utah □	**163**	39 30N	111 30W
Utah, L.	**163**	40 10N	111 58W
Uthai Thani	**94**	15 22N	100 3 E
Utica	**164**	43 5N	75 18W
Uto	**108**	32 41N	130 40 E
Utrecht	**40**	52 5N	5 8 E
Utrecht □	**40**	52 6N	5 7 E
Utrera	**50**	37 12N	5 48W
Utsunomiya	**107**	36 30N	139 50 E
Uttar Pradesh □	**92**	27 0N	80 0 E
Uttoxeter	**28**	52 53N	1 50W
Uusikaupunki	**66**	60 47N	21 25 E
Uvalde	**161**	29 15N	99 48W
Uvs Nuur	**74**	50 20N	92 30 E
Uwajima	**109**	33 10N	132 35 E
Uzbekistan ■	**70**	41 30N	65 0 E

V

Place	Page	Lat.	Long.
Vaal →	**137**	29 4S	23 38 E
Vaals	**41**	50 46N	6 1 E
Vaasa	**67**	63 6N	21 38 E
Vác	**58**	47 49N	19 10 E
Vach →	**69**	60 45N	76 45 E
Vadodara	**91**	22 20N	73 10 E
Vadsø	**67**	70 3N	29 50 E
Váh →	**59**	47 55N	18 0 E
Vaigach	**69**	70 10N	59 0 E
Val d'Or	**151**	48 7N	77 47W
Valahia	**57**	44 35N	25 0 E
Valcheta	**192**	40 40S	66 8W
Valdés, Pen.	**192**	42 30S	63 45W
Valdez	**142**	61 14N	146 17W
Valdivia	**190**	39 50S	73 14W
Valdosta	**170**	30 50N	83 20W
Valence	**37**	44 57N	4 54 E
Valencia, Spain	**51**	39 27N	0 23W
Valencia, Venezuela	**184**	10 11N	68 0W
Valencia □	**51**	39 20N	0 40W
Valencia, Albufera de	**51**	39 20N	0 27W
Valencia, G. de	**51**	39 30N	0 20 E
Valencia de Alcántara	**50**	39 25N	7 14W
Valenciennes	**38**	50 20N	3 34 E
Valentia I.	**35**	51 54N	10 22W
Valera	**184**	9 19N	70 37W
Valkenswaard	**41**	51 21N	5 29 E
Valladolid, Mexico	**177**	20 41N	88 12W
Valladolid, Spain	**50**	41 38N	4 43W
Valle d'Aosta □	**46**	45 45N	7 22 E
Valle de la Pascua	**184**	9 13N	66 0W
Valle de Santiago	**177**	20 23N	101 12W
Vallecas	**50**	40 23N	3 41W
Vallejo	**172**	38 12N	122 15W
Valletta	**49**	35 54N	14 30 E
Valley City	**163**	46 57N	98 0W
Valley View	**155**	40 39N	76 33W
Valona = Vlóra	**52**	40 32N	19 28 E
Valparaíso, Chile	**190**	33 2S	71 40W
Valparaíso, Mexico	**175**	22 46N	103 34W
Valsad	**91**	20 40N	72 58 E
Van	**81**	38 30N	43 20 E
Van, L. = Van Gölü	**81**	38 30N	43 0 E
Van Buren, Canada	**148**	47 10N	67 55W
Van Buren, U.S.A.	**168**	35 28N	94 18W
Van Gölü	**81**	38 30N	43 0 E
Van Wert	**167**	40 52N	84 31W
Vancouver, Canada	**154**	49 15N	123 10W
Vancouver, U.S.A.	**171**	45 44N	122 41W
Vancouver I.	**154**	49 50N	126 0W
Vandalia	**166**	38 57N	89 4W
Vanderhoof	**154**	54 0N	124 0W
Vänern	**60**	58 47N	13 30 E
Vanier	**151**	45 27N	75 40W
Vankarem	**73**	67 51N	175 50 E
Vännäs	**66**	63 58N	19 48 E
Vannes	**36**	47 40N	2 47W
Vanua Levu	**122**	16 33S	179 15 E
Vanuatu ■	**122**	15 0S	168 0 E
Varanasi	**92**	25 22N	83 0 E
Varangerfjorden	**67**	70 3N	29 25 E
Varaždin	**52**	46 20N	16 20 E
Vardak □	**87**	34 0N	68 0 E
Vardø	**67**	70 23N	31 5 E
Värmland	**60**	60 0N	13 30 E
Varna	**53**	43 13N	27 56 E

268 Vascongadas

Name	Page	Lat°	Lat′	Lon°	Lon′
Vascongadas	50	42	50N	2	45W
Västerås	60	59	37N	16	38 E
Västmanlands län □	60	59	45N	16	20 E
Vatnajökull	64	64	30N	16	48W
Vatra-Dornei	57	47	22N	25	22 E
Vättern	60	58	25N	14	30 E
Vaygach, Ostrov	69	70	0N	60	0 E
Veendam	41	53	5N	6	52 E
Vega, La	180	19	20N	70	30W
Veghel	41	51	37N	5	32 E
Vegreville	155	53	30N	112	5W
Vela, La	184	11	27N	69	34W
Vellore	90	12	57N	79	10 E
Venado Tuerto	190	33	50S	62	0W
Vendôme	39	47	47N	1	3 E
Véneto □	47	45	40N	12	0 E
Venézia	47	45	27N	12	20 E
Venézia, Golfo di	47	45	20N	13	0 E
Venezuela ■	184	8	0N	65	0W
Venezuela, Golfo de	184	11	30N	71	0W
Vengurla	91	15	53N	73	45 E
Venice = Venézia	47	45	27N	12	20 E
Venlo	41	51	22N	6	11 E
Venraij	41	51	31N	6	0 E
Ventnor	24	50	35N	1	12W
Ventoux	37	44	10N	5	17 E
Ventura	173	34	16N	119	18W
Veracruz	177	19	10N	96	10W
Veracruz □	177	19	20N	96	40W
Verde, R. —►	175	15	59N	97	50W
Verdun	37	49	12N	5	24 E
Vereeniging	137	26	38S	27	57 E
Verkhoyansk	72	67	35N	133	25 E
Verkhoyanskiy Khrebet	72	66	0N	129	0 E
Vermilion	152	53	20N	110	50W
Vermont □	164	43	40N	72	50W
Verneuil-sur-Avre	39	48	45N	0	55 E
Vernon, Canada	155	50	20N	119	15W
Vernon, France	39	49	5N	1	30 E
Vernon, U.S.A.	161	34	10N	99	20W
Verona	46	45	27N	11	0 E
Versailles	39	48	48N	2	8 E
Vert, C.	130	14	45N	17	30W
Verviers	42	50	37N	5	52 E
Vest-Agder fylke □	60	58	30N	7	15 E
Vesterålen	64	68	45N	15	0 E
Vestfjorden	64	67	55N	14	0 E
Vestfold fylke □	60	59	15N	10	0 E
Vestspitsbergen	13	78	40N	17	0 E
Vesuvio	49	40	50N	14	22 E
Vesuvius, Mt. = Vesuvio	49	40	50N	14	22 E
Viacha	187	16	39S	68	18W
Viborg	61	56	27N	9	23 E
Vicenza	47	45	32N	11	31 E
Vichy	37	46	9N	3	26 E
Vicksburg	169	32	22N	90	56W
Victor Harbor	119	35	30S	138	37 E
Victoria, Canada	154	48	30N	123	25W
Victoria, Chile	190	38	13S	72	20W
Victoria, U.S.A.	158	28	50N	97	0W
Victoria □	117	37	0S	144	0 E
Victoria, L.	132	1	0S	33	0 E
Victoria de las Tunas	178	20	58N	76	59W
Victoria Falls	137	17	58S	25	52 E
Victoria I.	145	71	0N	111	0W
Victoria Ld.	15	75	0S	160	0 E
Victoriaville	148	46	4N	71	56W
Vidalia	170	32	13N	82	25W
Vidin	53	43	59N	22	50 E
Viedma	192	40	50S	63	0W
Vienna = Wien	45	48	12N	16	22 E
Vienne	37	45	31N	4	53 E
Vienne —►	36	47	13N	0	5 E
Vientiane	95	17	58N	102	36 E
Vientos, Paso de los	180	20	0N	74	0W
Vietnam ■	95	19	0N	106	0 E
Vigo	50	42	12N	8	41W
Vijayawada	92	16	31N	80	39 E
Vila Real de Santo António	50	37	10N	7	28W
Vilhelmina	66	64	35N	16	39 E
Vilhena	187	12	40S	60	5W
Villa Bella	187	10	25S	65	22W
Villa Bens = Tarfaya	126	27	55N	12	55W
Villa Cisneros = Dakhla	126	23	50N	15	53W
Villa Dolores	190	31	58S	65	15W
Villa Maria	190	32	20S	63	10W
Villa Montes	187	21	10S	63	30W
Villaguay	190	32	0S	59	0W
Villahermosa	177	17	59N	92	55W
Villanueva de la Serena	50	38	59N	5	50W
Villarreal	51	39	55N	0	3W
Villarrica	191	39	15S	72	15W
Villazón	187	22	0S	65	35W
Ville Platte	168	30	45N	92	17W
Villefranche-sur-Saône	37	45	59N	4	43 E
Villers-Cotterêts	39	49	15N	3	4 E
Vilnius	68	54	38N	25	19 E
Vilskutskogo, Proliv	72	78	0N	103	0 E
Vilyuy —►	74	64	24N	126	26 E
Vilyuysk	74	63	40N	121	35 E
Viña del Mar	190	33	0S	71	30W
Vincennes	167	38	42N	87	29W
Vindhya Ra.	91	22	50N	77	0 E
Vinh	95	18	45N	105	38 E
Vinita	168	36	40N	95	12W
Vinkovci	52	45	19N	18	48 E
Vinnitsa	68	49	15N	28	30 E
Viramgam	91	23	5N	72	0 E
Virden	153	49	50N	100	56W
Vire	36	48	50N	0	53W
Virgenes, C.	192	52	19S	68	21W
Virgin —►	173	36	50N	114	10W
Virgin Is.	180	18	40N	64	30W
Virginia	156	47	30N	92	32W
Virginia □	165	37	45N	78	0W
Virginia Beach	165	36	54N	75	58W
Visalia	173	36	25N	119	18W
Visby	60	57	37N	18	18 E
Viscount Melville Sd.	145	74	10N	108	0W
Višegrad	52	43	47N	19	17 E
Vishakhapatnam	92	17	45N	83	20 E
Vistula = Wisła —►	58	54	22N	18	55 E
Vitebsk	68	55	10N	30	15 E
Viti Levu	122	17	30S	177	30 E
Vitim —►	74	59	26N	112	34 E
Vitória, Brazil	189	20	20S	40	22W
Vitoria, Spain	50	42	50N	2	41W
Vitória da Conquista	189	14	51S	40	51W
Vizianagaram	92	18	6N	83	30 E
Vlaardingen	40	51	55N	4	21 E
Vladikavkaz	70	43	0N	44	35 E
Vladimir	68	56	15N	40	30 E
Vladivostok	75	43	10N	131	53 E
Vlieland	40	53	16N	4	55 E
Vlissingen	40	51	26N	3	34 E
Vlóra	52	40	32N	19	28 E
Vltava —►	59	50	21N	14	30 E
Vogelkop	113	1	25S	133	0 E
Vogels Berg	42	50	37N	9	30 E
Vohimena, Tanjon' i	137	25	36S	45	8 E
Voi	133	3	25S	38	32 E
Volendam	40	52	30N	5	4 E
Volga —►	68	48	30N	46	0 E
Volga Hts. = Privolzhskaya Vozvyshennost	17	51	0N	46	0 E
Volgograd	68	48	40N	44	25 E
Vollenhove	41	52	40N	5	58 E
Vologda	68	59	10N	40	0 E
Vólos	54	39	24N	22	59 E
Volsk	68	52	5N	47	22 E
Volta —►	130	5	46N	0	41 E
Volta, L.	130	7	30N	0	15 E
Volta Redonda	188	22	31S	44	5W
Voorburg	40	52	5N	4	24 E
Vopnafjörður	64	65	45N	14	40W
Voriai Sporádhes	55	39	15N	23	30 E
Voronezh	68	51	40N	39	10 E
Voroshilovgrad = Lugansk	68	48	38N	39	15 E
Vosges	37	48	20N	7	10 E
Vostochnyy Sayan	74	54	0N	96	0 E
Vrangelya, Ostrov	73	71	0N	180	0 E
Vranje	53	42	34N	21	54 E
Vratsa	53	43	13N	23	30 E

Vršac	52	45	8N	21	18 E
Vught	40	51	38N	5	20 E
Vulcan	155	50	25N	113	15W
Vyatka	69	58	35N	49	40 E
Vyborg	68	60	43N	28	47 E
Vychegda →	69	61	18N	46	36 E
Východné Beskydy	59	49	30N	22	0 E

W

Wa	130	10	7N	2	25W
Waal →	41	51	59N	4	30 E
Waalwijk	40	51	42N	5	4 E
Wabash	167	40	48N	85	46W
Wabash →	167	37	46N	88	2W
Wąbrzeźno	58	53	16N	18	57 E
Waco	168	31	33N	97	5W
Wâd Medanî	129	14	28N	33	30 E
Waddenzee	40	53	6N	5	10 E
Waddington, Mt.	154	51	23N	125	15W
Waddinxveen	40	52	2N	4	40 E
Wadena	152	51	57N	103	47W
Wadi Halfa	129	21	53N	31	19 E
Wageningen	41	51	58N	5	40 E
Wager Bay	146	65	56N	90	49W
Wagga Wagga	117	35	7S	147	24 E
Wagin	120	33	17S	117	25 E
Waigeo	113	0	20S	130	40 E
Waihi	122	37	23S	175	52 E
Waikerie	119	34	9S	140	0 E
Waikokopu	122	39	3S	177	52 E
Waimate	123	44	45S	171	3 E
Wainwright, Canada	152	52	50N	110	50W
Wainwright, U.S.A.	142	70	39N	160	1W
Waipara	123	43	3S	172	46 E
Waipu	122	35	59S	174	29 E
Waipukurau	122	40	1S	176	33 E
Wairoa	122	39	3S	177	25 E
Waitara	122	38	59S	174	15 E
Wajima	105	37	30N	137	0 E
Wajir	133	1	42N	40	5 E
Wakasa-Wan	106	35	40N	135	30 E
Wakatipu, L.	123	45	5S	168	33 E
Wakayama	106	34	15N	135	15 E
Wakefield, N.Z.	123	41	24S	173	5 E
Wakefield, U.K.	28	53	41N	1	31W
Wakkanai	103	45	28N	141	35 E
Wałbrzych	58	50	45N	16	18 E
Walcha	116	30	55S	151	31 E
Walcheren	40	51	30N	3	35 E
Wales □	26	52	30N	3	30W
Walgett	116	30	0S	148	5 E
Walkerton	151	44	10N	81	10W
Walla Walla	171	46	3N	118	25W
Wallaceburg	150	42	34N	82	23W
Wallachia = Valahia	57	44	35N	25	0 E
Wallangarra	116	28	56S	151	58 E
Wallaroo	119	33	56S	137	39 E
Wallasey	28	53	26N	3	2W
Wallerawang	117	33	25S	150	4 E
Wallis & Futuna	122	13	18S	176	10W
Wallowa, Mts.	171	45	20N	117	30W
Wallsend, Australia	117	32	55S	151	40 E
Wallsend, U.K.	28	54	59N	1	30W
Walney, Isle of	28	54	5N	3	15W
Walpole	120	34	58S	116	44 E
Walsall	24	52	36N	1	59W
Walvis Bay	136	23	0S	14	28 E
Wana	88	32	20N	69	32 E
Wanaka L.	123	44	33S	169	7 E
Wang Saphung	95	17	18N	101	46 E
Wanganui	122	39	56S	175	3 E
Wangaratta	117	36	21S	146	19 E
Wanxian	99	30	42N	108	20 E
Warabi	107	35	49N	139	41 E
Warangal	91	17	58N	79	35 E
Warburton	117	37	47S	145	42 E
Wardha	91	20	45N	78	39 E
Wardha →	91	19	57N	79	11 E

Warialda	116	29	29S	150	33 E
Warley	24	52	30N	2	0W
Warner Mts.	172	41	30N	120	20W
Waroona	120	32	50S	115	58 E
Warracknabeal	119	36	9S	142	26 E
Warragul	117	38	10S	145	58 E
Warrego →	116	30	24S	145	21 E
Warrego Ra.	121	24	58S	146	0 E
Warren, Australia	116	31	42S	147	51 E
Warren, Ark., U.S.A.	168	33	35N	92	3W
Warren, Mich., U.S.A.	167	42	31N	83	2W
Warren, Ohio, U.S.A.	164	41	18N	80	52W
Warren, Pa., U.S.A.	164	41	52N	79	10W
Warrenpoint	34	54	7N	6	15W
Warrensburg	166	38	45N	93	45W
Warrington, U.K.	28	53	25N	2	38W
Warrington, U.S.A.	169	30	22N	87	16W
Warrnambool	119	38	25S	142	30 E
Warsaw = Warszawa	58	52	13N	21	0 E
Warszawa	58	52	13N	21	0 E
Warta →	58	52	35N	14	39 E
Warthe = Warta →	58	52	35N	14	39 E
Warwick, Australia	116	28	10S	152	1 E
Warwick, U.K.	24	52	17N	1	36W
Warwick, U.S.A.	164	41	43N	71	25W
Warwick □	24	52	20N	1	30W
Wasatch Ra.	163	40	30N	111	15W
Wasco	173	35	37N	119	16W
Wash, The	29	52	58N	0	20 E
Washim	91	20	3N	77	0 E
Washington, D.C., U.S.A.	165	38	52N	77	0W
Washington, Ind., U.S.A.	167	38	40N	87	8W
Washington, Mo., U.S.A.	166	38	35N	91	1W
Washington, Pa., U.S.A.	164	40	10N	80	20W
Washington □	171	47	45N	120	30W
Wassenaar	40	52	8N	4	24 E
Waterbury	164	41	32N	73	0W
Waterford	35	52	16N	7	8W
Waterford □	35	52	10N	7	40W
Waterloo, Canada	151	43	30N	80	32W
Waterloo, U.S.A.	166	42	27N	92	20W
Watertown, N.Y., U.S.A.	151	43	58N	75	57W
Watertown, Wis., U.S.A.	167	43	15N	88	45W
Waterville	148	44	35N	69	40W
Watling I. = San Salvador	178	24	0N	74	40W
Watrous	152	51	40N	105	25W
Watson Lake	144	60	6N	128	49W
Watsonville	173	36	55N	121	49W
Watubela, Kepulauan	113	4	28S	131	35 E
Wauchope	116	31	28S	152	45 E
Waukegan	167	42	22N	87	54W
Waukesha	167	43	0N	88	15W
Wausau	166	44	57N	89	40W
Wauwatosa	167	43	6N	87	59W
Waveney →	25	52	24N	1	20 E
Wâw	129	7	45N	28	1 E
Waxahachie	168	32	22N	96	53W
Waycross	170	31	12N	82	25W
Waynesboro, Pa., U.S.A.	164	39	46N	77	32W
Waynesboro, Va., U.S.A.	165	38	4N	78	57W
Waynesville	165	35	31N	83	0W
Wazirabad	89	32	30N	74	8 E
Weald, The	25	51	7N	0	9 E
Webo = Nyaake	130	4	52N	7	37W
Weddell Sea	14	72	30S	40	0W
Wedderburn	117	36	26S	143	33 E
Wee Waa	116	30	11S	149	26 E
Weert	41	51	15N	5	43 E
Weesp	40	52	18N	5	2 E
Weifang	98	36	47N	119	10 E
Weiser	171	44	10N	117	0W
Welbourn Hill	118	27	21S	134	6 E
Welch	165	37	29N	81	36W
Welland	151	43	0N	79	15W
Welland →	29	52	43N	0	10W
Wellingborough	25	52	18N	0	41W
Wellington, Australia	116	32	35S	148	59 E
Wellington, N.Z.	123	41	19S	174	46 E
Wellington, Shrops., U.K.	28	52	42N	2	31W
Wellington, Somst., U.K.	27	50	58N	3	13W
Wellington □	123	40	8S	175	36 E
Wellington, I.	192	49	30S	75	0W

Wells, Norfolk, U.K.	29	52 57N	0 51 E
Wells, Somst., U.K.	27	51 12N	2 39W
Wells, U.S.A.	172	41 8N	115 0W
Wellsville, N.Y., U.S.A.	164	42 9N	77 53W
Wellsville, Ohio, U.S.A.	164	40 36N	80 40W
Welshpool	26	52 40N	3 9W
Wem	28	52 52N	2 45W
Wenatchee	171	47 30N	120 17W
Wenchow = Wenzhou	99	28 0N	120 38 E
Wensleydale	28	54 18N	2 0W
Wentworth	119	34 2S	141 54 E
Wenzhou	99	28 0N	120 38 E
Werribee	117	37 54S	144 40 E
Werris Creek	116	31 18S	150 38 E
Weser →	42	53 33N	8 30 E
West Bengal □	92	23 0N	88 0 E
West Bromwich	24	52 32N	2 1W
West Falkland	192	51 40S	60 0W
West Frankfort	166	37 56N	89 0W
West Glamorgan □	27	51 40N	3 55W
West Memphis	169	35 5N	90 11W
West Midlands □	24	52 30N	1 55W
West Palm Beach	170	26 44N	80 3W
West Schelde =			
Westerschelde →	40	51 25N	3 25 E
West Siberian Plain	76	62 0N	75 0 E
West Sussex □	25	50 55N	0 30W
West Virginia □	165	39 0N	81 0W
West Yorkshire □	28	53 45N	1 40W
Western Australia □	114	25 0S	118 0 E
Western Ghats	90	14 0N	75 0 E
Western Isles □	32	57 30N	7 10W
Western Sahara ■	126	25 0N	13 0W
Western Samoa ■	123	14 0S	172 0W
Westerschelde →	40	51 25N	3 25 E
Westerwald	42	50 39N	8 0 E
Westfriesche Eilanden	40	53 20N	5 10 E
Westland □	123	43 33S	169 59 E
Westland Bight	123	42 55S	170 5 E
Westlock	155	54 9N	113 55W
Westmeath □	34	53 30N	7 30W
Westminster	164	39 34N	77 1W
Weston	165	39 3N	80 29W
Weston-super-Mare	27	51 20N	2 59W
Westport	123	41 46S	171 37 E
Westray	33	59 18N	3 0W
Wetar	113	7 30S	126 30 E
Wetaskiwin	155	52 55N	113 24W
Wewaka	168	35 10N	96 35W
Wexford	35	52 20N	6 28W
Wexford □	35	52 20N	6 25W
Weyburn	152	49 40N	103 50W
Weymouth	27	50 36N	2 28W
Whakatane	122	37 57S	177 1 E
Whale Cove	145	62 11N	92 36W
Whalsay	30	60 22N	1 0W
Whangamomona	122	39 8S	174 44 E
Whangarei	122	35 43S	174 21 E
Wharfe →	29	53 55N	1 30W
Wheeler Pk.	172	38 57N	114 15W
Wheeling	164	40 2N	80 41W
Whernside	28	54 14N	2 24W
Whitby	29	54 29N	0 37W
Whitchurch	28	52 58N	2 42W
White →, Ark., U.S.A.	168	33 53N	91 3W
White →, Ind., U.S.A.	167	38 25N	87 45W
White →, S. Dak., U.S.A.	163	43 45N	99 30W
White Cliffs	118	30 50S	143 10 E
White Mts.	157	44 15N	71 15W
White Nile = Nîl el			
Abyad →	129	15 38N	32 31 E
White Russia = Belorussia ■	68	53 30N	27 0 E
White Sea = Beloye More	69	66 30N	38 0 E
Whitecliffs	123	43 26S	171 55 E
Whitehaven	28	54 33N	3 35W
Whitehorse	144	60 43N	135 3W
Whitney, Mt.	173	36 35N	118 14W
Whitstable	25	51 21N	1 2 E
Whitsunday I.	121	20 15S	149 4 E
Whittier	142	60 46N	148 48W
Whyalla	118	33 2S	137 30 E
Wichita	158	37 40N	97 20W
Wichita Falls	161	33 57N	98 30W
Wick	33	58 26N	3 5W
Wickepin	120	32 50S	117 30 E
Wicklow	35	53 0N	6 2W
Wicklow □	35	52 59N	6 25W
Wicklow Mts.	35	53 0N	6 30W
Widnes	28	53 22N	2 44W
Wieluń	58	51 15N	18 34 E
Wien	45	48 12N	16 22 E
Wiesbaden	42	50 7N	8 17 E
Wigan	28	53 33N	2 38W
Wight, I. of	25	50 40N	1 20W
Wigtown	31	54 52N	4 27W
Wigtown B.	31	54 46N	4 15W
Wilcannia	118	31 30S	143 26 E
Wildwood	164	38 59N	74 46W
Wilhelmshaven	42	53 30N	8 9 E
Wilkes Barre	164	41 15N	75 52W
Wilkes Sub-Glacial Basin	15	75 0S	130 0 E
Wilkie	152	52 27N	108 42W
Willamina	171	45 9N	123 32W
Willemstad	181	12 5N	69 0W
Williams L.	154	51 48N	90 45W
Williamsburg	165	37 17N	76 44W
Williamson	165	37 46N	82 17W
Williamsport	164	41 18N	77 1W
Williamstown	117	37 51S	144 54 E
Williston	163	48 10N	103 35W
Willits	172	39 28N	123 17W
Willmar	156	45 5N	95 0W
Wilmette	167	42 6N	87 44W
Wilmington, Del., U.S.A.	164	39 45N	75 32W
Wilmington, N.C., U.S.A.	165	34 14N	77 54W
Wilson	165	35 44N	77 54W
Wilsons Promontory	117	38 55S	146 25 E
Wilton	24	51 5N	1 52W
Wiltshire □	24	51 20N	2 0W
Wiluna	120	26 36S	120 14 E
Wimereux	38	50 45N	1 37 E
Winchester, U.K.	25	51 4N	1 19W
Winchester, Ind., U.S.A.	167	40 10N	84 56W
Winchester, Ky., U.S.A.	165	38 0N	84 8W
Winchester, Va., U.S.A.	164	39 14N	78 8W
Wind River Range	163	43 0N	109 30W
Windermere	28	54 24N	2 56W
Windermere, L.	28	54 20N	2 57W
Windhoek	136	22 35S	17 4 E
Windsor, Australia	117	33 37S	150 50 E
Windsor, Nfld., Canada	149	48 57N	55 40W
Windsor, Ont., Canada	150	42 18N	83 0W
Windsor, U.K.	25	51 28N	0 36W
Windward Is.	181	13 0N	63 0W
Windward Passage =			
Vientos, Paso de los	180	20 0N	74 0W
Winisk →	140	55 17N	85 5W
Winkler	153	49 10N	97 56W
Winnemucca	172	41 0N	117 45W
Winnfield	168	31 57N	92 38W
Winnipeg	153	49 54N	97 9W
Winnipeg, L.	153	52 0N	97 0W
Winnipegosis L.	153	52 30N	100 0W
Winona	166	44 2N	91 39W
Winooski	151	44 31N	73 11W
Winschoten	41	53 9N	7 3 E
Winslow	161	35 2N	110 41W
Winston-Salem	165	36 7N	80 15W
Winter Haven	170	28 0N	81 42W
Winter Park	170	28 34N	81 19W
Winterswijk	41	51 58N	6 43 E
Winterthur	44	47 30N	8 44 E
Wirral	28	53 25N	3 0W
Wisbech	29	52 39N	0 10 E
Wisconsin □	166	44 30N	90 0W
Wisconsin →	166	43 0N	91 5W
Wisconsin Rapids	166	44 25N	89 50W
Wishaw	31	55 46N	3 55W
Wisła →	58	54 22N	18 55 E
Witham →	29	53 3N	0 8W
Withernsea	29	53 43N	0 2 E
Witney	24	51 47N	1 29W
Włocławek	58	52 40N	19 3 E
Wodonga	117	36 5S	146 50 E

Place	Page	Lat.	Long.
Wokam	**113**	5 45S	134 28 E
Woking	**25**	51 18N	0 33W
Wolin	**58**	53 50N	14 37 E
Wollaston L.	**145**	58 7N	103 10W
Wollaston Pen.	**145**	69 30N	115 0W
Wollongong	**117**	34 25S	150 54 E
Wolverhampton	**24**	52 35N	2 6W
Wondai	**116**	26 20S	151 49 E
Wŏnsan	**98**	39 11N	127 27 E
Wonthaggi	**117**	38 37S	145 37 E
Woodburn	**116**	29 6S	153 23 E
Woodenbong	**116**	28 24S	152 39 E
Woodend	**117**	37 20S	144 33 E
Woodland	**172**	38 40N	121 50W
Woods, L. of the	**153**	49 15N	94 45W
Woodstock, N.B., Canada	**148**	46 11N	67 37W
Woodstock, Ont., Canada	**151**	43 10N	80 45W
Woolgoolga	**116**	30 6S	153 11 E
Woomera	**118**	31 30S	137 10 E
Woonsocket	**164**	42 0N	71 30W
Wooroloo	**120**	31 48S	116 18 E
Worcester, U.K.	**24**	52 12N	2 12W
Worcester, U.S.A.	**164**	42 14N	71 49W
Workington	**28**	54 39N	3 34W
Worksop	**29**	53 19N	1 9W
Wormerveer	**40**	52 30N	4 46 E
Worms	**42**	49 37N	8 21 E
Worthing	**25**	50 49N	0 21W
Worthington	**166**	43 35N	95 36W
Wou-han = Wuhan	**99**	30 31N	114 18 E
Woy Woy	**117**	33 30S	151 19 E
Wrangel I.	**138**	71 0N	180 0 E
Wrangell	**143**	56 30N	132 25W
Wrangell Mts.	**142**	61 40N	143 30W
Wrath, C.	**32**	58 38N	5 0W
Wrekin, The	**28**	52 41N	2 35W
Wrexham	**26**	53 5N	3 0W
Wrigley	**144**	63 16N	123 37W
Wrocław	**58**	51 5N	17 5 E
Września	**58**	52 21N	17 36 E
Wu Jiang →	**99**	29 40N	107 20 E
Wubin	**120**	30 6S	116 37 E
Wuhan	**99**	30 31N	114 18 E
Wuhsi = Wuxi	**99**	31 33N	120 18 E
Wuhu	**99**	31 22N	118 21 E
Wulumuchi = Ürümqi	**100**	43 45N	87 45 E
Wuppertal	**42**	51 15N	7 8 E
Würzburg	**42**	49 46N	9 55 E
Wutongqiao	**99**	29 22N	103 50 E
Wuxi	**99**	31 33N	120 18 E
Wuzhong	**98**	38 2N	106 12 E
Wuzhou	**99**	23 30N	111 18 E
Wyalkatchem	**120**	31 8S	117 22 E
Wyandotte	**167**	42 14N	83 13W
Wycheproof	**119**	36 0S	143 17 E
Wye →	**27**	51 36N	2 40W
Wyndham	**114**	15 33S	128 3 E
Wynnum	**116**	27 27S	153 9 E
Wynyard	**152**	51 45N	104 10W
Wyoming □	**163**	42 48N	109 0W
Wytheville	**165**	37 0N	81 3W

X

Place	Page	Lat.	Long.
Xánthi	**55**	41 10N	24 58 E
Xapuri	**187**	10 35S	68 35W
Xenia	**167**	39 42N	83 57W
Xiamen	**99**	24 25N	118 4 E
Xi'an	**99**	34 15N	109 0 E
Xiangfan	**99**	32 2N	112 8 E
Xiangtan	**99**	27 51N	112 54 E
Xiao Hinggan Ling	**98**	49 0N	127 0 E
Xigazê	**101**	29 5N	88 45 E
Xingtai	**98**	37 3N	114 32 E
Xingu →	**188**	1 30S	51 53W
Xining	**98**	36 34N	101 40 E
Xinjiang Uygur Zizhiqu □	**100**	42 0N	86 0 E
Xinxiang	**99**	35 18N	113 50 E
Xinyang	**99**	32 6N	114 3 E
Xinzhu	**99**	24 49N	120 57 E
Xique-Xique	**188**	10 50S	42 40W
Xizang □	**101**	32 0N	88 0 E
Xuanhua	**98**	40 40N	115 2 E
Xuchang	**99**	34 2N	113 48 E
Xuzhou	**99**	34 18N	117 10 E

Y

Place	Page	Lat.	Long.
Ya'an	**99**	29 58N	103 5 E
Yablonovy Khrebet	**74**	53 0N	114 0 E
Yablonovy Ra. = Yablonovy Khrebet	**74**	53 0N	114 0 E
Yacuiba	**187**	22 0S	63 43W
Yaizu	**107**	34 52N	138 20 E
Yakima	**171**	46 42N	120 30W
Yaku-Jima	**104**	30 20N	130 30 E
Yakut Rep. □	**72**	62 0N	130 0 E
Yakutat	**143**	59 29N	139 44W
Yakutsk	**75**	62 5N	129 50 E
Yalgoo	**120**	28 16S	116 39 E
Yalinga	**129**	6 33N	23 10 E
Yamaga	**108**	33 1N	130 41 E
Yamagata	**103**	38 15N	140 15 E
Yamaguchi	**108**	34 10N	131 32 E
Yamal, Poluostrov	**69**	71 0N	70 0 E
Yamato	**107**	35 27N	139 25 E
Yamatotakada	**106**	34 31N	135 45 E
Yamazaki	**109**	35 0N	134 32 E
Yamba	**116**	29 26S	153 23 E
Yambol	**53**	42 30N	26 36 E
Yamdena	**113**	7 45S	131 20 E
Yame	**108**	33 13N	130 35 E
Yamma-Yamma, L.	**118**	26 16S	141 20 E
Yampa →	**163**	40 37N	108 59W
Yamuna →	**92**	25 30N	81 53 E
Yamzho Yumco	**101**	28 48N	90 35 E
Yana →	**72**	71 30N	136 0 E
Yanagawa	**108**	33 10N	130 24 E
Yanai	**109**	33 58N	132 7 E
Yanco	**117**	34 38S	146 27 E
Yangch'ü = Taiyuan	**98**	37 52N	112 33 E
Yangquan	**98**	37 58N	113 31 E
Yangtze Kiang = Chang Jiang →	**99**	31 48N	121 10 E
Yanji	**98**	42 59N	129 30 E
Yantai	**98**	37 34N	121 22 E
Yao	**106**	34 32N	135 36 E
Yaoundé	**131**	3 50N	11 35 E
Yaqui →	**174**	27 37N	110 39W
Yare →	**25**	52 36N	1 28 E
Yarensk	**69**	61 10N	49 8 E
Yarkand = Shache	**100**	38 20N	77 10 E
Yarmouth	**148**	43 50N	66 7W
Yaroslavl	**68**	57 35N	39 55 E
Yarram	**117**	38 29S	146 9 E
Yashiro-Jima	**109**	33 55N	132 15 E
Yass	**117**	34 49S	148 54 E
Yasugi	**109**	35 26N	133 15 E
Yatsushiro	**108**	32 30N	130 40 E
Yavari →	**186**	4 21S	70 2W
Yavatmal	**91**	20 20N	78 15 E
Yawatahama	**109**	33 27N	132 24 E
Yazd	**85**	31 55N	54 27 E
Yazoo →	**169**	32 35N	90 50W
Yazoo City	**169**	32 48N	90 28W
Ye Xian	**98**	37 8N	119 57 E
Yegros	**191**	26 20S	56 25W
Yekaterinburg	**69**	56 50N	60 30 E
Yelizavetgrad	**68**	48 35N	32 20 E
Yell	**30**	60 35N	1 5W
Yellow Sea	**99**	35 0N	123 0 E
Yellowhead P.	**155**	52 53N	118 25W
Yellowknife	**145**	62 27N	114 29W
Yellowstone →	**163**	47 58N	103 59W
Yellowstone National Park	**163**	44 35N	110 0W
Yemen ■	**82**	15 0N	44 0 E
Yenisey →	**69**	71 50N	82 40 E
Yeniseyskiy Zaliv	**69**	72 20N	81 0 E

Yeo →	27	51 10N	3	0W
Yeola	91	20 0N	74	30 E
Yeovil	27	50 57N	2	38W
Yeppoon	121	23 5S	150	47 E
Yerevan	70	40 10N	44	31 E
Yes Tor	27	50 41N	3	59W
Yetman	116	28 56S	150	48 E
Yezd = Yazd	85	31 55N	54	27 E
Yiannitsa	54	40 46N	22	24 E
Yibin	99	28 45N	104	32 E
Yichang	99	30 40N	111	20 E
Yichun	98	47 44N	128	52 E
Yilan	99	24 51N	121	44 E
Yinchuan	98	38 30N	106	15 E
Yingkou	98	40 37N	122	18 E
Yingtan	99	28 12N	117	0 E
Yining	100	43 58N	81	10 E
Yithion	54	36 46N	22	34 E
Yiyang	99	28 45N	112	16 E
Yogyakarta	111	7 49S	110	22 E
Yōkaichiba	107	35 42N	140	33 E
Yokkaichi	106	35 0N	136	38 E
Yokohama	107	35 27N	139	28 E
Yokosuka	107	35 20N	139	40 E
Yokote	103	39 20N	140	30 E
Yonago	109	35 25N	133	19 E
Yoneshiro →	103	40 15N	140	15 E
Yonezawa	103	37 57N	140	4 E
Yongji	99	34 52N	110	28 E
Yonkers	164	40 57N	73	51W
York, Australia	120	31 52S	116	47 E
York, U.K.	29	53 58N	1	7W
York, U.S.A.	164	39 57N	76	43W
Yorke Pen.	119	34 50S	137	40 E
Yorkshire Wolds	29	54 0N	0	30W
Yorkton	152	51 11N	102	28W
Yosemite National Park	172	38 0N	119	30W
Youghal	35	51 58N	7	51W
Young	117	34 19S	148	18 E
Younghusband Pen.	119	36 0S	139	25 E
Youngstown	164	41 7N	80	41W
Yuba City	172	39 12N	121	37W
Yūbari	103	43 4N	141	59 E
Yūbetsu	103	43 13N	144	5 E
Yucatán □	177	20 50N	89	0W
Yucatán, Canal de	178	22 0N	86	30W
Yucatan Str. = Yucatán, Canal de	178	22 0N	86	30W
Yuci	98	37 42N	112	46 E
Yugoslavia ■	52	44 0N	21	0 E
Yukon →	142	65 30N	150	0W
Yukon Territory □	144	63 0N	135	0W
Yuma	173	32 45N	114	37W
Yunnan □	101	25 0N	102	30 E
Yuribei	69	71 8N	76	58 E
Yurimaguas	186	5 55S	76	7W
Yushu	101	33 5N	96	55 E
Yuzhno-Sakhalinsk	75	46 58N	142	45 E
Yvetot	38	49 37N	0	44 E

Z

Zaandam	40	52 26N	4	49 E
Zabaykalskiy	74	49 40N	117	25 E
Zabid	82	14 0N	43	10 E
Zābol	85	31 0N	61	32 E
Zābol □	87	32 0N	67	0 E
Zabrze	58	50 18N	18	50 E
Zacapa	177	14 59N	89	31W
Zacatecas	175	22 47N	102	35W
Zacatecas □	175	23 0N	103	0W
Zacatecoluca	177	13 29N	88	51W
Zadar	52	44 8N	15	14 E
Zadetkyi Kyun	94	10 0N	98	25 E
Zagreb	52	45 50N	16	0 E
Zāhedān	86	29 30N	60	50 E
Zahlah	80	33 52N	35	50 E
Zaïre ■	134	3 0S	23	0 E
Zaïre →	134	6 4S	12	24 E
Zákinthos	54	37 47N	20	57 E

Zambeze →	135	18 55S	36	4 E
Zambezi = Zambeze →	135	18 55S	36	4 E
Zambia ■	135	15 0S	28	0 E
Zamboanga	112	6 59N	122	3 E
Zamora, Mexico	175	20 0N	102	21W
Zamora, Spain	50	41 30N	5	45W
Zandvoort	40	52 22N	4	32 E
Zanesville	167	39 56N	82	2W
Zanjan	81	36 40N	48	35 E
Zante = Zákinthos	54	37 47N	20	57 E
Zanzibar	135	6 12S	39	12 E
Zaouiet El-Kala = Bordj Omar Driss	127	28 10N	6	40 E
Zaouiet Reggane	127	26 32N	0	3 E
Zapadnaya Dvina →	68	57 4N	24	3 E
Západné Beskydy	59	49 30N	19	0 E
Zapala	190	39 0S	70	5W
Zaporozhye	68	47 50N	35	10 E
Zaragoza, Mexico	174	28 29N	100	55W
Zaragoza, Spain	51	41 39N	0	53W
Zaranj	87	30 55N	61	55 E
Zaria	131	11 0N	7	40 E
Zaruma	184	3 40S	79	38W
Zaskar Mountains	89	33 15N	77	30 E
Zavitinsk	75	50 10N	129	20 E
Zaysan, Oz.	71	48 0N	83	0 E
Zayü	101	28 48N	97	27 E
Zduńska Wola	58	51 37N	18	59 E
Zeebrugge	42	51 19N	3	12 E
Zeeland □	40	51 30N	3	50 E
Zeila	133	11 21N	43	30 E
Zeist	40	52 5N	5	15 E
Zemlya Frantsa Iosifa	13	81 0N	55	0 E
Zentsūji	109	34 14N	133	47 E
Zeya	75	53 48N	127	14 E
Zêzere →	50	39 28N	8	20W
Zhanghua	99	24 6N	120	29 E
Zhangjiakou	98	40 48N	114	55 E
Zhangzhou	99	24 30N	117	35 E
Zhanjiang	99	21 15N	110	20 E
Zhdanov = Mariupol	68	47 5N	37	31 E
Zhejiang □	99	29 0N	120	0 E
Zhengzhou	99	34 45N	113	34 E
Zhenjiang	99	32 11N	119	26 E
Zhenyuan	99	27 4N	108	21 E
Zhijiang	99	27 27N	109	42 E
Zhitomir	68	50 20N	28	40 E
Zhumadian	99	32 59N	114	2 E
Zhupanovo	73	53 40N	159	52 E
Zhuzhou	99	27 49N	113	12 E
Zibo	98	36 47N	118	3 E
Zielona Góra	58	51 57N	15	31 E
Zierikzee	40	51 40N	3	55 E
Zigong	99	29 15N	104	48 E
Žile	80	40 15N	35	52 E
Žilina	59	49 12N	18	42 E
Zimbabwe	137	20 16S	30	54 E
Zimbabwe ■	137	20 0S	30	0 E
Zinder	131	13 48N	9	0 E
Zipaquirá	184	5 0N	74	0W
Zitácuaro	175	19 24N	100	22W
Zlatograd	53	41 22N	25	7 E
Zlatoust	69	55 10N	59	40 E
Zlin	59	49 14N	17	40 E
Zomba	137	15 22S	35	19 E
Zonguldak	80	41 28N	31	50 E
Zorritos	186	3 43S	80	40W
Zoutkamp	41	53 20N	6	18 E
Zrenjanin	52	45 22N	20	23 E
Zufar	83	17 40N	54	0 E
Zug	44	47 10N	8	31 E
Zuid-Holland □	40	52 0N	4	35 E
Zuidhorn	41	53 15N	6	23 E
Zungeru	131	9 48N	6	8 E
Zunyi	99	27 42N	106	53 E
Zürich	44	47 22N	8	32 E
Zutphen	41	52 9N	6	12 E
Zuwārah	127	32 58N	12	1 E
Zvolen	59	48 33N	19	10 E
Zwickau	43	50 43N	12	30 E
Zwolle	41	52 31N	6	6 E
Zyryanovsk	71	49 43N	84	20 E